2016

the best campsites
in Britain
& Ireland

over 650 independent reviews

Compiled by: Alan Rogers Travel Ltd

Designed by: Vine Design Ltd

Additional photography: T Lambelin, www.lambelin.com
Maps created by Customised Mapping (01769 540044)
contain background data provided by GisDATA Ltd

Maps are © Alan Rogers Travel Ltd and GisDATA Ltd 2015

© Alan Rogers Travel Ltd 2015

Published by: Alan Rogers Travel Ltd,
Spelmonden Old Oast, Goudhurst, Kent TN17 1HE
www.alanrogers.com Tel: 01580 214000

British Library Cataloguing-in-Publication Data:
A catalogue record for this book is available
from the British Library.

ISBN 978-1-909057-78-4

Printed In Great Britain by Stephens & George Print Group

Contents

Alan Rogers - in search of 'the best'

Alan Rogers Guides were first published almost 50 years ago. Since Alan Rogers published the first campsite guide that bore his name, the range has expanded and now covers 27 countries in five separate guides. No fewer than 20 of the campsites selected by Alan for the first guide are still featured in our 2016 editions.

There are well over 5,000 camping and caravanning parks in Britain and Ireland of varying quality: this guide contains impartially written reports on over 650, including many of the very finest, each being individually inspected and selected. We aim to provide you with a selection of the best, rather than information on all – in short, a more selective, qualitative approach. New, improved maps and indexes are also included, designed to help you find the choice of campsite that's right for you.

We hope you enjoy some happy and safe travels – and some pleasurable 'armchair touring' in the meantime!

" ...the campsites included in this book have been chosen entirely on merit, and no payment of any sort is made by them for their inclusion."

Alan Rogers, 1968

How do we find the best?

The criteria we use when inspecting and selecting campsites are numerous, but the most important by far is the question of good quality. People want different things from their choice of site so we try to include a range of campsite 'styles' to cater for a wide variety of preferences: from those seeking a small peaceful park in the heart of the countryside, to visitors looking for an 'all singing, all dancing' park in a popular seaside resort. Those with more specific interests, such as sporting facilities, cultural events or historical attractions, are also catered for.

The size of the park, whether it's part of a chain or privately owned, makes no difference in terms of it being required to meet our exacting standards in respect of its quality and it being 'fit for purpose'. In other words, irrespective of the size of the park, or the number of facilities it offers, we consider and evaluate the welcome, the pitches, the sanitary facilities, the cleanliness, the general maintenance and even the location.

Understanding the entries

Facilities

Toilet blocks

Unless we comment otherwise, toilet blocks will be equipped with WCs, washbasins with hot and cold water and hot showers with dividers or curtains, and will have all necessary shelves, hooks, plugs and mirrors. We also assume that there will be an identified chemical toilet disposal point, and that the campsite will provide water and waste water drainage points and bin areas. If not the case, we comment. We do mention certain features that some readers find important: washbasins in cubicles, facilities for babies, facilities for those with disabilities and motorcaravan service points. Readers with disabilities are advised to contact the site of their choice to ensure that facilities are appropriate to their needs.

Shop

Basic or fully supplied, and opening dates.

Bars, restaurants, takeaway facilities and entertainment

We try hard to supply opening and closing dates (if other than the campsite opening dates) and to identify if there are discos or other entertainment.

Children's play areas

Fenced and with safety surface (e.g. sand, bark or pea-gravel).

Swimming pools

If particularly special, we cover in detail in our main campsite description but reference is always included under our Facilities listings. We will also indicate the existence of water slides, sunbathing areas and other features. Opening dates, charges and levels of supervision are provided where we have been notified.

Leisure facilities

For example, playing fields, bicycle hire, organised activities and entertainment.

Dogs

If dogs are not accepted or restrictions apply, we state it here. Check the quick reference list at the back of the guide.

Off site

This briefly covers leisure facilities, tourist attractions, restaurants etc. nearby.

Charges

These are the latest provided to us by the parks. In those cases where 2016 prices have not been provided to us by the parks, we try to give a general guide.

Opening dates

These are advised to us during the early autumn of the previous year – parks can, and sometimes do, alter these dates before the start of the following season. If you intend to visit shortly after a published opening date, or shortly beforethe closing date, it is wise to check that it will actually be open at the time required. Similarly some parks operate a restricted service during the low season, only opening some of their facilities (e.g. swimming pools) during the main season; where we know about this, and have the relevant dates, we indicate it – again if you are at all doubtful it is wise to check.

Sometimes, campsite amenities may be dependant on there being enough customers on site to justify their openingand, for this reason, actual opening datesmay vary from those indicated.

Non-geographic telephone numbers

In this guide we do not include any numbers that impose an extra charge on callers to that number (e.g. 084x or 03xx). Where Freephone numbers appear (0800 or 0808), calls to these numbers are free of charge.

Taking a tent?

In recent years, sales of tents have increased dramatically. With very few exceptions, the campsites listed in this guide have pitches suitable for tents, caravans and motorcaravans. Tents, of course, come in a dazzling range of shapes and sizes. Modern family tents with separate sleeping pods are increasingly popular and these invariably require large pitches with electrical connections. Smaller lightweight tents, ideal for cyclists and hikers, are also visible on many sites and naturally require correspondingly smaller pitches. Many (but not all) sites have special tent areas with prices adjusted accordingly. If in any doubt, we recommend contacting the site of your choice beforehand.

Our Holiday Home section

308 Over recent years, more and more parks in Britain and Ireland have added high quality holiday home accommodation in the form of caravan holiday homes, chalets and lodges. In response to feedback from many of our readers, and to reflect this evolution in campsites, we have decided to introduce a separate section on caravan holiday homes and chalets (see page 308). If a park has decided to contribute to this section, it is indicated above our site report in the main body of the guide with a page reference where the full details are given. We feature parks offering some of the best accommodation available and have included full details of one or two accommodation types at these parks.

Please note however that many other campsites listed in this guide may also have a selection of accommodation for rent.

You're on your way!

Whether you're an 'old hand' in terms of camping and caravanning or are contemplating your first trip, a regular reader of our Guides or a new 'convert', we wish you well in your travels and hope we have been able to help in some way.

We are, of course, also out and about ourselves, visiting parks, talking to owners and readers, and generally checking on standards and new developments.

We wish all our readers thoroughly enjoyable Camping and Caravanning in 2016 – favoured by good weather of course!

The Alan Rogers Team

Scotland
page 248

Northern
Ireland
page 275

Northumbria
page 214

Cumbria
page 203

Yorkshire
page 177

North West
England
page 195

Republic of Ireland
page 283

Heart of England
page 150

Wales
page 221

East of England
page 133

Southern
England
page 101

South West England
page 14

South East
England
page 116

London
page 129

Channel Islands
page 303

9

The Alan Rogers Awards

The Alan Rogers Campsite Awards were launched in 2004 and have proved a great success.

Our awards have a broad scope and before committing to our winners, we carefully consider more than 2,000 campsites featured in our guides, taking into account comments from our site assessors, our head office team and, of course, our readers.

Our award winners come from the four corners of Europe, from Spain to Croatia, and this year we are making awards to campsites in ten different countries.

Needless to say, it's an extremely difficult task to choose our eventual winners, but we believe that we have identified a number of campsites with truly outstanding characteristics.

In each case, we have selected an outright winner, along with two highly commended runners-up. Listed below are full details of each of our award categories and our winners for 2015.

Alan Rogers Progress Award 2015

This award reflects the hard work and commitment undertaken by particular site owners to improve and upgrade their site.

Winner		
ES84800	Camping Resort Sanguli Salou	*Spain*

Runners-up		
FR31000	Sites et Paysages Le Moulin	*France*
UK2450	The Orchards Holiday Caravan and Camping Park	*England*

Alan Rogers Welcome Award 2015

This award takes account of sites offering a particularly friendly welcome and maintaining a friendly ambience throughout readers' holidays.

Winner		
FR35080	Domaine du Logis	*France*

Runners-up		
ES88020	Camping Cabopino	*Spain*
NL5840	Veluwecamping de Pampel	*Netherlands*

Alan Rogers Active Holiday Award 2015

This award reflects sites in outstanding locations which are ideally suited for active holidays, notably walking or cycling, but which could extend to include such activities as winter sports or watersports.

Winner

| AU0180 | Sportcamp Woferlgut *Austria* |

Runners-up

| DE30030 | Camping Wulfener Hals *Germany* |
| IT62040 | Camping Seiser Alm *Italy* |

Alan Rogers Innovation Award 2015

Our Innovation Award acknowledges campsites with creative and original concepts, possibly with features which are unique, and cannot therefore be found elsewhere. We have identified innovation both in campsite amenities and also in rentable accommodation.

Winner

| IT60200 | Camping Union Lido Vacanze *Italy* |

Runners-up

| FR29010 | Castel Camping Ty Nadan *France* |
| FR24350 | RCN Le Moulin de la Pique *France* |

Alan Rogers Small Campsite Award 2015

This award acknowledges excellent small campsites (less than 75 pitches) which offer a friendly welcome and top quality amenities throughout the season to their guests.

Winner

| IT64045 | Camping Tenuta Squaneto *Italy* |

Runners-up

| FR02020 | Camping Les Etangs du Moulin *France* |
| DE34380 | Camping Am Möslepark *Germany* |

Alan Rogers Seaside Award 2015

This award is made for sites which we feel are outstandingly suitable for a really excellent seaside holiday.

Winner

| FR17010 | Camping Bois Soleil *France* |

Runners-up

| NL6870 | Kennemer Duincamping de Lakens *Netherlands* |
| CR6782 | Zaton Holiday Resort *Croatia* |

Alan Rogers Country Award 2015

This award contrasts with our former award and acknowledges sites which are attractively located in delightful, rural locations.

Winner

| AU0265 | Park Grubhof *Austria* |

Runners-up

| FR12160 | Camping Les Peupliers *France* |
| SW2630 | Röstånga Camping & Bad *Sweden* |

Alan Rogers Family Site Award 2015

Many sites claim to be child friendly but this award acknowledges the sites we feel to be the very best in this respect.

Winner

| ES80400 | Camping Las Dunas *Spain* |

Runners-up

| UK0845 | Hillhead Caravan Club Site *England* |
| LU7620 | Europacamping Nommerlayen *Luxembourg* |

Alan Rogers Readers' Award 2015

We believe our Readers' Award to be the most important. We simply invite our readers (by means of an on-line poll at www.alanrogers.com) to nominate the site they enjoyed most.

The outright winner for 2015 is:

Winner

| FR38010 | Camping Le Coin Tranquille *France* |

Our warmest congratulations to all our award winners and our commiserations to all those not having won an award on this occasion.

The Alan Rogers Team

What are you looking for?

Best of British, a group of high quality, family owned touring and holiday parks, provides you with a choice of 55 prestigious parks throughout the UK offering a variety of accommodation. You can take your tent, touring caravan or motorhome or, if you prefer, you can book a caravan holiday home, chalet or lodge for your holiday – the choice is yours! Go to **www.bob.org.uk** for full details of our member parks – some offer online booking facilities – or you can email the parks you are interested in direct from their individual page on **www.bob.org.uk** if you prefer.

A warm welcome wherever you go

Whichever Best of British park you choose, you can be sure that you will receive the warmest of welcomes and a very high standard of customer service.

Visit the Best of British website

Go to **www.bob.org.uk** to register for a **FREE** Best of British loyalty card and see details of the special offers available on the parks, sign up for the e-newsletter, or to request a full colour brochure.

A brochure and/or loyalty card can also be obtained by writing to
PO Box 28249, Edinburgh, EH9 2YZ

Visit www.bob.org.uk

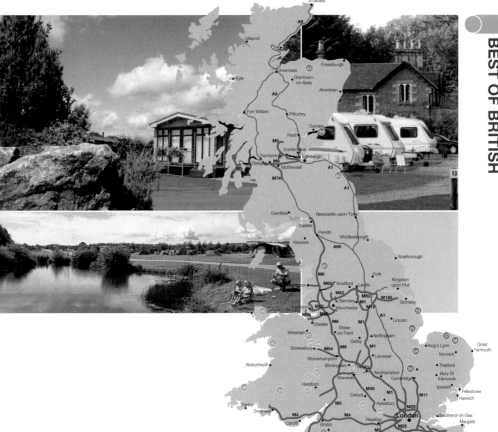

South West England

4 Bath Chew Valley Caravan Park
5 Beverley Park
6 Dolbeare Park
7 Dornafield
8 East Fleet Farm Touring Park
9 Green Hill Farm Caravan **NEW**
and Camping Park
10 Hendra Holiday Park
11 Hidden Valley Park
12 Highlands End Holiday Park
13 Ladram Bay Holiday Park **NEW**
14 Oakdown Country Holiday Park
15 The Old Oaks Touring Park
16 Polmanter Touring Park
17 Ross Park Caravan Park
18 Shamba Holidays
19 South Lytchett Manor
20 Trethem Mill Touring Park
21 Trevalgan Touring Park
22 Trevornick Holiday Park
23 Wareham Forest Tourist Park
24 Waterrow Touring Park
25 Webbers Park
26 Wilksworth Farm Caravan **NEW**
Park
27 Wood Farm
28 Wooda Farm Holiday Park
29 Woodlands Grove Caravan
and Camping Park
30 Woodovis Park

South East England

32 Broadhembury Caravan
and Camping Park
33 Concierge Camping **NEW**
34 The Orchards Holiday Park
35 Tanner Farm Touring Caravan
and Camping Park
36 Whitefield Forest Touring **NEW**
Park

Wales

38 Cenarth Falls Holiday Park
39 Erwlon Caravan and
Camping Park
40 Home Farm Caravan Park
41 Plassey
42 Trawsdir Touring Caravans
and Camping Park

Central England

44 Beaconsfield
45 Lincoln Farm Park Oxfordshire
46 Oxon Hall Touring and Holiday
Home Park
47 Poston Mill Park
48 Somers Wood Caravan Park
49 Swiss Farm Touring and Camping
50 Townsend
51 Westbrook Park

Eastern England

53 Cherry Tree Touring Park
54 Fields End Water Caravan Park
55 Long Acres Touring Park
56 Stroud Hill Park
57 The Old Brick Kilns
58 Two Mills Touring Park

Nortern England

60 Ord House Country Park
61 Riverside Caravan Park

Scotland

63 Aberlour Gardens Caravan
and Camping Park
64 Riverview Caravan Park

THE SOUTH WEST COMPRISES: CORNWALL, DEVON, SOMERSET, BATH, BRISTOL, SOUTH GLOUCESTERSHIRE, WILTSHIRE AND DORSET

The West Country is a region of contrasts, with windswept moorlands and dramatic cliffs towering above beautiful sandy beaches. Its bustling cities are a fascinating mix of history and contemporary culture.

With its dramatic cliffs pounded by the Atlantic ocean, and beautiful coastline boasting warm waters, soft sandy beaches and small seaside towns, Cornwall is one of England's most popular holiday destinations. The coast is also a surfers' paradise, while inland the wild and rugged Bodmin Moors dominate the landscape. In Devon, the Dartmoor National Park has sweeping moorland and granite tors where wild ponies roam freely. Much of the countryside is gentle, rolling, green fields, dotted with pretty thatched cottages. The coastline around Torbay is known as the English Riviera which, due to its temperate climate, allows palm trees to grow. Stretching across East Devon and West Dorset is the fossil-rich Jurassic Coast, a World Heritage Site. Dorset boasts several popular seaside resorts including Swanage, and Bournemouth, with its seven miles of golden sand. This stretch of coast is also home to Europe's largest natural harbour at Poole Bay. Famous for its cider and cheese, Somerset is good walking country, with the Exmoor National Park, which also straddles Devon. Wiltshire's natural attractions include the Marlborough Downs, Savernake Forest and the River Avon. It also boasts one of the most famous prehistoric sites in the world, the ancient stone circles of Stonehenge.

Places of interest

Bath: Roman and modern spas; Fashion Museum housing costumes from the 16th century. Bath Abbey with 212 steps to the top of the tower.

Bristol: Brunel's Clifton Suspension bridge; St Nicholas Market and the old city; vibrant harbourside area with bars, restaurants and cultural events.

Cornwall: historic Tintagel Castle, reputed birthplace of King Arthur; Tate Gallery, St Ives; Barbara Hepworth Museum and Sculpture Garden.

Devon: Exeter Cathedral; World Heritage Jurassic Coast; the granite rocks of Dartmoor; pretty harbours at Clovelly and Ilfracombe.

Dorset: Monkey World near Wareham; village of Cerne Abbas, with Cerne Giant. Dorchester, home of Thomas Hardy.

Somerset: Weston-Super-Mare; Wells Cathedral; Glastonbury; Cheddar Gorge and Wookey Hole caves.

Wiltshire: Longleat stately home and safari park; Stourhead House and gardens; the historic market town of Devizes.

Did you know?

Longleat pioneered the first drive-through safari park outside of Africa in 1966.

Silbury Hill dates back to around 2,400 BC and is the largest Neolithic mound of its kind in Europe.

Cornwall has over 300 beaches, including Fistral Beach, a magnet for surfers and the largest in Cornwall.

Pulteney Bridge in Bath is one of only a few bridges in the world with shops built into it.

Avebury houses the largest stone circle in Europe, believed to be 4,500 years old.

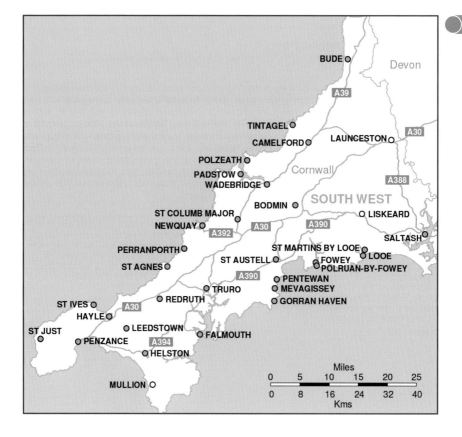

Bodmin
Eden Valley Holiday Park

Lanlivery, Lostwithiel, Bodmin PL30 5BU (Cornwall) T: 01208 872277.

E: enquiries@edenvalleyholidaypark.co.uk **alanrogers.com/UK0280**

Eden Valley Holiday Park is a pleasant, peaceful, family run touring park with plenty of sheltered lawns and a natural, uncommercialised atmosphere. This has been enhanced by careful planting of trees and shrubs to form a series of linked grassy areas with an unfenced stream running through. There are 56 numbered touring pitches spread around the perimeter of small glades. There are 16 pitches on neatly mown grass and 40 hardstandings, all with 16A electricity. Awning groundsheets must be lifted on alternate days. A separate field contains 39 private caravan holiday homes. A large, well equipped activity play area with adventure-style equipment is set out on grass. Families and couples are welcome to enjoy their surroundings with colourful trees, grassy paddocks and a stream. The owners are developing one field with log cabins for sale or rent. The village pub is within walking distance and there are several good local restaurants. Indoor tennis courts (Bodmin) and a swimming pool are nearby. The Eden Project is very close. The nearest beach is four miles away at Par.

Facilities

The smart, heated log cabin toilet block has en-suite facilities. A more traditional block has individual cubicles. Unit for disabled visitors. Laundry room. Motorcaravan services. Shop. Gas supplies. Large play area. Games room. Bicycle hire (delivered to site). WiFi over site (charged). Off site: Golf 2 miles. Beach 3.5 miles. Fishing 4 miles. Riding 6 miles.

Open: 1 April - 31 October.

Directions

Park approach road leads off A390 road 1.5 miles southwest of Lostwithiel. Follow white or brown camping signs. Do not follow signs for Lanlivery. GPS: 50.40162, -4.69742

Charges guide

Per unit incl. 2 persons and electricity	£ 14.00 - £ 18.00
extra person	£ 2.00
child (4-15 yrs)	£ 1.50
dog	£ 1.00 - £ 2.00

No single sex groups (excl. bona fide organisations).

For latest campsite news visit
alanrogers.com

Bodmin

Mena Caravan & Camping Park

Lanivet, Bodmin PL30 5HW (Cornwall) T: 01208 831845. E: mena@campsitesincornwall.co.uk

alanrogers.com/UK0270

A pleasant family run park, tucked away in the Cornish countryside, yet close to the main routes. It is open all year and a warm welcome awaits visitors. Set in 15 acres of secluded countryside with rural views, it is spacious and never crowded, offering only 25 level grass pitches on well drained, slightly sloping grass. There are 21 electricity connections (10A) and three hardstandings. Next to reception is a popular, reasonably priced café serving breakfast, afternoon tea and evening meals. Essential items can be purchased in reception. There is a small fishing lake and a wooded area. Mena means 'hilltop' in the Cornish language, and the site is actually situated at the geographical centre of Cornwall, overlooked by Helman's Tor, one of the highest points on Bodmin Moor. With its position visitors can choose between beaches on the north or south coast. Lanivet village has a shop and a pub serving meals. Children will love the chickens and two large Kune pigs.

Facilities

Toilet blocks with some en-suite cubicles and facilities for disabled campers. Family shower room. Laundry. Shop (1/1-31/1). Takeaway (1/5-30/9). Large games room with TV, a three-quarter size snooker table and darts. Swings, etc. for children in the central grass area. Fishing lake (licence required). Two mobile homes for hire. Caravan storage. WiFi (charged). Dog kennel facilities. Off site: Riding 1.5 miles. Lanivet village with shop and pub 2 miles. Golf and bicycle hire 3 miles. Eden Project 4 miles. Nearest beach 8 miles.

Open: All year.

Directions

Leave A30 Bodmin bypass, take A389 north (Lanivet, Bodmin). After 0.5 miles take first right (filter lane) and pass under A30. First left (Lostwithiel, Fowey) and in 0.25 miles turn right at top of hill (by Celtic cross). Continue for 0.5 miles and take first right into lane and site in 100 yds. GPS: 50.430267, -4.757167

Charges guide

Per unit incl. 2 persons and electricity	£ 19.00 - £ 24.00
extra person	£ 5.00 - £ 6.00
child (3-16 yrs)	£ 1.00 - £ 2.50
dog	free

Bodmin

South Penquite Farm

South Penquite, Blisland, Bodmin PL30 4LH (Cornwall) T: 01208 850491. E: thefarm@bodminmoor.co.uk

alanrogers.com/UK0302

South Penquite offers real camping with no frills. It is set on a 200-hectare hill farm, high on Bodmin Moor between the villages of Blisland and Saint Breward. The farm achieved organic status in 2001 and runs a flock of 100 ewes and a herd of 20 cattle and horses. The camping is small scale and intended to have a low impact on the surrounding environment. Fifty tents or simple motorcaravans (no caravans) can pitch around the edge of three walled fields, roughly cut in the midst of the moor. You can find shelter or a view. Four yurts are available to rent in one field, complete with wood burning stoves – quite original. Campfires are permitted with wood available from the farmhouse. You will also find horses, ponies, chickens, geese, ducks and turkeys which show their approval (or not) by the skin around their necks changing colour! A walk of some two miles takes you over most of the farm and some of the moor, taking in a Bronze Age hut settlement, the river and a standing stone. It is also possible to fish for brown trout on the farm's stretch of the De Lank river, a tributary of the Camel. The farm's website offers a fascinating insight into life and work at South Penquite.

Facilities

A smart new pine-clad toilet block, with a separate provision of four family-sized showers, with solar-heated rainwater. Washing machine and dryer. Small fridge and freezer. Home produced lamb, burgers and sausages available. Facilities for field studies and opportunities for educational groups and schools to learn about the local environment. Bush craft days. Arts workshops. Fishing (requires an EA rod licence and tokens available from the West Country Rivers Trust). Dogs are not accepted. Off site: Riding and cycling 1 mile. Pubs 1.5 and 2.5 miles. Beach 16 km. Sustrans Route 3 passes close by. North and south coasts within easy reach.

Open: 1 April - 31 October.

Directions

On A30 Bodmin Moor pass Jamaica Inn and sign for Colliford Lake and watch for St Breward sign (to right) immediately at end of dual carriageway. Follow narrow road over moor for 2 miles ignoring any turns, including right turn to St Breward just before South Penquite sign. Follow track over stone bridge through farm gate, then bear left to camping fields. Book in at Farm House. GPS: 50.5445, -4.671833

Charges guide

Per person	£ 8.00
child (5-15 yrs)	£ 4.00

Less 10% for stays of 5 nights or more. No credit cards.

For latest campsite news visit
alanrogers.com

Bodmin

Ruthern Valley Holidays

Ruthernbridge, Bodmin PL30 5LU (Cornwall) T: 01208 831395. E: holidays@ruthernvalley.com

alanrogers.com/UK0306

This is a little gem of a site set in eight acres of woodland, tucked away in a peaceful little valley not far from Bodmin. Run by Andrew and Nicola Johnson, the park was landscaped over 30 years ago with an amazing range of trees and shrubs, and there is plenty of animal wildlife. There are just eight touring pitches in a tree-lined field, informally spaced but numbered in the main, all with 10A electricity. There are three caravan holiday homes, four wigwams and three camping huts. The bubbling stream is an attraction for children and now there are some chickens and farm animals in an additional field, not to mention some adventure-type play equipment in an area set away from the pitches. A toilet block and a little shop complete the provision. Ruthern is a special place to unwind and enjoy the simple pleasures of life. Go walking, cycling or birdwatching (38 different species of bird have been recorded).

Facilities

The small, fully equipped toilet block has gas- and solar-heated water. Washing machines and dryer. Shop with basic provisions shares with reception (reduced hours in low season). Barbecue hire. Play area including five-a-side goal posts. Field with farm animals. Bicycle hire. Wetsuit and bodyboard hire. Free WiFi. Dogs are not accepted. Off site: Fishing 2 miles. Nearest pub 3-4 miles. Riding, pony trekking and golf 4 miles. Coast 10 miles.

Open: All year.

Directions

Do not use satnav which suggests unsuitable roads. From A30 St Austell/Innis Downs junction turn right to Lanivet, through town then towards Bodmin. After about 1 mile turn left and follow brown chalet sign to Nanstallon. Just before Nanstallon turn left for 100 m. then left again and following road into Ruthernbridge. At Ruthernbridge turn left just before stone bridge and site is on left in 300 m. GPS: 50.46455, -4.8019

Charges guide

Per unit incl. 2 persons and electricity	£ 16.00 - £ 25.00
extra person (over 3 yrs)	£ 3.50 - £ 5.00

Bude

Wooda Farm Holiday Park

Poughill, Bude EX23 9HJ (Cornwall) T: 01288 352069. E: enquiries@wooda.co.uk

alanrogers.com/UK0380

Wooda Farm is spacious and well organised with some nice touches. A quality, family run park, it is part of a working farm set within 40 acres, under two miles from the sandy, surfing beaches of Bude. In peaceful farmland with plenty of open spaces (and some up and down walking), there are beautiful views of the sea and countryside. The 220 large touring pitches are spread over four meadows on level or gently sloping grass. There are 142 with 16A electricity connections, and 83 hardstanding, hedged premier pitches (electricity, water, waste water), linked by tarmac roads. A 28-day field with electricity provides extra grass pitches for the peak season. A late arrivals area has electricity. A member of the Green Tourism Scheme and Best of British group and Caravan Club affiliated. Beside the shop and reception at the entrance are 55 caravan holiday homes for let. A takeaway service is available near reception and an attractive courtyard bar and restaurant with home cooking is popular. A few friendly farm animals are popular with children. Tractor and trailer rides, archery and clay pigeon shooting with tuition are provided according to season and demand, plus woodland (find the pixies) and orchard walks and excellent coarse fishing. There is much to do in the area – sandy beaches with coastal walks, and Tintagel with King Arthur's castle and Clovelly nearby.

Facilities

Three well maintained and equipped toilet blocks, one with private cubicles. A unit suitable for disabled campers, two baby rooms and five family bathrooms for hire (small charge). Dog washing area. Two laundry rooms. Motorcaravan services. Self-service shop with off-licence (all season). Courtyard bar/restaurant and takeaway (reduced hours out of season). Play area in separate field. 9-hole fun golf course (clubs provided). Games room with TV, table tennis and pool. Badminton. Tennis. Fitness suite. Coarse fishing in 1.5-acre lake (permits from reception, £2 per half day, £3 per day). Certain breeds of dog not accepted. Caravan storage. Caravan workshop with accessories. Internet access. WiFi over site (charged). Off site: Local village inn is five minutes walk. Riding, bicycle hire and boat launching all within 1.5 miles. Leisure Centre and Splash Pool in Bude.

Open: 28 March - 1 November.

Directions

Park is north of Bude at Poughill and well signed; turn left off A39 on north side of Stratton on minor road for Coombe Valley, following camp signs at junctions. GPS: 50.84359, -4.51795

Charges guide

Per unit incl. 2 persons and electricity	£ 19.00 - £ 30.00
extra person	£ 5.00 - £ 7.00
child (3-15 yrs)	£ 3.00 - £ 4.50
incl. water and drainage	£ 24.00 - £ 35.00

For latest campsite news visit

alanrogers.com

Bude

Pentire Haven Holiday Park

Stibb Road, Kilkhampton, Bude EX23 9QY (Cornwall) T: 01288 321601. E: holidays@pentirehaven.co.uk

alanrogers.com/UK0385

Pentire Haven is a quiet family site, under new management, located close to the popular resort of Bude. The original part of the site has 220 touring pitches with 16A electrical connections, and some with hardstanding; 54 are terraced super pitches with electricity, water and drainage. The more open area near reception has 100 level, grassy tent pitches in separate fields. The use of natural wood for the swimming pool area and fencing gives it a range-style feel. The park has an arrangement with the adjacent residential site (Penstone Manor) to share its amenities, including a bar/restaurant and a pool. Bude is renowned for the variety of holiday experiences on offer and can be reached in five minutes. It is a great centre for exploring Cornwall, with many opportunities for walking, cycling, fishing, golf and birdwatching. Coastal walks around Bude and Kilkhampton are always rewarding and the quaint seaside towns of Padstow and Perranporth are within easy reach, as are historic sites such as King Arthur's legendary castle at Tintagel.

Facilities

One new toilet block plus two older, renovated blocks are heated and have preset showers and some washbasins in cubicles. Facilities for disabled visitors (shower in 1 block). Washing machine. Motorcaravan services. Shop. Swimming pool (heated 21/7-1/9). Play area. TV room. Free WiFi over site. Entertainment next door at Penstone Manor. Off site: Nearest beach 5 minutes. Riding nearby. Shops and restaurants in Bude. Walking and cycle trails. Fishing 3 miles. Golf, bicycle hire and boat launching 5 miles. Surfing.

Open: All year.

Directions

Approaching from the south (Bude), head north on the A39. Turn right towards Stibb just before entering Kilkhampton and site entrance is almost immediately on right. GPS: 50.869086, -4.494175

Charges guide

Per unit incl. 2 persons and electricity	£ 17.00 - £ 30.50
extra person	£ 3.00 - £ 6.00
child (3-13 yrs)	£ 2.50 - £ 4.50
dog	£ 1.50 - £ 2.00

Bude

Budemeadows Touring Park

Widemouth Bay, Bude EX23 0NA (Cornwall) T: 01288 361646. E: holiday@budemeadows.com

alanrogers.com/UK0370

Budemeadows is a friendly, family run park catering for touring outfits. The park is beautifully landscaped and the pitches are arranged in small groups, separated by colourful shrubs and hedging offering just a little shade. There are 145 large, level pitches all for touring, 120 have 16A electricity and 35 are on hardstandings. The large play areas with swings, slides and a football field will delight the younger children. For the intellectuals, there is an outdoor giant chess set! There is a well stocked shop and at Whitsun and summer school holidays, a bar offers meals and takeaways. This area has a great deal to offer the holidaymaker – wonderful scenery, a challenging coastal path and many cycle routes down the small lanes. The wonderful beaches are a magnet for lovers of watersports, particularly surfing.

Facilities

Two older style, well appointed heated toilet blocks include a family bathroom and a separate building with en-suite facilities for disabled visitors. Small shop and bar (Whitsun-31/9), takeaway (Whitsun and July/Aug). Outdoor heated swimming pool and paddling pool. Play area. Games/TV room. Hedged barbecue areas. WiFi throughout (free in bar). Off site: Widemouth Bay 1 mile, Bude 3 miles. Fishing, bicycle hire, boat launching and riding 5 miles. Golf 7 miles.

Open: All year.

Directions

Leave M5 at exit 27, signed Barnstable. Take A361 then A39 signed Bideford and Bude. Continue on A39 3 miles beyond Stratton. Look for layby just beyond crossroads to Widemouth Bay. Enter layby, Budemeadows is first park on left. GPS: 50.783878, -4.53525

Charges guide

Per unit incl. 2 persons and electricity	£ 17.00 - £ 29.50
extra person	£ 6.25 - £ 7.75
child	£ 3.00 - £ 4.75
dog	£ 1.00 - £ 2.50
Pitch and awning included.	

For latest campsite news visit
alanrogers.com

Bude

Widemouth Bay Caravan Park

Widemouth Bay, Bude EX23 0DF (Cornwall) T: 01288 361208.

alanrogers.com/UK0373

Widemouth has a wonderful situation on the edge of Widemouth Bay amidst rural farmland. Covering 50 acres in total, a number of areas have mobile homes carefully fitted into the hillside. There are some 180 touring pitches on undulating meadowland at the top of the hill, with 16A electricity available and some level hardstandings. The views are magnificent. The sandy beach, just a 15 minute walk away, is very popular with bathers and surfers and the indoor heated swimming pool is a bonus. This is a big and lively park in season, very well catered for with a well stocked shop, a bar serving food and nightly entertainment for children and parents.

Facilities

Two traditional, fully equipped toilet blocks. Facilities for babies and an en-suite unit for visitors with disabilities. Launderette. Microwave. Shop, bar with food, and takeaway (limited hours). Indoor heated pool with lifeguard. Entertainment, quizzes, disco. Kids' club. Amusement arcade. Play area. Internet café/WiFi. Minigolf. Bus service. Mobile homes to rent. Off site: Tennis and riding nearby. Fishing and boat trips from Bude.

Open: 5 March - 31 October.

Directions

Using the A39 bypass Bude and after 3 miles watch for right-hand turning for Widemouth Bay. Follow to beach and continue south alongside beach. Turn left by the Manor Hotel. Lane to site on right. GPS: 50.78033, -4.5613

Charges guide

Per unit incl. 2 persons
and electricity   £ 14.00 - £ 41.00

Camelford

Lakefield Caravan Park

Lower Pendavey Farm, Camelford PL32 9TX (Cornwall) T: 01840 213279.

E: enquiries@lakefieldcaravanpark.co.uk alanrogers.com/UK0360

Lakefield is a small touring park on what was a working farm. Now the main focus is on the BHS-approved equestrian centre. With only 40 pitches, it is no surprise that the owners, Maureen and Dennis Perring, know all the campers. The well spaced pitches backing onto hedges and with 34 electric hook-ups (16A) are in view of the small, fenced lake watched over by one of Cornwall's first wind farms. The white-washed café/reception, converted from one of the old barns, is open all day between Easter and October. Children will love the goats and 'Wabbit World'.

Facilities

Simple but adequate toilet block. Washing machine and dryer in the ladies. Toilet for disabled visitors at riding centre. Café in reception. Gas supplies (Calor). Torches may be useful. WiFi (free). Off site: Golf 2 miles. Fishing: sea 4 miles, coarse 5 miles.

Open: 1 April - 30 September.

Directions

Follow B3266 north from Camelford. Park access is directly from this road on the left just before the turning for Tintagel, clearly signed. GPS: 50.635058, -4.687648

Charges guide

Per unit incl. 2 persons
and electricity   £ 15.50 - £ 18.50
extra person (5 yrs and over)   £ 1.00

Falmouth

Pennance Mill Farm Chalet & Camping Park

Maenporth, Falmouth TR11 5HJ (Cornwall) T: 01326 317431. E: jewell5hj@btinternet.com

alanrogers.com/UK0450

Pennance Mill Farm has been in the hands of the Jewell family for three generations and is listed as a typical Cornish farmstead in an Area of Outstanding Natural Beauty where you can enjoy a woodland walk beneath 200-year-old beech trees. In high season, skittles, country games and barbecue evenings are organised, all in keeping with the relaxed and friendly atmosphere generated by the owners. The camping area is naturally set out in four sheltered, slightly sloping fields with views over the countryside. There are 75 pitches, 60 with 16A electricity and 12 are fully serviced on hardstanding.

Facilities

Two basic toilet blocks have all necessary facilities. Washing machine and dryer. Gas supplies. Small play meadow. Weekly skittles and games nights (July/Aug). Bus to Falmouth and beach. Off site: Tennis courts, golf course, pitch and putt within walking distance. Beach 0.5 miles. Watersports and indoor heated pool 2 miles. Riding 4 miles. Bar/restaurant/takeaway 5 miles. New Maritime Museum. Coastal footpath to the Helford River.

Open: Easter - November.

Directions

From Truro take A39 towards Falmouth. In Penryn pass ASDA, turn right at next roundabout signed Maenporth. Follow brown camping signs for 1.5 miles. Site on left just before Maenporth. GPS: 50.134983, -5.092667

Charges guide

Per unit incl. 2 persons
and electricity   £ 23.00 - £ 26.00
extra person   £ 7.00 - £ 8.00
No credit cards.

For latest campsite news visit

alanrogers.com

Fowey

Penmarlam Caravan & Camping Park

Bodinnick-by-Fowey, Fowey PL23 1LZ (Cornwall) T: 01726 870088. E: info@penmarlampark.co.uk

alanrogers.com/UK0195

Penmarlam is situated high above the estuary opposite Fowey, close to the village of Bodinnick which is famous for being the home of Daphne du Maurier. The original field is level and sheltered with 29 pitches which are semi-divided by bushes. The newer field with 34 pitches has a slight slope, is divided with wild banks and enjoys good countryside views. Both fields have circular access roads. All pitches have 16A electricity and 14 also have water and drainage. The modern reception, shop and the toilet facilities are well situated between the two fields. Reception is fitted with a loop system for deaf visitors and the owner can 'sign' as well as speaking French, Spanish and some German! Internet access is provided here, with wireless access from the pitches.

Facilities	Directions
The modern, colourful and heated toilet block is fully equipped including a baby and toddler room in the ladies' and a separate en-suite unit for disabled visitors, which doubles as a family room with baby changing. Laundry facilities. Well stocked, licensed shop with fresh fruit and vegetables. Coffee machine (extended hours in high season). Video, DVD and book library. WiFi (charged). Off site: Fishing and boat launching 500 yds. Beach 1 mile. Riding 3 miles. Golf 6 miles. Car and passenger ferry for Fowey.	From the main A390 road at East Taphouse take B3359 towards Looe. After 4 miles fork right, signed Bodinnick and ferry. Site is signed on the right 1 mile past village of Lanteglos Highway, just before Bodinnick village. GPS: 50.34434, -4.62289

Charges guide

Per unit incl. 2 persons	
and electricity	£ 17.50 - £ 29.50
extra person	£ 5.50 - £ 9.00
child (3-15 yrs)	£ 2.25 - £ 3.25
dog	free

Open: 1 April - 31 October.

Fowey

Penhale Caravan & Camping Park

Fowey PL23 1JU (Cornwall) T: 01726 833425. E: info@penhale-fowey.co.uk

alanrogers.com/UK0285

Located in an Area of Outstanding Natural Beauty, Penhale is a traditional campsite on four and a half acres of rolling farmland, with magnificent views across the countryside to Saint Austell Bay. The Berryman family run an arable and beef farm alongside the campsite. The atmosphere here is relaxed and there is plenty of room in the touring fields. The fields do slope, but a number of pitches have been levelled. In total, there are 56 pitches for all types of units, 41 with 16A electricity hook-ups. Ten holiday caravans occupy a separate field. It is possible to walk to Polkerris beach a mile away, and Fowey is just a mile and a half.

Facilities	Directions
One fully equipped toilet block at the bottom of the touring fields. Laundry room. Games room. Reception at the farmhouse stocks basics. WiFi. Off site: Garage with shop 600 yds. Sandy beach, pub and watersports centre at Polkerris beach 1 mile (windsurfing, sailing, paddle surf, kayak). Fishing, boat launching and shops and restaurants in Fowey 1.5 miles. Bicycle hire 5 miles. Three golf courses within 7 miles.	Take A390 almost to St Austell, then east on A3082 towards Fowey. The site entrance is on the right 1 mile before Fowey and 600 yds. before a roundabout and petrol station. GPS: 50.34309, -4.66848

Charges guide

Per unit incl. 2 persons	
and electricity	£ 17.00 - £ 25.00
extra person	£ 5.00 - £ 6.50
child (4-15 yrs)	£ 2.60

Open: Easter/1 April - 8 October.

Gorran Haven

Sea View International

Boswinger, Gorran Haven, Saint Austell PL26 6LL (Cornwall) T: 01726 843425. E: seaviewinternational.com

alanrogers.com/UK0150

Sea View is an impressive, well cared for park; its quality is reflected in the many awards it has won. Located at the gateway to the Roseland Peninsula on the south coast of Cornwall, with views of the sea and nearby Dodman Point, this park offers quality camping pitches, luxury self-catering lodges and caravan holiday homes. There are 227 pitches, 189 for touring, some on grass, some hardstanding, and all with 16A electricity. They vary in size (80-170 sq.m) and 69 are fully serviced. Some of the pitches are on open grass meadows while others are in their own large, hedged bays.

Facilities

Excellent heated toilet and shower blocks are well maintained including facilities for disabled visitors. Luxury en-suite rooms, one with bath. Fully equipped campers' kitchens. Launderette. Motorcaravan services. Good shop and off-licence (all season). Café/takeaway (May-Oct, free WiFi). Heated outdoor swimming pool. Large play area. Tennis and badminton courts, pitch and putt (all free). Extensive dog walk area. Off site: Community bus picks up at the park. Fishing. Boat launching and riding 2 miles. Bicycle hire 5 miles. Golf 9 miles.

Open: Easter - 31 October.

Directions

From St Austell take the B3273 towards Mevagissey for 3 miles. At top of steep hill turn right, signed Lost Gardens of Heligan and Sea View International. Follow road and brown signs to park. Last half mile down narrow lane. Do not go through Mevagissey. GPS: 50.2369, -4.820033

Charges guide

Per unit incl. 2 persons	
and electricity	£ 12.00 - £ 44.00
extra person	£ 3.00 - £ 6.00
child (3-15 yrs)	£ 4.00 - £ 6.00

Hayle

Beachside Holiday Park

Beachside, Hayle TR27 5AW (Cornwall) T: 01736 753080. E: reception@beachside.co.uk

alanrogers.com/UK0049

With its own access to one of Britain's most attractive beaches, 3.5 miles long, with golden sand washed daily by the incoming tide, Beachside is understandably popular with guests of all ages. The park, which has been family owned for over 50 years, has 87 slightly sloping grass touring pitches, most with 16A electricity, situated towards the back of the site from where there are views across St Ives Bay. Whether one wants to sit and enjoy the views, stroll along the miles of sandy beach or have a go at kite surfing, surfboarding or other forms of watersports the opportunity is there. The efficient reception has an abundance of useful advice and tourist information. Dogs are not accepted.

Facilities

Modern, well maintained sanitary block with controllable hot showers and facilities for babies and disabled visitors (access to the beach itself challenging). Launderette. Motorcaravan services. Shop with takeaway. Bar with live entertainment (mid May-mid Sept, from 7pm). Heated outdoor swimming pool with paddling pool (mid May-Sept). Games room with pool tables. Large grass playing field. Playgrounds. Surf school. WiFi (free by main building). Off site: Bus stop on request. St Ives. Land's End. The Eden Project. Gardens, galleries and museums. Watersports. Golf. Pony trekking. Theme Parks.

Open: Easter - 30 October.

Directions

Site is 1 mile northeast of Hayle. From A30 take exit for Hayle (Loggans Moor Roundabout). Head towards Hayle and go straight ahead at double mini roundabouts. Turn right at petrol station following brown tourist sign to Beachside. Site entrance is approximately 0.25 miles on right. GPS: 50.19613, -5.41023

Charges guide

Per unit incl. 2 persons	
and electricity	£ 15.00 - £ 41.00
extra person	£ 5.00
child	£ 3.00

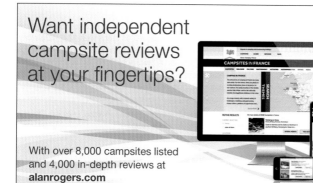

Helston
Silver Sands Holiday Park

Gwendreath, Ruan Minor, Helston TR12 7LZ (Cornwall) T: 01326 290631.
E: info@silversandsholidaypark.co.uk **alanrogers.com/UK0070**

Silver Sands is a small, peaceful 'away-from-it-all' park on the beautiful Lizard Peninsula, the most southerly part of mainland Britain. It is in an Area of Outstanding Natural Beauty and the beautiful beaches of Kennack Sands are within a half mile walk. The park has 35 pitches with 15 pitches for touring, all with 10/16A electricity. The caravan pitches are large, attractively situated and divided into individual bays by flowering shrubs and bushes. The adjoining tent field has large grassy pitches, some slightly sloping. There is plenty of free space for children to play and there is a very good play area.

Facilities

Fully equipped and very clean toilet block includes an en-suite room for families. Washing machine. TV room. Good play equipment. A three-acre field can be used for games, kite flying, etc. WiFi over part of site (charged). Off site: Restaurant nearby, pub within walking distance. Kennack Sands 0.5 miles. Fishing 1.5 miles. Boat launching 2 and 7 miles. Riding and bicycle hire 2 miles. Golf 9 miles. Interesting villages of Coverack and Cadwith.

Open: End March - end October.

Directions

From Helston take A3038 Lizard Road. After Culdrose turn left on B3293 passing Goonhilly after 4 miles. At next crossroads turn right (Kennack Sands), continue for 1.5 miles signed Gwendreath down single track narrow lane for 1 mile to site. GPS: 50.00900, -5.16900

Charges guide

Per unit incl. 2 persons, 2 children and electricity	£ 14.50 - £ 23.00
extra person	£ 3.50 - £ 4.00

Helston
Chy Carne Holiday Park

Kuggar, Ruan Minor, Helston TR12 7LX (Cornwall) T: 01326 290200. E: enquiries@chycarne.co.uk
alanrogers.com/UK0075

Situated on the Lizard Peninsula, the first impression of Chy Carne is of a traditional site with little stone bungalows and mobile homes at the entrance, but from the touring fields there are spectacular views of the sea and cliffs at Kennack Sands. In season, the owners erect large marquees so that the bar and takeaway have their own internal area to eat, drink and relax in. There is plenty of entertainment and music provided. The caravan field is level but the tent field is sloping with some terracing. The 150 pitches are marked by low, white chain fencing, some 100 with 10/16A electricity, and 60 with hardstanding. Some mobile homes and chalets are available to rent.

Facilities

One quite large toilet block is near the touring fields, with a small one at the far end. Fully equipped with showers (pink for ladies and blue for men) on payment (50p/5 mins). Double sized shower for use by families and disabled visitors. Laundry/washing up room. Shop, bar and takeaway selling pizzas (July/Aug when the marquees are put up). Games room with arcade games. Play area. Mobile fire baskets and chimneys available to hire. WiFi.

Open: March - November.

Directions

From Helston take A3083 towards the Lizard. Pass sign for Mullion then watch for left turn for Ruan Minor, (signed) for Kuggar. Site almost immediately on left on road to Kennack Sands. Bear right in Kuggar to site. GPS: 50.00404, -5.17625

Charges guide

Per unit incl. 2 persons	£ 12.00 - £ 17.00
incl. electricity	£ 17.25 - £ 22.25
extra person	£ 4.00 - £ 6.00

Helston
Lower Polladras Touring Park

Carleen, Helston TR13 9NX (Cornwall) T: 01736 762220. E: lowerpolladras@btinternet.com
alanrogers.com/UK0475

Lower Polladras is a small, friendly park located north of Helston in beautiful rolling Cornish countryside. There are 60 pitches, 44 reasonably level, grass touring pitches, 40 of them with 16A electricity. The remaining pitches are for mobile homes and seasonal campers. The site has a strong conservation interest and is actively working towards carbon neutral status. A two-acre area adjoining the park accommodates play equipment for children and a sports area. The upper level here is reserved for 28-day camping in the peak season. A nature and dog walk has been developed around the perimeter.

Facilities

Two refurbished toilet blocks, both clean and light. Large family shower room and en-suite facilities for disabled visitors. Baby changing area. Motorcaravan services. Small shop for basics (newspapers to order). Playground. Sports area. Nature and dog walk. Mobile homes for rent. WiFi (donation to charity). Off site: Golf 3 miles. Helston (shops and restaurants) 4 miles. Fishing 4 miles.

Open: 1 April - 4 January.

Directions

Take A394 from Helston towards Penzance. On edge of Helston, turn right onto B3302, signed Hayle. Take 2nd left to Carleen. In village take 2nd right and follow signs. GPS: 50.130156, -5.337199

Charges guide

Per unit incl. 2 persons and electricity	£ 17.25 - £ 23.25
extra person	£ 2.50 - £ 3.50

For latest campsite news visit
alanrogers.com

Helston

Franchis Holiday Park

Cury Cross Lanes, Near Mullion, Helston TR12 7AZ (Cornwall) T: 01326 240301. E: enquiries@franchis.co.uk
alanrogers.com/**UK0485**

A small rural site, Franchis is ideally situated for exploring the Lizard Peninsula in an Area of Outstanding Natural Beauty. Mature trees edge the site's two fields (a total of four acres) that slope slightly, with 57 pitches arranged around the perimeters, 57 with 10A electricity. Natural woodland areas and a stream will keep children occupied. Continuing past the fields into a wooded area are five small bungalows and seven static caravans, some privately owned and some to rent. There is a small toilet block for each field and a small shop that opens morning and evening.

Facilities

Two traditional small toilet blocks with showers. Two washing machines and two dryers. Freezer for ice blocks. Small shop (mid July-mid Sept). Small library. Play area. Dog exercise field (high season max. 1 dog). Mobile homes and chalets for rent. WiFi (charged). Off site: Golf, riding, beach, fishing and boat launching 2 miles. Sailing 4 miles. Helston 5 miles.

Open: 1 April - 15 October.

Directions

From Helston take the A3083 road towards Mullion and the Lizard. After 5 miles and passing the Wheel Inn, watch for site directly on the left. GPS: 50.039, -5.21843

Charges guide

Per unit incl. 2 persons and electricity	£ 20.00
extra person	£ 1.50 - £ 2.00

Leedstown

Calloose Caravan Park

Leedstown, Hayle TR27 5ET (Cornwall) T: 01736 850431. E: sales@calloose.co.uk
alanrogers.com/**UK0110**

A family touring park, Calloose is quietly situated in an inland valley, covering 12 acres. It is about four miles from Hayle with an extra half a mile to the beaches beyond, nine to Saint Ives on the north coast and six to Helston and Praa Sands on the south. Attractively landscaped, the terrain is dry and mainly flat with two slightly raised areas on terraces where 25 caravan holiday homes are located. There are 145 touring pitches (113 with 16A electricity, 35 with gravel hardstanding). Close together with individual markers, the pitches are mostly arranged around the perimeter with some free space in the middle.

Facilities

Both toilet blocks are well kept, providing washbasins in cubicles. Family shower room. Baby room. En-suite unit for disabled visitors. Laundry room. Motorcaravan services. Well stocked shop and off-licence (high season, including gas). Bar with bar meals (daily high season, w/ends early season). Takeaway (high season). Swimming pool (40x20 ft. mid May-mid Sept). TV lounge. Crazy golf. Adventure playground. Mountain bike hire (delivered to site). WiFi throughout (free). Off site: Village within 1 mile.

Open: 28 March - 3 October.

Directions

From crossroads of B3280 and B3302 in Leedstown take the B3302 towards Hayle. First right, then left on 0.5 miles access road to park. GPS: 50.169033, -5.360617

Charges guide

Per unit incl. 2 persons and electricity	£ 23.00 - £ 31.00

Looe

Tencreek Holiday Park

Polperro Road, Looe PL13 2JR (Cornwall) T: 01503 262447. E: reception@tencreek.co.uk
alanrogers.com/**UK0006**

Situated within walking distance of Cornwall's beautiful south coast, Tencreek is a family owned campsite with a friendly welcome which quite rightly justifies its description as a complete holiday park. Of the 350 pitches, about 100 are occupied by mobile homes, but the rest are reserved for touring units and tents, with most having hardstanding. The site gently slopes towards the coast and it is claimed that every pitch has a sea view. Although close to many local attractions, there is plenty on offer on site. Over the years the Joce family has continually invested in the park and the result is a well run site with clean, modern facilities, including a heated indoor pool, a bar and an all-weather multisports pitch.

Facilities

Two modern, well kept blocks provide toilets, showers and open style washbasins, plus 12 family washrooms. Facilities for disabled visitors. Full launderette. Shop. Bar with bar meals and takeaway, large screen TV and entertainment. Games room. Indoor pool with lifeguard. Multisports pitch. Play area. Organised entertainment for all ages. WiFi in bar area (free). Caravan holiday homes for rent. Off site: Beach, sailing, fishing and golf 2 miles. Polperro. Shark fishing in Looe. Eden Project.

Open: All year.

Directions

From Plymouth take A38, after 10 miles at big roundabout turn left towards Looe. Follow signs to Looe on A387 and B3253. In Looe turn right across bridge for Polperro. After 1.25 miles Tencreek is signed on left. The 400-yd. lane is narrow but there are passing places. GPS: 50.346191, -4.483177

Charges guide

Per unit incl. 2 persons and electricity	£ 16.50 - £ 35.00
extra person (over 3 yrs)	£ 2.00 - £ 3.50

For latest campsite news visit
alanrogers.com

Looe

Trelay Farmpark

Pelynt, Looe PL13 2JX (Cornwall) T: 01503 220900. E: stay@trelay.co.uk

alanrogers.com/UK0400

This quiet, small but spacious site is located in an Area of Outstanding Natural Beauty, and easily accessed from the B3359. It lies a little back from the coast, just over three miles from the lively port of Looe and the pretty fishing village of Polperro. Despite the name, there is no farm. On your right as you drive in, and quite attractively arranged amongst herbaceous shrubs, are caravan holiday homes (15 privately owned, some let by the park). The touring area has 30 pitches, six with hardstanding and all with 16A Europlug, in addition to some holiday homes and a play area. The coastal path is nearby and sandy beaches are within easy reach.

Facilities

Good, fully equipped, heated toilet block. En-suite unit with ramp for disabled visitors (key from reception). Baby bath. Washing machine and dryer. Gas supplies. Free use of fridge/freezer and ice pack service. WiFi (free). Off site: Village with pub, shops and bus service 0.5 miles. Looe and Polperro within 3 miles. Fishing, riding and boat launching 3 miles. Golf 6 miles.

Open: 30 March - end October.

Directions

From A390 Liskard-Lostwithiel road at East Taphouse, take B3359 south towards Looe. Site is on left (signed) 0.5 miles south of Pelynt. GPS: 50.36225, -4.518883

Charges guide

Per unit incl. 2 persons and electricity	£ 14.50 - £ 20.50
extra person	£ 3.50
child (0-17 yrs)	£ 1.50 - £ 2.50

Mevagissey

Tregarton Park

Gorran, Mevagissey, Saint Austell PL26 6NF (Cornwall) T: 01726 843666. E: reception@tregarton.co.uk

alanrogers.com/UK0155

Run by the welcoming Hicks family, the Tregarton Park estate itself dates back to the 16th century. The family have done well with their conversions to create a pleasing environment. The 12-acre caravan park is made up of four meadows with wonderful rural views. The 125 pitches, all with 10A electric hook-ups, 30 on hardstanding, are of a generous size with most separated by either hedges or fencing. All have been terraced as the park itself is quite hilly. Reception has a well stocked shop, tourist information and a takeaway service in season, offering freshly cooked food including a daily delivery of Cornish pasties.

Facilities

The fully equipped toilet block has been completely revamped and includes some excellent features. Facilities for disabled visitors. Laundry room. Well stocked shop with camping supplies (21/5-9/9), takeaway (28/5-9/9). Gas supplies. Heated swimming pool (21/5-9/9). Dog exercise meadow. Adventure playground. All weather tennis. WiFi (charged). Max. 2 dogs. Off site: Bus stop at entrance. Heligan Gardens, Mevagissey and beaches all 2 miles. Bicycle hire 3 miles. Golf 5 miles.

Open: 1 April - 3 October.

Directions

Leave St Austell travelling south on the B3273 and pass through London Apprentice and Pentewen. Follow Tregarton Park's brown tourist signs by turning right at the crossroads at the top of the hill towards Heligan and Gorran Haven. Do not go into Mevagissey. GPS: 50.2588, -4.829417

Charges guide

Per unit incl. 2 persons, electricity and awning	£ 19.00 - £ 46.00
extra person (over 17 yrs)	£ 4.00 - £ 8.00

Mevagissey

Sun Valley Holiday Park

Pentewan Road, Saint Austell Bay, Mevagissey PL26 6DJ (Cornwall) T: 01726 843 266.
E: hello@sunvalleyresort.co.uk **alanrogers.com/UK0255**

This very neat and tidy, family run holiday park sits in the sheltered grounds of a country house and is being extensively upgraded by its new owners. Sun Valley has the appearance of a beautiful park, helped by the wonderful cedar trees that are over 250 years old. The 72 caravan holiday homes have been carefully landscaped into the 20 acres, together with 28 level touring pitches (10A electricity), ten on hardstanding. Excellent facilities include a bar and restaurant where regular entertainment is arranged. There is an indoor heated swimming pool and tennis courts.

Facilities

Heated en-suite toilet facilities. Launderette. Shop (limited hours in low season). Bar/restaurant with regular entertainment. Takeaway. Activities and club for children. Indoor pool and paddling pool (all season). Play areas. Tennis. Bicycle hire. WiFi. Off site: Beach 1 mile. Golf 1.5 miles. Riding 5 miles. Bus stop at park entrance (hourly service).

Open: 22 March - 1 November.

Directions

From the St Austell ring road take B3273 south towards Mevagissey. After London Apprentice, watch for site entrance on right (about 1 mile). GPS: 50.3005, -4.801167

Charges guide

Per unit incl. 2 persons and electricity	£ 10.00 - £ 35.00
extra person	£ 1.00 - £ 3.00

For latest campsite news visit

alanrogers.com

Newquay
Trevella Holiday Park

Crantock, Newquay TR8 5EW (Cornwall) T: 01637 830308. E: holidays@trevella.co.uk

alanrogers.com/UK0170

Trevella has a longer season than most parks and is one of the best known and respected of the Cornish parks. It has many colourful flowerbeds and is a regular winner of a Newquay in Bloom award. Well organised, the pitches are in a number of adjoining meadows. The 150 slightly sloping touring pitches are in three different categories, all have 10A electricity. Some of the super pitches are on hardstanding and are fully serviced. For an extra charge some can be individually reserved. Trevella is essentially a quiet family touring park. Ready erected tents are available to hire. The accent is on orderliness and cleanliness with on-site evening activities limited, although Andy's Kitchen offers good home-cooked food. Access to two fishing lakes is free, (permits from reception); with some fishing instruction and wildlife talks for youngsters in season. There is a pleasant walk around the lakes, which are a haven for wildlife and the area is a protected nature reserve. It is possible to walk to Crantock beach, but check the tides first.

Facilities

Three blocks provide good coverage with individual washbasins in cabins, hairdressing room, baby rooms and large en-suite family rooms. Laundry. Freezer pack service. Well stocked supermarket (Easter-Oct). Café (including breakfast) and takeaway. Heated outdoor pool. Games room. Separate TV room. Crazy golf. Large adventure playground. Play and sports area. Pets' corner. Fishing. Caravan storage. WiFi. Off site: Shuttle bus to Newquay in high season. Beach 0.5 miles on foot, 1 mile by car. Riding 1 mile. Pubs at Crantock 1 mile.

Open: Easter - 31 October.

Directions

To avoid Newquay leave A30 at Indian Queens. Take A392 west to south of Newquay. At roundabout take A3075 (first exit) then first right. Follow signs to site. GPS: 50.3973, -5.096133

Charges guide

Per unit incl. 2 persons and electricity	£ 18.80 - £ 37.45
extra person	£ 4.95 - £ 9.35
child (3-14 yrs)	£ 1.60 - £ 6.75

Families and couples only.

Trevella Park

One of Cornwall's Finest Parks

For magical holiday memories, stay with us at Trevella Holiday Park near Newquay

- 5* holiday park close to the fantastic beaches of Crantock & Newquay
- Superb touring & camping facilities
- Ready tents and safari tents for hire
- Luxury caravans for hire & sale
- Play areas, TV & games room, cafe, takeaway & launderette
- Heated outdoor swimming pool
- Fishing lakes with free fishing
- Free Ranger activities for the kids during the school summer holidays

To book your short break or holiday
Call 01637 830 308 or visit trevella.co.uk

Newquay
Newperran Holiday Park

Rejerrah, Newquay TR8 5QJ (Cornwall) T: 01872 572407. E: holidays@newperran.co.uk

alanrogers.com/UK0160

Newperran is a large, level park in rural Cornish countryside. Being on high ground, it is quite open but this also gives excellent views of the coast and surroundings. The owners, Keith and Christine Brewer, have rebuilt the reception, shop and pub to a very high standard. The traditional layout of the park provides several flat, well drained meadows divided into over 500 individual pitches with 10/16A electricity. Some fields have larger and reservable spaces with more free space in the centre. There are 77 fully serviced pitches, some with hardstanding and a TV point. Newperran is only 2.5 miles from Perranporth beach, but there is an indoor heated swimming pool and paddling pool on the park.

Facilities

Four clean toilet blocks, two heated and refurbished, are well equipped with washbasins in cabins, family rooms, baby room, hairdressing room and a unit for disabled visitors. Laundry room. Well stocked, licensed shop, bar and café (all July/Aug). New indoor heated swimming pool with paddling pool (Whitsun-Sept). Adventure playground. Toddlers' play area. Games room. TV room. WiFi (free).

Open: 22 March - 31 October.

Directions

Leave Newquay south on A3075. After 7 miles site is signed, just north of Goonhavern village. GPS: 50.350433, -5.101817

Charges guide

Per pitch incl. 2 persons and electricity	£ 22.25 - £ 36.30
extra person	£ 6.15 - £ 10.15

For latest campsite news visit
alanrogers.com

Newquay
Treloy Touring Park
Newquay TR8 4JN (Cornwall) T: 01637 872063. E: stay@treloy.co.uk
alanrogers.com/UK0205

Treloy is a family owned and run park just three miles from the wonderful beaches around Newquay, yet peacefully located away from the crowds. There are 197 large pitches (120-190 sq.m), some slightly sloping, all with 16A electricity (new system) and 30 fully serviced; 130 are used for touring units on a site with a relaxed family atmosphere. There are some concrete hardstandings for caravans which are attractively interspersed with shrubs and form a pleasant landscape feature. Elsewhere, hydrangea edge the roads around the more open pitches and the new trees have grown well. Saint Mawgan, the RAF air sea rescue base, and Newquay's airport are nearby but there is little disturbance. There is an hourly bus service to Newquay from the park entrance which means the coast and beaches can be enjoyed without taking the car. On return to Treloy there is the Park Chef and the Surfrider's Bar for meals and drinks. If you do not fancy the beach there is a pool in the park. This is a real family park providing for all ages.

Facilities

Good quality toilet blocks. Baby room with bath and three family shower rooms. En-suite facilities for disabled visitors (key). Laundry. Gas. Shop with all necessities. Bar (20/5-15/9). Pleasant café including breakfast (July/Aug and weekends). Takeaway. Heated outdoor swimming pool (25/5-15/9). Fenced play areas and field with goal posts. Nature trail. Family entertainment such as magic shows, bingo, various musical acts. WiFi on part of site (charged). Off site: Golf 1 mile. Fishing 1.5 miles. Beach and boat launching 3 miles. Riding 5 miles. Many sandy beaches within a short car journey. Bus to Newquay.

Open: 29 March - 30 September.

Directions

From A39 St Columb Major take B3059 towards Newquay. Park is signed on right after 4 miles. GPS: 50.432867, -5.0125

Charges guide

Per unit incl. 2 persons	
and electricity	£ 17.75 - £ 27.75
extra person	£ 5.50 - £ 8.75
child (3-14 yrs)	£ 3.50 - £ 5.50
dog	£ 3.25

The friendly park in beautiful Cornwall

Telephone: **01637 872063**

Website: www.treloy.co.uk

Email: stay@treloy.co.uk

Address: Newquay, Cornwall TR8 4JN

Newquay
Monkey Tree Holiday Park
Rejerrah, Newquay TR8 5QR (Cornwall) T: 01872 572032. E: enquiries@monkeytreeholidaypark.co.uk
alanrogers.com/UK0165

A busy family park some three miles from the beach, Monkey Tree covers 56 acres and boasts an impressive entrance and smart reception. There are 750 pitches with 500 for touring units, 400 of which have 10/16A electrical connections. There are some hardstanding pitches and the 24 extra large ones with water and waste water include the use of private facilities in the toilet block. The park is broken up into a number of hedged fields, the older ones with mature trees and shrubs. Some 50 caravan holiday homes to rent have their own fields as do a number of seasonal caravans. The park has now developed an animal enclosure around the fishing lake. Alpacas can be seen peering at you, along with pygmy goats and some smaller, cuddly animals. During the holiday season there is much going on at Monkey Tree and all the family should find something to keep them happy.

Facilities

The original block (refurbished) supplements seven new modern timber blocks with heating, providing for all needs including facilities for babies and disabled visitors. Private en-suite facilities for use with the super pitches. Laundry. Motorcaravan services. Gas supplies. Shop (mornings only in low season). Club with entertainment, bar and restaurant (main season and B.Hs). Takeaway (high season). Outdoor pool and paddling pool (Whitsun-end Sept). Trampolines (supervised, with charge). Bouncy castles. Three adventure play areas. Amusement arcade. Fishing lakes. Animal enclosure. Local bus stops in car park. Caravan storage. Off site: Beach 3 miles. Golf 4 miles. Riding, boat launching and sailing 5 miles.

Open: All year.

Directions

Follow the A30 ignoring all signs for Newquay. At Carland Cross (windmills on the right) carry straight over following signs for Perranporth. After 1 mile turn right at Boxheater Junction on B3285 signed Perranporth and Goonhavern. Follow for 0.5 miles then turn right into Scotland Road for 1 mile to park on the left. GPS: 50.352218, -5.091659

Charges guide

Per unit incl. 2 persons	
and electricity	£ 16.85 - £ 49.45
extra person	£ 5.45 - £ 9.75
child (3-14 yrs)	free - £ 6.15
dog	£ 3.85

For latest campsite news visit
alanrogers.com

Newquay

Hendra Holiday Park

Newquay TR8 4NY (Cornwall) T: 01637 875778. E: enquiries@hendra-holidays.com

alanrogers.com/UK0210

Hendra, one of Newquay's most popular parks, is now over 40 years old, but still at the forefront in providing a wide range of facilities and entertainment, which makes for a memorable holiday experience. It is a large park with 280 caravan holiday homes to rent and 548 touring pitches on well mown, mostly terraced, grass fields with country views and mature trees, some pitches are more sheltered than others. With tarmac roads and lighting, 311 pitches have 16A electricity and 28 pitches are fully serviced including water, electricity, light, sewer drainage, satellite TV connections and some innovative awning pads (dogs are not accepted on these pitches). Ten camping pods have been added this year. This is an excellent, well maintained site with extremely helpful staff. The main attraction is perhaps the Oasis complex (open to the public) comprising an indoor fun pool with flumes, river rapids and beach. The outdoor heated pool with sunbathing area is free to campers. A wide variety of entertainment is on offer: comedians, bands, cabaret, dancing, bingo, discos, as well as the bar and restaurant, a pizzeria and fish and chip shop. The park is only 1.5 miles from Newquay and its fabulous surfing beaches; a bus to the town passes the gate. Hendra welcomes families and couples. A member of the Best of British group.

Facilities

Three modern fully equipped toilet blocks with facilities for babies and disabled visitors. Launderette. Motorcaravan services. Gas supplies. Well stocked shop. Various bars, restaurants and takeaway, open all season (limited hours in early season). Pizzeria (July/Aug). Outdoor swimming pool. Indoor pool complex (£2.99 pp/£15.90 for 7 tickets). Play areas including one for soft play. Games field. Skate and scooter park. Amusements. Comprehensive evening entertainment. Bicycle hire. Minigolf. Bowling. WiFi.

Open: 27 March - 2 November.

Directions

Park is on left side of A392 Indian Queens-Newquay road at Newquay side of Quintrell Downs.
GPS: 50.402433, -5.04915

Charges guide

Per unit incl. 2 persons	
and electricity	£ 17.65 - £ 27.48
extra person	£ 5.65 - £ 9.99
child (3-14 yrs)	£ 1.70 - £ 6.75

Minimum charges apply at peak times.

01637 875778
www.hendra-holidays.com
Hendra Holidays, Newquay, Cornwall, TR8 4NY

Newquay

Trevornick Holiday Park

Holywell Bay, Newquay TR8 5PW (Cornwall) T: 01637 830531. E: bookings@trevornick.co.uk

alanrogers.com/UK0220

Trevornick, once a working farm, is a busy and well run family touring park providing a very wide range of amenities, close to one of Cornwall's finest beaches. The park is well managed with facilities and standards constantly monitored. It has grown to provide pitches for caravanners and campers (no holiday caravans but 55 very well equipped Eurotents). There are 636 large grass pitches (600 with 16A electricity and 140 fully serviced) including TV connection, laid out on five level fields and two terraced areas. There are few trees but some good views. A member of the Best of British group.

Facilities

Five modern toilet blocks provide showers, two family bathrooms, baby bath, laundry facilities and provision for disabled visitors. Supermarket. Hire shop. Bars, café, restaurant and takeaway. Pool complex with heated outdoor pool and paddling pool. Fun park, adventure playground, Kids' club. Amusement arcade and bowling alley. Par 3 golf course. 18-hole pitch and putt. Bicycle hire. Coarse fishing with three lakes. WiFi (free).

Open: 10-24 April, 18 May - 13 September.

Directions

From A3075 approach to Newquay-Perranporth road, turn towards Cubert and Holywell Bay. Continue through Cubert to park on the right.
GPS: 50.384983, -5.128933

Charges guide

Per unit incl. 2 persons	
and electricity	£ 15.67 - £ 51.25
extra person	£ 6.59 - £ 13.16

For latest campsite news visit
alanrogers.com

Newquay
Sun Haven Valley Holiday Park

Mawgan Porth, Newquay TR8 4BQ (Cornwall) T: 01637 860373. E: mark1@sunhavenvalley.com

alanrogers.com/UK0215

An attractive, well maintained holiday park, Sun Haven Valley is on the edge of a small valley with views of the opposite hills. Owned and thoughtfully run by the Tavener family, it caters mainly for couples and families with children whose parents are said 'to play with their children'. On a gently sloping hillside, 37 caravan holiday homes for rent border the top field with a central area of neatly cut grass left free for play. The lower field is edged by a small trout stream (unfenced) and provides 109 level, grass touring pitches, 96 with 10A electricity and eight with hardstanding, marked by tram lines and accessed by a circular road. In peak season, extra pitches are provided in the field on the other side of the road. The facilities and play area are situated between the two fields and some up-and-down walking is required. A footpath involves a 15-20 minute walk to reach the beach and the small village of Mawgan Porth, which was buzzing with surfers and families out to enjoy the beach when we visited.

Facilities

Large, central and fully equipped toilet block, a smaller one in the far corner. Two en-suite family rooms double as facilities for disabled visitors. Laundry. Fridge and freezer. Microwave, toaster and oven. Basic foodstuffs available in reception (some supermarkets will deliver). Takeaway food (Aug). Play area. TV room. Games room with computers and amusement machines. Bicycle hire arranged. Tourist information centre. WiFi by reception (charged). Mobile reception poor. Max. 1 dog in high season. Mobile homes and chalets for rent.
Off site: Organic farm shop next door. Pubs, restaurant, bistro, takeaway and small supermarket in village.

Open: Easter - 31 October.

Directions

From B3276 at Mawgan Porth take narrow unclassified road between surf shop and minigolf (signed St Mawgan 2 miles) for 1 mile. Site is on the left. GPS: 50.46203, -5.01385

Charges guide

Per unit incl. 2 adults and electricity	£ 16.50 - £ 33.50
extra person	£ 5.00 - £ 7.00
child (5-13 yrs, first one free)	£ 2.00 - £ 4.50

Newquay
Summer Lodge Country Park

Whitecross, Newquay TR8 4LW (Cornwall) T: 01726 860415. E: salesenquiries@piranmeadows.co.uk

alanrogers.com/UK0325

Set some five miles back from Newquay in a rural situation (there is another park nearby), Summer Lodge has facilities for touring units along with some 56 privately owned mobile homes and an additional 35 for rent. Seventy touring pitches (12A electricity) are pleasantly situated in a large, sloping, grassy field with rural views. There is also room for a further 70 tenting places. The mobile homes are situated nearer the entrance in regular rows, close to where the bar and fish and chip café are to be found. Entertainment is offered all season and there is a largish heated swimming pool.

Facilities

Toilet facilities consist of prefabricated units which, though somewhat cramped, were clean but provided only one shower per sex. Facilities for disabled visitors. Laundry room. Shop, fish and chip café with takeaway. Bar with evening entertainment. Swimming pool with paddling pool (heated May-Oct). Play area. TV in bar. WiFi over site (charged). Off site: Fishing and golf 1 mile. Beach 5 miles.

Open: March - October.

Directions

From A30 at Indian Queens take A392 Newquay road and site is signed off to left at White Cross. GPS: 50.398322, -4.971258

Charges guide

Contact the site for details.

Newquay
Porth Beach Holiday Park

Porth, Newquay TR7 3NH (Cornwall) T: 01637 876531. E: info@porthbeach.co.uk

alanrogers.com/UK0235

The park is just across the road from Porth Beach with its beautiful bay, sandy shoreline and rock pools. Situated in a small, rural valley with a gentle stream to one side you can enjoy the ducks and the wildlife. The 182 good sized grass pitches stretching up the valley in parallel lines accessed by tarmac roadways are level, marked by tram lines and back on to open fencing. Most have 16A electricity, there are also a few with hardstandings. A well equipped toilet block is to be found half way up, heated in cold weather and with air conditioning for warmer times. There is a seasonal shop near the entrance, a pub across the road and a restaurant two doors up. Watergate Bay is just around the corner, and Newquay a couple of miles down the road, so if you are a surfer you will be in paradise. For walkers, Porth Headland and the South West Coastal path offer some outstanding views. Porth Beach is said to be the safest beach for swimming in the Newquay area. Altogether a super place for a family holiday.

Facilities

One modern, heated and fully equipped toilet block. Baby bath and facilities for disabled visitors. Launderette. Play area. WiFi over site (charged). Mobile homes to rent. Off site: Beach 100 m. Fishing 500 m. Golf, riding and boat launching 1.5 miles.

Open: 5 March - 31 October.

Directions

From Newquay take the B3276 to Padstow. Site is half a mile on right. GPS: 50.426071, -5.0534

Charges guide

Per unit incl. 2 persons and electricity	£ 16.00 - £ 44.00
dog	£ 2.00

Newquay
Trethiggey Touring Park

Quintrell Downs, Newquay TR8 4QR (Cornwall) T: 01637 877672. E: enquiries@trethiggey.co.uk

alanrogers.com/UK0530

Trethiggey is a garden-like park with an enjoyable, informal style and a ten month season, set some three miles back from the busy Newquay beaches and nightlife. With natural areas including a small wildlife pond and fishing lakes to enjoy, conservation is high on the agenda. There are 157 pitches, 110 with 16A electricity, 25 on hardstandings and six are fully serviced. Some level pitches are formally arranged, whilst others are on gently sloping grass amidst 12 caravan holiday homes. A more open field provides extra pitches and room for tents.

Facilities

Two fully equipped, heated shower blocks, one in traditional style. En-suite facilities for families and disabled visitors. Motorcaravan services. Laundry facilities and wetsuit wash. Games room with TV and amusement machines. Shop (all season). Café, bar and takeaway (June-Sept). Adventure play area and recreation field. Coarse fishing. WiFi (charged). Off site: Riding 2 miles. Golf and bicycle hire 3 miles. All the delights of Newquay within 3 miles with nightly minibus service (book in shop). Pub within walking distance.

Open: 2 March - 2 January.

Directions

Leave A392 at roundabout in Quintress Downs. Turn south on A3058 and site is shortly on left. GPS: 50.396833, -5.0283

Charges guide

Per unit incl. 2 persons and electricity	£ 15.15 - £ 26.10
extra person	£ 5.10 - £ 8.55
child (3-15 yrs)	£ 1.80 - £ 5.65
dog	£ 2.95 - £ 3.00

For latest campsite news visit

alanrogers.com

Newquay

Carvynick Motorhome Touring Park

Summercourt, Newquay TR8 5AF (Cornwall) T: 01872 510716. E: info@carvynick.co.uk

alanrogers.com/UK0540

Carvynick is unique in having been specially created and developed for American motorhomes. As you approach, you catch a glimpse of large, colourful 'monsters' through the trees. The RVs are parked in fully serviced, landscaped bays which include sewerage connections. In the Paddock area there is also parking for the tow car, whilst in the Copse there are decking and patio areas. A newer area built on a section of the existing golf course has similar facilities and amazing views across to the sea at Newquay. The reception complex is impressive and boasts a heated indoor pool, a badminton court and a small fitness centre with sauna, solarium and hot tub. A number of purpose built cottages provide extra accommodation overlooking the club's five-hole, par 3 golf course. An extra luxury is an impressive bar and restaurant run by a highly rated Michelin chef. This is almost a resort in itself, attractively laid out and very well organised. The site only accepts fully self-contained units that can utilise the provisions of the serviced pitches. There are no sanitary facilities for tourers.

Facilities

Restaurant and bar, separate bar. Indoor heated pool and toddler pool with spectators' lounge. Sauna, solarium and fitness suite. Golf course (5 hole). Badminton court. Games room. Pool table. WiFi (charged). Off site: North and south Cornwall coasts nearby. Eden Valley project 14 miles. St Ives and Tate Gallery within easy reach.

Open: All year.

Directions

From Bodmin on A30 continue until you pass a McDonalds and petrol station on right at Fraddon. Take next exit, A3058 (Summercourt). Continue into Summercourt, turn right at lights over A30 and take first turning left for site. GPS: 50.368736, -4.983035

Charges guide

Per motorhome incl. 4 persons, electricity, water and drainage	£ 22.00 - £ 27.00
extra person	£ 3.00

Padstow

Mother Ivey's Bay Holiday Park

Trevose Head, Padstow PL28 8SL (Cornwall) T: 01841 520990. E: info@motheriveysbay.com

alanrogers.com/UK0425

Mother Ivey's Bay has a wonderful cliff top location with amazing sea views and its own sandy beach. It is a well established family park located to the west of Padstow and features low, Cornish walls and colourful displays of plants. The site has been owned by the Langmaid family for over 20 years and is extremely well cared for and maintained. One hundred grassy touring pitches are in two well tended fields with 16A electricity, one slightly sloping, with a further field for 100 in high season. Ten super pitches are also available with electricity, water and drainage. There are some 100 attractively arranged, privately owned mobile homes, plus 58 to rent. On-site amenities include a well stocked shop and an adventure playground, but the emphasis is on peace and quiet, so there is no bar or restaurant.

Facilities

Two clean toilet blocks have all necessary facilities, including preset showers and open washbasins. Six family shower rooms. Facilities for babies and disabled visitors. Large laundry room. Licensed shop sells fresh bread. Sandy beach. Adventure playground. Mobile homes and chalets for rent. WiFi (charged). Off site: Golf 0.5 miles. Bar and restaurant within 1 mile. Riding 1.5 miles.

Open: 31 March - 4 November.

Directions

Follow A30 dual carriageway to Indian Queens. Follow signs firstly for Wadebridge (A39), then Padstow (B3274). After 3 miles, turn left (St Merryn). Follow signs to Trevose Golf Club and then Mother Ivey's Bay. GPS: 50.541334, -5.013923

Charges guide

Per unit incl. 6 persons and electricity	£ 19.00 - £ 44.00

Padstow
Carnevas Holiday Park
Saint Merryn, Padstow PL28 8PN (Cornwall) T: 01841 520230. E: carnevascampsite@aol.com

alanrogers.com/UK0428

Family run for over 55 years, Carnevas Holiday Park is an attractive, well maintained site close to the beaches and coastal paths. Of the 195 pitches, 95 have 10A electricity connections; they are set out on grass, some backing on to low walls, others positioned against hedges or in open fields. From most pitches there are wide ranging views over the surrounding countryside. With its friendly reception, homely bar with terrace serving snacks and takeaway dishes, the site is an ideal place to relax inbetween exploring the region by car or nipping into Padstow to try out its pasty shops and seafood restaurants.

Facilities

One large, well maintained sanitary block with free hot showers, hair washing room and family bathrooms. Facilities for babies and disabled visitors. Fully equipped laundry. Dishwashing under cover. Motorcaravan services. Well stocked shop (end May-early Sept). Bar serving meals and takeaway food. Games room. Playing field. Playground. Mobile homes and chalets to rent. WiFi over site (charged). Off site: Beaches and coastal paths including The Camel Trail (also for cycling). Eden Project.

Open: End of May - 20 September.

Directions

Leave A30 at Queens Junction and head north on A39 (Wadebridge). At Winnards Perch roundabout, left onto B3274 towards Padstow. After 2 miles take 2nd left towards St Merryn. Before town follow signs for Porthcothen Bay (narrow road). After 2 miles turn right at site sign opposite The Tredrea Inn. GPS: 50.51452, -5.01731

Charges guide

Per unit incl. 2 persons and electricity	£ 15.00 - £ 22.50

Padstow
Padstow Touring Park
Padstow PL28 8LE (Cornwall) T: 01841 532061. E: bookings@padstowtouringpark.co.uk

alanrogers.com/UK0430

With wonderful views over the surrounding countryside and easy access from the A389 Padstow road, this award-winning site is both a comfortable place to unwind and an ideal base from which to tour the region. The park's own colourful and well written brochures contain a wealth of useful information. The park has 150 pitches on grass or hardstanding, some in hedged bays and others on terraces, some without electricity, others with 10A electricity, and all with shared water and waste water. Your stay is made that much more convenient by the park's own bakery (freshly baked bread and pastries every morning), visiting vans selling takeaway foods Monday to Friday and a shop.

Facilities

Two toilet blocks, one new with underfloor heating, have a family room and facilities for disabled visitors. Full laundry facilities. Shop in reception with essentials, gas and camping equipment. Coffee lounge. Play area. WiFi throughout (charged). Off site: Supermarket 0.5 miles. Nearest beach is at Padstow, others are within 2 miles. Access from Padstow to the Camel Trail cycle route.

Open: All year.

Directions

Park is on main A389 road to right, 1 mile south of Padstow. NB: if towing or in a motorcaravan avoid A389 between Wadebridge and St Issey; instead take B3274. GPS: 50.52705, -4.949183

Charges guide

Per unit incl. 2 persons and electricity	£ 17.00 - £ 35.00

Pentewan
Pentewan Sands Holiday Park
Pentewan, Saint Austell PL26 6BT (Cornwall) T: 01726 843485. E: info@pentewan.co.uk

alanrogers.com/UK0250

Pentewan Sands is a very popular, well managed family park with an ideal position right beside a wide sandy private beach. A busy, 32-acre holiday park with lots going on, there are 584 pitches, 462 for touring, 412 with 16A electricity. The good sized pitches are marked and numbered on level grass but with nothing between them. A modern, heated indoor pool with a paddling pool is inside the Beach Club, with a gym, kids' zone and a new bar and restaurant. The bar and restaurant are open all day and serve food in high season.

Facilities

Four main toilet blocks receive heavy use in peak season. Two bathrooms, baby room and facilities for disabled campers. Launderette. Motorcaravan services. Shop with off-licence. Bistro (Easter-mid Sept). Seahorse restaurant. Swimming pools (supervised, Whitsun-mid Sept). Tennis. Playground. Games room. Entertainment. Bicycle hire. WiFi around reception and bar. Dogs are not accepted.

Open: 1 April - 31 October.

Directions

From St Austell ring road take B3273 towards Mevagissey. Park is on left in 3.5 miles, where the road is next to the sea. GPS: 50.288283, -4.78575

Charges guide

Per unit incl. 2 persons and electricity	£ 19.00 - £ 38.65
extra person	£ 4.00 - £ 6.50
child (3-15 yrs)	£ 1.75 - £ 4.50

For latest campsite news visit

alanrogers.com

Penzance

Wayfarers Camping & Caravan Park

Relubbus Lane, Saint Hilary, Penzance TR20 9EF (Cornwall) T: 01736 763326.
E: elaine@wayfarerspark.co.uk alanrogers.com/UK0065

Wayfarers is a neat and tidy, garden-like park reserved for adults only, and only accepts visitors with a reservation. Sheltered by perimeter trees and consisting of two finely mown fields, interspersed with shrubs and palm-like trees, 25 pitches are available for caravans (up to 24 ft. single axle), and motorcaravans up to 21 ft. There is a separate area for tents, and three holiday caravans are available to rent. All have 16A electricity, with hardstanding available on 23. Should you enjoy walking, you can follow the River Hayle down to Saint Erth. There are many more suggestions with maps and a good display of leaflets in the information room, including a star chart. The owners, Elaine and Steve, live on site and make you very welcome, maintaining the park to a high standard. Do look at the doll's house in the shop; built by Elaine's father, the detail and furniture are amazing. The Lizard and Land's End with the Minack Theatre wait to be explored, and Saint Michael's Mount is only two miles away.

Facilities	Directions
The modern toilet block is fully equipped. Ladies have a wash cubicle and there are two smart en-suite shower rooms (key system). Fully equipped laundry. Shop stocks basics. Dogs are not accepted. Off site: Two pubs serving food in Goldsithney 1 mile. Fishing and riding 1 mile. Golf 1.5 miles. Beach 2 miles. Bicycle hire, sailing and boat launching 5 miles.	Site is 6.5 miles north west of Helston. Following A30 Penzance road take A394 Helston road after St Ives turning. After 1 mile turn left on B3280 and pass through Goldsithney, site is in 1 mile on left. Do not use sat nav. GPS: 50.133167, -5.416833

Open: 8 May - 28 September.

Charges guide

Per unit incl. 2 persons and electricity	£ 19.50 - £ 27.00
extra person	£ 7.00

Perranporth

Perran Sands Holiday Park

Perranporth TR6 0AQ (Cornwall) T: 01872 573551. E: enquiries@haven.com
alanrogers.com/UK0135

A large, bustling, commercial site set out amongst grassy sand dunes with over 1,100 pitches; 640 of these are for touring and there are numerous mobile homes dotted amongst the dunes. The dedicated touring area has its own wardens and a separate reception in high season. The park is a holiday village, with everything that you could need – shops, restaurants, bars and entertainment. The entertainment centre is the heart of the site and is a long way from the camping areas. Pitches are on sandy grass, marked by fencing, some level, some sloping, many with rabbit holes. Most have 10A electricity and a few are hardstanding. A magnificent sandy beach is a stiff walk over some tall dunes. It is popular with surfers, but for something a little more relaxing there are indoor and outdoor heated pools on site.

Facilities	Directions
Three basic toilet blocks, 2 family rooms, facilities for babies and disabled campers. Launderette. Motorcaravan services. Supermarket. Gift shop. Café/bar/grill. Sports bar. Heated outdoor pool (20/5-1/9) and heated indoor fun pool with flume. Multisports court. Mini 10-pin bowling. Amusement arcade. Pool tables. Surf school (equipment hire). Two entertainment bars (one July/Aug only). Kids' club. Soft play area. Playland. Road train. WiFi in bar area.	From Goonhaven take road for Perranporth. Site entrance on right before going down the hill. GPS: 50.359357, -5.143635

Open: 20 March - 2 November.

Charges guide

Per unit incl. 2 persons and electricity	£ 8.00 - £ 61.00
extra person	free - £ 2.00
dog	£ 3.00

For latest campsite news visit
alanrogers.com

Polruan-by-Fowey

Polruan Holidays Camping & Caravanning

Townsend, Polruan, Polruan-by-Fowey PL23 1QH (Cornwall) T: 01726 870263. E: polholiday@aol.com

alanrogers.com/UK0190

Polruan is a rural site in an elevated position on the opposite side of the river to Fowey and 200 metres from the Coastal Path. There are marvellous sea views. This is a well maintained, delightful little site with just 37 touring pitches and six holiday caravans to let. The holiday homes are arranged in a neat circle, with a central area for seven adults only tourer pitches on gravel hardstanding, all with 16A electricity and one fully serviced. An adjacent meadow has 15 pitches for motorcaravans and tents, all with electricity and a third area has 10 tent only pitches (eight with electricity). This park is in a popular tourist area, within walking distance down a steep hill to the village and the passenger ferry to Fowey. A raised picnic area gives more views across the estuary to Fowey. A member of the Countryside Discovery group.

Facilities

The fully equipped, heated toilet block has modern, controllable showers large enough for an adult and child. Laundry room. Range of recycling bins. Reception with a small terrace and shop for everyday items. Gas. Microwave. Hot drinks machine and freezer for ice packs. Sloping field area with swings for children. Max. 2 dogs. Free phone charging. WiFi throughout (free). Off site: Coastal path 200 yds. Fishing 0.5 miles. Riding and bicycle hire 3 miles. Golf 10 miles. Local bus to Looe.

Open: 1 April - 27 September.

Directions

From main A390 at East Taphouse take B3359 towards Looe. After 5 miles fork right signed Bodinnick and ferry. Watch for signs on left for Polruan and site to left. Follow these carefully along narrow Cornish lanes to site on right just before village. GPS: 50.32759, -4.62515

Charges guide

Per unit incl. 2 persons and electricity	£ 17.00 - £ 27.00
extra person	£ 5.00 - £ 8.00
child (2-15 yrs)	£ 2.00 - £ 4.00
dog	£ 1.00 - £ 2.00

Polruan Holidays
Caravanning, Camping & Holiday Homes
Fowey • Cornwall • PL23 1QH
Tel: +44 (0)1726 870 263
polholiday@aol.com
www.polruanholidays.co.uk

Polzeath

Polzeath Beach Holiday Park

Trenant Nook, Polzeath PL27 6ST (Cornwall) T: 01208 863320.

alanrogers.com/UK0345

Set in the village of Old Polzeath with its shops, post office and pub, Polzeath Beach Holiday Park is ideally situated for enjoying the wealth of attractions on offer in Cornwall. There are no touring pitches at this site, but visitors have a choice of fully furnished static caravans, and there is a three-bedroom bungalow sleeping five people. A major attraction of this site is its proximity (300 yards) to a beautiful, Blue Flag beach whose enormous stretch of golden sand opens onto the Atlantic, just by the Camel Estuary. This is an excellent location for a family holiday and very popular with surfers at all levels. The site does not accept groups or visitors under the age of 21.

Facilities

Laundry facilities. Off site: Beach 300 yds. Shops, pubs and restaurants in Polzeath. Beautiful fishing village of Port Isaac.

Open: 28 March - 31 October.

Directions

From Bodmin take A389 to Wadebridge. Turn left at 1st traffic island (town centre), then right onto B3314 following signs for Polzeath (7 miles). Descend hill into Polzeath, turn right by Ann's Cottage Surf Shop, cross car park and follow lane to right for 60 yds. to park. GPS: 50.57391, -4.91429

Charges guide

Contact the site for details.

For latest campsite news visit
alanrogers.com

Redruth

Tehidy Holiday Park

Harris Mill, Illogan, Redruth TR16 4JQ (Cornwall) T: 01209 216489. E: holiday@tehidy.co.uk
alanrogers.com/UK0115

Tehidy is a rather special small park with an emphasis on the environment, so wild flowers abound and a note is kept of all bird sightings. Richard and his family have worked hard to ensure that the facilities on offer are of a high standard. Their newest development, in a secluded area at the top of the park, provides wigwam camping cabins, rather like a wooden tent with a hexagonal open cooking shelter. Tehidy also offers 28 level touring pitches (all with 10A electricity, two with hardstanding) plus 20 mobile homes and five bungalow-style cottages to rent. The pitches are terraced where necessary and some are hedged, with others part fenced and with views across the countryside. The owners live on site and are constantly looking for ways to make improvements and to provide a relaxing environment. The setting on a wooded hillside is peaceful, with a stream at the bottom and direct access to a woodland walk alive with primroses and bluebells in spring. Whilst the grass is neatly cut, the banks are left for nature to develop. The nearest beach is at Portreath, which has a deep rock pool for swimming at low tide. There is a request bus stop outside the entrance for Truro, Saint Ives and Newquay. This is surfing country but you can also windsurf at Saint Stithian's reservoir. Tehidy Country Park (250 acres of woodland) is nearby, together with Tehidy Golf Club.

Facilities

Modern fully equipped toilet block. Very smart en-suite family room doubles as a facility for disabled visitors. Laundry facilities. Reception with shop area. Games room and tourist information. Play area with small trampoline. Netball. Picnic tables. Woodland walk. Local takeaway delivery. WiFi over site (charged). Dogs are not accepted. Cottages and mobile homes for rent. Off site: Pub and restaurant within walking distance. Cycle routes. Golf and bicycle hire 1 mile. Beach and riding 2.5 miles.

Open: 28 March - 1 November.

Directions

Leave A30 at Porthtowan and Portreath exit. Right on roundabout to Portreath. Left at North Country crossroads. Follow signs to site. GPS: 50.244939, -5.252935

Charges guide

Per unit incl. 2 persons and electricity	£ 19.00 - £ 26.00
extra person	£ 4.00

Redruth

Lanyon Holiday Park

Loscombe Lane, Four Lanes, Redruth TR16 6LP (Cornwall) T: 01209 313474.
E: info@lanyonholidaypark.co.uk **alanrogers.com/UK0016**

Lanyon's location is a pleasant surprise set amidst the former and now attractive industrial landscape found in parts of the tip of Cornwall. Tucked away down a lane, the holiday caravans are attractively situated with hedged touring fields beyond. A neat tarmac road curves around to reception, the pub and an indoor swimming pool. There are 25 large hedged touring pitches around the edge of two level fields and room for around 40 tents during high season in a separate field. There is a large play area for children. This is a pleasant, relaxed destination for a family holiday with something for everyone and splendid views across the surrounding countryside to the sea.

Facilities

One traditional toilet block is attached to reception with heating. Two others are of prefabricated type but well maintained. Baby changing. Showers may be in short supply at peak times. Laundry room. Bar serving meals (22/5-5/9). Heated indoor pool (10x4 m. April-Oct). TV room. Games room. Play area and trampoline. Caravan storage. WiFi (free). Off site: Watersports at Stithians Lake 1 mile. Riding, fishing and bicycle hire 2 miles. Golf and beach 5 miles.

Open: 1 April - 30 October.

Directions

Site is 10 miles southwest of Truro. Leave A30 at Pool A3047 exit. Keep to left-hand lane, straight on at next 2 sets of lights, passing Tesco Extra on left. Take next right over railway bridge (Four Lanes). Follow road up hill for 1.5 miles, at T-junction turn right. Take 2nd right at Pencoy village hall. Lanyon Park is on left in 400 yds. GPS: 50.20292, -5.24554

Charges guide

Per unit incl. 2 persons and electricity	£ 14.00 - £ 26.00
extra person	£ 3.00 - £ 5.00
child (under 2 yrs)	free
dog	£ 2.00 - £ 3.00

Minimum stay 5 nights in high season.

Redruth

Globe Vale Holiday Park

Radnor, Redruth TR16 4BH (Cornwall) T: 01209 891183. E: info@globevale.co.uk

alanrogers.com/UK0114

A family run, well maintained, 13-acre site located in countryside where the tin mine chimneys are a stark reminder of the past. The Owen family have worked hard in the past few years to upgrade the site. A number of mobile homes are to be found in the first part of the site amidst a mix of trees and shrubs. A further neatly grassed and sheltered area has serviced pitches on hardstanding. Two large, open fields with wonderful countryside views and Cornish stone walls have 138 touring pitches (all with 16A electricity) around the edges with a central open space. Reception, in the centre of the site, is part of the Owen's home. Many campers return year after year.

Facilities

Smart, well equipped sanitary facilities are in a heated prefabricated unit. Facilities for disabled campers, ramped access. Laundry room. Motorcaravan services. Bar, restaurant, takeaway. Play area. WiFi over part of site (charged). Mobile homes for rent. Off site: 'Conveyor belt' ski slope within walking distance. Bicycle hire 2 miles. Beach 3 miles. 9-hole golf course. Riding 5 miles.

Open: All year.

Directions

Heading west on A30 take Redruth/Porthtowan exit, then take Porthtowan exit at roundabout and follow site signs. GPS: 50.257212, -5.218644

Charges guide

Per unit incl. 2 persons and electricity	£ 21.00 - £ 31.00
extra person	£ 3.00
dog	£ 2.00

Saint Agnes

Beacon Cottage Farm Holidays

Beacon Drive, St. Agnes TR5 0NU (Cornwall) T: 01872 552347. E: beaconcottagefarm@lineone.net

alanrogers.com/UK0125

Amazing views greet you as you arrive at Beacon Farm. The stark remains of Wheal Coates tin mine stand out against the cliffs, and views over the sea extend as far as Saint Ives. Beacon Farm is a mixed beef and arable farm and has its own home bred herd of beef cows and calves. The buildings and the impressive stone walls are extremely well maintained. One large, sloping field and a smaller one enjoy sea views but can be less sheltered than the pitches in smaller paddocks which are sheltered by walls and trees. In all there are 70 pitches of varying sizes, 50 with 10A electricity.

Facilities

Stone built toilet blocks are fully equipped and include a family room. Baby bath and changing mat. Facilities for disabled visitors. Laundry room. Motorcaravan services. Bread and eggs are available from reception. Fish and chip van calls once a week. Play area with adventure type equipment. Dog exercise field. Caravan storage. WiFi. Off site: Fishing and beach 0.5 miles. Riding 1.5 miles. Bicycle hire 2 miles. Golf 3 miles.

Open: Easter/1 April - 30 September.

Directions

Leave A30 at Chiverton roundabout. Take B3277 west to St Agnes. At mini roundabout turn left towards Chapel Port, follow brown signs to site. GPS: 50.30567, -5.2249

Charges guide

Per unit incl. 2 persons and electricity	£ 18.00 - £ 28.00
extra person	£ 4.90

Min. 7 nights in school holidays.

Saint Austell

River Valley Holiday Park

London Apprentice, Saint Austell PL26 7AP (Cornwall) T: 01726 73533. E: mail@rivervalleyholidaypark.co.uk

alanrogers.com/UK0003

In the heart of the Cornish countryside, River Valley is close to the beaches. Walkers and cyclists can join the adjacent Pentewan Valley Trail (St Austell to Pentewan) and head off to beaches, coastal villages and the gardens at Heligan. It is a family run park that prides itself on being quiet and well tended. The site falls into two halves, one with 40 static caravans for hire and the second with 45 level, hardstandings for touring, all with 10A electricity. The park is adjacent to the River Winnick and an energetic walk away from Pentewan village and beach.

Facilities

Well equipped heated central toilet block with facilities for disabled visitors. Laundry room. Small shop. Heated, covered pool. Games room with pool table and arcade games. Play area with zip wire, climbing frames, swings and an area for smaller children. Pets' corner with pigs, chickens and ducks. Bicycle hire. Internet room and WiFi. Off site: Small local shop at site entrance (milk, basic groceries and newspapers). Bus stop. St Austell 2 miles. Lost Gardens of Heligan 3 miles. Mevagissey 4 miles.

Open: Easter - October.

Directions

From A30 west of Bodmin turn south on A391 then B3274 to St Austell. Continue south on B3273 towards Pentewan and Mevagissey. Park is on left in 2 miles at village of London Apprentice. GPS: 50.31862, -4.7996

Charges guide

Per unit incl. 2 persons and electricity	£ 14.00 - £ 35.00
extra person	£ 3.00 - £ 4.00
child (5-15 yrs)	£ 2.00 - £ 3.00

For latest campsite news visit

alanrogers.com

Saint Austell

Carlyon Bay Caravan & Camping Park

Cypress Avenue, Carlyon Bay, Saint Austell PL25 3RE (Cornwall) T: 01726 812735.
E: holidays@carlyonbay.net **alanrogers.com/UK0290**

Tranquil, open meadows edged by mature woodland, well cared for by the Taylor family who live on site, provide a beautiful holiday setting with the nearest beach five minutes' walk from the top gate. The original farm buildings have been converted and added to, providing an attractive covered, central area with a certain individuality of design which is very pleasing. Pitches are in five spacious areas and allow for a family meadow and a dog-free meadow (high season only). There are 180 marked pitches, 150 with 10/16A electricity, some with hardstanding and eight are fully serviced. All are on flat, terraced or gently sloping grass with flowers and flowering shrubs or edged with trees. The impressively tiled toilet blocks are of good quality and design. In addition to the attractive kidney shaped pool and paddling pool there is now a large rectangular pool (also heated) within a walled and paved area which is excellent for sunbathing. This forms part of the central area which is the place to enjoy family entertainment in high season. There is also a pleasant family pub and Kidsworld for children within walking distance.

Facilities

Three individually designed, modern toilet blocks (one heated) provide a full range of comfortable facilities including some private cubicles. Fully equipped laundry room. Modern reception with little shop. Takeaway (May-mid Sept). Heated swimming and paddling pools (Whitsun-Sept). TV lounge. Crazy golf. Play areas (including adventure type). Eden Project tickets. WiFi on part of site (free). Off site: Bus service on main road. Coastal footpath nearby. Buses to St Austell and Fowey from park entrance. Beach 0.5 miles. Pub 1 mile.

Open: Easter/1 April - 28th September.

Directions

From Plymouth on A390, pass Lostwithiel and 1 mile after village of St Blazey, turn left at roundabout beside Britannia Inn. After 400 yds. turn right on a concrete road and right again at site sign. GPS: 50.34085, -4.737217

Charges guide

Per unit incl. 2 persons	
and electricity	£ 17.00 - £ 32.00
incl. services	£ 21.00 - £ 35.00
extra person	£ 5.00 - £ 6.00
child (3-15 yrs)	£ 4.00 - £ 5.00

For a colour brochure call: 01726 812735 • holidays@carlyonbay.net • www.carlyonbay.net

Saint Austell

Heligan Woods Camping & Caravan Park

Saint Ewe, Saint Austell PL26 6EL (Cornwall) T: 01726 844414. E: heligan@pentewan.co.uk
alanrogers.com/UK0410

A peaceful, attractive park in a mature garden setting, Heligan Woods complements its sister site, Pentewan Sands with its busy beach life and many activities. One can enjoy the mature trees and flowering shrubs here which have been further landscaped to provide an attractive situation for a number of holiday homes (17 to rent). These face out over a part of the 'Lost Valley' of Heligan fame with the touring pitches below on sloping grass, some terraced and others in a more level situation (some with handstanding) amongst trees and shrubs. In all, there are 100 good sized touring pitches, 89 with 16A electricity.

Facilities

Fully equipped and well kept, the modern, heated toilet block includes a unisex room with bath and small size bath. Extra showers in separate block. Fully equipped laundry room. Small shop. Adventure playground. Off site: Beach/sailing 1.5 miles. Riding 2 miles. Golf 3.5 miles. Bicycle hire/boat launching. Lost Gardens of Heligan next door.

Open: Mid January - end November.

Directions

From St Austell ring road take B3273 for Mevagissey. After 3.5 miles, pass Pentewan Sands, continue up hill and turn right following site signs. GPS: 50.288833, -4.812083

Charges guide

Per unit incl. 2 persons	
and electricity	£ 10.00 - £ 32.70
extra person	£ 2.50 - £ 4.75

Saint Austell
Meadow Lakes

Hewas Water, Saint Austell PL26 7JG (Cornwall) T: 01726 882540. E: info@meadow-lakes.co.uk

alanrogers.com/UK0415

Meadow Lakes is a well equipped park set on the side of a hill in 56 acres of rolling Cornish countryside, with woodland and lakes making it a wonderful place for a family holiday. There are over 200 pitches, the 159 touring pitches are sloping, on grass or hardstanding. Ninety-three have 10A electricity, and all have views of the lakes or surrounding rural countryside. The central farm buildings house all the amenities, including playbarn, games room and shop. There is a heated outdoor swimming pool, four coarse fishing lakes (each stocked with different fish), a pets' corner and outdoor play area. A proportion of the site is given over to smart wooden lodges available to buy and holiday caravans and small bungalows to rent or buy. In one corner there are two camping pods to rent. The owners encourage a happy and friendly atmosphere.

Facilities

New toilet block containing en-suite units, one with a bath. Launderette. Shop. Heated outdoor swimming pool (27/5-4/9). Indoor and outdoor play areas. Tennis court. Fishing (free, but rod licence needed). Play areas. Pets' corner. Bicycle hire (delivered to site). WiFi by reception (free). Off site: Golf 3 miles. Riding and nearest beach 4 miles. Shipwreck rescue and heritage centre 5 miles. The Lost Gardens of Heligan 4 miles. Eden Project 8 miles.

Open: 14 March - 1 November.

Directions

Site is 4.5 miles west of St Austell bypass. Take A390 towards Truro. Turn left on B3287 signed Tregony, site is in 1 mile on left. GPS: 50.30075, -4.85708

Charges guide

Per unit incl. 2 persons	
and electricity	£ 10.50 - £ 28.00
extra person	£ 5.50
child (4-16 yrs)	£ 3.50
dog (1st free)	£ 2.00

Saint Columb Major
Trewan Hall Campsite

Saint Columb Major TR9 6DB (Cornwall) T: 01637 880 261. E: enquiries@trewan-hall.co.uk

alanrogers.com/UK0305

Not so much camping as living in the gardens of a beautiful 350-year-old house. Trewan Hall's 36 acres have been slowly and carefully developed over 50 years by its owners and visitors cannot fail to be impressed by the idyllic setting. The modern facilities are housed mainly within the hall's former outbuildings, and the colourful, well maintained floral gardens are dispersed between the camping areas. The grassy, open plan pitches are set out in level fields with a minimum of six metres between each pitch, most of which are equipped with 10A electricity. Although the site never appears overcrowded, campers seeking an especially tranquil holiday might consider a visit in spring when the rhododendrons are in bloom, or in late summer. Hidden behind the beautiful stonework of the house and its outbuildings are all that is needed for a comfortable holiday. This is a site that will appeal to those seeking a rest from the hectic pace of daily life and where they can enjoy the beauty of the past combined with the comfort of the present.

Facilities

Three modern, well maintained sanitary blocks with free controllable showers and provision for disabled visitors. Family shower rooms with baby changing area. Rooms with baths. Laundry with washing machines and dryers. Drying room. Well stocked shop in reception serves takeaway snacks. Large covered swimming pool (high season, charged). Play area. Theatre with local entertainment for children (July/Aug). Children's nature workshop. Games rooms. Full sized billiard/snooker table for adults. Library in part of the main house with free WiFi. Off site: Beaches and surfing 4 miles. Coastal walks. National Trust properties.

Open: 5 May - 15 September.

Directions

Site is 7 miles southwest of Wadebridge. Leave A30 at Indian Queens junction and follow A39 towards Wadebridge. After 3 miles (shortly after bypassing St Column Major) turn left, signposted Talskiddy. Site entrance is 300 yds. on left. GPS: 50.44537, -4.94355

Charges guide

Per unit incl. 2 persons	
and electricity	£ 19.00 - £ 27.00
extra person	£ 7.00 - £ 11.00
child (5-15 yrs)	£ 3.50 - £ 6.00
dog	£ 1.50

For latest campsite news visit
alanrogers.com

Saint Ives
Ayr Holiday Park

Higher Ayr, Saint Ives TR26 1EJ (Cornwall) T: 01736 795855. E: recept@ayrholidaypark.co.uk

alanrogers.com/UK0030

Ayr Holiday Park has an unparalleled position overlooking Saint Ives Bay and Porthmeor beach and is a popular, well cared for site. On arrival it may seem to be all caravan holiday homes, but behind them is a series of naturally sloping fields with marvellous views providing a total of 90 pitches, of which 40 are for touring caravans and motorcaravans. These pitches are on grass, all with 16A electricity and several fully serviced with hardstanding. An extra field for tents is open in July and August.

Facilities

The excellent toilet block includes two family shower rooms and facilities for baby changing and disabled visitors. Wetsuit showers. Fully equipped laundry room. Motorcaravan point. Indoor swimming pool, sauna and bar in hotel (charged). Games room with TV, hot drinks and snack machines. Adventure play area. Max. 1 dog, contact site first. Bus calls. WiFi (charged). Off site: Tate Gallery and beaches within walking distance. Spar shop and leisure centre with indoor pool nearby. Golf 1 mile.

Open: All year.

Directions

From A30 follow heavy vehicles signs for St Ives (not town centre). After 2 miles join B3311 then B3306 1 mile from St Ives. Still heading for St Ives, turn left at mini-roundabout following camping signs through residential areas. Park entrance is 600 yds. at Ayr Terrace. GPS: 50.21261, -5.48928

Charges guide

Per unit incl. 2 persons and electricity	£ 24.00 - £ 43.75
extra person	£ 5.00 - £ 8.25

Saint Ives
Trevalgan Touring Park

Saint Ives TR26 3BJ (Cornwall) T: 01736 791892. E: reception@trevalgantouringpark.co.uk

alanrogers.com/UK0040

Trevalgan is a quiet, traditional style of park, on the cliffs two miles from Saint Ives. It is a truly rural location where you can enjoy spectacular views, an abundance of flora and fauna and plenty of space for children. The present owners, who took over in 2013, have made developments to the site including new sanitary facilities with underfloor heating, some pitches have hedging for privacy and a security barrier at the entrance. There are 135 clearly marked pitches (112 with 16A electricity and some with water as well) in two level fields edged by Cornish stone walls – it could be exposed on a windy day.

Facilities

A fully equipped heated toilet block includes family shower rooms, a baby room and facilities for disabled visitors. New reception and shop (fresh bread, coffee and local produce). Laundry room. Motorcaravan services. Gas supplies. Games field, adventure play area. Purpose built games room. Off site: Riding and golf within 2 miles. Fishing 3 miles. Bicycle hire 8 miles. Bus service to St Ives and back (Whitsun-mid Sept). As well as the coastal path, a path leads to St Ives across the fields (30-40 mins).

Open: 28 April - 30 September.

Directions

Take St Ives exit from A30, then 1st exit at 2nd mini roundabout. At T-junction turn right onto B3311 and through Halsetown. Turn left at next T-junction onto B3306 (St Just). After 0.5 miles, turn right at brown sign and follow single-track lane (passing bays) for 0.5 miles. Keep right at small triangle. Site is on right. Do not use sat nav. GPS: 50.20769, -5.51882

Charges guide

Per unit incl. 2 persons and electricity	£ 20.50 - £ 33.50

Saint Ives
Polmanter Tourist Park

Halsetown, Saint Ives TR26 3LX (Cornwall) T: 01736 795640. E: reception@polmanter.com

alanrogers.com/UK0050

A popular and attractively developed park, Polmanter is located high up at the back of Saint Ives with wonderful sea and countryside views. The Osborne family has worked hard to develop Polmanter as a complete family base. Converted farm buildings provide a cosy lounge bar with a conservatory overlooking the heated swimming pool. The 250 touring pitches (no caravan holiday homes) are well spaced in several fields divided by established shrubs and hedges giving large, level, individual pitches with connecting tarmac roads. There is a choice of grass and hardstanding multi-serviced pitches, serviced pitches with 16A electricity and non-serviced tent pitches.

Facilities

Three modern, fully equipped toilet blocks with underfloor heating include en-suite family rooms. Facilities for disabled visitors. Baby rooms. Fully equipped laundry. Motorcaravan services. Well stocked shop. Bar with food and family area (all Whitsun-mid Sept). Takeaway. Heated swimming pool (Whitsun-mid Sept). Some entertainment (peak season). Tennis. Putting. Play area. Sports field. Games room. WiFi (charged).

Open: 1 April - 31 October.

Directions

Take A3074 to St Ives from A30, then first left at a mini roundabout taking Holiday Route (B3311) to St Ives (Halsetown). At T-junction, turn right for Halsetown, right again at the Halsetown Inn then first left. GPS: 50.196183, -5.491017

Charges guide

Per unit incl. 2 persons and electricity	£ 20.00 - £ 36.00
extra person	£ 5.00 - £ 9.00

For latest campsite news visit
alanrogers.com

Saint Just

Roselands Caravan & Camping Park

Dowran, Saint Just, Penzance TR19 7RS (Cornwall) T: 01736 788571. E: info@roselands.co.uk
alanrogers.com/UK0025

Roselands is a small, family owned park situated on the Cornish moors overlooking the village of Saint Just and with marvellous views of the sea and countryside around Lands End. In all there are 19 holiday homes to let, 25 level, grassy touring pitches (all with 16A electricity) and some provision for tents. The owner's home, providing a bar and conservatory along with reception and a small shop, sits in the centre of the park. The conservatory acts as a community family room with games, Internet facility and tourist information with a play area outside and a games room nearby. This area is very popular with walkers and birdwatchers. The park itself originated in 1972 in old clay pits – the area where most of the holiday homes are located was one of the pits and is consequently very sheltered. Subsequent owners have added to the house and the current owners, Craig and Kerry with their young family, do everything themselves. Craig is very knowledgeable about the area and will also organise fishing trips.

Facilities

Small traditional toilet block, fully equipped and can be heated. Laundry facilities. Small shop mainly for basics and gas, plus a bar (1/5-31/8). Conservatory with TV and Internet access. Play area. Games room. WiFi throughout (free). Off site: Fishing and golf 1 mile. Riding, beach and surfing at Sennen Cove 2 miles. Boat launching 5 miles. Nearby Land's End and Cape Cornwall. Minack Outdoor Theatre.

Open: 1 March - 31 October.

Directions

Take the A3071 from Penzance for St Just. Follow for 5.5 miles then 0.5 miles before St Just turn left at sign for site. GPS: 50.11323, -5.658

Charges guide

Per unit incl. 2 persons	
and electricity	£ 13.50 - £ 19.50
extra person	£ 3.00
child (under 12 yrs)	£ 2.00
dog	£ 1.00

Saint Martins by Looe

Looe Country Park Caravan & Campsite

Bucklawren Road, No Mans Land, Looe PL13 1QS (Cornwall) T: 01503 240265.
E: info@looecountrypark.co.uk **alanrogers.com/UK0320**

Looe Country Park is a lovely all year site that will appeal to those who prefer a quiet, well kept small family site to the larger ones with many on-site activities. With good countryside views, 31 touring units can be accommodated on well tended grass. Good sized pitches are marked with some hedging between pairs of pitches to give privacy, and most have 16A electricity connections. There are several hardstandings and 17 serviced pitches. Five mobile homes and two camping pods are available to rent. The owners, Amanda and Dale Byers, live on the park and make everyone very welcome, creating a relaxed and happy atmosphere. The nearest beach is a 20-25 minute walk from a gate in the corner of the park. This is a good area for walking with links to the coastal path through Duchy woodlands. The Monkey Sanctuary is also nearby.

Facilities

Laminated teak with chrome fittings and black surfaces make an unusual but stylish and fully equipped, heated sanitary block. Family room. Laundry. Shop (April-Oct.) for gas and basics, and some camping accessories. New play area. Tourist information in reception. WiFi (charged). Off site: Restaurant 1.5 miles. Fishing, golf and boat launching within 2 miles. Diving school at Seaton 2 miles. Scuba centre and fishing trips Looe 2.5 miles. Riding 6 miles.

Open: All year.

Directions

Park is less than half a mile south of the B3253. Turn off 2 miles east of Looe and follow signs to park and Monkey Sanctuary at junctions. NB: the approach roads are narrow (6'6" width limit) and require caution. GPS: 50.377217, -4.4185

Charges guide

Contact site for details.
Less 10% for senior citizens for weekly bookings.

For latest campsite news visit
alanrogers.com

Saltash

Dolbeare Caravan & Camping Park

Saint Ives Road, Landrake, Saltash PL12 5AF (Cornwall) T: 01752 851332. E: reception@dolbeare.co.uk

alanrogers.com/UK0440

Dolbeare Park has a countryside setting, but is very easily accessible from the main A38 road. The site is surrounded by trees and farmland and slopes slightly at the top. Connected by a gravel road, there are 60 hardstanding and gravel pitches, all with 16A electricity connections. A four-acre camping paddock can also be used for rallies. For children there is a low level adventure play area and a separate area for games. Giant chess and Connect 4 games will entertain families. Dogs are accepted and a small dog walk is provided at the top of the park. Reception supplies leaflets on local attractions and amenities with a good supply of tourist information and maps. A member of the Best of British group.

Facilities

A modern, bright sanitary block has underfloor heating, family rooms and a room for visitors with disabilities. Small drying room. Laundry next to reception. Fridge and freezer in camping field. Motorcaravan services. Reception doubles as a small licensed shop for basics including takeaway and gas (limited hours out of main season). Low level adventure play area. Giant chess. Connect 4. WiFi (charged). Site barrier (card system, £10 deposit). Off site: Fishing 0.5 miles. Golf 5 miles. Nearest beach 8 miles. Looe 20 minutes. Plymouth 20 minutes. Polperro 30 minutes. Rame Peninsula, Whitesand Bay and Tamar Valley nearby.

Open: All year.

Directions

After crossing the Tamar Bridge into Cornwall, continue on A38 for a further 4 miles. In Landrake village turn right following signs and site is 0.75 miles on the right. GPS: 50.43064, -4.30551

Charges guide

Per unit incl. 2 persons and electricity	£ 19.00 - £ 25.00
extra person	£ 5.50
child (5-15 yrs)	£ 3.00
dog	£ 1.00 - £ 2.00

Dolbeare Park caravan & camping
caravan~camping~eurotents
Best of British
AA

South East Cornwall
A quality quiet relaxing and friendly park
01752 851332
www.dolbeare.co.uk

Tintagel

Trewethett Farm Caravan Club Site

Trethevy, Tintagel PL34 0BQ (Cornwall) T: 01840 770222. E: trewethettfarm@caravanclub.co.uk

alanrogers.com/UK0058

This site can boast some of the most dramatic views of any site in the country, overlooking Bossiney Cove and beyond to the ever changing seascape of the Atlantic Ocean. Vans can be positioned either front or back first, ensuring your own panoramic (and occasionally wild and windy) view. The 146 open pitches (most with 16A electricity) are well laid out and of a good size, some on slightly sloping ground (levelling blocks may be required). They are mainly on grass, but 69 are hardstanding. The whole site has the well tended appearance that one associates with the Caravan Club. Trewethett Farm will particularly suit those who are looking to experience the landscape of the Cornish coastline and who enjoy the open air. The coastal path runs alongside the site and both Boscastle and Tintagel are accessible on foot. There is a footpath to the beach below but the descent is challenging and could be difficult for small children. Polzeath beach is within ten miles and is a popular choice for families. The site is also very well located as a base for exploring North Cornwall with Rock, Padstow and the Camel estuary not too far away.

Facilities

Two modern sanitary blocks (closed 10.30-12.00), but one is only opened in high season. Facilities are of a very high standard with good sized showers and washbasins in cubicles. Facilities for babies (key) and disabled visitors. Laundry. Motorcaravan services. Small shop in reception. Play area. WiFi over site (charged). Off site: Shops, bars and restaurants in Tintagel. Port Isaac (location of the TV series 'Doc Marten'). Fishing 2 km. Riding 3 km. Golf 5 miles. Bicycle hire 12 km.

Open: 20 March - 2 November.

Directions

From A30 south of Launceston take A395 for 11 miles, turn right on A39 towards Bude. In one mile turn left before transmitter, then in 2.5 miles turn right on B3266 towards Boscastle. After 2.5 miles at junction on bend continue on to B3263. The site is visible on the right down a drive 2 miles further on. No arrivals before 12.00. GPS: 50.67396, -4.72664

Charges guide

Per person	£ 5.90 - £ 7.90
child (5-17 yrs)	£ 1.70 - £ 2.90
pitch incl. electricity (non-member)	£ 17.20 - £ 20.20

For latest campsite news visit
alanrogers.com

Truro

Chacewater Park

Cox Hill, Chacewater, Truro TR4 8LY (Cornwall) T: 01209 820762. E: enquiries@chacewaterpark.co.uk

alanrogers.com/UK0010

For those who want to be away from the hectic coastal resorts and to take advantage of the peace and quiet of an adults only park, this will be an excellent 'value for money' choice. Chacewater has a pleasant rural situation and the site is run with care and attention by Richard Peterken and his daughters Debbie and Mandy. It provides 100 level touring pitches - only two persons per pitch are allowed and tents are not accepted. All pitches have 10A electricity and 90 have hardstanding; they are set in two large fields (slight slope) edged with trees or in small bays formed by hedges. There are 29 serviced pitches (electricity, water and drainage connections) and an area for dog owners.

Facilities

The main toilet block provides well equipped showers and two en-suite units. Laundry room. Second fully equipped block near reception providing roomy showers open direct to outside. Gas supplies. Library and small shop in reception. Only adults are accepted. Max. 1 dog, contact site first. WiFi (charged). Off site: Golf, riding and bicycle hire within 3 miles. Bus stop 100 yds.

Open: 25 April - 4 October.

Directions

From A30, 28 miles west of Bodmin take A3047 (Scorrier), at roundabout go left towards St Day. After 500 yds. turn right at crossroads onto B3298 for 1 mile. Turn left at the crossroads, continue for 0.75 miles, then left at crossroads with blue camping sign (by Truro Tractors). Chacewater Park is the next right. GPS: 50.250802, -5.172557

Charges guide

Per unit incl. 2 persons and electricity	£ 20.00 - £ 28.00

Truro

Trevarth Holiday Park

Blackwater, Truro TR4 8HR (Cornwall) T: 01872 560266. E: info@trevarth.co.uk

alanrogers.com/UK0011

Trevarth Holiday Park is a friendly, well managed, family run site with very easy access from the A30, making it an ideal base from which to tour this very attractive area of Cornwall. In addition, a bus stop just outside of the campsite, and the park and ride only two miles away allow easy access to Truro. This well maintained 4.5-acre site has 33 level pitches on grass or loose stone, 28 of which have 16A electricity supply. Set in two meadows separated by hedges and tall trees, they are protected from the wind. A large playing field is located opposite the reception area.

Facilities

Well maintained sanitary block with free showers, laundry room and baby changing facilities. Motorcaravan services. Playground. Games room. Large sports field. WiFi (first 30 mins. free). Off site: Truro with its magnificent Cathedral. Cycling, fishing, surfing, golf, tennis and riding.

Open: 1 April - 31 October.

Directions

Site is 5 miles northwest of Truro. From A30 roundabout take B3277 towards St. Agnes, after 200 yds. at small roundabout take second exit. Site is in 200 yds. on right. GPS: 50.27719, -5.16877

Charges guide

Per unit incl. 2 persons and electricity	£ 13.00 - £ 21.00

Truro

Killiwerris Camping & Caravan Park

Penstraze, Chacewater, Truro TR4 8PF (Cornwall) T: 01872 561356. E: killiwerris@aol.com

alanrogers.com/UK0012

Tucked down a Cornish lane, Killiwerris is a rare find. This adults only park has been developed from a large garden and field surrounding the house into a small and delightful touring park which provides 18 good sized, fully serviced pitches for caravans and motorcaravans. Those in the front field are on hardstanding, have flowering shrubs and are sheltered by trees. The birds love it, as do the visitors, and this very peaceful park is open all year. Three further pitches are found in the back field. Electricity (10A) is available for all the pitches with water points between two.

Facilities

Excellent heated toilet block in a log cabin with en-suite facilities to a very high standard. Separate provision for disabled visitors has ramped access. Separate laundry room. Max. 2 dogs. Off site: Bus stop 8 minutes level walk. Chacewater village (shop, pub, etc) 1 mile. Riding 1.5 miles. Fishing and golf 2 miles. Bicycle hire 2-3 miles. Beach 4.5 miles.

Open: All year.

Directions

Site is 5 miles northwest of Truro. On A30 towards Penzance, exit at Chiverton Cross roundabout (28 miles west of Bodmin signed for Truro and St Agnes). Take 3rd exit for Blackwater and in 500 yds. turn left into Kea Down Road. Park is 1 mile on right. GPS: 50.2655, -5.155

Charges guide

Per unit incl. 2 persons, electricity and awning	£ 20.00 - £ 24.00
No credit cards.	

For latest campsite news visit

alanrogers.com

Truro
Porthtowan Tourist Park
Mile Hill, Porthtowan, Truro TR4 8TY (Cornwall) T: 01209 890256. E: admin@porthtowantouristpark.co.uk
alanrogers.com/UK0014

This delightful and sheltered park is set a mile back from the pretty seaside village of Porthtowan, a haven for surfers but enjoyed by families who can explore the rock pools and coves. The beach has Blue Flag status. In an Area of Outstanding Natural Beauty, tall chimney stacks, stark against the sky, remain a reminder of the tin mining for which this area of Cornwall was once renowned. This is now a peaceful spot with plenty of space on the park and tall trees surrounding the three camping fields. The facilities were spotless when we visited in high season. There are 72 pitches around the edges of the fields, on level grass, all with 10A electricity. There are three hardstandings. The park is attractively laid out with tarmac roads and flowering shrubs. There is a recycling box for odds and ends left behind by holidaymakers but of potential use to future visitors. A large adventure-type play area in the centre of the large top field is popular. There is a waiting list for seasonal pitches and caravan storage. The Coast to Coast Tramway trail passes within half a mile. The Newquay-Saint Ives bus stops at the site entrance.

Facilities
Modern fully equipped toilet block with two en-suite family rooms also suitable for disabled visitors. Washing machine and dryer. Shop in reception. Games room with tourist information. Adventure type play area. Fish and chip van calls once a week (variable day). WiFi throughout (charged). Off site: Riding 200 yds. Nearest beach 1 mile. Fishing and golf 8 miles.

Open: 23 March - 30 September.

Directions
From the A30 take exit for Redruth, Porthtowan and Portreath and follow signs for Porthtowan for 2 miles. At T-junction turn right and the park is half a mile on the left. GPS: 50.27374, -5.23768

Charges guide
Per unit incl. 2 persons	
and electricity	£ 15.00 - £ 23.50
extra person	£ 4.00
child (3-16 yrs)	£ 2.50
dog	£ 1.00

Mile Hill, Porthtowan, Truro, Cornwall, TR4 8TY
www.porthtowantouristpark.co.uk
01209 890256

Tranquil family park only minutes from a Blue Flag surfing beach

Truro
Trethem Mill Touring Park
Saint Just-in-Roseland, Saint Mawes, Truro TR2 5JF (Cornwall) T: 01872 580504. E: reception@trethem.com
alanrogers.com/UK0090

The three generations of the Akeroyd family are proud of their superb park and they work hard to keep it really well maintained. They have been recognised for their commitment to high standards by many gold awards. They aim to attract couples and families who seek peace and tranquillity, and who enjoy making their own entertainment. Trethem is strictly a touring park with all 84 pitches having 16A electricity, 66 with hardstanding and TV connections and 21 with water and waste water. All are large, most on slightly sloping lawns, with the lower area more level and sheltered. All are individual or in bays, divided by neat hedging, giving everyone some privacy. At Trethem Mill you can be sure of a warm welcome and it is ideally placed for sailing, walking the coastal path around the peninsula, visiting the gardens of Trelissick and Heligan, or simply lazing on the nearby beaches. A member of the Best of British group.

Facilities
The excellent central toilet block is kept spotlessly clean and is heated in cooler weather. Three new shower suites, underfloor heating, en-suite facilities for disabled visitors (doubles as family room). Baby room (under 4s). Launderette. Motorcaravan services. Small well stocked shop in reception. Freezer for ice packs (free). Picnic tables. Pick-your-own herb garden. Small library. Well equipped adventure playground (closed at 21.00). Large field for ball games. Extra field for dog walking and nature walks. WiFi (charged). Off site: Fishing 1.5 miles. Beach, sailing, boat launching and bicycle hire 2 miles. Golf 6 miles. Riding 8 miles.

Open: 24 March - 9 October.

Directions
From Tregony follow A3078 to St Mawes. After passing through Trewithian (about 2 miles), follow camping signs to site. GPS: 50.19003, -5.00096

Charges guide
Per unit incl. 2 persons	
and electricity	£ 19.00 - £ 31.00
extra person	£ 6.00
child (3-14 yrs)	£ 4.00
dog	£ 1.00

For latest campsite news visit
alanrogers.com

Truro
Silverbow Park

Goonhavern, Truro TR4 9NX (Cornwall) T: 01872 572347. E: silverbowhols@btconnect.com

alanrogers.com/UK0120

Silverbow has been developed by the Taylor family over many years and they are justifiably proud of their efforts. It is a small, unashamedly upmarket park catering for the discerning who seek a truly relaxing holiday (unaccompanied teenagers are not accepted). Hard work, planting and landscaping have created a beautiful environment set in 21 acres. There are 108 pitches with 90 good sized touring pitches; some are slightly sloping and many have attractive views. These include 77 much larger super pitches in a newly developed area along with Eco lodges and leisure homes. All are fully serviced (10A electricity). Much free space is not used for camping, including an excellent sports area with two all-weather tennis courts, as well as a wild meadow and wooded areas ideal for walks. A natural area with ponds has been created to encourage wildlife (Silverbow was the first in Cornwall to gain the coveted '5-year Bellamy Gold' award for conservation). The park is two and a half miles from the long sandy beach at Perranporth and six miles from Newquay.

Facilities

Two good toilet blocks include private cabins, four family shower/toilet rooms (two accessible by wheelchair). Laundry room. Motorcaravan services. Shop for basics (mid May-mid Sept). Covered, heated swimming pool and small paddling pool (mid May-mid Sept). Games room. Play field. Tennis. Off site: Beach, fishing, golf, riding and bicycle hire within 2.5 miles. Concessionary green fees at Perranporth golf club. Pub within walking distance.

Open: 23 April - 30 September.

Directions

Entrance is directly off the main A3075 road 0.5 miles south of Goonhavern.
GPS: 50.336567, -5.120633

Charges guide

Per unit incl. 2 persons	£ 18.00 - £ 31.00
extra person under 50 yrs	£ 3.00 - £ 6.00
child (2-12 yrs) or adult over 50 yrs	£ 2.50 - £ 4.50
dog	£ 2.00

Children over 12 yrs with or without parents not accepted. Discounts available.

Truro
Carnon Downs Caravan & Camping Park

Carnon Downs, Truro TR3 6JJ (Cornwall) T: 01872 862283. E: info@carnon-downs-caravanpark.co.uk

alanrogers.com/UK0180

Carnon Downs is an excellent all year park run personally and enthusiastically by Simon Vallance, a very forward thinking owner. It has been thoughtfully laid out in a series of fields covering 20 acres so that all pitches back onto attractive hedging or areas of flowering shrubs and arranged to provide some pleasant bays or other, more open grass areas. Gravel roads connect the 150 pitches, most with 10/16A electricity and over 70 with hardstanding. Of these, 55 are serviced, with the newer ones being exceptionally large and surrounded by young shrubs. On arrival you will receive a warm welcome, a neatly presented layout plan of the park and a touring information pack. Affiliated to the Caravan Club.

Facilities

Two excellent modern, light and airy, heated blocks include en-suite units and facilities for disabled visitors. Another well maintained block, also heated, includes some washbasins in cubicles and showers (unisex). Three good family bath/shower rooms, one suitable for use by disabled campers or families. Mother and toddler room, two baby sinks and full sized bath. Two laundries with freezers. Motorcaravan services (ask at reception). Good adventure-type play area. Football field. Gas, newspapers and caravan accessories. General room with TV. Good dog walks. Caravan storage. Off site: Walks direct from site. Bus outside site for Truro/Falmouth. Pub/restaurant 100 yds. across the road. Golf 1 mile. Riding and bicycle hire 2 miles. Fishing 5 miles.

Open: All year.

Directions

From Truro take A39 Falmouth road. After 3 miles, park entrance is directly off the Carnon Downs roundabout. GPS: 50.22529, -5.08012

Charges guide

Per unit incl. 2 persons and electricity	£ 23.00 - £ 33.00
extra person	£ 4.00
child (5-16 yrs)	£ 3.50
all-service hardstanding	£ 2.50

For latest campsite news visit
alanrogers.com

Truro

Cosawes Park

Perranarworthal, Truro TR3 7QS (Cornwall) T: 01872 863724. E: info@cosawes.com

alanrogers.com/UK0185

Cosawes is set in a beautiful wooded valley where there are woodland and river walks and the park offers a quiet and relaxing holiday. The Fraser family have owned the site since 1948 and the recent upgrading of the facilities is excellent, particularly for a site that is open all year. Cosawes now offers 31 large, serviced pitches on gravel hardstandings, each in its own fenced space. These are particularly popular with motorcaravan owners and very useful for twin-axle vans. This still leaves another 25 grass pitches which are slightly sloping, most with 16A electricity. A separate large residential area is private and away from the touring section.

Facilities	Directions
Excellent, modern block (with ground source heat pump) beside the new serviced pitches provides two en-suite family rooms also suitable for disabled visitors. Toilets, laundry and dishwashing are downstairs, upstairs are showers and washbasins in cubicles. Fish and chips weekly. Dog walking field. WiFi (charged). Walks from site. Off site: Two pubs within walking distance. Supermarket 3 miles. Bicycle hire 3 miles. Beach at Falmouth 7 miles.	Site is midway between Truro and Falmouth. Approaching from Truro via A39, after village of Perranarworthal, the park is clearly signed on right, and is 300 yds. up the lane on left. Use second entrance. GPS: 50.197026, -5.128319

Open: All year.

Charges guide

Per unit incl. 2 persons and electricity	£ 16.00 - £ 26.00
extra person	£ 3.00

Truro

Summer Valley Touring Park

Shortlanesend, Truro TR4 9DW (Cornwall) T: 01872 277878. E: res@summervalley.co.uk

alanrogers.com/UK0510

Summer Valley is a quiet and mature, but very pleasant, small rural park suitable for visiting both the north and south coast of Cornwall. South facing, the park comprises two large, well kept grass areas with reception and facilities to one side. A tarmac road circles this and mature trees edge the whole site providing shelter but still allowing rural views. Caravans go on the central area which slopes gently and is divided down the centre with more mature trees and shrubs. The pitches around the perimeter area are semi-divided by shrubs and used more for tents. There is provision for 60 units of all types, 45 with 10/16A electricity connections. A Countryside Discovery site.

Facilities	Directions
A good quality, solid toilet block is well maintained with ladies to the left and men to the right, plus unisex showers. Washbasins in cubicles and one shower/toilet en-suite. Laundry facilities. Rest room for campers with library. Reception/licensed shop (basics in high season) with freezer pack service. Gas supplies. Small play area hidden in one corner. WiFi (free). Off site: Shortlanesend with post office and pub within walking distance.	Site is 2 miles northwest of Truro. From A30 take B3284 southeast towards Truro. After 1.5 miles site is signed just before village of Shortlanesend. Entrance lane leading directly to the site is to the right. GPS: 50.29098, -5.08823

Open: 31 March - 31 October.

Charges guide

Per unit incl. 2 persons and electricity	£ 12.50 - £ 17.00
extra person	£ 3.50

Wadebridge

Saint Mabyn Holiday Park

Longstone Road, Saint Mabyn PL30 3BY (Cornwall) T: 01208 841677. E: info@stmabyn.co.uk

alanrogers.com/UK0230

The beaches of north Cornwall and the wilds of Bodmin Moor are all an easy drive from the site. The park has been extensively improved and is now carefully maintained by the Lloyd family and it provides a spacious and relaxed atmosphere. There are 110 level pitches, 97 with 16A electricity, on well drained and well mown grass with 50 hardstandings. There are caravan holiday homes and lodges to let. A nice, sheltered outdoor pool is an added attraction. Although there is no bar, the local village inn, one mile away, has a good reputation for food. The Camel Trail is only two miles away.

Facilities	Directions
The fully equipped modern toilet block includes one en-suite unit per sex. A second, newly renovated block has family rooms and fully equipped facility for disabled visitors. Indoor dishwashing area with fridge/freezer and microwave. Laundry. Heated outdoor swimming pool and paddling pool (late May-early Sept). Good, fenced adventure play area. Play area for small children. Games room. Caravan storage. WiFi over site.	From Bodmin or Wadebridge on A389, take B3266 north signed Camelford. At village of Longstone turn left signed St Mabyn and brown camping sign. Site is 400 yds. on right. Ignore all other signs to St Mabyn. GPS: 50.5278, -4.745183

Open: Mid March - end October.

Charges guide

Per unit incl. 2 persons and electricity	£ 12.00 - £ 24.00
extra person	£ 5.00

For latest campsite news visit

alanrogers.com

Wadebridge

Trewince Farm Holiday Park

Saint Issey, Wadebridge PL27 7RL (Cornwall) T: 01208 812830.

alanrogers.com/UK0500

A well established and popular park, Trewince Farm is four miles from Padstow and has been developed around a dairy farm with magnificent countryside views. Careful landscaping with flowering shrubs and bushes makes this an attractive setting. There are 35 caravan holiday homes discreetly terraced, some privately owned, some to let. Two touring areas on higher ground provide both hardstanding and level grass pitches with a sheltered tent area. Over half of the 120 touring pitches have 10A electricity and 34 have water and drainage. The park's main feature is an excellent sheltered, walled and heated swimming pool with paddling pool and paved sunbathing area. Farm rides are organised in high season.

Facilities

Two fully equipped, well maintained toilet blocks include washbasins in cabins, hair care rooms and laundry rooms. Family bathroom and facilities for disabled visitors. Well stocked shop (all season) by reception. Fish and chip man calls twice weekly, and pizza van (July/Aug). Swimming pool. Play area. Games room. Crazy golf. Natural lake and woodland walk. Off site: Pubs and restaurants in nearby village of St Issey. Riding 3 miles. Beach 4.5 miles.

Open: 1 April - 31 October.

Directions

From Wadebridge follow A39 towards St Columb and pick up the A389 for Padstow. Site is signed on left in 2 miles. Follow for short distance to park entrance on right. GPS: 50.506604, -4.911692

Charges guide

Per unit incl. 2 persons	
and electricity	£ 16.50 - £ 22.50
extra person	£ 3.50 - £ 4.50
child (3-15 yrs)	£ 2.50 - £ 3.50

Wadebridge

The Laurels Holiday Park

Padstow Road, Whitecross, Wadebridge PL27 7JQ (Cornwall) T: 01209 313474.
E: info@thelaurelsholidaypark.co.uk **alanrogers.com/UK0505**

Convenient for the A39, this is a small park in a garden-like setting of which the managers are very proud. It is very well maintained and provides 32 level pitches with 16A electricity. Some have hardstanding and some are extra large. Neat hedging marks the pitches and the central area with shrubs and plants is kept clear for enjoyment. A good play area for children is well fenced from the A39 which could be the cause of some road noise. The Camel Trail for walking or cycling is close and follows the estuary from Wadebridge to Padstow. A bus stops outside the site.

Facilities

Well kept fully equipped sanitary block. Family shower room. Laundry. Facilities for drying wetsuits. Freezer and communal fridge. Play area with trampoline. WiFi (free). Off site: Shops 2 miles. Riding, bicycle hire, boat launching 3 miles. Beach 4 miles. Fishing 5 miles. Camel Trail (walking/cycling).

Open: 1 April - 30 October.

Directions

The Park is two miles southwest of Wadebridge beside the A39 road at its junction with the A389 Padstow road. Site entrance is on the A389, some 30 yds. from its junction with the A39. GPS: 50.50827, -4.88192

Charges guide

Per unit incl. 2 persons	
and electricity	£ 14.00 - £ 26.00

Wadebridge

Tristram Camping Park

Polzeath, Wadebridge PL27 6TP (Cornwall) T: 01208 862215. E: info@tristramcampsite.co.uk

alanrogers.com/UK0525

Polzeath has one of the most spectacular surfing beaches in Cornwall and is just round the corner from the popular resorts of Rock and Padstow. The campsite is situated on the cliff just above the bay on sloping grass and a footpath leads to the beach. This is a popular and compact site for families so booking is essential in high season. A few units up to 26 feet can be accommodated but most of the pitches take 20 foot units. In total there are 107 marked pitches with a smaller area for two-man tents. Two toilet blocks serve the site and 16A electricity is available over most of the site. The coastal path runs along the front of the site.

Facilities

Two solid toilet blocks are fully equipped. 50p token required for showers. Washing machines and dryers. Restaurant. Surf hire (by day/hour). Off site: Shops in village (10 mins. walk). Two golf courses nearby. Foot ferry from Rock for the Camel Trail and Padstow (with Rick Stein's restaurants). Wadebridge 15 miles.

Open: March - October.

Directions

Follow directions to Polzeath from Wadebridge. Go downhill into village then keep left up hill. Site entrance is to right through a gate you must open and close yourself, just before the public parking barriers. The descent into the site is quite steep, so difficult for large units. GPS: 50.572947, -4.918816

Charges guide

Per unit incl. 4 persons	
and electricity	£ 37.50 - £ 42.50

For latest campsite news visit

alanrogers.com

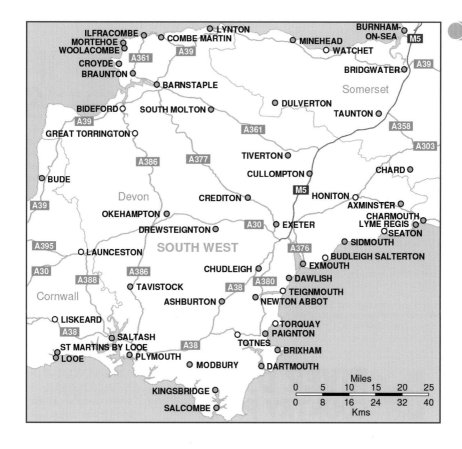

Ashburton

Parkers Farm Holiday Park

Higher Mead Farm, Ashburton, Newton Abbot TQ13 7LJ (Devon) T: 01364 654869.

E: parkersfarm@btconnect.com **alanrogers.com/UK0960**

Well situated with fine views towards Dartmoor, Parkers Farm is a modern, friendly touring site offering a unique chance to experience Devon country life at first hand, with pigs, sheep, goats, calves and rabbits to feed and touch. The 128 pitches (100 for touring) are on broad terraces giving groups of slightly sloping pitches, some with good views across the valley. Electricity (10A) is provided throughout and 11 pitches are fully serviced on hardstanding. Trees and hedges have matured nicely on the terraces, with many more planted. Caravan holiday homes are available to hire. There is some traffic noise. American motorhomes are accepted by prior arrangement. A family bar hosts entertainment during the main season (live singers, family bingo, children's entertainers) and a restaurant using locally sourced ingredients. Farm walks and tractor rides are tremendously popular and take place three evenings a week in high season, on request at other times. Parker's Farm provides a warm welcome – in the words of one camper, 'You come here and feel you belong'.

Facilities

Two modern, fully equipped toilet blocks with family rooms, baby bathroom and en-suite room for disabled visitors. Laundry. Shop (Easter-mid Oct). Restaurant, bar with family room (Easter, then Whitsun-mid Sept) and entertainment. Games room. Indoor play and TV area. Large outdoor play area. Trampolines. 6 acres of fields for dog walking. Caravan storage. Caravan holiday homes to hire. Rallies welcome. WiFi (charged). Off site: Golf 4 miles. Riding and bicycle hire 5 miles. Coast 12 miles.

Open: Easter - 31 October.

Directions

From Exeter on A38 turn left at Alston Cross signed Woodland Denbury. Site is 400 yds. GPS: 50.527646, -3.723459

Charges guide

Per unit incl. 2 persons and electricity	£ 12.00 - £ 25.00
extra person	£ 3.00
child (3-15 yrs)	£ 2.00
dog	£ 1.50

For latest campsite news visit

alanrogers.com

Ashburton

River Dart Country Park

Holne Park, Ashburton TQ13 7NP (Devon) T: 01364 652511. E: info@riverdart.co.uk

alanrogers.com/UK0950

The River Dart Country Park offers a great range of adventure experiences suitable for campers of all ages. Also open to the public, it does become busy at weekends and during school holidays so booking is essential. The camping and caravanning area is in open parkland overlooking the woods and is mainly on a slight slope with some shade from mature trees. There are 261 individual pitches of a reasonable size and in different locations. There are 136 pitches with electrical connections (10/16A) and 35 with hardstanding. Once part of a Victorian estate with mature woodland on the edge of Dartmoor in the beautiful Dart valley, the park features a variety of unusual adventure play equipment arranged amongst and below the trees, Lilliput Land for toddlers, Jungle Fun, woodland streams and a lake with a 'pirate ship' for swimming, and inflatables, fly fishing and marked nature and forest trails – all free to campers except fishing. There is a Commando assault course, Dare Devil activities (high ropes course across the river, water zorbs, mega zip wire, fee payable), while falconry displays are organised in high season.

Facilities

Two main sanitary blocks. A Biomass heating system provides hot water throughout. Washbasins in cubicles. Facilities for babies and children. En-suite unit for disabled visitors. Family bathroom. Drying room. Laundry. Freezer. Motorcaravan services. Shop, restaurant, bar, Sunday carvery and takeaway (all 25/3-29/9). TV and games room. Indoor climbing room. Tennis. Bicycle hire. Free WiFi in bar area. Max. two dogs. Off site: Ashburton with shops 2 miles. Golf 6 miles. Totnes 8 miles.

Open: 27 March - 26 September.

Directions

Signed from the A38 at Peartree junction, park is 1 mile west of Ashburton, on the road to Two Bridges. Disregard advisory signs stating 'no caravans' as access to the park is prior to narrow bridge. GPS: 50.51698, -3.78869

Charges guide

Per unit incl. 2 persons and electricity	£ 17.50 - £ 32.00
extra person (over 3 yrs)	£ 4.00 - £ 9.00
dog (max. 2)	£ 3.50

Axminster

Andrewshayes Holiday Park

Dalwood, Axminster EX13 7DY (Devon) T: 01404 831225. E: info@andrewshayes.co.uk

alanrogers.com/UK1252

The Lawrences have been developing the park for over 50 years so it is well established with visitors returning every year. Extra fields have been added providing 230 pitches in total. As the site is on the side of the valley with views across to the Blackdown Hills, most of the pitches have been terraced with central or circular access roads. One field is dedicated to privately owned mobile homes, the other two fields contain some 112 seasonal and 34 touring pitches (all with 10A electricity), some super pitches, some all weather and a few on grass. There is a summer camping field for tents (no electricity).

Facilities

Two fully equipped toilet blocks with family rooms and facilities for disabled visitors. Launderette. Microwave. Bar (weekend evenings only low season). Takeaway (mid July-end Aug). Shop in reception for essentials. Covered, heated swimming pool. Play area. Games room and new soft play area for young ones. WiFi (charged). Off site: Seaton Tramway 3 miles. Fishing and bicycle hire 5 miles. Riding 6 miles. Golf 9 miles.

Open: 20 March - 31 October.

Directions

Site is 3 miles northwest of Axminster on A35. From Axminster follow A35 towards Honiton for 3 miles. Watch carefully for road sign for village of Dalwood, turn right and right again almost immediately for Dalwood. Site is well signed 150 yds. on right. GPS: 50.782995, -3.069477

Charges guide

Per unit incl. 2 persons and electricity	£ 18.50 - £ 26.50
extra person	£ 3.00 - £ 6.00

For latest campsite news visit
alanrogers.com

Barnstaple
Greenacres Touring Caravan Park

Bratton Fleming, Barnstaple EX31 4SG (Devon) T: 01598 763334. E: stephenrj@hotmail.co.uk

alanrogers.com/UK0700

A delightful rural park on the edge of Exmoor, Greenacres is managed and run alongside, but separately from, the farm owned by the family. Drive through the farm access to the park (clearly signed) – you will need to go back and call at the house to book in. No tents are taken. The site has 30 very large, well drained pitches (all with 16A electricity) with connecting gravel paths to the road. The top area is level, the lower part next to the beech woods provides six pitches on hardstanding and some are separated by low hedging. There are marvellous views outside the beech hedge that shelters the site. To the west of Exmoor, the park is very suitable for the coast at Ilfracombe and Combe Martin, or for exploring the moor. There is a woodland walk through newly planted trees and across the fields to a secluded valley picnic area beside a stream to take advantage of the beautiful views and surroundings. The West Country cycle way passes within a mile of the park.

Facilities

The neat, clean toilet block with showers (20p). Units for disabled visitors. Laundry facilities. Gas supplies. Area for children with football and volleyball nets. Two-acre dog exercise field. Tourist information. Off site: North Devon coast and Exmoor within easy reach. Pubs, restaurants and takeaways within 3 mile radius. Fishing 3 miles. Riding 6 miles. Bicycle hire 12 miles.

Open: 1 April - 16 October.

Directions

From North Devon link road A361 (M5, exit 27) turn north at South Molton onto A399. Continue for 9 miles, past turning for Exmoor Steam Centre and on to Stowford Cross. Turn left towards Exmoor Zoological Park and Greenacres Farm is on the left. GPS: 51.147633, -3.917517

Charges guide

Per unit. 2 persons and electricity	£ 10.00 - £ 16.50
extra person (over 7 yrs)	£ 2.00 - £ 3.00
dog	free

No credit cards.

Braunton
Hidden Valley Touring & Camping Park

West Down, Ilfracombe EX34 8NU (Devon) T: 01271 813837. E: info@hiddenvalleypark.com

alanrogers.com/UK0710

The Legg family run this attractive and aptly named family park to very high standards. In a sheltered valley setting between Barnstaple and Ilfracombe, beside a small stream and a lake (with ducks), it is convenient for several resorts, beaches and the surrounding countryside. The park is divided into two sections. The older section has pitches of varying size on three sheltered terraces, all with electricity and a TV point and many are fully serviced. The other section, the Kingfisher Meadow, is more open and has spacious grass pitches more suitable for campers with tents, also with electricity and a TV point. Two good adventure play areas have wooden equipment and safe bark surfaces (one near a fast flowing stream which is fenced). Essentially this is a park for those seeking good quality facilities in very attractive, natural surroundings, without too many man-made distractions – apart from some traffic noise during the daytime. A member of the Best of British group.

Facilities

Two modern heated toilet blocks, one in each section with facilities for disabled visitors. The Kingfisher Meadow block has some washbasins with toilets in cubicles and a bathroom. Baby room. Laundry facilities. Motorcaravan service point. Gas supplies. Shop. Restaurant/coffee shop. Play areas. WiFi throughout (charged). Dog walk. Caravan storage. Off site: Fishing and golf 2 miles. Riding and bicycle hire 3 miles. Beach 4 miles.

Open: All year.

Directions

Park is on A361 Barnstaple-Ilfracombe road, 3.5 miles north of Braunton. GPS: 51.146533, -4.14555

Charges guide

Per unit incl. 2 persons and electricity	£ 10.00 - £ 40.00
extra person	£ 3.00 - £ 5.00
child (2-15 yrs)	£ 2.00 - £ 4.00
dog	£ 1.50

Discounts for over 50s.

For latest campsite news visit
alanrogers.com

Braunton

Lobb Fields Caravan & Camping Park

Saunton Road, Braunton EX33 1HG (Devon) T: 01271 812090. E: info@lobbfields.com

alanrogers.com/UK1140

Lobb Fields has two camping areas providing 180 pitches on sloping grass, with a few hardstandings. Twelve pitches are reserved for seasonal caravans, and 98 have 16A electricity hook-ups. A third field is open for campers for 28 days only in high season. The pitches are marked and grass roads lead to the amenities. As the two toilet blocks are at the very bottom or very top of the fields, some up and down walking is inevitable. Lobb Fields may be close to many holiday activities, but it is also a peaceful retreat for those wanting a quiet holiday. Braunton village, Saunton Sands, the famous Tarka Trail for cycling, Baggy Point for walking, the biosphere at Braunton Burrows (one of only 13 similar special reserves in the country), Marwood Gardens, and windsurfing and water skiing on the Taw estuary are just some of the many attractions within a short distance of Lobb Fields.

Facilities

Two rather dated toilet blocks (one in each field) have all the usual facilities. Two family/baby rooms. Laundry. Cleaning and maintenance can be variable. The lower block can be heated and has good facilities for disabled visitors. Hair dryers and irons available from reception (£5 deposit). Takeaway (all season). Play area. Surf shop. WiFi (charged). Off site: Nearest shops less than a mile. Beach, fishing, golf, riding and bicycle hire 1 mile. Boat launching 1.5 miles.

Open: 27 March - 1 November.

Directions

Take A361 Barnstaple-Braunton road, then B3231 (signed Croyde) to Braunton. Park is 1 mile from Braunton on the right. Take care through Braunton as roads are quite narrow and busy.
GPS: 51.11165, -4.181233

Charges guide

Per unit incl. 2 persons	
and electricity	£ 15.00 - £ 30.00
extra person	£ 6.00 - £ 8.00
child (5-15 yrs)	£ 2.00 - £ 4.00
dog	£ 2.00 - £ 3.00

Brixham

Hillhead Caravan Club Site

Hillhead, Brixham TQ5 0HH (Devon) T: 01803 853204.

alanrogers.com/UK0845

alan rogers

Runner up
2015 Awards

Hillhead is set in 22 acres of beautiful Devon countryside. It comprises 256 pitches, all with 16A electrical hook-ups and many with fine views of Torbay and the surrounding countryside. There are 111 pitches with hardstanding and 13 attractive and sheltered pitches for tents. Amenities are to a uniformly high standard, notably the main complex based around a pleasant courtyard and housing a shop, bar, games room and Nico's restaurant serving freshly cooked meals using local produce and a Sunday carvery. The site offers an entertainment programme from Whitsun onwards. The children's play area is outstanding, with a range of imaginative items including a large wooden fort. The swimming pool is sheltered by hedges and has been well placed to catch the sun all day. Timed sessions may be necessary during busy periods. With its range of pitches, levels and open spaces, the site has a village-like feel.

Facilities

The two sanitary blocks are maintained to a high standard. Each block includes three private family bathrooms (key from reception) and facilities for disabled visitors. Laundry facilities. Motorcaravan services. Shop. Bar and restaurant with takeaway. Swimming pool (June-Sept) with paddling pool adjacent. Large play area. Games room. TV. Entertainment in season. Games field. Dog walking area. WiFi throughout (charged). Off site: Bus stop at site entrance. Nearest beach and coastal path 2 miles. Golf (18 holes) and riding 2 miles. Bicycle hire 2.5 miles. Brixham 2 miles. Dartmouth and ferry 3 miles. Supermarket 4 miles. Torquay 6 miles. Numerous local attractions include South Devon Railway, River Dart boat trips and Paignton Zoo.

Open: 20 March - 4 January.

Directions

Site is well signed from the A379 Paignton-Dartmouth road and is on the B3205 (Slappers Hill Road). Entrance is on the left after 400 yds.
GPS: 50.36969, -3.54476

Charges guide

Per person	£ 6.20 - £ 11.30
child (5-17 yrs)	£ 0.01 - £ 4.90
pitch incl. electricity (non-member)	£ 15.80 - £ 22.90

For latest campsite news visit

alanrogers.com

Brixham

Galmpton Touring Park

Greenway Road, Galmpton, Brixham TQ5 0EP (Devon) T: 01803 842066.
E: enquiries@galmptontouringpark.co.uk **alanrogers.com/UK0850**

Within a few miles of the lively amenities of Torbay, Galmpton Park lies peacefully just outside the village of Galmpton, overlooking the beautiful Dart estuary just upstream of Dartmouth and Kingswear. A family park, now under new ownership, with 120 pitches (60 marked for caravans) which are arranged on a wide sweep of grassy, terraced meadow with some hedging. Each pitch has its own wonderful view of the river. Some fully serviced deluxe pitches are also available. Situated on the hillside, some parts have quite a slope but there are flatter areas (the owners will advise and assist). There are 90 electricity connections (10A) and 23 pitches have water and drainage. There is a separate tent field.

Facilities	Directions
A central toilet block provides clean facilities, including three washbasins in cabins, a very attractive under 5s bathroom and baby unit. En-suite unit for disabled visitors. New laundry facilities. Motorcaravan services. Shop selling essentials. Adventure play equipment. Max. 2 dogs. Motorcaravans over 26 ft. are not accepted. Torches useful. Off site: Local pub is 5 mins. walk. Bus 15 mins. walk on main road. Golf 1 mile. Beach 2 miles.	Take A380 Paignton ring road towards Brixham until junction with Paignton-Brixham coast road. Right towards Brixham, then second right (Manor Vale Road). Continue through village, past school and site is 500 yds. on right. GPS: 50.391650, -3.568070

Charges guide

Per unit incl. 2 persons and electricity	£ 17.50 - £ 23.50
extra person	£ 3.50 - £ 4.00

Open: 25 March - 1 November.

Chudleigh

Holmans Wood Holiday Park

Harcombe Cross, Chudleigh TQ13 0DZ (Devon) T: 01626 853785. E: enquiries@holmanswood.co.uk
alanrogers.com/UK0940

This attractive, neat park is close to the main A38 Exeter-Plymouth road and makes a good, sheltered base for touring south Devon and Dartmoor. The hedged park is arranged on well kept grass surrounding a shallow depression, the floor of which makes a safe, grassy play area for children. There are many trees and the park is decorated with flowers. In two main areas and accessed by tarmac roads, there are 150 level pitches with 115 for touring, 100 equipped with 10A Europlugs. Seventy fully serviced pitches are on hardstanding, while 25 are reserved for tents. There is some traffic noise.

Facilities	Directions
The single, well maintained toilet block includes facilities for babies and disabled visitors. Laundry room. Play area. Caravan storage. Woodland and meadow walks. WiFi over site (charged). Off site: Bus stop outside gate. Pub/restaurant nearby in Chudleigh village. Spar shop 5 minutes walk. Sunday market at Exeter Racecourse 2 miles. Haldon Forest for walks 2 miles. Golf and riding 4 miles. Beach and Dartmoor 7 miles.	From Exeter on A38 Plymouth road, 0.5 miles after the racecourse and just after a garage, take Chudleigh exit (signed). Park is immediately on the left. From Plymouth turn off A38 for Chudleigh/Teign Valley, then right for Chudleigh. Continue through the town and park is 1 mile. GPS: 50.61941, -3.58295

Charges guide

Per unit incl. 2 persons and electricity	£ 19.00 - £ 29.00
extra person	£ 3.50

Open: Mid March - 5 January.

Combe Martin

Newberry Valley Park

Woodlands, Combe Martin EX34 0AT (Devon) T: 01271 882334. E: relax@newberryvalleypark.co.uk
alanrogers.com/UK0685

Newberry Valley Park is set in a tranquil, semi-wooded valley that slopes down towards the rugged North Devon coast, on the edge of Combe Martin. Three wide terraces and several sheltered fields provide 110 good sized touring pitches (105 with 16A electricity), with views to the surrounding hills. These vary from 26 fully serviced, large pitches (16 with hardstanding) with picnic tables to simple grass areas more suitable for tents. Combe Martin Bay has two beaches with rock pools and caves, and Newberry Beach is only a five minute walk from the site down a small path.

Facilities	Directions
Central modern toilet block with underfloor heating and all the usual facilities including those for disabled visitors and family shower room. Laundry facilities. Motorcaravan services. Play area. Fishing. Small shop (Mar-Oct) in reception. WiFi throughout (charged). Off site: Beach 0.5 miles. Shops/restaurants in Combe Martin 0.5 miles. Riding 4 miles. Golf 7 miles.	Leave M5 at exit 17. Take A361 west bypassing South Molton then A399 north to Combe Martin. Site is on the left as you leave Combe Martin. GPS: 51.204191, -4.042599

Charges guide

Per unit incl. 2 persons and electricity	£ 16.00 - £ 38.00
extra person	£ 4.00 - £ 5.00

Open: 14 March - 31 October.

For latest campsite news visit
alanrogers.com

Crediton

Yeatheridge Farm Caravan Park

East Worlington, Crediton EX17 4TN (Devon) T: 01884 860330. E: yeatheridge@talk21.com

alanrogers.com/UK1060

Yeatheridge is a friendly, family park with riding, fishing lakes, and indoor pools. Based on a 200-acre farm, nine acres have been developed over many years into an attractive touring park. Around the site there are views of the local hills and Dartmoor away to the south, and Exmoor lies to the north. The touring area is very neat and tidy with a spacious feel as units are sited around the perimeter or back onto hedges, leaving open central areas. The 100 good sized, numbered pitches are flat or gently sloping with some on low terraces. Most have 10A electricity. Three woodland walks are possible ranging from 1 to 2.5 miles along the banks of the River Dalch. There are two deep coarse fishing lakes (bring your own rod), the top one offering family fishing and the lower one for serious fishing. Horse riding is available on site with 45-minute and park rides available. The owners, Geoff and Liz, are constantly upgrading the park and they try very hard to make everyone feel at home.

Facilities

Two superb toilet blocks provide family rooms, facilities for babies and disabled visitors. Laundry. Motorcaravan service point. Shop. Bar, restaurant and snack bar (hours vary acc. to season). Indoor swimming pools, paddling pool and water slide (10.00-20.00). Fenced play area with fort for under 10s. Football field. TV room. Games room. Fishing. Riding. WiFi (charged). Off site: Many marked walks and cycle routes. Interesting villages and towns to explore right in the centre of Devon. Two national parks.

Open: 15 March - 3 October.

Directions

Leave Tiverton west on B3137. Shortly before Witheridge turn left on B3042 for 3 miles to site on left. Well signed. GPS: 50.8887, -3.7501

Charges guide

Per unit incl. 2 persons and electricity	£ 13.00 - £ 27.00
extra person (over 4 yrs)	£ 3.50
dog	£ 1.00

Croyde

Ruda Holiday Park

Parkdean Holidays, Croyde Bay, Croyde EX33 1NY (Devon) T: 01271 890671.
E: rudatouring@parkdeanholidays.com alanrogers.com/UK1150

Ruda Holiday Park is a recent addition to Parkdean Holidays, now comprising 12 parks in Scotland, Wales and southwest England. Ruda is right beside a Blue Flag beach and provides 312 camping and touring pitches in two distinct areas. A large camping area divided into four sections is reserved for tents and small motorcaravans, there are some electricity hook-ups around the perimeter and it is served by two clean toilet blocks. Touring caravan and motorcaravan pitches, all with 16A connections, are in a separate field across the road with direct access to the beach. Here, there are modern toilet facilities. A central complex (well away from the camping fields) houses a supermarket, laundry, food outlets and all of the entertainment clubs and bars. The Cascade Tropical Pool, a fun pool with flume and water features is supervised at all times (children under five must wear the arm bands provided). There's plenty of walking on the sand dunes and around the park and Croyde Bay is renowned for surfing.

Facilities

Two blocks in the camping fields provide all facilities, including those for disabled campers. A modern building serves the touring field. Laundry. Bar, restaurant, snack bar and takeaway. Amusement arcade. Cascade Tropical pool. Adventure playground. Tennis court. Sports field. Fishing lake. Supermarket, boutique and hire centre. Surfing equipment for hire. Direct access to sheltered beach. WiFi. Dogs are not accepted. Off site: Golf 3 miles. Bicycle hire 8 miles. Surfing. Lundy Island excursion.

Open: March - November.

Directions

From Barnstaple, take A361 signed Braunton and Ilfracombe. At Braunton, take sharp left (narrow road) towards Croyde (signed) and follow the road to the beach. Entrance to Ruda is on the right. GPS: 51.135183, -4.2352

Charges guide

Per unit incl. 4 persons	£ 13.00 - £ 46.00
pitch with services	£ 19.00 - £ 49.50

Prices are for pitch and up to four persons; maximum of eight persons per pitch.

For latest campsite news visit

alanrogers.com

Cullompton
Forest Glade Holiday Park

Kentisbeare, Cullompton EX15 2DT (Devon) T: 01404 841381. E: enquiries@forest-glade.co.uk
alanrogers.com/UK1000

Forest Glade, owned and run by the Wellard family, is set in eight hectares of the Blackdown Hills (designated an Area of Outstanding Natural Beauty), deep in mid Devon away from the hectic life on the coast. A sheltered site set amongst woodland with extensive walking opportunities, there are 80 level touring pitches, 62 of which have 10A electricity connections, two with full services and 39 with hardstanding. Touring caravans must book in advance when the easiest route will be advised (phone bookings accepted). Although set in the countryside, the beaches of East Devon are a fairly easy drive away. There is a small, heated, covered pool with a paddling pool, sauna and patio area outside, and a large games room (up a flight of steps, so not suitable for visitors with disabilities). The surrounding 300 acres of forest makes this a nature- and dog-lovers' paradise (dogs are accepted).

Facilities

There is one main toilet block, heated in cold weather, with some washbasins in cubicles. Family shower room. Separate suite for disabled visitors. Laundry facilities. Facilities for babies. Extra prefabricated unit with toilets, washbasins and showers at the swimming pool. Well stocked shop includes gas and a takeaway (evenings except Sun). Microwave in campers' kitchen. Heated swimming pool (free). Sauna (on payment). Adventure play area with access to woodland. Games room. All-weather tennis court. WiFi over site (charged). Caravan storage. Wildlife information room. Off site: Fishing and riding 1.5 miles. Golf 6 miles. Beach 17 miles.

Open: 20 March - 2 November.

Directions

Caravans MUST approach from Honiton on the Dunkeswell road to avoid a steep hill. Call park or see website for full directions. Other vehicles take M5 exit 28, then A373 for 2.5 miles, continue past Keepers Cottage pub on right, then take next left towards Sheldon. Park is on left after 2.5 miles. GPS: 50.857833, -3.277517

Charges guide

Per unit incl. 2 persons	
and electricity	£ 16.50 - £ 21.50
extra person	£ 7.50
child (4-18 yrs)	£ 1.90 - £ 3.80

Dartmouth
Woodlands Grove Caravan & Camping Park

Blackawton, Dartmouth, Totnes TQ9 7DQ (Devon) T: 01803 712598. E: holiday@woodlandsgrove.com
alanrogers.com/UK0840

Woodlands is a pleasant surprise – from the road you have no idea of just what is hidden away deep in the Devon countryside. To achieve this, there has been sympathetic development of farm and woodland to provide a leisure park with a falconry centre and zoo park which is open to the public and offers a range of activities and entertainment appealing to all ages. Taking 350 units, the camping and caravan site overlooks the woodland and the leisure park. The original, main field has been fully terraced to provide groups of four to eight flat, very spacious pitches with hedging, the majority hardstanding (90% have 10A electricity and a shared water tap, drain and rubbish bin). The newest field has 120 pitches (with electricity) designed with a more open feel to provide space for larger groups or rallies. A popular park, early reservation is advisable. A member of the Best of British group.

Facilities

Three modern, heated toilet blocks, include private bathrooms (coin-operated, 20p) and 16 family shower cubicles. En-suite facilities for disabled visitors. Two laundry rooms. Motorcaravan services. Freezer for ice packs. Baby facilities. The leisure park café provides good value meals and a takeaway service. Café opening hours and camping shop (with gas and basic food supplies) vary according to season and demand. TV and games room. WiFi throughout (charged). Dogs are accepted on the campsite but not in the leisure park (unstaffed day kennels available). Caravan storage. Off site: Dartmouth and the South Hams beaches are nearby. Golf 0.5 miles. Riding 7 miles. Beach 6 miles. Fishing 9 miles.

Open: 28 March - 2 November.

Directions

From A38 at Buckfastleigh, take A384 to Totnes. Before the town centre turn right on A381 Kingsbridge road. After Halwell turn left at Totnes Cross garage, on A3122 to Dartmouth. Park is on right after 2.5 miles. GPS: 50.357898, -3.675001

Charges guide

Per unit incl. 2 persons	
and electricity	£ 15.50 - £ 24.00
extra person (over 2 yrs)	£ 7.75
awning or extra small pup tent	£ 3.50
large tent or trailer tent (120 sq. ft. plus) extra	£ 3.50
dog (contact site first)	£ 3.00

Free entry to leisure park for stays 2 nights or more.

For latest campsite news visit
alanrogers.com

Dawlish
Lady's Mile Holiday Park

Exeter Road, Dawlish EX7 0LX (Devon) T: 01626 863411. E: info@ladysmile.co.uk
alanrogers.com/UK1010

Lady's Mile is a popular, large family touring park, open all year and great for children. It has extensive grassy fields with some shade and a landscaped camping area, partly arranged on terraces. There are 550 good sized pitches (450 for touring) all with 10A electricity, and 59 fully serviced on hardstandings. You can walk to Dawlish (ten minutes) and to the sandy beaches at Dawlish Warren (20 minutes). The park also has a good sized, free outdoor swimming pool with a long slide and splash zone, a paddling pool and a super heated indoor pool with flume and separate paddling pool. A large bar complex has a family area overlooking the indoor pool and a daily entertainment programme caters for all ages. A new soft play area has been developed for children with a café/snack bar for parents. The park is popular over a long season with reservations necessary for high season.

Facilities

Four good toilet blocks of various ages and styles and an additional heated shower block. Facilities for disabled visitors. Four family bathrooms (50p). Two launderettes. Supermarket with camping accessories (March-end Oct). Fish and chip takeaway (July/Aug). Restaurant and carvery, café with pizzeria and snack bar. Bars and entertainment. Indoor and outdoor (25/5-1/9) pools. Gym and sauna. Adventure play area. Indoor soft play area, bowling alley and arcade machine. Games room. Ball area with nets. Bicycle hire. Late arrivals area. WiFi (free in clubhouse, rest of site charged). Off site: Golf 2.5 miles. Fishing and riding 3 miles. Bus stop on main road.

Open: All year.

Directions

Park is 1 mile north of Dawlish with access off the A379 (Exeter-Teignmouth) road.
GPS: 50.59525, -3.459467

Charges guide

Per unit incl. 2 persons	£ 15.00 - £ 29.50
extra person (over 2 yrs)	£ 2.50 - £ 4.75
dog	free - £ 4.75

Low season special offers.
Low season discount for OAPs.

Dawlish
Leadstone Camping

Warren Road, Dawlish Warren, Dawlish EX7 0NG (Devon) T: 01626 864411.
E: stay@leadstonecamping.co.uk **alanrogers.com/UK1095**

Leadstone provides traditional camping at its best in a series of hedged grass fields, sloping in parts, in a natural, secluded bowl. In a designed Area of Outstanding Natural Beauty, the Blue Flag beach and sand dunes of Dawlish Warren are only a half mile walk. The area can get somewhat frenzied in peak holiday times but Leadstone provides a haven of peace and tranquillity. Owned by the same family since 1974, the Leadstone welcome is personal and the site totally relaxed. In all, there are 137 pitches, 75 for touring, with 16A electricity. An impressive timber-clad building houses showers, toilets, a dishwashing room and launderette facilities. It is sympathetically designed in keeping with the site's location on the seaward side of the Warren road where it is subject to Coastal Preservation regulations. Extra toilet pods are brought in for peak times. The site is only open for a short season but is popular and well run.

Facilities

The fully equipped, centrally located new building with showers and toilets is well kept. Unisex showers (20p for 5-6 minutes). Facilities for disabled visitors. Laundry facilities. Motorcaravan services. Basic supplies and gas from reception. Play area with real tractor. Indoor pool. WiFi over site (charged). Off site: Beach with shops, cafés, etc. at Dawlish Warren 0.5 miles. Golf 0.5 miles. Bicycle hire 2 miles. Riding 5 miles. Boat launching 7 miles.

Open: 22 May - 7 September.

Directions

From Exeter follow the A379 Teignmouth road (M5 exit 30). After Starcross watch for left turn to Dawlish Warren and site is on right after 0.5 miles.
GPS: 50.59396, -3.45162

Charges guide

Per unit incl. 2 persons and electricity	£ 24.00 - £ 30.00
extra person	£ 8.00 - £ 11.00
child (3-13 yrs)	£ 3.00 - £ 3.50
dog	£ 2.75 - £ 3.50

For latest campsite news visit
alanrogers.com

Dawlish
Cofton Country Holidays

Starcross, Dawlish EX6 8RP (Devon) T: 01626 890111. E: info@coftonholidays.co.uk
alanrogers.com/UK0970

A popular and efficient family run park, Cofton is 1.5 miles from a sandy beach at Dawlish Warren. It has space for 450 touring units, including large motorcaravans, on a variety of fields and meadows with beautiful country views. Although not individually marked, there is never a feeling of overcrowding and there are some pre-bookable, accessible pitches. The smaller, more mature fields, including a pleasant old orchard for tents only, are well terraced. While there are terraces on most of the slopes of the larger, more open fields, there are still some quite steep gradients to climb, rewarded by the views. There are some 450 electrical connections (10A), 63 hardstandings and 20 'super' pitches. Self-catering accommodation on site includes holiday homes, cottages and apartments. A well designed, central complex overlooking the pool and decorated with flowers and hanging baskets houses reception, a shop and off-licence and a traditional bar, the Cofton Swan. An extension to this complex provides another two bar areas suitable for daytime dining and evening entertainment, plus an indoor pool, sauna, steam room and gym, as well as a soft play area for children and a centrally located arcade. The extension is open all year round except for Christmas and Boxing Day. The outdoor pool with a paddling pool has lots of grassy space for sunbathing. Coarse fishing is available in five lakes on the park. The adjoining unspoilt woodland of 50 acres provides wonderful views across the Exe Estuary and a woodland trail of two miles to Dawlish Warren.

Facilities

Six amenity blocks are well placed for all areas across the park. Facilities for disabled visitors. Family bathrooms and shower room. Hair dryers. Two launderettes. Gas available. Ice pack hire service. Bar (all year except Christmas Day and Boxing Day). Shop and fish and chip takeaway (25/3-30/10). Outdoor pool (27/05-11/09). Indoor pool (open all year excl. Christmas Day and Boxing Day). Arcade. Adventure playground, children's play areas and sports wall. Coarse fishing (from £5 per day). Caravan storage. WiFi (charged). Off site: Woodland walks and pub 0.5 miles. Beach 3 miles. Golf 3 miles. Riding 5 miles. Bicycle hire in Dawlish.

Open: All year.

Directions

Access to the park is off the A379 road 3 miles north of Dawlish, just after Cockwood Harbour village. GPS: 50.6126, -3.460467

Charges guide

Per unit incl. 2 persons and electricity	£ 18.50 - £ 34.00
serviced pitch	£ 23.00 - £ 43.00
extra person (over 2 yrs)	£ 2.65 - £ 5.50
dog	free - £ 4.00

Small discount for senior citizens outside peak season.

Drewsteignton

Woodland Springs Touring Park

Venton, Drewsteignton EX6 6PG (Devon) T: 01647 231695. E: enquiries@woodlandsprings.co.uk

alanrogers.com/UK1250

Hidden away in a corner of the Dartmoor National Park, Woodland Springs is a haven of peace and tranquillity. Set in a dip, it is sheltered by woodland with some views across the rural countryside. It provides 81 fairly level pitches, 50 with hardstanding, of which ten are fully serviced, 31 on grass and 69 with electricity (16A). There is a circular gravel access road and a central toilet block. There is a small shop and off-licence; bread is baked daily. A large field provides good dog walking. The resident owners provide a warm welcome on this quiet park that only accepts adults.

Facilities	Directions
Award-winning toilet block including full facilities for disabled visitors. Shop (limited hours). Coffee machine. Freezer. Dog kennels for rent. Torches useful. WiFi (charged). Off site: Fishing 3 miles. Riding 7 miles. Bicycle hire 8 miles. Golf 9 miles. Castle Drogo, Spinster's Rock, Finch Foundery and the Stone Lane Gardens nearby. Many walking and adventure opportunities on Dartmoor and in the Teign Valley.	From M5 exit 31 follow A30 (Okehampton). After 15 miles at Whiddon Down junction turn on A382 Moretonhampstead road for 0.5 miles then left at roundabout. After 1 mile turn left at caravan sign, then left to park. GPS: 50.706417, -3.850667

Open: All year.

Charges guide

Per unit incl. 2 persons and electricity	£ 20.00 - £ 23.00
extra person	£ 5.00

Exeter

Teign Valley Barley Meadow Camping & Caravanning Club Site

Crockernwell, Exeter EX6 6NR (Devon) T: 01647 281629. E: dartmoor.site@thefriendlyclub.co.uk

alanrogers.com/UK0760

This peaceful little park is located on the northern edge of Dartmoor with easy access from the A30. It is sheltered from the weather by good hedging and, although not always visible from the pitches, there are open views across the moorland to the south. The 63 pitches are mostly on level grass, well spaced, with 25 hardstandings and 38 electric hook-ups (10A). Shrubs divide some of the pitches. This is a Club site, but non-members are welcome. The site would be a suitable base for visiting Exeter, Okehampton and Plymouth, hiking over the moors or just enjoying the local area.

Facilities	Directions
The single heated toilet block provides all facilities including a well equipped room for babies and disabled campers. Laundry. Motorcaravan services. Small shop for basic groceries. Breakfast menu and newspapers to order for following day. Games room. Playground. Small library. WiFi. Only small American RVs (up to 30 ft) accepted. Off site: Fishing 2 miles (river) or 6 miles (lake). Golf 4.5 miles. Riding 8 miles.	From M5 exit 31, take A30 (Okehampton). After 10 miles turn left (Cheriton Bishop). After 0.5 miles pass through village and on for 1 mile (Crockernwell), Site entrance on left. GPS: 50.717533, -3.78325

Open: 10 March - 7 November.

Charges guide

Per unit incl. 2 persons and electricity	£ 19.25 - £ 22.65
extra person	£ 7.75 - £ 9.45
Non-member prices are higher.	

Exeter

Webbers Caravan & Camping Park

Castle Lane, Woodbury, Exeter EX5 1EA (Devon) T: 01395 232276. E: reception@webberspark.co.uk

alanrogers.com/UK1100

Set in a lovely location in East Devon, with beautiful views of the Haldon Hills, this large family run park (ten hectares) has developed over 20 years and offers spacious, modern facilities, yet still retains its relaxed, rural atmosphere. The 115 marked, grass pitches are large (100 with electricity, 10/16A), with the majority level and a few gently sloping. Some of the higher pitches have views across the Exe river valley. The park is surrounded by fields and visitors can watch the wildlife and grazing sheep from a fenced walk around the park perimeter. A member of the Best of British group.

Facilities	Directions
Three modern sanitary blocks, one a light and airy building with four family shower rooms, a bathroom (£1) and a unit for disabled visitors (WC, shower and washbasin). Laundry facilities. Motorcaravan services. Small shop at reception for essentials. Play area and games field. All-year caravan storage. Off site: Woodbury village within walking distance with pub/restaurant, post office, etc. Fishing and golf 1 mile. Riding 4 miles. Bicycle hire and boat launching 5 miles. Exeter 6 miles.	From M5 exit 30 take A3052 (Sidmouth) for 5 miles. Turn right at Halfway Inn. From A30, Daisymount exit, take B3180 for 3 miles to Halfway Inn and on at crossroads. Follow B3180 (Exmouth). After 2 miles turn right (Woodbury, golf and caravan parks). Park on left in 1 mile. GPS: 50.678083, -3.392017

Open: 14 March - 31 October.

Charges guide

Per unit incl. 2 persons and electricity	£ 14.00 - £ 20.00
Min. booking of 3 nights in high season.	

For latest campsite news visit

alanrogers.com

Exeter

Crealy Meadows Caravan & Camping Park

Sidmouth Road, Exeter EX5 1DR (Devon) T: 01395 234888. E: stay@crealymeadows.co.uk

alanrogers.com/UK1125

Crealy Meadows is a new park in rural Devon developed by the owners of Crealy Adventure Park and situated adjacent to it. The multi-million pound investment has resulted in a well planned, purpose built park with excellent facilities. At present there are 99 serviced touring pitches (16A electricity, water and drainage) on neatly cut, level grass, and 21 hedged 'super' pitches (144 sq.m) with hardstanding. There are also pre-sited lodge tents in superbly themed safari camp and medieval village settings. These are really rather special and very well equipped with woodburning stoves and sinks. The safari tents even boast a sleeping cupboard. There is direct gated access to the adventure park by means of pass cards. There is no doubt that this is the main attraction at Crealy Meadows. Exmouth with its sandy beaches is about five miles away.

Facilities

Two modern fully tiled toilet blocks with underfloor heating. Roomy showers, family bathrooms and facilities for disabled visitors. Baby changing facilities. Two laundry rooms. Shop. Bar, restaurant and takeaway (2/6-1/9). Family entertainment (high season evenings). Two play areas. WiFi (free). Dog walk. Safari and medieval tents to rent. Access to Adventure Park – pay admission charges once, and receive free entry to the park for the following six days. Unique 'own a pony' experience on Adventure park (booking required). Fishing. Off site: Greendale Farm shop. Woodbury Common and castle. Family pub within 2 miles. Exmouth and beaches 6 miles. Exeter 7 miles. Golf and riding 2 km.

Open: 27 March - 1 November.

Directions

From M5 exit 30 take A3052 signed Sidmouth, Seaton and Crealy. Keep straight on following Crealy signs. Site is on the right in under 2 miles. Using the A30/A303 from the east, join the M5 at exit 29 and travel south to exit 30, then as above.
GPS: 50.703606, -3.414967

Charges guide

Per unit incl. 2 persons	
and electricity	£ 10.00 - £ 35.00
extra person (over 1 yr)	£ 7.00 - £ 9.00
dog	£ 3.00 - £ 4.00

Exmouth

Devon Cliffs Holiday Park

Haven Holidays, Sandy Bay, Exmouth EX8 5BT (Devon) T: 01395 226226.

alanrogers.com/UK1260

Haven Holiday's flagship park, Devon Cliffs at Exmouth, is a very large, vibrant holiday resort dominated by the static accommodation, complete with its own, almost private, sandy beach. There are over 1,600 caravan holiday homes arranged around a central complex with a wide range of top class amenities. Overlooking this complex is a small, modern touring area providing 43 very small, marked and numbered pitches, all fully serviced (electricity, aerial point, water and drain) and on hardstanding. Tents are accepted in a separate area, but only in high season. The site is unsuitable for outfits over 6 m. Comprehensive and very lively, the excellent amenities include an indoor multi-level pool complex, a spa centre, sports facilities, entertainment programmes, a huge noisy hall with amusements and games and much more. Sandy Bay has a safe, sandy beach with lifeguards in high season.

Facilities

Clean, modern toilet facilities with open washbasins and preset showers. Excellent room for disabled campers. Family bathroom. Launderette. Shopping arcade. Buffet and grill, two café/bars, fish and chips, Burger King, pizzas, Starbucks Coffee. Two indoor 'show bars'. Indoor pool complex. Spa centre. Sports facilities. Amusements hall. Evening entertainment and clubs for children. Adventure play areas. Beach (lifeguards in high season). Tents accepted 24/7-4/9. Off site: Exmouth 2.5 miles with hourly bus. Bicycle hire 2.5 miles. Golf and riding 6 miles.

Open: 20 March - 2 November.

Directions

From M5 exit 30, take A376 signed Exmouth. On the outskirts of the town (just after a garage), turn left at traffic lights following signs for Budleigh Salterton, Littleham, Sandy Bay and the park.
GPS: 50.615645, -3.366387

Charges guide

Per unit incl. up to 4 persons	
and services	£ 17.00 - £ 46.50
extra person	£ 2.00 - £ 3.00

For latest campsite news visit

alanrogers.com

Ilfracombe
Stowford Farm Meadows

Berry Down, Combe Martin, Ilfracombe EX34 0PW (Devon) T: 01271 882476. E: enquiries@stowford.co.uk
alanrogers.com/UK0690

Stowford Farm is a very large, friendly, family run park set in 500 acres of the rolling North Devon countryside, good for recreation and walking and within easy reach of five local beaches. The touring park and its facilities have been developed in the fields and farm buildings surrounding the attractive old farmhouse and provide a village-like centre with a comfortable, spacious feel. There are 710 marked pitches, separated by beech and ash hedges, on five slightly sloping meadows. Most have 10/16A electricity, nine are on hardstanding and all are accessed by hard roads. Stowford also provides plenty to keep the whole family occupied without leaving the park, including woodland walks and horse riding from the park's own stables. In low season some facilities may only open for limited hours. A good base for exploring the North Devon coast and Exmoor.

Facilities

Five toilet blocks are fully equipped and include laundry facilities. The newest block (in field 5) has underfloor heating. Facilities for disabled visitors and private family washrooms beside reception. Well stocked shop. Bars, restaurant and takeaway (April-Oct). Entertainment (high season). Indoor pool (heated Easter-Oct, charged). Riding. 18-hole pitch and putt. Crazy golf. 'Kiddies kar' track (all charged). Games room. Play area. Organised games and activities (high season). WiFi on part of site. ATM. Woodland walks. Off site: Fishing and boat launching 4 miles. Bicycle hire 10 miles.

Open: All year.

Directions

From Barnstaple take A39 towards Lynton. After 1 mile turn left (B3230). Turn right at garage on A3123. Park is 1.5 miles on the right. GPS: 51.16498, -4.05995

Charges guide

Per unit incl. 2 persons and electricity	£ 10.80 - £ 28.20
extra person	free - £ 4.80
child (5-12 yrs)	free - £ 2.70
dog	£ 1.80 - £ 2.80

Low season discounts for over 50s.

Ilfracombe
Napps Touring Holiday Park

Old Coast Road, Berrynarbor, Ilfracombe EX34 9SW (Devon) T: 01271 882557. E: info@napps.fsnet.co.uk
alanrogers.com/UK1120

Set in an idyllic location in North Devon, this popular, family run site offers peace and quiet on site, with plenty to see and do off site. A path just outside the gates leads down to a private beach with safe bathing; although it is only 200 yards to the gate, there are 200 steps down to the beach so it is not suitable for wheelchair users or those with walking difficulties. Combe Martin and Ilfracombe beaches are also close by. The 200 touring pitches (100 hardstandings), most with views of Watermouth Bay, are terraced and spacious, 95 are serviced with electricity, water tap and waste point, and another 70 have a 16A hook-up. The toilet blocks are a long way from the pitches. An outdoor heated swimming pool with shallow section for children is unsupervised, but there is a terrace with table and chairs for non-swimmers to watch or enjoy a meal from the Bistro.

Facilities

Two modern toilet blocks include open plan washbasins, showers and family wash cubicles. Laundry. Licensed shop. Bar with terrace and light entertainment during high season. Restaurant (open mornings and evenings). Takeaway. Heated outdoor pool with paddling pool (Easter-end Sept). Tennis. Games room. Adventure play area. Caravan storage. Off site: Beach and fishing 200 yds. Combe Martin, golf and boat launching 1.5 miles. Ilfracombe 3.5 miles. Bicycle hire and riding 5 miles.

Open: 1 March - 31 October.

Directions

Leave M5 at exit 27, take A361 to South Molton and then A399 through Combe Martin. Site is 1.5 miles west of Combe Martin on the A399 (signed). GPS: 51.208517, -4.064083

Charges guide

Per unit incl. 2 persons and electricity	£ 16.00 - £ 30.00
extra person (over 5 yrs)	£ 3.00 - £ 5.00
dog	£ 2.00 - £ 3.00

No credit cards.

For latest campsite news visit
alanrogers.com

Ilfracombe

Hele Valley Holiday Park

Hele Bay, Ilfracombe EX34 9RD (Devon) T: 01271 862460. E: holidays@helevalley.co.uk

alanrogers.com/UK1145

Hele Valley is a well established park located a mile from Ilfracombe in a wooded valley and only a few minutes' walk from Hele Bay beach. The park caters for tents, motorcaravans and smaller caravans only, because of the difficult access. Of the 118 pitches, 50 are available for touring units and 30 are for tents. Some of the pitches are on terracing, strung out along a valley and surrounded by trees and hedges. All have 16A electricity, 16 are fully serviced and 16 have hardstanding. Parents must keep children away from the steep-sided stream running the length of the park.

Facilities	Directions
Modern heated toilet block provides all the usual facilities including those for babies and disabled visitors. Two adventure play areas. Play field. WiFi throughout (charged). Off site: Bus service on main road. Beach and golf 400 yds. Minimarket, pubs and cafés 5 minutes' walk. Fishing, sea fishing, sailing, bicycle hire and many shops in Ilfracombe 1 mile. Riding 4 miles.	From Ilfracombe, take A399 east (Combe Martin). With Ilfracombe pool on the left, go down hill for 400 yds. and, at Hele Valley sign, sharp right turn (easier from Combe Martin). Go down steep road and on to T-junction (right-angled and narrow). Turn right to the park. GPS: 51.205404, -4.101202

Open: 1 April - 31 October.

Charges guide

Per unit incl. 2 persons and electricity	£ 22.00 - £ 38.00

No credit cards.

Kingsbridge

Karrageen Caravan & Camping Park

Bolberry, Malborough, Kingsbridge TQ7 3EN (Devon) T: 01548 561230. E: phil@karrageen.co.uk

alanrogers.com/UK0825

Karrageen is a quiet and peaceful park in a wonderful area of Devon, near Kingsbridge and Salcombe, with a mixture of rolling countryside, hidden coves, cliff tops and sandy beaches. This is a small family park, run personally by the Higgin family, situated in the hamlet of Bolberry, one mile up the lane from Hope Cove. The main camping field slopes gently with either sea or rural views. It has been terraced with hedging to provide 95 pitches, 70 are on grass for tourers and 54 have 10A electricity. A number of caravan holiday homes to let complete the provision in a separate field.

Facilities	Directions
Modern toilet block includes showers (20p). En-suite provision for disabled visitors. Large family shower room. Laundry. Separate dishwashing (20p). Freezer for ice packs. Shop including some basic camping equipment. Fresh baguettes and croissants daily. Gas. Two open areas for ball games. Off site: Fishing, boat launching and beach 1 mile. Golf 3 miles. Salcombe, sailing Mecca and fishing port with sandy beaches 3.5 miles. Riding 6 miles. Kingsbridge, ancient market town, 6 miles.	From Totnes follow A381 bypassing Kingsbridge via Churchstow towards Salcombe at Malborough turn sharp right through village. Site is on right, and reception on left just beyond Bolberry (narrow lanes). GPS: 50.23929, -3.84004

Open: 27 March - 27 September.

Charges guide

Per unit incl. 2 adults, 2 children and electricity	£ 18.00 - £ 30.00
extra person	£ 4.00 - £ 8.00

No credit cards.

Kingsbridge

Higher Rew Caravan & Camping Park

Malborough, Kingsbridge TQ7 3BW (Devon) T: 01548 842681. E: enquiries@higherrew.co.uk

alanrogers.com/UK0826

Over the last 50 years, the Squire family have developed this rural park on their farm, which is located near Salcombe, about a mile from South Sands, along a single track lane. South Sands is ideal for boating, sailing and windsurfing as well as providing safe bathing. A large, gently sloping, open field has been slightly terraced to provide 90 grass pitches, 70 of which have 16A electricity. The rural views from the park are amazing, but you have to climb a little higher to see the sea. The estuary stretching between Salcombe and Kingsbridge is a local nature reserve famed for its birdwatching opportunities.

Facilities	Directions
Good quality toilet facilities. Unisex showers in a separate building. Showers are metered (20p for 4 minutes). Freezer for ice packs. Reception with shop for basics (open main season). Play area. Tennis court. Skittle alley. Caravan storage. Hog roast on Thursdays at 18.00 (high season). WiFi on part of site (free). Off site: Beach, fishing and sailing 1 mile. Boat launching 3 miles. Golf 4.5 miles.	Park is clearly signed from Malborough. Follow signs to Soar, 1 mile. Turn left at Rew Cross, then first right towards Higher Rew. Follow single track lane to site. GPS: 50.230174, -3.805647

Open: 27 March - 2 November.

Charges guide

Per unit incl. 2 persons and electricity (16A)	£ 18.00 - £ 24.00

No credit cards.

For latest campsite news visit

alanrogers.com

Lynton

Channel View Caravan & Camping Park

Manor Farm, Barbrook, Lynton EX35 6LD (Devon) T: 01598 753349. E: relax@channel-view.co.uk
alanrogers.com/UK0680

Channel View is a quiet, family run park situated in a sunny, south-facing position overlooking Lynton and Lynmouth. The gently sloping ground provides fairly level pitches which are mostly on hardstandings. The park is divided into two areas, an open area that is sheltered by bushes and trees, and one that is more exposed but enjoys panoramic views over the coast. Of the 75 touring pitches, 60 have 16A electricity and the remainder are fully serviced. The grass is well cared for and there is site lighting, although a torch would be useful. The Country Inn pub next door serves bar food.

Facilities	Directions
The modern and very clean toilet and shower block is partly tiled. Showers are free (there are three steps down to the ladies' showers from the toilets). Baby changing/family washroom. Facilities for disabled visitors (Radar key). Laundry with washing machines, dryers and iron. Small shop. Play area. WiFi. Off site: Lynton and Lynmouth, Exmoor and the Doone Valley are nearby. Many walks can be started from the site. Riding and fishing 1 mile. Beach 2 miles. Golf 15 miles. Open: 15 March - 15 November.	Take A399 travelling east from Ilfracombe. Turn left onto A39 and continue for 6 miles to Barbrook, where road forks to left for Lynton. Continue straight on up hill. Site is on left in 1 mile. Do not use GPS. It is not advised to approach from Lynton/Lynmouth. GPS: 51.21800, -3.82930

Charges guide

Per unit incl. 2 persons and electricity	£ 16.00 - £ 21.00
extra person	£ 6.00

Modbury

Moor View Touring Park

California Cross, Modbury PL21 0SG (Devon) T: 01548 821485. E: info@moorviewtouringpark.co.uk
alanrogers.com/UK0820

Moor View is a very popular, adults only site with individual, level, terraced pitches, many with marvellous views across to the Dartmoor Tors. This is a park in a lovely corner of Devon, run personally by the enthusiastic managers. A member of the Countryside Discovery group, it provides 106 pitches with 68 touring pitches of varying sizes, all with 10A electricity. Sixty-six are on hardstandings with water and drainage also. Bushes and shrubs planted between the pitches are growing well, giving the park a very attractive appearance. A two-acre field provides space for tents, but there is no electricity.

Facilities	Directions
Traditional style, heated and well maintained sanitary facilities have access from a courtyard area. Laundry room. Motorcaravan services. Shop. Takeaway in season (to order, 18.30-20.30). TV room. WiFi (charged). Off site: A local country pub is within walking distance. The small town of Modbury is 3 miles. Golf and bicycle hire 5 miles. Fishing 6 miles. Beach 8 miles. Open: All year.	On A38 from Exeter, pass exit for A385 (Totnes) and continue for 2 miles. Just past Woodpecker Inn leave A38 at Wrangaton Cross, (Modbury and Yealmpton). Turn left and over at crossroads for 3 miles to California Cross. Leave garage on left and follow B3207 (Modbury). Park is 0.5 miles on left. GPS: 50.35618, -3.82731

Charges guide

Per unit incl. 2 persons and electricity	£ 10.95 - £ 26.95

Mortehoe

Warcombe Farm Camping Park

Station Road, Mortehoe EX34 7EJ (Devon) T: 01271 870690. E: info@warcombefarm.co.uk
alanrogers.com/UK0725

This park is set in a quiet position on a hill above Woolacombe. It is a large, fairly open site on gently sloping land. There are 250 level or fairly level pitches, some secluded, others extra large with hardstanding and electricity, and others fully serviced. Shrubs and trees help to divide some of the pitches. Two hardstanding pitches are designed to provide facilities and access for disabled campers. In total, 160 pitches have 16A electricity hook-ups. The site has panoramic views across to the sea.

Facilities	Directions
Two modern toilet blocks are spotlessly clean, with underfloor heating and free preset showers. Family bathrooms and facilities for disabled visitors (coded locks). Laundry facilities. Motorcaravan services. Shop. Play area. Fishing also for children. Torches useful. WiFi (charged). Off site: Public footpaths and cycle trails (the Tarka Trail) is on the doorstep. Riding and golf 1.5 miles. Woolacombe beach is 1.5 miles. Bicycle hire 4 miles. Open: 13 March - 30 October.	Approaching from Barnstaple on A361 follow signs for Ilfracombe. At Mullacott Cross (10 miles from Barnstaple) turn left. Follow B3343 for Woolacombe. After 1.8 miles turn right for Mortehoe. Park is first on right in 500 yards. GPS: 51.190441, -4.180639

Charges guide

Per unit incl. 2 persons and electricity	£ 16.00 - £ 34.00
extra person	£ 4.00

For latest campsite news visit
alanrogers.com

Newton Abbot
Dornafield

Two Mile Oak, Newton Abbot TQ12 6DD (Devon) T: 01803 812732. E: enquiries@dornafield.com
alanrogers.com/UK0880

The entrance to Dornafield leads into the charming old courtyard of a 14th-century farmhouse giving a mellow feeling that is complemented by the warm welcome from the Dewhirst family. It is a haven for those seeking a quiet, restful holiday. There are 135 touring pitches with 119 fully serviced on hardstandings (10A Europlug), and 16 reasonably level grass pitches for tents in a walled orchard. At the top of the site are large luxury pitches with all facilities, including cleverly concealed TV connections. There are two super, well maintained woodland adventure play areas. Dornafield is a member of the Caravan Club's Affiliated Site scheme. The rural situation is delightful and this park is well worth consideration. A member of the Best of British group.

Facilities

Two excellent, modern, heated toilet blocks. The newer block has underfloor heating and a heat recovery system. Both blocks have facilities for babies and disabled visitors. Laundry rooms. Shop. Gas supplies. All-weather tennis court. 7 acres for dog walking. Games room. Play areas. WiFi (charged). Off site: Local inn and bus stop 0.5 miles. Golf 1 mile. Fishing 2.5 miles.

Open: 13 March - 3 November.

Directions

Park is northwest of A381 Newton Abbot-Totnes road. Leave A381 (turning west) at Two Mile Oak Inn opposite garage (site signed), after half a mile turn left at crossroads. Entrance is shortly on the right. GPS: 50.50032, -3.63717

Charges guide

Per unit incl. 2 persons and electricity	£ 15.00 - £ 33.00
extra person	£ 4.00 - £ 8.00
child (5-16 yrs)	£ 2.00 - £ 4.00

Newton Abbot
Ross Park

Park Hill Farm, Ipplepen, Newton Abbot TQ12 5TT (Devon) T: 01803 812983.
E: enquiries@rossparkcaravanpark.co.uk **alanrogers.com/UK0910**

Ross Park continues to impress us with the care and attention to detail and the amazing floral displays which are a feature of the park and must be seen to be appreciated. These are complemented by the use of a wide variety of shrubs which form hedging for most of the pitches to provide your own special plot, very much as on the continent. Every pitch has hardstanding and many have wonderful views over the surrounding countryside. All have 16A electricity. For those who prefer the more open style, one small area has been left unhedged. The park covers 32 acres but 21 acres are managed specifically as conservation areas providing a haven for wildlife which visitors can enjoy. The owners, Mark and Helen Lowe, are rightly proud of their park and strive to provide quality facilities and maintain standards. A member of the Best of British group.

Facilities

Thirteen well equipped, heated en-suite bathrooms, two with baby facilities, one suitable for disabled campers. Everything is built to a very high standard with underfloor heating. Further separate shower, washbasin and toilet facilities. Laundry room. Motorcaravan services. Reception with licensed shop. Gas supplies. Bar, bar snacks and restaurant with à la carte menu. Conservation and tourist information room. Games room. Seven-acre park area for recreation. Separate areas for dog walking. Croquet green. Badminton. Volleyball. Playground. WiFi (free). Electric barbecues not accepted. Caravan storage. Off site: Dainton Park 18-hole golf course is adjacent. Bus stop for Totnes and Newton Abbot 100 yds. Riding 1 mile. Fishing 3 miles. Lake/river 5 miles. Beach 10 miles.

Open: 7 March - 2 January

Directions

From A381 Newton Abbot-Totnes road, park is signed towards Woodland at Park Hill crossroads and Texaco filling station. GPS: 50.491940, -3.634240

Charges guide

Per unit incl. 2 persons and electricity	£ 16.25 - £ 29.50
extra person	£ 3.25 - £ 5.50
child (4-16 yrs)	£ 1.50 - £ 3.20

Christmas packages available.
No credit cards.

For latest campsite news visit
alanrogers.com

Newton Abbot
Woodville Caravan Park

Totnes Road, Ipplepen, Newton Abbot TQ12 5TN (Devon) T: 01803 812240. E: info@woodvillepark.co.uk

alanrogers.com/UK0915

A lovely little site exclusively for adults, Woodville is in a sheltered situation, attractively laid out with a variety of shrubs and trees. There are 26 pitches all with hardstanding and 16A electricity. They are accessed by a circular roadway which provides a central lawned area. A caravan storage area is to one side. This is a quiet site with few services, although the park is adjacent to Fermoys Garden Centre with farm shop and café. Dainton Park golf course is directly opposite and Ipplepen village is within walking distance and has a small supermarket and a pub. The owners live on the site and take a pride in their park. This small site has been family owned and run for the last 14 years and is ideal for touring couples.

Facilities

A fully equipped toilet block also provides a separate unit for visitors with disabilities. Washing machine and freezer. Vans selling fish and chips and eggs calls weekly. Library. Tourist information. Reception is in the house (limited opening hours). Off site: Shop with café and golf course adjacent. Ipplepen village with pub and shops within walking distance. Bus service on main road. Newton Abbot 3 miles. Riding 3 miles. Fishing 5 miles. Beach and boat launching 7 miles. Torquay 12 miles. Dartmoor 15 miles. Exeter 20 miles.

Open: 1 March - 2 January.

Directions

From Newton Abbot follow A381 Totnes road for 3 miles. Site is on the right just after Fermoys Garden Centre. The site gate is kept closed. GPS: 50.49505, -3.62965

Charges guide

Per unit incl. 2 persons	£ 13.20 - £ 17.80
extra person	£ 4.50 - £ 5.00
dog	£ 0.50
Electricity on meter.	

Newton Abbot
Lemonford Caravan Park

Bickington, Newton Abbot TQ12 6JR (Devon) T: 01626 821242. E: info@lemonford.co.uk

alanrogers.com/UK0980

Lemonford is a well run, neat and tidy site for families of all ages. It is some three miles from both Ashburton and Newton Abbot on the southern edge of the national park. The site is attractively landscaped with a mixture of trees and shrubs covering 7.5 acres. Although close to the main road, it is set in a sheltered, peaceful dip bordered by the pretty River Lemon. There are 142 pitches, with 87 reasonably level pitches for touring, of which 76 are fully serviced (10A electricity). Access is good for large outfits, but commercial vehicles are not accepted. A good pub is within walking distance along the banks of the river. There are several holiday homes in the centre of the touring area and in separate areas at the back of the site, some available for rent.

Facilities

Two modern toilet blocks, one heated. Bathrooms in each block (£1) and a family room with facilities for disabled visitors. Laundry facilities. Shop. Gas supplies. Freezer service. Play area. WiFi (charged). Off site: Pub within walking distance. Golf 2 miles. Riding and bicycle hire 3 miles. Fishing 4 miles. Leisure pool in Newton Abbot.

Open: All year.

Directions

Southwest of Exeter, leave A38 Plymouth road at A382 exit (Drumbridges). At roundabout take 3rd exit to Bickington. Continue for 3 miles and park is on left at bottom of hill. GPS: 50.54026, -3.70384

Charges guide

Per unit incl. 2 persons and electricity	£ 14.00 - £ 23.50
extra person (over 16 yrs)	£ 4.00
child (3-15 yrs)	£ 2.50
dog	£ 1.50
Special low season offers.	

For latest campsite news visit
alanrogers.com

Okehampton
Appledore Park

Sampford Courtenay, Okehampton EX20 2SR (Devon) T: 01837 659767. E: info@appledorepark.co.uk
alanrogers.com/UK0784

Appledore is a new, small but spacious, attractive, family run campsite ideal for couples and families with young children and open for a long season. It is close to the Dartmoor National Park and only 2.5 miles from Okehampton. The pitches are on terraces surrounding the toilet block and have wonderful views over fields and woods. There are 40 good sized pitches, all for touring, laid out in small groups giving campers plenty of space; 25 unmarked pitches are on grass, 15 are on hardstanding and 35 have 16A electricity. There is a late arrival area with electricity and water. Bus to Okehampton stops nearby.

Facilities

Excellent new central toilet block with underfloor heating and all necessary facilities, including those for babies and disabled campers. Motorcaravan services. Fire pit for hire. Dog walk. WiFi (free). Electric vehicle charging. Off site: Shops, bars, cinemas in market town of Okehampton 2.5 miles. Bicycle hire 2.5 miles.

Open: 1 March - 12 January.

Directions

From Okehampton take B3215 northeast, site on left in approx. 2.5 miles. Keep to main roads, no short cuts advised. GPS: 50.76248, -3.96876

Charges guide

Per unit incl. 2 persons and electricity	£ 17.00 - £ 24.00
extra person	£ 6.00

Okehampton
South Breazle Holidays

Bratton Clovelly, Okehampton EX20 4JS (Devon) T: 01837 871752. E: louise@southbreazleholidays.co.uk
alanrogers.com/UK0785

Tucked away down a half mile long bumpy lane is a rather special campsite. Built by Steve and Louise, who own South Breazle farm, the site is spacious with large pitches around the edge of a well mown field. They are marked with young hedging and are named, e.g. Squirrel's Secret. This relaxed site is a haven for stargazers and lovers of nature and the magnificent tall trees which edge the field are full of birds. There are only 29 large pitches, 23 with 16A electricity and water, and some with hardstanding. There are places for backpackers. The local pub at Bratton Clovelly is recommended for meals.

Facilities

Good toilet block with facilities for children and disabled visitors. Washing machine and dryer. Fun fountain. Recycling. Games field. Walks from site. Free WiFi on every pitch. Barbecues off ground. Caravan storage. Seasonal pitches available. Torches advised. Off site: Roadford Lake 2 miles. Watersports centre 4 miles (far side of lake). Riding and golf 10 miles.

Open: 1 March - 31 October.

Directions

West of Okehampton leave A30 at Stowford Cross. Follow signs for Roadford Lake. At top of hill turn right signed Bratton Clovelly. Take second left signed Germansweek. Site signed first right, follow narrow lane to site (0.5 mile). GPS: 50.70007, -4.20982

Charges guide

Per unit incl. 2 persons, electricity and water	£ 15.00 - £ 22.50
extra person	£ 4.00 - £ 5.50

Okehampton
Lydford Caravan & Camping Park

Lydford, Devon, Okehampton EX20 4BE (Devon) T: 01822 820497. E: info@lydfordsite.co.uk
alanrogers.com/UK0786

Lydford Caravan and Camping Park, a Caravan Club affiliated site, is known by its regular visitors for its sense of peace, beauty and tranquillity. It offers a host of stunning views of the nearby Dartmoor Tors and is set in three main areas divided by hedgerows and trees. There is a choice of 80 level and gently sloping touring pitches, either hardstanding or grassy, most with 16A electricity. Within easy reach from the site is Lydford village. Amongst its many attractions are a charming Norman castle and an ancient church, which boasts original ninth-century connections. No arrivals accepted before 12 noon.

Facilities

Heated toilet block. Family room. Facilities for disabled visitors. Laundry. Motorcaravan services. Shop. Dog walk. Electric barbecues not permitted. Free WiFi over site. Off site: Bicycle hire 0.5 miles. Fishing 2 miles. Public transport 1 mile. National Cycle Network within 5 miles. Golf and riding 5 miles. Supermarket in Tavistock 8 miles.

Open: 13 March - 2 November.

Directions

Use these directions for final approach, not sat nav (unsuitable roads for towing). Leave A30 dual-carriageway onto A386 (Plymouth, Tavistock). In 4 miles pass the Fox and Hounds pub on the left. In 1 mile turn right (Lydford village, sign by phone box). In centre of Lydford village turn sharp right at war memorial. In 50 yds. fork right. The site is on the left in 100 yds. GPS: 50.6486, -4.10623

Charges guide

Per unit incl. 2 persons and electricity	£ 17.30 - £ 22.80
tent pitch (no electricity)	£ 14.70 - £ 17.40

For latest campsite news visit
alanrogers.com

Paignton
Whitehill Country Park

Stoke Road, Paignton TQ4 7PF (Devon) T: 01803 782338. E: info@whitehill-park.co.uk
alanrogers.com/UK0860

Whitehill Country Park is beautifully situated in rolling Devon countryside, just 2.5 miles from the nearest beaches. Extending over 40 acres, a definite sense of space characterises this park and ten acres of ancient woodland are available for walks and attract a great deal of wildlife. Whitehill is a friendly park with 250 large grassy pitches which are located in separate fields around the site with evocative names, such as Nine Acres, Sweethill and Coombe Meadow. Most pitches have electrical connections (16A, 15 m. cable). Sixty pitches are used for caravan holiday homes. A new upmarket development of wooden lodges is now completed in Nine Acres field with views across the rural landscape. These luxurious homes are for private ownership and more may be added. The park was once a stud farm where shire horses were bred for showing and field work. Now the stables and farm buildings are used for the wide range of park facilities providing a craft centre for children. There is also an amusement barn, the Hayloft bar, a café and an extensive decking area for outside eating. An outdoor pool, woods to explore and cycling and walking trails to follow make a marvellous holiday venue for all the family.

Facilities

Good well equipped sanitary provision includes private, individual washing facilities for ladies and facilities for disabled visitors. Laundry facilities. Gas supplies. Shop. Bar. Café/takeaway (Easter then various dates until 13 Sept.) Swimming and paddling pools (heated 1/5-25/9). Play areas. Electronic games and amusement machines. Craft centre, treasure nature trail and letterboxing for children. Walking and cycle route maps available from reception. WiFi over site (charged). Off site: Fishing and golf 2 miles. Paignton 2.5 miles. Beach 3 miles. Riding 4 miles.

Open: Easter - 26 September.

Directions

Turn left at The Parkers Arms off the A385 Paignton to Totnes road, signed Stoke Gabriel. Site is 1 mile along this road. GPS: 50.417867, -3.609

Charges guide

Per unit incl. 2 persons and electricity	£ 16.50 - £ 30.45
tent pitch incl. 2 persons	£ 14.35 - £ 26.55
extra person	£ 4.30
child (4-14 yrs)	£ 3.30

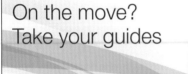

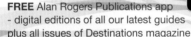
Paignton
Widdicombe Farm Tourist Park

The Ring Road, Compton, Paignton TQ3 1ST (Devon) T: 01803 558325. E: info@widdicombefarm.co.uk
alanrogers.com/UK0900

Widdicombe Farm is an adults only park, just three miles from Torquay and with easy access from the A380. There are 200 numbered pitches, all with 10A electricity of which most have hardstanding and 48 are fully serviced. Situated on a hillside and surrounded by farmland, the pitches are on terraces with open views across the countryside. Many trees have been planted and there are tarmac access roads and steps linking the terraces. There may be some background traffic noise but it is not too intrusive.

Facilities

Three toilet blocks are kept very clean. The original block by reception has recently been refurbished and includes facilities for disabled visitors and laundry room. Shop. Restaurant. Bar with singers and comedy acts (Easter, then Spring B.H-mid Sept). Certain breeds of dog are not accepted. Caravan storage. WiFi over site (charged). Off site: Golf 1.5 miles. Fishing 2 miles. Beach 2.5 miles.

Open: 15 March - 25 October.

Directions

From Newton Abbot take A380 south for 5 miles. On outskirts of Torquay turn right at roundabout onto ring road. Site is a further 2 miles. Access by continuing to next roundabout and returning back along dual carriageway. GPS: 50.467081, -3.586797

Charges guide

Per unit incl. 2 persons and electricity	£ 13.50 - £ 27.50

For latest campsite news visit
alanrogers.com

Paignton

Beverley Holidays

Goodrington Road, Paignton TQ4 7JE (Devon) T: 01803 661978. E: info@beverley-holidays.co.uk

alanrogers.com/UK0870

Beverley Park is an amazing holiday centre catering for every need. It has been developed and run by the Jeavons family for over 50 years to very high standards. It is popular, busy and attractively landscaped with marvellous views over Torbay. The pools, a cabaret area, bars and entertainment, are all run in an efficient and orderly manner. The park has 190 caravan holiday homes and 21 lodges, mainly around the central complex. There are 159 touring pitches in the lower areas of the park, all reasonably sheltered, some with views across the bay and some on slightly sloping ground. All pitches can take awnings and 87 have 16A electricity (15 m. cable), 42 have hardstanding and are fully serviced. Tents are accepted and a limited number of tent pitches have electrical connections. The park is open all year and reservations are essential for caravans in high season. There are indoor and outdoor pools, each one heated and supervised. The Oasis fitness centre provides a steam room, jacuzzi and an excellent fitness room. The park is in the heart of residential Torquay, with views across the bay to Brixham and the English Riviera, and sandy beaches less than a mile away. A member of the Best of British group.

Facilities

Good toilet blocks, well maintained and heated, include roomy showers, some with washbasins en suite. Baths on payment. Unit for disabled visitors. Facilities for babies. Laundry. Gas supplies. Motorcaravan services. General shop, restaurant, bars and takeaway (all 27/3-31/10). Heated swimming pools, outdoor 1/5-13/9, indoor all year. Fitness centre. Tennis. Crazy golf. Playground. Soft play area. Nature trail. Amusement centre. Children's room. WiFi over site (charged). No dogs. Off site: Fishing, bicycle hire, riding and golf all within 2 miles.

Open: All year.

Directions

Park is south of Paignton in Goodrington Road between A379 coast road and B3203 ring road and is well signed on both. GPS: 50.413533, -3.568667

Charges guide

Per unit incl. 2 persons and electricity	£ 18.15 - £ 35.50
tent pitch incl. 2 persons	£ 14.35 - £ 33.00
extra person	£ 5.00
child (4-14 yrs)	£ 4.00

Max. 6 persons per reservation.

Beverley HOLIDAYS

Paignton, South Devon

www.beverley-holidays.co.uk

01803 661961

Salcombe

Bolberry House Farm Caravan & Camping

Bolberry, Malborough, Kingsbridge TQ7 3DY (Devon) T: 01548 561 251. E: enquiries@bolberryparks.co.uk

alanrogers.com/UK0824

Five generations have farmed the land at Bolberry and the present owner's grandfather started the campsite in the field on top of the hill; this main field enjoys marvellous views of the surrounding countryside and out to sea. This is a traditional campsite, which caters for all units in three fields connected by grass paths with some up and down walking. There are 95 touring pitches with extra allowed in the peak period, well spaced around the edges of fairly level fields with plenty of central space for children to play. Eighty have 10A Europlugs. There are a few static vans to let in a separate area.

Facilities

Two dated toilet blocks fully equipped. Coin operated showers (20p). Laundry. Play area. Shop (mid July and Aug), fish and chip van (Sun), hog roast (Weds), all main season. Four different takeaways will deliver to site. Hope Cove holiday weekend (entertainment, events, music etc) last weekend in August. Off site: Pubs, farmhouse teas all within walking distance. Coastal paths half a mile.

Open: 27 March - 3 October.

Directions

From Totnes follow A381 bypassing Kingsbridge via Chuchstow, following signs for Salcombe. At Malborough turn sharp right through village. Follow signs for Bolberry until you come to park on right (narrow lanes). GPS: 50.238221, -3.831081

Charges guide

Per unit incl. 2 persons and electricity	£ 17.00 - £ 31.00

For latest campsite news visit

alanrogers.com

Plymouth

Riverside Caravan Park

Leigham Manor Drive, Marsh Mills, Plymouth PL6 8LL (Devon) T: 01752 344122.
E: office@riversidecaravanpark.com **alanrogers.com/UK0810**

As you leave the A38 for Plymouth, negotiate the Marsh Mills roundabout and approach through a light industrial estate, you can have no idea that there is a lush green touring park tucked away from the modern, out-of-town shopping units in a quiet green valley. Part of the park is being developed to provide a residential area alongside the River Plym which has therefore meant a reduction in the number of touring pitches. However, there are still some 200 spaces available for touring, 130 of which have 10A electricity, and 65 are on hardstanding. There are also 59 grass pitches for tents. Hidden behind a high, evergreen hedge are an attractive swimming pool and children's pool. A play area is nearby and a pleasant restaurant with a bar and games room provide welcome facilities and entertainment in high season. Over 30 years ago this park was a corn field but, with careful development by its owner, it now provides a welcome oasis from which to explore Dartmoor, to enjoy the amazing views from Plymouth Hoe or even to overnight quietly before catching the ferry to France. The wooded valley sides give way to level grass where the trees and shrubs planted all those years ago have matured to give a park-like feel. The River Plym runs down one side of the site but it is carefully fenced.

Facilities

Three modern, fully equipped toilet blocks include cubicles with toilets and washbasins. Facilities for disabled visitors. Laundry room. Motorcaravan services. Gas supplies. Some basics are kept in reception (more in high season). Bar, restaurant and takeaway (B.Hs and high season) with family entertainment included. Heated swimming pool and paddling pool (end May-12/9). Games room with TV. Play area. WiFi part site (free). Dogs accepted (max. 2). Off site: Fishing possible in River Plym (licence required). Dry ski slope, supermarket and retail park within walking distance. Bus stop 10 minutes. Bicycle hire 1 km. Sea fishing and boat launching 3.5 miles. Riding 4 miles. Golf 5 miles. Beach 10 miles.

Open: All year.

Directions

From the A38 Marsh Mills roundabout for Plymouth take the third exit. After a few yards turn left following caravan signs, then right alongside the River Plym to the park. GPS: 50.398167, -4.087333

Charges guide

Per unit incl. 2 persons and electricity	£ 15.50 - £ 30.50
tent pitch without electricity	£ 11.50 - £ 21.50
extra person	£ 5.00
child (0-16 yrs)	free - £ 3.00
dog (max. 2)	£ 2.50

Sidmouth

Oakdown Touring & Holiday Caravan Park

Weston, Sidmouth EX10 0PT (Devon) T: 01297 680387. E: enquiries@oakdown.co.uk

alanrogers.com/UK1020

Oakdown is a very attractive, well planned park that will celebrate its 65th birthday in 2016. Run by the Franks family, they and their team continue to work hard carrying out developments in keeping with the environment. The attention to detail is evident at this award-winning park as soon as you arrive and you can be sure of a warm welcome. The park has easy access, beautiful floral displays and a spacious feel. There are 100 level touring pitches arranged in landscaped bays, screened by a wide variety of trees and shrubs and linked by a circular road. All have 10/16A electricity and hardstanding and many have water and drainage. An additional touring area near the golf course, Beech Grove, provides a further 50 large pitches with hedging and 16A electricity. There is a new, fully equipped toilet block here. A member of the Best of British group.

Facilities

The original central toilet block has been completely renewed. Well maintained, fully equipped and heated facilities include a private cabin for ladies. Two unisex family bathrooms (bath, shower, toilet, washbasin and coin operated entry), double as units for disabled visitors. Laundry facilities plus free freezer and microwave. New facilities in Beech Grove include a room for families and disabled visitors, and a laundry area. Motorcaravan services. New café/shop selling essentials and snacks (mid May-mid Sept). Internet room. Fax service. Centrally heated TV/pool room with book exchange. Two excellent adventure play areas and castle. Lake. Dew pond. No cycling, skate-boarding or kite flying. WiFi over site (charged). Off site: Golf course adjacent. Swimming 1 mile. Beach 2 miles (Branscombe). Riding 6 miles.

Open: 20 March - 31 October.

Directions

Turn south off the A3052 (Exeter-Lyme Regis) road between Sidford and Colyford, 2.5 miles east of the A375 junction and park is on left.
GPS: 50.7056, -3.18063

Charges guide

Per unit incl. 2 persons and electricity	£ 16.70 - £ 24.20
with water and drainage	£ 22.50 - £ 30.25
extra person (5 yrs and over)	£ 3.20
dog	£ 2.60

Less 80p for senior citizens in low season.

Sidmouth

Salcombe Regis Camping & Caravan Park

Salcombe Regis, Sidmouth EX10 0JH (Devon) T: 01395 514303. E: contact@salcombe-regis.co.uk

alanrogers.com/UK1110

This spacious 16-acre park is under new ownership. It is on the edge of Salcombe Regis, 1.5 miles from Sidmouth and less than a mile from the sea. It is surrounded by farmland with views of the combe and the sea beyond. The reception and some pitches are arranged around a large green, all connected by a tarmac road. The pitch and putt and play area are on this green. The 110 pitches (100 for touring) are sloping and have their own water supply. Ninety-eight have 10A electricity and 52 are on hardstanding. A 25-minute walk across the fields takes you to a small, secluded beach, but the walk is fairly steep with around 130 steps. There are many footpaths and coastal walks nearby, protected by the National Trust and with views of Sidmouth and Weston Mouth.

Facilities

The traditional style toilet block (to one side of the site and a longer walk for some) is kept spotlessly clean and has a bathroom for families and disabled visitors. Laundry room with washing machines, dryers and ironing board. Motorcaravan services. Basic shop at reception sells local produce. Play area. Pitch and putt. Caravan storage. Torches useful. WiFi (charged). Off site: Fishing, bicycle hire and golf 1.5 miles. Sidmouth and beach 1.5 miles. Riding 3 miles. Free bus from site to Salcombe Regis.

Open: Easter - 28 October.

Directions

Park is signed from A3052 Exeter-Lyme Regis road. Take first left 0.25 miles after Donkey Sanctuary. From west climb hill out of Sidford. Do not take first road signed Salcombe Regis, take next right at top of hill (signed Camping and Golf Centre). Site on left in 0.25 miles. GPS: 50.695717, -3.205367

Charges guide

Per unit incl. 2 persons and electricity	£ 18.25 - £ 24.65
extra person	£ 4.60
child (5-15 yrs)	£ 3.00

For latest campsite news visit

alanrogers.com

South Molton

Riverside Caravan & Camping Park

Marsh Lane, North Molton Road, South Molton EX36 3HQ (Devon) T: 01769 579269.

E: relax@exmoorriverside.co.uk **alanrogers.com/UK0745**

A very impressive purpose built campsite beside the River Mole, Riverside is set in 70 acres of meadow and ten acres of woodland. There are 54 pitches with hardstanding, 16A electricity connection, water, drainage and TV aerial socket and some large tent pitches with or without electricity. Neat grass, tarmac roads and growing trees and hedges contribute to the attractive, overall impression. The heated toilet block gleams and visitors will appreciate the hairdryers, hand-dryers and shaver points. The owners, Joe and Nicky Penfold, are not resting on their laurels and have developed fishing lakes with specimen carp down by the river and a play area on the opposite bank. There is easy access from the A361 road, so noise can be expected. The ancient market town of South Molton is a mile away and a bus stops outside the site entrance. Exmoor is on hand to explore, as are the North Devon resorts of Woolacombe, Ilfracombe, Combe Martin and Lynton, not to mention the surfing paradise of Croyde Bay.

Facilities

Two modern, fully equipped and heated toilet blocks accessed by code. Facilities for disabled visitors. Family shower room. Laundry room. Shop (limited hours in low season). Restaurant/bar (Easter-end Oct). Play area. Entertainment (B.Hs and high season). Fishing. Swimming in river. WiFi throughout (charged). Accommodation to rent. Off site: Market town of South Molton with all facilities 1 mile. Riding 2 miles. Golf 5 miles. Boat launching 10 miles. Bicycle hire and beach 12 miles.

Open: All year.

Directions

Site is 1 mile northeast of South Molton. From M5 exit 27 take the North Devon Link road A361 northwest for 25 miles. Near South Molton watch for site signs on right (direction North Molton). GPS: 51.02918, -3.823467

Charges guide

Per unit incl. 2 persons	
and electricity	£ 17.00 - £ 30.00
extra person	£ 6.00
child (under 16 yrs)	£ 4.00

Tavistock

Harford Bridge Holiday Park

Peter Tavy, Tavistock PL19 9LS (Devon) T: 01822 810349. E: stay@harfordbridge.co.uk

alanrogers.com/UK0790

Harford Bridge has an interesting history – originally the Wheal Union tin mine until 1850, then used as a farm campsite from 1930 and taken over by the Royal Engineers in 1939. It is now a quiet, rural, mature park inside the Dartmoor National Park. It is bounded by the River Tavy on one side and the lane from the main road to the village of Peter Tavy on the other, with Harford Bridge, a classic granite moorland bridge, at the corner. With 16.5 acres, the park provides 125 touring pitches well spaced on a level grassy meadow with some shade from mature trees and others recently planted; 52 pitches have 16A electrical hook-ups and 12 have multi-services, five with hardstanding.

Facilities

The single toilet block has been modernised and is fully equipped and well kept, with some private cabins, free hot water and showers. Facilities for disabled visitors and babies. Launderette and drying room. Motorcaravan services. Shop. Games room. TV room. Play area with new equipment. Tennis. Two communal barbecue areas. Fly fishing (by licence, £3/day, £10/week). WiFi over site (charged). Replica 19th-century shepherd's hut for hire. Off site: Bicycle hire, riding and golf within 2.5 miles.

Open: 15 March - 14 November.

Directions

Two miles north of Tavistock, off A386 Tavistock-Okehampton road, take the road to Peter Tavy. GPS: 50.5713, -4.114

Charges guide

Per unit incl. 2 persons	
and electricity	£ 19.25 - £ 24.35
dog	£ 1.80
extra person	£ 6.00
child (3-16 yrs)	£ 3.00

Tavistock
The Old Rectory Caravan & Camping Park

Gulworthy, Tavistock PL19 8JA (Devon) T: 01822 832927. E: info@tamarvalleycamping.co.uk
alanrogers.com/UK0795

The Old Rectory is a neat little park where hedging provides bays to give you your own space and shelter. You can share the larger bays with friends or family. The hedging will be taken down a foot or two in the Autumn to allow more enjoyment of the panoramic views across to Dartmoor. There are just eleven touring pitches, eight with 16A electricity, 20 tent pitches, and four timber camping pods are to rent. A small toilet block has recently been extended to double the facilities. There is no reception office, you simply contact the owners by phone when you arrive. Children will enjoy watching the miniature Shetland ponies; hopefully in the future they may be able to pull a little cart to give rides. The market town of Tavistock on the edge of Dartmoor is just three miles away. Possible road noise from A390 during the day.

Facilities

New fully equipped toilet block with free hot showers and facilities for disabled visitors. Washing machine and dryers. Small freezer for ice blocks. Wash bay to clean down bikes or wet suits etc. Eggs, bacon and sausages for sale. Bicycle hire arranged. Caravan storage. Camping pods to rent. Torches useful. Off site: Nearby activities include canoeing on Tamar river, tree surfing, mountain biking, or walking on Dartmoor. Golf 2 miles. Fishing 3 miles. Boat launching 4 miles. Riding 5 miles.

Open: All year.

Directions

From Tavistock follow A390 for Liskeard. After 3 miles turn left at Gulworthy roundabout signed Bere Alston. Site on left past school and church hall. GPS: 50.532675, -4.190927

Charges guide

Per unit incl. 2 persons and electricity	£ 16.00 - £ 20.00
extra person (over 5 yrs)	£ 5.00
dog	£ 1.00

Tavistock
Langstone Manor Holiday Park

Moortown, Tavistock PL19 9JZ (Devon) T: 01822 613371. E: jane@langstonemanor.co.uk
alanrogers.com/UK0802

Situated on the southwest edge of Dartmoor, this holiday park has been developed in the grounds of the old Langstone Manor house. The touring pitches are tucked into various garden areas with mature trees and flowering shrubs, or in the walled garden area with views over the moor. In all there are 42 level grass pitches which vary in size (30 with 10A electricity). A new camping area is popular and has been terraced with open views over farmland and the moor. You pass by a number of holiday caravans on the way to reception and the touring pitches, where you will also find some holiday cottages and flats for rent. The 'pièce de resistance' is the unexpected traditional bar and restaurant in the Manor House, complete with a terrace that catches the evening sun. Open in high season and on demand in low season, it has an open fire (if needed) and games room.

Facilities

The facilities have been refurbished to a very high standard and include a bathroom and private cabins. Showers are now free. Laundry. Changing mats for babies now in both the men's and ladies' rooms. Basic supplies kept in reception (order bread the day before). Bar/restaurant with terrace. Games room. Play area. Camping pods for hire. Off site: Golf 1 mile. Leisure centre and pool 2 miles. Fishing and bicycle hire 2 miles. Riding 5 miles. Boat launching 10 miles. Sailing 15 miles.

Open: 15 March - 15 November.

Directions

From Tavistock take B3357 Princetown road. After 2 miles turn right at crossroads (site signed). Pass over cattle grid onto the moor and follow site signs. GPS: 50.5449, -4.084167

Charges guide

Per unit incl. 2 persons and electricity	£ 18.00 - £ 23.00
extra person	£ 4.25
child (3-16 yrs acc. to age)	£ 2.75 - £ 3.25
dog	free

For latest campsite news visit
alanrogers.com

Tavistock

Woodovis Park

Woodovis House, Gulworthy, Tavistock PL19 8NY (Devon) T: 01822 832968. E: info@woodovis.com

alanrogers.com/UK0805

Woodovis Park is set in the grounds of Woodovis House, nestling in a sheltered wooded position covering 14 acres, by the edge of the Tamar Valley on the borders of Devon and Cornwall. John and Dorothy Lewis have been running Woodovis Park since 1999, helped by their very welcoming staff. There are 39 good sized pitches, all with 10A electricity. You have a choice of grass, all weather and 11 super pitches (with 16A, water, waste and TV hook-ups too). Split over two fields and landscaped inbetween are 35 caravan holiday homes, 24 for hire. A member of the Best of British group.

Facilities	Directions
Heated toilet block. Bathroom (coin operated). Family cubicles. Toilet for disabled visitors at the pool. Laundry. Motorcaravan services. Shop with fresh bread daily plus basics with off-licence, doubles with reception. Indoor heated swimming pool, spa and sauna. Weekly hog roast. Games room. Fenced play area. New large dog exercise meadow. Pétanque. Archery and 'water-walking' (during school holidays). WiFi over site (first 30 minutes free). New play equipment. Bicycle hire. Off site: Pub with restaurant.	From Tavistock follow A390 for Liskeard. After 3 miles turn right at Gulworthy roundabout signed Chip Shop, Lamerton and Caravan Park. After 1 mile entrance is signed on left. GPS: 50.548867, -4.21585

Open: 20 March - 30 October.

Charges guide	
Per unit incl. 2 persons and electricity	£ 24.00 - £ 41.00
extra person (over 5 yrs)	£ 4.00 - £ 12.50

Tiverton

Minnows Touring Caravan Park

Sampford Peverell, Tiverton EX16 7EN (Devon) T: 01884 821770. E: admin@minnowstouringpark.co.uk

alanrogers.com/UK0750

Minnows is an attractive, neat, small park with views across the Devon countryside, separated by hedging from the Grand Western Canal. Easily accessible from the M5, it is an ideal touring centre for Devon and Somerset or for breaking a long journey. The area is ideal for cycling, walking, fishing and canoeing. Open for eight months of the year, it provides 59 level pitches, all with 16A electricity and hardstandings, 15 with water and waste water (two for continental units and RVs). A further 3.5 acres have been added to the park providing space for extra larger pitches, a grass tent area, and a play area.

Facilities	Directions
Well maintained, heated toilet block. Facilities for babies and disabled visitors. Laundry facilities. Motorcaravan services. Shop. Newspaper delivery. Play area. Bicycle hire (delivery to site). American RVs accepted (up to 36 ft, advance booking necessary). Gates closed 20.00-07.30. WiFi throughout (charged). Off site: Boat slipway, golf driving range and 9-hole course 400 yds, full course 4 miles. Pubs and shops within walking distance.	From M5 exit 27 take A361 (Tiverton). After 600 yds. take first exit (Sampford Peverell). After 100 yds. turn right at roundabout and cross bridge over A361 to 2nd roundabout. Straight on, park is ahead. From North Devon A361 go to M5 exit 27 and return back up A361 as above. GPS: 50.925017, -3.364517

Open: 2 March - 2 November.

Charges guide	
Per unit incl. 2 persons and electricity	£ 15.50 - £ 22.00

Woolacombe

North Morte Farm

Mortehoe, Woolacombe EX34 7EG (Devon) T: 01271 870381. E: info@northmortefarm.co.uk

alanrogers.com/UK0703

North Morte Farm is a family run park adjoining National Trust land and is only 500 yards from Rockham beach. The site has 250 pitches (there are 150 pitches for tents in a separate field) of which 30 are for touring, with hardstanding and their own 16A electricity point. Some have a TV connection and a water point close by. The toilet block is modern and there is a well stocked shop/off-licence with gas exchange and a well designed play area for children. This is a good site for a family holiday with plenty to do and see in the vicinity. Other popular resorts, such as Ilfracombe, are within easy reach.

Facilities	Directions
Clean, modern toilet block with free hot water and hairdryers can be heated. Facilities for disabled visitors. Launderette with ironing facilities. Shop/off-licence with gas exchange. Play area. Public telephone. Off site: Direct access to the southwest coastal path. Shops, post office and restaurants in Mortehoe 5 minutes walk. Fishing 800 yds. Golf and riding 1.6 miles.	From Barnstable take A361 (Ilfracombe). At Mullacott Cross roundabout take first left (Woolacombe, Mortehoe). After 2 miles turn right (Mortehoe). In Mortehoe turn right opposite car park (lighthouse) and site is 500 yds. Lanes are narrow. GPS: 51.188343, -4.203939

Open: 27 March - 31 October.

Charges guide	
Per unit incl. 2 persons and electricity	£ 15.50 - £ 24.00

For latest campsite news visit
alanrogers.com

Woolacombe

Woolacombe Bay Holiday Park

Sandy Lane, Woolacombe EX34 7AH (Devon) T: 01271 870221. E: goodtimes@woolacombe.com

alanrogers.com/UK1070

Woolacombe Bay Holiday Park has a range of holiday accommodation, from touring pitches, caravan holiday homes, luxury lodges to apartments and villas. It has numerous on-site amenities including pools, restaurants and bars, and provides a wide choice of entertainment. There are 391 pitches with 150 level, grass pitches for tourers, 97 with 10/16A electricity. A separate section caters for tents and trailer tents only. Partly laid on terraces and partly on the hilltop, it has some original pine trees and many more trees planted for landscaping. Some up-and-down walking is required to reach the toilet block. The site has magnificent views out across the bay. A bus service (£4/week) runs to the other three sites in the group and the beach during the main season, although there is a footpath to the beach from the site. The three larger parks have plenty of entertainment and children's clubs for campers to enjoy.

Facilities

A good central toilet block has all necessary facilities including those for families, children and disabled campers. Laundry rooms. Two units for disabled visitors. Supermarket, bars, restaurant and takeaway. Indoor (all season and heated) and outdoor pools (21/5-15/9) with flumes and slides. Sauna, steam room and gym. Beauty and holistic treatments. Sporting activities. Tennis. ATM. WiFi throughout. Off site: Fishing and beach 1 mile. Riding 2 miles. Golf 3 miles. Bicycle hire 6 miles.

Open: 21 March - 3 November.

Directions

Take A361 Barnstaple-Ilfracombe road through Braunton. Turn left at Mullacott Cross roundabout towards Woolacombe then right towards Mortehoe. Follow the camping signs by turning left and park is on the left. GPS: 51.177117, -4.191317

Charges guide

Per unit incl. 8 persons and electricity	£ 19.00 - £ 70.00

Woolacombe

Golden Coast Holiday Park

Station Road, Woolacombe EX34 7HW (Devon) T: 01271 866766. E: goodtimes@woolacombe.com

alanrogers.com/UK1075

The Golden Coast Holiday Village is part of the Woolacombe Bay Holiday Parks group that includes Woolacombe Bay, Twitchen Park and Easewell Farm. Golden Coast's main interest is a range of brick-built bungalows, lodges and apartments, plus a variety of caravan holiday homes, all of good quality and well equipped. Two touring areas provide 101 pitches, all with electricity, most with hardstanding and some super pitches. There are indoor and outdoor pools, spa facilities, a cinema and a range of sports facilities for active visitors. Guests at the park can enjoy extensive entertainment and nightly cabaret; a programme of daily activities is arranged for adults and children. A shuttle bus runs between the four parks and to the beach several times a day (it costs £4 per person over 5 yrs per week, family tickets available). A visit to the Old Mill Inn should not be missed; it serves bar meals, and has an excellent beer garden with adventure play area for the children. The range of amenities and facilities at this large park will suit families looking for a lively holiday filled with activities and entertainment.

Facilities

Unisex toilet block. Washing machine and dryer. Well stocked supermarket (all season). Boutique. Heated indoor (all season) and outdoor (21/5-15/9) swimming pools, outdoor flume, sauna and solarium. Bar, club, Inn, restaurant and takeaway (all season). Floodlit tennis. Adventure playgrounds. Snooker. Games room. Soft play area. Ceramics studio. Swim classes. 9-hole golf course. Bowls, ten-pin bowling. Evening entertainment. Activities and clubs for children. Surfing simulator. Fishing. Woodland walks. WiFi (charged). Dogs only accepted in selected accommodation. Off site: Golf, riding and bicycle hire 0.5 miles. Woolacombe beach about 2 miles. For walkers there is the coastal path. Amenities at sister parks available to all visitors, with shuttle bus.

Open: 13 February - 24 November.

Directions

From Barnstaple, take A361 (Braunton and Ilfracombe). Turn left on B3343 (Woolacombe) and follow the road towards the town. The park is on the left near the top of the hill. GPS: 51.1725, -4.172767

Charges guide

Per unit incl. 8 persons and electricity	£ 11.00 - £ 75.00

For latest campsite news visit

alanrogers.com

Woolacombe
Easewell Farm Holiday Park

Mortehoe, Woolacombe EX34 7EH (Devon) T: 01271 870343. E: goodtimes@woolacombe.com
alanrogers.com/UK0720

Easewell Farm Holiday Village is near the sandy beaches of Woolacombe and is part of the Woolacombe Bay Holiday Park group which also owns three other nearby parks. A shuttle bus runs between the four holiday villages and to the beach (tickets £4 per person per week). The largest camping field is sloping with superb views across the headland to the sea. Two smaller fields are terraced and one area has upgraded hardstandings with new landscaping. Together they provide 330 pitches (248 for touring), 207 with 16A electricity and 20 also with TV and water connections. The shop is well stocked (gas available), there is a takeaway and restaurant and an attractive bar with patio overlooking a small duck pond. The park has its own, very well maintained, professional nine-hole golf course which is popular, and there are reduced fees for campers. One of the huge redundant farm buildings has been divided into three areas providing table tennis and pool, a skittle alley and two lanes of flat green bowling. There are walks to the local village and along the coastal path from the site. A bus to Ilfracombe and Barnstaple stops 100 yards from the entrance.

Facilities

Central heated toilet block with all necessary facilities, including those for babies and disabled campers. Laundry. Motorcaravan services. Shop. Bar. Restaurant and takeaway. Small heated indoor swimming pool. TV and games rooms. Golf. Fenced play area. Indoor skittle alley. Off site: Fishing and riding 1 mile. Bicycle hire 6 miles. Tarka Trail for walking and riding. Boat trips to Lundy Island.

Open: 20 March - 2 November.

Directions

From Barnstaple, take A361 Ilfracombe road through Braunton. Turn left at Mullacott Cross roundabout on B3343 to Woolacombe, turning right after 2-3 miles to Mortehoe. Park is on right before village. GPS: 51.1853, -4.198933

Charges guide

Per unit incl. 8 persons	from £ 6.00

Woolacombe
Twitchen House Holiday Park

Mortehoe Station Road, Woolacombe EX34 7ES (Devon) T: 01271 870848. E: goodtimes@woolacombe.com
alanrogers.com/UK0730

Set in the landscaped grounds of an attractive Edwardian country house, Twitchen House Holiday Park is owned by Woolacombe Bay Holiday Parks. Its most recent additions include a £2.5 million, state-of-the-art family entertainment centre featuring attractions such as a 10-pin bowling alley, a 3D cinema, an innovative craft centre and an exciting new indoor soft play area. The new Show Lounge provides a venue for daytime fun and varied evening entertainment, and a poolside terrace with coastal themed café and retro milkshake bar. Of the 600 pitches, 367 are for touring, 228 with 16A electricity, 120 on hardstanding, mostly arranged around oval access roads in hedged areas. The superb amenities include a swimming pool complex that incorporates indoor and outdoor heated pools where lessons and other fun activities are organised, plus a steam room and sauna. Twitchen House is very popular for families with children. There are excellent beaches nearby with a footpath down to the sea (20 minutes walk). All the facilities of the three other Woolacombe Bay Holiday Villages are free to visitors at Twitchen House, with a bus (£4 per week) running regularly between the four parks and to the beach. There is a surf school here with equipment for hire.

Facilities

Two toilet blocks include family bathrooms and saunas. Laundry facilities. Motorcaravan services. Shop. Club, bars, restaurant. Takeaway. Entertainment for adults and children, day and evening. Outdoor pool with flume and terrace, and splash pad water play area (19/5-14/9). Indoor pool, sauna, paddling pool and fountain. Ten pin bowling. Climbing wall. Adventure golf. Games rooms. Good adventure play area. Indoor soft play area. WiFi in bars and cafés (free). Off site: Beach and golf 1 mile. Fishing and riding 2 miles. Bicycle hire and sailing 6 miles.

Open: 20 March - 2 November.

Directions

From Barnstaple take A361 towards Ilfracombe and through Braunton. Turn left at Mullacott Cross roundabout towards Woolacombe and then right towards Mortehoe. Park is on the left before village. GPS: 51.184683, -4.1977

Charges guide

Per unit incl. max. 6 persons and electricity	£ 18.00 - £ 68.00
Special offers available.	

For latest campsite news visit
alanrogers.com

Escape to North Devon

Right next to Woolacombe's three miles of golden sandy beach

Britain's best beach
WOOLACOMBE BAY HOLIDAY PARKS

You won't believe how high I climbed, I could see for miles!

What we've got to offer...

- Sea view touring & super pitches
- 400 all weather pitches
- 16 amp electric hookups
- Modern amenity blocks
- Level pitches with easy access
- 4 award winning Holiday Parks
- Outstanding leisure facilities
- Activities for all ages

Call **0844 7700 363**
or visit **woolacombe.com/ar**

WOOLAC MBE BAY
HOLIDAY PARKS

We're here

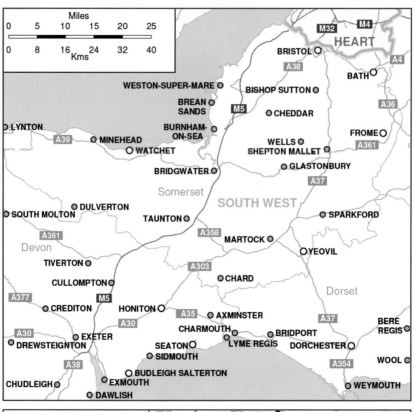

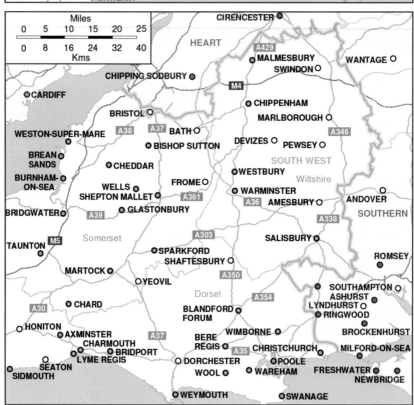

Bere Regis

Rowlands Wait Touring Park

Rye Hill, Bere Regis BH20 7LP (Dorset) T: 01929 472727. E: enquiries@rowlandswait.co.uk

alanrogers.com/UK2050

Rowlands Wait is in a designated Area of Outstanding Natural Beauty and part of the park is officially of Special Scientific Interest. The top of the park, edged by mature woods (full of bluebells in spring) is a haven for tents (and squirrels) with marvellous views and provides 30 areas in three descending fields. The rest of the park is a little more formal and nearer to the central toilet block. Most pitches back on to hedging or trees and they are generally level. There are 71 pitches in total with 23 seasonal pitches. Many walks are possible from the park with information leaflets available from reception. It is also possible to walk into the village of Bere Regis. The owners Ivor and Stevie Cargill are keen to welcome nature lovers who enjoy birdwatching, walking and cycling. Sightings of various owls and two pairs of buzzards have been reported on the park. The park is a member of the Countryside Discovery group and is open in winter by arrangement. Rallies are welcome.

Facilities

The refurbished toilet block is fully equipped. New family room and facilities for disabled visitors. Laundry room. Recycling bins. Shop (reduced hours in low season) providing basic essentials and a freezer for ice packs. Play area. Games room. Bicycle hire arranged. Torch useful. WiFi (free). Off site: Village (10 minute walk) with shops, two pubs, etc. plus a bus service for Dorchester and Poole. Golf 3 miles. Fishing 5 miles. Riding 9 miles.

Open: All year (31 October - 16 March by arrangement).

Directions

Park is 0.5 miles south of Bere Regis on the road to Wool. GPS: 50.743683, -2.22405

Charges guide

Per unit incl. 2 persons	
incl. electricity	£ 17.25 - £ 22.75
extra person	£ 3.75 - £ 5.25
child (3-16 yrs)	£ 2.50 - £ 3.50
dog	free - £ 2.50

Blandford Forum

The Inside Park Touring Caravan & Camping Park

Blandford Forum DT11 9AD (Dorset) T: 01258 453719. E: mail@theinsidepark.co.uk

alanrogers.com/UK2070

The Inside Park is set in the grounds of an 18th-century country house that burned down in 1941. Family owned and carefully managed alongside an arable farm, this is a must for those interested in local history or arboriculture and it is a haven for wildlife and birds. The nine-acre camping field, a little distant, lies in a sheltered, gently sloping dry valley containing superb tree specimens – notably cedars, with walnuts in one part – and a dog graveyard dating back to the early 1700s under a large Cedar of Lebanon. In total there are 125 spacious pitches, 90 with 10A electricity and some in wooded glades. The six acres adjoining are the old pleasure gardens of the house. The reception/toilet block and games room block are respectively the coach house and stables of the old house. No vehicle access to the park is allowed after 22.30 (there is a separate late arrivals area and car park). Extensive, marked walks are provided through the farmland and a guide is available in the shop.

Facilities

The toilet block provides some washbasins in cubicles, comfortably sized showers and facilities for disabled visitors and babies. Laundry room. Shop with basics, gas and camping provisions. Spacious games room. Adventure play area. Day kennelling facilities for dogs. Mountain bike course. Winter caravan storage. Free WiFi around reception. Off site: Blandford leisure and swimming centre (temporary membership possible) 2 miles. Fishing and riding 2 miles. Golf 3 miles. Beach 25 miles.

Open: Easter - 31 October.

Directions

Park is 2 miles southwest of Blandford and is signed from the roundabout junction of A354 and A350 roads. Do not use postcode in sat nav. GPS: 50.841333, -2.19515

Charges guide

Per unit incl. 2 persons	
and electricity	£ 22.45 - £ 25.45
extra person	£ 4.50 - £ 5.00
child (3-15 yrs)	£ 1.00 - £ 2.00
dog	£ 1.00 - £ 1.50

THE INSIDE PARK
Blandford, Dorset
So Relaxing You Won't Want To Leave!
- Extra Large Pitches
- All modern Facilities
- Ideal Family Site
- Quiet & Secluded
- Children's Play Area
- Country Walks
- Caravan Storage
www.theinsidepark.co.uk 01258 453719

Bishop Sutton

Bath Chew Valley Caravan Park

Ham Lane, Bishop Sutton BS39 5TZ (Somerset) T: 01275 332127. E: enquiries@bathchewvalley.co.uk

alanrogers.com/UK1510

A small and secluded garden site for adults only, Bath Chew Valley has been developed with much tender love and care by the Betton family and is now affiliated to the Caravan Club. Caravans are sited on hardstanding pitches amongst colourful beds of flowers, shrubs and trees. Cars are tucked away on the nearby car park, providing a tranquil and restful atmosphere. An area of woodland is adjacent with an enclosed dog walking area called Puppies' Parade. The warden will assist you in placing your caravan. There are neat hardstandings for all pitches and 27 spacious, fully serviced pitches, all with 16A electricity connections. This park will particularly appeal to garden and nature lovers. Next to reception there is a good library, also providing tourist information. Chew Valley lake is a walk of about half a mile with trout fishing available and is popular for birdwatching. There are several circular walks in the area – visitors may borrow the route plans and a walking stick from reception or take advantage of the on-site car hire. Bristol and Bath are within easy driving distance and Cheddar Gorge or Longleat make excellent days out. A member of the Best of British group.

Facilities

The heated toilet block (with a 'home from home' feel), provides all the fittings that make life comfortable. Separate en-suite units each with WC, basin and shower. One unit has facilities for disabled visitors. Useful utility room with sinks, coin-operated washer/dryers and ironing facilities, together with a service wash facility for those who do not want to watch their laundry on holiday. Free use of freezer. Motorcaravan services. Internet access. WiFi over site (charged). Car hire. Max. 2 dogs. Off site: Village 200 m. with useful general store, newsagent, post office, pub and restaurant. Supermarkets within 15 minutes drive. Fishing lake 800 yds. Golf 5 miles. Riding 8 miles. Beach 15 miles.

Open: All year.

Directions

From the A37 or A38 take the A368 (which links them) to Bishop Sutton. Ham lane is opposite the Red Lion Public House, and the park is 800 yds. along Ham Lane on the left. GPS: 51.336583, -2.597183

Charges guide

Per unit incl. 2 persons and electricity	£ 24.00 - £ 31.00

Brean Sands

Northam Farm Holiday Park

South Road, Brean Sands, Burnham-on-Sea TA8 2SE (Somerset) T: 01278 751244.
E: stay@northamfarm.co.uk **alanrogers.com/UK1570**

Brean has been a popular holiday destination for decades and many large campsites have evolved. Northam Farm, owned by the Scott family, is one of them. It is a large family park with good facilities, but not overly commercial and still retaining a family feel. There are 350 pitches for seasonal units and these are separated from the four touring fields. The 553 touring pitches (most with 16A electricity) are well established and many have block paved hardstanding. The owners and staff are always available to help visitors enjoy their stay. A monthly newsletter is published giving details of 'what's on' both on and off site. There are two play areas for youngsters, a playing field, bicycle track and football pitch for teenagers, and fishing on the lake for adults and supervised children. About 600 yards down the road is The Seagull, which is also owned by Northam Farm. Here you will find an excellent restaurant, bar and nightly live entertainment, even during the low season at weekends. Just along the road is Brean Leisure Park with its swimming complex, funfair, golf and much more.

Facilities

Three good toilet blocks, well maintained and within reasonable distance of all pitches, provide ample toilets, washbasins and spacious showers (50p). Bathrooms (£1 charge). Baby room. Rooms for disabled visitors (radar key access). Good launderette. Motorcaravan services. Dog shower and two exercise areas. Licensed shop well stocked with food, holiday gear and accessories. Snack bar/takeaway. Free entry to live entertainment at The Seagull Inn. Fishing lake (license required for over 12s). On-site caravan workshop for repairs and servicing. Caravan storage. Dogs are not accepted in some of the fields. Off site: Bus stop for Burnham and Weston at entrance. Beach 200 m. across road. Golf, bicycle hire and riding 0.5 miles. Burnham-on-Sea 4 miles. Weston-Super-Mare 8 miles.

Open: March - October.

Directions

From M5 exit 22 follow signs to Burnham-on-Sea, Berrow and then Brean. Continue through Brean and Northam Farm is on the right, 0.5 miles past Brean Leisure Park. GPS: 51.2949, -3.010167

Charges guide

Per unit incl. 2 persons and electricity	£ 9.00 - £ 27.50
extra person	free - £ 2.00
child (0-15 yrs)	free - £ 1.00
dog, awning, fishing	free
No credit cards.	

For latest campsite news visit

alanrogers.com

Brean Sands
Warren Farm Holiday Centre

Warren Road, Brean Sands, Burnham-on-Sea TA8 2RP (Somerset) T: 01278 751227.
E: enquiries@warren-farm.co.uk **alanrogers.com/UK1580**

Warren Farm is an easily accessible holiday destination set on the Somerset Levels. It is a popular venue for family campers who want the beach, fun and entertainment available at Brean Sands. Family run, the park is divided into several fields, and includes 500 pitches for touring units. Pitches are mainly grassed and level, with 16A electric hook-ups. In addition, there are seasonal pitches and privately owned caravan holiday homes, with a small hire fleet set on an elevated park facing Bridgwater Bay and its own access to five miles of beach. Play equipment is arranged in a line through the camping fields.

Facilities

Several accessible toilet blocks of varying styles provide WCs, showers (on payment), open style washbasins and hairdressing stations. Facilities for babies and disabled visitors. Laundry facilities. Motorcaravan services. Two shops, snack bar and Chinese takeaway (opening times vary). Fish bar. Beachcomber Inn and restaurant with entertainment and WiFi. Play equipment. Indoor play centre. Sports field. Fishing lakes. No dogs in field six.

Open: April - October.

Directions

Leave M5 at exit 22 and follow the B3140 to Burnham-on-Sea, then to Berrow and Brean. Continue through Brean and Warren Farm is on the right 1.5 miles past Brean Leisure Park. GPS: 51.30251, -3.00944

Charges guide

Per unit incl. 2 persons and electricity	£ 12.00 - £ 22.00

Bridgwater
Mill Farm Caravan & Camping Park

Fiddington, Bridgwater TA5 1JQ (Somerset) T: 01278 732286.
alanrogers.com/UK1306

On the edge of the village of Fiddington, in a countryside location at the foot of the Quantock Hills, Mill Farm is just seven miles from Bridgwater and four miles from the sea. This is an extensive and popular family holiday park with three main fields, each taking 50-60 units with a toilet block, a playground and a plentiful supply of water points. Extra fields are opened for the peak season allowing a total capacity of 400 units, all with 10A electricity. The site has a large swimming pool complex with indoor and outdoor pools, free to campers, and also a new gym and fitness suite. There is a licensed riding school, rowing boats on the little lake and entertainment during high season and at weekends during mid-season. A well stocked mini-market provides all the usual items. American motorhomes accepted, motorcyclists at the management's discretion. Mill Farm is a good family holiday base, very much children orientated with a wide range of activities to keep them happy.

Facilities

Several toilet blocks include facilities for disabled visitors (Radar key). Bathrooms (charged) and baby rooms. Launderette. Shop. Large club room with bar, takeaway (weekends and peak seasons), games room and family entertainment (high season). Sports bar and fitness centre. Heated indoor pool with whirlpool and paddling pool (Mid May-early Nov) and outdoor pool with giant waterslide (15/5-31/9). Pony riding and trekking, canoe hire, and trampolining (charged). Boating lake. WiFi over site (charged). Off site: Golf 3 miles. Beach 4 miles.

Open: 1 March - 1 December.

Directions

From M5 exit 23 or 24, turn west and pass through Bridgwater and continue on A39. After 6 miles turn right towards Fiddington. Continue through narrow lane with passing places for 1 mile to site entrance. GPS: 51.16092, -3.11670

Charges guide

Per unit incl. 2 persons and electricity	£ 16.00 - £ 28.00
extra person	£ 4.00
child (2-14 yrs)	£ 3.00

No credit cards.

For latest campsite news visit
alanrogers.com

Bridport
Golden Cap Holiday Park

Seatown, Chideock, Bridport DT6 6JX (Dorset) T: 01308 422139. E: holidays@wdlh.co.uk
alanrogers.com/UK1740

Golden Cap, named after the adjacent high cliff (the highest in southern England) which overlooks Lyme Bay, is only 150 m. from a shingle beach at Seatown and is surrounded by National Trust countryside and the Heritage Coastline. The park is arranged over several fields on the valley floor, sloping gently down towards the sea. It is in two main areas, having once been two parks, each separated into fields with marvellous panoramic views and providing 108 touring pitches. All have electricity and 30 also have hardstanding with drainage and gravel awning area. An extra sloping tent area with 159 pitches is used for peak season (torch useful), although it is a five minute walk from here to the toilet blocks and shop. There are 219 caravan holiday homes in their own areas. A small but attractive lake is used for coarse fishing and the heated indoor pool and gym at Highlands End (under the same ownership, three miles away) is open for campers at Golden Cap on payment. Beaches are nearby, sea fishing, boat launching, riding or fossil hunting are possible in the area, plus good walks including access to the coastal path.

Facilities

The modern toilet block is of good quality with spacious shower cubicles (some with toilet and washbasin). Facilities for disabled visitors. Baby room. Two other smaller blocks around the park. Laundry room. Motorcaravan services. Useful and well stocked shop. Takeaway (1/7-6/9). Gas supplies. Small play area. Coarse fishing lake (day tickets from shop). American motorhomes are not accepted. WiFi throughout (charged). Camping pods to rent. Off site: Bus stop in village 10 mins walk. Pub serving food nearby. Beach 150 yds. Golf 2 miles. Bicycle hire, boat launching 3 miles.

Open: 1 March - 30 November.

Directions

Turn off A35 road at Chideock (a bigger village) 3 miles west of Bridport, at sign to Seatown opposite church. Park is less than 1 mile down narrow lane. GPS: 50.72333, -2.82221

Charges guide

Per unit incl. 2 persons	
and electricity	£ 16.50 - £ 33.00
extra person	£ 5.00
child (4-17 yrs)	£ 3.50
all service pitch	£ 18.50 - £ 35.00
dog	£ 3.00 - £ 3.50

Bridport
Highlands End Holiday Park

Eype, Bridport DT6 6AR (Dorset) T: 01308 422139. E: holidays@wdlh.co.uk
alanrogers.com/UK1750

On slightly sloping ground with superb open views, both coastal and inland, Highlands End is quietly situated on the Dorset Heritage Coastline. A path in front of the park runs along the cliff top and then leads down to a shingle beach a little further along. It is a good quality park with 180 caravan holiday homes, mostly privately owned, and 195 touring pitches in two areas nearest to the sea – one has to travel through the holiday homes to reach them. The field for tents has 73 pitches, ten with electricity, and the field for touring is all electric with 45 pitches, also having water, drainage and hardstanding. A further area is used for tents in high season. A modern, attractive building houses a lounge bar, excellent good value restaurant with takeaway facility, family room and games room with some musical evenings in high season. The park's amenities also include an excellent, air-conditioned indoor heated pool, a tennis court and a nine-hole pitch and putt (all charged). The park is run to high standards and is a member of the Best of British group.

Facilities

Two good quality toilet blocks near the touring sections are well maintained and can be heated. Some washbasins in cubicles with toilets, large, roomy showers. En-suite facilities for disabled visitors. Baby care room. Laundry room. Motorcaravan services. Well stocked shop (opening times vary), including gas supplies. Bar and restaurant/takeaway (evenings and Sunday lunch). Indoor pool (20x9 m), gym, sauna/steam room. Tennis (charged). Games room. 9-hole pitch and putt. Excellent adventure play area. Large sloping field for ball games. All facilities open all season. WiFi throughout (charged). Off site: Beach 0.5 miles. Bicycle hire and golf 2 miles. Fishing 3 miles.

Open: 1 February - 30 November.

Directions

Follow Bridport bypass on A35 around the town and park is signed to south (Eype turning), down narrow lane. There is a new exit road. GPS: 50.72104, -2.77767

Charges guide

Per unit incl. 2 persons	
and electricity	£ 16.50 - £ 33.00
all services and hardstanding	£ 21.00 - £ 37.00
extra person	£ 5.00
child (4-17 yrs)	£ 3.50
dog (max. 2)	£ 3.00 - £ 3.50

For latest campsite news visit
alanrogers.com

Bridport

Bingham Grange Touring & Camping Park

Melplash, Bridport DT6 3TT (Dorset) T: 01308 488234. E: enquiries@binghamgrange.co.uk

alanrogers.com/UK1770

Bingham Grange is a very well maintained, purpose built park for adults only, attractively laid out and with a very comfortable restaurant. In a pleasant, rural situation two miles from the market town of Bridport, there are views seaward towards West Bay and inland across Beaminster Downs and Pilsdon Hill. There are over 135 individually landscaped pitches, more than 118 with 10A electricity and 83 with hardstanding, 26 serviced. Shrubs and trees are fully developed in the original field and have been planted in the newer field. Pitches here are level and terraced and have super views. Some without electricity are for tents. Paths have been created through the woods to the river and there is access to public footpaths (Bridport 20 minutes). Good dog walks are provided. A limited bus service runs on the main road. The Brit Valley is an unspoilt area of West Dorset with an ancient heritage and coastal West Bay is only a couple of miles. The facilities at this park are good, having been converted from original farm buildings. The excellent restaurant has a resident chef and is good value. The present owners are working hard to maintain and improve their park.

Facilities

Well equipped toilet block, with underfloor heating with a separate, fully equipped room for disabled visitors with ramped access, and seven luxury en-suite shower rooms. Laundry room with microwave and freezer. Reception with small shop. Popular bar/restaurant with good value menu (closed two days each week). Gas available. WiFi throughout (charged). Only adults (over 18 yrs) are accepted and only two per unit at B.Hs. Off site: Leisure centre 2.5 miles. Sea fishing and golf 3 miles. Boat launching 4 miles. Riding and bicycle hire 5 miles.

Open: Mid March - end October.

Directions

At the roundabouts on the A35 road, on the east side of Bridport, follow signs for Beaminster on the A3066. After 2 miles watch for site entrance on the left. GPS: 50.765076, -2.740911

Charges guide

Per unit incl. 2 persons and electricity (10A)	£ 19.50 - £ 28.50
extra person	£ 7.50
dog	£ 2.50

Bridport

Freshwater Beach Holiday Park

Burton Bradstock, Bridport DT6 4PT (Dorset) T: 01308 897317. E: office@freshwaterbeach.co.uk

alanrogers.com/UK1780

Family run parks for families with direct access to their own private beach are rare in Britain and this one has the added advantage of being in beautiful coastal countryside in West Dorset. It now offers the Jurassic Fun Centre with pools, gym, bowling and a café. This building has a living, 'green' roof supporting native species of salt-tolerant grass and wildflowers which helps the complex merge into the landscape and includes many eco-friendly features. The park is next to the sea and a beach of fine pebbles, sheltered from the wind by pebble banks. Approached by a fairly steep access road, the park itself is on level, open ground. The 500 touring pitches, 400 with 10A electricity, are on an open, undulating grass field connected by tarmac or hardcore roads. Caravan pitches are marked and evenly spaced in lines. Some tent pitches are in the main field, with others well spaced on a terraced field. There are 260 caravan holiday homes, with 60 for hire in a separate area. This lively holiday park has an extensive range of facilities, including an outdoor pool, a good value, licensed restaurant and main bar with evening entertainment in season. Daytime entertainment caters for all ages. Footpaths lead to the thatched village of Burton Bradstock and West Bay and the coastal path. The overall impression is of a large, busy holiday park with a friendly reception and happy atmosphere. Units over 23' long can have extra space at no extra cost during non-peak periods.

Facilities

Three fully equipped toilet blocks – good provision for a busy beach park. Facilities for disabled visitors (Radar key). Baby care room (key system). Launderette. Bars with wide variety of entertainment and evening shows. Café. Good value supermarket and takeaway. Leisure complex with indoor pool, water play area for young children, gym and 10-pin bowling (family tickets available). Heated, supervised outdoor swimming and paddling pools (24/5-1/9). Activities for children. Two play areas. WiFi (charged). Off site: Bus stop on main road. Golf course 0.5 miles. Fishing possible from Chesil Bank. Abbotsbury Subtropical Gardens and Swannery 8 miles.

Open: 15 March - 9 November.

Directions

Park is immediately west of the village of Burton Bradstock, on the Weymouth-Bridport coast road (B3157). GPS: 50.70500, -2.73867

Charges guide

Per unit incl. up to 6 persons, car and awning	£ 16.00 - £ 44.00
car or boat	£ 2.00
electricity	£ 2.00
small tent incl. 2 persons walking or cycling	£ 5.00 - £ 17.00
dog (max. 3)	£ 2.50
Single sex groups not admitted.	

For latest campsite news visit
alanrogers.com

Burnham-on-Sea

Home Farm Holiday Park & Country Club

Edithmead, Burnham-on-Sea TA9 4HD (Somerset) T: 01278 788888. E: enquiries@hfhp.co.uk

alanrogers.com/UK1480

Home Farm is neatly and attractively laid out covering 44 acres and is convenient for those using the M5. There are 650 level pitches in total including 170 privately owned holiday homes and a number of seasonal units. These are laid out on level grass, all clearly marked and accessed by tarmac roads. They are divided into various sections, one of which is an area specifically for those with dogs. The 120 hardstanding pitches include 20 serviced pitches for RVs and motorcaravans. Electricity connections (10A) are available everywhere. A large, modern outdoor pool with paved surrounds and a paddling section is neatly walled and an indoor pool and leisure centre which includes access for disabled visitors. There is early evening entertainment for children, plus amusement machines and pool tables. The club house (with free membership) is a feature of the site providing meals, a range of entertainment, wide screen TV, an attractive conservatory and outside barbecue area. In all, it is a site with a lot to offer.

Facilities

Two main, refurbished toilet blocks are heated and well situated for touring areas. Bathrooms (key with £5 deposit). Baby room. Well equipped laundry. Facilities for disabled visitors. Dog shower. Shop with groceries, camping accessories and camping gas (April-end Nov). Club house with TV and entertainment. Restaurant and takeaway (April-October). Bar (all season). Outdoor swimming pool (June-Sept). Leisure centre with heated pool, gym, sauna, steam room and massage (charges apply). Play area. Fishing lake. Free WiFi over part of site. Security patrols at night. Barrier card (£2). Overnight parking for late arrivals. Off site: Beach 1 mile. Golf 2 miles. Riding 3 miles.

Open: 10 February - 6 January.

Directions

Home Farm is 400 yds. from M5 exit 22 and the A38, signed from the B3140 into Burnham-on-Sea. GPS: 51.23875, -2.964167

Charges guide

Per unit incl. 2 persons, electricity and awning	£ 10.95 - £ 31.95
extra person	£ 3.25 - £ 5.50
child (4-17 yrs)	£ 1.75 - £ 4.75
dog	£ 1.00 - £ 2.50

Club membership included in pitch fee; leisure centre extra. Special offers available.

Chard

Alpine Grove Touring Park

Forton, Chard TA20 4HD (Somerset) T: 01460 63479. E: stay@alpinegrovetouringpark.com

alanrogers.com/UK1415

This peaceful woodland site is owned by Richard and Helen Gurd who go the extra mile to ensure you enjoy your stay here. The pitches vary in size (20-70 sq.m) and are on flat ground served by gravel roads giving easy access. Some informally marked pitches are tucked away in dense foliage and are very private. Electricity (10A) is supplied to 38 of the 40 touring pitches (16 hardstandings). All the standard facilities are near reception, including a free fenced and heated swimming pool (10x5 m). A play area is provided for children under the canopy of mature trees which shade the site. Campers can barbecue on the pitches and use the picnic tables provided or perhaps hire a fire pit for cooking their supper. Torches are essential at night. It is well placed for visiting Devon, Dorset and Somerset, and many places of interest close by. There are many fascinating things to do and see in the area and details are provided by reception. This is a pleasant 'back to nature' park, which is highly suitable for families who enjoy this type of camping. Four charming log cabins are also for hire.

Facilities

A modest, modern sanitary building provides all usual facilities and is kept clean and smart. There are facilities for disabled campers which double as a family bathroom. Washing machine and dryers. Reception doubles as the shop selling some fresh food, milk, bread and essentials. Heated outdoor swimming pool (20/5-20/9). Play area with trampoline (outside). Planned walks and some day activities. Bicycle hire. Four log cabins for hire. Barbecues allowed (not electric). WiFi (charged). Off site: Public transport in Forton 0.5 miles. ATM and supermarket at Chard (the birthplace of powered flight) 2 miles. Fishing and golf 2 miles. Forde Abbey 2.5 miles. Beaches 9 miles.

Open: Easter - 30 September.

Directions

From M5 exit 25 take the A358 signed Chard. From Chard take the Forton road where the site is well signed. From the A35, take A358 via Axminster to Chard, and then Forton. Ignore GPS and approach through Chard. GPS: 50.85779, -2.93597

Charges guide

Per unit incl. 2 persons and electricity	£ 14.50 - £ 23.50
extra person	£ 5.50 - £ 8.50
dog	£ 2.00

For latest campsite news visit

alanrogers.com

Charmouth
Wood Farm Caravan Park

Axminster Road, Charmouth DT6 6BT (Dorset) T: 01297 560697. E: holidays@woodfarm.co.uk
alanrogers.com/UK1760

Wood Farm is an excellent, family run park, maintained to high standards on sloping, well landscaped ground with rural views across the Marshwood Vale. With an indoor heated pool, tennis court, fishing lakes and a rather good café open all day, it is well worth consideration. All 184 pitches for touring units have hardstanding and 10A electricity (ten for camping), while 57 have water and waste water. The ground slopes, so most pitches are terraced with some divided by distinctive, box-like leylandii hedging. Around 80 privately owned caravan holiday homes are in separate areas at the bottom of the site. Three are available to let. Excellent provision is made for disabled visitors, although there is considerable up and down walking due to the terrain. Situated on the western side of Charmouth beside the A35 (some road noise may be expected), the park is only a mile or two from Lyme Regis and its beaches. This area is now part of England's first natural World Heritage site, the Jurassic Coast. Wood Farm is part of the Caravan Club's Affiliated Scheme (non-members are also very welcome). Wood Farm has been in the hands of the same family for over 40 years. A member of the Best of British group.

Facilities

Four modern, well equipped, heated toilet blocks include some excellent, new en-suite shower rooms. Good facilities for disabled campers and children. Baby care unit. Two laundry rooms. Motorcaravan services. Shop by reception. Super conservatory café with sun terrace and viewing area for the swimming pool serving food all day, including breakfasts, and supper on 2/3 nights per week. Fish and chip van calls. Good heated indoor pool and outdoor tennis court (charged). Games room with soft ball area, table tennis and snooker tables. Bridge club. Outdoor draughts. Play field. Two coarse fishing ponds (carp, rudd, roach, tench, perch) adjacent – day and weekly tickets (licence required from park). WiFi (charged).

Open: 19 March - 1 November.

Directions

Park is 0.5 miles west of Charmouth village with access near the roundabout at the A35 and A3052 (Lyme Regis) junction. GPS: 50.74216, -2.91588

Charges guide

Per person	£ 5.00 - £ 8.00
child (5-16 yrs acc. to age)	£ 2.50 - £ 5.50
pitch incl. 10A electricity	£ 7.00 - £ 14.00
'premium' pitch	£ 13.00 - £ 20.00
pup tent, dog, extra car	£ 2.00

Weekly offer in low and mid season.

- Breathtaking countryside views
- Superb indoor swimming pool
- Idyllic fishing ponds
- Tennis court
- 'Offshore' Cafe

Woodfarm
Charmouth, Dorset DT6 6BT
Tel: (01297) 560697
www.woodfarm.co.uk

Charmouth
Monkton Wyld Caravanning & Camping Park

Scotts Lane, Monkton Wyld, Charmouth DT6 6DB (Dorset) T: 01297 631131.
E: holidays@monktonwyld.co.uk **alanrogers.com/UK1730**

Monkton Wyld combines pitches for the independent camper and for members of The Camping and Caravanning Club. The park prides itself on its conservation efforts and the space and landscaping provided. Every pitch backs against a hedge or flower bed; 150 pitches, of which 92 are hardstanding, have 16A electricity. A further 50 tenting pitches are available in the school holiday period. A number of privately owned holiday homes have a separate area. There is also a range of self-catering accommodation, including a safari tent, cottages, a flat and a large farmhouse. This family run park has matured into an attractive, comfortable, garden-like park with trees and flowering shrubs and is maintained to a high standard.

Facilities

Two well built, heated toilet blocks are fully equipped. Family room with baby changing facilities (can also be accessed by wheelchairs). Laundry area. Gas supplies. Shop (Easter-end Oct). Takeaway (May-Aug). Play areas. Caravan storage. Gate locked at 23.00. Caravan holiday homes for private purchase and other self-catering accommodation available. WiFi over site (charged). Off site: Shops and local pubs within 1 mile. Fishing and riding 2 miles. Bicycle hire, golf and boat launching 3 miles. Charmouth and Lyme Regis 3 miles (buses leave from just along the road to both towns).

Open: 9 March - 29 October.

Directions

Park is signed on A35 between Charmouth and Axminster, 2.5 miles west of Charmouth. Turn right at Greenway Head (B3165 signed Marshwood) and park is on the left. Do not go to Monkton Wyld hamlet as the road is very steep. GPS: 50.765333, -2.9525

Charges guide

Per unit incl. 2 persons and electricity	£ 19.25 - £ 27.45
extra person	£ 7.70 - £ 11.30
child (6-17 yrs)	£ 3.35 - £ 5.65

Charmouth

Newlands Caravan Park

Charmouth DT6 6RB (Dorset) T: 01297 560259. E: enq@newlandsholidays.co.uk

alanrogers.com/UK1810

Newlands is well situated on the Jurassic Coast, the first natural World Heritage site in England. A family owned park, it is run with care and enthusiasm by Jackie and Rex Ireland and their daughter, Natalie. It occupies a prominent position beside the road into Charmouth village with rural views southwards to the hills across the valley. The terrain is terraced in two fields to provide over 200 well spaced places for touring units, some for seasonal units and over 80 for caravan holiday homes (36 for hire). The mainly sloping tent field, with some terracing, also has super views towards the sea and Lyme Regis. Electricity (10A) is provided on 160 pitches and 30 have hardstanding, water and drainage. Other accommodation includes smart pine lodges, apartments and motel rooms. This is a comfortable site for families with the beach and village within easy walking distance, and some evening and family activities.

Facilities	Directions
Two modern, heated toilet blocks provide roomy showers. Baby room. Well stocked shop (Mar-Nov). Licensed club bar (limited hours Nov-Mar). Restaurant (18.00-21.00. mid March-early Nov) including takeaway. Outdoor heated pool (supervised in high season; the entrance is key coded). Indoor pool and adventure play areas. Family entertainment. WiFi over site (charged). Off site: Bus stop outside site. Beach 0.5 miles. Fishing 1 mile. Golf 2 miles. Riding 3 miles. Fishing trips and fossil hunting trips. Charmouth is known for its fossil finds and its connection with Jane Austen.	Approaching from Bridport leave the A35 at first sign for Charmouth at start of the bypass and site almost directly on your left. GPS: 50.7385, -2.889833

Open: Mid February - early November.

Charges guide

Per unit incl. up to 6 persons and awning	£ 14.00 - £ 34.00
incl. electricity	£ 17.00 - £ 37.00
fully serviced pitch	£ 24.00 - £ 42.00
dog (max. 2)	£ 2.00 - £ 4.00
extra person	£ 3.00

Only one van or tent per pitch.
Max. unit size applies.

Cheddar

Cheddar Bridge Touring Park

Draycott Road, Cheddar BS27 3RJ (Somerset) T: 01934 743048. E: enquiries@cheddarbridge.co.uk

alanrogers.com/UK1545

Within easy walking distance of Cheddar village, this is an adult only (over 18 yrs) park. A compact site, there are 65 pitches, mostly on level grass, with 40 electricity hook-ups (16A) and 35 gravel hardstandings. A separate area for 20 tents is on the river bank, with its own toilet facilities. Ten caravan holiday homes are now also available to rent. Reception keeps basic supplies and gas cylinders. Cream teas are available (which you prepare yourself) and profits go to charity. Note: the site access is over a fairly narrow bridge with low stone walls, passable for double-axle caravans, but more difficult for very large motorcaravans. Cheddar village has two good supermarkets with a garage, pubs, restaurants, ATM and a leisure centre with an indoor pool. Cheddar Gorge is easily accessed on foot, without the difficulty and expense of parking a vehicle in the Gorge itself. Further opportunities for walking include the nearby Mendips. Weston-super-Mare, Wells and Glastonbury are all within 20 minutes by car.

Facilities	Directions
Heated sanitary block (close to site entrance, some distance from most of the pitches) with washbasins in cubicles, large showers, and family bathroom with shower over the bath. Utility room with sinks, washing machine and dryer. Hot water is restricted to 07.00-12.00 and 16.00-21.00. Fishing. WiFi over part of site (charged). Off site: Swimming pool 0.5 miles. Golf and riding 3 miles. Cheddar Gorge and village.	Site entrance is 100 yds. south of village on A371, on right hand side, next to Cheddar Football Club. GPS: 51.27315, -2.774583

Open: 1 March - end October.

Charges guide

Per unit incl. 2 persons and electricity	£ 13.00 - £ 22.00
extra person	£ 5.00
dog	£ 2.00

Special offers available.

For latest campsite news visit

alanrogers.com

Cheddar
Bucklegrove Caravan & Camping Park

Wells Road, Rodney Stoke, Cheddar BS27 3UZ (Somerset) T: 01749 870261. E: info@bucklegrove.co.uk

alanrogers.com/UK1550

Bucklegrove is set right in the heart of Somerset on the southern slopes of the Mendip Hills and close to the tourist attractions of Cheddar Gorge, Wookey Hole and Wells. There are 110 individually marked and numbered touring and tenting pitches, most of which have 10A electricity connections. The site is made up of the Grove, a level and terraced field, joined by a woodland walk to the lower field. There is also a summer camping meadow just for tents (no electricity here), with plenty of space and great views. The play area (for under 14s) has a safety surface and includes a multiplay unit, slide and spring riders. Heated indoor swimming pool and separate children's pool.

Facilities

Two toilet blocks house all the usual amenities including some washbasins in cubicles and some spacious showers. The larger, heated block near reception also provides bathrooms (£1) with baby changing facilities, and a room for visitors with disabilities. Laundry rooms. Freezer for ice packs. Well stocked shop (Easter-Oct). Indoor swimming pool and paddling pool (28/3-2/11). Licensed café with toddlers' soft play area for 2015. Dogs are accepted in certain fields. WiFi (charged). Luxury log cabins for hire. Off site: Wookey Hole and riding 2 miles. Golf 3 miles. Cheddar 3 miles. Wells Cathedral 4 miles. Fishing 5 miles. Beach at Weston-Super-Mare 12 miles. A bus to Wells and Cheddar stops regularly at the park entrance.

Open: 1 March - 30 November.

Directions

Please do not use GPS for large or towing vehicles. Park is on the A371 3 miles east of Cheddar and 4 miles west of Wells. Take care as the road between Wells and Cheddar is rather narrow through some of the villages. GPS: 51.24296, -2.73178

Charges guide

Per unit incl. 2 persons and electricity	£ 10.00 - £ 35.00
extra person	£ 3.00 - £ 6.00
child (5-12 yrs)	£ 1.00 - £ 4.00
dog (max. 2)	free - £ 5.00

Chippenham
Piccadilly Caravan Park

Folly Lane West, Lacock, Chippenham SN15 2LP (Wiltshire) T: 01249 730260. E: piccadillylacock@aol.com

alanrogers.com/UK1660

Piccadilly Caravan Park is set in open countryside close to several attractions, notably Longleat, Bath, Salisbury Plain, Stourhead, and the picturesque village of Lacock itself. You will receive a warm welcome from the owner at this small, quiet family owned park that is beautifully maintained. Well kept shrubs, flowers and trees have been landscaped to provide three separate areas and create a very pleasant ambience. There are 45 well spaced, clearly marked pitches, 12 of which have hardstanding, and 42 have electricity (10A). Two areas have been made available for tents. A bus service runs from Lacock village to Chippenham (entry to the Chippenham museum and Heritage centre is free of charge). Lacock Abbey was once the home of Henry Fox-Talbot, pioneer of photography, and there is now a museum in the village.

Facilities

Two heated toilet blocks are well maintained and equipped. No facilities for disabled visitors. Laundry room. Ice pack service. Playground and a large, grass ball play area. Limited gas supplies. Newspapers can be ordered. WiFi (free). Off site: Fishing 1 mile. Riding 4 miles. Golf 3 miles. Bicycle hire 6 miles. Chippenham 5 miles.

Open: Easter/1 April - October.

Directions

Turn right off A350 Chippenham-Melksham road approx. 5 miles south of Chippenham (signed Gastard and site). Entrance on left in 300 yds. GPS: 51.4138, -2.129683

Charges guide

| Per unit incl. 2 persons and electricity | £ 21.00 |
| extra person (over 5 yrs) | £ 2.00 |

No credit cards.

For latest campsite news visit
alanrogers.com

Chippenham
Plough Lane Caravan Site

Plough Lane, Kington Langley, Chippenham SN15 5PS (Wiltshire) T: 01249 750146.
E: enquiries@ploughlane.co.uk **alanrogers.com/UK1680**

Catering for adults only (over 18 years), this is a good example of a well designed, quality, modern touring site; booking is essential. The 50 pitches (all for touring units) are attractively laid out over four acres, access roads are gravel and the borders are stocked with well established shrubs and trees. The pitches are half grass, half hardstanding and all have 16A electricity, with 25 having full services. The site entrance has a barrier system for security. This site is an ideal base for visiting Bath and the Cotswolds, Avebury and Stonehenge, the Caen Hill locks at Devizes and Bristol.

Facilities

The sanitary building is heated, spacious, light and airy, and has all the usual facilities including some washbasins in cubicles, and a hairdressing area for ladies. Separate en-suite room for disabled visitors with ramp access. Fully equipped heated laundry. Max. 2 dogs per unit, a gravel dog walking path is provided. This park is for adults only (over 18 yrs). Barrier card deposit. WiFi throughout. Off site: Supermarket, two public houses, and one garage (with gas). Golf less than 1 mile.

Open: 16 March - 2 November.

Directions

Site is 2 miles north of Chippenham. From M4 exit 17 turn south on A350 for 2 miles, then left at lights (site signed). From Chippenham head north on A350 (towards M4), approaching lights (Kington Langley) take right hand lane. GPS: 51.486367, -2.1257

Charges guide

Per unit incl. 2 persons and electricity	£ 23.00 - £ 25.00
extra person (max. 2 extra)	£ 5.00

No credit cards.

Christchurch
Grove Farm Meadow Holiday Park

Meadowbank Holidays, Stour Way, Christchurch BH23 2PQ (Dorset) T: 01202 483597.
E: enquiries@meadowbank-holidays.co.uk **alanrogers.com/UK2130**

Grove Farm Meadow is a quiet, traditional park with caravan holiday homes and a small provision for touring units. The grass flood bank which separates the River Stour from this park provides an attractive pathway. The river bank has been kept natural and is well populated by a range of water birds. It is popular with bird watchers and there is fishing in the river. There are just under 200 caravan holiday homes (75 for hire), sited in regular rows. For touring units there are 41 level pitches (21 fully serviced and with hardstanding), all clearly numbered with 10A electricity, backing on to fencing or hedging and accessed by tarmac roads. This site is ideally located for visiting the New Forest, just 15 minutes by car.

Facilities

The new heated toilet block provides a bathroom for each sex (50p). Separate toilets, washbasins and showers. Facilities for disabled visitors with ramped access. Baby room. Laundry facilities. Well stocked shop. Games room with pool table and electronic games. Adventure play area beside the river bank. Fishing (permits from reception). Free WiFi throughout. Dogs are not accepted. No tents.

Open: 1 March - 31 October.

Directions

From A388 Ringwood-Bournemouth road take B3073 for Christchurch. Turn right at the first roundabout and Stour Way is the third road on the right. GPS: 50.750336, -1.807938

Charges guide

Per unit incl. 2 persons and electricity	£ 12.00 - £ 28.00
extra person (over 5 yrs)	£ 1.00 - £ 2.00

Christchurch
Harrow Wood Farm Caravan Park

Poplar Lane, Bransgore, Christchurch BH23 8JE (Dorset) T: 01425 672487.
E: harrowwood@caravan-sites.co.uk **alanrogers.com/UK2160**

Harrow Wood Farm Caravan Park is a small family park, set in 80 acres of farmland in the village of Bransgore, just within the New Forest National Park. It has 63 hardstanding pitches for tourers, all with 10A electricity. They are not hedged and have little shade. The on-site coarse fishing lake, stocked with roach, bream and carp, is free to residents, and has a one mile circular walk. Harrow Wood is an ideal base for camping and caravanning in the New Forest and a local bus service runs to the local towns of Christchurch, Ringwood and Lymington. There is also a train station five miles away.

Facilities

Two small and one large heated toilet blocks are clean and have preset showers and vanity style washbasins. Hairdryers. Facilities for disabled visitors. Laundry. Large fishing lake. Tourist information. WiFi over site (charged). Caravan storage. Dogs are not accepted. Off site: Village shop 10 mins. walk. Restaurant 1 mile. Tennis 1 mile. Bicycle hire 4 miles. Golf and riding 5 miles.

Open: 1 March - 6 January.

Directions

From Lyndhurst take A35 towards Christchurch. When you see Cat and Fiddle pub ahead, turn right into Christchurch Road for Bransgore. After 2 miles enter village, turn right after Church and Three Tuns pub into Poplar Lane. GPS: 50.779107, -1.728551

Charges guide

Per unit incl. 6 persons	£ 17.50 - £ 26.50
awning	£ 4.00

For latest campsite news visit
alanrogers.com

Dulverton
Exe Valley Caravan Site

Mill House, Bridgetown, Dulverton TA22 9JN (Somerset) T: 01643 851432. E: info@exevalleycamping.co.uk
alanrogers.com/UK1590

Occupying a prime position in a wooded valley alongside the River Exe, within the National Park, Exe Valley Caravan Site is ideally situated for visiting Tarr Steps, Dulverton, the North Somerset coast and many other beautiful places in the area. This quiet, four-acre, adult only campsite is owned and managed by Paul and Christine Matthews and their excellent wardens. Set beside the River Exe, or the millstream, there are 50 large pitches (mostly grass but with some hardstandings at the top end and one near the entrance), of which 47 have 10A electricity and TV hook-ups (cable provided on loan). Reception is now at the entrance. The owner's home is an old mill, complete with working water wheel and millstones, that opens to visitors most Sundays at 10 am. CCTV has been installed, so campers may watch the bat colony in the loft from a screen in the mill. A small shop run by the wardens stocks local produce and some camping requirements. Fly fishing along the River Exe is possible from the site or at Wimbleball Reservoir, just over four miles away. This part of Somerset is a haven for walking, cycling, pony trekking, or as a place to just sit and relax.

Facilities

The refurbished toilet block houses the usual facilities and an en-suite room for disabled visitors (short steep ramp to enter). Excellent laundry with domestic washing and drying machines, plus a microwave and freezer. Motorcaravan services. Small shop. Bicycle hire. Gas supplies. Free fly fishing. Free WiFi. This is an adult only park. Off site: Riding 4 miles. Golf 12 miles. Pub at Bridgetown. Winsford village has a general stores and tea rooms.

Open: 12 March - 18 October.

Directions

Bridgetown is roughly midway between Dunster and Tiverton on the A396. On entering Bridgetown from Tiverton, look for site sign and turn left on minor road. Site is 50 yds. on the right.
GPS: 51.0882, -3.53875

Charges guide

Per unit incl. 2 persons, electricity and TV hook-up	£ 13.00 - £ 22.00
extra person	£ 5.00
awning	£ 1.00
dog	£ 1.00

No credit cards.

Dulverton
Exmoor House Caravan Club Site

Kemps Way, Dulverton TA22 9HL (Somerset) T: 01398 323268.
alanrogers.com/UK1585

This pleasant site, reserved for motorcaravans and caravans, is well situated on the outskirts of the charming country town of Dulverton, alongside the River Barle. It is professionally run and all facilities are maintained to a very high standard. The site is well landscaped with tarmac roads and a choice of 67 pitches, 53 on gravel hardstandings. They are quite small but certainly not cramped. All have 16A electricity hook-ups, and eight are fully serviced. Walls and hedges divide the site into smaller areas. It is ideal for those who simply want to relax and enjoy the birdsong, but there are numerous opportunities for an adventurous stay, with canoeing and kayaking on the doorstep and sailing and fishing at Wimbleball Lake, just five miles away.

Facilities

The single heated sanitary block has good modern showers and washing cubicles. Indoor dishwashing area and a well equipped laundry. Facilities for disabled visitors. Motorcaravan services. Shop. No play area and no ball games allowed, but a small park is nearby. WiFi over site (charged). Off site: Bus service to Minehead and Taunton 200 m. Small park with play house 300 m. Fishing and riding 3 miles. Exmoor National Park Centre in Dulverton, with information, exhibitions, art gallery and library. Beach 17 miles.

Open: 20 March - 4 January.

Directions

From M5 exit 27 take dual carriageway A361 (Barnstable). After 6 miles turn right at roundabout onto A396 (Minehead). After a further 8 miles at Exebridge turn left onto B3222 (Dulverton). At outskirts of Dulverton, turn right over a bridge. The site is signposted down a road on the left, just before the Bridge Inn. Towing a caravan through Dulverton is not advised. Earliest arrival time is 13:00. GPS: 51.04144, -3.55284

Charges guide

Per person	£ 5.60 - £ 7.80
child (5-17 yrs)	£ 0.01 - £ 2.90
pitch incl. electricity (non-member)	£ 15.70 - £ 19.60

For latest campsite news visit
alanrogers.com

Glastonbury
The Old Oaks Touring Park

Wick Farm, Wick, Glastonbury BA6 8JS (Somerset) T: 01458 831437. E: info@theoldoaks.co.uk

alanrogers.com/UK1390

The Old Oaks, an adults only park (over 18 years), is tucked below the Glastonbury Tor in a lovely secluded setting with views across to the Mendips. The grounds are immaculate with a great deal of attention to cleanliness throughout. In total there are 100 large pitches in a series of paddocks, 91 with 16A electricity, on hardstandings and 50 are fully serviced. Mainly backing on to hedges, they are attractively arranged and interspersed with shrubs and flowers in a circular development or terraced with rural views. There is a quiet orchard area for camping and six camping cabins provide a luxurious alternative to tents, but retain that 'outdoor feel'. A member of the Best of British group.

Facilities

Two blocks (one a new facility) are both of excellent quality with fully fitted individual shower rooms and a bathroom (£1). Disabled visitors have three rooms. Two fully equipped laundry rooms. Motorcaravan services. Freezer for ice packs (free). Useful dog wash. Licensed shop selling local produce, freshly baked cakes and bread (pre-ordered). Pool table. Fishing. Painting holidays. Internet access at reception. Free WiFi over site.

Open: 13 February - 22 November.

Directions

Park is north off A361 Shepton Mallet-Glastonbury road, 2 miles from Glastonbury. Take the narrow unclassified road signed Wick for 1 mile and park is on the left. GPS: 51.152633, -2.6803

Charges guide

Per unit incl. 2 persons	
and electricity	£ 18.00 - £ 31.00
with full services	£ 20.00 - £ 35.00
extra person	£ 9.00 - £ 14.00

Lyme Regis
Shrubbery Caravan & Camping Park

Rousdon, Lyme Regis DT7 3XW (Dorset) T: 01297 442227. E: info@shrubberypark.co.uk

alanrogers.com/UK1720

Three miles south of historic Lyme Regis, in a good situation to explore the Jurassic Coast, this well cared for park has distant views of the surrounding countryside. There are 120 generous pitches, 28 with hardstanding and more than enough room to pitch for most units. On slightly sloping, neatly cut grass which undulates in places, they are accessed by tarmac roads and all have 10A electricity. The pitches back on to square-cut shrubs or the perimeter trees. A modern reception area is welcoming and stocks basic supplies and local provisions. This is a comfortable park where couples and families with young children are welcomed.

Facilities

Excellent, well maintained, heated toilet blocks, the newest (part of the reception building) with en-suite units, bathroom and laundry facilities. Two further blocks nearer the top of the park, fully equipped and well maintained. Facilities for disabled visitors. Motorcaravan filling point. Simple shop at reception specialising in local produce. Large play area. Crazy golf. Off site: Fishing 1 mile. Golf, beach and boat launching 3 miles. Riding 5 miles

Open: 1 April - 31 October.

Directions

From the A35 near Axminster follow the A358 towards Seaton. At T-junction turn left on A3052 signed Rousdon and Lyme Regis. Site entrance is on the left a few yards after Rousdon Garage. GPS: 50.71734, -2.99521

Charges guide

Per unit incl. 2 persons	
and electricity	£ 16.25 - £ 21.75
extra person	£ 3.75

Malmesbury
Burton Hill Caravan Park

Arches Lane, Malmesbury SN16 0EH (Wiltshire) T: 01666 826 880. E: stay@burtonhill.co.uk

alanrogers.com/UK1665

The owners of this park, Robert and Ali Simmons, tend it with pride. It is a flat, grassy site surrounded by hedges with open views across farmland on the outskirts of historic Malmesbury. The approach is through a well tended 'village' of park homes. There are 28 numbered touring pitches each with 16A electricity, with eight more for tents. There are limited amenities on-site but you will find a choice of shops, inns and restaurants in the town which is a short walk (10-15 minutes) across the river. Here you can also visit the Abbey House Gardens, Abbey and 15th-century market place.

Facilities

Modern, well equipped and well maintained heated toilet block with free hot water. Family shower room. Separate well equipped facilities for disabled visitors. Washing machine. Motorcaravan services. Fishing. Max. 2 dogs. Off site: Malmesbury also has a new sports centre and swimming pool. Golf 6 miles.

Open: 1 April/Easter - 31 October.

Directions

From M4 exit 17 follow A4129 towards Cirencester (5 miles). Approaching Malmesbury at international caravan sign, turn left into Arches Lane, and follow signs. GPS: 51.579083, -2.097321

Charges guide

Per unit incl. 2 persons and electricity	£ 20.00
extra person	£ 5.00
child (5-15 yrs)	£ 3.00
dog (max. 2)	free

For latest campsite news visit
alanrogers.com

Martock

Southfork Caravan Park

Parrett Works, Martock TA12 6AE (Somerset) T: 01935 825661. E: info@southforkcaravans.co.uk

alanrogers.com/UK1420

Michael and Nancy Broadley now own and run this good, modern, well drained site just outside the lovely village of Martock. There are 25 touring pitches on grass with a gravel access road, 22 with 10A electricity and two with water and drainage. It is an orderly, quiet park on two acres of flat, tree lined meadow near the River Parrett. Despite the rural setting, the A303 trunk road is just five minutes away making this a good stopover or for a longer stay to explore this very interesting area. Also, there is an on-site NCC-approved caravan repair/servicing centre. This area of south Somerset contains much of interest, including gardens, historic houses and sites, the Fleet Air Arm Museum and Haynes Motor Museum. Information about access to many cycle routes and numerous walks, including the Parrett Trail, is available from reception.

Facilities

One heated and well maintained toilet block is fully equipped and includes some washbasins in cabins and free hot showers. No facilities for disabled visitors. Washing machine and dryer. Small shop with local produce, local cider and beer. Play area. Fishing permits from reception. Enclosed dog exercise area. Off site: Fishing (with licences) on the River Parrett a few yards from the park. Pubs with good food in South Petherton and Martock, less than 2 miles. Golf 5 miles. Bicycle hire 8 miles. Riding 10 miles.

Open: All year.

Directions

From A303 between Ilchester and Ilminster turn north at roundabout signed South Petherton. At T-junction in middle of village, turn right towards Martock. Park is at Parrett Works midway between the two villages (about 1.5 miles from South Petherton). GPS: 50.965367, -2.789817

Charges guide

Per unit incl. 2 persons	
and electricity	£ 18.00 - £ 26.00
extra person	£ 3.00
child (under 5 yrs)	free
dog	£ 1.00

Minehead

Westermill Farm

Exford, Minehead TA24 7NJ (Somerset) T: 01643 831238. E: info@westermill.com

alanrogers.com/UK1301

This superbly located farm campsite can be found nestling in a valley beside the River Exe. The working farm provides four meadows, all without electricity, and is ideal for 'back to basics' style touring. Uniquely, open fires are permitted in one field with logs being available to purchase. You can marvel at the wildlife, wander around the working farm and sample the farm's own produce in the shop, which also stocks basic provisions. Walking maps can be found at reception which is located in the old dairy. The Edwards Family are helpful and friendly and encourage you to explore their farm. The site also has six self-catering holiday cottages to let.

Facilities

The unheated toilet block houses the usual facilities including showers and washbasins and hot water is provided by solar energy. Laundry facilities. Farm shop (end May-early Sept). Gas supplies. Facility for freezer packs (20p). Fishing in the River Exe. The river is also used for bathing. Off site: Village 2.5 miles. Bicycle hire 6 miles. Riding 15 miles. Beach 15 miles.

Open: All year.

Directions

Leave Exford on Porlock Road with Post Office on right. At Y fork turn left down single track road. Farm is 2 miles on right. Do not use sat nav. GPS: 51.14485, -3.67687

Charges guide

Per person	£ 6.50
child	£ 3.50
car	£ 2.50
dog	£ 2.50
No credit cards.	

For latest campsite news visit
alanrogers.com

Minehead
Burrowhayes Farm Caravan & Camping Site

West Luccombe, Porlock, Minehead TA24 8HT (Somerset) T: 01643 862463. E: info@burrowhayes.co.uk

alanrogers.com/UK1370

This delightful park with riding stables on site, is on the edge of Exmoor. The stone packhorse bridge over Horner Water beside the farm entrance sets the tone of the park, which the Dascombe family have created over the last forty years having previously farmed the land. The farm buildings have been converted into riding stables with escorted rides available (from Easter). Touring and tent pitches are on a partly sloping field with marvellous views, or a flatter location in a clearing by the river, while 20 caravan holiday homes are in a separate area. Electrical hook-ups are available (16A), although some require long leads (25 m). There are six fully serviced pitches. With walking, birdwatching, plenty of wildlife to observe, pretty Exmoor villages and Lorna Doone country nearby there is much to do. Children can ride, play in the stream or explore the woods at the top of the site. Limited trout fishing is available in Horner Water (NT permit) alongside the park.

Facilities

The very well equipped, heated toilet block provides controllable hot showers and washbasin cubicles for each sex, hairdressing and shaving areas, laundry room, unit for disabled visitors and babies. A second older block is opened in high season with extra WCs and washbasins. Motorcaravan services. Well stocked shop doubles with reception (from 1/4). Riding stables. Dogs must be kept on a lead at all times and exercised off site. Free WiFi. Off site: Beach and fishing 2 miles. Minehead and bicycle hire 5 miles. Golf 6 miles. Local pub 20 minutes walk.

Open: 15 March - 31 October.

Directions

From A39, 5 miles west of Minehead, take first left past Allerford to Horner and West Luccombe. Site is on right after 400 yds. GPS: 51.203533, -3.5778

Charges guide

Per unit incl. 2 persons and electricity	£ 17.00 - £ 23.50
extra person	£ 6.00
child (3-16 yrs)	£ 2.50
dog	free

In the heart of Exmoor Country
Burrowhayes Farm
Caravan & Camping Site
Riding Stables
Tel: 01643 862 463
www.burrowhayes.co.uk

Minehead
Halse Farm Touring Caravan & Camping Park

Winsford, Minehead TA24 7JL (Somerset) T: 01643 851259. E: ar@halsefarm.co.uk

alanrogers.com/UK1360

A truly rural park with beautiful, moorland views, you may be lucky enough to glimpse red deer across the valley or see ponies and foals grazing outside the main gate which is adjacent to the moor. Two open, neatly cut fields (level at the top) back onto traditional hedging and slope gently to the middle and bottom where wild flowers dominate. One field provides 10A electricity points and is used for motorcaravans, caravans and tents requiring electricity, the other is for tents. Reception is in the farmhouse – leave your unit by the toilet block and walk down to the farm kitchen to book in. The pretty village of Winsford is one mile away (footpath from farm) with a post office, shop, pub and restaurant. A member of the Countryside Discovery group.

Facilities

The recently refurbished central toilet block is heated, well equipped and maintained. It includes a toilet, washbasin and shower for visitors with disabilities, washing machine, dryer and iron, and tourist information. Gas is available at the farm. Play equipment. Free WiFi over site. Off site: Winsford village 1 mile. Riding 2 miles. Tarr Steps and Barle Valley 3 miles. Fishing 4 miles. Bicycle hire 15 miles.

Open: 14 March - 31 October.

Directions

Turn off A396 Tiverton-Minehead road for Winsford. In Winsford village turn left in front of Royal Oak (avoiding ford), continue uphill for 1 mile. Cross cattle grid onto moor and turn immediately left to farm. Caravans should avoid Dulverton – keep to the A396 from Bridgetown. GPS: 51.097717, -3.579983

Charges guide

Per unit incl. 2 persons and electricity	£ 17.00 - £ 19.00
extra person	£ 7.00 - £ 8.00
child (5-16 yrs)	£ 2.00
dog	free

Less 10% for 7 days paid on booking, or at least 14 days before arrival.

For latest campsite news visit
alanrogers.com

Minehead

Hoburne Blue Anchor

Blue Anchor Bay, Minehead TA24 6JT (Somerset) T: 01643 821360. E: enquiries@hoburne.com

alanrogers.com/UK1380

Although mainly a holiday park with over 300 caravan holiday homes, Blue Anchor nevertheless offers good facilities for 103 touring units. Trailer tents are accepted but not other tents (other than pup tents with a touring booking). Virtually in a separate touring area, the level pitches all have 10A electricity and hardstanding for cars and motorcaravans (with caravans going on the adjacent grass). A feature of the park is a good sized, irregularly shaped indoor swimming pool with an area for small children complete with a mushroom shaped fountain. With views of the sea from the pool, it is heated and supervised. Although not within the park itself, there are restaurants and takeaways within easy walking distance.

Facilities	Directions
Toilet facilities provide large, free hot showers (with pushbutton). Fully equipped launderette in a single, modern block serving just the touring area. Well stocked shop. Indoor heated swimming pool (free). Excellent adventure-style play area in a copse. NB: unfenced river runs along one boundary of the park. Crazy golf. Large motorhomes accepted (max. 36 ft). WiFi in reception. **Open:** 27 February - 31 October.	From M5 exit 25, take A358 (Minehead). In 12 miles turn left onto A39 at Williton. After 4 miles turn right onto B3191 at Carhampton signed Blue Anchor. Park is 1.5 miles on right. GPS: 51.1822, -3.397283
	Charges guide
	Contact the park for details. Short breaks available.

Poole

Pear Tree Holiday Park

Organford Road, Holton Heath, Poole BH16 6LA (Dorset) T: 01202 622434. E: enquiries@peartreepark.co.uk

alanrogers.com/UK2110

Pear Tree is a neat, landscaped and well cared for park, set in 7.5 acres with mature trees and views across to Wareham Forest. There are 155 pitches in total, of which 87 are for touring units with hardstanding, 10A electricity, water and drainage. Only breathable groundsheets are permitted for awnings. The tent area is a tranquil, secluded spot with many mature trees. Reception, incorporating tourist information and a small shop supplying milk, bread, gas and other basics, is at the park entrance. The park is well situated for visiting Poole, Corfe Castle, Swanage and the Purbecks.

Facilities	Directions
The main heated toilet block (opened by key and recently refurbished) provides some washbasins in cubicles, baby changing unit, two new family rooms with Belfast sink, baby bath and a wet room for disabled visitors. Laundry. Separate small prefabricated unit near the tent area. All is kept spotlessly clean. Shop for basics. Play area. All-year caravan storage. Off site: The Clay Pipe Inn 500 m. Bicycle hire 0.5 miles. Golf 2.5 miles. Beach 9 miles. **Open:** 1 March - 31 October.	From the A351 (Wareham-Poole) road, turn west at traffic lights in Holton Heath (signed Organford and Sandford Park). Park is on left after 550 yds. past Sandford Park and the Clay Pipe Inn. GPS: 50.724033, -2.086967
	Charges guide
	Per unit incl. 2 persons and electricity £ 19.50 - £ 28.00
	extra person £ 6.50

Poole

South Lytchett Manor Caravan & Camping Park

Dorset Road, Lytchett Minster, Poole BH16 6JB (Dorset) T: 01202 622577. E: info@southlytchettmanor.co.uk

alanrogers.com/UK2120

Joanne and David are rightly proud of what they have achieved at South Lytchett Manor and, along with their staff, try hard to meet all your needs and make you very welcome. It has an unusual situation on parkland either side of what was once one of the driveways to the manor itself with impressive gates at the entrance. The 150 touring pitches are level, of a good size, with TV connections and electricity. There are 85 available with gravel hardstanding and a good number also have water, waste water connections and a picnic bench. They are neatly landscaped with rural views. Poole is just three miles away and a 20 minute drive will take you to Bournemouth. A member of the Best of British group.

Facilities	Directions
Three modern, fully equipped sanitary blocks have piped music, fresh flowers and can be heated in winter. They include family rooms and facilities for disabled visitors. Motorcaravan services. Laundry. Well stocked shop with off-licence and gas. Games room. Fenced play area. Playing field. Woodland walk. Off-lead dog walking field. Bicycle hire. WiFi throughout (free). Off site: Shops, pubs, ATM 1 mile. Beach and sailing 2 miles. Ferry port 3 miles. **Open:** 1 March - 2 January.	At roundabout at eastern end of A35 west of Poole, turn north on B3067 to Lytchett Minster. Go through village to site on left 0.5 miles past church, through wrought-iron gates. GPS: 50.73959, -2.05542
	Charges guide
	Per unit incl. 2 persons and electricity £ 17.50 - £ 33.25
	pitch fully serviced £ 20.75 - £ 37.50
	extra person £ 4.75 - £ 8.00

89

For latest campsite news visit

alanrogers.com

Salisbury
Stonehenge Campsite & Glamping Pods

Berwick St James, Salisbury SP3 4TQ (Wiltshire) T: 07786 734732. E: Stay@stonehengecampsite.co.uk
alanrogers.com/UK1610

A small, very attractive family run park tucked away in the beautiful Wiltshire countryside, yet with easy access to the A303 and Stonehenge. There are 15 pitches (11 for touring) laid out in three separate areas. The 13 nearest reception, in a garden setting, are for caravans and motorcaravans, all with 16A electricity and ten on hardstandings. The 20 pitches for tents and small motorcaravans are around the edge of two large open meadows, 12 have 16A electricity. There is plenty of room in the meadows to play games. Those with caravans and motorcaravans should phone ahead for availability.

Facilities	Directions
Small, modern, heated toilet blocks near reception with some en-suite shower units. Family room. Washing machine/dryer. Very well appointed campers' kitchen. No facilities for disabled campers. Small shops with local produce. Takeaways deliver. WiFi over site (charged). Campfire pits for hire. Off site: Bus stop at park entrance (Salisbury and Devizes). Stonehenge 2 miles. Longleat House, Bath, Salisbury. Nature reserve.	Leave A303 1.7 miles southwest of roundabout at Stonehenge Visitor Centre. Turn left, B3083, signed Berwick St James. Site is shortly on left. GPS: 51.16265, -1.89658

Open: 1 February - 30 November.

Charges guide

Per unit incl. 2 persons and electricity	£ 19.00 - £ 29.00
extra person	£ 5.00

Salisbury
Greenhill Farm Caravan & Camping Park

New Road, Landford, Salisbury SP5 2AZ (Wiltshire) T: 01794 324117. E: info@greenhillholidays.co.uk
alanrogers.com/UK1640

Located on the northern edge of the New Forest National Park, this site occupies 14 out of a total of 50 acres of beautiful forest owned by the family. It is an uncommercialised hideaway and has two distinctive areas: the 'adults only' area, fenced, gated and set around two small lakes, one of which is reserved for coarse fishing; and the 'family' area with a playground, views over the meadow, sightings of deer and a generally open aspect. There are 160 pitches in total, with 50 for tents in a separate hilltop meadow with views over the nearby forest and its own fishing lake. The remainder are for touring units with some seasonal pitches and a number of hardstandings. All pitches are level and with 16A electricity.

Facilities	Directions
Two new toilet blocks and two prefabricated units with excellent facilities include provision for families and disabled visitors. Laundry with washing machine and dryer. Reception/shop. Gas supplies. Takeaway in high season in family area. Room for special events. Bicycle hire. Coarse fishing lakes (£4.00 per rod per day). Grazing for horses. Torches useful. Off site: Bus services to Salisbury and Southampton. Several pubs serving meals are nearby. Landford village 15 mins. walk. Golf 3 miles.	From M27 exit 2 take A36 north towards Salisbury for 6 miles. Pass through West Wellow and after passing a B.P. garage on left, take next left into New Road and continue for 0.9 miles to site entrance on left. GPS: 50.96445, -1.62575

Open: All year.

Charges guide

Per unit incl. 2 persons and electricity	£ 17.50 - £ 27.50
extra person	£ 5.00 - £ 7.00

Salisbury
Coombe Touring Park

Coombe Nurseries Race Plain, Netherhampton, Salisbury SP2 8PN (Wiltshire) T: 01722 328451.
E: enquiries@coombecaravanpark.co.uk **alanrogers.com/UK1650**

A touring park with outstanding views over the Chalke Valley, Coombe is close to Salisbury racecourse. There are 100 spacious pitches all on level, well mown grass, 73 with 10A electricity. Tent pitches are generally around the outer perimeter and there are four caravan holiday homes to rent. Many pitches are individual and sheltered by mature hedging. Reception also has a small shop, there are supermarkets in Salisbury (4.5 miles) and pubs in Netherhampton and Coombe Bissett (2 miles), both serving meals.

Facilities	Directions
A well built, modern, heated sanitary unit provides an ample supply of WCs, spacious pushbutton showers, washbasins in cubicles for the ladies. Family room (with bath) with facilities for disabled visitors, babies and toddlers. Laundry. Small shop (May-July). Open grass play area with slide and new adventure feature. Good tourist information chalet. Off site: Golf 400 yds. Riding and tennis in Wilton 2.5 miles. Indoor pool, leisure centre and cinema in Salisbury 4.5 miles.	From A36 two miles west of Salisbury turn south on A3094 (Netherhampton). After 0.5 miles on sharp, left hand bend turn right to Stratford Tony and racecourse. By racecourse entrance, turn left on narrow lane behind racecourse for 700 yds. to site entrance. GPS: 51.05428, -1.86092

Open: All year.

Charges guide

Per unit incl. 2 persons and electricity	£ 17.00 - £ 20.00
No credit cards.	

For latest campsite news visit
alanrogers.com

Salisbury

Church Farm Caravan & Camping Park

Sixpenny Handley, Salisbury SP5 5ND (Wiltshire) T: 01725 552563. E: churchfarmcandcpark@hotmail.co.uk

alanrogers.com/UK1655

Sixpenny Handley is a Saxon hilltop village with Saint Mary's church dating back some 900 years; from the site you can hear the bells and the chimes of its clock. Church Farm, next to the village centre, offers 35 partly sheltered, level, spacious pitches including some hardstandings, all with 10A, arranged around the perimeter of two fields, plus a tent field. It is in an Area of Outstanding Natural Beauty and the views and many walks are an absolute delight. Not forgetting the hundreds of tumuli and prehistoric remains, there are many places for the visitor to discover the delights around this junction of Dorset, Hampshire and Wiltshire. Arrivals to the park should be after 2 pm. Reception is well stocked with tourist infomation leaflets and timetables for local transport to Salisbury and Blandford. Maps of walks are available starting from the village and one starts from the park. Nearby attractions include the Royal Signals museum (on the bus route) and Bovington tank museum.

Facilities

A spacious and modern eco building houses reception, a seasonal café/bar and up-to-date heated toilet facilities. Dedicated room for disabled visitors. Baby changing. Laundry with washing machine and dryer. Freezer for ice packs. Gas supplies. Motorcaravan services. Play area with new adventure type equipment. Two holiday caravans for rent. Off site: The village has a bus stop, a number of small shops, a small supermarket and Post Office. The Roebuck Inn offers a varied menu. Tennis courts (hire equipment from site). Golf 4 miles. Riding 5 miles. Fishing 10 miles.

Open: All year.

Directions

To avoid the village centre, 1 mile southwest of the Handley Cross roundabout on A354 turn towards Sixpenny Handley, then right by the school and site in 300 yds. by the church.
GPS: 50.955317, -2.006883

Charges guide

Per unit incl. 2 persons and electricity	£ 21.50 - £ 22.50
extra person	£ 9.00 - £ 9.50
child (3-16 yrs)	£ 2.00 - £ 3.50

Shepton Mallet

Batcombe Vale Campsite

Batcombe Vale, Shepton Mallet BA4 6BW (Somerset) T: 01749 372373. E: stay@batcombevale.co.uk

alanrogers.com/UK1540

Set in a secluded valley with fields gently rising around it, contented cows grazing with watchful buzzards cruising above and views across the distant hills, this is a very special place. Descending slowly down the steep, narrow drive you see the pitches, attractively set and terraced where necessary, in an oval with the lakes below. The grass is left natural around the 32 pitches (20 have 10A electricity) and paths are mown where needed. Batcombe Vale House is an attractive, mellow building covered with wisteria, to one side of the valley overlooking the lakes and the wilder landscape. Trees and shrubs have been skilfully placed to enhance the natural environment providing a range of colours and shapes. Designated an Area of Outstanding Natural Beauty, there are 120 acres around the valley where you are welcome to wander and picnic in the fields – a haven for wild flowers, birds and butterflies. There are many places to visit nearby, from Glastonbury with the Tor, to Cheddar Gorge and the Caves.

Facilities

The small rustic toilet block covered in honeysuckle meets all needs, including a freezer (ice packs only) and hot water to dishwashing sinks. Launderette. Groundsheet awnings must be lifted daily. Fishing. Rowing boats. Caravan storage. B&B in Batcombe Vale House. Max. 1 dog (unless by prior arrangement). Off site: Bruton and Evercreech (for shops, etc.) 2 miles. Golf and leisure facilities 9 miles.

Open: 1 April - end September.

Directions

Bruton is south of Shepton Mallet and Frome and north of Wincanton where the A359 intersects the B3081. Access to the site must be via Evercreech or Bruton (B3081), then follow the brown and white camping signs. Access drive is steep.
GPS: 51.136467, -2.453167

Charges guide

Per unit incl. 2 persons and electricity	£ 22.50
extra person	£ 6.00
child (3-15 yrs)	£ 3.50
dog	£ 1.00

No commercial vehicles or motorcycle 'packs' – family groups only. No credit cards.

For latest campsite news visit
alanrogers.com

Shepton Mallet

Greenacres Camping

Barrow Lane, North Wootton, Shepton Mallet BA4 4HL (Somerset) T: 01749 890497.
E: stay@greenacres-camping.co.uk **alanrogers.com/UK1490**

Greenacres is a rural site in the Somerset countryside for tents, trailer tents and small motorcaravans only. Hidden away below the Mendips and almost at the start of the Levels, it is a simple green site, a true haven of peace and quiet. The grass is neatly trimmed over the 4.5 acres and hedged with mature trees, though there is a view of Glastonbury Tor in one direction and of Barrow Hill in the other. All of the 40 pitches are around the perimeter of the park, leaving a central area safe for children to play. At the south side of the site, 13 pitches with 10A electricity are ideal for birdwatchers and those without children. There are now six pitches on the north part of the site with electricty (10A).

Facilities

The central wooden toilet block is kept very clean and includes facilities for children. Small shop. Van calls in high season with local produce. Play equipment, football, badminton net and play house. Crafts/entertainment for children (July/Aug and busy w/ends). Gloworm safaris (summer evenings). The park office and bicycle hire across the lane. Cabin with fridges and freezers for campers' use (free). Library. WiFi (charged). No dogs.

Open: April - September.

Directions

From A361 Glastonbury-Shepton Mallet road follow camp signs from Pilton or Steanbow. (Roads are narrow with few passing places).
GPS: 51.172367, -2.641883

Charges guide

Pitch incl. 2 persons and electricity	£ 22.50
child (2-14 yrs)	£ 4.50

Sparkford

Long Hazel Park

High Street, Sparkford, Yeovil BA22 7JH (Somerset) T: 01963 440002. E: longhazelpark@hotmail.com
alanrogers.com/UK1500

Pamela and Alan Walton are really enthusiastic about their small, beautifully kept, adults only park in the Somerset village of Sparkford where they will make you most welcome. This level, landscaped site is surrounded by attractive beech hedging, silver birch and many other ornamental trees and the park has a relaxed, comfortable feel. It provides 50 touring pitches for all types of units (max. 12 m) with 16A electricity hook-ups (32A on request), 30 pitches with hardstanding, some extra long with grass lawns at the side, and the entrance has been widened for easier access. Part of the park is being developed with holiday lodges for private ownership or rent. American-style motorhomes are welcome.

Facilities

Clean, well equipped and heated sanitary block. En-suite facilities for disabled visitors. Washing machine and dryer. Motorcaravan waste water discharge. Shop (all year). Gas supplies. Details of safe cycle routes and walks available at reception. Seasonal pitches available. WiFi over part of site (charged). Off site: Bus service, village inn 100 yds. Spar shop and McDonalds 400 yds. International Motor Museum 1 mile.

Open: All year.

Directions

At roundabout on A303 take road into village of Sparkford and park is signed on the left 100 yds. before the inn. GPS: 51.0344, -2.568633

Charges guide

Per unit incl. 2 persons and electricity	£ 24.00
extra person	£ 5.00
dog	£ 1.00
No credit cards.	

Swanage

Ulwell Cottage Caravan Park

Ulwell, Swanage BH19 3DG (Dorset) T: 01929 422823. E: enq@ulwellcottagepark.co.uk
alanrogers.com/UK2020

Nestling under the Purbeck Hills on the edge of Swanage, Ulwell Cottage is a family run holiday park with an indoor pool and a wide range of facilities. A good proportion of the park is taken by caravan holiday homes (140), but an attractive, undulating area accessed by tarmac roads is given over to 79 numbered touring pitches interspersed with trees and shrubs. All have 10A electricity, 12 are fully serviced and 14 are hardstanding. The colourful entrance area is home to the Village Inn with a courtyard adjoining the heated, supervised indoor pool complex (both open all year and open to the public; limited pool supervision in winter months) and the modern reception.

Facilities

The modern, cheerful toilet block at the top of the site is heated and includes a unit for disabled visitors and baby changing. Laundry room. Well stocked shop with gas (Easter-end Oct). Bar snacks and restaurant meals with family room. Takeaway (July/Aug). Indoor pool with lifeguard (times vary acc. to season). Playing fields and play areas. WiFi throughout (charged).

Open: 1 March - 7 January.

Directions

From A351 Wareham-Swanage road, turn onto B3351 Studland road just before Corfe Castle. Follow signs to right (southeast) for Swanage and drop down to Ulwell. Park is on right 100 yds. after 40 m.p.h. sign. GPS: 50.626460, -1.969403

Charges guide

Per unit incl. up to 6 persons	£ 16.00 - £ 47.50
full services incl. hardstanding	£ 16.00 - £ 50.50

For latest campsite news visit
alanrogers.com

Taunton
Cornish Farm Touring Park
Shoreditch, Taunton TA3 7BS (Somerset) T: 01823 327746. E: info@cornishfarm.com
alanrogers.com/UK1340

This neat little park, which opened for its first full season in 2006, is on level ground and located close to the M5 motorway. There are 49 pitches, all with 10A electricity, 25 are on gravel hardstanding. Most are accessed from a gravel road (one-way system) with plenty of fresh water taps, site lighting and some picnic tables. A separate area for tents is close to the toilet block. Light power cables cross the site and there is some background motorway noise. Maximum length for motorcaravans is 30 ft, unless by prior arrangement with the wardens. With its old apple trees this park makes a very pleasant stopover. Off to the left are the barns that house the Van Bitz workshops producing security systems for motorcaravans along with accessories for both motorcaravans and caravans. A cycle path and a footpath will take you into the town centre, just two miles away. Taunton, the county town of Somerset, is worth a visit with its Castle, museum, a variety of livestock and produce markets and an annual flower show.

Facilities	Directions
One central block has underfloor heating and modern fittings and you can listen to the local radio. Large, dual-purpose room providing facilities for disabled visitors and small children. Dusk to dawn low energy lighting. Laundry room. Motorcaravan services. Camping supplies for sale and plenty of tourist information available. Calor Gas bottle exchange. Free WiFi. Off site: Village pub 2 miles. Shops 10 mins. Tesco Express 1 mile. Golf, fishing and bicycle hire 2 miles. Riding 4 miles.	From M5 exit 25 follow signs for Taunton. At 1st set of lights turn left onto Bridgwater Rd. Take 3rd left into Ilminster Rd. Right at roundabout, left at next roundabout into Chestnut Dr and follow to T-junction (B3170). Turn right then next left (Killams Dr). Take 2nd left and cross motorway. Site entrance is after the bridge on left. GPS: 50.99200, -3.09257

Open: All year.

Charges guide

Per unit incl. 2 persons and electricity	£ 16.00 - £ 19.00
extra person (over 5 years)	£ 2.25 - £ 3.75

Taunton
Quantock Orchard Caravan Park
Crowcombe, Taunton TA4 4AW (Somerset) T: 01984 618618. E: member@flaxpool.freeserve.co.uk
alanrogers.com/UK1350

Quantock Orchard nestles at the foot of the Quantocks in quiet countryside, close to many of the attractions of the area. Attractively developed, mature apple trees, recently planted trees, shrubs and pretty flower beds with a nice use of heathers, make a pleasant environment. The clock tower on the wooden sanitary block and a dovecote at the entrance add interest. With access from fairly narrow gravel roads, there are 60 touring pitches, part separated by growing shrubs and hedging, of which 40 can also be used for tents. Of various sizes, all touring pitches have 15A electricity hook-ups, 15 have hardstanding and six are fully serviced (two extra large, with patio and barbecue). Levelling blocks may be required on some pitches. Only 'air-flo' style groundsheets are permitted on grass pitches.

Facilities	Directions
The central, heated sanitary block is very well maintained. Some washbasins in curtained cubicles for ladies, family bathroom and baby rooms. Microwave. Laundry. Facilities for disabled visitors (no shower). Drain for motorcaravans. Well stocked licensed shop. Swimming pool (40x20 ft, May-Sept). Games/Sky TV room. Fenced play area. Mountain bike hire. WiFi on part of site (free).	Park is west off A358 road (Taunton-Minehead), signed 1 mile south of Crowcombe village. GPS: 51.1084, -3.22645

Open: All year.

Charges guide

Per unit incl. 2 persons and electricity	£ 15.00 - £ 28.50
extra person	£ 6.00

For latest campsite news visit
alanrogers.com

Taunton
Lowtrow Cross Caravan Site
Upton, Wiveliscombe, Taunton TA4 2DB (Somerset) T: 01398 371199. E: info@lowtrowcross.co.uk
alanrogers.com/UK1355

Lowtrow Cross is a small, adults only park situated just inside Exmoor National Park and is ideal for owners of well behaved dogs. It is quietly located on a hillside giving lovely views north towards the Brendon Hills. There are 28 mixed pitches, four occupied by caravan holiday homes (two for hire) and six seasonal, and all the remaining touring pitches are hardstanding with grass surround, with 16A electricity and TV socket. An adjacent meadow with stunning views over the rolling countryside can be used for tents. Lowtrow Cross Inn by the gate stocks local cask beers and excellent food.

Facilities	Directions
Well equipped, heated toilet block but no facilities for disabled visitors. Excellent laundry room. Freezer and microwave. Motorcaravan services. Small shop in reception selling basic foodstuffs; milk, bread, free range eggs, frozen meals, local produce, toiletries and Calor gas. Maps for sale and book exchange. Free WiFi over site. Off site: Lowtrow Cross Inn at gate. Garage 750 m. Fishing and boating 3 miles. Golf and riding 10 miles.	From M5 exit 25 follow signs for Minehead (A358) via Taunton, then 5 miles from Taunton turn west (left) on B3224 (Raleigh Cross). Shortly after passing Raleigh Cross Inn on left continue south on B3190 signed Bampton. Site is on right in 4 miles just before Upton village. GPS: 51.053342, -3.419923

Open: March - October.

Charges guide

Per unit incl. 2 persons and electricity	£ 17.00 - £ 21.00
extra person	£ 5.00

Taunton
Waterrow Touring Park
Wiveliscombe, Taunton TA4 2AZ (Somerset) T: 01984 623464. E: info@waterrowpark.co.uk
alanrogers.com/UK1520

This is an award-winning site beside the River Tone, in a pretty part of South Somerset. Tony and Anne Taylor have enthusiastically developed Waterrow into a charming, landscaped touring park for adults only. Nestling in a little sheltered valley, it is very peaceful and suitable either for an overnight stop (just over 30 minutes from M5) or ideal as a base for exploring nearby Exmoor and the Brendon Hills. There are 48 touring pitches, most of which are on level hardstandings, including five with full services. All have 16A electricity, spring and mains water are available and TV aerial points have been installed (long leads sold on site). A small area has been set aside for tent campers. A member of the Best of British group.

Facilities	Directions
A modern, heated, clean sanitary unit provides some washbasins in curtained cubicles. Heated shower block. Facilities for disabled visitors (key). Laundry facilities. Motorcaravan services. Limited provisions are available in reception. Regular watercolour painting and drawing courses are run (May-Oct) at the in-house studio. Additional fly fishing holidays can be arranged at certain times. WiFi (charged). Caravan storage with 'store and stay' system. No American motorhomes. Max. 2 dogs.	From M5 exit 25 take A358 (signed Minehead) round Taunton for 4 miles, then at Staplegrove onto B3227 for 11.5 miles to Wiveliscombe, straight over at lights to Waterrow. Park is on left shortly after Rock Inn. Do not use sat nav. GPS: 51.0165, -3.352717

Open: All year.

Charges guide

Per unit incl. 2 persons (adults only) and electricity	£ 18.00 - £ 27.00
with full services	£ 18.00 - £ 38.50
extra person	£ 8.00

Wareham
Lookout Holiday Park
Stoborough, Dorset, Wareham BH20 5AZ (Dorset) T: 01929 552546. E: lookout@caravan-sites.co.uk
alanrogers.com/UK1953

The Lookout Holiday Park is a peaceful family caravan park two miles from the ancient town of Wareham. It is within easy reach of the seaside resorts of Swanage, Sandbanks and Bournemouth, and one of England's finest beaches at Studland. This is a mixed park of 240 pitches, 50 for tourers are in two areas, one with hardstandings, the other a mixture of hard and grassy pitches with a large play area. Both areas have 10A electricity hook-ups and spacious heated toilet blocks. The well stocked shop and off-license can cater for all your daily needs, and hot takeaway rolls and light snacks are also available.

Facilities	Directions
Two heated toilet blocks have controllable hot showers, vanity style washbasins and hairdryers. Facilities for disabled visitors and limited facilities for children. Well equipped laundry room. Basic motorcaravan services. Well stocked, licensed shop with gas supplies and hot food. Large play area. Games room. Football pitch. WiFi over site (charged). Caravan storage. No dogs.	From A352 at Wareham take A351 south towards Swanage. Ignore first Stoborough sign, but continue on to next island. Turn north on B3075 Corfe Road. Site is on right. GPS: 50.67003, -2.10363

Open: 22 March - 4 January.

Charges guide

Per unit incl. up to 6 persons and electricity	£ 18.00 - £ 28.00

For latest campsite news visit
alanrogers.com

Warminster
Longleat Caravan Club Site

Warminster BA12 7NL (Wiltshire) T: 01985 844663. E: longleat@caravanclub.co.uk

alanrogers.com/UK1690

What a magnificent situation in which to find a caravan park, next to Longleat House, gardens and Safari Park. The site is well managed by Caravan Club wardens and is situated in ten acres of lightly wooded, level grassland within walking distance of the house and gardens. There are 164 generous pitches (151 with hardstanding and ten on grass), all with 16A electricity connections. Water points and recycling bins are neatly walled with low night lighting. Two new buildings provide immaculate facilities, whilst an amenity block houses a family room and tourist information. Tents are not accepted (except trailer tents). Admission charges now apply to all of the Longleat attractions and grounds. Discounts are available to Caravan Club members.

Facilities

Two heated toilet blocks provide washbasins in cubicles, controllable showers and a vanity section with mirrors and hairdryers. Baby/toddler room, suite for disabled visitors, laundry room and a family room with a DVD player. Two motorcaravan service points. Play area. Office is manned 09.00-17.30 and stocks basic food items, papers can be ordered and gas is available. Paperback exchange library. Fish and chip van calls some evenings. WiFi over site (charged). Late arrivals area with hook-up. Off site: Longleat House. Frome 7 miles.

Open: 20 March - 4 January.

Directions

All arrivals must now enter Longleat from A362 (Warminster-Frome). Turn left off A36 Warminster bypass at roundabout onto A362. In 500 yds. at roundabout take third exit (Frome). After some 2 miles turn into Lane End by White Hart pub, pass Safari Park entrance and Stalls Farm, then left again. Site entrance is 200 yds. on left. GPS: 51.19053, -2.27835

Charges guide

Per person	£ 6.60 - £ 8.50
child (5-16 yrs)	£ 0.01 - £ 3.30
pitch incl. electricity (non-member)	£ 16.70 - £ 20.30

Wells
Cheddar, Mendip Heights Camping & Caravanning Club Site

Townsend, Priddy, Wells BA5 3BP (Somerset) T: 01749 870241. E: cheddar.site@thefriendlyclub.co.uk

alanrogers.com/UK1430

Mendip Heights is a Camping and Caravanning Club site, but non-members are welcome. It is a well kept park half a mile from the village. There are picturesque views across the Mendip fields with their characteristic dry stone walling. It has a simple charm with field margins kept natural to encourage wildlife, and nest boxes in the mature trees edging the three fields which make up the site. These provide space for 90 units, some on slightly sloping short grass, with 76 electric hook-ups (16A), 37 with hardstanding. Historic Priddy is the highest village in the Mendips and is famed for its annual Sheep Fair in August and a popular folk festival in July. Nearby are extensive Roman lead-workings, Bronze Age burial mounds, the Priddy Circle and access to Swildons Hole, one of the popular cave systems in the Mendips. The park is also on the Padstow-Bristol Sustrans Route 3. Many tourist attractions are within a 20-mile radius.

Facilities

The refurbished toilet block with all facilities is bright, cheerful and heated. Two family rooms (one with high and low toilet and shower). Facilities for disabled visitors. Laundry facilities. Motorcaravan services. The reception with licensed shop doubles as the village shop (open all season selling locally produced meat, cheese, groceries, Calor gas, etc). Fresh bread and pastries are baked each morning (pre-order). Play house, swings and table tennis for children. Torches useful. WiFi throughout (charged). Off site: Two traditional village pubs with very different characters stand by the village green within walking distance (0.5 miles). Riding 2 miles. Bicycle hire and golf 5 miles. Fishing 6 miles.

Open: 11 March - 7 November.

Directions

From M5 exit 21 take A371 to Banwell. Turn left on A368, right on B3134 and right on B3135. After 2 miles turn left at camp sign. From M4 westbound exit 18, A46 to Bath, then A4 towards Bristol. Take A39 for Wells and right at Green Ore traffic lights on B3135; after 5 miles turn left at camp sign. GPS: 51.2636, -2.685383

Charges year

Per unit incl. 2 persons and electricity	£ 20.70 - £ 34.90
extra person	£ 7.90 - £ 13.30
child	£ 3.95 - 6.65

Non-member prices are higher.
No credit cards.

For latest campsite news visit
alanrogers.com

Wareham

Wareham Forest Tourist Park

North Trigon, Wareham BH20 7NZ (Dorset) T: 01929 551393. E: holiday@warehamforest.co.uk

alanrogers.com/UK2030

This peacefully located and spacious park, on the edge of Wareham Forest, has 200 pitches and is continually being upgraded by its enthusiastic owners, Tony and Sarah Birch. The focal point of the park is the modern reception and shop, located by the pools. Four main areas provide a wide choice of touring pitches from grass to hardstanding and luxury, all with 16A electricity. Tent campers have their own choice of open field or pinewood. The site has provided direct access for walkers into the forest or the seven miles of the Sika cycle trail may be used. The lovely market town of Wareham is accessible by bike without having to use the roads. This park has an almost continental feel, with plenty of space. Even when it is busy, it is calm and peaceful in its forest setting. In low season you may be lucky enough to spot the herd of Sika deer which live in the forest. The park is well situated to explore the Dorset coast and Thomas Hardy country. A member of the Best of British group.

Facilities

Two well maintained toilet blocks are of a good standard with some washbasins in cubicles and several family bathrooms (one with baby bath). Main block was recently refurbished and both blocks are centrally heated. Facilities for disabled visitors. Well equipped laundry rooms. Motorcaravan services. Small licensed shop with gas. Swimming pool (60x20 ft, heated 20/5-15/9). Large adventure play area. Barrier closed 23.00-07.00. Resident wardens on site. Caravan storage. WiFi. Off site: Cycle trail and walking in the forest. Bicycle hire and golf 3 miles. Fishing 5 miles. Riding 8 miles.

Open: All year.

Directions

From A31 Bere Regis, follow A35 towards Poole for 0.5 miles and turn right where signed to Wareham. Drive for a further 1.5 miles. First park on the left as you enter forest. GPS: 50.721733, -2.156217

Charges guide

Per unit incl. 2 persons	
and electricity	£ 17.60 - £ 37.50
'superior' pitch fully serviced	£ 21.10 - £ 41.40
extra person	£ 3.30 - £ 6.00
child (5-15 yrs)	£ 2.00 - £ 4.15
dog	free - £ 1.75

Couples and families only.

Westbury

Brokerswood Country Park

Brokerswood, Westbury BA13 4EH (Wiltshire) T: 01373 822238. E: info@brokerswoodcountrypark.co.uk

alanrogers.com/UK1630

This countryside campsite is situated in an 80-acre country park with ancient broadleaf woodland, plenty of marked walks and a woodland railway. There are 69 pitches arranged around an open meadow area, served by a circular gravel roadway, with low level site lighting. There are 25 hardstanding pitches, and 44 electricity hook-ups (10A). Although fairly recently laid out, the site is maturing well. American RVs and other large units should use the coach entrance and they (and all other arrivals after 18.00) are asked to phone ahead. Cycling is possible on site but not in the country park. The park has adventure playgrounds and play trails amongst its many activities for the family. On-site activities include archery, tree climbing, walking in the trees and canoeing (subject to booking).

Facilities

Two well insulated and heated sanitary buildings are at one end of the site. Some washbasins in cubicles, large, controllable hot showers. Family bathrooms (charged). Fully equipped suite for disabled campers. Laundry facilities. Motorcaravan service point. Gas available. Milk, bread, newspapers to order from reception/shop. Takeaway food (peak times). Fishing. Archery. Tree climbing. Walking in the trees. Canoeing. Cycling (on site). Ready erected tents for hire. Archery. A high ropes course. Off site: Nearest shops are at Dilton Marsh and Westbury 2 miles. Golf and Longleat House 6 miles. Bath 12 miles.

Open: March - October.

Directions

From Trowbridge take A361 south for 2 miles, turning left (east) at Southwick, and follow signs to Country Park. GPS: 51.270283, -2.231417

Charges guide

Per unit incl. 4 persons	
and electricity	£ 16.00 - £ 32.00
extra person (aged 1 or more)	£ 4.95
dog	£ 1.00

No credit cards.

For latest campsite news visit

alanrogers.com

WAREHAM FOREST
TOURIST PARK

Wareham Forest Tourist Park
North Trigon, Wareham, Dorset. BH20 7NZ

Best of British

01929 551393

 WiFi Available

www.warehamforest.co.uk

 DORSET
from the scenery to the coast

AA
▶▶▶▶▶
♦ ⛺ Å

~ **ONLINE BOOKING AVAILABLE** ~

SPECIAL OFFERS ~ OPEN ALL YEAR ~ LICENCED SHOP

Weston-super-Mare
West End Farm Touring Park
Locking, Weston-super-Mare BS24 8RH (Somerset) T: 01934 822529. E: robin@westendfarm.org
alanrogers.com/UK1305

West End Farm is situated close to the M5 motorway yet in a quiet position. It is set in ten acres and offers a true country setting. There are 80 touring pitches, all with 10A electricity, of which 30 are fully serviced. All serviced pitches benefit from having hardstanding. A separate field caters for 30 tents. The site is open all year round and has tarmac roadways with lighting throughout the site. There is a lack of shade from trees but as a result there are open views. With good public transport links, cycle tracks and footpaths this site provides a base from which to explore this fascinating area. There are two local pubs – The Landing Light, just a short walk from the park and The Coach House, one mile away. The historic town of Weston-super-Mare with its famous pier is only two miles away. For aircraft enthusiasts, the world's largest helicopter museum is worth a visit and is only a short stroll away.

Facilities

Two toilet blocks (one heated), are located at the site entrance and include toilets, showers, laundry (with hairdryers) and dishwashing area. Seasonal pitches and caravan storage. Sloping games field. Dog walking area. Off site: Helicopter Museum 0.5 miles. Weston-super-Mare and beaches 2 miles. Bath, Cheddar and Glastonbury all within easy driving distance. Good public transport links.

Open: All year.

Directions

From M5 motorway leave at exit 21. Follow signs for International Helicopter Museum. Turn first right past Museum into Laneys Drove and follow signs to West End Farm. Park is at the top of the hill. GPS: 51.334965, -2.929122

Charges guide

Per unit incl. 2 persons and electricity	£ 20.00 - £ 24.00
extra person	£ 5.00

Debit cards accepted.

West End Farm
CARAVAN & CAMPING PARK

Locking • Weston-super-Mare • North Somerset BS24 8RH
tel: 0044 (0)1934 822529 • email: robin@westendfarm.org
WWW.WESTENDCARAVAN.COM

Weymouth
East Fleet Farm Touring Park
Fleet Lane, Chickerell, Weymouth DT3 4DW (Dorset) T: 01305 785768. E: enquiries@eastfleet.co.uk
alanrogers.com/UK1800

East Fleet Farm has a marvellous situation on part level, part gently sloping meadows leading to the shores of the Fleet, with views across to the famous Chesil Bank with the sea beyond. This park has been developed by the Whitfield family within the confines of their 300-acre organic arable farm in keeping with its surroundings, yet with modern amenities. It is maturing well as bushes and trees grow. The 400 pitches back onto hedges and are a comfortable size so there is no feeling of crowding. Of these, 350 are level and marked with 10/16A electricity, over 70 also have hardstanding. The large shop has a very good range of camping equipment and outdoor gear. A member of the Best of British group.

Facilities

Three fully equipped toilet blocks, the two latest providing en-suite facilities. Unit for disabled visitors. Laundry room. Motorcaravan services. Reception plus shop with groceries, bread, papers, gas and camping accessories. Bar serving food with terrace (w/ends only in low season). Large play barn with table tennis and gym equipment. Fenced play area (remember, elsewhere this is a working farm). Games field. Nature watch boards. WiFi throughout (charged). Off site: Bus service from the main road. Riding and golf 2 miles. Sandy beach 3 miles.

Open: 15 March - 31 October.

Directions

Park is signed at traffic lights on B3157 Weymouth - Bridport road, 3 miles west of Weymouth beside a Territorial Army base. Fleet Lane has been widened and resurfaced with passing places and speed bumps (20 mph). GPS: 50.61927, -2.50040

Charges guide

Per unit incl. 2 persons and electricity	£ 19.00 - £ 33.50
extra person	£ 1.00 - £ 5.00
child (5-12 yrs)	£ 1.00 - £ 2.50

For latest campsite news visit
alanrogers.com

Weymouth
Bagwell Farm Touring Park

Chickerell, Weymouth DT3 4EA (Dorset) T: 01305 782575. E: ar@bagwellfarm.co.uk

alanrogers.com/UK1820

A friendly, welcoming, family park, Bagwell Farm is open all year. It is situated between Weymouth and Abbotsbury, close to Chesil Beach. Set in a valley, yet with an attractive open aspect, there are 320 numbered pitches, 280 for touring units, the remainder taken up by seasonal units. All have 10A electricity connections and 34 serviced pitches with hardstanding have a 16A supply. Some of the terraced pitches have beautiful views of Chesil Bank and the sea. In addition there is a traditional camping field where a campers' shelter is provided. An attractive bar serves meals.

Facilities	Directions
Modern, heated toilet block with four en-suite family rooms and a unit for disabled visitors (Radar key). Two traditional blocks have two family bathrooms (£1). Laundry room. Wetsuit wash. Very well stocked shop (open all day). Bar and restaurant (Easter-Oct). Good fenced play area. Campers' shelter. Communal barbecue. WiFi over site (charged). Access to coastal path.	From A354 follow signs for Weymouth town centre. Turn onto B3157 (Chickerell) and continue towards Bridport. Park is 1 mile west of Chickerell on this road. GPS: 50.63088, -2.51999

Open: All year.

Charges guide

Per unit incl. 2 persons and electricity	£ 16.50 - £ 27.00
extra person	£ 5.00

Weymouth
Sea Barn & West Fleet Holiday Farms

Fleet Road, Fleet, Weymouth DT3 4ED (Dorset) T: 01305 782218. E: enquiries@seabarnfarm.co.uk

alanrogers.com/UK1830

Sea Barn and West Fleet are just half a mile apart in delightful countryside overlooking the Fleet Lagoon, Chesil Bank and Lyme Bay – all part of the Jurassic coast. Only tents, trailer tents and motorcaravans with tents and awnings are accepted. The parks share some facilities. West Fleet has 250 pitches, 112 with electricity. Sea Barn has the same number of pitches but only 68 electric hook-ups. These are situated in grassy meadows, some sloping, some protected by trees and hedging, many with wonderful views. West Fleet has a newly rebuilt Clubhouse with bar, which serves good local steaks.

Facilities	Directions
A modern block at both sites with en-suite room for disabled visitors and two bathrooms and traditional block, each for peak season. Laundry facilities at both sites. Heated pool at West Fleet (May-Sept). Bigger shop offering wider range at West Fleet which also has the Club House (peak season and w/ends) with refurbished bar. Breakfast served. Family entertainment. Adventure play area at Fleet, smaller area at Sea Barn. Games field. Torches useful. WiFi most areas (charged).	From Weymouth take the B3157 coast road for Abbotsbury. Pass Chickerell and turn left at mini-roundabout to Fleet. Pass church on right and continue to top of hill. Sea Barn is to the left, West Fleet to the right. GPS: 50.62539, -2.53865

Open: West Fleet Easter - September;
Sea Barn 16 March - October.

Charges guide

Per unit incl. 2 persons and electricity	£ 17.00 - £ 28.00
extra person	£ 4.00 - £ 6.00
child (2-15 yrs)	£ 1.00 - £ 3.00

Wimborne
Wilksworth Farm Caravan Park

Cranborne Road, Wimborne BH21 4HW (Dorset) T: 01202 885467.
E: rayandwendy@wilksworthfarmcaravanpark.co.uk **alanrogers.com/UK2060**

First opened by the parents of the present owners, the careful and sympathetic development of Wilksworth continues with the aim of providing all the 'mod cons' while remaining in keeping with the environment. It is a spacious, quiet park, well suited for families, with a heated outdoor pool which has been totally refurbished in a beautiful Spanish style. The rural situation is lovely, just outside Wimborne and around 12 miles from the beaches between Poole and Bournemouth. The park takes 60 caravans and 25 tents, mainly on grass. All pitches have electricity, ten also have water and drainage. There are 77 privately owned caravan holiday homes in a separate area. A member of the Best of British group.

Facilities	Directions
The central, well equipped toilet block has washbasins in cubicles, family bathroom and facilities for children and disabled visitors. Laundry room. Modern reception and shop (basics only, limited hours, Easter-30/9). Gas supplies. Coffee shop with takeaway service. Heated swimming pool (unsupervised, May-Sept). Small paddling pool with slide. Upgraded play area. BMX track. Two tennis courts, one full and one short size. WiFi (charged).	Park is 1 mile north of Wimborne, west off the B3078 road to Cranborne. GPS: 50.8167, -1.9904

Open: 1 April - 30 October.

Charges guide

Per unit incl. 2 persons and electricity	£ 16.00 - £ 33.00
full services	£ 2.00
extra person	£ 5.00

Wimborne
Merley Court Touring Park

Merley, Wimborne BH21 3AA (Dorset) T: 01590 648331. E: holidays@shorefield.co.uk

alanrogers.com/UK2080

Merley Court is part of the Shorefield Group and all aspects of this well planned, attractively landscaped park are constantly maintained to the highest of standards. Tarmac roads connect 162 touring pitches, all of which have 16A electricity, on neat lawns or one of the many hardstandings. This provision includes 19 serviced pitches with water, waste disposal and satellite TV. The entire park is interspersed with a variety of shrubs, plants and the odd ornamental urn. Twelve lodges, seven with hot tubs, are located in a wooded valley. A well furnished club complex provides a lounge bar with meals.

Facilities

Three heated toilet blocks, two with showers, are of good quality. Separate facilities for disabled visitors and babies. Laundry facilities. Motorcaravan services. Well stocked shop sells gas. Café and takeaway. Bar with food (limited hours in low and mid season). Outdoor pool (30x20 ft) with section for children (Whitsun-early Sept). Tennis and short tennis courts. Play area. Games room with pool tables. Barrier card £5 deposit. WiFi throughout (free).

Open: All year excl. 3 January - 5 February.

Directions

Site clearly signed at the junction of A31 and A349 roads (roundabout) on the Wimborne bypass. GPS: 50.785733, -1.98525

Charges guide

Per unit incl. 6 persons and electricity	£ 14.00 - £ 42.00
all service pitch	£ 19.00 - £ 45.00
dog	£ 1.50 - £ 3.00

Wimborne
Woolsbridge Manor Farm Caravan Park

Three Legged Cross, Wimborne BH21 6RA (Dorset) T: 01202 826369. E: woolsbridge@btconnect.com

alanrogers.com/UK2150

Close to the Moors Valley Country Park, this friendly, family run site is within easy reach of the south coast, the resorts of Christchurch, Bournemouth and Poole, and the ancient market town of Wimborne Minster. Entry is restricted to couples and families. The seven-acre camping meadow has 100 large, level pitches (51 seasonal) all with 16A electricity and arranged on either side of a central tarmac road. Reception has a well stocked shop and a good selection of tourist information. The site is part of a working beef cattle farm, so parents should be aware of moving farm machinery and tractors.

Facilities

The neat, refurbished toilet block is well maintained and has ample facilities. Four newly built family rooms each with shower, WC, basin, handrails and ramped access provided for disabled visitors, babies and toddlers. Washing machine, dryer and ironing facilities. Shop. Gas. Playground. Fishing. American RVs accepted, advance booking appreciated. Torches useful. Caravan storage. Off site: Old Barn Farm inn and restaurant 400 yds. Riding, golf and bicycle hire 0.5 miles. Boat launching and sailing 5 miles.

Open: 1 March - 31 October.

Directions

From Ringwood take A31 southwest to Ashley Heath roundabout (junction of A31 and A338). Take left hand slip road to roundabout, avoiding throughway, and turn right (north) onto unclassified road signed for Moors Valley Country Park. Follow signs to Country Park, pass entrance on right, continue for 400 yds. to site. GPS: 50.842982, -1.859982

Charges guide

Per unit incl. 2 persons and electricity	£ 17.50 - £ 24.50
extra person	£ 6.50 - £ 7.00

Wool
Whitemead Caravan Park

East Burton Road, Wool BH20 6HG (Dorset) T: 01929 462241. E: whitemeadcp@aol.com

alanrogers.com/UK2090

The Church family continue to make improvements to this attractive little park which is within walking distance of the village of Wool, between Dorchester and Wareham. Very natural and with open views over the Frome Valley water meadows, it provides 95 numbered pitches on flat grass sloping gently north and is orchard-like in parts. The 76 touring pitches are well spaced, mostly backing onto hedges or fences and all have 10A electrical connections. All roads are now tarmac. There are no caravan holiday homes but 19 pitches are seasonal. There is some rail noise but this is not intrusive at night.

Facilities

The toilet block provides showers, private cubicles and a baby room. Washing machine and dryer. Shop (limited hours) with off-licence, gas supplies and information room/library. Games room with pool table and darts. Playground. WiFi throughout (free). Off site: The Ship Inn 300 yards. Bicycle hire 2 miles. Riding, fishing and golf 3 miles.

Open: 15 March - 31 October.

Directions

Turn off main A352 on eastern edge of Wool, just north of level crossing, onto East Burton road. Site is 350 yds. on right. GPS: 50.68164, -2.22595

Charges guide

Per unit incl. 2 persons and electricity	£ 17.00 - £ 24.00
extra person (over 5 yrs)	£ 4.50 - £ 5.00
dog	£ 0.75 - £ 2.00

For latest campsite news visit

alanrogers.com

THIS REGION INCLUDES: HAMPSHIRE, ISLE OF WIGHT, OXFORDSHIRE, BERKSHIRE AND BUCKINGHAMSHIRE

Rich in maritime heritage and historical attractions, the Southern region comprises tranquil English countryside boasting picture postcard villages, ancient cities and towns, formidable castles and grand stately homes, coupled with a beautiful coastline and lively seaside resorts.

Rural Southern England comprises green, rolling hills and scenic wooded valleys, with numerous walking and bridle paths passing through picturesque villages with quintessential English pubs. The New Forest, well known for its wild roaming ponies, is a distinctive, peaceful retreat. Across the water is the Isle of Wight, easily reached via a short ferry trip across the Solent. It has always been a popular destination for those seeking a traditional beach holiday in one of the bucket-and-spade resorts. The long stretches of sand at Shanklin and Sandown are family favourites and have plenty of other attractions. Don't miss historic Carisbrooke Castle, and Osborne House, the favourite retreat of Queen Victoria. The River Thames weaves its way through the Thames basin and Chilterns area, passing charming riverside villages, castles, stately homes and beautiful countryside, including that around Oxford. This 'city of dreaming spires' has lovely scenic walks, old university buildings to explore, plus a huge selection of restaurants, pubs and shops. Along the river you can go punting, hire a rowing boat, or take one of the many river-boat trips available.

Places of interest

Hampshire: Winchester, ancient capital of England; Portsmouth's historic dockyard and Spinnaker Tower; Southampton's West Quay shopping complex and city art gallery.

Isle of Wight: Cowes; Sandown with Dinosaur Isle; Shipwreck Centre in Ryde; Smuggling Museum in Ventnor; Carisbrooke Castle in Newport.

Oxfordshire: Blenheim Palace; Oxford University buildings; Ashmolean Museum, Oxford; River and Rowing Museum, Henley-on-Thames; Bicester Shopping Village.

Berkshire: Windsor with Legoland, Windsor Castle; Reading.

Buckinghamshire: Bletchley Park and Stowe Landscape Gardens near Milton Keynes; Waddesdon Manor, Aylesbury; Bekonscot Model Village and Railway, Beaconsfield.

Did you know?

The Ashmolean Museum, Oxford was the first museum to be opened to the public in 1683.

There are over 200 scheduled ancient monuments within the New Forest National Park.

The first Cowes regatta was held in 1812, and 'Cowes Week' is now the world's biggest international yachting event.

Quar stone from the Isle of Wight was used in the construction of the Tower of London.

The Spitfire aircraft, used to great effect during the Battle of Britain, was devised in Southampton.

The first ever dry dock was constructed in Portsmouth in 1495.

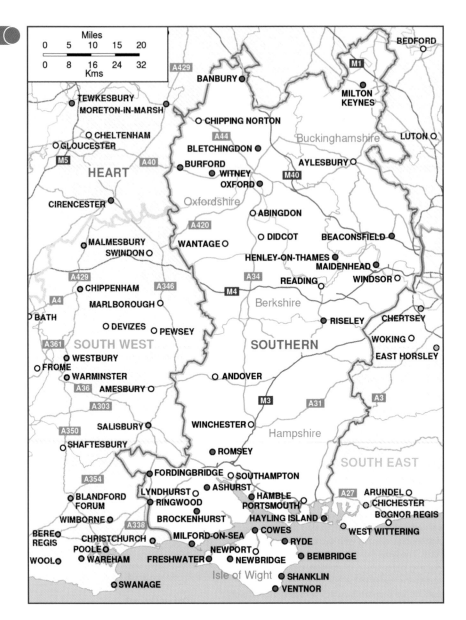

Ashurst
Camping In The Forest Ashurst
Lyndhurst Road, Ashurst SO40 7AR (Hampshire) T: 023 8029 2097. E: info@campingintheforest.co.uk
alanrogers.com/UK2300

Camping in the Forest is a partnership between The Forestry Commission and The Camping and Caravanning Club. An attractive site, Ashurst is on the fringe of the New Forest, set in a mixture of oak woodland and grass heathland which is open to the grazing animals of the Forest. It provides 280 pitches, some of which have been gravelled to provide semi-hardstanding; otherwise you pitch where you like, applying the three-metre rule on ground that can be uneven. There are no electricity connections. Some noise must be expected from the adjacent railway line – the station is just five minutes' walk away. A stay here is unique as you will be amongst the ponies all year round.

Facilities	Directions
The single well kept central toilet block (may be under pressure in main season) provides everything necessary, including a family room, hairdryers and a unit for visitors with disabilities. Laundry room. Motorcaravan services. Bicycle hire. Torches useful. No dogs. Off site: Nearby pub via footpath. Shops within a five-minute walk.	From Southampton, follow A35 west through village of Ashurst, continue over railway bridge and site is 200 yds. on left. GPS: 50.88810, -1.52846

Charges guide

Per unit incl. 2 persons	£ 16.00 - £ 30.50
extra person	£ 5.50 - £ 10.00

Open: 26 March - 28 September.

Banbury
Barnstones Caravan & Camping Park
Great Bourton, Banbury OX17 1QU (Oxfordshire) T: 01295 750289.
alanrogers.com/UK2600

Three miles from Banbury and open all year round, this small, neat park provides an excellent point from which to explore the Cotswolds, Oxford and Stratford-upon-Avon. There are 49 level pitches of which 44 have gravel hardstanding with a grass area for awnings (only breathable groundsheets are allowed) and 10A electricity; 20 of these are fully serviced. Shrubs, flowers and an oval tarmac road convey an attractive, tidy impression throughout. The park provides a pleasant environment for couples and young families, but it is near the main road so some traffic noise is to be expected.

Facilities	Directions
The toilet block is small, but clean, heated and well maintained. It is quite adequate for the number of visitors it serves. New tiled, adjustable showers. Laundry room and washing up area. Freezer. Gas supplies. Enclosed play area. Boules. American-style motorhomes by prior arrangement. WiFi. Off site: Pub 150 yds. Nearest shop 1 mile. Supermarket, fishing, bicycle hire, golf and riding, all within 3 miles.	From M40 take exit 11 for Banbury. Follow signs for Banbury and Southam. On two small roundabouts follow signs for Southam and Great Bourton. At third roundabout turn right on A423, Southam is 2.5 miles. Turn right (Great Bourton and Cropredy) and site is on the right. GPS: 52.104966, -1.338868

Charges guide

Per unit incl. 2 persons and electricity	£ 13.00
extra person	£ 1.50
No credit cards.	

Open: All year.

Banbury
Bo Peep Caravan Park
Aynho Road, Adderbury, Banbury OX17 3NP (Oxfordshire) T: 01295 810605. E: warden@bo-peep.co.uk
alanrogers.com/UK2610

Set amongst eighty-five acres of farmland and woodland, there is an air of spacious informality about this delightful, friendly park which blends perfectly with the surrounding views. Cotswold stone buildings, dovecotes and the planting of trees, shrubs and hedges enhance the natural environment of the park. There are 104 numbered pitches, all with 16A electricity, for caravans and motorcaravans, in several areas, each with a different character. A separate four-acre field for tents provides a further 40 pitches, including four electricity points. One area is now being landscaped as a formal garden.

Facilities	Directions
The two toilet blocks are clean and heated. Large showers and hairdryers. Laundry rooms. Motorcaravan services. Low-level lighting. Excellent small shop with off-licence, gas and basic supplies. Information centre and Internet access. Fishing. Caravan storage. Caravan cleaning area. WiFi over site. Off site: Adderbury is a lovely English village with several pubs. Golf 1 mile. Banbury 3 miles. Riding 10 miles. Blenheim Palace 15 miles. Silverstone 16 miles.	Adderbury village is on A4260 Banbury-Oxford road. From north on M40 use exit 11, A422 (Banbury) then A4260. At traffic lights in Adderbury turn on B4100 (Aynho). Park is signed 0.5 miles on right. From the south on the M40 use exit 10 onto A43, then B4100 (Aynho and Adderbury). GPS: 52.01585, -1.299433

Charges guide

Per unit incl. 2 persons and electricity	£ 19.00 - £ 22.00
No credit cards.	

Open: 20 March - 29 October.

For latest campsite news visit
alanrogers.com

Beaconsfield

Highclere Farm Country Touring Park

Newbarn Lane, Seer Green, Beaconsfield HP9 2QZ (Buckinghamshire) T: 01494 874505.
E: highclerepark@aol.com **alanrogers.com/UK2750**

A magnificent sweeping drive provides the entrance to this peaceful park that backs onto fields and woodland. Originally developed around a working farm, the owners continue to keep chickens. There are 115 level pitches all with 10A electricity. Of these, 60 with gravel hardstanding are reserved for caravans and motorcaravans, the remainder being mainly used for tents. The atmosphere is friendly and informal, with reception doubling as a small shop supplying freshly laid eggs. At the top of the park is an open play area and a footpath leading to walks in the surrounding fields.

Facilities	Directions
The toilet and shower block is fully equipped and can be heated. Large showers (20p). Unit with toilet and washbasin for disabled visitors. Baby changing. Two new units (in former stables) provide extra large facilities including showers at 50p. Launderette. Basic shop in reception. Play area. WiFi. Freeview and Sky connections. Off site: Pub serving food 0.25 miles. Golf 0.5 miles. Open: All year excl. February.	From M40 exit 2 follow signs for Beaconsfield at first roundabout. Take A355 (Amersham) and after 1 mile turn right (Seer Green) following signs to park. GPS: 51.625617, -0.590867

Charges guide

Per unit incl. 2 persons and electricity	£ 23.00 - £ 33.00

Bembridge

Whitecliff Bay Holiday Park

Hillway, Whitecliff Bay, Bembridge PO35 5PL (Isle of Wight) T: 01983 872671. E: holiday@whitecliff-bay.com
alanrogers.com/UK2510

Whitecliff Bay is a very large complex divided by a road, with a holiday home and chalet park on the right-hand side (230 units), and a touring site on the left-hand side (379 pitches). The large touring site is on a sloping hillside with commanding views over the surrounding countryside. The pitches are spread over three fields, the top and second fields are terraced, but field three is quite level. Most of the pitches have 16A electricity hook-ups, and there are 42 gravel hardstandings, 12 in the top field, the remainder in the lowest field. There are just 13 multi-serviced pitches available, so book early if these appeal. On the opposite side of the lane, in the holiday home park, you will find all the main entertainment and leisure facilities. These include The Culver Club with a bar and evening entertainment, several snack bars and takeaways, supervised swimming pools, sunbed and soft play zone. Close to the outdoor pool, a very steep path leads down to a sandy beach where there is a small café. It is possible to launch a boat from this beach (four-wheel drive vehicle essential, advance booking necessary).

Facilities	Directions
Three sanitary units. Showers and a suite (with shower) for disabled campers. A second suite with a hip bath/shower is at the lower block with a similar facility to serve as a baby/family room. Motorcaravan services. Small shop at reception. Playground. At the holiday home park: launderette, hairdresser and second larger shop. The Culver Club. Snack bars. Swimming pool (18x18 m, Whitsun-end Aug). Indoor fun pool and soft play zone. Most facilities open Mar-Oct. Free WiFi on main site. Activities and entertainment for all. Fully equipped tents to rent. Off site: Riding 2 miles. Bicycle hire 4 miles. Open: 22 March - 4 November.	Bembridge is at the eastern end of the island. From A3055 between Ryde and Sandown, turn east at Brading on B3395 for 2 miles passing the Airfield and Propeller Club, fork right (site signed). Follow signs to site, first entry on right is static area, touring entrance is on left immediately after. GPS: 50.67498, -1.09606

Charges guide

Per unit incl. up to 6 persons and electricity	£ 6.00 - £ 54.00
dog	£ 2.00

Bletchingdon

Greenhill Farm Caravan & Camping Park

Greenhill Farm, Station Road, Bletchingdon OX5 3BQ (Oxfordshire) T: 01869 351600.
E: info@greenhill-leisure-park.co.uk **alanrogers.com/UK2590**

Greenhill is a gently sloping site at the heart of a working farm in a rural setting. A tarmac path round the park gives access to 100 pitches, all with 16A electricity and 49 with hardstanding. Young trees and hedges partition the site and screen the water stands. An adjacent field is available for rallies and a second smaller field for tents. There are now two fishing lakes (carp, roach, bream and tench) and fishing is possible on the Cherwell and the Oxfordshire Canal that runs through the farm. This is a pleasant park with plenty going on, modern facilities, and a variety of animals.

Facilities

Three toilet blocks, two of which have ramp access to facilities for disabled visitors and families. Separate laundry room. Shop selling camping equipment, groceries and own farm produce between April-Sept. Play area with assault course and football nets. Fishing lakes. Games/meeting room. Well behaved dogs accepted 1/3-30/9 (on leads while on farm). Caravan storage. WiFi. Off site: Canal walks 1 mile. Golf 2 miles.

Open: All year.

Directions

From M40 exit 9 take A34 to Newbury and Oxford. After 5 miles turn left on B4027 signed Bletchingdon. After 2.5 miles park is on left just past the village. GPS: 51.85754, -1.29142

Charges guide

Per unit incl. 2 persons and electricity	£ 18.00 - £ 20.00
extra person	£ 3.00

Brockenhurst

Camping in the Forest Hollands Wood

Camping in the Forest, Lyndhurst Road, Brockenhurst SO43 7QH (Hampshire) T: 01590 622967.
E: info@campingintheforest.co.uk **alanrogers.com/UK2310**

Camping in the Forest is a partnership between the Forestry Commission and The Camping and Caravanning Club. This is a large, spacious, 168-acre, secluded site in a natural woodland setting (mainly oak). It is set in the heart of the New Forest with an abundance of wildlife. The site is arranged informally with 600 level unmarked pitches but it is stipulated that there must be at least 20 feet between each unit. There are no electrical connections and traffic noise is audible from the busy A337 which runs alongside one boundary. Brockenhurst village is only half a mile away for shops, trains and buses.

Facilities

Three refurbished toilet blocks provide all necessary requirements including for disabled visitors and babies. Good laundry room. All these may be under pressure at peak times. Motorcaravan services. Freezer packs and charging of batteries (fee). Maps and guides. Barbecues allowed (off ground). Milk stocked. Barrier closed 22.30-07.00. Night security. Torches essential. Off site: Bicycle hire and riding 2 miles. Golf 3 miles.

Open: 26 March - 28 September.

Directions

Site entrance is on east side of A337 Lyndhurst-Lymington road, 0.5 miles north of Brockenhurst. GPS: 50.83655, -1.56952

Charges guide

Per unit incl. 2 persons	£ 16.00 - £ 30.50
extra person	£ 5.50 - £ 10.00
Discounts available including 15% for Camping and Caravanning Club members.	

Burford

Wysdom Touring Park

The Bungalow, Burford School, Burford OX18 4JG (Oxfordshire) T: 01993 823207. E: geoffhayes@fsmail.net
alanrogers.com/UK2620

You'll have to go a long way before you find anything else remotely like this site! The land is owned by Burford School and the site was created to raise money for the school. It really is like stepping into their own private garden. This adults only park is screened from the main school grounds by trees and provides 25 pitches (six seasonal), separated by hedges, all with 16A electricity. This is a lovely location for exploring the Cotswolds – Burford calls itself the 'Gateway to the Cotswolds'. The turn into the site off the school drive is narrow and the site is not therefore considered suitable for large motorcaravans. It is best to avoid school pick-up and drop-off times when the school can be congested.

Facilities

The heated sanitary building is clean and well maintained with two unisex showers (payable by token) – there may be a queue at peak times. (Max. 2 dogs per pitch). Off site: Burford is yards away with its famous hill full of antique shops, old coaching inns and quaint shops. Burford Golf Club is next door. Fishing 750 yds.

Open: All year.

Directions

From roundabout on A40 at Burford, take A361 towards Lechdale on Thames. Park is a few yards on right signed Burford School. Once in drive watch for narrow entrance to site on right in 100 yds. GPS: 51.801983, -1.639367

Charges guide

Per unit incl. 2 persons and electricity	£ 13.00 - £ 16.00

For latest campsite news visit
alanrogers.com

Cowes

Waverley Park Holiday Centre

51 Old Road, East Cowes PO32 6AW (Isle of Wight) T: 01983 293452. E: sue@waverley-park.co.uk

alanrogers.com/UK2530

This delightful small park, with 33 pitches in addition to a large camping area, is family owned and set in the grounds of an old country house which was once frequently visited by Dr Arnold, the subject of Tom Brown's Schooldays. Watch out for the red squirrels! The owners have terraced the grass area for touring units and have created 26 large and level, well spaced, fully serviced hardstanding pitches all with impressive views over the Solent. The remaining 14 pitches on a sloping grass area are for caravans and tents – these have no electricity. To one side there are 46 holiday homes. At the bottom of the park, a gate leads onto the promenade and the beach which is sand, shingle and seaweed, so popular sailing, windsurfing, fishing and crabbing.

Facilities

At the top of the park, a heated toilet block provides the usual facilities including some spacious cubicles with washbasins en-suite. Good suite for disabled visitors with baby changing. Laundry facilities. Heated outdoor pool and paddling pool with sun terrace (22/5-14/9). Club with restaurant, bar and outdoor terrace serving good value meals (mostly home made, 1/5-20/9), plus family entertainment in season (23/5-29/8). Small adventure-style playground. Games room. WiFi throughout (free). Off site: Tennis courts nearby. East Cowes with two supermarkets is within walking distance. Fishing and golf 0.5 miles.

Open: All year.

Directions

Immediately after leaving Southampton-Cowes car ferry, take first left, then right into Old Road, and park entrance is 200 yds. on left. GPS: 50.76088, -1.28366

Charges guide

Per unit incl. 2 persons and electricity	£ 17.00 - £ 23.00
extra person	£ 6.50 - £ 10.00
child (5-13 yrs)	£ 3.00 - £ 5.00
dog	£ 1.00 - £ 2.00

During Cowes Week min. pitch fees apply. Packages incl. ferry travel and other offers available from site.

Fordingbridge

Sandy Balls Holiday Village

Godshill, Fordingbridge SP6 2JZ (Hampshire) T: 0333 251 5241. E: post@sandyballs.co.uk

alanrogers.com/UK2290

Sandy Balls sits high above the sweep of the Avon river near Fordingbridge, amidst woodland which is protected as a nature reserve. It has been in these guides for over 30 years and the entertainment facilities have been improved and developed. Very well run and open all year, the 120-acre park has many private holiday homes as well as 220 lodges for rent. In August, there is an additional unmarked area for 200 tents. The touring areas have 240 marked, hedged, serviced pitches for caravans and tents on part-hardstanding and part-grass, with 10/16A electricity and TV connections. A woodland leisure trail allows wild animals and birds to be observed in their natural surroundings and the attractions of the New Forest are close at hand.

Facilities

Three toilet blocks have underfloor heating and washbasins in cubicles. Prefabricated units with hot water for the tent field. Toilets for disabled visitors and baby facilities. Excellent central launderette. Motorcaravan services. Entertainment and activity programme (high season). Outdoor pool (25/5-1/9). Indoor pool (66x30 ft). Well equipped gym, jacuzzi, steam room, sauna and hair and beauty suite. Games room. Adventure playground and play areas including indoor soft play area. Tents for rent. River fishing (permit). Bicycle hire. Archery. Dogs only allowed on certain fields. Off site: Riding stables. Golf 6 miles. Beach 20 miles. Dry ski slope 20 km.

Open: All year.

Directions

Park is well signed 1.5 miles east of Fordingbridge on the B3078. GPS: 50.930267, -1.7602

Charges guide

Per unit incl. 2 persons and electricity	£ 10.00 - £ 65.00
extra person	free - £ 5.00
child	free
dog	free - £ 5.00

For latest campsite news visit
alanrogers.com

Fordingbridge
Hill Cottage Farm Camping & Caravan Park

Sandleheath Road, Alderholt, Fordingbridge SP6 3EG (Hampshire) T: 01425 650513.
E: hillcottagefarmcaravansite@supanet.com **alanrogers.com/UK2360**

This mature, well maintained site is set in 40 acres of beautiful countryside on the Dorset and Hampshire border. There are 95 touring pitches, 32 on hardstandings with 10/16A electricity hook-ups, water taps and drainage. They are screened by hedges and arranged around a circular gravel roadway. The remaining numbered pitches are on grass in a level, open area with some new planting. There is also a rally field, space for ball games and a small playground. There are three small lakes for coarse fishing, and many woodland walks in the area. This is an excellent park for dog owners. It is more suitable for adults and young children rather than active teenagers.

Facilities

A large modern barn-style building provides excellent heated facilities. Laundry room. Facilities for disabled visitors and babies. Motorcaravan services. Facilities for tent pitches. First floor games room with full size snooker table, two pool tables and dart board, plus a separate function room. Shop. Playground. Free WiFi. Shepherd's hut for hire. Rallies welcome. Off site: Village centre with pub, church, Post Office and store is a 20-minute woodland walk. Local attractions include Rockbourne Roman Villa, Cranborne Chase, The Dolls Museum at Fordingbridge, Salisbury and Ringwood with its Wednesday market.

Open: 1 March - 30 November.

Directions

From Fordingbridge take B3078 westwards for 2 miles to Alderholt. On entering the village, at left hand bend, turn right towards Sandleheath (site signed) and site entrance is 300 yds. on the left. GPS: 50.919017, -1.832783

Charges guide

Per unit incl. 2 persons	
and electricity	£ 21.00 - £ 27.00
extra person	£ 5.00
child (3-15 yrs)	£ 2.00 - £ 4.00
dog	£ 1.00

Freshwater
Heathfield Farm Camping

Heathfield Road, Freshwater PO40 9SH (Isle of Wight) T: 01983 407822. E: web@heathfieldcamping.co.uk
alanrogers.com/UK2500

Heathfield is a pleasant contrast to many of the other sites on the Isle of Wight in that it is a 'no frills' sort of place, very popular with tent campers, cyclists and small camper vans. Despite its name, it is no longer a working farm. A large, open meadow provides 60 large, level pitches, all with 16A electricity. Two small fenced areas provide traffic free zones for backpackers and cyclists' tents. There is no shop as you are only eight minutes walk from the centre of Freshwater. The site overlooks Colwell Bay and across the Solent towards Milford-on-Sea and Hurst Castle. A playing field for ball games also has three picnic tables and two communal barbecues. There is a wild flower meadow with the perimeter mown for dog walking. It is ideal for visiting attractions on the western side of the island including Totland and Freshwater Bays, The Needles and Old Battery, Compton Down and Mottistone Manor Garden. The Military road which runs from Freshwater Bay to Saint Catherine's Point gives spectacular coastal views.

Facilities

The main sanitary facilities are housed in a modern, ingeniously customised, prefabricated unit and include hot showers and baby changing. A second similar unit has WCs and washbasins in cubicles plus facilities for disabled visitors. Laundry facilities. Motorcaravan services. Gas supplies. Ice pack service. Playing field. Bicycle hire arranged. WiFi throughout (charged). No commercial vehicles are accepted. Gate locked 22.30-07.00. Off site: Bus stop 20 m. Riding, beach and fishing 0.5 miles. Golf 1.25 miles.

Open: 12 April - 30 September.

Directions

From A3054 north of Totland and Colwell turn into Heathfield Road where site is signed. Site entrance is on right after a short distance. GPS: 50.68940, -1.52704

Charges guide

Per unit incl. 2 persons	
and electricity	£ 15.50 - £ 25.00
extra person	£ 7.50 - £ 9.50
child (3-15 yrs)	£ 3.50 - £ 5.50
dog	£ 3.00

For latest campsite news visit
alanrogers.com

Hamble

Riverside Holidays

Satchell Lane, Hamble, Southampton SO31 4HR (Hampshire) T: 02380 453220.
E: enquiries@riversideholidays.co.uk **alanrogers.com/UK2315**

What makes Riverside so special is its location; close to the River Hamble, Mecca for the international yachtsman. The site is family owned and covers five acres surrounded by trees and hedges; it has 123 pitches of which 52 are level for touring caravans, all with 16A electricity hook-ups. There are also 25 tent pitches. The remaining pitches are used for caravan holiday homes on slightly rising ground, well spaced and with plenty of grass so they are not too obtrusive. A warden-run log cabin reception, with tourist information, including local bus and rail times, is at the entrance. Hamble village, one mile away, with its cobbled streets, pubs and restaurants, is famed the world over for its association with yachting. This is an ideal base for the Southampton Boat Show, Cowes Week and its very own Hamble Week Regatta. At the marina adjacent to the site, a mere two minutes' walk, is Oyster Quay with a bar and restaurant overlooking hundreds of yachts worth millions.

Facilities

A brand new lodge contains the sanitary facilities, including family and baby changing rooms. The old prefabricated unit has been kept for busy periods. Small laundry room alongside. All these facilities could be under pressure in high season. Caravan storage. WiFi throughout (charged). Off site: Fishing, sea fishing, sailing, supermarket, buses and trains in village 1 mile. Bicycle hire 2 miles. Riding 3 miles. Golf 4 miles. You can catch a small ferry across to Warsash on the other bank or take a boat up to the Upper Hamble Country Park. The New Forest, Winchester and Portsmouth are nearby.

Open: 1 March - 31 October.

Directions

From M27 exit 8 follow signs for Hamble. Take the B3397 with Tesco on the left, continue 1.9 miles through traffic lights until Hound roundabout. After 50 yds. turn left into Satchell Lane (signed Mercury Marina) and site is on left in 1 mile. GPS: 50.868835, -1.313586

Charges guide

Per unit incl. 2 persons and electricity	£ 17.00 - £ 46.00
extra person	£ 4.00
child (4-16 yrs)	£ 3.00

Hayling Island

Fishery Creek Caravan & Camping Park

100 Fishery Lane, Hayling Island PO11 9NR (Hampshire) T: 023 924 621654. E: camping@fisherycreek.co.uk
alanrogers.com/UK2221

Fishery Creek is set in a beautiful and quiet location adjoining a tidal creek of Chichester harbour. Of the 150 pitches, 90 are for touring and the remainder are seasonal. All have 10A electricity connections and are individually marked on level grass. From the park you can enjoy a paddle, a spot of fishing, or launch a small boat from the private slipway. Local shops, restaurants and pubs and a coastal path are all within easy reach and there is a new nautical-themed bistro near reception. Access is shared with the local household amenity tip which can cause congestion at weekends. The south coast has many interesting places to visit including nearby Portsmouth with its naval base and historic dockyard.

Facilities

The toilet and shower facilities are housed in separate blocks and have both been recently refurbished. The shower block has underfloor heating. Toilet facility for disabled visitors. Excellent laundry room with TV and a seating area. Motorcaravan services. Small shop for basics. Play areas. Fishing. Slipway to launch small boats. Off site: Golf and bicycle hire 2 miles. Riding 3 miles.

Open: 1 March - 31 October.

Directions

From A27, follow A3023 onto Hayling Island. At first roundabout turn left then follow brown signs to park. GPS: 50.784205, -0.958565

Charges guide

Per unit incl. 2 persons and electricity	£ 19.85 - £ 30.46
extra person	£ 4.00
child (4-14 yrs)	£ 3.30

For latest campsite news visit
alanrogers.com

Henley-on-Thames
Swiss Farm Touring & Camping
Marlow Road, Henley-on-Thames RG9 2HY (Oxfordshire) T: 01491 573419. E: info@swissfarmhenley.co.uk
alanrogers.com/UK2572

Nestling at the foot of the Chiltern Hills and just a short stroll from Henley-on-Thames, Swiss Farm is ideally located for those seeking either a relaxing or an active break. The site can offer quiet, communal style pitches or the more family orientated field type. Of the 187 pitches, 156 have 10A electricity, 62 are hardstandings and 31 are fully serviced with 16A electricity and a TV point. This park boasts a heated outdoor, supervised pool, bar and patio barbecue. Reception includes a small shop selling basic provisions. There is an adventure-style wooden children's play area. Just ten minutes walk on a footpath is Henley-on-Thames and there is a bus stop at the site entrance providing services to Wycombe, Marlow, Reading and Henley.

Facilities

Two fully equipped toilet blocks. One private bathroom. Free showers. Facilities for disabled campers. Baby facilities. Launderette. Basic shop in reception. Bar. Supervised swimming pool. Play area. Patio barbecue. Coarse fishing. WiFi. Dogs welcome in low season only. Off site: Boat launching 0.5 miles. Bicycle hire 1 mile. Golf 2 miles. Toad Hall. Henley-on-Thames. London's Paddington Station 40 minutes.

Open: 1 March - 31 October.

Directions

From M4 exit 8/9 or M40 exit 4A, take A404, A4130 to Henley-on-Thames. Follow Henley-on-Thames signs and site is signed on left just before town. GPS: 51.54594, -0.90504

Charges guide

Per unit incl. 2 persons	
and electricity	£ 19.00 - £ 27.00
extra person	£ 5.00 - £ 6.00
child (5-15 yrs)	£ 2.50 - £ 3.00

Maidenhead
Hurley Riverside Park
Hurley, Maidenhead SL6 5NE (Berkshire) T: 01628 824493. E: info@hurleyriversidepark.co.uk
alanrogers.com/UK2700

On the banks of the Thames, not far from Henley-on-Thames, you will find the picturesque village of Hurley where some buildings date back to 1086. Just outside the village is Hurley Riverside Park providing facilities for holiday homes, touring units, tents and moorings for boats. The touring area is flat and separated into smaller fields. With the pitches arranged around the outside of each field and the centre left free, the park has a spacious feel even during busy periods. There are 200 touring pitches, 146 with 10-16A Europlug, including 13 fully serviced and some on long hardstandings especially for American-style RVs. A camping field provides 62 tent pitches including some with electric hook-ups. A very popular park, there is also a large rally field. You can enjoy walks along the banks of the Thames or visit the various pubs and restaurants in the village for a good meal and a pint. Local pizza and takeaway outlets will deliver for free. A nature trail has been installed along the length of the touring park and there are large riverside picnic grounds alongside the Thames. Nearby Windsor has its famous castle or for younger members of the family, Windsor is the home of Legoland. At Henley you can watch the regatta. Alternatively, you can just relax in the peaceful settings of the site.

Facilities

Three wooden toilet blocks (raised on legs) include a very good new unisex block with private bathrooms (shower, washbasin, toilet). The other blocks have been renovated and are well equipped. Family shower rooms in one block (shower, WC, washbasin). Separate shower and toilet facilities for disabled visitors at reception. Baby area. Launderette. Motorcaravan services. Shop at reception. Play area. Fishing. Temporary moorings. Nature and wildlife trail, riverside picnic grounds, slipway and fishing in season. WiFi. Discounted tickets for family attractions. American RVs accepted. Accommodation to rent. Off site: Golf 2 miles. Bicycle hire 4 miles. Legoland at Windsor, Thorpe Park. Henley and Marlow for Thames cruises.

Open: 1 March - 31 October.

Directions

From M4 exit 8/9 take A404M towards Wycombe. After 3 miles take A4130 (Henley). Go down steep hill. Hurley village signed on right, but ignore this turning and take next right (site signed from here). GPS: 51.5466, -0.8248

Charges guide

Per unit incl. 2 persons	£ 15.00 - £ 28.00
full services	£ 19.00 - £ 30.00
extra person	£ 4.00
child (5-17 yrs)	£ 2.00
dog	£ 2.00

For latest campsite news visit
alanrogers.com

Southern England

Milford-on-Sea
Lytton Lawn Touring Park
Lymore Lane, Milford-on-Sea SO41 0TX (Hampshire) T: 01590 648331. E: holidays@shorefield.co.uk
alanrogers.com/UK2280

Lytton Lawn is the touring arm of Shorefield Country Park, a nearby holiday home park and leisure centre. Set in eight acres, it provides 135 marked pitches with some seasonal available. These include 53 premier pitches (hardstanding, 16A electricity, pitch light, water and waste water outlet) in a grassy, hedged area – this section, with its heated toilet block, is open for a longer season. The rest of the pitches, all with electricity, are in the adjoining, but separate, sloping field, edged with mature trees and hedges and with a further toilet block. A good, comfortable, self-sufficient site.

Facilities

Two modern toilet blocks are well fitted. Washing machine and dryer. Baby changing. Facilities for disabled visitors (Radar key). Motorcaravan services. Large shop (Feb-Dec). Small fenced play area and hedged field with goal posts. Tents for rent. Games room with free WiFi. Off site: Village pub 10 minutes walk. Bicycle hire 1 mile. Sailing, windsurfing and boat launching facilities 1.5 miles.

Open: All year excl. 3 January - 4 February.

Directions

From M27 follow signs for Lyndhurst and Lymington on A337. Continue towards New Milton and Lytton Lawn is signed at Everton, entrance down narrow lane (Shorefield is signed at Downton). GPS: 50.73885, -1.58695

Charges guide

Per unit incl. 6 persons
and electricity £ 11.00 - £ 21.00

Milton Keynes
Cosgrove Park
Main Street, Cosgrove, Milton Keynes MK19 7JP (Buckinghamshire) T: 01908 563360.
E: enquiries@cosgrovepark.co.uk **alanrogers.com/UK2755**

This beautifully laid out 180-acre site encompasses no less than 13 (unfenced) fishing lakes and a central watersports lake too. Not far from the M1 and the A5, Cosgrove Park offers active family holidays as well as peaceful relaxation for anglers. Motorised craft are not allowed on the main lake, but oars, paddles and sails are encouraged, with tuition available if required. Of the 400 pitches, 350 are occupied by seasonal campers, leaving just 50 for tourers. These are pleasingly sited on the top terrace and have 10A Europlugs. Early bookings are strongly advised, especially for holiday periods.

Facilities

Five toilet blocks. Two blocks with facilities for disabled campers. Baby room in restaurant. Laundry facilities. Superb shop. Excellent restaurant and coffee bar. Takeaway and fish and chips. TV in restaurant. Heated outdoor swimming pool with lifeguard. Large playground and separate football/ball games field. Dog walking field. Fishing. Watersports. Slipways. Crazy golf. Public telephone. WiFi (charged). Off site: Grand Union Canal and towpath cycle track. Indoor ski centre.

Open: 1 April - 1 November.

Directions

From A5 at Milton Keynes, take A508 towards Northampton. Turn right to Cosgrove Village and follow brown signs to site. GPS: 52.074401, -0.840787

Charges guide

Per unit incl. 2 persons and electricity £ 27.00

Newbridge
The Orchards Holiday Caravan & Camping Park
Newbridge, Yarmouth PO41 0TS (Isle of Wight) T: 01983 531331.
E: info@orchards-holiday-park.co.uk **alanrogers.com/UK2450**

In a village situation in the quieter western part of the island, The Orchards is a family owned holiday park with stunning countryside views and high quality facilities. The park's neat 11-acre touring area has 160 marked pitches suitable for tents, caravans and motorcaravans, on terraced or gently sloping paddocks broken up by apple trees, mature hedges and fences. All pitches have 10A electricity, 62 have hardstandings and 22 are 'all service' pitches, also with hardstanding. A separate area contains 65 caravan holiday homes. The Orchards is a good base from which to explore the island. The park is part of the Caravan Club's affiliated scheme and a member of the Best of British group.

Facilities

An excellent sanitary block with underfloor heating provides shower and washbasin cubicles, family bathroom and shower room. Facilities for babies and disabled visitors. Laundry facilities. Motorcaravan services. Shop. Gas supplies. Indoor heated pool (Mar-Nov). Outdoor heated pool (May-Sept). Coffee shop. Takeaway. Play areas. Pool room. Dog walking area. WiFi throughout (charged). Off site: Beach 4 miles. Bicycle hire 5 miles.

Open: 28 March - 3 November.

Directions

Park is in Newbridge village, signed south from B3054 (Yarmouth-Newport) road. GPS: 50.687967, -1.419967

Charges guide

Per unit incl. 2 persons
and electricity £ 19.50 - £ 35.50
extra person £ 5.40 - £ 7.75
child £ 2.05 - £ 3.60

For latest campsite news visit
alanrogers.com

Oxford

Diamond Farm Caravan & Camping Park

Islip Road, Bletchingdon, Oxford OX5 3DR (Oxfordshire) T: 01869 350909. E: warden@diamondpark.co.uk
alanrogers.com/UK2595

Diamond Farm is a spacious site five miles north of Oxford and within easy reach of the Cotswolds and Chilterns. The attractive, 300-year-old Cotswold stone farmhouse is at the heart of the site, along with a games room, bar and new restaurant. This is a small site with just 37 touring pitches. The new managers are keen to make improvements to the site including increasing the size of pitches by cutting back the mature hedges. The pitches are level and all equipped with 16A electricity. A number of hardstandings are also available. A separate field is used for tents and caravans (with some electrical connections). On-site amenities include a bar, a well equipped play area and a heated swimming pool.

Facilities

Two modern sanitary blocks with heated family bathroom and laundry area with freezer, microwave and iron. Facilities for disabled visitors. Shop. Bar (Fri & Sat. eves, May-Sept). Restaurant with takeaway. Solar-heated swimming pool (May-Sept). Games room. Play area. WiFi (free). Off site: Oxford city centre, Blenheim Palace and Bicester Shopping Village all 6 miles. Silverstone 24 miles.

Open: All year.

Directions

Diamond Farm is on the B4027, 1 mile from the A34 (clearly signed) and 3 miles south of exit 9 of the M40. GPS: 51.84897, -1.25518

Charges guide

Per unit incl. 2 persons and electricity	£ 18.00 - £ 21.00
extra person	£ 3.00
child	£ 3.00

Ringwood

Shamba Holidays

Ringwood Road, Saint Leonards, Ringwood BH24 2SB (Hampshire) T: 01202 873302.
E: enquiries@shambaholidays.co.uk **alanrogers.com/UK2340**

Shamba is a family run, very modern park although the aim remains to create a relaxed, pleasant atmosphere. There are 150 pitches, most used for touring units (45 are on a seasonal basis). Surrounded by trees, the camping area is on flat, open grass with 10/16A electricity available on all pitches. A Scandinavian-style building forms the focal point and here you will find reception, a bar/restaurant, takeaway and a shop. The indoor swimming pool has walls and a roof which can be opened in good weather. The park's location is excellent for a family holiday on the edge of the New Forest and for visits to the resorts of Bournemouth and Poole. Within easy reach are the Jurassic Coast, the Sealife Centre and beaches at Weymouth, the Tank Museum at Bovington and Monkey World, as well as the Purbecks and Corfe Castle. Take a trip to Brownsea Island where Baden-Powell started the Scouting movement.

Facilities

Sanitary facilities with underfloor heating include modern showers, washbasins and toilets and family changing rooms. Baby rooms with bath and facilities for disabled visitors. Launderette. Motorcaravan services. Restaurant (high season and B.Hs). Bar with meals and takeaway (weekends only off season). Indoor swimming pool (12x6 m, heated) and paddling pool. Large play area. Amusements room. Adjacent field for dog walking and football/sports pitch. Off site: Moors Valley Country Park and riding 1 mile. Golf 2 miles. Ringwood, fishing and bicycle hire 2.5 miles. Beach 8 miles.

Open: 1 March - 31 October.

Directions

Take A31 westbound from Ringwood. After 3 miles, at second roundabout, turn back on yourself and after only 20 yds. turn left at park sign. GPS: 50.825067, -1.853117

Charges guide

Per unit incl. 2 persons and electricity	£ 25.00 - £ 35.00
extra person	£ 5.00
child (3-15 yrs)	£ 4.00
dog	£ 2.50

A minimum advance booking policy applies at peak periods.

For latest campsite news visit
alanrogers.com

Ringwood

Oakdene Forest Park

Saint Leonards, Ringwood BH24 2RZ (Hampshire) T: 01202 865601. E: holidays@shorefield.co.uk

alanrogers.com/UK2270

This park, part of the Shorefield Group, is a large holiday complex with many caravan holiday homes, but also with a small, basic area set aside for 13 tents, all with 10A electricity (no trailer tents). These pitches are on a rather uneven, grassy field with no shade, but only a short walk from the central facilities. The park provides a wide range of activities and entertainment, both outdoor and indoor, not forgetting the heated, indoor pool with its 34-metre flume and toddlers' beach area. With bars, supermarket, bakery and café, this is ideal for families with children of all ages. Alongside, and with direct access, is Hurn Forest - great for walking and cycling, with the 26 km. Castleman Trailway.

Facilities	Directions
Prefabricated sanitary unit has WCs, showers, washbasins and dishwashing facilities. Launderette. Shop. Restaurant and bars. Takeaway. Indoor pool (all year). Outdoor pools (May-Sept). Gym. Table tennis and pool table. Crazy golf. Compact bowling. Amusement arcade. Play area. Free Squirrel's Club for children. Bicycle hire. ATM. Free WiFi in main building. Off site: Forest walks. Market, supermarket and restaurant 3 miles. Golf and riding 3 miles. Fishing 5 miles. Beach 9 miles.	From Ringwood take A31 westbound for 4.5 miles (just after Forest Edge) and site is on left. GPS: 50.811936, -1.858323

Open: April - October.

Charges guide

Per pitch incl. 6 persons and electricity	£ 14.50 - £ 37.00
extra person	£ 4.00

Riseley

Wellington Country Park

Riseley, Reading RG7 1SP (Berkshire) T: 01189 326444. E: info@wellington-country-park.co.uk

alanrogers.com/UK2690

This campsite is situated within the very popular 350-acre Wellington Country Park, which is open to the public from February to November. The park contains a wide range of amenities: a shop, a café, play areas, twelve-hole mini golf, animal farm and petting barn, miniature railway (charged), four nature trails, a deer park and a host of play equipment. Entrance to the park is included in the campsite fees. There are 87 pitches, 57 with 6A electricity and 50 on hardstanding. Thirty non-electric pitches are for tents; a few premium pitches offer slightly more privacy. It is a very pleasant setting and once the park closes at 18.00 all is much quieter. You should aim to arrive before 16.30 (low season) and 17.30 (high season) when the main reception centre closes. Access to the site is through a locked gate (key from reception on check-in). The design of the site with generous individual pitches and some small groups, all within woodland clearings, gives a very rustic and relaxed ambience. The warden lives on the site.

Facilities	Directions
The central toilet block provides washbasins and well equipped showers with good dry areas. Ample laundry. Shop stocks basics. Café (during park hours). Calor gas exchange. Country Park with nature walks, deer field, minigolf, play areas and miniature railway (£1.50 extra). Family events are held all year round. Twin-axle caravans by arrangement. WiFi over site (charged). Torch useful. Off site: Local shops, bars and entertainment including swimming, cinema, ice-skating, all within a short drive. Wellington Riding School nearby. Golf 6 miles. Major attractions such as Legoland, Thorpe Park, Windsor etc. all within easy reach.	From M4 take exit 11 (A33) south towards Basingstoke. At first roundabout turn left onto B3339 and park is off next roundabout. From M3 take exit 5 onto B3349 towards Reading and stay on this road directly to the roundabout at the site entrance. Do not use sat navs. GPS: 51.36001, -0.95513

Open: 18 March - 1 November.

Charges guide

Per unit incl. 2 persons and electricity	£ 17.00 - £ 33.00
extra person	£ 7.50 - £ 9.00
child (3-15 yrs)	£ 6.50 - £ 8.00
dog	£ 3.00

Ringwood
Red Shoot Camping Park

Linwood, Ringwood BH24 3QT (Hampshire) T: 01425 473789. E: enquiries@redshoot-campingpark.com

alanrogers.com/UK2350

Red Shoot is set in the heart of the New Forest, on four acres of level and slightly sloping grass meadows. A simple, rural retreat with panoramic views of the surrounding countryside and forest, it is very popular in high season. A cattle grid at the entrance keeps the New Forest animals outside the park. There are 120 good sized pitches, 45 with 10A electricity, served by a gravel access road. There is no site lighting so a torch would be useful. The adjacent Red Shoot Inn serves meals and brews its own real ales. There are ample opportunities for walking, cycling and naturalist pursuits in the area.

Facilities

The toilet and shower facilities have been upgraded to a high standard with underfloor heating including a family shower room/baby bath and changing area. Well equipped laundry room. Good unit for disabled visitors. Licensed shop with fresh bread and croissants. Bar. Fenced adventure-style playground. Off site: Fishing and riding 5 miles. Golf 7 miles. Beach 12 miles.

Open: 1 March - 31 October.

Directions

From A338, 1.75 miles north of Ringwood, turn east (signed Linwood and Moyles Court). Follow signs, over a staggered crossroads, and continue straight on for another 1.75 miles to Red Shoot Inn and park. GPS: 50.883917, -1.7347

Charges guide

Per unit incl. 2 persons and electricity	£ 17.00 - £ 28.00
extra person	£ 8.00

Romsey
Hill Farm Caravan Park

Branches Lane, Sherfield English, Romsey SO51 6FH (Hampshire) T: 01794 340402.
E: joe@hillfarmpark.com **alanrogers.com/UK2380**

This 11-acre rural park is ideal for those seeking a quiet base but one that is within easy reach of all the main tourist attractions of Hampshire and Dorset. There are 120 pitches, of which 50 for seasonal units are located in a separate area. The touring area is a large open field surrounded by trees and hedges. All pitches are well marked, numbered and mainly level. All have 10/16A electricity hook-ups, are fully serviced with electricity and water and 60 are available with hardstanding. Adding to the attractiveness of the site is a pitch and putt golf course set in a sizeable and well landscaped area. This is a dog-friendly park with kennels available. For anyone interested in roses, nearby Mottisfont Abbey (National Trust) has a unique collection of old fashioned varieties. The New Forest with Beaulieu Estate and National Motor Museum is just a short drive away. A trip to the Isle of Wight makes a good excursion – the ferry terminal is within a 30 minute drive. Paulton's Park and Peppa Pig World are nearby.

Facilities

Two very clean, traditionally built toilet blocks include washbasins, both open style and in cubicles, and controllable showers. Facilities for families, babies and disabled visitors. Motorcaravan services. Shop in reception for gas supplies and basics. Bread and pasties are cooked on the premises. Café serving breakfast, lunch, Sunday roast and afternoon tea. Play area. Pitch and putt golf. WiFi (charged). Off site: Riding, golf and fishing 3 miles. Bournemouth and Southampton for shopping, leisure and family entertainment nearby.

Open: 1 March - 31 October.

Directions

From Romsey, drive north on the A27 for 3.5 miles, turning right into Branches Lane and site is a further 0.5 miles on right. GPS: 51.00627, -1.57682

Charges guide

Per unit incl. 2 persons and electricity	£ 18.00 - £ 30.00
extra person	£ 7.00
child (4-16 yrs)	£ 2.50 - £ 5.00

Minimum booking requirement for B.Hs, July and August weekends. No credit cards.

HILL FARM Caravan Park Near Romsey, ten minutes north of the New Forest, we are an ideal base for exploring Southern England and approximately 1 hour from London. Welcome

Hill Farm Caravan Park • *Branches Lane* • *Sherfield English* • *Romsey* • *Hampshire SO51 6FH*
Tel +44 (0)1794 340402 • *E-mail info@hillfarmpark.com* • *www.hillfarmpark.com*

For latest campsite news visit
alanrogers.com

Ryde

Whitefield Forest Touring Park

Brading Road, Ryde PO33 1QL (Isle of Wight) T: 01983 617069. E: pat&louise@whitefieldforest.co.uk

alanrogers.com/UK2495

This family run park, opened in May 2007, has been sympathetically developed by the owners working closely with the Forestry Commission to maintain the natural beauty of the ancient woodland, Whitefield Forest. There is a mixture of well drained, all-weather hardstanding and grass pitches (90 in total) all with 16A electricity hook-up; 14 are fully serviced. Varying in size (100-170 sq.m), the pitches are level and sheltered with some on terraces. They are all suitable for tents, caravans and motorcaravans. Some slight road noise is audible from a few pitches. A member of the Best of British group.

Facilities

The excellent, well appointed, heated toilet block has private cubicles. Family shower rooms. Baby changing and facilities for disabled visitors. Laundry facilities. Motorcaravan services. Paperback book exchange. Adventure type play area. Nature walk. WiFi (free in reception). Charcoal barbecues only; strictly no fires. Off site: Supermarket 600 yds. Golf 1 mile. Riding 3 miles.

Open: 18 March - 3 October.

Directions

From Fishbourne and East Cowes follow A3054 to Ryde. Follow the A3055 to Brading. Site is 800 yds. on left (signed). From Yarmouth follow A3054 to Newport, then to Ryde. Follow the A3055 to Brading and as above. GPS: 50.70049, -1.14574

Charges guide

Per unit incl. 2 persons and electricity	£ 17.00 - £ 24.00

Shanklin

Ninham Country Holidays

Ninham, Shanklin PO37 7PL (Isle of Wight) T: 01983 864243. E: office@ninham-holidays.co.uk

alanrogers.com/UK2465

Ninham is an attractive, well maintained park tucked in a wooded valley but only ten minutes' drive to the bustling resort of Shanklin with its long, sandy beaches and good shops and restaurants. Two touring areas, one open all season, have spacious grass and gravel pitches, some open and some separated by hedges, with water and electrical hook-ups. There are two (unfenced) lakes for carp fishing and numerous cycle paths which can be used to access local amenities. The site will appeal in particular to walkers and cyclists who can take full advantage of the beautiful countryside.

Facilities

Clean and well maintained sanitary facilities in two buildings, one traditional used in high season, the second a high quality, modern block with solar-heated water. Facilities for disabled visitors. Space for baby changing. Laundry facilities. No shop but supermarkets nearby. Small outdoor pool (end May-Sept). Games room with TV for special events. Play areas. Coarse fishing (charged). Bicycle hire. WiFi (charged). Dogs welcome in one area. Mobile homes and self-catering houses to rent. Off site: Beach 2 miles. Golf 2 miles. Riding 4 miles.

Open: May - end of September.

Directions

From Newport/Cowes direction pass park entrance and continue 400 yds. to Morrison's roundabout. Return to filter off left onto private drive. From Ryde-Fishbourne (A3055) turn onto A3056 at lake. Entrance is on left after Morrison's roundabout. Sat navs use PO36 9PJ. GPS: 50.640607, -1.192424

Charges guide

Per unit incl. 2 persons and electricity	£ 18.50 - £ 25.75
extra person	£ 6.25 - £ 8.75

Shanklin

Lower Hyde Holiday Park

Landguard Road, Shanklin PO37 7LL (Isle of Wight) T: 01983 866131. E: lower.hyde@park-resorts.com

alanrogers.com/UK2475

This site is located on the edge of Shanklin within walking distance of shops and services and only 1.5 miles from the beach. Lower Hyde is a large holiday park complex with 198 caravan holiday homes for rent and 167 privately owned. The separate touring area has 85 well spaced and numbered pitches, all with 16A electricity and 26 with full services. There is a further area for tents (no electricity). The touring area is in an elevated position with good views over the surrounding countryside. The pitches are large and flat, easily accessed, with tarmac roads and low-level lighting.

Facilities

The toilet block has WCs, open washbasins, showers, a family shower room and two bathrooms. Separate baby room. Suite for disabled visitors. Launderette. Well stocked shop. Bar. Restaurant and takeaway. Indoor and outdoor pools. Adventure playground. Clubs for children. Entertainment. All-weather multisports court. Soccer. Archery. Fencing. Tennis. ATM. Bicycle hire. WiFi (charged). Off site: Fishing and boat launching 1.5 miles. Golf 2.5 miles. Riding 5 miles.

Open: Easter - 2 November.

Directions

From East Cowes ferry take A3021 for 2.5 miles to roundabout and turn right on A3054 to Newport. From Newport take A3020 (Shanklin). At Blackwater go straight on joining A3056 to Sandown. After Lidl supermarket go straight on turn right into Whitecross Lane (signed Lower Hyde Camping). Follow signs to touring reception. GPS: 50.633317, -1.180983

Charges guide

Per unit incl. up to 4 persons and electricity	£ 7.00 - £ 29.00

Ventnor

Appuldurcombe Gardens Holiday Park

Wroxall, Ventnor PO38 3EP (Isle of Wight) T: 01983 852597. E: info@appuldurcombegardens.co.uk

alanrogers.com/UK2480

Originally part of the grounds of an historic house, this pretty family holiday park is situated in 14 acres of beautiful countryside in the valley of Stenbury Downs and Saint Martin's Downs, close to the sandy beaches at Sandown, Shanklin and Ventnor. The camping field is set in a grassy meadow through which a stream meanders with a tranquil seating area close by. With hard access roads, there are 135 spacious marked pitches for touring units and tents, all with 14A electricity. There are 38 fully serviced pitches, 22 with hardstanding. The old walled orchard contains 40 good quality caravan holiday homes. There is also the access-friendly Orchard Lodge (all accommodation on one level with ramp access to outside) plus two self-contained apartments.

Facilities

Two good sanitary blocks with hot showers. Facilities for disabled visitors (but not for children). Launderette. Drying room and secure cycle storage. Motorcaravan services planned. Shop. Café. Bar and family entertainment room. All amenities open from Spring B.H.-early Sept. Outdoor swimming pool (8x18 m) and toddlers' pool. Play area. Crazy golf. Football pitch. WiFi (charged). Off site: Fishing, golf, riding, bicycle hire, boat launching, beach, sailing, all within 2-3 miles.

Open: March - November.

Directions

From Newport take A3020 towards Shanklin. 2 miles past Godshill turn right at Whiteley Bank roundabout towards Wroxall (B3320). Pass Donkey Sanctuary and turn right into Appuldurcombe Road. Park entrance (narrow road) is second on right. Do not use sat nav. GPS: 50.61891, -1.22657

Charges guide

Per unit incl. 2 persons and electricity	£ 16.95 - £ 29.35
extra person	£ 4.95 - £ 7.45
child (3-15 yrs)	£ 2.95 - £ 5.25
dog	£ 1.50 - £ 2.00

Witney

Lincoln Farm Park Oxfordshire

High Street, Standlake, Witney OX29 7RH (Oxfordshire) T: 01865 300239. E: info@lincolnfarmpark.co.uk

alanrogers.com/UK2570

From its immaculately tended grounds and quality facilities to the efficient and friendly staff, this park is a credit to its owner. Situated in a small, quiet village it is well set back and screened by mature trees, and has wide gravel roads, hedged enclosures, brick pathways and good lighting. All 92 numbered, level touring pitches are generously sized and have 10/16A electricity connections, 75 with gravel hardstanding and grass for awnings and 23 are fully serviced. Gazebos or extra tents are not permitted on pitches. Although only a relatively small site its leisure facilities are quite outstanding. The indoor leisure centre boasts two heated pools plus a pool for toddlers, spa pools, saunas, steam room, sunbed and a fitness suite. A member of the Best of British group.

Facilities

Two heated toilet blocks are well maintained and exceptionally clean with showers and washbasins in cubicles. A well equipped, separate unit for disabled visitors. Two family bathrooms (with baby bath and changing facilities). Laundry facilities. Freezers, fridges and microwaves (free). Motorcaravan services. Well stocked shop. Information kiosk. Outdoor chess/draughts, putting green and adventure play area. Indoor swimming pools (charged). WiFi (charged). Games room with pool, table football and electronic games machines. Battery charging room. Off site: Bird hides 250 yds. Fishing (lake and river) 300 yds. and 5 miles. Riding centre and watersports nearby. Golf 5 miles. Oxford 14 miles.

Open: 1 February - mid November.

Directions

Take A415 Witney-Abingdon road and turn into Standlake High Street by garage; park is 300 yds. on the right. GPS: 51.7232, -1.428783

Charges guide

Per unit incl. 2 persons and electricity	£ 22.30 - £ 33.80
extra person	£ 5.20
child (5-14 yrs)	£ 3.60
dog	£ 1.30
Low season offers.	

For latest campsite news visit

alanrogers.com

THE SOUTH EAST COMPRISES: EAST SUSSEX, WEST SUSSEX, SURREY AND KENT

Land of 1066, the South East is brimming with historical sights as castles, stately homes and cathedrals abound. It also boasts miles of footpaths and cycle routes through some of the best landscapes in England, passing chalk downland, wooded valleys and dramatic white-faced cliffs.

The chalk countryside of golden downland in Sussex offers many opportunities for an active holiday, from walking and cycling to more adventurous pursuits such as rock climbing or ballooning. Once an ancient forest, much of the Weald is now taken up with farmland but some areas still remain, including Ashdown Forest, a walkers' paradise with stunning views of the High Weald and South Downs. The many rivers of the county have cut their way through gaps in the chalk landscape ending spectacularly in white cliffs on the coast. Here you will find the Regency resorts of Bognor Regis and Brighton with its Royal Pavilion, famous pier and quirky shops. Often referred to as the 'Garden of England', Kent is a richly fertile region flourishing with hop gardens, fruit orchards and flowers. It is also home to the world-renowned Canterbury Cathedral, several splendid castles, hidden towns, and quaint villages with oast houses. Surrey too boasts a rich heritage with numerous stately homes and National Trust sites plus large areas of ancient woodland. With a network of rivers, an enjoyable way to explore the beautiful countryside is by boat, stopping off at a riverside pub – or two!

Places of interest

East Sussex: Royal Pavilion, Brighton; the cinque ports towns of Hastings and Rye; Eastbourne with its Victorian pier.

West Sussex: Chichester cathedral; Arundel, with its Norman castle and charming antique shops; Goodwood Racecourse.

Surrey: Guildford castle and cathedral; Mole Valley; Royal Horticultural Society's gardens at Wisley; Chessington World of Adventures; Dorking, a renowned centre for antiques; Runnymede; Thorpe Park in Chertsey.

Kent: Leeds Castle and gardens with maze; Canterbury cathedral, Roman museum and river tours; Dover, with museum and castle; traditional seaside resort of Broadstairs; Chartwell, family home of Sir Winston Churchill; Turner Art Gallery, Margate.

Did you know?

The Battle of Hastings was actually fought six miles away at Senlac Hill.

Brighton is home to Britain's oldest electric railway, opened by Marcus Volks in 1883.

The modernist De La Warr Pavilion, Bexhill, was designed by Serge Chermayeff and Erich Mendelsohn and opened in 1935.

Fishbourne Palace, covering six acres, is the largest Roman site discovered in Britain.

Runnymede takes its name from the meadow where the Magna Carta, the great charter of English liberties, was sealed by King John in 1215.

Oscar Wilde wrote The Importance of Being Earnest in 1895 while living in Worthing.

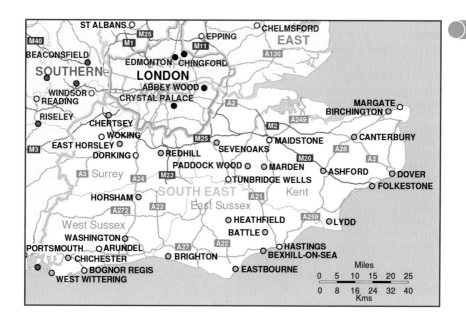

Ashford

Broadhembury Caravan & Camping Park

Steeds Lane, Kingsnorth, Ashford TN26 1NQ (Kent) T: 01233 620859. E: holidaypark@broadhembury.co.uk
alanrogers.com/UK3040

In quiet countryside just outside Ashford and within easy reach of London, Dover, Folkestone and the Kent coast, this sheltered park is attractively landscaped. There are areas for family camping with play areas and amenities designed with children in mind and separate quiet meadows just for adults with new luxury facilities. In total the park takes 110 touring units of any type. The well kept pitches are on level grass and backed by tall, neat hedges; 105 with electricity connections (10/16A). In addition, six pitches are fully serviced and ten more have double hardstanding plus a grass area for an awning. The welcome is friendly at this popular park and it is often full in the main season. Security arrangements are excellent with coded entry through the gates and onto the park. A trip to France is easily possible with the International railway terminal at Ashford (Paris in two hours) – take your passport. A member of the Best of British group.

Facilities

Well equipped toilet block for the family areas and new, ecologically considered block for the couples meadows, both kept very clean. Underfloor heating. Private cabins. High quality facilities for disabled visitors. Laundry room. Good campers' kitchen. Motorcaravan services. Well stocked shop with local produce, wine and beer (bread and papers to order). Internet access. Pool room. Games room. Two play areas with wood-chip bases. Play field away from the touring area. Campers' herb garden. WiFi over site (charged). Dog exercise field – up to two dogs per pitch are accepted. Large units are accepted if pre-booked. Off site: Ashford International offers a direct link to London and Eurostar services to Paris, Brussels and Lille. Fishing 300 m. Golf 1 mile. Riding 2 miles.

Open: All year.

Directions

From M20 exit 10 take A2070. After 2 miles follow sign for Kingsnorth. Turn left at second crossroads in Kingsnorth village. GPS: 51.10647, 0.86809

Charges guide

Per unit incl. 2 persons	
and electricity	£ 23.00 - £ 52.00
extra person	£ 6.50
child (5-16 yrs)	£ 2.00 - £ 5.00
tent incl. 2 persons	£ 20.00 - £ 25.00

Less 10% for bookings of 7 nights or more.

Battle

Brakes Coppice Park

Forewood Lane, Crowhurst, Battle TN33 9AB (East Sussex) T: 01424 830322. E: brakesco@btinternet.com
alanrogers.com/UK2965

Brakes Coppice Park is a small and secluded site set in woodland just a mile away from historic Battle. Reached by an uneven, winding private track, it is signed to prevent visitors taking a wrong turn to the nearby farm of the same name. Ideal for tents, but welcoming any type of unit, the site has 60 grass pitches, 22 with 6A electricity and TV aerial points, in a gently sloping field. A further area near a small fishing lake provides a few extra pitches. As well as fishing, visitors can enjoy walking in the surrounding woods. There is a play area for younger children in the centre of the main field. Booking is advisable.

Facilities

The single heated toilet block is simple but adequate. Facilities for disabled visitors. Laundry. Well stocked shop. Gas supplies. Fishing permits from reception. WiFi in reception (charged). Accommodation to rent. Off site: Pubs and shops in Crowhurst and Battle. Crowhurst station 10 minutes walk.

Open: 1 March - 31 October.

Directions

From Battle follow the A2100 towards Hastings for 2 miles. Turn right on Telham Lane (Crowhurst). Continue into Forewood Lane and turn left on private track shortly after passing sign for Crowhurst village. GPS: 50.89065, 0.507083

Charges guide

Per unit incl. 2 persons	£ 15.00 - £ 19.00
incl. electricity	£ 17.00 - £ 21.00

Bexhill-on-Sea

Chestnut Meadow Camping & Caravan Park

Ninfield Road, Sidley, Bexhill-on-Sea TN39 5JG (East Sussex) T: 01424 892361.
E: info@chestnutmeadow.co.uk **alanrogers.com/UK2945**

In a peaceful country location near Bexhill, with Hastings and rural East Sussex to explore close by, a family, long used to camping themselves, have developed this into an attractive park. The well drained, sheltered meadow is virtually surrounded by trees with a glimpse of the sea. Flowers and shrubs enhance the entrance and buildings. The 75 large touring pitches (up to 150 sq. m) are marked by posts with numbered buckets which you can use for recycling. Electricity (16A) is available on 74 pitches and 22 have hardstanding beneath the grass, eight with their own water and drainage. They are well spaced with the central area kept free for children to play and adults to gather and relax.

Facilities

Excellent heated sanitary building. Facilities for disabled visitors double as family room. Launderette. Motorcaravan services. Shop with local produce at reception. Bar, café (good value, serving breakfast through to evening meal) and takeaway (all high season and weekends). Games hall with snooker, pool, table tennis, air hockey, table football. Large, new, fenced play area. WiFi (charged). Off site: Golf and riding 1 mile. International fishing lakes 5 miles.

Open: Mid March - mid September.

Directions

The park is northwest of Bexhill on the A269 Ninfield Road between Sidley and Ninfield with a 110-yd. entrance drive. GPS: 50.865412, 0.447312

Charges guide

Per unit incl. 2 persons and electricity	£ 20.00 - £ 29.00
extra person	£ 5.00
Barrier card £10 deposit.	

Bexhill-on-Sea

Kloofs Camping & Caravan Park

Sandhurst Lane, Whydown, Bexhill-on-Sea TN39 4RG (East Sussex) T: 01424 842839.
E: camping@kloofs.com **alanrogers.com/UK2955**

This peaceful, rural park is situated in a quiet, country lane with rural views, yet within easy reach of several well known towns on the East Sussex coast. Set in three acres, Kloofs is owned and run by Terry and Helen Griggs who have taken great care in making this a most attractive and well maintained park. There are 50 level, generously sized touring pitches in two separate areas. Most are on hardstanding making them suitable for all-weather touring and have 10/16A electricity, water and drainage. It is evident that considerable investment has been made to ensure visitors have a comfortable stay.

Facilities

One main, centrally heated toilet block is modern and spotlessly clean. Washbasins in cubicles and spacious hot showers. Large shower room for families and en-suite facility for disabled visitors. The lower paddock offers additional toilet and shower facilities. Heated kitchen area. Laundry facilities. Small shop in reception for basics. Adventure-style play area. Small library. Off site: Footpath from site to village 1.4 miles. Watersports, golf, riding and fishing all nearby. Beach 2 miles. Bexhill-on-Sea 3 miles.

Open: All year.

Directions

From Battle, take A269 and turn right into Pear Tree Lane, then right at crossroads. Sandhurst Lane is 300 yds. on left and site is signed on right. From Hastings, take A259 to Little Common roundabout. Turn off right into Pear Tree Lane, then left at crossroads. Then as above. GPS: 50.8560, 0.4271

Charges guide

Per unit incl. 2 persons, electricity and water	£ 27.50
extra person	£ 8.50

For latest campsite news visit
alanrogers.com

Birchington
Quex Caravan Park

Park Road, Birchington CT7 0BL (Kent) T: 01843 841273. E: info@keatfarm.co.uk

alanrogers.com/UK3110

Although there is a large number of privately owned holiday homes at Quex, they do not intrude on the touring area which is in a sheltered glade under tall trees. Here, there are 40 shady touring pitches all with 10A electricity. This park accepts trailer tents but not other tent campers. This is an attractive and well maintained park. As with the other parks in the Keat Farm group, there is a strong commitment to conservation here. 'Bugingham Palace' and other such insect houses are a fascinating feature on the park. Local attractions include Quex House and gardens and, of course, the popular seaside resorts of Margate, Ramsgate and Broadstairs. Reception provides a good selection of tourist information and can provide a map of the local area. Quex House is the home of the Powell-Cotton family and houses an extraordinary museum with a collection of treasures from around the world. There are also 15 acres of beautiful gardens. Margate is close at hand and is a lively resort now undergoing something of a revival with the Turner Contemporary gallery and the recently reopened Dreamland Amusement park.

Facilities

The central sanitary unit is in a heated chalet style building with all the usual facilities. Laundry room with washing machine and dryer. Well stocked shop (all season). Café and takeaway (all season). Playground. Conservation features including insect houses. WiFi throughout (charged). More than one dog per pitch is accepted by prior arrangement only. Off site: Supermarkets close by. Fishing, golf and riding 3 miles.

Open: 15 February - 15 December.

Directions

From roundabout at junction of A28 and A299, take A28 east towards Birchington and Margate. At Birchington carry straight on at roundabout by church then next right. Turn right again and left at mini-roundabout. Site is on right in half a mile (well signed). GPS: 51.367583, 1.3324

Charges guide

Per unit incl. 2 persons and electricity	£ 18.00 - £ 27.00
extra person	£ 4.00
child (5-16 yrs)	£ 3.00
dog	£ 2.00

Less 10% for 4 nights booked and paid for in advance.

Brighton
Brighton Caravan Club Site

East Brighton Park, Brighton BN2 5TS (East Sussex) T: 01273 626546.

alanrogers.com/UK2930

Brighton is without doubt the South of England's most popular seaside resort, and Brighton Caravan Club's site is a first class base from which to enjoy the many and diverse attractions, both in the town and this area of the south coast. A wide tarmac road winds its way through the site from reception, with gravel pitches on either side, leading to terraces with grass pitches on the lower slopes of the valley. The 215 pitches all have 16A electricity; 123 have hardstanding and 12 have water, drainage and TV sockets. Three grass terraces take 57 tents and these have hard parking nearby as a low fence prevents cars being taken onto the camping areas. The site fully lives up to the very high standards expected from the Caravan Club and provides a high quality venue both for a quiet holiday and as a base for sightseeing.

Facilities

Two heated sanitary blocks include all washbasins in private cabins. In the main season a third timber-clad building provides additional services near the tent area. Well equipped room for wheelchair users, another one for walking disabled, and two baby and toddler washrooms. Laundry facilities. Motorcaravan services. Gas available. Shop. Play area with safety base. WiFi throughout (charged). Off site: Brighton is 2 miles with a bus service from the entry road. Extensive recreation grounds adjacent.

Open: All year.

Directions

From north (London) on M23/A23, join A27 (Lewes). Exit via slip road for B2123 (Falmer/Rottingdean). At roundabout turn left on B2123. Continue for 2 miles then turn right at traffic lights by Downs Hotel into Warren Road. After 1 mile turn left at traffic lights into Wilson Ave, crossing racecourse. In 1.75 miles at foot of hill (just before lights) turn left and follow lane to site. GPS: 50.82229, -0.09737

Charges guide

Per person	£ 6.50 - £ 8.80
child (5-17 yrs)	£ 0.01 - £ 3.40
pitch incl. electricity (non-member)	£ 16.60 - £ 21.10

For latest campsite news visit
alanrogers.com

Canterbury
Canterbury Fields Holiday Park

Stone Street, Petham, Canterbury CT4 5PL (Kent) T: 01227 700306. E: enquiries@canterburyfields.co.uk

alanrogers.com/UK3060

Canterbury Fields has beeen acquired by the Darwin Leisure group. This a small, quiet site located in the heart of the Kent countryside overlooking the Chartham Downs. Just five miles south of Canterbury and eight miles north of the M20, it is ideally placed either to explore the delights of the ancient city or the many attractions of eastern and coastal Kent. With some caravan holiday homes, the site also has 45 pitches for touring units and tents. The 27 pitches with 10A electricity are marked on mainly level grass either side of the entrance road, the remainder unmarked on a rather attractive, sloping area, left natural with trees and bushes creating cosy little recesses in which to pitch.

Facilities

Two sanitary blocks (one for each sex) can be heated. Washbasins and four showers (on payment). Extra toilets on the edge of the camping area. Toilet/shower room for families and disabled visitors. Laundry facilities. Gas supplies. Play area. Torches may be useful. Dogs are not accepted. WiFi (free). Off site: Pub (serving food) 100 m. Riding and County cricket ground 4 miles. Bicycle hire 5 miles. Golf 6 miles.

Open: Easter - September.

Directions

From south, take exit 11 from the M20. From Canterbury, ignore signs to Petham and Waltham on B2068 and continue towards Folkestone. From either direction, turn into road beside the Chequers Inn, turn left into park and follow road to owners' house/reception. GPS: 51.2168, 1.058183

Charges guide

Per unit incl. 2 persons and electricity	£ 19.00 - £ 24.50

Canterbury
Canterbury Camping & Caravanning Club Site

Bekesbourne Lane, Canterbury CT3 4AB (Kent) T: 01227 463216. E: canterbury.site@thefriendlyclub.co.uk

alanrogers.com/UK3070

Situated just off the A257 Sandwich road, about 1.5 miles from the centre of Canterbury, this site is an ideal base for exploring Canterbury and the north Kent coast, as well as being a good stopover to and from the Dover ferries and the Folkestone Channel Tunnel terminal. There are 200 pitches, 120 with 16A electric hook-ups and, except at the very height of the season, you are likely to find a pitch although not necessarily with electricity. Most of the pitches are on well kept grass with hundreds of saplings planted, but there are also 65 pitches with hardstanding. Note: power lines cross the site.

Facilities

Two recently refurbished sanitary blocks, the main one with a laundry room, family room and facilities for disabled visitors. Motorcaravan services. Reception stocks a small range of essential foods, milk and gas. Excellent tourist information room. Play area with equipment on bark chippings. Bicycle hire. Dog walk. WiFi throughout (charged). Off site: Golf adjacent. Shop 0.5 miles. Bicycle hire 2 miles. Canterbury 1 mile.

Open: All year.

Directions

From the A2 take exit for Canterbury and follow signs for Sandwich (A257). Pass military barracks and turn right into Bekesbourne Lane opposite golf course. Do not use sat nav (narrow approach lanes). GPS: 51.2769, 1.113533

Charges guide

Per unit incl. 2 persons and electricity	£ 6.45 - £ 10.95

Non-member prices are higher.

Chertsey
Chertsey Camping & Caravanning Club Site

Bridge Road, Chertsey KT16 8JX (Surrey) T: 01932 562405.

alanrogers.com/UK2810

This attractive site is ideally located on the banks of the River Thames, only a few minutes' walk from two riverside pubs with restaurants close to the shops and amenities of Chertsey. There are 150 pitches including 56 new serviced pitches with hardstanding and 16A electricity, and 15 super service pitches which have TV aerial points, water and waste drainage. Fishing is possible and canoes can be launched from the site. There has been extensive landscaping and the existing Thames creek has been extended to flow through the site with marshland areas to support the local wildlife environment.

Facilities

Two older style sanitary blocks can be heated and include washbasins in cabins and facilities for disabled visitors. Hairdryers. Laundry. Motorcaravan services. Essentials in reception (shop opposite site). Snack van selling burgers and breakfast (Fri.-Sun). Recreation hall. Play area on bark. Fishing (adults £1.70, NRA licence needed). Short dog walk areas. Caravan storage. Torches are necessary. WiFi throughout (charged). Off site: Riverside pubs 5 mins.

Open: All year.

Directions

Suggested: from M25 use exit 11. Turn left at roundabout on A317 (Shepperton) and continue to 2nd set of traffic lights. Turn right then look for green Club camp sign, turn left just before Chertsey bridge; the opening is narrow. GPS: 51.38986, -0.49008

Charges guide

Per unit incl. 2 persons and electricity	£ 22.55 - £ 37.90

Non-member prices are higher.

For latest campsite news visit
alanrogers.com

Chichester
Chichester Camping & Caravanning Club Site

345 Main Road, Southbourne PO10 8JH (West Sussex) T: 01243 373202.

alanrogers.com/UK2320

This small, neat site is just to the west of Chichester and north of Bosham harbour. Formerly an orchard, it is rectangular in shape with 58 pitches on flat, well mown lawns on either side of gravel roads. All pitches have 16A electricity, 42 with level hardstanding. Although the A27 bypass takes most of the through traffic, the site is by the main A259 road so there may be some traffic noise in some parts (not busy at night). Opposite the park are orchards through which paths lead to the seashore. Arrival must be before 20.00 unless prior arrangements have been made with the site manager.

Facilities

The well designed, brick built toilet block is of first class quality. Fully tiled and heated in cool weather with facilities for campers with disabilities (key access). Washing machines and dryers. Gas supplies. No ball games permitted. Dogs can be walked in the lane opposite the entrance. WiFi throughout (charged). Off site: Shops, restaurants and pubs within easy walking distance in the nearby village. Bicycle hire 1 mile.

Open: 4 February - 14 November.

Directions

Park is on A259 Chichester-Havant road at Southbourne, 750 yds. west of Chichester Caravans. Coming from the west, it is 2.8 miles from the A27/A259 junction near Havant. GPS: 50.84498, -0.90299

Charges guide

Per unit incl. 2 persons and electricity	£ 15.05 - £ 25.25

Non-member prices are higher.

Chichester
Chichester Lakeside Park

Vinnetrow Road, Chichester PO20 1QH (West Sussex) T: 01243 218520. E: lakeside@ParkHolidays.com

alanrogers.com/UK2875

Located just outside the historic city of Chichester, this large site is a member of the Park Holidays group. Set amidst ten fishing lakes, it is within easy access of a sandy beach and the resort of Bognor Regis. The 115 touring pitches with 16A electricity are on three sides of a large, level and grassy field, the fourth side being used for seasonal units and storage. The central, unmarked space is for tents and caravans with no electric hook-ups and a large, fenced area provides space for sports and organised events for the whole park. The larger part of the park is occupied by 400 holiday caravans.

Facilities

Two dated toilet blocks are likely to be under pressure at busy times. Facilities for disabled visitors. Shop. Dated bar and snack bar. Entertainment complex. Swimming pool. Fishing. Playing field. Club for children (high season). Mobile homes for rent. WiFi throughout (charged). Off site: Riding 2 miles. Golf 2.5 miles. Beach 3 miles. Bognor Regis (cafés, restaurants and shops).

Open: 1 March - 4 November.

Directions

The park is well signed on either side of a roundabout at the junction of the A27 and A259. Turning south on Vinnetrow Road, the park is 200 yds. on the right. GPS: 50.823885, -0.75119

Charges guide

Per unit incl. 2 persons and electricity	£ 10.00 - £ 32.00
extra person	£ 2.00 - £ 4.00

Chichester
Warner Farm Touring Park

Warner Lane, Selsey, Chichester PO20 9EL (West Sussex) T: 01243 604499. E: touring@bunnleisure.co.uk

alanrogers.com/UK2885

This site is a member of the Bunn Holiday Villages group, owners of several large holiday home parks which surround the pretty holiday town of Selsey. Warner Farm is a top quality touring park with 174 large grassy pitches and 47 on hardstanding, all with electrical connections. Pitches have a generally open aspect and there is a large area at the back of the site, the 'camping field', which offers an unmarked camping area as well as providing picnic tables and barbecues. There are 42 serviced pitches with electricity, water and waste water. The site is modern and well maintained and benefits from free access to the extensive leisure facilities on offer at the neighbouring holiday villages.

Facilities

Modern toilet block with facilities for disabled visitors. Preset showers in large cubicles. Washing machines and dryers. Small shop. Takeaway. Play area. Multisports area. Communal barbecues, picnic area and dog walking area. Free shuttle bus to neighbouring parks. WiFi throughout (charged). Off site: Nearest beach 900 m. Oasis Pool and Leisure Complex, indoor pools, funfair, bars, restaurants, entertainment and kids' club. Bicycle hire. Tennis.

Open: 1 March - 7 January.

Directions

Head for Chichester on A27. At Whyke roundabout join B2145 and follow signs to Selsey. At Selsey go across mini-roundabout and continue past entrance to Bunn Leisure. After next mini-roundabout take 2nd right (School Lane), right again (Paddock Lane) and then first left into Warner Lane. Follow signs to park (signed from Selsey). GPS: 50.73815, -0.79913

Charges guide

Per unit incl. up to 4 persons and electricity	£ 25.00 - £ 60.00

For latest campsite news visit

alanrogers.com

Dover

Hawthorn Farm Caravan & Camping Site

Martin Mill, Dover CT15 5LA (Kent) T: 01304 852658. E: info@keatfarm.co.uk

alanrogers.com/UK3100

Hawthorn Farm is a large, relaxed park near Dover. Set in 28 acres, it is an extensive park taking 226 touring units of any type on several large meadows which could accommodate far more, plus 160 privately owned caravan holiday homes in their own areas. Campers not requiring electricity choose their own spot, most staying near the toilet blocks, leaving the farthest fields to those liking solitude. There are 112 pitches with 10/16A electricity, 46 of which are large and separated by hedges, with the remainder in glades on either side of tarmac roads. There are 15 hardstandings available. A well run, relaxed park with plenty of room, mature hedging and trees make an attractive environment. A torch would be useful. Being only four miles from Dover docks, it is a very useful park for those using the ferries and is popular with continental visitors. Close to the sea at Saint Margaret's Bay, it is a fairly quiet situation apart from some rail noise (no trains 23.30-05.30).

Facilities

Two heated toilet blocks are well equipped and of good quality. Facilities for disabled visitors. Baby room. Launderette. Motorcaravan services. Breakfast and other meals are served at the shop (all season). Gates close at 20.00 (22.00 in July/Aug), £10 deposit for gate card. Caravan storage. WiFi throughout (charged). Off site: Martin Mill railway station 500 yds. Riding 0.5 miles. Golf 3 miles. Bicycle hire, fishing and boat launching 4 miles. Dover cliffs and castle. Walmer Castle.

Open: All year.

Directions

Park is north of the A258 road (Dover-Deal). Park and Martin Mill are signed at the turn, 4 miles from Dover. GPS: 51.16855, 1.346333

Charges guide

Per unit incl. 2 persons	
and electricity	£ 18.00 - £ 22.00
extra person	£ 4.00
child (5-16 yrs)	£ 3.00
dog	£ 2.00

Less 10% for 4 nights booked and paid in advance.

East Horsley

Horsley Camping & Caravanning Club Site

Ockham Road North, East Horsley KT24 6PE (Surrey) T: 01483 283273.

alanrogers.com/UK2820

London and all the sights are only 40 minutes away by train, yet Horsley is a delightful, quiet, unspoilt site with a good duck and goose population on its part lily-covered lake (unfenced). It provides 130 pitches, of which 73 have 10A electricity connections and 64 are on hardstandings. Seventeen pitches are around the bank of the lake (persons over 12 years only), the remainder are further back in three hedged, grass fields with mostly level ground but with some slopes in places. There is a range of mature trees and a woodland dog walk area (may be muddy). The soil is clay based so rain tends to settle – sluice gates remove extra water from the lake area when the rain is heavy.

Facilities

Two purpose built, heated sanitary blocks (main one undergoing refurbishment in August 2015), with good design and fittings, have some washbasins in cabins, a Belfast sink and parent and child room with vanity style basin and WC. Laundry room and new drying areas. Well designed facilities for disabled visitors. Small shop in reception. New play area. Recreation hall with table tennis. Two fully equipped tents for hire (sleep 6). Fishing is possible from 1/5 (adult £7/children £3.50 per day, NRA licence required). WiFi (charged). Off site: Shops and the station are 1 mile. Pubs 1.5-2 miles. Golf 1.5 miles. Riding 2 miles.

Open: 24 March - 31 October.

Directions

From M25 exit 10, towards Guildford, after 0.5 miles take first left B2039 to Ockham and East Horsley, continuing through Ockham towards East Horsley. After 2 miles start to watch for brown site sign (not easy to see) and site is on right in 2.5 miles (along a private lane). GPS: 51.28504, -0.44869

Charges guide

Per unit incl. 2 persons and electricity	£ 18.70 - £ 31.85
extra person	£ 7.15 - £ 12.15
child (6-18 yrs)	£ 3.55 - £ 6.00

Non-member prices are higher.

Eastbourne

Fairfields Farm Caravan & Camping Park

Eastbourne Road, Westham, Pevensey BN24 5NG (East Sussex) T: 01323 763165.

E: enquiries@fairfieldsfarm.com **alanrogers.com/UK2915**

Part of a working, family run farm, this is a simple peaceful park which is ideally located to enjoy the Sussex countryside and coast, just a short distance from Eastbourne. A single, rectangular meadow is split by a line of attractive silver birch trees and provides 66 large grass pitches, all but four with electricity connections. The farm and its rural landscape stretch towards the sea at Pevensey Bay. Beyond the camping field there is a duck pond with grassy surrounds and picnic benches, pens with numerous small animals and pets and a pleasant walk to a fishing lake. Children are invited to feed the animals (with special food on sale). Within walking distance are the villages of Westham and Pevensey with a choice of pubs and restaurants, as well as Pevensey Castle which has a history spanning 16 centuries. Eastbourne has a promenade, beautiful beaches and a retail complex and cinema at the Sovereign Centre.

Facilities

The single, central toilet block is traditional in style and very clean. An adjacent building houses showers and toilets for disabled visitors. Laundry facilities. Well stocked farm shop selling local produce. Small animals and pets. Fishing lake (licence required). WiFi throughout (free). Vans, commercial or sign-written vehicles are not accepted. Off site: Pubs, restaurants and fish and chip shop within walking distance. Beach 1.5 miles. Sailing 2 miles. Golf 4 miles. Eastbourne 5 miles.

Open: 1 April - 31 October.

Directions

From the roundabout junction of the A27 and A259 (petrol station) take exit to Pevensey and the castle. Go around the castle walls and into Westham village. At end of high street turn left (B2191), over level crossing and park is on left. GPS: 50.81358, 0.32448

Charges guide

Per unit incl. 2 persons and electricity	£ 22.00 - £ 25.00
extra person	£ 3.00
child (3-13 yrs)	£ 2.50
dog	£ 2.50

FREE WiFi

FAIRFIELDS FARM

CARAVAN & CAMPING PARK

This seasonal touring park provides good, clean facilities in peaceful surroundings. On site you will find a duck pond, farm pets, beautiful lakeside walk and free fishing.

Eastbourne Road - Westham - Pevensey - East Sussex - BN24 5NG
Tel: 01323 763165 - enquiries@fairfieldsfarm.com - www.fairfieldsfarm.com

For latest campsite news visit
alanrogers.com

Eastbourne
Bay View Park

Old Martello Road, Pevensey Bay BN24 6DX (East Sussex) T: 01323 768688. E: holidays@bay-view.co.uk

alanrogers.com/UK2920

This friendly, beachside park is located at the end of a private road right beside the beautiful Sussex coast and its pebble beach and the park's own brand new 9-hole golf course. Two separate areas of grass (some areas are a little uneven) are surrounded by low banks and hedges to give some shelter if it is windy. Careful use of wooden fencing adds to the attractiveness whilst also keeping the rabbits off the flowers. The 94 touring pitches (80 sq.m, most with 16A electricity and some with hardstanding) are neatly marked and numbered. Several caravan holiday homes for hire are positioned at the back of the park. This is an ideal park for a family beach holiday. Couples and families only.

Facilities

Each area has toilet facilities, one fully equipped block has private cubicles (shower, washbasin and WC) and facilities for babies and disabled visitors. Heated when required, both blocks are kept very clean. Laundry room. Motorcaravan services. Shop. Golf (9 holes). Clubhouse for tea, coffee and snacks. Gas. Play area. Winter caravan storage. Free WiFi on part of site. Off site: Sailing club. Sea fishing. Indoor swimming pool 1 mile. Riding 5 miles.

Open: 1 March - 31 October.

Directions

From the A27/A259 roundabout at Pevensey take A259 through Pevensey Bay. Park and golf course are signed after 1 mile (private access road) to the left. GPS: 50.79998, 0.33797

Charges guide

Per unit incl. 2 persons and electricity	£ 21.00 - £ 26.00
extra person	£ 5.00

No commercial vehicles, large vans or pick-ups.

Folkestone
Black Horse Farm Caravan Club Site

385 Canterbury Road, Densole CT18 7BG (Kent) T: 01303 892665.

alanrogers.com/UK3090

This neat, tidy and attractive six-acre park, owned by The Caravan Club, is situated amidst farming country in the village of Densole on the Downs, just four miles north of Folkestone, eight west of Dover and 11 south of Canterbury. Accessed directly from the A260, the entrance road leads towards the top field which has gravel hardstanding pitches with a grass area for awnings (there is some road noise from the A260), past hedging to the smaller middle area, then to the large bottom field which has been redeveloped to give some larger pitches (15 for tents) and some to accommodate larger motorcaravans. There are 119 pitches in total, 95 with hardstanding, all with 16A electricity and 11 serviced.

Facilities

Two sanitary blocks have washbasins in private cabins with curtains, good sized shower compartments, a baby room and facilities for disabled visitors and laundry facilities, all well heated in cool weather. Motorcaravan services. Gas supplies. Play area. A fish and chip van calls on Thurs. (April-Sept). Caravan storage. WiFi throughout (charged). Off site: Riding 1 mile. Golf and fishing 5 miles. Battle of Britain Museum 2 miles.

Open: All year.

Directions

Directly by the A260 Folkestone-Canterbury road, 2 miles north of junction with A20. Follow signs for Canterbury. GPS: 51.13307, 1.15716

Charges guide

Per person	£ 4.80 - £ 7.00
child (5-17 yrs)	£ 0.01 - £ 2.50
pitch incl. electricity (non-member)	£ 15.50 - £ 19.10

Folkestone
Little Satmar Holiday Park

Winehouse Lane, Capel-le-Ferne, Folkestone CT18 7JF (Kent) T: 01303 251188. E: info@keatfarm.co.uk

alanrogers.com/UK3095

Capel-le-Ferne is a relatively little known seaside town midway between Dover and Folkestone. Little Satmar is a quiet site a short walk from the delightful cliff top paths which run between these towns and which offer fine views across the English Channel. The site is a member of the Keat Farm group and is located about a mile from the village. There are 61 touring pitches, 51 of which have 10A electricity. The pitches generally have a sunny, open setting, a few with rather more shade. Privately owned mobile homes occupy 78 pitches near the entrance but these are quite separate from the touring field.

Facilities

Two toilet blocks (one with toilets only) are kept very clean. The main block is heated. Washing machines and dryers. Motorcaravan services. Gas (with gas). Play area. 'Bug Garden'. WIFi in part of site (charged). For more than 1 dog per unit, contact park. Off site: Bus at end of lane to Dover and Folkestone. Battle of Britain Memorial. Dover Castle. Port Lympne Zoo.

Open: 15 February - 15 December.

Directions

Leave A20 Dover-Folkestone road at Capel-le-Ferne exit and follow signs to the village. Site is clearly signed to right after 0.75 miles. GPS: 51.10718, 1.22068

Charges guide

Per unit incl. 2 persons and electricity	£ 18.00 - £ 22.00
extra person	£ 4.00

For latest campsite news visit
alanrogers.com

Heathfield

Horam Manor Touring Park

Horam, Heathfield TN21 0YD (East Sussex) T: 01435 813662. E: camp@horam-manor.co.uk

alanrogers.com/UK2900

This family run park is situated on a manor estate, perfect for touring East Sussex. The first field now offers level pitches throughout, all with 16A hook-ups and including 20 hardstandings. In total there are 100 spacious pitches, 65 with electricity. A brand new toilet block has underfloor heating, large showers, private washing cubicles and carefully designed facilities for disabled visitors. The park is set back from the main road and is a haven of peace and tranquillity, although in high season it becomes busy. For younger visitors there is a play area. On the manor estate, amenities include horse riding, fishing, the Lakeside Café and peaceful walks through the woods.

Facilities

Two toilet blocks, one of which is new and heated and includes private cubicles, large showers and a room for disabled visitors. Family room with shower, washbasin, toilet and baby bath. Gas supplies. Shop (1/3-31/10). WiFi throughout (free). Off site: Horam Manor adjacent with café, fishing and riding. Shops and inns within walking distance. Tennis 200 yds. Golf within 1 mile. Brighton, Hastings and Eastbourne are within easy reach.

Open: 1 March - 31 October.

Directions

Horam is on the A267 between Tunbridge Wells and Eastbourne and entry to the park is signed at the recreation ground at southern edge of the village. GPS: 50.931783, 0.240167

Charges guide

Per unit incl. 2 adults, 2 children and electricity	£ 24.50 - £ 28.25
extra person	£ 3.50 - £ 7.00

Horsham

Sumners Ponds Campsite and Fishery

Chapel Road, Barns Green, Horsham RH13 0PR (West Sussex) T: 01403 732539.
E: bookings@sumnersponds.co.uk **alanrogers.com/UK2935**

Established around a farm and fishing lake in the glorious Sussex countryside, Sumners Ponds has been developed into a first class campsite, offering tranquil surroundings for the angler and fun camping for the family. Over 100 standard (53 hardstanding) and 15 premium lakeside pitches are supplemented by a selection of imaginative wooden pods and chalets. The newer areas of the site and the children's playground are at a safe distance from the main lake. Sumners is a working farm with a herd of beef cattle – a source of fascination and education for younger campers.

Facilities

Two toilet blocks with hot water, heated sanitary block. Washing machines and dryers. Motorcaravan services. Gas. Caravan storage. Shop for angling supplies and camping essentials. Café open all day with takeaway and small bar. WiFi. Off site: Supermarket and a pub within 1 mile. Golf, riding and watersports within 5 miles. The south coast is approximately 20 miles.

Open: All year.

Directions

Barn Green lies approximately 3 miles northeast of Billingshurst. From A29, just north of Billingshurst take New Road, signed to Barn Green and arriving at village turn left into Chapel Road and left again into site. GPS: 51.028521, -0.398517

Charges guide

Per unit incl. 2 persons and electricity	£ 21.50 - £ 34.50
extra person	£ 4.50 - £ 7.50

Horsham

Honeybridge Park

Honeybridge Lane, Dial Post, Horsham RH13 8NX (West Sussex) T: 01403 710923.
E: enquiries@honeybridgepark.co.uk **alanrogers.com/UK2940**

This 15-acre park is situated amidst beautiful woodlands and countryside on the edge of the South Downs, within an Area of Outstanding Natural Beauty. Of the 150 pitches, 97 are for touring, some are on hardstandings and all have 16A electricity. The remaining pitches are occupied by holiday homes but these are in a separate area. Some pitches are hedged for privacy, others are on slightly sloping grass, well spaced and generously sized. A large wooden, adventure-style playground is provided for children away from the pitches and simple family entertainment is organised on special occasions.

Facilities

Two modern toilet facilities are heated in cool weather and include spacious facilities for disabled visitors (Radar key). Laundry facilities. Motorcaravan services. Licensed shop and café (1/3-31/10). Play area. Games room with library. Security barrier (card access) is locked 23.00-07.00. Caravan for hire. WiFi at café. Off site: Bus 0.5 miles. Pub/restaurant in nearby Dial Post village. Old Barn Nurseries serves meals during the day. Fishing 1 mile.

Open: All year.

Directions

Two miles south of the junction of A24 and A272 at Dial Post, turn east by Old Barn Nurseries. Follow signs to site (about 0.5 miles). GPS: 50.94864, -0.35274

Charges guide

Per unit incl. 2 persons and electricity	£ 19.60 - £ 28.40
extra person	£ 3.40 - £ 7.80
Barrier card (£10 deposit).	

For latest campsite news visit

alanrogers.com

Lydd

Romney Farm Caravan & Camp Site

Romney Road, Lydd, Kent TN29 9LS (Kent) T: 01797 361499. E: info@romneyfarm.com

alanrogers.com/UK3076

Situated just off the A259 coast road on Romney Marsh, this is an ideal base for exploring the south coast area as well as making a good stopover to and from the Dover ferries and the Folkestone Channel Tunnel terminal. There are 47 level grass pitches, 17 with 10A electricity hook-ups. The site also has three camping pods for rent. Romney Farm is a small, family run site with a homely and charming atmosphere – the local steam railway can be seen and heard from your pitch. Although the busy A259 is close, there is minimal noise from the traffic.

Facilities

Single wooden toilet block includes basic facilities for disabled campers. Two unisex units are in the nearby barn and open in peak season. Motorcaravan services. Fridge and freezer available for use. Privately owned café open peak times. Excellent tourist information room. WiFi (free). Off site: RSPB Dungeness. Romney, Hythe and Dymchurch steam railway. Dungeness lighthouse. Historic churches. Local pubs.

Open: April - September.

Directions

From Dover follow Folkestone A259 through New Romney, turn left B2075, site is 700 yds on right. From Hastings follow coast road A259 through Rye to Lydd on B2075, past Lydd airport, site is 1 mile on left. GPS: 51.17666, 0.968055

Charges guide

Per unit incl. 2 persons and electricity	£ 15.00 - £ 25.00
extra person	£ 4.00 - £ 6.50

Marden

Tanner Farm Touring Caravan & Camping Park

Goudhurst Road, Marden TN12 9ND (Kent) T: 01622 832399. E: enquiries@tannerfarmpark.co.uk

alanrogers.com/UK3030

Tanner Farm is a quality park, surrounded by arable farmland and orchards, oast houses, lovely countryside and delightful small villages in the beautiful Weald of Kent. The park extends over 15 acres, most of which is level and part is a gentle slope. The grass meadowland has been semi-landscaped by planting saplings, which units back onto, as the owners do not wish to regiment pitches into rows. There are 120 pitches, all with 16A electricity, 40 with hardstanding and 12 with water and waste water. A member of Best of British and Countryside Discovery groups.

Facilities

Two heated, well cared for toilet blocks include some washbasins in private cubicles. Facilities for disabled visitors. Family shower room and baby/toddler facilities in the newer block (not open Nov-Easter). Launderette. Motorcaravan services. Reception, shop and tourist information building (limited hours and stock in winter). Play area. WiFi over site (charged). Off site: Riding and golf within 6 miles. Leisure centres nearby.

Open: All year.

Directions

Park is 2.5 miles south of Marden on B2079 towards Goudhurst. GPS: 51.1471, 0.47482

Charges guide

Per person	£ 6.30 - £ 8.30
child (5-16 yrs)	£ 1.85 - £ 2.95
pitch incl. electricity (non-member)	£ 6.15 - £ 13.35
tent pitch incl. electricity	£ 6.80 - £ 13.35
Only one car per pitch permitted.	

Paddock Wood

The Hop Farm Touring & Camping Park

Maidstone Road, Paddock Wood TN12 6PY (Kent) T: 01622 870838. E: touring@thehopfarm.co.uk

alanrogers.com/UK3055

Set in 400 acres of the Garden of England, The Hop Farm is a popular family visitor attraction. There are plenty of activities to entertain children including adventure play areas (indoor and outdoor), a driving school, funfair rides, the Magic Factory and the Great Goblin Hunt. This is also the venue for many special events throughout the summer including music festivals, shows and other gatherings. To one side, and overlooking all this activity and the attractive cluster of oasts, is the touring park, which provides over 300 grass and hardstanding pitches on flat, open fields. Electricity (16A) and water are available. There is also plenty more space for tents.

Facilities

Brick built toilet block with open washbasins, preset showers (with curtain) and toilets. Further prefabricated units when the park is full for events. Small shop (in reception) for essentials. Free entry for campers and caravanners to the Family Park, with restaurant and café. Nature walks. Boat launching. Fishing. Dogs accepted but not permitted inside the visitor attraction. Off site: Shops, restaurants and golf courses nearby.

Open: 1 March - 31 October.

Directions

The Hop Farm is located on the A228 near Paddock Wood. Follow the brown tourist signs from exit 4 of the M20 or exit 5 of the M25 onto the A21 south. GPS: 51.200725, 0.39333

Charges guide

Per unit incl. 4 persons and electricity	£ 19.50 - £ 23.50
extra person (over 3 yrs)	£ 2.75
dog	£ 1.75

For latest campsite news visit

alanrogers.com

Redhill

Alderstead Heath Caravan Club Site

Dean Lane, Merstham, Redhill RH1 3AH (Surrey) T: 01737 644629. E: aldersteadheath@caravanclub.co.uk
alanrogers.com/UK2800

Alderstead Heath is a surprisingly rural site given that it lies just 35 minutes from central London by train. It is also well located for exploring the North Downs and is situated on the Pilgrim's Way. There are 161 touring pitches, all with 16A electricity connections. Most pitches are on well kept grass and there are also 68 hardstandings. Given the proximity of the M25 and M23 motorways, this is a convenient stop en route to and from Dover. There are numerous walks and cycle routes to explore in the area. Part of the site is used for seasonal pitches.

Facilities

Two well maintained toilet blocks include a family bathroom. The main block houses facilities for disabled visitors. Laundry facilities. Motorcaravan services. Reception stocks a small range of essential foods, milk and gas. Two small play areas. Football field. Good tourist information room. WiFi throughout (charged). Off site: Golf 2 miles. Fishing 3 miles.

Open: All year.

Directions

Leave M25 at exit 8 and join A217 (Reigate). Fork left after 300 yds (Merstham). After a further 2.5 miles turn left at T-junction and join A23. After 500 yds, right on B2031 Shepherd's Hill (Caterham) and after 1 mile left into Dean Lane. Site on right after 175 yds. Avoid sat nav route via M23/A23 (J7) where Dean Lane is very narrow. GPS: 51.2832, -0.13888

Charges guide

Per person	£ 5.00 - £ 6.90
pitch incl. electricity (non-member)	£ 15.70 - £ 19.00

Sevenoaks

Thriftwood Holiday Park

Plaxdale Green Road, Stansted, Sevenoaks TN15 7PB (Kent) T: 01732 822261.
E: info@thriftwoodholidaypark.com **alanrogers.com/UK3038**

Thriftwood Holiday Park is a well located base for exploring Kent and has good access to a major motorway network. London can be reached in around 50 minutes from Borough Green station (two miles). There is an attractive touring area here with a good number of hardstandings available and grassy tent pitches around the edge. Some pitches may require the use of levelling blocks. Around 150 pitches have electrical connections. The toilet block has recently been refurbished to a very high standard. Amenities include a swimming pool and a convivial bar/club house where meals may be ordered. There is some entertainment, mainly in high season. The historic town of Sevenoaks is within easy reach along with its magnificent Elizabethan place, Knole House. Tonbridge and Royal Tunbridge Wells are also close at hand, and, by way of contrast, the large shopping centres at Bluewater and Lakeside are easily accessible, as well as Brands Hatch racing circuit.

Facilities

Recently refurbished toilet block with facilities for disabled visitors. Shop (in reception). Bar/snack bar/club house. Swimming pool (Easter-end Sept). Play area. Games arcade. Nature walks. Mobile homes for rent. Off site: Hotel/restaurant 150 yds. All amenities and railway station in Borough Green 2 miles. Brands Hatch 2 miles. Fishing 3 miles. Golf 5 miles.

Open: All year.

Directions

Leave M20 motorway at exit 2 and take northbound A20 towards West Kingsdown and Brands Hatch. After passing across 2 roundabouts, turn right into Labour in Vain Road and follow signs to the site. GPS: 51.324233, 0.292382

Charges guide

Per unit incl. 2 persons and electricity	£ 25.00 - £ 30.00
extra person	£ 5.00
child (5-12 yrs)	£ 2.00 - £ 5.00

For latest campsite news visit
alanrogers.com

Sevenoaks
Gate House Wood Touring Park

Ford Lane, Wrotham Heath, Sevenoaks TN15 7SD (Kent) T: 01732 843062.
E: contact@gatehousewoodtouringpark.com **alanrogers.com/UK3120**

This sheltered park has been created in a former quarry where all the pitches are on well drained grass. A spacious paved entrance with an attractive reception building and well stocked shop leads on to the park itself. The 54 pitches are level and open with a few small trees, two brick built barbecue units and 36 electricity hook-ups (10A). A playground has swings, a seesaw and a slide, all set on a safety base, and the entire site is enclosed by grassy banks on three sides with a wild flower walk around the top.

Facilities

Comprehensive toilet facilities are well maintained, including a well equipped room which is designed for disabled visitors. Laundry facilities. Shop (in reception) has fresh bread daily. Play area. WiFi (charged). No dogs or other pets. Caravans/motorcaravans greater than 28 ft. overall are not admitted. Commercial vehicles are not accepted. Off site: Within walking distance are three pubs and a good Cantonese restaurant. Golf 1 mile. Riding 3 miles. Fishing 7 miles.

Open: 1 March - 31 October.

Directions

From M26 exit 2a, take A20 eastwards towards Wrotham Heath and Maidstone. Just past junction with A25, and opposite the Royal Oak pub, turn left into Ford Lane and park is immediately on left. GPS: 51.300133, 0.345383

Charges guide

Per unit incl. 2 persons and electricity	£ 18.50 - £ 23.50
extra person	£ 5.00

No credit cards.

Washington
Washington Caravan & Camping Park

Old London Road, Washington RH20 4AJ (West Sussex) T: 01903 892869.
E: washingtoncampsite@yahoo.co.uk **alanrogers.com/UK2950**

Washington is a pleasant campsite to the north of Worthing with a bias towards tenting families and groups. It provides only 21 hardstanding pitches for caravans and motorcaravans and a large gently sloping grassy field with enough space for 40 tents. There are 23 electric hook-ups (16A, on meter £1.00). There is some road noise from the A24. Local attractions (all with free admission, check opening times) include Highdown Chalk Gardens at Worthing, Nutbourne Vineyard near Pulborough, and Steyning Museum. Parham House is another beautiful privately owned house and garden worthy of a visit. Brighton with its famous Pavilion, plenty of shops and seafront is within easy reach.

Facilities

A heated, wooden chalet-style building houses the sanitary facilities including spacious shower rooms (20p) and indoor dishwashing and laundry facilities. No on-site shop but eggs available from the reception office. Hot drinks machine and freezer. Off site: Bus stop 200 yds in village. Local pub and a nearby restaurant. Beach 9 miles.

Open: All year.

Directions

Site entrance is just east of the junction of A24 and A283 at Washington, 6 miles north of Worthing. GPS: 50.90875, -0.4056

Charges guide

Per unit incl. 2 persons	£ 21.00
extra person	£ 5.00
electricity on meter	£ 1.00

West Wittering
Nunnington Farm Campsite

Rookwood Road, West Wittering PO20 8LZ (West Sussex) T: 01243 514013.
E: enquiries@nunningtonfarm.com **alanrogers.com/UK2895**

This no-frills, basic, family run farm site for touring units only, can be found on the coast a mere seven miles from Chichester. There are 200 touring pitches, 110 with 15A electricity connections. The pitches are large, level and grassy, providing a comfortable feeling, even when the site is full. The safe, sandy beaches of The Witterings, only a mile away, make this an especially good venue for families in the holidays and a quieter one for off-season visitors. The easily accessible pets' corner is an attraction for children of all ages. Visitors with tents are very welcome here and a second field is opened in busy periods, but has no electricity.

Facilities

Three clean, central toilet blocks provide all facilities including showers in cubicles, open washbasins, baby bath, washing machines and ramped facilities for disabled visitors (key access). Motorcaravan services. Gates closed 23.00-07.00. WiFi (free). Off site: Local shops 300 yds. Bus service to Chichester every 30 minutes. Beach and boat mooring 1 mile. Bicycle hire 2 miles. Golf 3 miles.

Open: Easter - second week October.

Directions

From A27 at Chichester, take A286 signed The Witterings and continue to roundabout. Take second exit on B2179 for West Wittering and site is on left after 2 miles. NB Continue to site entrance, do not turn into farm access. GPS: 50.78377, -0.88588

Charges guide

Per unit incl. 2 persons and electricity	£ 22.00 - £ 25.00
extra person	£ 5.00

No credit cards.

For latest campsite news visit
alanrogers.com

WE HAVE CHOSEN FIVE PARKS WHICH HAVE EASY ACCESS TO CENTRAL LONDON, INCLUDING ONE IN HERTFORDSHIRE

The largest city in Europe, covering over 600 square miles, London is jam packed with hundreds of magnificent museums, impressive art galleries, historic buildings and monuments, beautiful parks, bustling shopping centres and markets; it really has something to offer everyone.

Despite its size, London is relatively easy to explore, largely thanks to the efficient underground service. Buses are also very useful and allow you to see the famous sights as you travel, in particular, the open-top tourist buses which ply the streets offer a good introduction to the city. Among London's many landmarks are the Tower of London, Trafalgar Square, Piccadilly Circus, Buckingham Palace, Big Ben and the Houses of Parliament, to name but a few! Running through the heart of London is the River Thames, dividing north and south; over the years many attractions, restaurants and chic bars have appeared along its banks. Being one of the most multicultural cities in the world, there is a huge choice of restaurants offering a diverse variety of cuisine; food markets are dotted all around the capital. Shopping is another major feature of the city, from the famous Harrods store and Harvey Nichols, to commercial Oxford Street and the street markets of Camden Town and Portobello Road. If all the crowds become too much then head to one of London's beautiful parks such as St. James's Park next to Buckingham Palace, or Hyde Park, where you can take a boat trip along the Serpentine.

Places of interest

London Eye: world's highest observation wheel, reaching 443 feet. With 32 capsules, carrying 25 passengers in each, it offers breathtaking views.

Tower of London: home of the Crown Jewels and the Yeoman Warders.

Tate Modern: contemporary art gallery housed in the converted Bankside Power Station.

Natural History Museum: over 70 million items relating to the life and earth sciences.

Kew Gardens: beautiful botanical gardens, with over 40,000 varieties of plants.

Imperial War Museum: charting the impact of conflict from WWI to the present day.

Hampton Court Palace: one of the best palaces in Britain, with a maze.

British Museum: houses a treasure trove of objects from all over the globe.

Did you know?

One in eight of the UK population live in London and over 300 languages are spoken.

Following expansion in the 1930s and '40s, less than 50% of London's Underground railway is actually below ground.

Founded in 1753, the British Museum is the oldest public museum in the world.

The Great Fire of London destroyed over 13,000 houses and 87 churches.

London's licensed taxi drivers have to pass a test known as the Knowledge, which requires them to learn over 300 routes in the centre of the city.

At over 900 years old, the Tower of London has been a palace, prison, treasury, arsenal and even a zoo.

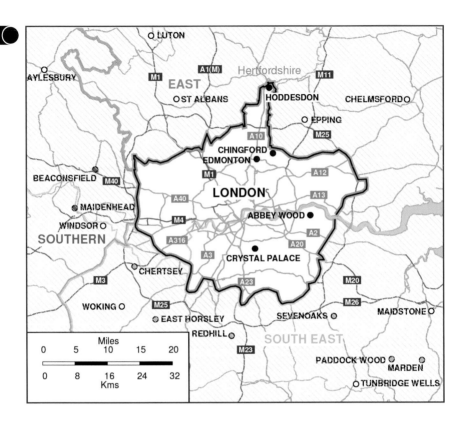

Abbey Wood
Abbey Wood Caravan Club Site

Federation Road, London SE2 0LS (London) T: 02083 117708.

alanrogers.com/UK3260

Situated close to Abbey Wood, it is hard to believe that this park is in London and the wardens have made every effort to create an attractive environment. There are 156 level caravan pitches, all with 16A electricity and TV aerial connections; of these, 73 are hardstanding. A tent area provides 50 pitches. Many benefit from the shade of mature trees. A secure fence around the perimeter is linked to closed-circuit TV cameras, and just outside is a late arrivals area with electricity and toilets, also protected by cameras. A number of camping pods are now available to rent. This park attracts many UK and overseas visitors as it offers a very good base from which to visit central London. A train service runs every 15 minutes from Abbey Wood station (5 minutes' walk) to either Charing Cross or Cannon Street (around 35 minutes).

Facilities

Three modern, fully equipped sanitary blocks, two with underfloor heating, one designed to be open all year, include washbasins in cubicles, generous showers and baby/toddler washroom. Good private facilities for disabled visitors. Laundry facilities. Motorcaravan services. Gas. Bread, milk and cold drinks from reception (high season). Play area. Good travel and information centre. WiFi over site (charged). Off site: Sports centre 1 mile. Golf 4 miles. National Cycle Network.

Open: All year.

Directions

From east on M2/A2 or from central London: on A2 (third exit) turn off at A221 into Danson Road (Bexleyheath, Welling, Sidcup). Follow Bexleyheath sign to Crook Log (A207 junction); at lights turn right and immediately left (Brampton Road). In 1.5 miles at lights turn left into Bostal Road (A206); in 0.75 miles at traffic lights turn right into Basildon Road (B213). In 300 yds. turn right into McLeod Road, in 0.5 miles at roundabout turn right into Knee Hill; in 100 yds. take second right into Federation Road. Site on left in 50 yds. From M25, north, west or south approach: leave at exit 2 onto A2 (signed London), then as above. GPS: 51.48635, 0.11971

Charges guide

Per person	£ 6.50 - £ 8.60
child (5-17 yrs)	£ 0.01 - £ 3.50
pitch incl. electricity (non-member)	£ 17.60 - £ 21.00

Tent campers apply to site.

Chingford
Lee Valley Campsite

Sewardstone Road, Chingford, London E4 7RA (London) T: 020 8529 5689.
E: sewardstonecampsite@leevalleypark.org.uk **alanrogers.com/UK3250**

This attractive site provides an excellent base from which to visit London, having both easy access to the M25 and excellent public transport links into the centre of London. Close to Epping Forest in the heart of the Lee Valley, this site is on a hillside overlooking the King George reservoir in a very pleasant and relaxed setting. Like its sister sites, it is understandably very popular with foreign tourers. With capacity for 160 units, the site is mostly level, with several bush sheltered avenues and plenty of trees throughout providing shade. There are 65 pitches with hardstanding and 80 with 10A electricity. American motorhomes are welcome. Just outside the gate is a bus stop (May-September; reception have full details of good value Travelcard schemes). Staff are very pleasant and helpful.

Facilities

Two recently refurbished blocks offer good facilities (one is heated in low season). Good en-suite room for disabled visitors. Baby changing area. Laundry. Motorcaravan services. Well stocked shop. Takeaway food van 3 times a week. Gas available. Playground. Accommodation for rent. WiFi (charged). Off site: Fishing 500 yards. Shops within 2 miles. Riding 1 mile. 9-hole golf 1 mile, 18-hole golf 3 miles. Waltham Abbey 3 miles. River Lee Country Park and Epping Forest nearby.

Open: 1 March - 31 January.

Directions

From M25 take exit 26 on A112 to Chingford and site is on right in 3 miles.
GPS: 51.653983, -0.006517

Charges guide

Per unit incl. 2 persons	
and electricity	£ 18.00 - £ 26.00
extra person	£ 7.00 - £ 11.00
child (under 18 yrs)	£ 2.50 - £ 5.50
dog	£ 2.00

Min. charge £14 per unit/night.

Crystal Palace
Crystal Palace Caravan Club Site

Crystal Palace Parade, London SE19 1UF (London) T: 02087 787155. E: crystalpalace@caravanclub.co.uk
alanrogers.com/UK3270

The Caravan Club's site at Crystal Palace in south London provides easy access to the city centre and its many attractions. The 89 pitches are pleasantly arranged in terraces adjacent to the ruins of the old Crystal Palace, its park and National Sports Centre, and are allocated by the site warden. It is surprisingly quiet given its location (with the exception of police sirens and over-flying aircraft). Advance booking is advisable all year round. Sixty pitches are on gravel hardstandings, useful for stays out of season. There are places for 71 caravans and motorcaravans, all with 16A electricity, and 18 for tents. The Crystal Palace park is extensive and provides open spaces for strolls and picnics.

Facilities

The main sanitary block can be heated in cool weather and has curtained washbasins for ladies. Another seasonal block provides basic unisex showers and toilets. Facilities for disabled visitors. Laundry room. Motorcaravan services. Small shop in reception. Gas. WiFi over site (charged). Off site: Shops, pubs, etc. 400 yds. Many buses stop outside the site, including services to central London (all-night service). National Cycle Network.

Open: All year.

Directions

On A205 South Circular travelling east, pass Dulwich College and golf course, turn right at traffic lights. Within 400 yds, at lights, turn right into Sydenham Hill. In 350 yds. at roundabout turn right. Site is 1 mile opposite mini-roundabouts. Travelling west on A205 South Circular, immediately after passing under Catford railway bridge, keep left onto A212 (Crystal Palace). After 2.75 miles, site is on left.
GPS: 51.42503, -0.07315

Charges guide

Per person	£ 5.00 - £ 8.80
child (5-17 yrs)	£ 1.30 - £ 3.50
pitch incl. electricity (non-member)	£ 21.00 - £ 26.00

Tent campers apply to site.

For latest campsite news visit
alanrogers.com

Edmonton
Lee Valley Camping & Caravanning Park

Meridian Way, Edmonton, London N9 0AR (London) T: 020 8803 6900.
E: edmontoncampsite@leevalleypark.org.uk **alanrogers.com/UK3230**

Certainly one of the only sites in this guide with a multiplex cinema just outside the gate, you are greeted here by a very attractive entrance with flower displays. The site offers 160 spacious level pitches, 44 with hardstanding and 100 with 10A electricity hook-ups. The pitches are well laid out around a large field and there is a tent area just behind two grassy mounds. The grass and gardens are well trimmed and kept very tidy. The site also offers hook-up points for tents. The adjacent sports complex has been rebuilt and was used for the 2012 Olympics. From the cinema complex you can hop on a bus to Edmonton Green or Ponders End station from where there is a regular service into central London (journey time around 40 minutes). This is a popular site, very well looked after and kept clean and tidy by site managers. It provides a peaceful stop within easy reach of the city.

Facilities

Two modern, heated toilet blocks include spacious showers and two large en-suite units for disabled visitors. Baby changing area. All facilities are accessed by combination locks. Laundry. Motorcaravan services. Shop. Play area. Accommodation available to rent. WiFi throughout (charged). Off site: Cinema at entrance. Golf adjacent. Supermarket and fishing 0.5 miles. Riding 4 miles.

Open: All year.

Directions

From M25 take exit 25. Follow signs for the city. At first set of traffic lights turn left (Freezywater). Continue on for 6 miles. Follow signs for Lee Valley Leisure Complex. After roundabout (where A110 crosses) turn left at second set of traffic lights onto the complex. Follow site signs.
GPS: 51.632383, -0.038383

Charges guide

Per unit incl. 2 persons and electricity	£ 32.00 - £ 48.00
extra person	£ 7.00 - £ 11.00
child (under 18 yrs)	£ 2.50 - £ 5.50
dog	£ 2.00

Min. charge £14 per unit/night.

Hoddesdon
Lee Valley Caravan Park

Essex Road, Dobbs Weir, Hoddesdon EN11 0AS (Hertfordshire) T: 01992 447988.
E: dobbsweircampsite@leevalleypark.org.uk **alanrogers.com/UK3210**

This large (27-acre) camping park is ideally situated in the Lee Valley for fishing, walking and cycling activities. It is divided into two sections: one for private static caravans with a large fenced caravan storage area, the other for touring. The 34 level touring pitches are numbered, but not separated; all have 10A electricity and 22 are hardstanding. There is an area for tents, with a field adjacent to the River Lee for tents requiring electricity. The whole complex is very flat with little shade. There is no public transport but a 25-minute walk along a towpath takes you to Broxbourne railway station for travel along the Lee Valley to London. Reception has a range of maps showing walking routes. Many of the villages and towns in the region are of historic interest and worth visiting.

Facilities

One modern, heated toilet block with controllable showers, open washbasins and facilities for disabled campers. Washing machines and dryers. Motorcaravan services. Small shop (open all season). Small play area. River fishing. Bicycle hire. WiFi over site (charged). Off site: Lee Valley Regional Park for watersports, fishing, walking and cycling. Golf 3 miles. Riding 9 miles. Olympic park and London (trains from Broxbourne 1.5 miles).

Open: 1 March - 31 January.

Directions

On M25 take exit 25 for Waltham Abbey, go north on A10 signed Hoddesdon, and exit on A1170 following signs for industrial area, then pick up signs for Dobbs Weir, the site is just before the weir on the right. GPS: 51.75374, 0.000134

Charges guide

Per person	£ 7.00 - £ 11.00
child (under 18 yrs)	£ 2.50 - £ 5.50
minimum charge	£ 14.00 - £ 22.00
dog	£ 2.00

Min. charge £13.50 (backpackers accepted). Checking out time 12 noon.

For latest campsite news visit
alanrogers.com

THIS REGION INCLUDES THE COUNTIES OF ESSEX, SUFFOLK, NORFOLK, CAMBRIDGESHIRE, HERTFORDSHIRE AND BEDFORDSHIRE

The East of England is a perfect mix of gentle countryside, ancient cities, historical towns and storybook villages. It is an unspoilt region with endless skies and a maze of inland waterways ideal for birdwatching and boating, while the traditional beach resorts offer old-fashioned seaside fun.

Bedfordshire and Hertfordshire are the smallest counties in the region, with peaceful canals, undulating countryside with chalk downs, and some of the greatest stately homes in the country. Essex is full of quaint villages with a smattering of old towns and traditional seaside resorts, including Colchester and Southend-on-Sea. The River Cam winds its way through Cambridgeshire; punting along the river in Cambridge is a good way to relax and take in the university buildings that dominate the waterfront along the 'Backs'. Further along the river is the ancient city of Ely, once an island before the Fen drainage. The flat Fenland has a network of rivers and canals, ideal for narrowboat trips, as are the Norfolk Broads. Norfolk itself is very flat, sparsely populated and tranquil, popular with walkers and cyclists, while the numerous nature reserves attract a variety of wildlife. It also has a beautiful coastline; the seaside towns of Great Yarmouth and Hunstanton are major draws. This unspoilt coastline stretches into Suffolk, 'Constable Country'. Full of space, with picturesque villages set amongst lush green countryside, dotted with timbered cottages and ruined abbeys, the county is home to Newmarket, the horse racing capital of the world.

Places of interest

Essex: Clacton-on-Sea; Walton-on-the-Naze, with nature reserve; Waltham Abbey; Epping; Chelmsford; Colchester.

Suffolk: Ipswich; Lowestoft; market town of Bury St Edmunds with Georgian theatre; Aldeburgh with its annual festival.

Norfolk: bustling city of Norwich; seaside resort of Great Yarmouth; waterways of the Norfolk Broads; Sandringham Palace near King's Lynn; Banham Zoo.

Cambridgeshire: museums, historic college buildings and punting in Cambridge; Ely cathedral and stained glass museum; Imperial War Museum in Duxford; St Ives riverside town with popular Monday market; Wildfowl & Wetlands Trust near Wisbech.

Hertfordshire: St Albans and nearby Butterfly World project; historic Knebworth House with gardens and miniature railway.

Bedfordshire: Wrest Park gardens; Woburn with abbey and safari park; Whipsnade Wild Animal Park; Shuttleworth Collection near Biggleswade with birds of prey.

Did you know?

Newmarket has been recognised as the Headquarters of Racing for over 300 years.

The tractor was invented in Biggleswade, Bedfordshire, in 1901 by Daniel Albone.

Danbury Common, Essex, is home to Britain's largest population of adders.

The artist, John Constable, was born in 1776 in the village of East Bergholt. Nearby Flatford Mill, was portrayed in his most famous scene, 'The Haywain'.

Oliver Cromwell's head is buried in an unmarked grave close to the entrance of Sidney Sussex College chapel, Cambridge.

Epping Forest was the haunt of the renowned highwayman, Dick Turpin.

Aldeburgh

Church Farm Holiday Park

Church Farm Road, Aldeburgh IP15 5DW (Suffolk) T: 01728 453433. E: aldeburgh@amberleisure.com

alanrogers.com/UK3350

This area of the Suffolk coast has always been a popular destination for visitors and Church Farm Holiday Park has an enviable location on the outskirts of Aldeburgh. The park includes a large area designated for caravan holiday homes as well as a separate touring area situated to the front of the park. The touring area provides 68 pitches for caravans and motorcaravans (tents and trailer tents are not accepted). Pitches are separated by attractive hedging that blends in well with the natural environment. Sixty-four pitches have 16A electricity, water, waste water and night light.

Facilities

The single toilet block has been fully upgraded with heating, free hot showers, toilets and washbasins (entry card with £10 deposit). Access to the toilets and showers are via two steps making it unsuitable for wheelchair users. Laundry room. Motorcaravan services. Large units by prior arrangement. WiFi over site. Off site: Beach 5 mins walk. Bus service 0.5-1 mile. Shops, pubs, etc. 15 mins. walk. Fishing 1 mile. Golf 2 miles. Bicycle 6 miles. Riding 15 miles.

Open: 1 April - 2 January.

Directions

On arrival at Aldeburgh, site is signed at roundabout towards Thorpeness. Where road meets seafront, site is on left. From town centre follow road along seafront to site on left at end of town. GPS: 52.15827, 1.60330

Charges guide

Per pitch incl. all persons	£ 12.00 - £ 26.00
incl. services	£ 20.00 - £ 34.00

Cheques are not accepted.
Credit cards 2.5% surcharge.

Banham
Applewood Countryside Holidays

Banham Zoo, The Grove, Banham NR16 2HE (Norfolk) T: 01953 888370. E: caravanpark@banhamzoo.co.uk
alanrogers.com/UK3385

Applewood is a 13-acre touring park adjacent to the famous Banham Zoo. One day's entrance fee gives unlimited access whilst on the campsite. Applewood has 200 pitches with 190 on level grass and ten on hardstanding; 120 have 10A electric hook-ups. The large central area has unmarked pitches for those who do not need electricity. Other pitches surrounding this area are in small groups separated by neat laurel hedges. There is a further area with pitches and a large field for rallies. A small number of camping pods are available for hire. Just four minutes walk from the park is a small supermarket, a pub with a restaurant, a fish and chip shop and gift shops.

Facilities

Two toilet blocks, one new and one refurbished, provide clean and adequate facilities. Room for disabled visitors. Washing machine and dryer. Motorcaravan services. Gas supplies. Rally field and function room. Play area. Free WiFi. Off site: Zoo adjacent. The Appleyard with shops and restaurant. Snetterton race circuit 3 miles.

Open: 14 February - 2 November.

Directions

Leave A11 at Attleborough, take B1077 south. Follow signs to Banham Zoo. At T-junction with B1113 turn west. Continue through Banham. Park is on the left, entrance through Banham Zoo (not clearly signed). GPS: 52.44636, 1.02514

Charges guide

Per unit incl. electricity	£ 18.50 - £ 23.95

Beccles
Waveney River Centre

Staithe Road, Burgh St Peter, Beccles NR34 0BT (Norfolk) T: 01502 677 343.
E: info@waveneyrivercentre.co.uk **alanrogers.com/UK3380**

Set in the Norfolk Broads adjacent to the River Waveney, this site has something for everybody but will particularly suit those interested in boating. There are 14 mainly level, grass touring pitches all with 16A electric hook-up, plus 35 large tent pitches, many with electricity. The facilities are of the highest standard and include an indoor swimming pool complex with a café. There is a recently refurbished pub that serves local Adnams ales and locally sourced food. A games arcade for children (in the pub), a wildlife garden and an adventure play area will keep children busy. There is boat hire available and launching facilities for own boats. A foot ferry service is available across to the marshes.

Facilities

Two very clean toilet blocks (both key access), one superbly fitted with 9 private rooms (WC, shower sink, hairdryer). Well equipped facilities for disabled visitors and families. A second smaller block has toilets and washbasins. Laundry facilities. Fully stocked shop. Pub serving food. Indoor heated swimming pool, café with pool viewing area and outside decking. Play area. Evening entertainment. Fishing allowed in open season (charged). Boat hire. WiFi. Luxury holiday lodges and pods for rent.

Open: All year.

Directions

Follow A143 (Beccles-Great Yarmouth) into Haddiscoe. Turn right at village hall into Wiggs Road, signed Waveney River Centre. After 2 miles turn left into Burgh Road. Proceed for 2.5 miles to site (with care along single track road with passing places). GPS: 52.481911, 1.6696

Charges guide

Per unit incl. 2 persons and electricity	£ 16.00 - £ 37.00
dog (max. 2)	£ 2.00

Bury Saint Edmunds
The Dell Caravan & Camping Park

Beyton Road, Thurston, Bury Saint Edmunds IP31 3RB (Suffolk) T: 01359 270121.
E: thedellcaravanpark@btinternet.com **alanrogers.com/UK3345**

Close to the A14 and surrounded by farmland, this small touring site, four miles east of Bury Saint Edmunds, provides a convenient base to explore the nearby town and surrounding villages, or as a stopover point. The owners have created 50 spacious pitches within the main touring area, which is divided into two sections – one of which is reserved for adults only. All pitches have 10A electricity. A separate field with a further ten pitches situated under trees is available for contractors working locally as well as any visitors who prefer shaded areas. The main touring field has some shade from well maintained hedges and the trees bordering the site. All pitches have access to the site's facilities.

Facilities

Excellent and ample toilets and spacious shower facilities (free) are provided within a purpose built sanitary block. Ladies' toilets include a private bathroom and toilet. Family bathroom with bath, shower and baby changing facilities. Separate toilet/shower for disabled visitors. Laundry room. Motorcaravan services. Off site: Bus service to Bury St Edmunds from outside park.

Open: 1 March - 31 October.

Directions

From A14 take exit for Thurston and Beyton, 4 miles east of Bury St Edmunds. Follow signs to Thurston. Park is on left, shortly after arriving at Thurston and signed from Beyton. GPS: 52.24053, 0.82437

Charges guide

Per unit incl. 2 persons and electricity	£ 16.00 - £ 20.00
extra person	£ 3.00

For latest campsite news visit
alanrogers.com

Cambridge

Cambridge Cherry Hinton Caravan Club Site

Lime Kiln Road, Cherry Hinton, Cambridge CB1 8NQ (Cambridgeshire) T: 01223 244088.
alanrogers.com/UK3562

Cherry Hinton is a compact, quiet and peaceful site, open to non members. It is set in a disused quarry surrounded by tall trees and wild flowers, yet close to the university city of Cambridge, with a frequent bus service just a few minutes' walk away. The site has 56 small to medium sized pitches mostly shaded by mature trees and shrubs. Six grass pitches are reserved for tents, 48 are on hardstanding and all have 16A electricity and a TV aerial point. There is an excellent heated sanitary block and a small shop but no other facilities. Cycling is very popular here.

Facilities

Clean and very well equipped, heated sanitary block has pushbutton showers and some washbasins in cubicles. Facilities for disabled campers. Baby room. Washing machine and dryer. Motorcaravan services. Basic shop sells camping supplies. WiFi over site (charged). Off site: Playground 400 yds. 24-hour supermarket 1 mile. Wide range of shops, bars, restaurants, museums, churches and ancient colleges in Cambridge.

Open: All year.

Directions

Leave M11, exit 11. east towards Cambridge on A1309. After 1.5 miles, at traffic lights, turn right (Long Road), signed Hospital. Cross roundabout, in 1 mile just before traffic lights turn sharp right (Lime Kiln Way). Site is on right. GPS: 52.18089, 0.16798

Charges guide

Per person	£ 5.90 - £ 7.90
child (5-17 yrs)	£ 0.01 - £ 2.80
pitch incl. electricity (non-member)	£ 16.00 - £ 19.70

Clacton-on-Sea

Homestead Lake Park

Thorpe Road, Weeley, Clacton-on-Sea CO16 9JN (Essex) T: 01255 833492.
E: lakepark@homesteadcaravans.co.uk **alanrogers.com/UK3300**

This well laid out, 25-acre park was opened in 2002. It is hidden from the road at the rear of Homestead Caravans' sales area and workshops in the countryside of the Tendring district, at Weeley near Clacton. It offers 50 fully serviced, hardstanding pitches on gently sloping ground overlooking a fishing lake and recently built holiday lodge accommodation on the other side of the lake. Tents accepted for short stays only on a limited number of pitches. The park makes an ideal spot to stay either for fishing, for a relaxing weekend or as a base for touring this part of Essex.

Facilities

The toilet block offers clean and spacious facilities including an en-suite unit for disabled visitors with baby changing facilities. Coffee shop/café and snack bar. Fishing lake. Woodland walks. Caravan sales, workshops and accessory shop. A large rally field is also available. Off site: The towns of Clacton-on-Sea, Frinton, Harwich and Brightlingsea are all within a 10-mile radius and the heart of 'Constable Country', with Flatford Mill and Dedham, is a short drive away.

Open: 1 March - 31 October.

Directions

From Colchester take A120, then A133 signed Clacton. At roundabout, turn left on B1033 into Weeley and site and showrooms are on left just past council offices. GPS: 51.85989, 1.12021

Charges guide

Per unit incl. 2 persons and electricity	£ 21.00 - £ 24.50
extra person	£ 5.00
child (under 18 yrs)	£ 3.00

Colchester

Fen Farm Caravan & Camping Site

Moore Lane, East Mersea, Colchester CO5 8FE (Essex) T: 01206 383275. E: havefun@fenfarm.co.uk
alanrogers.com/UK3290

Tents were first pitched at Fen Farm in 1923 and since then the park has 'grown rather than developed' – something of which owners Ralph and Wenda Lord and their family are proud. The 70 touring pitches are all unmarked, on level grass and within four fields that have a spacious feel to them. An area for 90 holiday homes is separate and screened from the touring area. All pitches have 10A electricity connections and three have hardstanding and are fully serviced. A limited number of seasonal pitches are available on the smaller field with outstanding views and direct access to the beach. This is an attractive well laid out site with trees and two ponds.

Facilities

The very good toilet block in the main touring field includes a family room and shower/toilet for disabled visitors. Laundry room. Gas supplies. Two play areas. Caravan and boat storage. WiFi throughout (charged). Off site: Well stocked shop adjacent sells groceries, bread and milk. 'Pick your own' fruit farm and tea room. Shops, pubs, restaurants and banks in West Mersea.

Open: 13 March - 31 October.

Directions

From Colchester, take B1025 to Mersea Island. Cross (tidal) causeway, take left fork to East Mersea. Follow road for 2.75 miles to Dog and Pheasant pub. Site entrance is next right. GPS: 51.78996, 0.98460

Charges guide

Per unit incl. up to 6 people and electricity	£ 18.00 - £ 27.00

For latest campsite news visit
alanrogers.com

Cambridge
Highfield Farm Touring Park

Long Road, Comberton, Cambridge CB23 7DG (Cambridgeshire) T: 01223 262308.
E: enquiries@highfieldfarmtouringpark.co.uk **alanrogers.com/UK3560**

The welcome is always warm from the friendly, family owners at this delightful eight-acre park. Situated only five miles from Cambridge, yet in a wonderfully quiet touring location, it is close to major routes around the city. The pitches are fairly level with 60 numbered pitches for caravans and motorcaravans, 42 with hardstanding, and 60 for tents. All have 10A electricity. The facilities are of high quality and the grass and hedges are well cared for. Conifer hedges divide the site into five areas. There are also some shady glades for those who wish to retreat even further and one area is reserved for those without children. A good dog walk is provided, which can be extended to a pleasant 1.5 mile walk, with seats, around the farm perimeter. The site is a very good base for visiting the famous university town of Cambridge and a walking tour around the town exploring the colleges is highly recommended. The town can be accessed by car (park and ride recommended), by bus or by bike via a special cycle route.

Facilities

Three heated toilet blocks provide good facilities, all very clean and well maintained. No dedicated provision for disabled visitors, although one block has extra wide doors and easy access. Laundry room. Motorcaravan services. Shop. Gates closed 23.00-07.30. Off site: Comberton village with bus stop 0.5 miles. Golf 2 miles. Fishing 3.5 miles. Cambridge 5 miles. Bicycle hire 8 miles. National Trust Wimpole Estate 7 miles. Duxford War Museum.

Open: 30 March - 31 October.

Directions

From M11 exit 12, take A603 towards Sandy. After 0.5 miles turn right, B1046 to Comberton. Turn right just before village signed Madingley (also caravan sign). Site on right just north of village.
GPS: 52.194981, 0.031103

Charges guide

Per unit incl. 2 persons and electricity	£ 20.00 - £ 25.00
extra person	£ 4.00
child (5-16 yrs)	£ 2.50
dog	£ 1.00

No credit cards.

Highfield Farm Touring Park

PREMIER PARK 2016
The finest campsites, independently assessed

A warm welcome awaits you at our popular award winning park with its excellent facilities, set in peaceful farming countryside. It is close to the historic University City of Cambridge, the Imperial War Museum, Duxford and ideally suited for touring East Anglia.

Comberton, Cambridge CB23 7DG Tel/Fax: 01223 262308
www.highfieldfarmtouringpark.co.uk

137

For latest campsite news visit
alanrogers.com

Cromer

Woodhill Park

Cromer Road, East Runton, Cromer NR27 9PX (Norfolk) T: 01263 512242. E: info@woodhill-park.com

alanrogers.com/UK3500

Woodhill is a seaside site with good views and a traditional atmosphere. It is situated on a clifftop in a large, gently sloping, open grassy field with 250 marked touring pitches. Of these, 205 have electricity (16A), 17 are fully serviced, and have a TV booster socket; many have wonderful views over the surrounding coastline and countryside. A small number of holiday homes are available with magnificent sea views. Although the site is fenced, there is access to the clifftop path which takes you to the beach. Locally, it is possible to take a boat trip to see the seals off Blakeney Point. Nearby attractions include the Shire Horse Centre at West Runton and the North Norfolk Steam Railway. Green technology plays a major role with solar panels added to one of the block roofs to heat the water. Access to nearby towns and resorts is available using the local bus stop outside the entrance, or by the tourist railway.

Facilities

Three modern toilet blocks with all necessary facilities including two family rooms with bath, showers, basin and WC, and four rooms with shower, basin and WC. Washing machine and dryer. Well stocked shop. Good, large adventure playground and plenty of space for ball games. Crazy golf. Giant chess and golf course adjacent to the site. Bicycle hire. Free WiFi throughout. Off site: Bus stop outside entrance for 'Coast Hopper'. Beach 0.5 miles. Fishing and shop 1 mile. Golf and riding 2 miles. Bird Reserve at Cley. National Trust properties.

Open: 1 March - 30 November.

Directions

Site is beside the A149 coast road between East and West Runton. GPS: 52.93742, 1.26250

Charges guide

Per unit incl. 2 persons and electricity	£ 11.05 - £ 18.60
extra person	£ 2.65 - £ 3.00
child (4-16 yrs)	£ 1.10 - £ 1.35
dog	£ 2.20 - £ 3.95

NORTH NORFOLK... naturally

Woodhill Park

Relax in your touring caravan or tent enjoying peace and tranquillity with magnificent views of the sea and surrounding North Norfolk countryside. Multi-service, electric pitches and amenity buildings available. Luxurious centrally heated holiday homes for hire.

Bookings or **brochure 01263 512242**
or online **www.woodhill-park.com**
Cromer Road, East Runton, Cromer,
Norfolk NR27 9PX

East Harling

The Dower House Touring Park

Thetford Forest, East Harling NR16 2SE (Norfolk) T: 01953 717314. E: info@dowerhouse.co.uk

alanrogers.com/UK3390

Set on 20 acres in the heart of Britain's largest forest on the Suffolk and Norfolk borders, The Dower House provides quiet woodland walks and cycleways, with an abundance of wildlife. David and Karen Bushell continue to upgrade the facilities without compromising the park's natural features. There are 160 large pitches; 72 with 10A electricity. Most are reasonably level, although given the forest location there are a few tree roots. Six pitches for visitors with mobility problems are linked by a path to the main facilities. Torches are recommended as the site is unlit at night (ideal for stargazing!).

Facilities

Two toilet blocks, one with a baby room. A separate building houses the showers and a unit for disabled visitors. Washing machine and dryer. Well stocked shop. Information room. Quiet rooms (no games machines). Heated outdoor swimming pool (23/5-1/9, under 16s must be with an adult). Paddling pool. Caravan storage. Torches necessary. WiFi on part of site (free). Off site: Fishing nearby 1.5 miles. Riding 1 km. Snetterton motor racing circuit and Sunday market 2-3 miles. Many walks and cycle rides in the forest. Golf 10 km.

Open: 28 March - last weekend in September.

Directions

From A11 (Thetford-Norwich) road, 7 miles east of Thetford, turn right on B1111 to East Harling. Drive through village, round a right hand bend to crossroads. Turn right and site is signed just under 1 mile. Turn right onto unpaved road and entrance in 0.8 miles. GPS: 52.42829, 0.89631

Charges guide

Per unit incl. 2 persons and electricity	£ 17.50 - £ 29.50
extra person	£ 5.00
child (4-15 yrs)	£ 2.00 - £ 2.50

For latest campsite news visit
alanrogers.com

Fakenham

The Old Brick Kilns Caravan & Camping Park

Little Barney Lane, Barney, Fakenham NR21 0NL (Norfolk) T: 01328 878305.
E: enquiries@old-brick-kilns.co.uk **alanrogers.com/UK3400**

This is an excellent tranquil, family run park and a friendly, helpful atmosphere prevails. The park's development on the site of old brick kilns has resulted in land on varying levels. This provides areas of level, well drained pitches with many on hardstanding. There are 65 pitches in total, all with 16A electricity and 30 are fully serviced. A wide range of trees and shrubs provide shelter and are home for a variety of wildlife. There are garden areas, including a butterfly garden, and a conservation pond is the central feature. There is a large, comfortable bar area and restaurant open five days a week. Drinking water is supplied by a 285 ft. bore and excellent roofed service areas provide water and waste disposal. As the park is only eight miles from the coast, it is ideally situated to explore north Norfolk. Strictly no arrivals before 13.30. A member of the Best of British group.

Facilities

Very good heated toilet blocks provide very clean facilities. Baby room. Facilities for disabled guests (Radar key). Laundry room. Motorcaravan services. Good shop with gas supplies. Bar/restaurant (5 days a week, April-Oct) and takeaway (July/Aug) with patio area outside. TV/games room. Giant chess. Small library. Fenced play area. Fishing. WiFi (charged). B&B also available. Caravan storage. Off site: Thursford collection 2 miles. Golf 5 and 8 miles. Riding and bicycle hire 6 miles. Beach 7 miles. Boat launching 8 miles. Stately homes. Birdwatching.

Open: All year excl. 2 January - 14 March.

Directions

From Fakenham take A148 Cromer road northeast. After 6 miles, at Thursford, fork right on B1354 signed Melton Constable. In 0.4 miles, turn right to Barney, and then first left along a narrow country lane with passing places for 0.5 miles.
GPS: 52.85804, 0.97583

Charges guide

Per unit incl. 2 persons	
and electricity	£ 17.00 - £ 23.00
'super pitch'	£ 21.00 - £ 27.00
extra person	£ 4.00
child (0-15 yrs)	£ 1.00 - £ 3.00
dog (max. 2)	£ 1.50

Great Yarmouth

Rose Farm Touring Park

Stepshort, Belton, Great Yarmouth NR31 9JS (Norfolk) T: 01493 780896.
E: myhra@rosefarmtouringpark.fsnet.co.uk **alanrogers.com/UK3382**

Rose Farm is open all year and, although close to Great Yarmouth, is quietly situated offering campers space, peace and tranquillity. There are 145 reasonably level pitches, 20 on hardstanding and the remainder on grass; 100 have 16A electricity, and some of these also have water and drainage. The park is split into three separate areas; the first is large and open, surrounded by fencing, the second area is long with pitches either side of the road and beyond this is an open area mainly for tents. Recent landscaping of the site includes a new walkway along the bank with picnic tables. With nearby attractions such as Fritton Lake Country Park, Pleasure Wood Hills Theme Park and, of course, Great Yarmouth with its fun fair and amusement arcades, your holiday in Norfolk could be full of busy days. Sue and Tora Myhra are very proud of Rose Farm and what has been achieved in the few years since taking over what was quite a run-down campsite.

Facilities

Three sanitary blocks (two main with excellent facilities, one more basic for the tent area). Two family rooms with shower, toilet and basin. Laundry facilities. Facilities for disabled visitors (pitching can be arranged in advance). Café (eat in or takeaway). Adventure playground. TV/information room. Dog walk. WiFi (free). Off site: Shops nearby. Bus stop. Sailing 2 miles. Fishing and golf 3 miles. Riding and bicycle hire 4 miles. Beach 5 miles.

Open: All year.

Directions

From Great Yarmouth and Gorleston take A143 signed Beccles and Diss. At dual carriageway (Bradwell) turn right (signed Holiday Parks) to Burgh Castle. In 0.75 miles, take next right, site on right in 25 yds. GPS: 52.57136, 1.66876

Charges guide

Per unit incl. 2 persons	
and electricity	£ 19.50 - £ 25.00
tent with 2 persons	£ 12.00 - £ 15.00
extra person	£ 2.50 - £ 3.50
dog	£ 1.50

Special offers available.
No credit cards.

For latest campsite news visit
alanrogers.com

Great Yarmouth
Clippesby Hall

Hall Lane, Clippesby, Great Yarmouth NR29 3BL (Norfolk) T: 01493 367800. E: holidays@clippesby.com
alanrogers.com/UK3485

Set in the heart of the Broads National Park this is a spacious, high quality site where you can be sure of a warm welcome from the Lindsay family who have lived in the Hall for many years. Clippesby offers the choice of pitching amongst the shady woodland, on the gently sloping lawns of the hall with colourful mature trees and shrubs or in a new area, The Meadow, which offers fully serviced pitches with hardstanding. The 110 touring pitches are well spaced and clearly numbered (80 have 10A electricity). Children can roam at will in safety and parents can relax and unwind at this beautiful park.

Facilities

Three heated, timber toilet blocks provide very clean, modern facilities. Some cabins with washbasin and WC. En-suite room for disabled visitors. Family room with bath and baby changing. Laundry. Gas. Shop (Easter-end Oct). Café and family bar/restaurant (Easter-end Oct). Pizza takeaway. Small swimming pool and paddling pool (end May-end Sept). Adventure play area. Football. Bicycle hire. Max. 1 dog per pitch. Dog walk. WiFi (charged). Off site: Bus service 1.5 miles. Fishing and boat launching 2 miles. Riding 3 miles. Golf, beach and sailing 5 miles. Great Yarmouth 7 miles. Norwich 15 miles. The Broads for cycling, walking and boating.

Open: All year.

Directions

From the A47 Norwich-Great Yarmouth road at Acle roundabout take exit for Filby (A1064). After 1.5 miles fork left on B1152 signed Potter Heigham. Take first left and park is 100 yds. on the right. GPS: 52.67283, 1.58299

Charges guide

Per unit incl. 2 persons	
and electricity	£ 12.50 - £ 36.00
extra person	£ 6.50
child	£ 3.00
dog (max. 1)	£ 5.00

Great Yarmouth
The Grange Touring Park

Ormesby Saint Margaret, Great Yarmouth NR29 3QG (Norfolk) T: 01493 730306.
E: info@grangetouring.co.uk **alanrogers.com/UK3490**

This family touring site has a pleasant atmosphere and visitors are given a warm and friendly welcome by the resident wardens. There are 70 level pitches with 16A electricity, 14 with hardstanding, and ten pitches for tents, all arranged on well trimmed grass with tarmac access roads. There are some mature trees throughout the site providing shade to many of the pitches. Adjacent to the campsite is The Grange, a free house offering meals, beers and real ale, plus play equipment for children (open all year). The site owner also has a holiday campsite at Hemsby (four miles) with its own wide sandy beach, which guests at The Grange are welcome to use. There is a little road noise from the bypass. The nearest beach is a mile away and local attractions include Caister Castle and Motor Museum and the Norfolk Rare Breed Centre. Great Yarmouth centre with its many attractions and The Broads are within five miles.

Facilities

A modern, heated toilet building is spacious and well maintained housing all the usual facilities including free showers. Baby room in the ladies'. Family room. Two fully equipped wet rooms for disabled visitors. Motorcaravan services. Laundry room with washing machine and dryer. Washing lines are provided at the rear of the building. Gas supplies. Swings for children. Internet and copying facilities in reception and WiFi over site (£3 per hour or per 24 hours if using own computer). Off site: Bus service 250 yds. Beach, shops and supermarket 1 mile. Riding and bicycle hire 2 miles. Golf 3 miles. Fishing 4 miles. Great Yarmouth 5 minutes drive.

Open: Mid March - early October.

Directions

Site is just north of Great Yarmouth. Entrance is just south of the roundabout at the northern edge of the Caister bypass. GPS: 52.66812, 1.71097

Charges guide

Per unit incl. up to 4 persons	
and electricity	£ 13.50 - £ 25.50
extra person	£ 3.50
child (under 5 yrs)	free
dog	£ 3.50

For latest campsite news visit
alanrogers.com

Harleston
Little Lakeland Caravan Park
Wortwell, Harleston IP20 0EL (Norfolk) T: 01986 788646. E: information@littlelakeland.co.uk
alanrogers.com/UK3480

This peaceful hideaway, with its own fishing lake, is tucked behind the houses and gardens that border the village main street. It is a traditional, mature little park with just 58 pitches. There are several caravan holiday homes and long stay units, but there should always be around 22 places with 10A electricity for touring units. The pitches are mostly individual ones separated by mature hedges and trees giving varying amounts of shade. Fishing in the attractive lake is free of charge and solely for the use of campers (bream, tench, roach, perch and carp). A member of the Countryside Discovery group.

Facilities

A modern, heated toilet block provides washbasins all in cubicles for ladies and one for men. Fully equipped laundry. Separate en-suite room for disabled visitors also has facilities for baby changing. A further unit (also heated) by reception provides a shower, WC and basin per sex. Reception stocks gas and essentials (newspapers to order). Small play area. Library of paperback books in the summer house. Fishing (max. 4 rods per unit). WiFi (charged). Off site: Bus service on the main road 250 yds. Pub (with food) 500 yds. Harleston 2 miles. Golf 4 miles.

Open: 15 March - 31 October.

Directions

From Diss, leave A143 at roundabout signed Wortwell. Continue to village, pass The Bell pub, a garage on right, then turn right at first bungalow (Little Lakeland Lodge) watching carefully for signs. Site is down lane, 250 yds. on right. GPS: 52.41628, 1.35282

Charges guide

Per unit incl. 2 persons and electricity	£ 18.00 - £ 22.50
No credit cards.	

Hunstanton
Searles Leisure Resort
South Beach Road, Hunstanton PE36 5BB (Norfolk) T: 01485 534211. E: bookings@searles.co.uk
alanrogers.com/UK3520

This is a high quality, 'all in', family holiday park on the north Norfolk coast offering everything for a great seaside family holiday. There is a beach within walking distance, a covered 'town plaza' including a sports bar, Chinese restaurant and American diner plus fish and chip bar, club house, pools, Country Club, golf course and driving range, fishing lakes and bowling greens; there should be something to entertain everyone. There are 823 pitches with 323 of varying sizes for touring; 129 with 16A electricity. Some are on hardstanding and fully serviced, with others on grass. An open area is reserved for tents.

Facilities

Three large, modern, clean toilet blocks with washbasins and toilets in cubicles. Facilities for disabled visitors. Baby room. Launderette. Food hall. Shop. Restaurants, bars and cafés. Hair and beauty salon. Indoor and outdoor heated swimming pools. Gym. Tennis. Outdoor play area and indoor soft play area. Golf (9-hole course, driving range and putting course). Fishing lake. Bowling green. Bicycle and pedalo hire. WiFi. Off site: Beach 400 yds.

Open: All year, excl. 25 December.

Directions

From King's Lynn take A149 north to Hunstanton. At first roundabout take B1161. After 0.3 miles cross roundabout (supermarket), site immediately on left. GPS: 52.93033, 0.48289

Charges guide

Per pitch	£ 14.00 - £ 58.00
fully serviced pitch	£ 11.00 - £ 62.00
dog	£ 3.25

Hunstanton
Deepdale Backpackers & Camping
Deepdale Farm, Burnham Deepdale PE31 8DD (Norfolk) T: 01485 210256.
E: info@deepdalebackpackers.co.uk **alanrogers.com/UK3525**

Deepdale Camping is a quiet, family friendly campsite on the north Norfolk coast welcoming tents and small campervans (caravans are not accepted). The 75 standard pitches are no larger than 6.5 m. (including guy ropes) while ten additional jumbo pitches accommodate larger tents up to 10 m. There are no electricity hook-ups and generators are not allowed. The site occupies five well kept paddocks in the heart of the beautiful village of Burnham Deepdale, in an Area of Outstanding Natural Beauty. Accommodation can also be hired in the form of four yurts, six teepees and two shepherd's huts. The complex also has two hostels for backpackers with full kitchen facilities and heating during the winter.

Facilities

Heated sanitary facilities with showers (including family shower), dishwashing and washing machine. Information centre with details of walking and cycling trails, camping gas and equipment and eggs from the resident chickens. Bicycle hire. WiFi (free). Off site: Supermarket, filling station and restaurant adjacent. Coast a short walk away.

Open: All year.

Directions

Burnham Deepdale is 25 miles northeast of King's Lynn via the A159 to Cromer. Site is at the eastern end of the village. GPS: 52.96553, 0.68465

Charges guide

Per person	£ 4.50 - £ 13.00
child	£ 2.50 - £ 6.00
dog	free

For latest campsite news visit
alanrogers.com

Huntingdon

Wyton Lakes Holiday Park

Banks End, Wyton, Huntingdon PE28 2AA (Cambridgeshire) T: 01480 412715. E: loupeter@supanet.com

alanrogers.com/UK3555

Wyton Lakes is a family run, adults only park with four well stocked fishing lakes, very close to the River Great Ouse, between Huntingdon and Saint Ives. There are 80 level pitches of medium size with 60 for caravans and motorcaravans and 20 for tents. The tent pitches are on grass, some with electricity. The other pitches are mainly on hardstanding with gravel for awnings and all have 16A electricity and a water tap. Most of the pitches border the lakes making fishing possible from the pitch. Well placed as a centre for touring, the park has easy access for large outfits. The old market towns of Huntingdon and Saint Ives are only three miles away and the delightful village of Houghton with its old mill, pub and riverside walks is just one mile. Just across the road is a large garden centre with restaurant and coffee shop.

Facilities

Heated toilet block with all necessary facilities including those for campers with disabilities. Laundry with washer and dryer. Coarse lake and river fishing on payment (carp, bream, tench, perch, roach and rudd). Small riverside walk. WiFi throughout (charged). Off site: Garden centre, restaurant and coffee shop opposite entrance. Interesting old village of Houghton, pub, shop, National Trust Houghton Mill, riverside walks 1 mile. Boat hire and golf 3 miles. Huntingdon Race Course 4 miles. St Ives, Huntingdon, Cambridge (bus stop close). Paxton Pits Nature Reserve. Hinchingbrooke Park. National Trust Ramsey Abbey Gatehouse Ruins 12 miles.

Open: 18 March - 30 October.

Directions

From the A14 take exit 26 (St Ives). Take A1096 north towards St Ives over four roundabouts. Turn left onto A1123, signed Huntingdon and site entrance is on the left in 2 miles opposite garden centre. GPS: 52.33664, -0.13872

Charges guide

Per unit incl. 2 persons and electricity	£ 22.00
tent pitch incl. 2 adults	£ 18.00
extra adult	£ 2.00
dog	£ 1.00

Adults only (over 18 yrs).
No credit cards.

Wyton Lakes Holiday Park
Banks End, Wyton
Huntingdon Cambs PE28 2AA
Tel: 01480 412 715 *or* 07785 29 44 19
loupeter@supanet.com
www.wytonlakes.com
Adults only

Ipswich

Orwell Meadows Leisure Park

Priory Lane, Ipswich IP10 0JS (Suffolk) T: 01473 726666. E: recept@orwellmeadows.co.uk

alanrogers.com/UK3315

This popular, family park is set on the edge of the Orwell Country Park, near Ipswich, with its many miles of walks and the famous Orwell Bridge with views of the Suffolk countryside. The park is run by David and Sally Miles and offers an ideal spot for a family holiday with an outdoor swimming pool and a good clubhouse with a bar, restaurant and a shop. Spacious pitches are around the edges of several separate meadows (surrounded on three sides by earth banks), all offering 16A electricity hook-ups. There is much to see and do in the area. Visit towns such as Ipswich and Colchester or unspoilt villages such as Framlingham (with its castle) and Aldeburgh, plus the rest of Constable country.

Facilities

The modern toilet block includes clean and spacious free showers. It is kept to a very high standard. En-suite facilities for disabled visitors (key entry). Washing machine and dryer.Well stocked shop in office. Bar and restaurant (evenings). Outdoor swimming and paddling pools (from end May). Play area. TV/family room. Max. 2 dogs. WiFi (charged). Off site: Market town of Bury St Edmunds.

Open: All year excl. February.

Directions

From A14 Ipswich bypass take Nacton/Ipswich exit (north of the A14) and follow signs for Orwell Country Park (narrow lane). Cross single-track bridge over the A14 to the site entrance 200 yds. on left. GPS: 52.02044, 1.19161

Charges guide

Per unit incl. 2 persons and electricity	£ 20.00 - £ 24.00
extra person	£ 5.00 - £ 6.50
child (3-12 yrs)	£ 3.50 - £ 4.50
dog	£ 2.00 - £ 2.50

Weekly specials available.

For latest campsite news visit

alanrogers.com

Ipswich
Westwood Park Caravan Park

Old Felixstowe Road, Bucklesham, Ipswich IP10 0BW (Suffolk) T: 01473 659637.
E: info@westwoodcaravanpark.co.uk **alanrogers.com/UK3335**

This park opened in Easter 2007 and has been developed on land previously owned by the neighbouring farm. The park is situated between Felixstowe and Ipswich and is within easy reach of the River Deben and Woodbridge. The 90 level grass and hardstanding pitches are of varying sizes to accommodate both small and large caravans, motorcaravans and tents. In addition, there is a considerable number of seasonal units. All pitches have 10A electricity. When they are available, the seasonal hardstanding super pitches, equipped with 16A electricity, can be used by touring units.

Facilities

A modern, but traditionally built, toilet block in the centre of the park includes facilities for disabled visitors (£5 deposit for key). Family shower room. Laundry. Purpose built reception sells a limited range of provisions e.g. milk. Recycling facilities. Grass play area for children. WiFi (charged). Off site: Free range eggs from a farm (short walk). Bus service to Ipswich nearby. Pubs serving meals in nearby Bucklesham and surrounding villages. Fishing 2 miles. Golf 3 miles. Beach 5 miles. Riding 10 miles.

Open: 29 February - 15 January.

Directions

Site is near Bucklesham. From the A12 (south) or A14(12) (north) take A14 towards Felixstowe. Continue for 5 miles and turn left signed Kirton, Bucklesham and Brightwell. Continue for 1 mile and park is on the right, immediately after Tenth Road on the left. GPS: 52.02316, 1.28389

Charges guide

Per unit incl. 2 persons and electricity	£ 18.00 - £ 21.00
extra person	£ 2.50

King's Lynn
The Garden Caravan Site

Barmer Hall, Syderstone, King's Lynn PE31 8SR (Norfolk) T: 01485 578220. E: nlmason@tiscali.co.uk
alanrogers.com/UK3460

In the quiet Norfolk countryside, this imaginative touring park is a sun trap set in an enclosed walled garden. Sheltered from the winds by the high walls, visitors can relax in peace and tranquillity. Attractive mature trees, shrubs and climbers provide shade at various times of the day. The Mason family run the site in a relaxed way and the atmosphere is superb. There are 30 pitches, all with 16A electricity and TV hook-up (cable supplied), but little shade. Some are slightly sloping and will require blocks. Reception is housed in a small kiosk (not always manned, so pitch yourself and pay later).

Facilities

The single toilet block (heated) has all the usual facilities including a toilet and washbasin for disabled campers. Spin dryer and iron. No shop, but ices, soft drinks and free range eggs are available. Off site: Golf and fishing 10 km. Boat launching 15 km. Royal Sandringham. Norfolk Lavender, Langham Glass and the Thursford collection of steam engines and mechanical organs.

Open: 1 March - 1 November.

Directions

About 6 miles west of Fakenham leave A148. Take B1454 (Docking, Hunstanton). After 3 miles turn right (Barmer Hall). Road marked 'unsuitable for motor vehicles' but continue for 0.3 miles. Beyond Barmer Hall turn left to site. GPS: 52.86414, 0.69116

Charges guide

Per unit incl. 2 persons	£ 16.00 - £ 18.00
No credit cards.	

King's Lynn
King's Lynn Caravan & Camping Park

New Road, North Runcton, King's Lynn PE33 0RA (Norfolk) T: 01553 840004. E: klcc@btconnect.com
alanrogers.com/UK3465

Set in ten acres of mature parkland, just off the A47, this friendly, family run camping and caravan park is spread over three level fields at the edge of the village of North Runcton. The well maintained site has 150 large, level, tidy grass pitches with 10A electricity connections. Eight holiday cottages, 'mega pods' and holiday lodges for rent. Benefiting from sustainable energy, the site boasts solar-powered heating and a rainwater flushing system. King's Lynn Caravan Park is ideally situated for touring north Norfolk and the Fens, both Areas of Outstanding Natural Beauty. It is also the nearest campsite to the historic port and market town of King's Lynn. A regular bus service runs past the site.

Facilities

Two modern, well maintained toilet blocks include showers and open washbasins. Family room, washing and dishwashing facilities. Facilities for disabled visitors (designated pitches available). Motorcaravan services. Small shop. WiFi over site (charged). Off site: Newsagent and Post Office in North Runcton 1 mile. Supermarkets 1 mile. Stock car and speedway at the Norfolk Arena 1 mile. Bowling and Clay pigeon shooting.

Open: All year.

Directions

From King's Lynn take A47 Swaffham-Norwich road about 1 mile from large roundabout where A10 and A47 meet. Turning right to North Runcton, campsite entrance is about 150 yards on left. GPS: 52.721093, 0.435105

Charges guide

Per unit incl. 2 persons and electricity	£ 19.00
extra person	£ 5.00
child (up to 16 yrs)	£ 3.00

For latest campsite news visit
alanrogers.com

Lowestoft

Heathland Beach Caravan Park

London Road, Kessingland, Lowestoft NR33 7PJ (Suffolk) T: 01502 740337.
E: heathlandbeach@btinternet.com **alanrogers.com/UK3371**

Owned and run by the Reader family, Heathland Beach is acclaimed as having one of the most perfect settings along the beautiful Suffolk Coastline, with the local award-winning sandy beach just a few minutes walk away. The location of the site, overlooking the secluded beach, makes it easy to explore both Suffolk and Norfolk. There are 64 generously sized grass pitches, all with 16A electricity and TV hook-ups. On site, there is everything for the family to enjoy, including fishing and three outdoor heated swimming pools with maxi-flume, play centre and licensed bar.

Facilities

Two modern toilet blocks, one at each end of the touring field, have all the usual facilities and were fairly clean when we visited. Facilities for disabled visitors including a designated pitch. Laundry. Motorcaravan services. Bar. Three outdoor heated swimming pools with maxi-flume. All-weather tennis court. Fishing (licence required). Football. Large area for ball games. Adventure-style play centre. Barbecue and picnic area. Max. 1 dog in peak periods. Free WiFi in bar. Off site: Nearest beach 700 yds.

Open: 1 March - 31 October.

Directions

From A12 south take second exit at the Out of Africa roundabout, onto B1437 London Road. Park is clearly signposted on right.
GPS: 52.429055, 1.723223

Charges guide

Per unit incl. 2 persons and electricity	£ 20.00 - £ 28.00
extra person (over 6 yrs)	£ 2.00
dog	£ 3.00

Mundesley-on-Sea

Sandy Gulls Caravan Park

Cromer Road, Mundesley-on-Sea NR11 8DF (Norfolk) T: 01263 720513. E: info@sandygulls.co.uk
alanrogers.com/UK3410

This is an adults only park on the outskirts of Mundesley-on-Sea. One of the only clifftop parks with space for touring units on this coastline, there are panoramic views from most pitches. All 40 pitches (14 on hardstanding) have 10A electricity and TV aerial hook-ups. The unmarked pitches are arranged on an unshaded sloping meadow so levelling blocks are advised. There is no reception for the touring area so visitors are invited to find a pitch and someone will come and find you. Primarily a caravan holiday home park, there are mobile homes to rent. The facilities are well maintained but some distance from the pitches. Access to the Blue Flag beach is via a large tarmac ramp.

Facilities

The heated toilet block is modern and spacious offering large shower rooms and open washbasins, all kept very clean. TV aerial hook-ups. Fish and chip van visits on Mon. at 18.00. Ice cream van daily (afternoons). WiFi (charged). Off site: Shops and pubs nearby. Mundesley-on-Sea 1 mile. Tennis, boat launching, riding and golf nearby. National Trust. Tourist railway.

Open: March - November.

Directions

Site is 1 mile north of Mundesley (7 miles south of Cromer) on the main coast road.
GPS: 52.88457, 1.42074

Charges guide

Per unit incl. up to 4 persons and electricity	£ 15.00 - £ 26.00
dog	free

North Walsham

Two Mills Touring Park

Yarmouth Road, North Walsham NR28 9NA (Norfolk) T: 01692 405829. E: enquiries@twomills.co.uk
alanrogers.com/UK3420

Two Mills is a quiet, adults only site with a long season. Set in the bowl of a former quarry, the park is a real sun trap. It is secluded, sheltered and terraced with birdsong to be heard at all times of the day. Neatly maintained with natural areas, varied trees, wild flowers and birds, the owners, Barbara and Ray Barnes, want to add their own touches to this popular park. Following the purchase of an adjacent field, there are now 81 average sized, level pitches for touring units on hardstanding, including 72 serviced pitches (patio, water and drainage). All have 10/16A electricity. A member of the Best of British group.

Facilities

Two neat, clean, central toilet blocks can be heated, and include some washbasins in cabins and en-suite facilities for disabled visitors. Washing machine, dryer and spin dryer. Motorcaravan services. Small shop at reception. TV room/library with tea and coffee facilities. WiFi (charged on part of site). Dogs are accepted by arrangement only. Off site: Hotel/pub 100 yds. North Walsham 20 mins. walk. Bicycle hire 1.5 miles. Fishing 3 miles. Golf and coast 5 miles.

Open: 1 March - 31 December.

Directions

From A149 Stalham-North Walsham road, watch for caravan sign 1.5 miles before North Walsham (White Horse Common). The road runs parallel to A149 and site is on right after 1.25 miles.
GPS: 52.80661, 1.41708

Charges guide

Per unit incl. 2 persons and electricity	£ 17.95 - £ 22.50
full service pitch	£ 19.95 - £ 25.50
extra person	£ 4.00

For latest campsite news visit
alanrogers.com

Norwich
Deer's Mead Caravan & Camping Park

The Street, Erpingham, Norwich NR11 7QD (Norfolk) T: 01263 768959. E: info@deersmead.co.uk

alanrogers.com/UK3450

Within easy reach of the north Norfolk coast and the Broads, this is a very attractive, peaceful little site with excellent facilities. Only adults are accepted. The park was re-opened in April 2014 following complete refurbishment of the pitches and the addition of a new, top quality shower block. There are 24 hardstanding pitches and 11 all grass pitches, all fully serviced with 16A electricity, TV, water and waste points. New hedging has been planted between the pitches. There is no shop but two pubs serving food and traditional ales are within walking distance. This is an ideal base for cycling and walking (the Weavers Way footpath is within half a mile) or just relaxing.

Facilities

The well maintained toilet block is heated and includes spacious hot showers and a covered dishwashing and laundry area. Off site: Bus service on the main A140 road. Fishing 3 miles. Bicycle hire 3 miles. Beach 6 miles. Riding and golf 6 miles.

Open: 1 March - 31 October.

Directions

From Norwich take the A140 towards Cromer, and 4 miles north of Aylsham, turn left signed Erpingham, plus camping sign (narrow road). Site is 175 yards on the right. GPS: 52.84208, 1.27090

Charges guide

Per unit incl. 2 persons, electricity and awning	£ 22.50 - £ 25.00

No credit cards.

Norwich
Deer's Glade Caravan & Camping Park

White Post Road, Hanworth, Norwich NR11 7HN (Norfolk) T: 01263 768633. E: info@deersglade.co.uk

alanrogers.com/UK3455

In 2003, David and Heather Attew decided that they had an area that would make a superb setting for a caravan park and that they could give up farming. In early 2004, they opened this top quality park, which has since developed into a very popular site. Not far from the Norfolk Broads and close to the East Anglia coast, the park is open all year round. There are 117 level pitches, some with hardstandings, plus eight pods, a shepherd's hut and two bell tents. There are 99 pitches with 16A electricity and TV aerial points. Hedging is established between the pitches, and WiFi access is available throughout.

Facilities

Two spacious toilet blocks are of a very high standard and include vanity style washbasins for ladies. Room for disabled visitors and families. Laundry. Motorcaravan services. Shop (all year). Play area. Fishing lake (charged). Bicycle hire. Dog kennels. WiFi (free). Off site: Bus service under 1 mile. Pub 1.5 miles. Woodland walks. Small supermarket 3 miles. Riding 4 miles. Beach and golf 5 miles. Blicking Hall. Felbrigg Hall. Birdwatching.

Open: All year.

Directions

From Norwich take A140 towards Cromer and 5 miles beyond Aylsham turn right towards Suffield Green (White Post Road). Park is 0.5 miles on the right. GPS: 52.85781, 1.28765

Charges guide

Per unit incl. 2 persons and electricity	£ 15.00 - £ 19.00
extra person	£ 7.25

Peterborough
Ferry Meadows Caravan Club Site

Ham Lane, Peterborough PE2 5UU (Cambridgeshire) T: 01733 233526. E: enquiries@caravanclub.co.uk

alanrogers.com/UK3580

Three miles from bustling Peterborough and closer to the East of England Showground, the immaculate Ferry Meadows is an ideal family holiday site occupying 30 acres of the 500-acre Nene Country Park. Open all year, the site provides 258 pitches (16A electricity) – grass pitches on one side of the park, informally laid out in small groups and surrounded by a variety of mature trees, and 132 gravel hardstandings just across the road for caravans and motorcaravans. A very small area (without electricity) is reserved for tents. Families with children may prefer the grass area from where they can keep a watchful eye on the well equipped playground.

Facilities

Two modern, well appointed and heated sanitary blocks are of the usual high standard with en-suite facilities for disabled visitors in one block. Baby/toddler washroom. Laundry room. Motorcaravan services. The office stocks basic provisions. Fish and chip van at weekends. Good play areas. TV socket and lead. WiFi (charged). Off site: Steam railway 500 yds. Bus service and pitch and putt 800 yds. Restaurants within 0.5 miles.

Open: All year.

Directions

Leave the A1 on A605, turn east, signed showground, Peterborough. At fourth roundabout turn left, signed Ferry Meadows. Entrance is on the left just beyond railway. GPS: 52.56053, -0.30593

Charges guide

Per person	£ 6.30 - £ 8.10
child (5-17 yrs)	£ 0.01 - £ 2.80
pitch incl. electricity (non-member)	£ 16.50 - £ 19.90

For latest campsite news visit
alanrogers.com

Pidley

Stroud Hill Park

Fen Road, Pidley PE28 3DE (Cambridgeshire) T: 01487 741333. E: office@stroudhillpark.co.uk

alanrogers.com/UK3575

Open all year round for adults only, Stroud Hill Park is a well designed, high quality park; a credit to its owners, David and Jayne Newman. The park has been landscaped to create a terraced effect and now incorporates a large fishing lake (well stocked with carp, tench, bream, rudd and roach) plus a superb tennis court. There are 60 large, slightly sloping pitches, fully serviced with 16A electricity, fresh water and drainage, 44 of which have hardstanding. Affiliated to the Caravan Club, non-members are equally welcome. A member of the Best of British group.

Facilities

Toilets and spacious en-suite shower facilities are in the main building. Well equipped room for disabled visitors. All spotlessly clean. Small, licensed shop stocks basic provisions, homemade cakes, local produce, gas and camping accessories. Attractive bar and superb café/restaurant. Fishing (£5 per day). All-weather tennis court. WiFi (charged). Off site: Golf course, 10-pin bowling and paintball adjacent to site. Riding 0.5 miles.

Open: All year.

Directions

Leave A1 near Huntingdon, take A14 east. Leave A14 at A141, signed March. In Warboys, at roundabout, turn right on B1040 signed Pidley. In Pidley turn left just beyond church, Fen Road. Site is 1 mile on right. GPS: 52.38926, -0.03966

Charges guide

Per unit incl. 2 persons and full services	£ 25.00 - £ 27.00
extra person	£ 2.50
Caravan Club Members discount £1.00 per night.	

Polstead

Polstead Camping & Caravanning Club Site

Holt Road, Bower House Tye, Polstead CO6 5BZ (Suffolk) T: 01787 211969.
E: polsteadtouring@hotmail.com alanrogers.com/UK3340

This lovely touring park in the peaceful Suffolk countryside (in the heart of Constable Country) is an ideal base from which to explore many places of interest. These include Flatford Mill, the scene for Constable's famous painting, Sudbury (the birthplace of Gainsborough), Long Melford with its Hall, and Colchester, Britain's oldest town. The very neat and well cared for park is attractively presented and offers 60 level pitches, 54 with 10/16A electricity. Well established hedges separate most of the pitches, 35 of which have gravel hardstanding. This is a Club site but non-members are welcome.

Facilities

Modern sanitary block with spacious hot showers. Facilities for disabled visitors consist of a wet room including a toilet with handrails; this doubles as a baby changing/family room. Laundry. Reception sells a range of supplies. Fish and chips delivered by arrangement on Sat. Rally field. Children's trim trail. Free WiFi over site. Caravan storage. Off site: Pub serving food, 3 mins. walk. Farm shop 100 yds. Riding 0.75 miles. Golf 2 miles.

Open: 13 February - 14 January.

Directions

From A1071 Hadleigh-Sudbury road, just past the Brewers Arms public house, turn left just before a water tower towards Polstead; park is 250 yds. on the right. GPS: 52.02865, 0.89569

Charges guide

Per unit incl. 2 persons and electricity	£ 18.70 - £ 31.85
extra person	£ 7.15 - £ 12.15
Non-member prices are higher.	

Sheringham

Woodlands Caravan Park

Holt Road, Upper Sheringham NR26 8TU (Norfolk) T: 01263 823802. E: info@woodlandscaravanpark.co.uk

alanrogers.com/UK3435

This pleasant caravan park is set in parkland in the beautiful surroundings of north Norfolk's protected heathland, next to Sheringham Park (National Trust). There are 180 grass pitches, around half of which are on a gentle slope, all with 10A electricity. They are in two main areas for caravans and motorcaravans (tents are not accepted). Static units (160) occupy the edge of the site on three sides and these are all privately owned. A major feature of this site is the superb new toilet block with electronically controlled showers and underfloor heating. There are many lovely local walks including one to the beach (1.5 miles). The park is within easy reach of Holt, Cromer and Sheringham, with the major birdwatching areas of Blakeney, Cley and Salthouse also within 30 minutes drive.

Facilities

One excellent new toilet block provides all the necessary facilities including those for disabled visitors, baby changing and laundry. Well stocked shop. Gas supplies. Lounge bar and family bar. Barbecues. Play area (fenced and gated). Off site: Leisure Club with indoor pool, gym, sauna. Bicycle hire and fishing 1.5 miles.

Open: 21 March - 31 October.

Directions

From Cromer take the A148 towards Holt, pass signs for Sheringham Park and site is on right (camping sign) just before Bodham village. GPS: 52.92093, 1.17445

Charges guide

Per unit incl. electricity	£ 20.00 - £ 31.00
awning	£ 3.50

For latest campsite news visit

alanrogers.com

Sheringham
Kelling Heath Holiday Park
Weybourne, Holt, Sheringham NR25 7HW (Norfolk) T: 01263 588181. E: info@kellingheath.co.uk
alanrogers.com/UK3430

Not many parks can boast their own railway station and Kelling Heath's own halt on the north Norfolk Steam Railway gives access to the beach at Sheringham. Set in 270 acres of woodland and heathland, this very spacious holiday park offers freedom and relaxation with 300 large, level, grass touring pitches, all with 16A electricity and six are fully serviced. Together with 384 caravan holiday homes (36 to let, the rest privately owned), they blend easily into the part-wooded, part-open heath. A wide range of facilities provides activities for all ages. 'The Forge' has an entertainment bar and a family room with comprehensive entertainment all season. The leisure centre provides an indoor and outdoor pool, spa pool, sauna, steam rooms and gym. An adventure playground with assault course is near. The central reception area is attractively paved to provide a village square with an open air bandstand where one can sit and enjoy the atmosphere. The park's natural environment allows for woodland walks, a nature trail and cycling trails, and a small lake for fishing (permit holders only). Other amenities include two hard tennis courts, a small, outdoor heated fun pool and play areas (some rather hidden from the pitches).

Facilities

Three toilet blocks include facilities for disabled visitors, a baby room and laundry facilities. Gas. Well stocked shop, bar, restaurant and takeaway. Indoor leisure centre with pool, gym, etc. with trained staff (membership on either daily or weekly basis). Outdoor heated pool (25/5-5/9). Adventure play area. Tennis. Fishing. Bicycle hire. Entertainment. Special environmental Acorn activities for the family. WiFi (charged). Torches useful.

Open: 10 February - 2 January.

Directions

On A148 road from Holt to Cromer, after High Kelling, turn left just before Bodham village (international sign) signed Weybourne. Follow road for 1 mile to park. GPS: 52.92880, 1.14953

Charges guide

Per unit incl. electricity £ 18.95 - £ 34.90
with full services £ 25.00 - £ 43.55
dog (max. 2) £ 3.20 - £ 5.25
Min. 7 days in high season. No single sex groups.

KELLING HEATH. THE NATURAL ESCAPE

Enjoy the beauty of Kelling Heath from your touring pitch set amongst rare open heathland with backdrops of pine and native woodland. A magnificent range of facilities and environmental activities await you. Lodges and holiday homes available for hire.

Bookings or brochure 01263 588 181 or online **www.kellingheath.co.uk** Kelling Heath, Weybourne, Holt, Norfolk NR25 7HW

Escape the normal routine...

Swaffham
Breckland Meadows Touring Park
Lynn Road, Swaffham PE37 7PT (Norfolk) T: 01760 721246. E: info@brecklandmeadows.co.uk
alanrogers.com/UK3470

Open all year, this compact, adult only park offers peace and tranquillity yet is only ten minutes walk from the historic market town of Swaffham. The site makes a good base to explore East Anglia and the local area with a wide range of diverse attractions. There are 40 average sized pitches with hardstanding, 16A electricity and TV hook-ups. There are two main roads close to the park but well established hedges and trees help minimise any noise. A small shop sells basic supplies and local produce, ices and drinks, and has a good library. Complimentary tea and coffee are in reception.

Facilities

The well maintained, heated toilet block provides all the usual facilities including showers and toilet facilities for disabled visitors. Laundry room. Gas supplies. WiFi over site (free). Off site: Swaffham with a range of shops, bars, restaurants, museums, Saturday market 0.5 miles. Bicycle hire 1 mile. Golf 2 miles. Riding 4 miles. Fishing 5 miles. Iceni village. Gooderstone Water Gardens.

Open: All year.

Directions

Park is 0.5 miles west of Swaffham on Low Road (old A47). Entrance on right just beyond garage. GPS: 52.65115, 0.67687

Charges guide

Per unit incl. 2 persons
and electricity £ 13.50 - £ 15.00
awning £ 1.00 - £ 2.00
dog £ 0.50
No credit cards.

For latest campsite news visit
alanrogers.com

Woodbridge
The Moon & Sixpence

Newbourne Road, Waldringfield, Woodbridge IP12 4PP (Suffolk) T: 01473 736650.
E: info@moonandsixpence.eu **alanrogers.com/UK3320**

This excellent site offers 60 large touring pitches that are positioned in the centre of an established and very spacious caravan holiday home park. The site is extremely well maintained and all 50 touring pitches are equipped with 10A electricity, TV point, water tap and a drain. In the centre of the site, and easily accessible to all, is an unsupervised lake with a sandy beach. An area at one end of the lake is set aside for ten pitches for adults only, all with views of the lake. Quiet is essential from 21.00-08.00.

Facilities	Directions
Exceptionally well finished, centrally placed unisex sanitary block consists of 11 fully equipped private rooms containing a selection of WCs, washbasins, showers, baths and wet rooms. No specific facilities for disabled visitors but access to the block is via a ramp. Laundry facilities. Well stocked shop. Bar and restaurant (main season). TV room. Two adventure play areas. Dog walking trails. Lake with beach. Tennis. Golf. WiFi (free).	From the A12 (Ipswich-Lowestoft) take third exit at roundabout, towards Waldringfield and follow signs to site. After one and a half miles, turn left at Waldringfield Golf Club to site, three-quarters of a mile on the left. GPS: 52.06252, 1.29858

Open: 1 April - 31 October.

Charges guide

Per unit incl. 2 persons	
and electricity	£ 22.00 - £ 34.00
extra person	£ 11.00 - £ 17.00

Woodbridge
Run Cottage Touring Park

Alderton Road, Hollesey, Woodbridge IP12 3RQ (Suffolk) T: 01394 411309. E: info@runcottage.co.uk
alanrogers.com/UK3322

This small and very attractive site in the heart of unspoilt Suffolk countryside offers an opportunity to explore many of the local attractions on Suffolk's Heritage Coast. Facilities on the site are limited but certainly adequate and the resident owners, Michele and Andy Stebbens, continue to add more features, such as a kitchen with washing machine and dryer, to ensure you have an enjoyable stay. The site is open all year round and all 45 pitches have 10-16A electricity, with 14 on hardstanding. All pitches have satellite TV connection. A new summerhouse provides a meeting area and is home to the tourist information. This is a popular site and advance booking is strongly recommended. We see it as being more suited to couples than families with children.

Facilities	Directions
New, well finished sanitary block with free hot water is easily accessed and is well equipped. Kitchen with washing machine, dryer and fridge freezer. A summer-house contains a comprehensive selection of tourist leaflets and details of local attractions. Off site: Excellent pubs and restaurants within 1 mile. Riding and Suffolk Punch Horse Trust 1 mile. Beach, fishing and bicycle hire 1.5 miles. Golf 5 miles.	From A12 (Ipswich-Lowestoft) take 2nd exit at roundabout at Melton onto A1152 (Bawdsey, Orford). In 1.5 miles, at roundabout, turn right onto B1083 (Bawdsey, Hollesley). Within 0.75 miles fork left to Hollesley. At Duck Corner cross road, turn right and continue through village to site, 100 yds. past Red Brick Bridge. GPS: 52.04503, 1.42683

Open: All year.

Charges guide

Per unit incl. 2 persons and electricity	£ 18.00
extra person (over 3 yrs)	£ 3.50

Woodbridge
Steadings Park Camping and Caravan Site

Ipswich Road, Newbourne, Woodbridge IP12 4NS (Suffolk) T: 01473 736505.
E: reception@steadingspark.co.uk **alanrogers.com/UK3324**

Steadings Park is a rural campsite bordering the Newbourne Spring Nature Reserve and the River Deben. This quiet retreat provides the perfect base for walkers and cyclists to explore the pleasant, rolling Suffolk countryside and coast. There are 90 pitches spread across 20 acres in five fields. The main touring field has spacious, flat pitches, 60 with 10-16A electricity on well drained ground. A further small sheltered field (5A electricity) for tents is conveniently located near the new sanitary block. A holiday home has been installed in a secluded garden area.

Facilities	Directions
Heated sanitary block with open washbasins, free hot showers and wet room for disabled visitors (key access). Family shower room. Washing machine and dryer. Fridge/freezer available. Shop. Two play areas. Dog walking area. WiFi over site (charged). Club rallies are welcome. Off site: The Fox Inn pub and restaurant. Restaurants, tea shops and shopping in Woodbridge.	From A14 travelling west take exit 58 signed A12N, Woodbridge. Continue along A12, at roundabout take 3rd exit towards Newbourne. After 800 yds. turn right, signed Fox Inn and Katie's Garden, then follow signs to park. GPS: 52.04129, 1.30217

Open: 1 March - 31 October.

Charges guide

Per unit incl. 2 persons and electricity	£ 20.00
extra person	£ 3.50

For latest campsite news visit
alanrogers.com

Woodbridge
Moat Barn Touring Caravan Park

Dallinghoo Road, Bredfield, Woodbridge IP13 6BD (Suffolk) T: 01473 737520.

alanrogers.com/UK3330

Mike Allen opened this small adults only touring park in April 2000 on the Suffolk Heritage Cycle Route and also the Hull-Harwich National Cycle Route. The main touring area is bordered by established hedging and incorporates a circular roadway. The park currently provides 34 level grass pitches, all with 10A electricity. The park is popular with both walkers and cyclists and provides a tranquil environment to explore nearby Woodbridge and surrounding areas. The park has limited provision for large units (for example, American motorhomes).

Facilities

The well equipped sanitary block can be heated. Motorcaravan services. Bicycle hire. Free WiFi. B&B accommodation available. Off site: Nearby pub serving food. Public footpath. Bus stops outside site.

Open: 1 March - 15 January.

Directions

Park is midway between Woodbridge and Wickham Market. From A12 take turning signed Bredfield (left from south, right from north). At village pump in Bredfield turn right and follow road past public house and church. Continue through S-bends and, after 200 yds, site entrance is on left, just after farm buildings. GPS: 52.13510, 1.31710

Charges guide

Per unit incl. 2 persons and electricity	£ 19.00
extra person	£ 3.00

For latest campsite news visit
alanrogers.com

THE REGION COMPRISES LINCOLNSHIRE, RUTLAND, NORTHAMPTONSHIRE, NOTTINGHAMSHIRE, WEST MIDLANDS, DERBYSHIRE, STAFFORDSHIRE, LEICESTERSHIRE, WARWICKSHIRE, HEREFORDSHIRE, WORCESTERSHIRE, GLOUCESTERSHIRE & SHROPSHIRE

Spanning central England, from the ancient borders of Wales in the west across to Lincolnshire on the east coast, the Heart of England is rich in glorious rolling countryside, magnificent castles, fine stately houses and beautiful gardens.

The diverse countryside of the Heart of England includes: the Lincolnshire Wolds, with the dramatic open landscape of the Fens; the ragged crags, dales and moorland of the Peak District National Park in Derbyshire and Staffordshire; the heathered hilltops of Shropshire; the famous Sherwood Forest in the heart of Nottinghamshire; and the miles of lush green countryside of Herefordshire, dotted with black and white timber houses. Rutland Water is a mecca for watersports and the whole region offers superb opportunities for walking, cycling and more daring activities such as rock climbing and caving. The Cotswolds to the west of the region is the largest Area of Outstanding Natural Beauty in England and Wales. Here you will find many traditional English villages with charming country pubs and cottage gardens. Other significant features of the region are the rivers and canals. Passing pretty towns and villages, a large canal network threads its way through the area, weaving through the Lincolnshire Fens, past the waterside bars and restaurants of Birmingham and along to the estuaries of the rivers Severn and Avon.

Places of interest

Lincolnshire: Skegness and seal sanctuary.

Rutland: market towns of Oakham and Uppingham; Rutland water outdoor centre.

Northamptonshire: Silverstone; Althorp House; Abington Park Museum.

Nottinghamshire: Nottingham Castle and city of caves; Sherwood Forest.

West Midlands: Birmingham; Cadbury World.

Derbyshire: Bakewell; Buxton; Peak District National Park; Chatsworth House.

Staffordshire: Alton Towers; Stoke-on-Trent.

Leicestershire: Snibston Discovery Park; Twycross Zoo. Great Central steam railway.

Warwickshire: Warwick Castle; Kenilworth Castle; Stratford-upon-Avon.

Herefordshire: Hereford Cathedral.

Worcestershire: Severn Valley Railway.

Gloucestershire: Gloucester cathedral and falconry; Cheltenham; Forest of Dean.

Shropshire: Shrewsbury and Whitchurch.

Did you know?

The last battle of the English Civil War was on 3 September 1651 at Worcester.

The World Toe Wrestling Championship, held every June in Wetton, is a registered international sport.

The hollow trunk of the 'Mighty Tree' in Sherwood Forest is reputedly where Robin Hood and his Merry Men hid from the Sheriff of Nottingham.

Rutland is the smallest county in Britain, measuring just 16 miles by 16 miles.

The Emperor Fountain at Chatsworth House, designed in 1844 by Joseph Paxton, is the tallest in Britain at just over 260 feet.

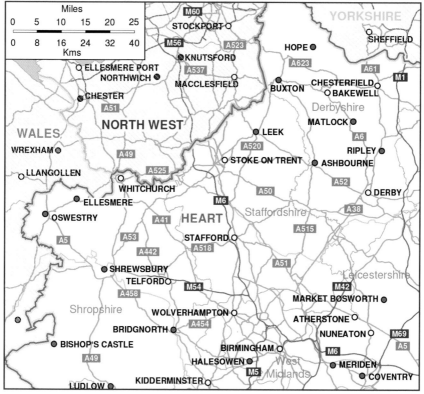

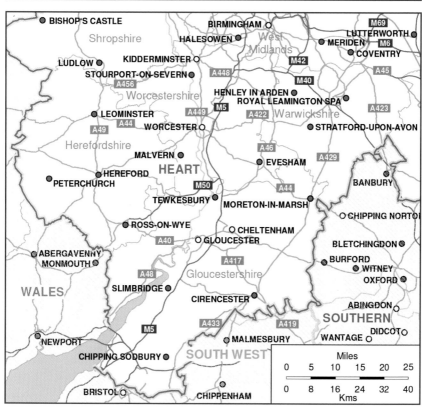

For latest campsite news visit
alanrogers.com

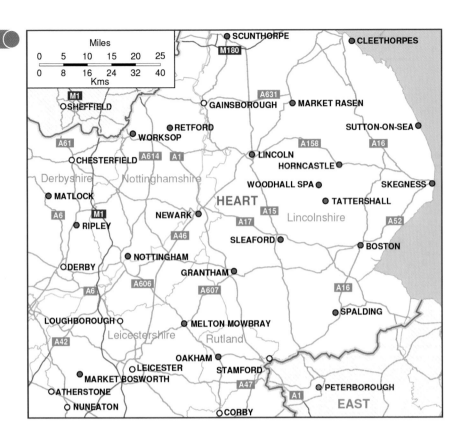

Ashbourne
Rivendale Caravan & Leisure Park

Buxton Road, Alsop-en-le-Dale, Ashbourne DE6 1QU (Derbyshire) T: 01335 310311.
E: enquiries@rivendalecaravanpark.co.uk **alanrogers.com/UK3850**

This unusual park has been developed in the bowl of a hill quarry which was last worked over 50 years ago. The steep quarry walls shelter three sides with marvellous views over the Peak District National Park countryside to the south. Near the entrance to the park is a renovated stone building which houses reception, shop, bar and a café/restaurant. Nearby are 102 level and landscaped pitches, mostly of a generous size with 16A electricity and a mix of hardstanding and grass. In two separate fields and a copse, there is provision for 50 tents and this area includes a fishing lake. The park takes up about 11 acres and a further 26 acres belong to the owners, with certain parts suitable for walking – a must to appreciate the Derbyshire countryside with its dry stone walls and wild flowers, as well as a little more of the quarry history. The park is situated almost on the Tissington Trail for walking or off-road cycling and links with the High Peak and Monsal Dale trails. Other spectacular walks and cycle rides run along the Manifold, Wye and Dove valleys.

Facilities

Good, heated toilet facilities include some washbasins in cubicles for ladies. Excellent en-suite room for disabled visitors. Laundry room. Motorcaravan services. Gas. Shop (all essentials). Bar (evenings) and café with homemade and local food (open mornings, lunch and evenings, w/ends only in low season). Special events monthly and games in main season. Hot tubs for hire, delivered to your pitch. Fly fishing lake. For rent are B&B rooms, camping pods, lodges and yurts. Two lodges adapted for wheelchair users. Torches useful. WiFi in some areas (charged). Off site: Riding and bicycle hire 5 miles. Sailing and boat launching 8 miles. Golf 10 miles. Alton Towers 35 minutes drive. Go Ape. National Tramway Museum. Chatsworth and Haddon Hall. Derwent Valley Mills.

Open: All year excl. 4-29 January.

Directions

Park is 7 miles north of Ashbourne on the A515 to Buxton, on the eastern side of the road. It is well signed between the turnings east to Alsop Moor and Matlock (A5012), but take care as this is a very fast section of the A515. GPS: 53.106383, -1.760567

Charges guide

Per unit incl. 2 persons	
and electricity	£ 19.00 - £ 27.00
extra person	£ 2.50
child (4-15 yrs)	£ 2.00
dog	£ 2.00

For latest campsite news visit
alanrogers.com

Ashbourne
Ashbourne Heights

Fenny Bentley, Ashbourne DE6 1LE (Derbyshire) T: 01335 350228. E: ashbourneheights@northdales.co.uk
alanrogers.com/UK3800

Ashbourne Heights is set on high, flat ground in the Peak District National Park with marvellous views. The site provides 260 spacious and carefully positioned pitches, of which 170 are for touring units. On grass or with hardstanding, most have 16A electricity. Privately owned caravan holiday homes (30) and 60 seasonal units occupy further fields. Amenities include an indoor, heated swimming pool which is open all season. The park is in the heart of the National Park – Dovedale and Ilam are only a mile or two by footpath and the Tissington Trail with access to the High Peak Trail passes by the park. The surrounding Derbyshire countryside provides breathtaking landscapes. Destinations for days out could include Buxton, Chatsworth House, the Crich Tram Museum or Alton Towers.

Facilities

Two heated, stone-built toilet blocks are well maintained and clean. No special facilities for children or disabled campers. Washing machine and dryer. Shop for basics and gas. Good play area. Heated indoor swimming pool (all season, charged). WiFi throughout (charged). Winter caravan storage. Torches useful. Off site: Pub and restaurant nearby. Golf 2 miles. Fishing, riding and bicycle hire 3 miles. Boat launching and sailing 7 miles.

Open: 1 March - 2 November.

Directions

Park is west off A515 Buxton - Ashbourne road, just north of Fenny Bentley village; the entrance is 100 yds. south of old railway bridge (take care at sharp turn to site road when approaching from Ashbourne). GPS: 53.054792, -1.747481

Charges guide

Per unit incl. 2 persons and electricity	£ 20.00 - £ 25.00
extra person	£ 3.00
dog	£ 3.00

Ashbourne
Callow Top Holiday Park

Buxton Road, Sandybrook, Ashbourne DE6 2AQ (Derbyshire) T: 01335 344020.
E: enquiries@callowtop.co.uk **alanrogers.com/UK3855**

Situated just north of the market town of Ashbourne, Callow Top has an attractive setting in an elevated countryside position. The park's location makes it well placed to allow visitors to explore the picturesque villages, bustling market towns and the many attractions of the Peak District. It is ideal for both walking and cycling holidays. Spread over seven separate areas at the top of a hill, there are 200 flat pitches of which 100 are for tents only. The touring pitches on hardstanding have 10A electricity, the grass pitches have no power supply. Water points tend to be rather scarce. Some of the pitches are rather small and on these, cars are parked away from the pitch. Day and evening visitors are not permitted.

Facilities

Three heated toilet blocks (only one open in low season) provide unisex showers (20p). Toilet for disabled visitors. Laundry room. Motorcaravan services. Calor gas. Shop. Inn/restaurant, snack bar and takeaway (w/ends only in low season). Heated swimming and paddling pools (May-Sept). Bicycle hire. Games room. Play area. Entertainment (w/ends and high season). Fishing. WiFi in some areas (free). Winter caravan storage. Off site: Ashbourne (supermarket, etc) 1 mile. Golf 1 miles. Riding 3 miles. Carsington Water (boat launching) 4 miles.

Open: 20 March - 8 November.

Directions

At Sandybrook, 0.5 miles north of Ashbourne, on the A515 (Ashbourne-Buxton) turn west into site road which becomes steep. Site is signed. GPS: 53.02693, -1.74646

Charges guide

Per unit incl. 2 persons and electricity	£ 22.50 - £ 32.00
extra person	£ 2.50
child (4-16 yrs)	£ 1.50
dog	£ 1.50

For latest campsite news visit
alanrogers.com

Ashbourne

Woodland Caravan Park

Windmill Lane, Snelston, Ashbourne DE6 2GT (Derbyshire) T: 01335 300598.

E: info@woodlandcaravanpark.co.uk **alanrogers.com/UK3860**

Set in woodland within the private grounds of the Snelston Estate, this site presents a charming, tranquil haven for those seeking a leafy retreat. The 52 pitches, constructed from local limestone, are level, each with 10A electricity hook-up. Expect to see shafts of light falling on irregularly arranged pitches allowing a sense of privacy within the tall trees that give the site its name. These trees help screen out low level traffic noise, which is much reduced at night. The modern, clean toilet block is tastefully coloured to blend with the surroundings. The 900-acre estate has plenty of walks on local footpaths.

Facilities

One modern, clean, heated toilet block has a room for disabled visitors. Ample low level lighting on site. Laundry. Microwave. No motorcaravan services. Separate, enclosed area for dog walking. Reception offers advice on waymarked walks. Site has eco-friendly water handling. WiFi over site (charged). Off site: Darley Moor Motorcycle Circuit 1 mile. Local Spa town of Ashbourne 2 miles. Tissington Trail with bicycle hire 5 miles.

Open: 13 March - 1 November.

Directions

NB: postcode is unreliable. Stay on the A515 until you see the brown caravan sign pointing to the village of Snelston. GPS: 52.98117, -1.753294

Charges guide

Per unit incl. 2 persons and electricity	£ 20.00 - £ 25.00
extra person	£ 4.00
dog	£ 1.00

Bishop's Castle

The Green Caravan Park

Wentnor, Bishop's Castle SY9 5EF (Shropshire) T: 01588 650605. E: karen@greencaravanpark.co.uk
alanrogers.com/UK4440

Remotely situated in a pleasant valley, in a designated Area of Outstanding Natural Beauty and sandwiched between the Stiperstones and The Long Mynd, The Green would make an ideal base for some serious walking; a footpath to the Stiperstones passes through the site. The 15-acre site is delightful and is divided into several fields. There are 160 pitches taking tourers, seasonal units and around 20 holiday homes (with 53 pitches having 16A electricity hook-ups for tourers). The main field has some hardstandings. The East Onny is a small, shallow river which runs through the site, much enjoyed by the youngsters who can spend many hours catching minnows

Facilities

One main sanitary block, built into the side of a large barn, provides adequate and plentiful facilities with spacious hot showers (20p), dishwashing and laundry facilities. There is no dedicated unit for disabled campers. Small shop in new reception building. Playground. WiFi (free by reception). Off site: Three pubs within 3 miles, direct access to one. Shop 200 yds. Fishing 3 miles. Riding 5 miles. Bishop's Castle with museums. Leisure Centre.

Open: Easter - 31 October.

Directions

Wentnor is southwest of Shrewsbury. From Shrewsbury take A49. Ignore sat nav instructions to turn right but continue and turn right onto A489 for 7 miles. Turn right off A489 at brown campsite sign. Site is immediately after The Inn on the Green. GPS: 52.53421, -2.91428

Charges guide

Per unit incl. 2 persons and electricity	£ 18.50
extra person	£ 6.00

Boston

Long Acres Touring Park

Station Road, Old Leake, Boston PE22 9RF (Lincolnshire) T: 01205 871555.

E: enquiries@longacres-caravanpark.co.uk **alanrogers.com/UK3695**

An attractive, adults only site on the Lincolnshire Fens north of Boston, yet only six miles from the coastline of the Wash, Long Acres is a purpose-built park opened in 2008 and attractively laid out to take maximum advantage of the great variety of trees and shrubs. Ranged on either side of the park's single road, the 40 pitches, all with 10A electricity hook-ups, are on hardstandings separated by well tended grass for tents and awnings. The beaches and attractions of Skegness are an easy drive away, whilst Gibraltar Point, Snipe Dales, Freiston Shore and Frampton Marshes are also within easy reach.

Facilities

A single well equipped, central toilet block provides preset showers, open-style washbasins with hairdryers, a small freezer for ice packs and an outstanding en-suite unit for disabled visitors. Motorcaravan services. Calor gas. Reception has tourist information, maps of walking and cycling routes, sample menus from local pubs and a small library. Area available for small rallies. Boules pitch. Dog exercise area. WiFi over site (charged). Off site: Fishing 1 mile. Golf 7 miles. Boston 9 miles. Bicycle hire 10 miles.

Open: 1 March - 8 January.

Directions

Old Leake is 8 miles northeast of Boston on A52. The site is best approached from the A16 Boston - Louth road. At Sibsey turn east on B1184 towards Old Leake. At T-junction turn left and in 1.7 miles turn right along Station Road to site on left. GPS: 53.057487, 0.063732

Charges guide

Per unit incl. 2 persons and electricity	£ 18.00 - £ 22.00

For latest campsite news visit
alanrogers.com

Bridgnorth

Stanmore Hall Touring Park

Stourbridge Road, Bridgnorth WV15 6DT (Shropshire) T: 01746 761761. E: stanmore@morris-leisure.co.uk

alanrogers.com/UK4400

This attractive park is situated in the former grounds of Stanmore Hall where the huge lily pond, fine mature trees and beautifully manicured lawns give a mark of quality. There are 131 generously sized pitches, 128 with 16A electricity, digital TV connection and a choice of grass or hardstanding. Thirty of these have water and waste. Also available are 23 standard pitches but most are on grass. Some pitches are reserved for adult only use (over 18 years). Access and internal roads are tarmac; site lighting is adequate and reassuring. The park is Caravan Club affiliated but non-members are very welcome. A size restriction of 30 ft. exists for motorcaravans. Reception is located within the shop. The adjacent conservatory (open during shop hours) allows guests to sit in comfort overlooking the lake and observe the wildlife. But there's something else too: this is a peaceful site with personality. Little wonder it needs advance booking and people keep returning to enjoy its atmosphere. Open all year round, there are even groups who spend Christmas and New Year at Stanmore Hall.

Facilities

The upgraded, centrally heated sanitary block is accessed by key. Facilities are excellent and provide washbasins in cubicles and a room for disabled guests and baby care. Full laundry facilities. Motorcaravan services. A well equipped shop stocks camping and caravan accessories. A digital TV booster with Freeview is available. Play area. Dogs are limited to two per unit. WiFi throughout (charged). Off site: Fishing at Bridgnorth 1.5 miles. Golf and riding 2 miles.

Open: All year.

Directions

Site is 1.5 miles from Bridgnorth on the A458 (signed Stourbridge). If using sat nav, approach from Bridgnorth only. GPS: 52.52715, -2.378617

Charges guide

Per unit incl. 2 persons and electricity	£ 25.70 - £ 28.30
extra person	£ 7.50 - £ 7.90
child (5-15 yrs)	£ 2.50
dog (max. 2)	£ 1.50

Buxton

Buxton Caravan Club Site

Grin Low Road, Ladmanlow, Buxton SK17 6UJ (Derbyshire) T: 01298 77735. E: buxton@caravanclub.co.uk

alanrogers.com/UK3805

Conveniently situated for the Peak District, yet nestling peacefully in the idyllic valley floor, Buxton Caravan Club Site is the ideal location for those looking to escape the hustle and bustle of modern life without sacrificing home comforts. It has 117 large, mainly hardstanding pitches, all with 16A electricity and TV hook-ups. The delightful town of Buxton, with its colourful Pavilion Gardens, is nearby. The Opera House is of great interest and is home to a wide range of events, including the world famous festival in mid July to August. Maximum unit length is 9 m. Only backpacking tents are accepted. This is the ideal destination for seeing the best of England's rolling countryside, either on foot or by bicycle. A choice of stately homes can be found close to the site and there are many local customs to discover, such as the folk art of 'well dressing', an ancient form of flower arranging dating from Pagan times.

Facilities

A centrally positioned, heated sanitary block provides free showers and facilities for children and disabled visitors (RADAR key). Laundry room. Motorcaravan services. Shop sells basics, including newspaper and milk. Woodland walks. Play area. Recycling facility. WiFi over site (charged). Security barrier. Public phone. Off site: Public transport 1 mile. Supermarket 3 miles. Golf 4 miles. Cinema 10 miles. Chatsworth House. Haddon Hall. Jodrell Bank Discovery Centre.

Open: 20 March - 2 November.

Directions

Turn left off A53 (Buxton-Leek) within 1.5 miles at signpost to Grin Low, Harpur Hill. In 300 yds. turn left into site road (signposted Grin Low). The site entrance is in 0.25 mile. Please follow these directions carefully, alternative routes are unsuitable for towing. The route from Congleton on A54 is narrow and steep. GPS: 53.24534, -1.92845

Charges guide

Per person	£ 5.50 - £ 7.00
child (5-17 yrs)	£ 1.40 - £ 2.40
pitch incl. electricity (non-member)	£ 16.20 - £ 18.90
dog	free

For latest campsite news visit

alanrogers.com

Buxton

Lime Tree Holiday Park

Dukes Drive, Buxton SK17 9RP (Derbyshire) T: 01298 22988. E: info@limetreeparkbuxton.com

alanrogers.com/UK3840

Lime Tree is in a convenient, edge of town location that makes a very good base for touring the Peak District. The site has three widely spaced main areas, touring pitches on two levels with a toilet block on the upper level, a caravan holiday home area which has the reception shop and games room, and above and a short distance away, a large, mainly sloping field for tents. The toilet block for the tents and a play area are above reception. The refitted, original unit serves the tent area. Both are heated and have top quality fittings. Laundry room. Shop. Play area. Games/TV room. WiFi area (free). Off site: Pub serving food 10 mins. walk. Swimming, riding and golf 1 mile. Bicycle hire 5 miles.

There are 40 seasonal pitches. With good views, the park is situated next to a thickly wooded limestone gorge and a magnificent old railway viaduct provides a dramatic backdrop.

Facilities	Directions
A modern toilet building serves the touring area including some washbasins in cubicles, controllable showers, baby room with modern baby bath and a family room with facilities for disabled visitors. The refitted, original unit serves the tent area. Both are heated and have top quality fittings. Laundry room. Shop. Play area. Games/TV room. WiFi area (free). Off site: Pub serving food 10 mins. walk. Swimming, riding and golf 1 mile. Bicycle hire 5 miles.	Park is on outskirts of Buxton. From town, just after hospital bear sharp left into Dukes Drive, go under railway viaduct and site is on right. From south watch out for sharp turn right at foot of hill (signed in advance). GPS: 53.250230, -1.896673

Open: 1 March - 31 October.

Charges guide

Per unit incl. 2 persons and electricity	£ 25.00 - £ 31.00
extra person	£ 5.00

Buxton

Clover Fields Touring Caravan Park

1 Heath View, Harpur Hill, Buxton SK17 9PU (Derbyshire) T: 01298 78731.
E: reservations@cloverfieldstouringpark.co.uk **alanrogers.com/UK3845**

The Redferns are more than happy to welcome you to their family owned, adults only park (over 18 yrs). It is located on the outskirts of the spa town of Buxton and within easy reach of the Peak District National Park. You will be able to relax here in the 'away from it all' atmosphere. There are just 45 pitches serviced by a first rate toilet block. The pitches are divided by low hedges, part hardstanding and part grass, all with 16A electricity, a water tap and a concealed dustbin. There is a little noise from the adjacent road. Recently added is a newly constructed and stocked fishing pond. The site has its own animals which are happy to be spoiled by visitors! The new café serves fresh food and takeaway dishes.

Facilities	Directions
The toilet and shower block is modern and clean with many complimentary toiletry items. Facilities for disabled visitors. Gas supplies. Laundry room. Motorcaravan services. Licensed shop selling essentials, local dairy produce, bacon and chutney and caravan accessories. Newspapers and milk delivered to your pitch. Barbecues allowed but no open fires. Small library. Fishing. Resident animals and birds. Torches recommended.	From Buxton, at Harpur Hill just to the southeast, turn right off A515 (Buxton-Ashbourne) onto B5053. Turn immediately right towards Harpur Hill. Site entrance is 0.5 miles on left (easily missed) at start of 40 mph limit. GPS: 53.23066, -1.8878

Open: All year.

Charges guide

Per unit incl. 2 persons and electricity	£ 23.00 - £ 25.00
extra person	£ 5.00

Chipping Sodbury

Little Wood Caravan Park

Mapleridge Lane, South Gloucestershire, Chipping Sodbury BS37 6PB (Gloucestershire) T: 01454 294256.
E: info@littlewoodcaravanpark.co.uk **alanrogers.com/UK4165**

Little Wood offers a relaxing venue with first class facilities. Previously a private members club, they are now pleased to welcome you to their attractive park set in seven acres of beautiful woodland with well groomed lawns. An adult only site, located just outside of the market town of Chipping Sodbury, it is ideal for a stopover or as a touring base. There are 22 level hardstanding touring pitches, all with 10A electricity hook-up. There is plenty of scope for relaxation with indoor and outdoor swimming pools, short tennis courts, boules and a nine-hole putting green.

Facilities	Directions
One heated sanitary block with clean, modern showers and vanity style washbasins. Laundry. Basic motorcaravan services. Outdoor and heated indoor swimming pools (May-Sept). Two short tennis courts. Boules. Croquet. 9-hole putting course. Communal barbeque areas. Pavilion with pool table, darts, table tennis, and TV. Free WiFi on part of site. Pets are not allowed. Torches handy.	From the north on M5, take exit 14 and join B4509. Continue on this road and B4060 towards Wickwar and Chipping Sodbury. Join Mapleridge Lane (on left south of Wickwar at crossroads). The site is then on your right. GPS: 51.56793, -2.39523

Open: 1 March - 31 October.

Charges guide

Per unit incl. 2 adults and electricity	£ 21.50 - £ 24.50

For latest campsite news visit

alanrogers.com

Cirencester
Hoburne Cotswold

Broadway Lane, South Cerney, Cirencester GL7 5UQ (Gloucestershire) T: 01285 860216.

E: enquiries@hoburne.co.uk **alanrogers.com/UK4100**

Since this park is adjacent to the Cotswold Water Park, those staying here will have easy access to the varied watersports available. On the park itself there is a lake with pedaloes for hire. The wide range of other amenities includes outdoor and indoor heated swimming pools and an impressive, large indoor leisure complex. There are 189 well marked touring pitches for any type of unit, all with hardstanding (fairly level) and a grass surround for awning or tent. Pitches are of a good size with low hedging between them, and very little shade; all have electricity (10A, some need long leads).

Facilities	Directions
Four small toilet blocks are clean and well maintained with preset showers and background heating. Baby changing facilities. Basic facilities for disabled visitors. The site has heavy weekend trade. Launderette. Supermarket. Indoor leisure complex including a pool with flume, spa bath, sauna, detox, steam room and mini-gym. Outdoor pool (mid May-early Sept). Clubhouse with bar, food and entertainment and free WiFi. Animals are not accepted.	Three miles southeast of Cirencester on A419, turn west towards Cotswold Water Park at new roundabout on bypass onto B4696 signed South Cerney. Continue past Water Park for 1.5 miles. Road leading to campsite is on right. Take second right and follow signs. GPS: 51.66018, -1.91910

Open: March - October.

Charges guide

Per unit incl. max. 6 persons and electricity	£ 18.00 - £ 41.00
serviced 'super' pitch	£ 20.00 - £ 43.00

Cleethorpes
Thorpe Park Holiday Centre

Humberston, Cleethorpes DN35 0PW (Lincolnshire) T: 01472 813395.

alanrogers.com/UK3655

Thorpe Park is a Haven Holiday Park at Cleethorpes on the north Lincolnshire coast. The touring site, although part of one of the largest caravan parks in Europe, is neat and compact. There are 81 landscaped Euro pitches with brick-built hardstandings, electricity, water and drainage, and a further 55 in an open area, most with electricity. A third area has 17 tent pitches (no electricity). There is direct access to the beach from a corner of the site and the park's main entertainment complex is a short walk away. A shuttle train will take you to more distant parts of the park including a nine-hole golf course.

Facilities	Directions
Three modern toilet blocks. The one in the main area has pushbutton showers in well fitted cubicles, open style washbasins and an excellent room (key access) for disabled visitors and families. Launderette. Motorcaravan services. Supermarket. Fish and chips. Entertainment complex with main 'show bar', café bar, amusements and games room. Heated indoor pool and outdoor flumes, splash zone and 'lazy river'. Play area. Crazy golf. Climbing wall. Tennis. Multisports court. Fishing lakes. Roller rink. Bicycle and buggy hire. WiFi over part of site.	Cleethorpes is 2 miles southeast of Grimsby. From M180 take A180 to Grimsby, turn south on A16 (Louth), then east on A1098 to Humberston and follow signs for Pleasure Island. Park is to right at roundabout. GPS: 53.5347, 0.00412

Open: Easter - 2 November.

Charges guide

Per unit incl. up to 4 persons	£ 17.00 - £ 67.00
extra person	£ 3.00

Charges for Sun-Thurs are 50-60% lower and discounts of 15-50% are available for longer stays.

Coventry
Hollyfast Caravan Park

Wall Hill Road, Allesley, Coventry CV5 9EL (Warwickshire) T: 024 7633 6411.

E: sales@hollyfastcaravanpark.co.uk **alanrogers.com/UK4075**

Hollyfast is situated in beautiful countryside on the outskirts of Coventry, part of the park being set within a lovely woodland area giving peace and tranquillity all year round. Located on the Birmingham side of Coventry, this means a short drive into the centre of Coventry and a fifteen minute drive to Birmingham's National Exhibition Centre. You will receive a friendly welcome and be directed to a very clean and well spaced site with 40 touring pitches of varying sizes with 16A electricity connections. Cars are parked away from pitches. Rallies are welcome and a club house is provided.

Facilities	Directions
One modern toilet block provides simple, clean facilities with good sized showers (3 per sex) and open washbasins. Toilet and shower for disabled campers. Shop. Club house for rallies. Large outdoor ranch style play centre and indoor games room. Deposit for barrier (£25). Torches useful. Off site: Shops, three pubs (hot and cold food), a golf course and a riding centre nearby.	From M1/M45 take A45 towards Birmingham. Turn right on A4114 and follow caravan signs. Turn off in front of White Lion pub, site is 0.5 miles on left. GPS: 52.44588, -1.55572

Open: All year.

Charges guide

Per unit incl. 2 persons and electricity (non member)	£ 20.00 - £ 22.00
extra person	£ 3.00

For latest campsite news visit
alanrogers.com

Ellesmere

Fernwood Caravan Park

Lyneal, Ellesmere SY12 0QF (Shropshire) T: 01948 710221. E: enquiries@fernwoodpark.co.uk
alanrogers.com/UK4380

Fernwood is set in an area known as the Shropshire Lake District – the mere at Ellesmere is the largest of nine meres – and the picturesque Shropshire Union Canal is only a few minutes walk. The landscaped park is tranquil and presented to a very high standard, the natural vegetation blending harmoniously with trees and shrubs. In addition to 163 caravan holiday homes, with two units for hire, there are 30 touring pitches (caravans, motorcaravans and trailer tents only) in several well cut, grassy enclosures (including 30 seasonal long stays). Some are in light woodland, others in more open, but still relatively sheltered situations. All pitches have 10A electricity and six also have water and drainage. One area is set aside for units with adults only.

Facilities

The small toilet block for touring units has background heating for cooler days and includes some washbasins in cabins and facilities for disabled visitors. Baby changing facilities. Basic motorcaravan services. Dishwashing facilities in laundry room, also additional sanitary facilities for ladies and men. Shop doubles as reception (from 1/4-30/10, hours vary). Coarse fishing lake. Forty acres of woodland for walking. Grassy play area for children. Off site: Shrewsbury, Oswestry and Chester are all within easy travelling distance.

Open: 1 March - 30 November.

Directions

Park is just northeast of Lyneal village, signed southwest off the B5063 Ellesmere-Wem road, 1.5 miles from junction of the B5063 with the A495. GPS: 52.89896, -2.81739

Charges guide

Per unit incl. 2 persons and electricity	£ 23.50 - £ 27.50
multi-service pitch	£ 27.00 - £ 31.00

One night free for every 7 booked in advance.
Midweek saver (mid and low season, 4 nights for price of 3, telephone bookings only).

Evesham

Ranch Caravan Park

Honeybourne, Evesham WR11 7PR (Worcestershire) T: 01386 830744. E: enquiries@ranch.co.uk
alanrogers.com/UK4180

This quiet, attractive caravan park set in the Vale of Evesham covers an area of 50 acres of flat, partly undulating, hedged meadows. The park lies between Bidford-on-Avon and Broadway and is only half an hour's drive from Stratford. The park takes 120 touring units – caravans, motorcaravans and trailer tents, but not other tents. The spacious pitches are not marked but the staff help to position units. All have 10A electrical connections and there are 21 hardstandings including eight fully serviced pitches (electricity, TV, water and drainage). There are 193 caravan holiday homes in their own section. The Vale of Evesham is often overshadowed by its next door neighbour, the Cotswolds. It is, however, populated by some of the prettiest villages in the area and is well worth exploring in its own right. Hidcote Manor Gardens, Broadway Tower and the Fleece Inn at Bretforton are all within a short drive. The riverside town of Evesham is an attractive market town some six miles to the west and is well worth a visit.

Facilities

Two very well appointed, modern sanitary blocks with free hot showers and heating, one with facilities for disabled visitors, plus baby changing area. Laundry facilities. Motorcaravan services. Shop. Clubhouse (w/ends only off season) offering wide range of good value meals with entertainment arranged throughout the season. Heated pool (55x30 ft; Spr. B.H-mid Sept). Spa (Mar-Nov). Gym and sauna (charged). Games room with TV. Playground. WiFi (charged). Off site: Riding and bicycle hire 2 miles. Fishing 4 miles. Golf 6 miles.

Open: 1 March - 30 November.

Directions

From A46 Evesham take B4035 towards Chipping Campden. After Badsey and Bretforton before Weston Subedge pass over the old railway bridge, turn east at the crossroads to Honeybourne. Park is through village on left before station. GPS: 52.09722, -1.83124

Charges guide

Per unit incl. 2 persons and electricity	£ 24.50 - £ 29.00
incl. water and drainage	£ 28.00 - £ 32.50
extra person (over 5 yrs)	free - £ 4.50
dog	free - £ 2.50

One free night for every 7 booked.

For latest campsite news visit
alanrogers.com

Grantham
Woodland Waters

Willoughby Road, Ancaster, Grantham NG32 3RT (Lincolnshire) T: 01400 230888.
E: info@woodlandwaters.co.uk **alanrogers.com/UK3765**

This attractive holiday park occupies 70 acres of woodland, gently sloping grassland and lakes, with the caravan park itself occupying about 20 acres. There are 120 pitches although only 60 are regularly used (all with 10A electricity and water taps nearby). There is a rally field of 20 pitches with hook-ups, plus areas for camping and for those not requiring electricity. The land slopes gently down to the 14-acre lake and the pitches nearer the water are more level, although probably not suitable for those with younger children since there is no fencing.

Facilities

A single, modern, heated toilet block is well maintained and kept clean. Open style washbasins and free showers (controllable for ladies, pushbutton for men). Facilities for disabled visitors. A second block provides extra facilities when the additional camping areas are fully occupied. Small laundry room with washing machine, tumble dryer and iron, but no laundry sinks. Motorcaravan services. Bar and restaurant with takeaway (all year). Play area. Four fishing lakes. Chalets and rooms to rent. WiFi.

Open: All year.

Directions

Ancaster is 8 miles northeast of Grantham and 19 miles south of Lincoln. The park entrance is off the A153 Grantham-Sleaford road, 600 yds. west of the junction with the B6403 High Dyke road (Ermine Street). GPS: 52.98053, -0.54698

Charges guide

Per unit incl. 4 persons and electricity	£ 18.00 - £ 20.00
extra person	£ 2.00

Grantham
Wagtail Country Park

Cliff Lane, Marston, Grantham NG32 2HU (Lincolnshire) T: 07814 481088. E: info@wagtailcountrypark.co.uk
alanrogers.com/UK3775

There has been a small campsite here for many years but the new owner has transformed the appearance of the original camping area alongside an attractive little fishing lake and has created a new, larger lake with additional pitches and facilities. There are now 76 touring pitches, all with electricity (16A), on gravel hardstanding and separated by grass borders, raised flower beds or timber beams. Tents are not accepted. A pleasant trail runs along the embankment bordering the (unfenced) main lake.

Facilities

Two small heated buildings near the original pitches each provide an en-suite controllable shower, washbasin and WC. A new heated and well equipped toilet block includes a WC for disabled visitors and laundry facilities. Motorcaravan services. Security barriers. Gas supplies. Secure caravan storage. Fishing (£5 per person). WiFi over site (charged). Off site: Shopping Outlet and Garden Centre 3 miles. Belton House and golf 5 miles.

Open: All year.

Directions

Site is off A1 between Grantham and Newark. Turn east towards Marston at filling station 1.2 miles north of Gonerby Services, Grantham (from south, move into right lane after passing services). In 500 yds. turn right into Green Lane towards Barkston, then right again in 0.75 miles into Cliff Lane where park is signed and on left. GPS: 52.961229, -0.667269

Charges guide

Per unit incl. 2 persons and electricity	£ 18.50 - £ 24.50
extra person	£ 6.00 - £ 7.50
No credit cards.	

Halesowen
Clent Hills Camping & Caravanning Club Site

Fieldhouse Lane, Romsley, Halesowen B62 0NH (West Midlands) T: 01562 710015.
alanrogers.com/UK4040

Two miles from the M5/M42 intersection, this site is a stunning surprise, being quiet, peaceful and very pretty with panoramic views of wooded hillsides. The site has partially sloping ground, but site staff are happy to assist where required. The roads through the site are lined with mature trees offering shade. The 95 pitches are mostly level (chocks recommended on some) and all of a good size; 76 have 16A electricity connections and 42 are hardstanding. There is a central grassy area for tents, with some hook-ups. This attractive site is a good base for a range of excursions, all within 15 miles.

Facilities

The central sanitary block is heated in cold weather and provides washbasins in cabins, hairdryers, child and parent room and a wet room for disabled campers. It was spotless when last visited. Washing machine, dryer and ironing facilities. Basic supplies in reception. Small play area with rubber safety surface. Gas supplies. Caravan storage. WiFi (charged). Off site: Pubs within 1 mile.

Open: 24 March - 31 October.

Directions

From M5 exit 4 take A491, branch right to Romsley on B4551 and watch for site signs in Romsley village by shops. Site is on left. GPS: 52.41469, -2.06814

Charges guide

Per unit incl. 2 persons and electricity	£ 15.05 - £ 25.70
Non-member prices are higher.	

For latest campsite news visit
alanrogers.com

Henley-in-Arden

Island Meadow Caravan Park

The Mill House, Aston Cantlow, Henley-in-Arden B95 6JP (Warwickshire) T: 01789 488273.
E: holiday@islandmeadowcaravanpark.co.uk **alanrogers.com/UK4090**

This peaceful, traditional, family run site is in a delightful rural location, surrounded by the River Alne and its mill race. A good base for walking, cycling and birdwatching, it has 80 pitches in total with 56 holiday homes (five for rent) located around the perimeter. The 24 touring pitches are on the spacious, central grassy area of the site, all have 10A electric hook-ups. Only environmentally friendly groundsheets are permitted. Note: The site is on an island, so parents will need to supervise children closely. There is an excellent playground in the village centre (five minutes walk via footpath across Mill Meadow).

Facilities	Directions
Two sanitary units, both heated. The original provides adequate WCs and washbasins for men and the more modern unit has been provided for women, with a separate access shower unit for the men, and a wet room-style suite for disabled visitors on one end. Laundry with washing machine, dryer and ironing facility. The millpond and its weir offer good coarse fishing. Off site: The village has its own Club (campers welcome) and the local pub serves a good range of meals. Golf 3 miles. Riding 4.5 miles. Bicycle hire 6 miles.	From A46 (Stratford-Alcester) follow signs for Mary Arden's House. At Wilmcote follow signs to Aston Cantlow and site. GPS: 52.23549, -1.80265

Directions (continued)

Charges guide

Per unit incl. 2 persons and electricity	£ 25.00
extra person	£ 2.00
child (5-12 yrs)	£ 1.00
tent (2 man)	£ 15.00

Gazebos only by prior arrangement.
No credit cards.

Open: 1 March - 31 October.

Hereford

Lucksall Caravan & Camping Park

Mordiford, Hereford HR1 4LP (Herefordshire) T: 01432 870213. E: karen@lucksallpark.co.uk
alanrogers.com/UK4310

Set in 17 acres and bounded on one side by the River Wye, and over 90 acres of woodland on the other, Lucksall has 139 large, well spaced and level touring pitches, all with 16A electricity and 70 with hardstanding. The river is open to the site with lifebelts and safety messages in evidence. Canoes are available for hire or bring your own (launching facilities); fishing permits may be obtained from reception. A large, fenced playground and a large grassy area for games are provided. A well stocked shop selling a variety of goods is in reception (a mini market is within 1.5 miles) and there is a café/takeaway. A member of the Countryside Discovery group.

Facilities	Directions
Three centrally heated toilet blocks provide top of the range facilities, two separate units with ramped entrances for disabled campers. Family room. Laundry room. Shop and licensed café/takeaway. Free WiFi. Only breathable groundsheets are permitted. Off site: Golf 5 miles. Bicycle hire 9 miles. Riding 10 miles. Sustrans cycle route nearby.	Between Mordiford and Fownhope, 5 miles southeast of Hereford on B4224, the park is well signed. GPS: 52.02302, -2.63052

Charges guide

Per unit incl. 2 persons and electricity	£ 21.00 - £ 33.00
extra person (over 17 yrs)	£ 3.50

Open: 1 March - 30 November.

Hereford

Hereford Camping & Caravanning Club Site

The Millpond, Little Tarrington, Hereford HR1 4JA (Herefordshire) T: 01432 890243.
alanrogers.com/UK4330

This attractive, peaceful site is situated between Hereford and Ledbury and is in an idyllic rural location. The site is next to the millpond after which it was originally named and has 102 large pitches, of which 38 are hardstanding and 84 have 10A electrical hook-ups. Attention has been given to the provision of good facilities for the visitor with disabilities. The large fishing lake (unfenced) is well stocked with coarse fish, has facilities for disabled fishermen and offers reduced rates for campers. Site lighting is minimal so a torch might be useful. There may be some noise at times from a railway track nearby. Dog owners are welcome and there is a designated walking area.

Facilities	Directions
The refurbished, modern building houses heated sanitary facilities, baby changing surface, an upgraded unit for disabled campers (with wet room shower). Laundry. Motorcaravan services. Shop. Information room. WiFi over site (charged). Off site: The local pub is 10 mins. walk, but there is no shop in the village.	Little Tarrington is between Hereford and Ledbury. The site is just north of A438 on eastern edge of Tarrington village. GPS: 52.065295, -2.545902

Charges guide

Per unit incl. 2 persons and electricity	£ 20.70 - £ 34.90
extra person	£ 7.90 - £ 13.30

Non-member prices are higher.

Open: 4 March - 7 November.

For latest campsite news visit
alanrogers.com

Hope

Laneside Caravan Park

Station Road, Hope Valley, Hope S33 6RR (Derbyshire) T: 01433 620215. E: laneside@lineone.net

alanrogers.com/UK3807

Laneside Caravan Park is in a beautiful location facing Win Hill, Lose Hill and the high gritstone hills of The Dark Peak, while the gentler rolling hills of The White Peak are to the south. The park is on the floor of Hope Valley with the River Noe running alongside. There are 160 marked level pitches, 95 on grass and 30 on hardstanding for touring units, while 35 are seasonal; 110 have 16A electricity hook-ups. The two toilet blocks have recently been refurbished. The site welcomes families (although there is no swimming pool on site) and quiet couples, but no young single-sex groups or unaccompanied teenagers. The river separates the site from Hope village – over the bridge and you are there.

Facilities	Directions
Two heated toilet blocks with free hot showers, washbasins in cubicles, large family room and new room for disabled campers (Radar key). Laundry room with baby changing unit. Motorcaravan services. Site shop with basics. Gas exchange and basic camping spares. Dog walk. Payphone. Picnic benches. Large riverside recreation area with picnic benches and boules courts. Security barriers and CCTV protection. WiFi (free). Off site: Shops, pub and restaurant in Hope. Caverns at Castleton 5 minutes. Golf 2 miles. Bicycle hire 4 miles.	From east via A619/A623, at Tideswell crossroads (Anchor pub), turn right onto B6049 (Castleton, Bradwell). Turn left at T-junction (A6187) opposite Travellers' Rest. 500 yds. after Travellers' Rest, just before Hope, look for sign (Laneside) on right directing left into park. GPS: 53.345159, -1.735706

Open: 13 March - 8 November.

Charges guide

Per unit incl. 2 persons and electricity	£ 17.50 - £ 23.50
extra person (over 5 yrs)	£ 2.75

Horncastle

Ashby Park

West Ashby, Horncastle LN9 5PP (Lincolnshire) T: 01507 527966. E: ashbypark@btconnect.com

alanrogers.com/UK3680

Ashby Park is a pleasant, well run park located in 70 acres of former gravel pits that now provide seven attractive fishing lakes. There is a series of clearings occupied by privately owned caravan holiday homes, seasonal caravans and 127 touring pitches. All have access to 16A electricity and 100 pitches also have hardstanding, water tap and drainage. Lakeside pitches will no doubt appeal to anglers, whereas families with young children will probably prefer to be further away from the lakes as they are unfenced. Nearby is the bustling market town of Horncastle renowned for its antique shops.

Facilities	Directions
Three toilet blocks are well maintained and equipped, with open style washbasins and controllable showers; all hot water is metered (20p). Good en-suite facilities for disabled visitors. Washing machine and dryer. Limited dishwashing (in the new block – a long walk from lakeside pitches). Motorcaravan services. Gas supplies. Fishing (day ticket £6). WiFi. Off site: Golf 0.5 miles. Shops, pubs and restaurants in Horncastle 2-3 miles. Riding 5 miles.	Horncastle is 22 miles east of Lincoln. Site is 2.6 miles north of town and signed to east from A158. Follow signs to site, turning north in 1 mile. Also signed to the west from A153 Sleaford-Louth road. GPS: 53.233293, -0.122426

Open: 1 March - 30 November.

Charges guide

Per unit incl. 2 persons and electricity	£ 22.60 - £ 28.30
extra person	£ 5.00

Leek

Glencote Caravan Park

Station Road, Cheddleton, Leek ST13 7EE (Staffordshire) T: 01538 360745. E: canistay@glencote.co.uk

alanrogers.com/UK3970

Nestled in the Churnet Valley, three miles south of the market town of Leek, a pleasant stay awaits you at this well managed, family run park of six acres. Each of the 84 level touring pitches, accessed via tarmac roads, has grass and a paved hardstanding, 16A Europlug and a dedicated water supply. Pretty flowerbeds, trees and varied wildlife make a very pleasant environment. Alongside a fenced coarse fishing pool is a grass play area and this whole corner is enclosed by banks with an abundance of attractive shrubs and flowers. Cheddleton station, with working steam trains, is a short walk away.

Facilities	Directions
The clean toilet block is centrally situated and can be heated. Facilities include one private cabin for ladies, combined shower and WC for disabled visitors, a small laundry room, two dishwashing sinks and one vegetable preparation sink under cover. Gas supplies. Takeaway services will deliver. Information centre and library. Play area. Fishing. Max. 2 dogs per unit. WiFi (charged).	Park is signed off A520 Leek-Stone road, 3.5 miles south of Leek on northern edge of Cheddleton Village. GPS: 53.06994, -2.02901

Open: 1 February - end December.

Charges guide

Per unit incl. 2 persons and electricity	£ 25.00
extra person	£ 5.00
child (5-16 yrs)	£ 3.00

Min. stay of 3 nights at B.Hs.

For latest campsite news visit
alanrogers.com

Leek

Blackshaw Moor Caravan Club Site

Leek ST13 8TW (Staffordshire) T: 01538 300203. E: blackshawmoor@caravanclub.co.uk

alanrogers.com/UK3975

Blackshaw Moor Caravan Club Site is situated on the southern edge of the Peak District National Park and non-members are very welcome. It is within walking distance of Tittesworth Reservoir and nature reserve, and the town of Leek is just three miles away with a range of antique and mill shops. The site offers 89 spacious touring pitches with 16A electricity and digital TV aerial connections. They are attractively laid out on terraces with level hardstandings separated by grass. Eight pitches are available with all services. The Peak District is a haven for nature lovers, walkers and cyclists.

Facilities

Two modern sanitary units provide showers and washbasins in cabins. En-suite facilities for disabled visitors, baby room with bath and changing area (both key access). Laundry facilities with drying room. Motorcaravan services. Reception sells some basic camping and food items. Calor gas. Tourist information room. Play area. WiFi over site (charged). Off site: Three Horseshoes pub and restaurant 300 yds. Roaches 800 yards. Fishing 3 miles.

Open: 1 March - 2 November.

Directions

From Leek on A53, site is on right within 3 miles (450 yards beyond the Three Horseshoes pub which is passed on your left). GPS: 53.13864, -1.98503

Charges guide

Per person	£ 5.60 - £ 7.60
child (5-17 yrs)	£ 1.50 - £ 2.60
pitch incl. electricity (non-member)	£ 16.20 - £ 19.60

Leominster

Townsend Touring & Caravan Park

Townsend Farm, Pembridge, Leominster HR6 9HB (Herefordshire) T: 01544 388527.
E: info@townsend-farm.co.uk **alanrogers.com/UK4345**

This is a modern, family run campsite hidden in a natural dip next to a working farm, but within a short walk of Pembridge. It has gravel roads, good lighting, well spaced pitches and drive-over motorcaravan services. There is plenty of open space and a small fishing lake. There are 60 pitches in total, 29 with gravel hardstanding and all have access to 16A electricity, water and drainage. Reception is at the farm shop by the entrance, stocking a wide variety of fresh fruit, vegetables and eggs; a butchery section has farm produced meats. One jumbo sized and three standard pods available for rent. Special fishing breaks with tuition are available. A member of the Best of British group.

Facilities

A modern sanitary building with warm air heating, accessed through a foyer with public telephone and tourist information. It is surrounded by wide decking with ramps giving easy access for wheelchairs to all facilities including the dishwashing area and laundry room. Spacious controllable showers, some washbasins in cubicles, a suite for disabled guests, family bathroom and baby changing facilities. Farm shop. Fishing lake.

Open: 1 March - mid January.

Directions

Site is beside the A44, 7 miles west of Leominster. Site is just inside the 30 mph. speed limit on the eastern edge of Pembridge village. GPS: 52.21792, -2.88845

Charges guide

Per unit incl. 2 persons, electricity, water and drainage	£ 19.00 - £ 26.00
extra person	£ 5.00

Lincoln

Hartsholme Country Park

Skellingthorpe Road, Lincoln LN6 0EY (Lincolnshire) T: 01522 873578. E: hartsholmecp@lincoln.gov.uk

alanrogers.com/UK3663

Set in an extensive Country Park, with Swanholme Lakes Local Nature Reserve a short walk away, this peaceful site is just three miles from the centre of the historic city of Lincoln, either via a dedicated cycle track or by bus. The 34 pitches are round the edge of two linked, well tended fields enclosed by trees, and are clearly marked by pegs. Twenty-six have electricity connections (10A), including three with hardstandings and paved paths for disabled visitors. Eight tent pitches are in a semi-circle at the far end of the site where two picnic tables are provided.

Facilities

One small, well maintained toilet block at site entrance provides open-style washbasins and spacious cubicles with controllable showers. Utility room with hot and cold water to dishwashing and laundry sinks. No specific facilities for disabled visitors but the block is accessible. Gas barbecues only. Off site: Café and Visitor Centre outside site entrance. Play area nearby. Waymarked paths through Country Park and Nature Reserve, including orienteering course. Fishing 300 yds. Lincoln 3 miles.

Open: 1 March - 31 October.

Directions

Hartsholme Country Park is southwest of the city centre and signed from the A46 Lincoln bypass. Turn southeast on B1378 Skellingthorpe Road towards city centre and park entrance is signed on right in 1.2 miles. GPS: 53.214616, -0.583458

Charges guide

Per unit incl. all persons and electricity	£ 16.10 - £ 18.50

For latest campsite news visit
alanrogers.com

Ludlow
Westbrook Park

Little Hereford, Ludlow SY8 4AU (Shropshire) T: 01584 711280. E: info@westbrookpark.co.uk
alanrogers.com/UK4390

A beautifully kept, traditional, quiet touring campsite in a working cider apple orchard, Westbrook Park is bordered on one side by the River Teme and is within walking distance of the village and pub. There are 60 level pitches with 10A electric hook-ups, gravel or concrete/gravel all-weather hardstandings with water and waste water drainage. Some pitches have semi-shade, others have none. Westbrook's policy of continuous improvement has resulted in the provision of spacious hardstanding pitches with new and improved electricity supply, digital TV aerial connections and innovative water and waste water provision. A member of the Best of British group.

Facilities

A modern, timber-clad, heated toilet block provides spacious hot showers (coin operated), washbasins in curtained cubicles, a basic laundry room. Full facilities for disabled visitors (WC and basin). Gas supplies. Playground (fenced, woodchip base). Fishing (£4/day). WiFi (free). Riverside walks. No gazebos. No cycling. Only well behaved dogs accepted. Off site: The Temeside Inn does not accept payment by cards but has a cash point. Burford House Gardens. Croft Castle.

Open: 1 March - 30 November.

Directions

From A49 midway between Ludlow and Leominster, turn east at Woofferton on A456 (Tenbury Wells, Kidderminster). After 2 miles turn right just before river bridge and Temeside Inn. Turn left in 150 yds. Park is on left. Access roads are narrow. GPS: 52.307377, -2.665815

Charges guide

Per unit incl. 2 persons and electricity	£ 22.00 - £ 25.00
extra person	£ 4.00

Ludlow
Ludlow Touring Park

Overton Road, Ludlow SY8 4AP (Shropshire) T: 01584 878788. E: ludlow@morris-leisure.co.uk
alanrogers.com/UK4395

Ludlow Touring Park opened in May 2012 and is the latest addition to the Morris Leisure Group. The 135 pitches are all level with 107 on hardstanding and the remainder on grass. They include some spacious, fully serviced pitches (16A electricity, TV connections, water, drainage and a small light). There is a small play area and plenty of space for dog walking. Some pitches are reserved for adults (over 16 years). Ludlow, in the shadow of its castle, is 2 miles to the north and has plenty to offer the visitor, including its Festival (last week in June and first week in July), antique shops, boutiques, River Teme and Saint Lawrence's Church. The delightful small town of Tenbury Wells is 15 minutes away by car.

Facilities

The modern, heated toilet block provides washbasins and showers in cubicles plus facilities for children and disabled visitors. Laundry. Motorcaravan services. Small shop (caravan accessories and basics). No bar or restaurant but fish and chip van visits Sat. evenings. Play area. WiFi over site (charged). Off site: Fishing, bicycle hire and riding 2 miles. Golf 3 miles. Acton Scott Victorian Farm 10 miles.

Open: All year.

Directions

From Bridgnorth take A49 (S) around Ludlow and follow signs for Livestock Market. At B4361 junction, follow signs for Ludlow Touring Park, turn right heading back toward Ludlow. Park entrance is 0.25 miles on right. GPS: 52.344365, -2.718183

Charges guide

Per unit incl. 2 persons and electricity	£ 25.20 - £ 28.30
extra person	£ 7.50 - £ 7.90

Lutterworth
Stanford Hall Caravan Park

Stanford Road, Swinford, Lutterworth LE17 6DH (Leicestershire) T: 01788 860387.
E: stanfordpark@yahoo.co.uk **alanrogers.com/UK3890**

Under new management, this picturesque and tranquil site is ideally situated for an overnight stop and you are guaranteed a warm welcome and a pleasant stay. Formerly a Caravan Club site, it is set in the rural grounds of the Stanford Hall Estate, just a mile from the M1/M6/A14 interchange. There are 123 pitches (30 of which are seasonal), 70 on grass and 56 on hardstanding, all with 16A electricity. Tents are not accepted. The site experiences high levels of repeat bookings so you are advised to contact them in advance of busy weekends to avoid disappointment.

Facilities

There are no toilets or shower facilities on site, so each unit must be totally self-contained. Tents are not accepted. Motorcaravan services. Well stocked shop. Gas supplies. Newspapers to order daily. Picnic tables. Information room. Rally field. Late arrivals area. CCTV.

Open: All year.

Directions

From south on M1, leave at exit 18 onto A428, A5 north and then follow signs for Stanford Hall. GPS: 52.4065, -1.149367

Charges guide

Per unit incl. electricity	£ 20.00
dog	£ 1.00

For latest campsite news visit
alanrogers.com

Malvern

Kingsgreen Caravan Park

Kingsgreen, Berrow, Malvern WR13 6AQ (Worcestershire) T: 01531 650272.

alanrogers.com/UK4190

An attractive, welcoming and well kept site with views of the Malvern Hills, Kingsgreen is in a lovely rural location. An ideal site for adults who like the quiet life, there are no amusements for children. The surrounding countryside is ideal for walking or cycling and the small, fenced fishing lakes on the site are well stocked (£5 per day). There are 45 level, grass and gravel pitches, all with 13A electricity, plus an additional area for tents. Some old orchard trees provide a little shade in parts. The site is seven miles from the market town of Ledbury with its half-timbered buildings. A barrier is closed at all times.

Facilities	Directions
Modern heated toilet facilities (key on deposit) provide hot showers (25p token from reception) and a separate unit for disabled visitors (WC and washbasin). No baby changing facilities. Laundry room with coin-operated washing machine and dryer. Payphone. Gas. Fishing. Off site: Nearest shop and pub 1.5 miles. Riding 3 miles. Golf 5 miles.	From M50 exit 2, take A417 towards Gloucester, then first left, where site is signed, also signed the Malverns, back over the motorway. Site is 2 miles from the M50. GPS: 52.00211, -2.33929

Charges guide

Per unit incl. 2 persons and electricity	£ 16.00 - £ 18.50
extra person (over 2 yrs)	£ 1.50

No credit cards.

Open: 1 March - 31 October.

Market Bosworth

Bosworth Caravan Park

The Gatehouse, Cadeby Lane, Cadeby CV13 0BA (Leicestershire) T: 01455 292259.

E: info@bosworthcaravanpark.co.uk **alanrogers.com/UK3898**

Bosworth Caravan Park is a friendly, family run site in the village of Cadeby near Market Bosworth and occupies buildings that were formerly the gatehouse to Bosworth Hall. The site has 22 fully serviced pitches on hardstanding and a further 20 grass pitches with electricity. Young hedges offer some shade and the perimeter of the ground is wooded. Tourists have flocked to the area since the discovery of the body of King Richard III in nearby Leicester. The battlefield where this last Plantagenet King lost his life is within walking distance of the campsite. Visitors can spend a fascinating day there enjoying the visitor centre and restaurant. The site itself is pleasantly landscaped with well maintained pitches.

Facilities	Directions
One traditional sanitary block serves all 42 pitches and has just one shower/WC cubicle for each sex, so could come under considerable pressure. Washing machine and dryer. WiFi (charged). Off site: Bosworth battle field 0.5 miles. Mallory Park race track, water park, Shenton heritage steam railway, all 2 miles. Drayton Manor Park. Twycross Zoo 9 miles. Leicester 11 miles.	Exit 1 from M69 continue North on Rugby Road. Take B4467, then A447 towards Cadeby. Park is on Cadeby Lane on right. GPS: 52.62398, -1.38339

Charges guide

Per unit incl. 2 persons and electricity	£ 15.00
extra person	£ 2.00
dog	free

Open: All year.

Market Rasen

Walesby Woodlands Caravan Park

Walesby, Market Rasen LN8 3UN (Lincolnshire) T: 01673 843285. E: walesbywoodlands@hotmail.co.uk

alanrogers.com/UK3660

Alongside the Lindsey walking trail and surrounded by Forestry Commission woodland, this small, attractive touring park is very peaceful. The new owners, John and Brenda, will make you very welcome. They have upgraded the facilities and have plans for further improvements whilst still maintaining the site's identity as a tranquil retreat. There are 60 well spaced pitches, 52 with 10A electricity, marked out in a single, mainly flat, grassy field divided by a central gravel road and with a double row of trees providing useful visual screening. About a mile away is the small town of Market Rasen.

Facilities	Directions
The single, heated toilet block is spacious and ample for the site. Pushbutton showers and open style washbasins. Toilet facilities for disabled visitors. Laundry room. Some basic supplies kept in reception. Coffee shop (w/ends 08.30-14.00 Easter-5/11). Battery charging. Gas supplies. No kite flying (overhead wires). Hardstandings. Seasonal pitches. Winter caravan storage. WiFi over site. Off site: Golf 1.5 miles. Shops, supermarkets, pubs and restaurants 1-2 miles. Riding and racecourse 2 miles.	Market Rasen is on the A46, 17 miles northeast of Lincoln. Park is just over a mile northeast of the town. Take B1203 towards Tealby, then turn left 800 yds. along Walesby Road. Site is on left. It is signed from all the main approach roads to town. GPS: 53.40135, -0.321

Charges guide

Per unit incl. 2 persons and electricity	£ 18.00 - £ 21.00
extra person	£ 2.50

Open: All year.

For latest campsite news visit
alanrogers.com

Matlock
Lickpenny Touring Park

Lickpenny Lane, Tansley, Matlock DE4 5GF (Derbyshire) T: 01629 583040. E: lickpenny@btinternet.com
alanrogers.com/UK3815

This spacious caravan park on a hill above Matlock has 122 terraced pitches, all on hardstandings and with 16A electricity. Most have good countryside views. There are some 80 touring pitches, 27 of which are fully serviced. Tents are not accepted. There are rows of mature trees and pitches are large and separated by shrubs and bushes. The enthusiastic owners have taken full advantage of the fact that this was previously a market garden. High standards have been maintained and some facilities improved.

Facilities

Two well equipped, heated toilet blocks include free preset showers and some washbasins in cubicles. Good facilities for disabled visitors. Family room. Bathroom for children. Laundry room. Motorcaravan services. Play area. Security barrier with keypad access. Tents are not accepted. WiFi throughout (charged). Off site: Bus service from end of the road. Woodland walk to garden centre with restaurant serving snacks and lunches (200 yds).

Open: All year.

Directions

Matlock is 18 miles west of M1 exit 28. From Matlock take A615, after Tansley fork left on B6014 (Clay Cross) and turn right at top of hill after Garden Centre. GPS: 53.134787, -1.491190

Charges guide

Per unit incl. 2 persons and electricity	£ 19.00 - £ 25.00
extra person	£ 5.00

Matlock
Middlehills Farm Caravan and Campsite

Grangemill, Matlock DE4 4HY (Derbyshire) T: 01629 650368. E: middlehillsfarm@yahoo.co.uk
alanrogers.com/UK3825

Middlehills Farm is close to the towns of Bakewell and Matlock. It is a well established, family run site to which visitors return year after year to enjoy the relaxed friendly atmosphere. It is well placed for visiting many of the local attractions, and the owners, Nick and Liz Lomas, are happy to provide local information. This secluded, 7.5-acre park is located on a family run former working farm within the Peak District National Park and comprises three separate, gently sloping fields – one with electric hook up points. Some 90 grass pitches include ten with electricity (16A). There are some pigs, ponies and chickens. The chickens are free roaming so dogs must be kept on a lead at all times.

Facilities

One small shower block with washbasins and showers in cubicles (£1/5 mins). A second new modern unit has toilets and washbasins. One block on the edge of a barn serves the upper field. All the units have dishwashing facilities as well as fridge freezers. No facilities for children or disabled visitors. No motorcaravan services. Small shop sells basics. No bar or restaurant. Adventure play area. Recycling facilities. Off site: Fishing 1 mile. Bicycle hire 3 miles. Supermarket 4 miles. Golf 5 miles.

Open: Easter - 31 October.

Directions

From M1 exit 28, take A38 heading for Ripley. Turn on A610 heading to Ambergate then A6 to Cromford. In Cromford turn left at lights then right on A5012 for 4 miles. Pass Holly Bush Inn, in 400 yds, turn left over cattle grid. Take care along single width drive (passing places). GPS: 53.116541, -1.64391

Charges guide

Per unit incl. 2 persons and electricity	£ 20.00
extra person	£ 8.00
child (4-16 yrs)	£ 4.00

Melton Mowbray
Eye Kettleby Lakes Caravan Touring & Camping Park

Eye Kettleby, Melton Mowbray LE14 2TD (Leicestershire) T: 01664 565900. E: info@eyekettlebylakes.com
alanrogers.com/UK3895

Set in the rolling Leicestershire countryside, this six-acre site with its seven lakes is a fishermen's paradise. The adults only touring area comprises 53 spacious, level, touring pitches set around a small lake. Forty-seven of these are hardstanding super pitches with 16A electricity, water and drainage. The toilet blocks are of an exceptionally high standard with individual en-suite shower rooms, and the facilities for disabled visitors are large and well appointed with underfloor heating. A number of luxury lodges, each with its own hot tub, are available for rent. There is an intimate bar and a restaurant that just serves breakfast. There are numerous walks from the site and in the area.

Facilities

Three superbly fitted, heated toilet blocks with free hot water and individual en-suite rooms. Laundry room. Large, well appointed wet room with en-suite facilities and hairdryer for disabled visitors. Dishwashing in heated room. Motorcaravan services. Shop. Bar with TV and free WiFi (open daily and evenings Thu-Sat). Breakfast (daily 08.00-10.00). Takeaway food delivered. Small games area with pool table. Fishing. Bicycle hire.

Open: All year.

Directions

From Melton Mowbray take A607 towards Leicester. After 1.5 miles turn left towards Great Dalby, site in 1 mile (signed). GPS: 52.74168, -0.90952

Charges guide

Per unit incl. 2 persons, electricity and water	£ 18.50 - £ 26.00
superior pitch	£ 23.00 - £ 31.50
extra person	£ 5.00

For latest campsite news visit
alanrogers.com

Meriden

Somers Wood Caravan Park

Somers Road, Meriden CV7 7PL (Warwickshire) T: 01676 522978. E: enquiries@somerswood.co.uk

alanrogers.com/UK4070

Somers Wood is a quiet, peaceful park, attractively situated amongst mixed conifers and deciduous trees. A very pleasant park which only accepts adults and does not take tents, it is especially convenient for those visiting shows at the NEC in Birmingham when it can get very busy. From the reception building at the entrance, an oval gravel road provides access to 48 pitches, all on hardstanding and with 10A electricity hook-ups. Areas of woodland, carpeted with flowers in summer, surround the site and partition it into small intimate areas that create a rural feel. A member of the Best of British group.

Facilities	Directions
The central, heated, completely refurbished sanitary block is fully equipped with facilities for disabled visitors. Shower cubicles are especially large. New laundry and drying room. WiFi (charged). Off site: Local shops and restaurant less than 1 mile and visitors also welcome to use the bar and restaurant at the golf club next door.	From M42 exit 6 (NEC) take A45 towards Coventry. Keep in left lane down to roundabout and exit on A452 (signed Leamington/Meriden), then turn left into Hampton Lane at the next roundabout, then left into Somers Road. Site is signed with golf and fishing centres. GPS: 52.43930, -1.66947
Open: All year.	**Charges guide**
	Per unit incl. 2 persons and electricity £ 19.00 - £ 25.00

Moreton-in-Marsh

Moreton-in-Marsh Caravan Club Site

Bourton Road, Moreton-in-Marsh GL56 0BT (Gloucestershire) T: 01608 650519.

alanrogers.com/UK4130

This excellent busy but rural site is attractively located within mature woodland in the heart of the Cotswolds and offers what one would hope for from a camping holiday. Within easy walking distance of the interesting market town of Moreton-in-Marsh, there is ample choice for food and pubs. The town's main street is part of the Roman Fosse Way. The site has 183 pitches, all with 16A electricity and TV sockets, 171 with hardstanding. A size limit of nine metres for motorcaravans and caravans exists. Milk and ice cream are available from reception. Family recreation facilities include crazy golf, five-a-side football, boules and an adventure climbing frame.

Facilities	Directions
The two main sanitary blocks have been renovated and offer excellent facilities. A separate toilet block has disabled toilet and baby room. Large laundry. Shop. Play area. Crazy golf. Volleyball. Boules. 5-a-side football. Adventure climbing frame. WiFi over site (charged). No kite flying (power cables). Off site: Shops, pubs and restaurants 400 yds. Tuesday street market.	From Evesham on A44, site on left after Bourton-on-the-Hill village, 150 yds. before town sign. From Moreton-in-Marsh take A44 towards Evesham and site is on right, 150 yds. past the Wellington museum. GPS: 51.98885, -1.710283
Open: All year.	**Charges guide**
	Per person £ 6.00 - £ 8.90
	pitch incl. electricity (non-member) £ 16.20 - £ 20.80

Newark

Smeaton's Lakes Touring Caravan & Fishing Park

Great North Road, South Muskham, Newark-on-Trent NG23 6ED (Nottinghamshire) T: 01636 605088.
E: lesley@smeatonslakes.co.uk **alanrogers.com/UK3940**

This 90-acre site is really ideal for anglers with four fishing lakes (coarse, carp and pike) and river fishing on the Trent. There are 130 pitches, of which 90 are for touring, all with 16A electricity connections. The remaining pitches are occupied by seasonal units. Non-anglers might choose this park if visiting antique fairs or events at nearby Newark Showground, or Newark town (1 mile) with its castle, air museum, National Civil War centre and various weekly markets. During your stay, you might visit Southwell Minster, Sherwood Forest, Clumber Park, Lincoln with its castle and cathedral, or Nottingham with its castle, caves and shopping centres.

Facilities	Directions
Two heated toilet blocks (keypad access) could be stretched in high season. Good unit for disabled visitors. Small shop with gas, soft drinks, dairy produce, etc. Newspapers can be ordered. On-site concessions for lake and river fishing. Entry barrier with key access. Security cameras and night-time height barrier (about 6 ft). Off site: Bus stop at the end of the entry lane. Boat launching 2 miles. Golf 3 miles. Riding 4 miles.	Park is 1 mile north of Newark. From south on A1, take A46 west (signed Newark, then Leicester) and turn north on A6065/A616 towards South Muskham. Pass through village and continue on A616 to site on the left. GPS: 53.0936, -0.820667
Open: All year.	**Charges guide**
	Per unit incl. 2 persons £ 16.00 - £ 20.00
	extra person £ 5.00
	child £ 2.00

For latest campsite news visit
alanrogers.com

Newark

Milestone Caravan Park

Great North Road, Cromwell, Newark NG23 6JE (Nottinghamshire) T: 01636 821244.
E: enquiries@milestonepark.co.uk **alanrogers.com/UK3945**

Situated just off the A1 north of Newark, Milestone has a good deal more to offer than simply a stopover option. Its 76 level touring pitches all have 16A electricity and nearby water points. Grass pitches are available but most are all-weather in a variety of locations. Six are outside the security barrier for those in transit (although key access is always available), then comes a pleasantly landscaped area and finally terraces overlooking an attractive fishing lake. An embankment built to muffle traffic noise provides a pleasant grassed walk with views across an adjoining lake and the surrounding countryside. This is a Caravan Club affiliated site.

Facilities	Directions
Two heated toilet blocks provide pushbutton showers and open-style washbasins (may be under pressure at busy times). Excellent en-suite facilities for disabled visitors. Washing machine, dryer and ironing facilities. Motorcaravan services. Tourist information, guides and children's quiz sheets on the site's wildlife. Fishing (charged). Lakeside cabin with nature and fishing displays. WiFi throughout (charged). Off site: Village has shop, small brewery and buses to Newark.	From the south on A1, 3.7 miles after A46 junction, take slip road to Cromwell and site is on the left after the village. From the north on A1, 9 miles after Markham Moor junction, take slip road for Cromwell, turn right over bridge and right again to site. GPS: 53.14985, -0.80693

Open: All year.

Charges guide

Per unit incl. 2 persons and electricity	£ 17.40 - £ 26.50
extra person	£ 5.80 - £ 8.20

Newark

Orchard Park

Marnham Road, Tuxford, Newark NG22 0PY (Nottinghamshire) T: 01777 870228.
E: info@orchardcaravanpark.co.uk **alanrogers.com/UK3950**

This well established touring and caravan park, with new owners and now open all year, has been created in an old fruit orchard in a quiet location, yet is very convenient for the A1. It has a friendly feel, with just 77 pitches, all with 10A electricity, 34 with hardstanding and about 15 occupied by seasonal units. There is also a spacious camping field with good views. Reception is on the left as you arrive and a nearby cabin has information on attractions including Sundown Adventureland, Laxton Medieval village and Victorian Times, Rufford Abbey, Clumber Park, Sherwood Forest and the Robin Hood Centre.

Facilities	Directions
The heated toilet block has pushbutton showers, open style washbasins and a well equipped room for disabled visitors. Family shower room. Laundry with washing machines, dryer, free spin dryer, iron and a freezer for ice packs. Small shop with basics and gas. Picnic area. Excellent adventure trail for children and nature walk. Apples, pears and blackberries can be picked in season. WiFi throughout (charged). No electric barbecues.	Park is east of A1. Leave at signs for Tuxford, turn east on A6075 towards Lincoln (A57), go through village, turn south towards Marnham for 0.5 miles. Site is on right 0.5 miles after railway bridge. Follow caravan signs. GPS: 53.2296, -0.8695

Open: All year.

Charges guide

Per unit incl. 2 persons and electricity	£ 19.00 - £ 22.00
extra person	£ 4.00

Nottingham

Thornton's Holt Camping Park

Stragglethorpe, Radcliffe-on-Trent, Nottingham NG12 2JZ (Nottinghamshire) T: 0115 933 2125.
E: camping@thorntons-holt.co.uk **alanrogers.com/UK3935**

Thornton's Holt is an attractively laid out, great family camping park at Stragglethorpe, a scattered rural hamlet 3.5 miles southeast of the city of Nottingham. The 155 spacious pitches (93 for touring) are arranged in four separate areas, including one with an orchard setting. With a mixture of grass and gravel hardstanding, most have access to 10A electricity. The owners encourage a friendly farm-type atmosphere with free range chickens, ducks and guinea fowl wandering around the park. You may also encounter Spike and Spartacus, the resident horses, as well as dogs and a cat.

Facilities	Directions
The old style sanitary block was being replaced when we visited (May 2015). Open washbasins, showers on payment (20p). Basic facilities for disabled visitors. Laundry. Small shop (1/4-1/11). Heated indoor swimming pool (1/4-1/11). Play area. Bungalow (4 persons) for rent. Caravan storage. Free WiFi on part of site. Off site: Pub with restaurant adjacent. Supermarket 1 mile.	From A46, join A52 westbound. Pass Radcliffe-on-Trent and after 1.5 miles turn left at traffic lights (white house) into Stragglethorpe Road signed Cotgrave and Cropwell Bishop. Site is on left just after railway bridge. GPS: 52.932024, -1.053404

Open: All year.

Charges guide

Per unit incl. 2 persons and electricity	£ 17.50 - £ 23.00

For latest campsite news visit
alanrogers.com

Oakham
Rutland Caravan & Camping Park
Park Lane, Greetham, Oakham LE15 7FN (Rutland) T: 01572 813520.
E: info@rutlandcaravanandcamping.co.uk **alanrogers.com/UK3903**

This family run site is situated in the heart of England's smallest county – Rutland. The family continue to invest in the site, with an indoor swimming pool and six luxury lodges opened recently. The pitches (118 for touring units, 13 for tents) have limited shade and are not fenced. There are two separate pitching areas, one reserved for adults and another for families. Electricity (10A) is available to all, 40 have full services and hardstanding is provided on 66 pitches. The site is beside the village of Greetham (with a footpath from the site), through which the Viking Way and other footpaths meander.

Facilities

Two modern heated toilet blocks. Baby changing facility. Facilities for disabled visitors. Laundry. Motorcaravan services. Small shop (essentials only, bread and papers to order). Gas and camping gas. Heated indoor swimming pool (charged). Play area. Small games room. Picnic tables. Security barrier (£10 deposit for card). WiFi throughout (charged). Extensive dog walk. Torches useful. Off site: Fishing, golf, riding and bicycle hire 3 miles.

Open: All year.

Directions

From A1 turn off on B668 towards Greetham Village. Turn right at crossroads before village and take the 2nd left. From Oakham, take B668 through Greetham. Turn left at crossroads at end of village and then take 2nd left. GPS: 52.72402, -0.63288

Charges guide

Per unit incl. 2 persons and electricity	£ 17.60 - £ 27.15
extra person	£ 5.40 - £ 8.05

Oakham
Greendale Farm Caravan & Camping Park
Pickwell Lane, Whissendine, Oakham LE15 7LB (Rutland) T: 01664 474516. E: enq@rutlandgreendale.co.uk
alanrogers.com/UK3904

This is a delightful little adults only park set in rolling countryside, ideal for those seeking peace and tranquillity. It is very eco-friendly and extremely well appointed for such a small site. There are only 12 pitches, four of which are suitable for tents or small units, so it is worth checking availability. All have 10/16A Europlug and pebbled hardstanding; there are plenty of water points and one pitch has its own tap and drain. Lawns are immaculately tended, while flower beds, shrubs and wild flower planting add to the appeal of the site. Birds and other wildlife are encouraged. No arrivals before 13.30.

Facilities

Each of the two rooms in the toilet block has a power shower, WCs and two washbasins (cubicles for ladies). All is beautifully appointed and immaculately kept. Washing machine and dryer. Small shop selling local produce and essentials. Cream teas. Small open-air, solar-heated swimming pool (6x3 m; June-Sept; £1) with summer house. Tourist information. Free WiFi over site. Off site: Village with bus service 0.5 miles. Pub and farm shop 1 mile. Fishing 3 miles. Supermarket 4 miles.

Open: Fully open May - October.

Directions

Whissendine is just off A606 Oakham-Melton Mowbray road. Approach from this road and NOT through village. From Oakham site is signed to northeast at second turning to Whissendine. From Melton take third turning to village. Park is on right in 0.6 mile. GPS: 52.711833, -0.788617

Charges guide

Per unit incl. two adults and electricity	£ 19.00 - £ 25.00
extra person	£ 5.00

Oswestry
Oswestry Camping & Caravanning Club Site
Cranberry Moss, Kinnerley, Oswestry SY10 8DY (Shropshire) T: 01743 741118.
alanrogers.com/UK4405

This family run Club site is set within rolling countryside and welcomes non-members. There are 65 pitches on a mixture of grass and hardstandings, 54 with 16A electricity hook-ups. The site is calm and well sheltered but pitches are open with flowerbeds interspersed with the grassed areas. Dogs are welcomed and provided with two designated walks. Oswestry, with its medieval buildings and an interesting mixture of shops, is a good base to explore the region. There is a bus stop at the gate for getting into Shrewsbury and Oswestry. A loop of the North Shropshire Way has been extended and is within one mile of the site, ideal for walking enthusiasts.

Facilities

The heated sanitary unit has a dedicated room for parent and child and disabled visitors. Laundry facilities. Motorcaravan services. Shop with local produce. Ice pack freezing. Storage facilities. Battery charging facility. WiFi (free). Social room with entertainment. Off site: Oswestry, Shrewsbury (park and ride) and Ellesmere.

Open: All year.

Directions

From north Chester/Wrexham on A5 towards Shrewsbury. At Wolfshead roundabout onto B4396 towards Knockin, site entrance is second left. GPS: 52.78335, -2.94011

Charges guide

Per unit incl. 2 persons and electricity	£ 20.70 - £ 34.90

Non-member prices are higher.

For latest campsite news visit
alanrogers.com

Peterchurch
Poston Mill Caravan Park
Golden Valley, Peterchurch HR2 0SF (Herefordshire) T: 01981 550225. E: info@poston-mill.co.uk
alanrogers.com/UK4300

Set in pleasant undulating farmland in the heart of the Golden Valley, Poston Mill Park is a mile from the delightful village of Peterchurch. It is an ideal location for relaxation or exploring. There are currently 43 touring pitches set on level grass or hardstanding with mature trees around the perimeter. Thirty have 16A electricity, while 21 are fully serviced (TV leads for hire). An area is set aside for tents, some with electricity hook-up. An attractive walk runs along one side of the park, edging the River Dore (fishing available). Adjoining the park is a licensed restaurant (takeaways available) and a general store selling a range of produce and newspapers; when this is closed, basics can be purchased from reception.

Facilities

One central sanitary block with a smaller, refurbished block near the holiday home area which includes private cubicles. Both are fully equipped and include units for disabled guests and families. Motorcaravan services. Play area. Pitch and putt. Tennis, pétanque and croquet. Games room. WiFi (charged).

Open: All year.

Directions

Park is 1 mile south of Peterchurch on the B4348 road. GPS: 52.02832, -2.9388

Charges guide

Per unit incl. 2 persons and electricity	£ 20.00 - £ 27.00
extra person	£ 4.00

Retford
Trentfield Farm Camping & Caravanning
Church Laneham, Retford DN22 0NJ (Nottinghamshire) T: 01777 228651. E: post@trentfield.co.uk
alanrogers.com/UK3955

A small, friendly, professionally run park. The owners of Trentfield Farm work on the policy of old-fashioned camping and caravanning with all the new amenities and mod cons! Located in north Nottinghamshire, Trentfield Farm is set between historic Lincoln, Newark, Worksop and Gainsborough, on the banks of the River Trent. It is just within the idyllic hamlet of Church Laneham, an old estate village of the Bishop of York, which is steeped in history. The campsite is level and free draining with just 25 grass pitches for touring, 16A electricity hook-ups and nearby taps. A further 20 pitches are for seasonals and six mobile homes are for rent. There is private river frontage with free coarse fishing.

Facilities

The heated toilet block (may be stretched at busy times) has push-button showers and open style washbasins. Family shower room. No facilities for disabled visitors. Laundry with washing machines, dryer and free spin dryer, iron and freezer for ice-packs. 24-hour vending machine with basics. Free WiFi over much of site. Off site: Ferry Boat Inn within walking distance. Sundown Adventure, Lincoln City and Cathedral, Sherwood Forest and Clumber park, Pureland Japanese Garden.

Open: Easter - 31 October.

Directions

From A1/A57 roundabout at Markham Moor follow A57 towards Lincoln for 6 miles. Follow signs for 'Sundown Adventure'. Take 2nd turning into Laneham and go 1.5 miles through village towards river and ferry. At Church Laneham, pass Ferry Boat Inn on left and river on right. Go past Manor House Residential Park, up small rise and park is 300 yds. on right. GPS: 53.287685, -0.777497

Charges guide

Per unit incl. 2 persons and electricity	£ 22.50 - £ 25.50

Ripley
Golden Valley Caravan & Camping Park
Coach Road, Golden Valley, Ripley DE55 4ES (Derbyshire) T: 01773 513881.
E: enquiries@goldenvalleycaravanpark.co.uk **alanrogers.com/UK3865**

Golden Valley Caravan & Camping Park is located in the beautiful hamlet of Golden Valley, alongside the Cromford Canal in the Amber Valley area of the Peak District. The site is situated within 26 acres of historic woodland, once a thriving industrial centre for coal, iron foundries and canal workers on the adjacent canal. This secluded woodland site has just 40 pitches on hardstanding for motorcaravans and caravans. There are 30 with independent water supply, electricity connection (16A) and mains drainage. There are also two wooded areas for tents and a communal barbecue area.

Facilities

A centrally positioned, heated utility block has hot showers, facilities for disabled visitors, a laundry room, heated jacuzzi, an indoor games room and a gym. Bar, café and takeaway (July/Aug). Fishing pond. Woodland walks. Play area. Bouncy castle. Sand pit. Quad bikes, zip wire and zorbing (all July/Aug). CCTV. Free WiFi.

Open: All year.

Directions

Leave M1 at exit 26, follow signs for Matlock (A610). At Codnor, turn right at lights, then first right onto Alfreton Road. After a further 2 miles turn left before passing the Newlands Inn to join Coach Road. Site entrance is on left. GPS: 53.05669, -1.37267

Charges guide

Per unit incl. 2 persons and electricity	£ 22.00 - £ 32.00
extra person	£ 5.00 - £ 10.00

For latest campsite news visit
alanrogers.com

Ross-on-Wye

Broadmeadow Caravan & Camping Park

Broadmeadows, Ross-on-Wye HR9 7BW (Herefordshire) T: 01989 768076. E: site@broadmeadow.info

alanrogers.com/UK4320

Ross-on-Wye town centre is within easy walking distance of this modern, spacious park complete with open views and its own fishing lake. The approach to the site is very unusual, passing through an industrial estate, but eventually you will arrive at a well laid out and pleasant site with facilities of the highest quality. There are 150 large pitches on a mixture of hardstanding and level, open grass; the site is especially good for tents. Each set of four pitches has a service post with water, drain, 16A electricity points and lighting. There may be some traffic noise from the A40 relief road. Seasonal pitches are now available. The market town of Ross-on-Wye is centrally placed for touring Herefordshire, the Wye Valley and the Forest of Dean. The town itself has many facilities such as an indoor swimming pool, putting greens and tennis courts, plus of course lots of good places to eat and drink. Shopping is excellent with a general market held on Thursdays and Saturdays with a farmers' market on the first Friday of each month.

Facilities

Two fully equipped, modern sanitary blocks with baby rooms, family bathrooms each with WC, washbasin and bath and a comprehensive unit for disabled visitors. Laundry at each block. Basic motorcaravan services. Small part-fenced playground. Fenced fishing lake (coarse fishing £8.50 per rod per day – fishing licence not available at reception). WiFi throughout (free). Off site: Supermarket 200 yds. Bicycle hire in town. Golf 3 miles. Riding 8 miles.

Open: Easter/1 April - 30 September.

Directions

From A40 relief road turn into Ross at roundabout on to Gloucester Road, take first right into industrial estate, then right in 0.5 miles before supermarket, where site is signed. GPS: 51.91801, -2.57575

Charges guide

Per unit incl. 2 persons	
and electricity	£ 26.00 - £ 30.00
extra person	£ 6.00
child (2-9 yrs)	£ 3.50
dog	£ 1.75

Ross-on-Wye

Doward Park Camp Site

Great Doward, Symonds Yat West, Ross-on-Wye HR9 6BP (Herefordshire) T: 01600 890438.

E: enquiries@dowardpark.co.uk **alanrogers.com/UK4360**

This site, which was created around 1997 in a disused quarry, has matured into a very pleasant, peaceful little site, partially terraced and in a sheltered location. The access roads and the physical proportions of the site make it suitable only for tents, trailer tents and campervans. This site is popular with couples, nature lovers, walkers and those with young families, but has nothing to offer teenagers. There is a children's play area in Bluebell Wood (unsupervised) at the top of the site with a rope swing and a 'Timber Trak'. Of the 27 pitches for touring (15 with 10/16A electricity), three are hardstanding for motorcaravans up to 23 feet in length, the remainder are on grass. Five hardstandings are used for seasonal units. Visit King Arthur's Caves and Seven Sisters Rocks or walk to Symonds Yat Rock and cross the River Wye on the suspension bridge.

Facilities

A neat central building provides the usual facilities including refurbished hot showers. No designated area for disabled visitors, but toilet facilities have wide access. Freezer for ice packs. Small shop selling basic supplies. Service washing and drying facilities available. Torches are advisable. Free WiFi over site. Off site: Variety of inns at both Symonds Yat West and East all offering meals. Fishing 1 mile. Shops and services in Monmouth 4 miles. Golf 4 miles. Bicycle hire 10 miles.

Open: 27 March - 10 October.

Directions

From A40 between Ross-on-Wye and Monmouth, turn for Symonds Yat West, and follow signs for Doward Park and Biblins. Turn into narrow lane for 1 mile and site is on right, on sharp left hand bend. Sat nav: use GPS, not postcode. GPS: 51.838517, -2.657

Charges guide

Per unit incl. 2 persons	
and electricity	£ 14.00 - £ 18.00
extra person	£ 3.50
child (4-15 yrs)	£ 3.00
dog	£ 1.00

Royal Leamington Spa
Harbury Fields Farm Touring Caravan Park
Middle Road, Harbury CV33 9JN (Warwickshire) T: 01926 612457. E: rdavis@harburyfields.co.uk
alanrogers.com/UK4065

This is a delightful, family run caravan park surrounded by a 222-acre arable and sheep farm. Peaceful and quiet, it is set in the unspoilt Shakespeare countryside and is a Caravan Club affiliated site. Located well away from main roads, it is just a mile from the lively village of Harbury, an ancient, prehistoric settlement on a hill near the Fosse Way Roman Road in Warwickshire. There are 58 fully serviced pitches, all with 16A electricity. Tents are not accepted. The surrounding area has a large number of old quarries that were historically used to extract lyas, a form of limestone used in the manufacture of cement. These quarries now make for unique family excursions.

Facilities

All the heated sanitary facilities have shower cubicles with washbasins. Facilities for families and disabled visitors. Washing machine and dryer. Motorcaravan services. No shop. Dog walk around the farm. Off site: Village with pubs, shops, post office and small supermarket 1.5 miles. Bus service at end of drive. Fishing and golf 4 miles. Leamington Spa 4 miles. Warwick Castle 6 miles. Stratford-upon-Avon 11 miles. NEC 17 miles.

Open: 12 February - 30 November.

Directions

From south on M40, take exit 12 and turn left. After 0.5 miles turn right, then in 3 miles at second roundabout take fourth exit onto B4455 Fosse Way (Harbury). After 2 miles turn right (Harbury) and site is 420 yds. GPS: 52.23985, -1.48689

Charges guide

Per unit incl. 2 persons
and electricity (non member)   £ 18.50 - £ 25.00

Scunthorpe
Brookside Caravan & Camping Park
Stather Road, Burton-upon-Stather, Scunthorpe DN15 9DH (Lincolnshire) T: 01724 721369.
E: brooksidecp@aol.com **alanrogers.com/UK3755**

Brookside is an immaculately kept, peaceful, adults only park on a bank of the River Trent, close to its confluence with the Humber. It is an ideal base from which to explore north Lincolnshire, and to cross the Humber Bridge to visit Hull and the Yorkshire coast. Of the 70 pitches, 35 are for touring on spacious hardstandings with grass verges separated by neat hedges. All have 10A electricity; a further 16 connections are available on unmarked grass pitches around the edge of a large, gently rising field on which 19 more units can be accommodated. Beyond this is an impressive bank of trees.

Facilities

A modern, well maintained and heated toilet block (with pictures and flowers, and music from local radio) has preset showers and open-style washbasins, plus one in cabins on each side, hair- and hand dryers. Excellent en-suite unit for disabled visitors. Dishwashing with tourist information and small exchange library. Washing machine, dryer and ironing facility. Motorcaravan services. WiFi over site (free). Four-acre field for dog walking.

Open: All year.

Directions

Burton-upon-Stather is 7 miles north of Scunthorpe. From M180 via M181 continue north and east on A1077, then turn north on B1430 following signs for Normanby Hall then Burton-upon-Stather and campsite. Site entrance is on right, 250 yds. after phone box on left. GPS: 53.6545, -0.69117

Charges guide

Per unit incl. 2 persons and electricity   £ 20.00
extra person   £ 5.00

Shrewsbury
Beaconsfield Farm Caravan Park
Battlefield, Shrewsbury SY4 4BE (Shropshire) T: 01939 210370. E: mail@beaconsfieldholidaypark.co.uk
alanrogers.com/UK4410

Just north of the historic market town, a drive through open fields leads to this purpose designed park for adults only (over 21 years). Neatly laid out in a rural situation, the park is well lit with a circular tarmac access road, beyond a security barrier. The grounds have been levelled and grassed to provide 80 well spaced pitches, all with 10A electricity connections, of which 50 are 'super' hardstanding pitches. Two further areas accommodate 49 caravan holiday homes. On site there are two well stocked coarse fishing pools, an indoor swimming pool and an excellent, fully-licensed à la carte restaurant, 'The Bothy', serving local produce. A member of the Best of British group.

Facilities

Heated toilet facilities (£5.00 key deposit) are of excellent quality, with roomy, preset showers and hairdryers. Excellent unit for disabled visitors. Laundry facilities. Motorcaravan services. Restaurant. Indoor heated swimming pool with daily open sessions (£3 per person, incl. steam room) and to hire privately at other times. Small library. Bicycle hire. WiFi part site (free).

Open: All year.

Directions

Site is north of Shrewsbury off A49 Whitchurch road. In Hadnall, turn right opposite New Inn at camping sign, towards Astley and park entrance is 400 yds. on right. Go down narrow access road with passing places for 800 yds. GPS: 52.770917, -2.704817

Charges guide

Per unit incl. 2 persons
and electricity   £ 20.00 - £ 26.00

For latest campsite news visit
alanrogers.com

Shrewsbury
Oxon Hall Touring Park
Welshpool Road, Shrewsbury SY3 5FB (Shropshire) T: 01743 340868. E: oxon@morris-leisure.co.uk
alanrogers.com/UK4430

Oxon Hall is a purpose-built park, well situated for visiting Shrewsbury. Under the same ownership as Stanmore Hall (UK4400) the site has been developed to a very high standard with mature trees and shrubs providing some shade and shelter. Of the 120 pitches, 105 are in use for touring units, all of which have 16A electric hook-ups, 65 are full service pitches (fresh and waste water facilities, TV hook-up), the others being either grass or with hardstanding. An area is set aside as an adults only section. Some pitches for RV-style units have 32A electric hook-ups. A member of the Best of British group.

Facilities

Toilet facilities here are first rate with washbasins in cubicles, ample showers, baby room, facilities for disabled visitors, dishwashing room and laundry, all situated at the entrance in a centrally heated building, also housing reception and the shop. Deposit for toilet block key £5. Motorcaravan services. Max. 2 dogs per pitch – dog walk on site. WiFi throughout (charged). Off site: Supermarket and pub within walking distance. Golf and fishing nearby.

Open: All year.

Directions

From junction of A5 and A458, west of Shrewsbury, follow signs for Oxon park and ride. Park is signed 0.5 miles from junction. GPS: 52.71540, -2.804917

Charges guide

Per unit incl. 2 persons	
and electricity	£ 25.20 - £ 31.30
extra person	£ 7.50 - £ 7.90
child (5-15 yrs)	£ 2.50

Skegness
Skegness Sands Touring Site
Winthorpe Avenue, Skegness PE25 1QZ (Lincolnshire) T: 01754 761484. E: info@skegness-sands.com
alanrogers.com/UK3730

This very well organised touring site is part of a much larger caravan holiday home park, but has its own entrance. It is a modern, well appointed site adjacent to the promenade and beach. There are 82 pitches, all level and with 16A electricity; 45 are grass and 37 on gravel hardstandings, four of which are fully serviced. Site lighting is good throughout and there are regular security patrols. The gate to the promenade is kept locked at all times, campers getting a key. The site is a Caravan Club affiliated site; members and non-members are all made welcome.

Facilities

The good quality, heated toilet block includes washbasins in curtained cubicles plus three family shower rooms and a well equipped room for disabled campers. Laundry room. Gas supplies. Hairdressing salon. Indoor heated swimming pool (Spr. B.H-30 Sept; charged). Small modern playground. Off site: Beach 50 yds. Well stocked shop/post office 500 yds. Pubs, fast food outlets and a supermarket are all within easy walking distance. Bus service to Skegness and Ingoldmells 500 yds.

Open: All year.

Directions

Site is off A52 Boston-Skegness-Mablethorpe road, north of Skegness town centre. Turn east opposite Garden City pub into Winthorpe Ave and entrance is on left at far end of road. New arrivals after 17.00 should contact site. GPS: 53.1668, 0.3495

Charges guide

Per unit incl. 2 persons	
and electricity	£ 17.60 - £ 25.70
extra person	£ 5.85 - £ 8.20

Sleaford
Low Farm Touring & Camping Park
Spring Lane, Folkingham, Sleaford NG34 0SJ (Lincolnshire) T: 01529 497322. E: lowfarmpark@sky.com
alanrogers.com/UK3770

This quiet, secluded park is a lovely spot to relax or to use as a base for touring the Lincolnshire countryside. Jane and Nigel Stevens work hard to make it a pleasant place to stay and have a well laid out park offering good quality facilities that are kept clean and tidy. The park offers 36 pitches (17 occupied by seasonal vans) with 10A electricity hook-ups and a field for tents and small rallies. Some hardstandings are available. The park is on the edge of the village of Folkingham with a pub (serving food), a shop selling an amazing range of produce and an artisan chocolate shop.

Facilities

Central, well maintained toilet block with controllable free showers and open style washbasins. Washing machine. Reception is at owners' house and a tourist information room with toilets is adjacent. Large field where children can play (also sometimes used by tent campers). Off site: Fishing 5 miles. Golf 10 miles. Shops and supermarkets in Bourne 9 miles and Sleaford, 10 miles.

Open: 2 April - 11 October.

Directions

Folkingham is 26 miles south of Lincoln on A15 to Peterborough, 2 miles south of roundabout junction with the A52 (Nottingham/Grantham-Boston). Park is on southern edge of village; at foot of hill at campsite sign, turn west and park is at end of lane. GPS: 52.88685, -0.411167

Charges guide

Per unit incl. 2 persons	
and electricity	£ 12.50 - £ 17.50
No credit cards.	

For latest campsite news visit
alanrogers.com

Slimbridge
Tudor Caravan & Camping Park
Shepherds Patch, Slimbridge GL2 7BP (Gloucestershire) T: 01453 890483. E: info@tudorcaravanpark.co.uk
alanrogers.com/UK4170

This attractive, peaceful campsite is adjacent to the Gloucester-Sharpness Canal. Located behind the Tudor Arms public house, a gate clearly identifies the entrance and the brand new reception is just inside on the right. There are many trees and hedges, particularly surrounding the site, so the canal is not visible. Attractively laid out on two separate fields, there are 75 pitches, all with 16A electricity hook-ups and 50 with hardstanding. The old orchard is for long stay or adults only units with gravel hardstandings, and more open grassy meadow for family touring units. There is a rally field beyond the meadow.

Facilities

A high quality shower block with underfloor heating provides large shower cubicles, private washing cubicles, baby changing room and facilities for disabled visitors. The other heated toilet building is located to one side of the orchard and provides all the usual facilities including pushbutton hot showers. Laundry. Gas available. Some site lighting but a torch would be useful. Gate locked 22.30-07.00. WiFi (charged). No charcoal barbecues.

Open: All year.

Directions

From A38 by junction with A4135 (Dursley), turn west, signed WWT Wetlands Centre Slimbridge. Continue for 1.5 miles turning left into car park of the Tudor Arms. Site entrance is at rear of car park. GPS: 51.735533, -2.395817

Charges guide

Per unit incl. 2 persons	
and electricity	£ 17.00 - £ 24.00

No credit cards.

Spalding
Delph Bank Touring Park
Old Main Road, Fleet Hargate, Holbeach, Spalding PE12 8LL (Lincolnshire) T: 01406 422910.
E: enquiries@delphbank.co.uk **alanrogers.com/UK3646**

A delightful, peaceful, adults only park, Delph Bank is ideally situated as a base from which to enjoy the delights of the southern Lincolnshire Fens and even to explore north Norfolk. It is conveniently located just off the A17 road from the East Midlands to Norfolk. There are just 45 pitches, all with electricity connections (16A), although usually only 35 are used, including 26 with hardstanding and grass verge; five of these also have individual water taps and drain. The park is beautifully tended, sheltered by surrounding hedges and with a few mature trees offering a little shade in places.

Facilities

Single well equipped sanitary block is immaculately maintained and offers modern electronically-controlled showers, washbasins (in cabins for the ladies), soap dispensers, hair- and hand dryers. Outstanding suite for disabled visitors. Dishwashing, washing machine and dryer in reception. Motorcaravan services. Small library. Tourist information. Dog walk. WiFi over site (charged). Off site: Licensed tea rooms and farm shop 400 yds.

Open: 20 March - 3 November.

Directions

Park is just off A17 Kings Lynn/Sleaford road between the turnings for Wisbech (A1101) and Spalding (A151). Turn southwest at brown campsite sign and immediately turn right to site on left in 100 yds. GPS: 52.801354, 0.071433

Charges guide

Per unit incl. 2 persons	
and electricity	£ 22.50 - £ 25.00
extra person	£ 5.00

Stourport-on-Severn
Lickhill Manor Caravan Park
Lower Lickhill Road, Stourport-on-Severn DY13 8RL (Worcestershire) T: 01299 871041.
E: excellent@lickhillmanor.co.uk **alanrogers.com/UK4210**

Lickhill Manor is a well managed touring and holiday site within easy walking distance of the town centre via a footpath along the River Severn. Opportunities exist for fishing and boating. The site is open all year for touring units and there are 62 pitches all with 10A electricity, 18 with hardstanding and some with water and waste water. A large 14-acre rally field with 68 hook-ups is also available for touring units. It is an attractive site with 125 private holiday homes which are well screened from the touring areas so they are not visually intrusive. There are two excellent play areas and a dog exercise field within the park. The site is well laid out, populated with native trees and shrubs and wildlife ponds.

Facilities

An additional sanitary building serves the touring pitches and complements the older unit at the far end of the park. These heated buildings provide good, modern facilities including a well equipped suite for disabled guests which doubles as a family washroom with facilities for baby changing. Drive-over motorcaravan service point. Recycling bins. Gas supplies. Fishing permits from site shop. Off site: Stourport shops and pub 10 mins. walk.

Open: All year.

Directions

From the A451 in Stourport take B4195 northwest towards Bewdley. After 1 mile turn left at crossroads (traffic lights), into Lickhill Road North where site is signed. GPS: 52.34558, -2.29743

Charges guide

Per unit incl. 4 persons	
and electricity	£ 19.00 - £ 25.00
extra person (over 2 yrs)	£ 3.00
dog	£ 2.00

For latest campsite news visit
alanrogers.com

Stratford-upon-Avon
Riverside Park
Tiddington Road, Tiddington, Stratford-upon-Avon CV37 7AB (Warwickshire) T: 01789 292312.
E: riverside@stratfordcaravans.co.uk **alanrogers.com/UK4080**

On the bank of the River Avon, this spacious site has 100 touring pitches (no tents) on grass, all with 10A electric hook-ups. A rally field has a further 60 pitches (30 with electricity). At the adjacent Rayford Park, which is under the same management, there is a bar and restaurant complex serving lunch and dinner, and breakfast in high season; club house facilities, including live entertainment, are available most weekends. There is a possible flood risk during periods of inclement weather. A river taxi runs to Stratford from the site. The site offers a choice of rental accommodation in camping pods, luxury lodges and caravans.

Facilities
The heated sanitary block has been refitted to modern standards and is bright and comfortable with spacious showers and some washbasins in cubicles. Wet room style facilities for disabled visitors. Laundry facilities. Motorcaravan services. Play area. Minigolf. Slipway and fishing on site. Gas supplies. No commercial vehicles are accepted. WiFi over site (charged). Off site: Bar, restaurant and club house adjacent. Buses to Coventry, Warwick, Leamington Spa and Stratford 5 mins. walk.
Open: 1 April - 1 November.

Directions
From Stratford take B4086 towards Wellesbourne. Site entrance is on left after one mile, just before Tiddington village (ignore entrance to Rayford Park C.P). GPS: 52.20023, -1.68213

Charges guide
Per unit incl. 2 persons	
and electricity	£ 19.00 - £ 26.00
extra person	£ 3.50
child (5-15 yrs)	£ 2.00

Sutton-on-Sea
Cherry Tree Site
Huttoft Road, Sutton-on-Sea LN12 2RU (Lincolnshire) T: 01507 441626. E: info@cherrytreesite.co.uk
alanrogers.com/UK3650

This is a delightful, tranquil, adult only site and is a fine example of a small, good value touring park. It is a 15-minute walk from a Blue Flag beach and a short drive from some of the attractive villages of the Lincolnshire Wolds. A very warm welcome awaits from Kevin and Sue Lannen whose pride in the park is evident everywhere. The site is level, the grass is neatly trimmed and well drained, and screening is provided by lines of evergreen hedging. There are 40 good sized touring pitches, all with 10A electricity and hardstanding (no tents) and ten with water and waste water drain. A shop and pub are within a ten-minute walk. A member of the Tranquil Touring Park and Best of British groups.

Facilities
The brick-built toilet block, recently extended and refurbished to a high standard, can be heated and is immaculately kept. Controllable hot showers. En-suite unit for disabled visitors (Radar key). Laundry room with washing machine, spin dryer and tumble dryer. Neat reception and separate tourist information cabin. Gas. WiFi over site (charged). Off site: Riding adjacent. Shop and pub 0.6 miles. Beach, bowls and fishing 1.5 miles.
Open: 7 March - 2 November.

Directions
Sutton-on-Sea is 15 miles north of Skegness and 40 miles east of Lincoln. The site is 1.5 miles south of the town on A52 coast road, with the entrance leading off a layby on the east. GPS: 53.29292, 0.28439

Charges guide
Per unit incl. 2 persons	
and electricity	£ 19.00 - £ 27.50
extra person	£ 5.00

Tewkesbury
Winchcombe Camping & Caravanning Club Site
Brooklands Farm, Alderton, Tewkesbury GL20 8NX (Gloucestershire) T: 01242 620259.
alanrogers.com/UK4140

This is a popular, high quality site, situated in a quiet and rural location, close to the Cotswold attractions. Some pitches surround a small coarse fishing lake, with others in a recently developed area of maturing bushes and shrubs with open views over the surrounding countryside. In total there are 80 touring pitches, 60 with 16A electricity hook-ups and 52 with gravel hardstanding. Two camping areas have also been provided and there are four lodges for hire. The reception building flanks a small gravel car park approached from a tarmac drive.

Facilities
The main heated sanitary unit is kept very clean and tidy to an extremely high standard. Room with disabled access. Separate parent and child room. Laundry facilities. Gas supplies. Recreation room. Small outdoor play area. WiFi throughout (charged). Fishing (on payment, licence required). Lodges to rent. Off site: Several pubs and restaurants in the area. Golf 7 miles.
Open: 4 March - 9 January.

Directions
From M5 exit 9, take A46 Evesham road for 3 miles to Toddington roundabout, then B4077 towards Stow-on-the-Wold for a further 3 miles to the site entrance on right. GPS: 51.9904, -1.990683

Charges guide
Per unit incl. 2 persons	
and electricity	£ 20.70 - £ 34.90
Non-member prices are higher.	

For latest campsite news visit
alanrogers.com

Tattershall

Tattershall Lakes Country Park

57 Sleaford Road, Tattershall LN4 4LR (Lincolnshire) T: 01526 348800.
E: tattershall.holidays@away-resorts.com **alanrogers.com/UK3685**

This extensive park with seven lakes of varying sizes is well kept, offers opportunities for enthusiasts of watersports and fishing, and the pleasant village of Tattershall is within walking distance. The touring fields are flat and rather featureless but with views across the main lake. There are 245 pitches, numbered but with no hedges or markings to separate them; all have 16A electrical connections and 25 also have an individual tap and drainage, plus hardstanding. Ten tent pitches are on a small peninsula in the lake. Fifty-five lodges and static caravans are for rent and a further 437 are privately owned. A large pub and eatery is close to the park entrance and the nearby village has a number of small shops and pubs. Tattershall Castle (NT) is just down the road and RAF Coningsby, home to the Battle of Britain Memorial Flight, is close by (so some daytime aircraft noise is inevitable).

Facilities	Directions
Sanitary block with preset showers and open-style washbasins will be under considerable pressure at busy times. En-suite unit for disabled visitors. Laundry. Two prefabricated units provide additional very basic en-suite units, though access is not easy. Small, well stocked shop. Coffee shop serving meals, snacks and takeaways. Bar with evening discos and entertainment. Upstairs bar with TV, electronic games and darts. New swimming pool and spa complex with hot tubs. Artificial beach. TV and games rooms. Water skiing and jet ski lakes. Four fishing lakes. Golf course. Archery. Bicycle and pedalo hire. Activities and entertainment. WiFi (free).	Tattershall is 22 miles southeast of Lincoln on the A153 Sleaford/Horncastle road, 14 miles northeast of Sleaford. Park is on the western edge of the village between the River Witham and Tattershall Castle. GPS: 53.09725, -0.20219

Open: 1 March - 31 October.

Charges guide

Per unit incl. 6 persons and electricity	£ 9.00 - £ 35.00
dog	£ 1.00

Tewkesbury

Croft Farm Leisure & Waterpark

Bredon's Hardwick, Tewkesbury GL20 7EE (Gloucestershire) T: 01684 772321.
E: enquiries@croftfarmleisure.co.uk **alanrogers.com/UK4150**

Croft Farm is an AALA licensed Watersports Centre with Royal Yachting Association approved tuition available for windsurfing, sailing, kayaking and canoeing. The lakeside campsite has 140 level pitches, of which 80 are for touring units with 10A electricity hook-ups. There are 70 gravel hardstandings with very little shade or shelter. Facilities include a fully equipped gymnasium with qualified instructors and sauna. Sports massage, aromatherapy and beauty treatments are available by appointment. The clubhouse has an attractive lakeside terrace and there is a new slipway to the River Avon.

Facilities	Directions
Excellent sanitary facilities with spacious hot showers. A heated unit in the main building is always open and best for cooler months; this provides further WCs, washbasins and showers, laundry and facilities for disabled visitors. Watersports centre. Café/bar (Fri-Sun low season, daily at other times). Takeaway. Gym. Playground. River fishing. Barrier and toilet block key (£5 deposit). Fenced dog exercise area. Free WiFi in the clubhouse.	From M5 exit 9 take A438 (Tewkesbury), at first lights turn right into Shannon Way. Turn right at next lights into Northway Lane, cross motorway bridge. Turn left into housing estate and cross 2nd bridge. At T-junction turn right on B4080, site is opposite Cross Keys Inn. GPS: 52.015967, -2.130267

Open: 1 March - mid November.

Charges guide

Per unit incl. 2 persons, electricity	£ 20.00
extra person (over 3 yrs)	£ 4.00

For latest campsite news visit
alanrogers.com

Woodhall Spa

Glen Lodge Touring Park

Glen Lodge, Edlington Moor, Woodhall Spa LN10 6UL (Lincolnshire) T: 01526 353523.

alanrogers.com/UK3692

This quiet, attractive and spacious site is ideal for couples and families who enjoy the rural lifestyle, yet it is only just over a mile from the thriving village of Woodhall Spa which retains much of its old-fashioned charm. All 35 pitches have hardstanding and 10A electricity hook-ups (one or two appeared to need long leads) and are served by shingle roads with some street lighting. The grass and flowerbeds are obviously tended by someone who enjoys gardening. In fact, the whole park has a much-loved feel.

Facilities

The modern heated toilet block (key-pad access) is kept spotlessly clean with controllable showers, vanity style washbasins and piped music. En-suite facilities for disabled visitors. Washing machine and dryer. Off site: Pub serving good food 0.5 miles. Open-air pool, tennis and bowls 1 mile. Shops in village 1.5 miles. Golf and fishing 2 miles. Tattershall Castle 5 miles.

Open: 1 March - 30 November.

Directions

Woodhall Spa is 18 miles southeast of Lincoln. From mini-roundabout in village turn northeast towards Bardney on B1190 (Stixwould Road) past Petwood Hotel. In just over 1 mile at sharp left bend, turn right. Site is 300 yds. on left. GPS: 53.166233, -0.22

Charges guide

Per unit incl. 2 persons and electricity	£ 17.00
extra person (over 4 yrs)	£ 3.00

No credit cards.

Woodhall Spa

Petwood Caravan Park

Off Stixwould Road, Woodhall Spa LN10 6QH (Lincolnshire) T: 01526 354799.

E: info@petwoodcaravanpark.co.uk **alanrogers.com/UK3693**

On the outskirts of the thriving inland 'resort village' of Woodhall Spa, Petwood is a newly-built, well maintained park in the heart of 'Bomber' County. A few of Lincolnshire's many Second World War airfields are now Aviation Heritage sites and RAF Coningsby is home to the Battle of Britain Memorial Flight; the Dambusters' pub is just down the road. There are 98 spacious, level pitches with electricity connections (16A) and water taps. They are divided into distinct areas by young shrubs and trees and include 67 grass touring pitches and eight gravel hardstandings with grass verges; the remainder are occupied by seasonal units.

Facilities

Two modern, spacious, well equipped and maintained sanitary blocks have preset showers and open style washbasins, baby changing and an excellent en-suite unit for disabled visitors. Laundry room with washing machine and dryer but no sinks. Dishwashing room including sink at wheelchair height. Motorcaravans use tap by pitch and drain by sanitary block. Large field for ball games. WiFi throughout (charged). Off site: Adjacent Jubilee Park has heated outdoor swimming pool (15/5-15/9), bowls, croquet, tennis and café. Village 500 yds. Golf 1 mile.

Open: 21 March - 2 November.

Directions

Woodhall Spa is southeast of Lincoln. From A15 (Lincoln-Sleaford) at Metheringham Heath turn east on B1189 to Metheringham, in 3.7 miles turn left on B1191 to Woodhall Spa. At mini-roundabout in village turn north on B1190 (Bardney). Jubilee Park is on left in 0.3 miles. NB Petwood is the first of two sites behind the park. GPS: 53.15477, -0.22314

Charges guide

Per unit incl. 2 persons and electricity	£ 20.00 - £ 24.00
extra person	£ 3.00

Worksop

Riverside Caravan Park

Central Avenue, Worksop S80 1ER (Nottinghamshire) T: 01909 474118. E: riversideworkshop@hotmail.co.uk

alanrogers.com/UK3920

A town centre touring park adjacent to the Worksop cricket ground, this excellent site is attractive and surprisingly peaceful. Riverside is within easy walking distance of the town centre, and the Chesterfield Canal runs close to its northern side offering delightful towpath walks and fishing (children would need to be watched). For those who cannot resist the thwack of leather on willow, this site is ideal. Of the 60 marked level pitches, ten are seasonal and 43 are for touring, mainly on gravel hardstanding, seven are on grass and some are separated by trees and low rails, and all have 10A electric hook-ups.

Facilities

The single sanitary unit near reception can be heated and has all the usual facilities, although showers are on payment (£1 coin). Limited facilities for disabled visitors. No laundry. Motorcaravan services. Gas supplies. WiFi over site (charged). Off site: Fishing 0.5 miles. Several golf courses 1 mile. Bicycle hire 4 miles. Squash and flat or crown green bowling nearby.

Open: All year.

Directions

Worksop is 7 miles west of M1 at exit 30 and 4 miles east of A1. Easiest approach is from A57/A60 roundabout west of town – third roundabout from A1. Turn east (at Little Chef) on B6024 towards town centre. Site is well signed. GPS: 53.30572, -1.12882

Charges guide

Per unit incl. 2 persons and electricity	£ 20.00 - £ 25.00

For latest campsite news visit
alanrogers.com

THE REGION IS DIVIDED INTO NORTH, SOUTH, EAST AND WEST YORKSHIRE

A beautiful and varied region of rolling hills and undulating moors, Yorkshire has an historic past with a wealth of new attractions. Its landscape has inspired famous authors and been the setting for some of Britain's best-loved television programmes.

The major attractions of this region are the parks: the Yorkshire Dales National Park comprises 680 square miles of unspoilt countryside with high fells, winding rivers, ancient castles and outstanding views of the surrounding landscapes, with their limestone plateaux and dry stone walls; while the North York Moors National Park has miles of open, heather-covered moorland and pretty villages in its valleys. These areas are ideal places for walking, cycling, horse riding and climbing. Or if you prefer to relax and take in the scenery, the North Yorkshire Moors Railway, starting at Pickering, is one of the many steam railways in the region. On the coast, traditional family resorts like Scarborough, Bridlington and Whitby offer the holidaymaker a wide range of activities. Also by the sea is Kingston-upon-Hull, a maritime city with powerful links to Britain's proud seafaring tradition, and the picturesque fishing port of Whitby, once home to Captain James Cook. Elsewhere in the region are the vibrant cities of York, with its wealth of ancient sites including the Minster, Leeds and Sheffield, plus the busy market town of Doncaster.

Places of interest

North: Harrogate; Wensleydale Creamery in Hawes; Jorvik Viking Centre in York; Lightwater Valley Theme Park, near Ripon; Castle Howard near York; Mother Shipton's Cave, Knaresborough; Skipton Castle.

South: Hatfield Waterpark near Doncaster; Tropical Butterfly House and Wildlife Centre in Anston; Sheffield Ski Village, Europe's biggest artificial ski resort; Magna science adventure centre in Rotherham.

East: Bempton Cliffs RSPB Nature Reserve near Bridlington, England's largest seabird colony; market town of Beverley; Captain Cook Museum and abbey in Whitby; Scarborough castle and sea life centre.

West: National Media Museum, Bradford; Royal Armouries Museum, Leeds; Saltaire Victorian village; Brontë Museum, Haworth.

Did you know?

The comedy series, Last of the Summer Wine, was filmed in the Pennine town of Holmfirth and its surrounding countryside.

York is the oldest city in Yorkshire, founded in AD71. The Minster is the largest Gothic cathedral in Northern Europe.

Saltaire was built as a model village during the industrial revolution by Sir Titus Salt.

Bradford was once known as the wool capital of the world. In 1841 there were 38 mills in the town.

Under the pseudonym Ellis Bell, Emily Brontë wrote Wuthering Heights in 1847 at Haworth Parsonage.

Rudston is said to be the oldest inhabited village in England, named after the Rood Stone, a mysterious 4,000-year-old monolith.

Whitby was the inspiration for the Gothic horror novel, Dracula, by Bram Stoker and now holds bi-annual Gothic weekends.

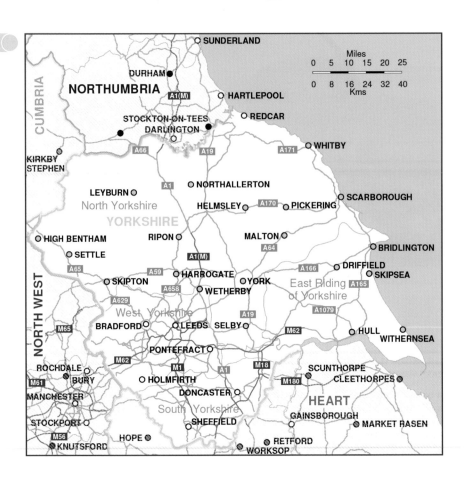

Bridlington

South Cliff Caravan Park

Wilsthorpe, Bridlington YO15 3QN (East Yorkshire) T: 01262 671051. E: southcliff@eastriding.gov.uk

alanrogers.com/UK4498

This traditional style caravan park is part of a large complex owned and operated by the East Riding of Yorkshire Council. There are 193 touring pitches, each with a 16A electricity post; 20 are for tents, the remainder have hardstanding surrounded by grass or, in a few cases, extended to the road. They are in rows across the field, so access for larger units can be tricky when the site is full. Direct access to the seafront is via a 'park and ride' system and from there a land train runs a mile along the shore to Bridlington. Here you can visit the historic old town, the harbour with its heritage museum, the Spa Theatre and Ballroom, Sewerby Hall and Gardens and Leisure World.

Facilities

Two toilet blocks (one traditional, one new) provide pushbutton showers, open washbasins (a few in cubicles for ladies). Excellent en-suite units for disabled visitors. Three bathrooms with washbasins and baby changing facilities. No motorcaravan service point. Franchised facilities include a launderette, a well stocked shop (1/3-8/10), a fish and chip shop and a leisure complex (bar, restaurant, clubroom, games room) offering entertainment evenings in high season and monthly themed weekends (outside August). Ten mobile homes for rent. Dogs are not accepted (except assistance dogs). Large motorcaravans are accepted by arrangement subject to availability. Off site: Golf 0.5 miles. Beach (by car), riding, sailing and boat launching 1 mile. Shops, pubs and restaurants within 2 miles. Fishing 2 miles.

Open: 1 March - 30 November.

Directions

Bridlington is 40 miles east of York via A166/A614. From M62 exit 37, take A614 to Bridlington and turn south on re-routed A165 towards Hull. At roundabout south of town, turn north on newly renumbered A1038; site is signed to right at next roundabout. GPS: 54.0641, -0.2132

Charges guide

Per unit incl. up to 5 persons
and electricity £ 20.00 - £ 33.00

Discounts in low season and mid seasons.

Bridlington

Bridlington Caravan Club Site

Flamborough Road, Sewerby, Bridlington YO15 1DU (East Yorkshire) T: 01262 672707.
alanrogers.com/UK4504

This Caravan Club site is set within 18 acres and offers 78 level and attractively laid out touring pitches, 70 on hardstanding, all with 16A electricity. Of these, eight are fully serviced. The site is just two years old and newly planted trees will eventually provide privacy between pitches. There are measures in place to make this an eco-friendly site including the use of solar heating and recycled water for flushing. The site is just three miles from Bridlington with its beautiful beaches and harbour. A bus service from outside the gate runs to Bridlington and Flamborough.

Facilities

A single, well appointed sanitary block is heated and includes facilities for babies and disabled visitors. Well equipped showers and most washbasins are in cabins. Laundry room with coin-operated washing machine and dryer. Small shop in reception with tourist information. Play area. WiFi throughout (charged). Off site: Golf adjacent. Bar and restaurant within 1 mile. Supermarkets 1.5 and 4 miles. Beach and fishing 1 mile.

Open: All year.

Directions

From the A165 in Bridlington at a roundabout, take the B1255 signed Flamborough. Site is on the left after 2.5 miles, just after you pass Sewerby Hall and Marton Holiday Park on the right. GPS: 54.11157, -0.15839

Charges guide

Per person	£ 5.90 - £ 8.70
child (5-17 yrs)	£ 0.01 - £ 3.40
pitch incl. electricity (non-member)	£ 16.80 - £ 21.00

Driffield

Thorpe Hall Caravan & Camping Site

Rudston, Driffield YO25 4JE (East Yorkshire) T: 01262 420393. E: caravansite@thorpehall.co.uk
alanrogers.com/UK4510

Just outside the village of Rudston, in the grounds of Thorpe Hall, this pleasant small touring park is six miles from the sea at Bridlington. Enthusiastically managed by Jayne Chatterton, it is set on flat grass, largely enclosed by the old kitchen garden wall. The 78 large pitches have 16A electrical hook-ups and TV connections. A separate field accommodates 14 tents. There are no caravan holiday homes or seasonal pitches. Tourist information leaflets on a range of local walks are provided and Sir Ian MacDonald takes visitors on walks around the estate.

Facilities

A solid, central toilet block can be heated. Some washbasins are in cabins. Bathroom for disabled visitors and families with young children. Laundry facilities. Small shop selling local produce. Games room with pool table, table football and table tennis. TV room. Play area. No ball games (field adjacent). Coarse fishing lake (charged). WiFi (charged). Off site: 4-acre games field adjacent. Footpath to the village and a garage. Bus service to Bridlington three times a week. Riding 2 miles. Beach, sailing and boat launching 4.5 miles. Bicycle hire and golf 5 miles.

Open: 1 March - 31 October.

Directions

Site is by the B1253 road, 4.5 miles from Bridlington, on east side of Rudston. GPS: 54.093817, -0.3125

Charges guide

Per unit incl. 2 persons and electricity	£ 13.00 - £ 25.00
tent pitch incl. 2 persons	£ 10.00 - £ 22.00
extra person (over 2 yrs)	£ 2.50
Single person discount available (tent field).	

Harrogate

Harrogate Caravan Park

Great Yorkshire Showground, Harrogate HG2 8NZ (North Yorkshire) T: 01423 546145.
E: enquiries@harrogatecaravanpark.co.uk **alanrogers.com/UK4625**

Comprising 66 mixed grass and hardstanding pitches, all with 16A electric hook-up, this attractive site at the edge of the Great Yorkshire Showground offers a convenient and pleasant base for exploring Harrogate. It is either a short drive or a bus ride into town. Parts of the showground can be seen from the site, set within the Crimple Valley. It is normally a very quiet site for nature lovers, but during July it is host to the Great Yorkshire Show. Although well placed for touring Yorkshire, it is ideal for visiting Harrogate with over 200 restaurants, a theatre and spa centre and excellent shopping.

Facilities

A single, modern and clean toilet block has open style vanity units and baby changing facilities in the ladies' area. Separate facilities for disabled campers in a prefabricated unit. Dishwashing and laundry facilities. Motorcaravan services. WiFi (free). Off site: Shop and café 50 yds. Fishing and golf 3 miles. Harrogate itself but Fountains Abbey, Harewood House, Lightwater Valley and Brimham Rocks are a short drive away as are the North York Moors.

Open: End March - 7 November.

Directions

From A661 Harrogate to Wetherby road turn into Railway Road at the traffic lights alongside Sainsburys. Drive to end of road and site is on the right. GPS: 53.98319, -1.49936

Charges guide

Per unit incl. 2 persons and electricity	£ 17.00 - £ 22.00
extra person	£ 5.00

For latest campsite news visit
alanrogers.com

Harrogate
Ripley Caravan Park
Ripley, Harrogate HG3 3AU (North Yorkshire) T: 01423 770050. E: info@ripleycaravanpark.com
alanrogers.com/UK4630

Peter and Valerie House are the friendly, resident owners of Ripley Park, a 25-acre grassed caravan park with an indoor heated pool. It accommodates 100 touring units, all with access to 10A electricity, on fairly level grass which undulates in parts. Connected by a circular gravel road, the pitches are marked or spaced (allowing the grass to recover). There are 50 hardstandings. The owners have planted 2,000 trees and these are developing well to provide individual areas and shelter. A pond with ducks provides an attractive feature (children should be supervised). In addition, 100 caravan holiday homes occupy a separate area. The park is situated at the gateway to the Yorkshire Dales National Park.

Facilities

At the edge of the touring area, the toilet block can be heated and includes some washbasins in curtained cubicles, 11 individual washing facilities, a baby bath and a separate unit with a shower for disabled visitors. Small laundry. Motorcaravan services. Shop with gas (limited hours in low seasons). Games room with TV. Nursery playroom. Adventure play equipment and football area. Heated indoor pool (charged) and sauna. Max. 2 dogs, some breeds excluded. Winter caravan storage. WiFi (charged). Off site: Bus service 150 yds. Fishing, bicycle hire, riding and golf 3 miles.

Open: Mid March - 31 October.

Directions

About 4 miles north of Harrogate, park access is 150 yds. down the B6165 Knaresborough road from its roundabout junction with the A61.
GPS: 54.0369, -1.558833

Charges guide

Per unit incl. 2 persons and electricity	£ 18.00 - £ 23.00
extra person	£ 4.00 - £ 5.00
child (3-16 yrs)	£ 1.50
dog	£ 1.00

Harrogate
Rudding Holiday Park
Follifoot, Harrogate HG3 1JH (North Yorkshire) T: 01423 870439. E: holiday-park@ruddingpark.com
alanrogers.com/UK4710

The extensive part wooded, part open grounds of Rudding Park are very attractive, peaceful and well laid out. One touring area is sloping but terraces provide level pitches. All 86 touring pitches have 10/16A electricity, 15 have hardstandings with water and a drain and a small number of super pitches are available for touring units. Further pitches are let on a seasonal basis; caravan holiday homes and chalets are in separate areas. On the outer edge of the park is The Deer House, a family pub serving bar meals, with limited opening outside the high season weeks. A heated outdoor swimming pool (charged), a ball play area and a play park for children are near the pub. This is an attractive park with something for all the family. A bus to Harrogate stops outside the main entrance.

Facilities

Two toilet blocks (heated when necessary and may be under pressure at peak times), some washbasins in private cubicles, baby room and bathroom. Laundry rooms. Facilities for disabled visitors. Motorcaravan services. Shop (6/3-7/11; limited hours). Gas. Restaurant and bar (limited hours outside high season). Heated outdoor swimming and paddling pools (25/5-30/8), supervised (extra charge). Spa and wellness centre at the hotel (charged). Adventure playground. Football pitch. Games room. Golf. WiFi throughout (charged). Off site: Buses to Harrogate and Knaresborough. Riding 1 mile. Fishing 2 miles.

Open: 4 March - 30 January.

Directions

From the junction of the A658 and A661 (roundabout), 3 miles southeast of Harrogate take the A658 (Leeds). After 0.5 miles turn sharp right onto a road that passes the golf course, holiday park and hotel. All have separate entrances.
GPS: 53.97307, -1.49720

Charges guide

Per unit incl. 2 adults, 2 children and electricity	£ 18.00 - £ 44.00
extra person	£ 7.25 - £ 12.50
child (5-16 yrs)	£ 4.25 - £ 9.00
dog	£ 3.75

Special offers - contact park.

For latest campsite news visit
alanrogers.com

Helmsley

Golden Square Caravan & Camping Park

Oswaldkirk, Helmsley, York YO62 5YQ (North Yorkshire) T: 01439 788269.
E: reception@goldensquarecaravanpark.com **alanrogers.com/UK4560**

Golden Square is a popular, high quality, family owned park. An exceptionally attractive caravan park has been created from an old quarry with a number of separate, level bays that have superb views over the North Yorkshire Moors. The pitches are individually marked with car parking alongside. In very dry weather the ground can be hard so rock pegs would be needed (even in wet weather the park is well drained). All pitches have 10A electricity, 24 have drainage and six are deluxe pitches (with waste water, sewerage, electricity, water and TV aerial connections). There are some seasonal pitches and holiday caravan homes for sale. A well stocked shop sells locally sourced produce, including homemade fresh bread and cakes, dairy produce, groceries, newspapers, gas, gifts and camping accessories. Visitors may use the Ampleforth College sports centre (charged), with its indoor pool, tennis and gym, etc. The area abounds with footpaths and three well known, long distance footpaths are nearby. Dog owners are welcome with two or three enormous fields for exercising alongside the park.

Facilities

Two stone-built toilet blocks are first rate, modern and well equipped with underfloor heating, with some washbasins in private cubicles. Showers are free. Bathroom (£1) also houses baby facilities. Both ladies and men have full facilities for disabled visitors. Laundry facilities. Motorcaravan services. Tourist information room also houses a microwave. Well stocked shop. Two excellent play areas. Games field and a barn with games. Bicycle hire. All year caravan storage. CCTV. WiFi throughout (charged). Off site: Golf 3 miles. Fishing and riding 5 miles. Outdoor pool at Helmsley, sports centre at Ampleforth with indoor pool, both have shops and pubs with food.

Open: 1 March - 31 October.

Directions

From York take B1363 to Helmsley. At Oswaldkirk Bank Top turn left on B1257 to Helmsley. Once on B1257 take second left signed Ampleforth and caravan route to site. Site is easily accessed from A170 leaving at Sproxton, near Helmsley, on to B1257 but caravans are prohibited on Sutton Bank (6 miles west of site). GPS: 54.209333, -1.073783

Charges guide

Per unit incl. 2 persons	
and electricity	£ 17.50 - £ 26.00
extra person	£ 3.50
extra child (5-15 yrs)	£ 1.50
dog (max. 2)	£ 1.50

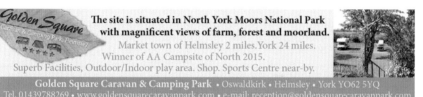

The site is situated in North York Moors National Park with magnificent views of farm, forest and moorland.
Market town of Helmsley 2 miles. York 24 miles.
Winner of AA Campsite of North 2015.
Superb Facilities, Outdoor/Indoor play area. Shop. Sports Centre near-by.
Golden Square Caravan & Camping Park • Oswaldkirk • Helmsley • York YO62 5YQ
Tel. 01439788269 • www.goldensquarecaravanpark.com • e-mail: reception@goldensquarecaravanpark.com

Helmsley

Foxholme Touring Caravan & Camping Park

Harome, Helmsley YO62 5JG (North Yorkshire) T: 01439 772336. E: reservations@riccalvalecottages.co.uk
alanrogers.com/UK4580

Foxholme is an adults only park, managed by an on-site warden. It would suit those who want a quiet holiday disturbed only by birdsong and passing deer. There are 30 touring pitches set either in an open, slightly sloping field, or between trees on grass. Both areas are attractive and well tended. A further 30 seasonal pitches are arranged amongst the trees. All the pitches have 6A electricity (a few need long leads) and six have hardstanding. Some picnic tables are provided. Wildlife abounds and poppies and other wild flowers enhance this tranquil site. The park is set in quiet countryside and would be a good base for touring, being within striking distance of the moors, the coast and York.

Facilities

The toilet block is an older style building and is clean but basic and showing signs of its age. Some private cubicles. Laundry facilities. Two further small blocks provide WCs only in other parts of the park. Basic motorcaravan service point. Very basic provisions are kept. Caravan storage. Torches useful. Off site: Riding and golf 3.5 miles. Shops and bicycle hire at Helmsley and Kirkbymoorside, both about 4 miles away.

Open: 1 March - 31 October.

Directions

Turn south off A170 between Beadlam (to west) and Nawton (to east) at sign to Ryedale School, then 1 mile to park on left (passing another park on right). From west turn right 400 yds. east of Helmsley, signed Harome, turn left at church, go through village and follow camping signs. Sat nav postcode: YO62 7SD. GPS: 54.23745, -0.990333

Charges guide

Per unit incl. up to 4 persons	
and electricity	£ 20.00
extra person	£ 1.00
No credit cards.	

For latest campsite news visit
alanrogers.com

High Bentham
Riverside Caravan Park

High Bentham, Lancaster LA2 7FJ (North Yorkshire) T: 01524 261272. E: info@riversidecaravanpark.co.uk
alanrogers.com/UK4715

The pretty, tree-lined approach to Riverside leads into an attractive park, owned by the Marshall family since the late 1960s. Nestling in beautiful countryside, alongside the River Wenning, the park has easy access to the Yorkshire Dales and the Lake District. For touring units there are 12 fully serviced pitches, 15 on hardstanding and 30 grass pitches. All have 16A electricity and TV hook-ups. An area has been developed for 50 seasonal pitches on gravel. Located away from the touring area are 206 privately owned holiday homes. Tents are not accepted. A member of the Best of British group.

Facilities

The modern toilet block with underfloor heating is centrally situated. Washbasins in cubicles. Unisex showers in a separate area. Toilet and shower room for disabled visitors (Radar key). Family shower/bathroom (charged). Motorcaravan services. Shop (all season). Play area for younger children. Large field for ball games. Family games room. The river can be used for fishing (permit from reception) swimming and small boats. Caravan storage. WiFi (free). Off site: Golf 1 mile. Riding 2 miles.

Open: 1 March - 2 January.

Directions

Leave M6 at exit 34, taking A683 (Kirkby Lonsdale). After 5 miles take B6480 (High Bentham). From the east, take A65 after Settle. Site is signed at B6480, turn left. At Black Bull Hotel follow caravan signs. Park on right after bridge. GPS: 54.11311, -2.51066

Charges guide

Per unit incl. 2 persons and electricity	£ 20.95 - £ 26.75
Min. charge per night £ 15.90.	

Hull
Burton Constable Holiday Park & Arboretum

The Old Lodges, Sproatley, Hull HU11 4LJ (East Yorkshire) T: 01964 562508. E: info@burtonconstable.co.uk
alanrogers.com/UK4500

The approach to this holiday park is set in the grounds of the stately home of Burton Constable, and is most impressive – one of the gatehouses acts as reception and tourist information room. The original 300-acre park, which was landscaped by Capability Brown in the 18th century, and the 90-acre holiday complex, with its well trimmed grass and hedges, has a spacious feel. Much of the park is devoted to holiday homes, but there is a separate touring area on grass, overlooking two sizeable lakes. There are 120 touring pitches, almost all with 10A electricity; there is a separate field for 40 tents and a large hardstanding area for four large motorcaravans.

Facilities

Two heated toilet blocks; one older and small with unisex showers, the newer block includes a laundry room with baby changing. Facilities for disabled visitors. Shop in the mobile home area. Bar with family room and tables outside overlooking the lakes. Snooker room. Adventure play area. Fishing. Sailing. Arboretum. Off site: Sproatley with pubs, a shop and the occasional bus 1 mile. Riding 3 miles. Golf 5 miles. Hull 7 miles. Beach 8 miles.

Open: 1 March - 30 November.

Directions

From south via M62 or Humber Bridge, take A63 into Hull, then follow signs to A165 Bridlington. On outskirts of Hull turn east on B1238 (Aldborough). At Sproatley, site is signed to left. GPS: 53.80265, -0.199

Charges guide

Per unit incl. 2 persons and electricity	£ 18.00 - £ 31.00
extra person	£ 2.00

Leyburn
Constable Burton Hall Caravan Park

Constable Burton Hall, Leyburn DL8 5LJ (North Yorkshire) T: 01677 450428.
E: caravanpark@constableburton.com **alanrogers.com/UK4690**

This tranquil park is in beautiful Wensleydale and the emphasis is on peace and quiet, the wardens working to provide a relaxing environment. Being in the grounds of the Hall, it has a spacious, park-like feel to it. On part level, and some a little uneven, well maintained grass, the 120 pitches (40 for touring units) are of a good size and all have 10A electrical connections. There are no pitches for tents. There is no shop on site but milk and newspapers are available to order and nearby Leyburn will provide all your needs. Opposite the park entrance is the Wyvill Arms for bar meals.

Facilities

Two toilet blocks have been refurbished recently, are well tiled, kept immaculately clean, and can be heated. Facilities for disabled visitors. Baby room. Laundry room and extra washrooms with washbasins for both men and women. Information leaflets and a few books for visitors can also be found here. Gas supplies. Gates closed 22.00-08.00. WiFi over site (charged). Off site: Irregular bus service from site gate. Fishing and golf within 5 miles.

Open: Early March - 31 October.

Directions

Park is by the A684 between Bedale and Leyburn, 0.5 miles from the village of Constable Burton on the Leyburn side. GPS: 54.3125, -1.754167

Charges guide

Per unit incl. 2 persons and electricity	£ 20.50 - £ 25.50
extra person	£ 5.00
No commercial vehicles.	

For latest campsite news visit
alanrogers.com

Malton
Wolds Way Caravan Park

West Farm, West Knapton, Malton YO17 8JE (North Yorkshire) T: 01944 728463. E: info@ryedalesbest.co.uk
alanrogers.com/UK4545

Opened in 2004, this park is located along the top of the Yorkshire Wolds with super panoramic views across the Vale of Pickering to the North Yorks Moors. The one and a half mile tarmac and gravel track from the road to the park is well worth while to reach this peaceful location set amongst glorious countryside. There are 80 level pitches (just 25 for touring units), most with 16A electricity and some with water points. Seating areas, picnic benches and barbecues are provided on the park. There are many footpaths and cycle ways in the area.

Facilities

A new toilet block is very well appointed and heated. Family bathrooms. Laundry facilities. Very large heated room with sinks, microwave, fridge/freezers, hot drinks machine and TV. Room for disabled visitors. Small shop in reception selling basic supplies. Play area. Areas to walk dogs. Caravan storage. A Finnish-style chalet for up to five people is available to rent. Off site: Bus stop 1 mile. Fishing 3 miles. Golf and riding 5 miles. Beach 15 miles.

Open: 1 March - 31 October.

Directions

Park entrance is on the south side of the A64 York-Scarborough road, just past the B1258 turn off and it is signed (may be hidden by foliage). GPS: 54.16633, -0.65425

Charges guide

Per unit incl. 2 persons and electricity	£ 15.00 - £ 25.00
extra person (over 15 yrs)	£ 4.00

Northallerton
Otterington Park

Station Farm, South Otterington, Northallerton DL7 9JB (North Yorkshire) T: 01609 780656.
E: info@otteringtonpark.com **alanrogers.com/UK4765**

This family owned, five-acre park is located on a former farm between Thirsk and Northallerton, in the Vale of York. It is ideally placed for visiting the Yorkshire moors and dales, along with local market towns, theme parks and stately homes. Predominantly, it is a flat grass site with gravel hardstandings for 30 touring pitches, with a separate paddock for a further 28 pitches, all with 16A electricity. Privately owned lodges and static caravans are located in an adjoining park, separated from the touring units by an old, well established, tall hedge. A family oriented park with grassy play areas for children.

Facilities

One purpose built, clean block in a heated building. Unisex en-suite style shower rooms with free showers. Facilities for disabled visitors. Family bathroom with a baby area. Laundry. Drinks/snacks vending machines in reception. Play area. WiFi throughout (charged). Off site: Fishing 250 yds. Golf 3 miles. Riding 5 miles. Local bus service to Thirsk and Northallerton run every 2 hours from park entrance (not Sun). Local country pubs serving meals within 1 mile. Large supermarkets 4 miles.

Open: 1 March - 31 October.

Directions

From A1M join A684 for Leeming Bar and Morton-on-Swale. At roundabout bear right on A167 signed South Otterington and Topcliffe. At South Otterington crossroads (pub) turn left signed Thornton-le-Moor to park in 500 yds. GPS: 54.28771, -1.42046

Charges guide

Per unit incl. 4 persons and electricity	£ 19.00 - £ 23.00
extra person	£ 3.00

Northallerton
Cote Ghyll Caravan & Camping Park

Osmotherley, Northallerton DL6 3AH (North Yorkshire) T: 01609 883425. E: hills@coteghyll.com
alanrogers.com/UK4775

This attractive, family run park is set in a secluded valley with the higher pitches terraced and the lower ones on a level grassy area either side of the small Cod Beck stream. Of the 80 pitches, 50 are for touring units, all with 10A electricity hook-ups, 12 fully serviced (eight reserved for seasonal), plus three larger super pitches. A further 18 pitches are used for caravan holiday homes and 30 are reserved for seasonal units. A simple site with a tranquil setting, Cote Ghyll is highly suited for lovers of peace and quiet, for birdwatching or for more energetic hobbies such as cycling and walking.

Facilities

Two well equipped, heated toilet blocks, one new, provide free power showers and vanity style washbasins. Baby room (bath only). Facilities for disabled visitors. Family bathroom. Laundry facilities. Drying room. Reception provides a small shop for essentials. Gas supplies. Two play areas. WiFi throughout (charged). Caravan storage. Off site: Shop and pubs 10 minutes walk. Fishing 1 mile. Leisure centre, bicycle hire 6 miles.

Open: 1 March - 31 October.

Directions

Osmotherley is east of the A19. Leave the A19 at A684 exit signed Northallerton and Osmotherley. Go to Osmotherley and site is at the northern end of the village, well signed. GPS: 54.37643, -1.29166

Charges guide

Per unit incl. 2 persons and electricity	£ 20.50 - £ 33.00
extra person	£ 4.50

For latest campsite news visit
alanrogers.com

Pickering

Rosedale Caravan & Camping Park

Rosedale Abbey, Pickering YO18 8SA (North Yorkshire) T: 01751 417272. E: info@flowerofmay.com

alanrogers.com/UK4770

In a beautiful location beneath Rosedale Moor and on the edge of a popular village in the National Park, this is a campsite that is highly suitable for walkers. The site gently rises alongside the river, nestling within the valley. There are 150 touring pitches, 50 with hardstanding and 10A electricity connections. There are some caravan holiday homes (private), six glamping pods for rent and seasonal touring pitches in their own areas. The majority have superb views of the surrounding hills. WiFi is now available; there is no mobile phone signal on the site. One field is set aside for tents only and many are sited near the river which runs along the edge of the park. The surrounding hillsides are a maze of public footpaths and these and nearby Cropton Forest can all be reached without using your car. In summer, the Dales Bus runs through the village connecting several of the popular villages. The 13-mile Rosedale circuit follows the route of the old iron ore railway giving magnificent views and reminders of bygone industries. There is a glass blower at the village blacksmith's and Ryedale Folk Museum at Hutton-le-Hole is 3.5 miles.

Facilities

Sanitary facilities with underfloor heating include free showers and hairdressing units. They may be under a little pressure when the site is very full and are at a distance from some pitches. Facilities for disabled visitors and baby changing. Laundry facilities. Reception provides some basic provisions, sweets, maps and a small selection of camping accessories. Gas supplies. Games room with pool and video games. Large play area with space for ball games. WiFi. Entrance barrier controlled by card (£10 deposit). Off site: The village has a general store with daily papers, a post office, bakery, pubs and a restaurant. 9-hole golf course (set on a picturesque hillside) 200 yards. Bicycle hire 200 yds. Fishing 6 miles.

Open: Easter - 3 November.

Directions

Rosedale is signed from the A170, 2 miles west of Pickering. Site is in the village of Rosedale Abbey, 8 miles north of the A170. Note: this park is adjacent to a Club site with a similar name.
GPS: 54.35366, -0.88795

Charges guide

Per unit incl. 4 persons	£ 22.00 - £ 28.00
extra person	£ 3.00
dog	£ 1.00

10% discount on pitch fee for weekly bookings.

Pickering

Overbrook Caravan Park

Maltongate, Thornton-le-Dale, Pickering YO18 7SE (North Yorkshire) T: 01751 474417.
E: enquiry@overbrookcaravanpark.co.uk **alanrogers.com/UK4534**

Situated on the edge of the very pretty village of Thornton-le-Dale, this most attractive, well cared for, adults only site has been developed on a disused railway station. The station building now provides holiday cottages and the caravan park toilet facilities. The site is level with 50 pitches (25 for touring units, the remainder used for seasonal units) arranged either side of a tarmac access road and backed by trees. All are on hardstanding and all have 16A electricity connections. Tents are not accepted. The owners will do all they can to assist you during your stay. A half mile, level walk brings you to the village. This is very convenient for shops, pubs, tearooms and even a chocolate factory. There is a good bus service to Pickering, Malton, Whitby, York and Scarborough.

Facilities

The toilet and shower facilities are situated in the old station house. Laundry facilities. Gas supplies. No tents accepted. Only adults are accepted (no children). Free WiFi. Off site: Village with bus stop, shops, pubs, fish and chips 800 yds. Bicycle hire 800 yds. Fishing 3 miles. Golf and riding 5 miles. Beach 25 miles.

Open: 1 March - 7 January.

Directions

Thornton-le-Dale is on the A170 Pickering-Scarborough road. In the village follow sign for Malton and park is 800 yds. on the left (follow the stream on the left). GPS: 54.228533, -0.7229

Charges guide

Per unit incl. 2 persons and electricity	£ 17.50 - £ 24.50
incl. awning	£ 19.00 - £ 25.50
extra person	£ 5.00
dog (max. 2)	£ 1.50

1% charge for credit cards.

Pickering
Upper Carr Caravan Park

Upper Carr Lane, Malton Road, Pickering YO18 7JP (North Yorkshire) T: 01751 473115.
E: info@uppercarrcaravanpark.co.uk **alanrogers.com/UK4620**

With a central location in the Vale of Pickering, Upper Carr is well placed for the many attractions the area has to offer. Part of the Flower of May group, the park is undergoing improvements and many changes are planned, including larger numbers of static homes. The park is surrounded by a high, well trimmed hedge which protects it from the wind and deadens the road noise. Upper Carr's six acres provide 86 level pitches, 45 for touring, with 10/16A electricity and some with hardstanding. Seasonal units use 28 pitches. The picturesque village of Thornton-le-Dale can be reached on foot or by bicycle along the Upper Carr nature trail. Three camping pods are available for rent.

Facilities

Recently refurbished, heated toilet blocks. Baby changing facilities. Separate room with WC and washbasin for disabled visitors. Laundry room. Motorcaravan services. Small shop in reception for basics. Play area. Games room with pool table, TV and electronic games. Nature trail. WiFi (charged). Off site: New pub and grill nearby. Golf and tennis adjacent. Swimming pool 1.5 miles.

Open: 1 March - 31 October.

Directions

Travelling on the Pickering-Malton A169 road, park is on the left 1.5 miles south of Pickering. GPS: 54.222967, -0.769

Charges guide

Per unit incl. 2 adults, 2 children and electricity	£ 14.00 - £ 31.00
extra adult	£ 1.00 - £ 2.50

Ripon
Sleningford Watermill Caravan & Camping Park

North Stainley, Ripon HG4 3HQ (North Yorkshire) T: 01765 635201.
alanrogers.com/UK4588

The watermill buildings are a focal point for this park and house the welcoming reception and some of the facilities. Eight hardstanding pitches plus 90 well spaced grass touring pitches (45 with 10A electricity) for tents, caravans and motorcaravans are set in 14 acres of mature riverside meadow in three distinct areas. Management of the natural habitat of the park is carried out with conservation in mind at all times. The beautiful riverside provides a beach and access for swimming, canoeing and a nature trail. River fishing is possible (fly only). The Ripon Rowel walk passes through the park. The park is very popular at the weekends and very much quieter mid-week. Please phone to check availability.

Facilities

Two toilet blocks, one with facilities for disabled visitors (doubles as a family room). Laundry room with local information and brochures. Ice pack freezing service. Shop (essentials and children's fishing nets). Independent canoe hire, trips and courses. Fly fishing. Max. 2 dogs per pitch. Off site: Pub and restaurant within walking distance. Golf and riding 5 miles. Ripon 5 miles.

Open: 1 April - 31 October.

Directions

The park is on the A6108 5 miles north of Ripon between the villages of North Stainley and West Tanfield and is clearly signed (brown tourist signs). GPS: 54.199925, -1.571883

Charges guide

Per unit incl. 2 persons and electricity	£ 24.00 - £ 29.00
extra person	£ 4.00

Ripon
Woodhouse Farm Caravan & Camping Park

Winksley, Ripon HG4 3PG (North Yorkshire) T: 01765 658309. E: info@woodhousewinksley.com
alanrogers.com/UK4660

This secluded family park on a former working farm is only six miles from Ripon and about four from the World Heritage site of Fountains Abbey. It is a very rural park with a spacious feel and various pitching areas are tucked away in woodland areas or around the edges of hedged fields with the centre left clear for children. There are hard roads and all of the pitches (60 for touring, 30 seasonal) have 10A electricity. There are 56 acres in total, 17.5 devoted to the site and 20 acres of woodland for walking. The 2.5 acre fishing lake is a big attraction and provides a pleasant area for picnics and walks.

Facilities

The clean toilet block has been upgraded and includes heating, roomy showers and some washbasins in cabins. Two bathrooms. Facilities for disabled visitors. Laundry facilities. Gas supplies. Bar and restaurant (daily in season except Mondays). Takeaway on request. New games room with TV. Outdoor play equipment. Fishing (day tickets from reception). Mountain bike hire. Caravan storage. WiFi (free). Off site: Twice daily bus service passes gate. Many villages with inns for food and drinks.

Open: Mid March - 31 October.

Directions

From Ripon take Fountains Abbey-Pateley Bridge road (B6265). After 3.5 miles turn right to Grantley and then follow campsite signs for further 1-2 miles. Do not use postcode for GPS directions. GPS: 54.13728, -1.63474

Charges guide

Per unit incl. 2 persons and electricity	£ 20.00 - £ 26.00
extra person	£ 4.00
child (under 16 yrs)	£ 1.00

For latest campsite news visit
alanrogers.com

Scarborough
Flower of May Holiday Park

310

Lebberston Cliff, Scarborough YO11 3NU (North Yorkshire) T: 01723 584311. E: info@flowerofmay.com

alanrogers.com/UK4520

Situated on the cliff tops, 4.5 miles from Scarborough and 2.5 miles from Filey, Flower of May is a large, family owned park for both touring caravans, caravan holiday homes and four Glamping Pods. The entrance to the park is very colourful and the reception office is light and airy. The park is licensed for 300 touring units of which 200 are fully serviced. The touring pitches are pretty level, arranged in wide avenues, mainly on grass and divided by shrubs. The range of leisure facilities grouped around reception includes an indoor pool with areas for both adults and children and a jacuzzi. The main building has two squash courts, ten-pin bowling, table tennis and amusement machines. The leisure centre is also open to the public (concessionary rates for campers) but during high season is only available to local regulars and the caravanners and campers on the park. There are cliff walks down to the beach but for those less able there is an easier walk from a car park a mile away. Riverside Meadows at Ripon, Rosedale Country Caravan Park near Pickering and Goosewood near York are under the same ownership.

Facilities	Directions
Three toilet blocks, all refurbished, provide showers and washbasins in both cabins and vanity style. Baby rooms. Facilities for disabled visitors. Laundry room. Well stocked and licensed shop. Two modern bar lounges, one for families and one for adults only, with discos in season. Café and takeaway fish and chips. Games room with TV. Large adventure playground. Indoor swimming pool. Skateboard ramps. Basketball. Dog exercise area but numbers and breeds are limited (one per pitch). WiFi throughout the park (charged). Funfarm indoor play area. Off site: The Plough Inn near the park entrance offers good bar meals. Fishing, boat slipway and riding 2 miles. Golf 3 miles. Bicycle hire 4 miles.	Park is signed from roundabout at junction of A165 and B1261 from where it is 600 yds. GPS: 54.2292, -0.3425

Open: Easter - 3 November.

Charges guide

Per unit incl. up to 4 persons (electricity metered)	£ 22.00 - £ 28.00
2 person tent (no electricity)	£ 11.00 - £ 28.00
extra person (over 3 yrs)	£ 3.00
dog	£ 1.00

10% discount on pitch fee for weekly advance bookings.

Ripon
Riverside Meadows Country Caravan Park

Ure Bank Top, Ripon HG4 1JD (North Yorkshire) T: 01765 602964. E: info@flowerofmay.com

alanrogers.com/UK4760

The approach to Riverside Meadows belies the fact that it is a rural park. The short approach from the main road passes houses and a factory but once they are passed the park opens up before you and you are once again back in the countryside. There are plenty of caravan holiday homes here but they are, on the whole, quite separate from the 20-25 touring pitches which are mixed amongst a number of seasonal pitches. These pitches, practically all with electrical hook-ups, are mainly on gently sloping grass with 10 hardstandings. A meadow separates the park from the River Ure, a favourite place for strolling and fishing (licences available). Close to Ripon is the Lightwater Valley theme park, and a little further are Fountains Abbey, Harrogate, Knaresborough, the Yorkshire Dales and Thirsk with its market and the James Herriot centre. There is plenty to do on and off the park for both families and couples.

Facilities	Directions
The tiled toilet block is quite new and includes a baby room and a fully fitted shower room for disabled visitors. Laundry facilities. Shop. Bar. Games room. Play area. Fishing. WiFi throughout (charged). Max. 2 dogs per pitch, contact park first. Off site: Fishing, bicycle hire and riding 800 yds. Golf 1.25 miles. The delightful market town (city) of Ripon with its cathedral is only 20 minutes walk.	At the most northern roundabout on the Ripon bypass (A61), turn onto the A6108 signed Ripon, Masham and Leyburn. Go straight on at mini-roundabout and park is signed on right. GPS: 54.15045, -1.515

Open: Easter/1 April - 31 October.

Charges guide

Per unit/tent incl. up to 4 persons (electricity metered)	£ 18.00 - £ 24.00
extra person	£ 3.00
dog	£ 1.00

10% discount on pitch fee for weekly bookings.

For latest campsite news visit

alanrogers.com

Scarborough
Saint Helens in the Park

Wykeham, Scarborough YO13 9QD (North Yorkshire) T: 01723 862771. E: caravans@wykeham.co.uk
alanrogers.com/UK4540

Saint Helens is a high quality touring park with pleasant views, set within 30 acres of parkland. The site is divided into terraces with trees screening each area (one of which is for adults only) and the 130 mainly level, touring pitches have a spacious feel. Electrical hook-ups (16A) are available to most pitches, also in the late arrivals area. A further 170 pitches are occupied seasonal units. Set on a hillside, the park's buildings are built in local stone and all is maintained to a high standard. The Downe Arms, a short stroll away, is known for its good food and friendly atmosphere. Some road noise can be expected.

Facilities

Four heated toilet blocks are well equipped and maintained to a high standard. Some washbasins in cabins, free showers and baby baths. Unit for disabled visitors. Good central laundry room. Well stocked shop. Café and takeaway. Small games room. Large dog walking area. Bicycle hire. Caravan storage. Internet café. WiFi throughout. Off site: Nearby Wykeham Lakes offer fishing, scuba diving and windsurfing 1 mile. Golf 2 miles.

Open: All year excl. 15 January - 13 February.

Directions

Park access road leads off the A170 (Pickering-Scarborough) road in Wykeham village 2 miles west of junction with B1262. GPS: 54.23795, -0.517044

Charges guide

Per unit incl. 2 persons and electricity	£ 17.00 - £ 29.50
extra person (over 3 yrs)	£ 2.00
dog	£ 1.80

Scarborough
Cayton Village Caravan Park

Mill Lane, Cayton Bay, Scarborough YO11 3NN (North Yorkshire) T: 01723 583171.
E: info@caytontouring.co.uk **alanrogers.com/UK4550**

Cayton Village Caravan Park can only be described as a gem. Just three miles from the hustle and bustle of Scarborough, it is a peaceful, attractive haven. Originally just a flat field with caravans around the perimeter, years of hard work have produced a park which is well designed and very pleasing to the eye with quality facilities. The 310 pitches, all with electricity (200 fully serviced) are numbered and everyone is taken to their pitch. A new development, The Laurels, provides 110 hardstanding pitches with 16A electricity, water, waste water, TV connection and WiFi.

Facilities

Four good toilet blocks can be heated. Some showers are preset, others are controllable. Two family shower rooms, family bathroom and baby facilities. Large room for disabled visitors. Two laundry rooms. Shop. Adventure playground. Football pitch. Nature trail and large area for dog walking. Caravan storage. WiFi at The Laurels. Off site: Cayton Bay 0.5 miles. Bicycle hire 3 miles.

Open: 1 March - 2 November.

Directions

From A165 Scarborough-Filey road, turn right at Cayton Bay roundabout into Mill Lane. The park is half a mile on the right as you approach the village. GPS: 54.235733, -0.376117

Charges guide

Per unit incl. 2 persons and electricity	£ 15.00 - £ 28.00
extra person	£ 1.00

Scarborough
Jasmine Park

Cross Lane, Snainton, Scarborough YO13 9BE (North Yorkshire) T: 01723 859240.
E: enquiries@jasminepark.co.uk **alanrogers.com/UK4740**

Jasmine is a very attractive, quiet and well manicured park with owners who go to much trouble to produce many plants to decorate a very colourful entrance. Set in the Vale of Pickering, the park is level, well drained and protected by a coniferous hedge. Of the 126 pitches, 71 are for touring units with 10/16A electricity connections. Fifty-one are super pitches and there are 70 separate pitches for tents. A field is provided for games. Tourist information is provided in a log cabin and the owners are only too happy to advise. This is an excellent, peaceful park for a restful holiday.

Facilities

The heated toilet block is of a high standard and is kept very clean. It includes a large room for families and disabled visitors containing a bath, shower, WC and washbasin (access by code). Laundry room with dishwashing sinks, washing machine, dryer and iron. Motorcaravan services. Licensed shop selling essentials and gas. New play area. Dogs are welcome but there is no dog walk. Caravan storage. WiFi (charged). Off site: Bus service in village 0.5 miles. Riding, golf driving range and 9-hole course 2 miles. Fishing 5 miles.

Open: 1 March - 31 October.

Directions

Snainton is on the A170 Pickering-Scarborough road and park is signed at eastern end of the village. Turn down Barker's Lane and at the small crossroads turn left and the park is 230 yds. on the left. GPS: 54.218583, -0.575567

Charges guide

Per unit incl. 4 persons and electricity	£ 22.00 - £ 37.00
extra person	£ 2.00
Min. stay at B.Hs.	
Supplement for credit card payments.	

For latest campsite news visit
alanrogers.com

Scarborough
Lebberston Touring Park

Filey Road, Lebberston, Scarborough YO11 3PE (North Yorkshire) T: 01723 585723.
E: info@lebberstontouring.co.uk **alanrogers.com/UK4780**

Lebberston Touring Park is a quiet, spacious touring site and is highly suitable for anyone seeking a quiet relaxing break, such as mature couples or young families (although tents are not accepted). There is no play area or games room, the only concession to children being a large central area with goal posts, so teenagers may get bored. The park itself has a very spacious feel – it is gently sloping and south facing and the views are superb. Of the 125 numbered pitches, 75 are for touring units. All have 10A (some 16A) electricity and 25 are on hardstanding.

Facilities

The toilet blocks are of high quality and kept very clean. Large shower cubicles and washbasins in cubicles with curtains. Family bathroom (20p). Good room for disabled visitors. Laundry facilities. Reception sells basics, plus papers, ice cream and gas. Only breathable groundsheets are permitted. WiFi throughout (charged). Max. 2 dogs. Off site: Golf 600 yds. Beach and fishing 2 miles. Riding 3 miles. Hourly bus 5 mins. walk.

Open: 1 March - 31 October.

Directions

From A64 Malton-Scarborough road turn right at roundabout (McDonald's, pub and superstore) signed B1261 Filey. Go through Cayton, Killerby and in 4.5 miles site signed on left (not easy to see). If you miss the turning, continue to roundabout and turn around. GPS: 54.22502, -0.34343

Charges guide

Per unit incl. 2 persons and electricity	£ 15.50 - £ 32.00
Minimum stay for B.Hs.	

Selby
Cawood Holiday Park

Ryther Road, Cawood, Selby YO8 3TT (North Yorkshire) T: 01757 268450. E: enquiries@cawoodpark.com
alanrogers.com/UK4635

An attractive site with a lake partly surrounded with privately owned caravan holiday homes. The touring section, with 28 fully serviced pitches on hardstanding, is beyond the lake. A variety of birds can be seen on and around the water and fishing is possible. Use of the heated indoor swimming pool is included in the price and a large bar and restaurant overlook the lake. The village is within easy walking distance. Due to the layout of the pitches, caravans manufactured in Europe are not accepted. Improvements are constantly being made and current work includes 23 additional holiday homes.

Facilities

One refurbished toilet block (can be heated) is kept very clean. Cubicles with washbasins, free preset showers. Baby changing area and facilities for disabled visitors. Washing machine. Shop in reception. Large bar and restaurant. Heated indoor swimming pool. Play area. Fishing. Off site: An hourly bus service runs from the village. York, Selby, the coast and North York Moors are all within easy reach. Riding 3 miles. Bicycle hire 4 miles.

Open: All year.

Directions

From the South leave the A1(M) at exit 42 taking the turning for Selby. Follow signs for Sherburn in Elmet and then Cawood. In Cawood take a left turn to Tadcaster (B1223). Site is half a mile on the left just past the lake. GPS: 53.838858, -1.139987

Charges guide

Per unit incl. 2 persons and electricity	£ 30.00 - £ 33.00
Minimum stay two nights.	

Settle
Knight Stainforth Hall Caravan & Camping Park

Little Stainforth, Settle BD24 0DP (North Yorkshire) T: 01729 822200. E: info@knightstainforth.co.uk
alanrogers.com/UK4720

In a very attractive setting, this park is located in the heart of the Yorkshire Dales; the whole area is a paradise for hill-walking, fishing and potholing and has outstanding scenery. The camping area is on slightly sloping grass, sheltered by mature woodland. There are 100 touring pitches (20 are seasonal), 60 with 16A electricity and water and 25 with hardstanding. A separate area contains 66 privately owned caravan holiday homes. A gate leads from the bottom of the camping field giving access to the river bank. This area is not fenced and children should be supervised.

Facilities

A modern, heated amenity block provides toilets and showers and includes some washbasins in cubicles. Facilities for disabled visitors and baby changing. Laundry facilities. Motorcaravan services. Small shop. Games/TV room. Play area with safety base. Fishing (permit from reception). Security barrier. Deposit for key to toilet block and barrier £10. WiFi throughout (charged). Off site: Bicycle hire and golf 3 miles. Riding 6 miles.

Open: 1 March - 31 October.

Directions

Drive to Settle from A65, through town centre and then west (Giggleswick). Ignore turning for Stainforth and Horton and after 200 yds. turn sharp right into Stackhouse Lane (Knight Stainforth). After 2 miles, right at crossroads. GPS: 54.10025, -2.284833

Charges guide

Per unit incl. 2 persons and electricity	£ 17.00 - £ 24.00
Min. stay at B.Hs 3 nights. Special offers.	

For latest campsite news visit
alanrogers.com

Skipsea

Skipsea Sands Holiday Park

Mill Lane, Skipsea YO25 8TZ (East Yorkshire) T: 01262 468634. E: skipsea.sands@park-resorts.com

alanrogers.com/UK4496

This well established holiday park is now owned by Park Resorts and is primarily dedicated to caravan holiday homes, of which there are 625 privately owned and 70 to rent. There is however a pleasantly laid out touring park occupying its own corner of the site and bordered by an attractive duck pond and a large playing area (both well fenced). The 90 marked, level pitches (some occupied by seasonal caravans) are separated by hedges and all have 16A electricity; some also have water, drainage and sewerage connections. The leisure facilities are outstanding and there are daily activities all season.

Facilities

Two heated toilet blocks with pushbutton showers, open washbasins and en-suite facilities for disabled visitors. Basic motorcaravan services. Laundry facilities. Shop. Bar, coffee shop and restaurant with takeaway. Leisure centre with sports hall, 10-pin bowling, heated indoor swimming pool, jacuzzi, sauna and steam room. Fitness centre. New entertainment complex. Fishing in duck pond (charged). WiFi (charged). Off site: Village with shops, pub, restaurant 1 mile. Beach 0.25 miles (on foot). Golf 3 miles.

Open: 20 March - 1 November.

Directions

From Humber Bridge or from M62, take A63 to Hull, east of city follow signs to join A165 towards Bridlington. After 18 miles, turn east on B1249 to Skipsea. In village, turn right then left to site (signed). GPS: 53.98957, -0.20716

Charges guide

Per unit incl. up to 4 persons and electricity	£ 6.00 - £ 32.00
will full services	£ 10.00 - £ 47.00

Skipton

Wood Nook Caravan Park

Skirethorns, Threshfield, Skipton BD23 5NU (North Yorkshire) T: 01756 752412. E: info@woodnook.net

alanrogers.com/UK4670

Wood Nook is a family run park in the heart of Wharfedale, part of the Yorkshire Dales National Park. The site includes six acres of woodland with quite rare flora and fauna. Reception is in the farmhouse. The gently sloping fields have gravel roads and provide 39 touring pitches (30 with gravel hardstanding). All have 10A electricity and nearby water and chemical disposal points. There is also room for 31 tents and there are some caravan holiday homes to let. The access road is narrow for a short distance, so care should be taken. This is a delightful base from which to explore the Yorkshire Dales.

Facilities

Converted farm buildings provide dated but clean sanitary facilities which can be heated. Washbasins in cubicles for ladies. Roomy showers (in another building – coin operated). Laundry facilities. Motorcaravan services. Licensed shop for basics and gifts (from Easter). Gas. Small play area. American motorhomes are taken by prior arrangement. Internet access in reception. WiFi throughout (free). Off site: Fishing and bicycle hire 2 miles. Riding 3 miles. Golf 9 miles. Leisure centre.

Open: 1 March - mid January (subject to weather).

Directions

Threshfield is 9 miles north of Skipton on the B6265. Continue through village onto B6160. After garage turn left (Skirethorns Lane). Follow signs for 600 yds, keeping left up narrow lane, then turn right up track for 300 yds. The last 900 yds. is single track – phone ahead to check it is clear. GPS: 54.07267, -2.04199

Charges guide

Per unit incl. 2 persons and electricity	£ 16.00 - £ 23.00

Skipton

Howgill Lodge Caravan & Camping Park

Barden, Skipton BD23 6DJ (North Yorkshire) T: 01756 720655. E: info@howgill-lodge.co.uk

alanrogers.com/UK4750

Howgill Lodge is a traditional family park set in the heart of the Yorkshire Dales. Arranged on a sloping hillside, the terraced pitches have fantastic views. It is a small park catering for the needs of walkers, tourers and people who like to just relax. The whole area is a haven for both experienced walkers or the casual rambler, without having to move your car. The 20 touring pitches at the upper part of the park are on hardstanding and have 10A electricity connections. A further 30 pitches on the lower part are mainly grass and for tents. Picnic tables and chairs are provided. Three mobile homes available to rent.

Facilities

Heated toilet facilities with large, controllable showers. Laundry room with four additional unisex showers. Two small blocks housing WCs are lower down the site for the convenience of tent campers. Shop. No play area. Fishing licences are available from reception. Off site: Bus service within walking distance (3 per day). Fishing 1 mile. Bolton Abbey with its beautiful riverside walks 3 miles. Golf, riding and bicycle hire 7 miles. Skipton 8 miles.

Open: 1 April (or Easter) - 31 October.

Directions

Turn off A59 Skipton-Harrogate road at roundabout onto B6160 Bolton Abbey, Burnsall road, through a low (10 ft. 4 in) archway. Three miles past Bolton Abbey at Barden Towers, bear right (Appletreewick and Pateley Bridge). Road narrow for 1.25 miles (with passing places). Park is signed on right at phone box. GPS: 54.025767, -1.909833

Charges guide

Per unit incl. 2 persons and electricity	£ 21.00

For latest campsite news visit
alanrogers.com

Wetherby

Maustin Caravan Park

Kearby with Netherby, Wetherby LS22 4BZ (North Yorkshire) T: 0113 2886234. E: info@maustinpark.co.uk

alanrogers.com/UK4755

A tranquil site for the whole family, this manicured park is set within the North Yorkshire National Park. It offers 25 well spaced pitches (10A electricity) sited on grass, all with peaceful, scenic views of the surrounding area. Caravan holiday homes are in a separate area. A bowling club on the site offers membership to all visitors and competitions are held throughout the season. Relax in the comfortable lounge or in the tasteful bar and restaurant area. A covered terrace overlooks the bowling green. There is an information building providing books, DVDs, videos and games, which you may borrow for free.

Facilities

One heated, well equipped toilet block has good showers, free hairdryers and roomy toilet and washing cubicles, all with non-slip flooring. Excellent facility for disabled visitors. Laundry room. Kitchen area with freezer. Bowling club with lounge, bar, restaurant and takeaway (weekends from March). Internet facilities. WiFi throughout (free). Off site: Fishing 2 miles. Riding 3 miles. Golf 4 miles.

Open: All year excl. February.

Directions

From north on A1 take exit 47 for Harrogate (A59). At roundabout take A658 left (Leeds). After 9 miles turn left at roundabout on A61 (Leeds). In 2 miles turn left (Kirkby Overblow) then after 0.5 miles right to Kearby and park is 1.5 miles on the right. From A1 south follow Harewood House signs through Collingham to join A61 (Harrogate). At lights turn right over River Wharfe, right for Kirkby Overblow, then as above. GPS: 53.917464, -1.497488

Charges guide

Per unit incl. 2 persons	£ 18.50
extra person	£ 2.50

Withernsea

Sand le Mere Holiday Village

Southfield Lane, Tunstall HU12 0JF (East Yorkshire) T: 01964 670403. E: info@sand-le-mere.co.uk

alanrogers.com/UK4480

Sand le Mere is an independently run holiday village ideally situated on the east coast of Yorkshire, nestling between beautiful countryside and sandy beaches. The park offers a wide range of facilities and activities to keep the whole family entertained, including a show lounge and an outdoor leisure area. The site is likely to prove popular with fishermen as both fresh water and sea fishing options are available. There are 60 new hardstanding pitches for tourers (all with 16A electricity), 18 of which are fully serviced. A new camping area has electricity hook-ups and new toilet and shower facilities. Just along the coast are the resorts of Hornsea, Bridlington and Scarborough; inland are York and Beverley with their beautiful churches.

Facilities

One new heated toilet block has excellent showers and WCs. A more dated one awaiting refurbishment is clean and well equipped. Facilities for disabled visitors. Launderette. Complex with shop, bar, restaurant and takeaway. Indoor swimming pool (March-Nov) with play areas, sauna and steam room. Indoor soft play area. Adventure playgrounds. Gym (charged). Children's club in high season (5-12 yrs). Sea fishing and freshwater fishing (charged). Max. 2 dogs per pitch. WiFi over site (charged). Off site: Public transport. Golf and riding 6 km.

Open: 1 March - 31 October.

Directions

From Hull take B1242 between Hornsea and Withensea. At Roos, take the turn for Tunstall, where site is signed. GPS: 53.761592, -0.011233

Charges guide

Per unit incl. 4 persons and electricity	£ 18.00 - £ 28.00
extra person	£ 1.00
dog	free

For latest campsite news visit

alanrogers.com

Whitby

Sandfield House Farm Caravan Park

Sandsend Road, Whitby YO21 3SR (North Yorkshire) T: 01947 602660. E: info@sandfieldhousefarm.co.uk
alanrogers.com/UK4528

Although it is set on a hill in undulating countryside on the low cliffs near Whitby, this park provides 200 level pitches, all with electricity. The views from the park are superb. There are 60 pitches for touring caravans, all on hardstanding, and these are mainly set to the front of the park giving wonderful views over the golf course and the sea. Three fully serviced pitches are available. Tents are not accepted here. Whitby is only a mile away and a quarter of a mile walk down a track from the park brings you to a two mile long sandy beach. From here it is a gentle stroll along the new promenade to Whitby harbour.

Facilities

Two toilet blocks, one of which has been replaced by a new block including facilities for disabled visitors. Laundry room with washing machines, dryers and iron. Motorcaravan services. Off site: Half-hourly bus service to town centre. Golf 200 yds. Fishing 400 yds. Shops and boat launching 800 yds. Railway station 1 mile.

Open: 1 March - 7 November.

Directions

From Whitby follow signs for Sandsend on A174. The park is on landward side of the road, opposite golf course. GPS: 54.491717, -0.642767

Charges guide

Per unit incl. up to 4 persons
and electricity   £ 25.00 - £ 30.00
No credit or debit cards.
Minimum stay supplements for bank holidays.

Whitby

Middlewood Farm Holiday Park

Middlewood Lane, Fylingthorpe, Robin Hood's Bay YO22 4UF (North Yorkshire) T: 01947 880414.
E: info@middlewoodfarm.com alanrogers.com/UK4532

Middlewood Farm is a level park, surrounded by hills and with views of the sea from some of the pitches. A short walk through the farm fields and wild flower conservation areas leads to the picturesque old fishing village of Robin Hood's Bay and the sea. The park has 30 touring pitches for caravans and motorcaravans with 10A electricity, 18 with hardstanding and the remainder on grass. There is space for around 130 tents in two areas with 41 electricity connections available and 30 caravan holiday homes to rent. Camping pods are also available to hire. A good beach is only a ten-minute walk.

Facilities

Two splendid toilet blocks have clean facilities and are modern, heated and tiled with free showers and private cabins. Fully equipped laundry room including iron and board. Facilities for babies and disabled visitors. Play area with base set amongst the tents. WiFi on part of site (charged). Off site: Sandy beach with fishing 0.5 miles (10 minutes walk). Boat launching 2 miles. Bicycle hire 3 miles. Golf 7 miles. Shop and public transport in village 5 minutes walk.

Open: 1 March - 31 October.

Directions

From A171 Scarborough-Whitby road turn right (Robin Hood's Bay and Fylingthorpe). Just past 30 mph sign bear right and after 100 yds. turn right into Middlewood Lane. GPS: 54.43012, -0.54670

Charges guide

Per unit incl. 2 persons
and electricity   £ 18.00 - £ 30.00
extra person   £ 3.00
awning   £ 3.00
dog   £ 2.00

York

York Caravan Park

Stockton Lane, York YO32 9UB (North Yorkshire) T: 01904 424222. E: mail@yorkcaravanpark.com
alanrogers.com/UK4609

A well maintained, family owned campsite with 55 large touring pitches close to the City of York. The majority of pitches are fully serviced with electricity (16A), water, waste point and TV hook-up. This is an adults only site with a large fishing lake and picnic area in the centre. Surrounded by open fields grazed by the family farm's organic cattle, it is conveniently located just two miles from York city centre. Access to the site is via a fob operated barrier for which a refundable £10 deposit is required. Some road noise may be experienced but it is not intrusive.

Facilities

The central toilet block has eight large unisex shower rooms each with toilet and basin. The toilets also have two smaller shower cubicles and vanity units. En-suite unit for disabled visitors. Laundry area. Motorcaravan services. WiFi (free). Off site: Golf, riding and bicycle hire all 1 mile. Boat launching 2 miles. The City of York with Yorvik Museum, Railway Museum, Castle Museum, The Shambles etc. The North York Moors, Scarborough, Whitby and Harrogate are a short drive or bus ride away.

Open: 20 March - 1 November.

Directions

From A64 (York bypass) take exit signed A1037 and stay in left hand lane to second roundabout, continue into A1036 (Malton Road). In 50 yds turn left into Hopgrove Lane South just before pub. Turn right at T junction at the end of Hopgrove Lane. Site is half a mile on right. GPS: 53.980383, -1.031658

Charges guide

Per unit incl. 2 adults,
electricity and water   £ 21.00 - £ 28.00
extra person   £ 7.00

For latest campsite news visit
alanrogers.com

Yorkshire

York
York Meadows Caravan Park
Sheriff Hutton, York YO60 6QP (North Yorkshire) T: 01347 878508.
E: reception@yorkmeadowscaravanpark.com **alanrogers.com/UK4605**

Set in a grassy meadow, this newly created park is surrounded by farmland, half a mile from Sherriff Hutton with its two pubs and village shops. A total of 45 pitches are available, 35 of which are for touring;30 with hardstanding and electricity (16A) and five super pitches with hardstanding and all services. A further area has room for 38 tents, some with electricity. These are separated from the touring section by trees and a children's play area. The park is a haven for wildlife with trees and meadows all around. It is very peaceful here yet within easy reach to visit the historic city of York, just eight miles away. You can be sure of a warm welcome from the park wardens who will offer advice and information on the local area. A motorcaravan service point and a late arrivals area with electricity are outside the barrier.

Facilities

The heated toilet facilities are in a single block along with reception and provide a mix of washbasins in cubicles and open vanity units. Separate shower room for disabled visitors. Laundry facilities. Small shop in reception selling essentials. Slides, swings and a zip wire frame for children (safety surface). WiFi (free but limited reception). Max. 2 dogs. Off site: Fishing 3 miles. Golf 4 miles. City of York 8 miles. Rievaulx Abbey, Castle Howard and Eden Camp within 10 miles. Over 500 square miles of the North York Moors National Park. Yorkshire coast within one hour's drive. North Yorkshire Moors Steam Railway at Pickering.

Open: 1 March - 31 October.

Directions

Join A64 between York and Scarborough. Approximately 8 miles beyond York, heading for Malton, turn left, signposted Flaxton and Sheriff Hutton. At West Lilling turn left for Strensall. Site entrance immediately opposite junction. GPS: 54.0797, -1.0166

Charges guide

Per unit incl. 2 persons	
and electricity	£ 17.50 - £ 26.00
extra person	£ 3.50
child (5-15 yrs)	£ 1.50
dog (max. 2)	£ 1.50

York
Moorside Caravan Park
Lords Moor Lane, Strensall, York YO32 5XJ (North Yorkshire) T: 01904 491865.
alanrogers.com/UK4610

Strensall is only a few miles from York, one of England's most attractive cities and Moorside Caravan Park will provide a peaceful haven after a day's sightseeing. Children (under 16) are not accepted at this park. It will impress you with its pretty fishing lake, many flowers and the tranquillity (except for the odd passing daytime train). There are 50 marked touring pitches on neat, well trimmed grass, with 6/10A electricity and 22 with paved hardstanding. The whole park is very well maintained making it a very pleasant environment. The small lake is well stocked for coarse fishing and the pitches bordering the lake are the most popular. Set in the heart of Strensall Common, with York golf course close to the site entrance.

Facilities

The purpose built toilet block can be heated and houses immaculately kept facilities with washbasins in cubicles for ladies. Separate facility for disabled visitors. Fully equipped laundry room. Tourist information and books to borrow. Coarse fishing (£3 per day). Caravan storage. WiFi (free). Off site: Strensall village with shops and places to eat is less than a mile. Golf 0.5 miles. Riding 3 miles.

Open: 13 March - 31 October.

Directions

From the A1237 York outer ring road, take the Strensall turn and head towards Flaxton, past York Golf Club for about half a mile and park is on left just before a cattle grid. GPS: 54.042733, -1.011683

Charges guide

Per unit incl. 2 persons	
and electricity	£ 14.00 - £ 17.00
extra person	£ 2.00
dog	£ 1.00
No credit cards.	

For latest campsite news visit
alanrogers.com

York

Alders Caravan Park

Home Farm, Alne, York YO61 1RY (North Yorkshire) T: 01347 838722. E: enquiries@homefarmalne.co.uk

alanrogers.com/UK4638

The Alders is located in the village of Alne, nine miles from the centre of York, and has been carefully developed and managed on a working farm in historic parkland. The drive from reception around the village cricket ground to the pitches gives a real feeling of space. The extra large pitches are arranged in small bays designed to give privacy and separate the 28 touring pitches (16 with 6/10A Europlug) from the seasonal units, storage and the camping pods. Service tracks throughout allow site maintenance without compromising privacy. Woodland walks and a water meadow with wild flowers enhance the wonderful peace and tranquillity. Occasional light aircraft noise. This park would especially suit couples or young families (no play area). The village centre is only a short stroll away.

Facilities

The first rate toilet blocks are heated with family sized shower rooms, one also has a bath (£1 for baths). The newer block includes en-suite bathrooms with bath or shower. Laundry facilities. Provision for disabled visitors. Motorcaravan services. Shop (serves as local village shop). Gas is sold at reception. Only 2 dogs accepted per pitch. Off site: Floodlit tennis courts in the village. Fishing 2 miles. Golf 3 miles. Riding and bicycle hire 4 miles.

Open: 1 March - 31 October.

Directions

From north on A19: after leaving Easingwold bypass take next right turn signed Alne. From south (A19), 5 miles north of Shipton turn left at sign for Alne. In 1.5 miles at T-junction turn left and in 0.5 miles site is signed in the centre of the village. GPS: 54.08185, -1.24105

Charges guide

Per unit incl. 2 persons and electricity	£ 19.50

York

Goosewood Holiday Park

310

Carr Lane, Sutton-on-the-Forest, York YO61 1ET (North Yorkshire) T: 01347 810829.
E: goosewood@flowerofmay.com **alanrogers.com/UK4640**

Part of the Flower of May group, Goosewood has a natural woodland setting. It provides a quiet, relaxed atmosphere from which to explore York itself and the surrounding Yorkshire Dales, Wolds and Moors. The park has a well kept air and a rural atmosphere, with 100 well spaced and marked pitches, all with metered 10A electricity on hardstanding (six also have water and drainage). A new leisure complex with a heated indoor swimming pool (charged), a bar serving food and a children's area was constructed for 2014. The park is popular with families in high season when it can be busy at weekends. A park and ride scheme for York operates from nearby all year, six days a week or there is a local bus every hour. The park is just over a mile from Sutton village. There are lodges in a separate area from the touring pitches.

Facilities

Tiled and heated, the modern toilet block is spacious and well maintained. An additional unit provides shower rooms, WC and washbasins in cubicles and extra dishwashing sinks. Full facilities for disabled visitors. Laundry room. Motorcaravan services. Well stocked shop (with gas). Bar and takeaway. Fishing lake. New large adventure playground. Outdoor table tennis. Dogs (max. two per pitch; no designated walking area). WiFi throughout (charged). Off site: Riding and golf 3 miles. Bicycle hire 6 miles. York 6 miles.

Open: March - 2 January.

Directions

Park is 6 miles north of York; from the A1237 York outer ring-road take the B1363 for Sutton-on-the-Forest and Stillington, taking the first right after the Haxby and Wigginton junction and follow park signs. N.B. Do not use postcode for sat navs; use GPS or Carr Lane. GPS: 54.0591, -1.0861

Charges guide

Per unit incl. 4 persons (electricity on meter)	£ 22.00 - £ 28.00
extra person	£ 3.00
dog	£ 1.00

For latest campsite news visit

alanrogers.com

THIS REGION INCLUDES: CHESHIRE, LANCASHIRE, MERSEYSIDE, GREATER MANCHESTER AND THE HIGH PEAKS OF DERBYSHIRE

The North West region boasts a wealth of industrial heritage with undiscovered countryside, the vibrant cities of Manchester and Liverpool, the seaside resorts of Blackpool and Morecambe, plus miles of glorious coastline, home to a variety of bird species.

The miles of beautiful north west countryside offers endless opportunities for recreation. For the more active, the peaceful plains of Cheshire are a walkers' haven with endless trails to choose from. Lancashire is also good walking country with waymarked paths passing through the outstanding Forest of Bowland, which affords marvellous views over the Lake District in Cumbria and the Yorkshire Dales. Birdwatchers are catered for too with the coast offering some of the best birdspotting activity in the country, most notably along the Sefton coast and around the Wirral Peninsula. The region's cities have their own charm. Manchester, with its fabulous shopping centres and vibrant nightlife, boasts a rich Victorian heritage; the maritime city of Liverpool has more museums and galleries than any other UK city outside London; Lancaster features fine Georgian buildings and an imposing Norman castle; while Chester is renowned for its medieval architecture and shopping galleries. And offering good, old-fashioned seaside fun is Blackpool. England's most popular seaside resort is packed full of lively entertainment and attractions, such as the white knuckle rides at the pleasure beach, amusement games on the pier and the observation decks in the famous Tower.

Places of interest

Cheshire: Tatton Park in Knutsford; Chester Cathedral and Zoo; Cheshire Military Museum; Lyme Park stately home in Macclesfield; Beeston Castle; Blue Planet Aquarium at Ellesmere Port.

Lancashire: Williamson Park, castle and leisure park in Lancaster; Camelot Theme Park; Blackpool tower and illuminations; Morecambe Bay; Hoghton Tower and National Museum of Football in Preston.

Merseyside: Liverpool Football Club Museum and Tour Centre; The Beatles Story Museum; Speke Hall garden and estate; The Wirral Country Park; Williamson Tunnels Heritage Centre.

Greater Manchester: Imperial War Museum North; Manchester United Football Club Museum; The Lowry; Corgi Heritage Centre in Rochdale; The Trafford Centre.

Did you know?

The first public gallery to open in England was in Liverpool in 1877.

Lancaster Castle is infamous as host to the Pendle witch trials of 1612.

The first passenger railway station was built in Manchester.

Carnforth station was the location for David Lean's 1945 film Brief Encounter.

Ramsbottom holds an annual, two-day chocolate festival in spring.

Morecambe Bay is notorious for its shifting sands and treacherous currents, but can be crossed on foot with a guide.

Opened in 1894, the Blackpool Tower was copied from the Eiffel Tower; the height to the top of the flagpole is 518 feet 9 inches.

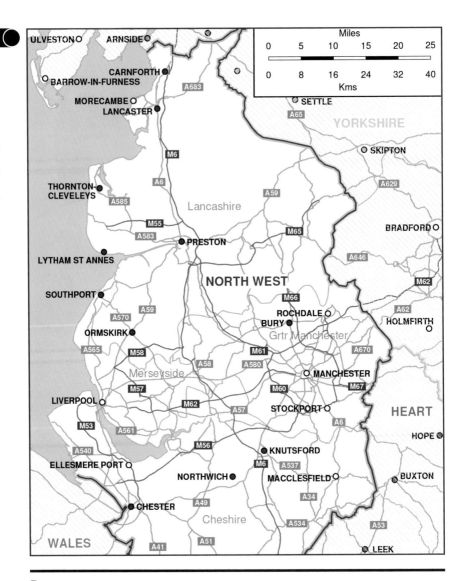

Bury

Burrs Country Park Caravan Club Site

Woodhill Road, Bury BL8 1DA (Greater Manchester) T: 01617 610489.

alanrogers.com/UK5265

Surrounded by a country park, and on an historic cotton mill site, this Caravan Club site is perfectly located for a relaxing holiday. There are no on-site facilities but there is a pub and an activity centre just yards from the entrance. There are 85 touring pitches available, 64 of which are on gravel hardstanding. Electricity (16A) is available to all and six pitches are fully serviced. The grounds and buildings are immaculately kept. A preserved steam railway runs alongside its boundary. The River Irwell runs through the Burr Country Park where you can enjoy plenty of pleasant walks.

Facilities

One centrally located sanitary block includes facilities for babies and disabled visitors. Showers are well equipped and washbasins are either open style or in cabins. Laundry room with coin-operated washing machine and dryer. Motorcaravan services. Small shop for basics and tourist information. WiFi throughout (charged). Off site: Pub serving food and children's activity centre 100 m. Fishing within 1 mile. Golf 5 miles. Bury 2 miles.

Open: All year.

Directions

From the M66 exit 2, take A58 (Bury). Continue through Bury on A58 towards Bolton. Turn right on B6214 (Tottington, Ramsbottom) keeping right. Follow signs for Country Park, turning right 300 m. past pub. GPS: 53.6105, -2.30541

Charges guide

Per person	£ 6.50 - £ 7.90
pitch incl. electricity (non-member)	£ 16.30 - £ 19.70

No credit cards.

For latest campsite news visit

alanrogers.com

Carnforth

Silverdale Caravan Park

Middlebarrow Plain, Cove Road, Silverdale LA5 0SH (Lancashire) T: 01524 701508. E: info@holgates.co.uk
alanrogers.com/UK5350

This attractive, very high quality park is in an outstanding craggy, part-wooded, hillside location with fine views over Morecambe Bay. It takes 80 touring units with 339 privately owned caravan holiday homes and 134 to rent located in woodland away from the touring pitches. With just six grassy pitches for tents (steel pegs required), the remaining large touring pitches are on gravel hardstandings, all with 16A electricity, free TV connection, individual drainage and water points. Eight family camping pods are for rent. The main complex with reception and the entrance barrier provides a well stocked supermarket, lounge bar, restaurant with good value meals and a terrace with views over the bay. There is also an indoor leisure centre. Children have a choice of two adventure playgrounds and plenty of space for ball games. Also on site is a small but challenging pitch-and-putt course.

Facilities

Two modern, heated toilet buildings with top quality fittings include some private cubicles with WC and washbasin. Provision for disabled visitors with a reserved pitch and parking bay adjacent. Launderette. Shop. Bar and restaurant. Indoor pool (17x17 m, with lifeguard) with spa pool, steam room and sauna. Gym (charged). Playgrounds. Games room. Pitch and putt (charged). WiFi (free around the clubhouse). Off site: Riding, cycling, golf and fishing all within 4 miles. Morecambe 12 miles.

Open: All year.

Directions

From traffic lights in centre of Carnforth take road to Silverdale under low bridge. After 1 mile turn left signed Silverdale and after 2.5 miles over level crossing, carry on and turn right at T-junction. Follow Holgates sign from here watching for left then right forks (narrow roads). GPS: 54.176603, -2.836034

Charges guide

Per unit incl. 2 persons and all services	£ 32.00
extra person	£ 8.00

Make the discovery
Holgates

Hollins Farm – Beautiful secluded Farm site with hard standing fully serviced pitches, seasonal pitches also available. AA Most Improved Campsite of the Year 2013

Bay View – Open all Year. 50 hard standing fully serviced pitches on the beautiful coastline of South Cumbria. Best Park in Lancashire 2013 & 14

Silverdale Caravan Park – Open all Year. Hard standing fully serviced pitches. Best Park in Cumbria 2014 & AA Campsite of the Year 2011

Contact us on
01524 701508,
info@holgates.co.uk
www.holgates.co.uk

Carnforth

Bay View Holiday Park

A6 Main Road, Bolton Le Sands, Carnforth LA5 8ES (Lancashire) T: 01524 732854.
E: info@holgatesleisureparks.co.uk **alanrogers.com/UK5270**

Bay View has been developed by the Holgate family into an excellent addition to their group. Situated on the north Lancashire coast, the park is an ideal base for exploring the Lake District, North Yorkshire and the Forest of Bowland. The park is divided into several grassy fields and many of the pitches have stunning views over Morecambe Bay, while others look towards the Lakeland Fells. It is a very open park with little shade. There are 20 fully serviced touring pitches with 6-15A electricity, a field accommodating 30 tents and a choice of rental accommodation. From the park there is direct access to the salt marshes and eventually the sea, although care must be taken in Morecambe Bay because of the quicksand. The bay can be crossed by joining an organised walk led by the Queen's Guide, Cedric Robinson.

Facilities

Four toilet blocks with facilities for disabled visitors. Good laundry. Motorcaravan services. Shop. An excellent new bar/restaurant situated in a barn conversion. A pool room and children's games room. Playground for younger children. Large field for ball games. Farm park (visitors can view the animals). WiFi (Free). Off site: Fishing 200 yds. Golf and riding 3 miles. Canal cruises on Lancaster Canal. Shopping in nearby Lancaster and Kendal 15 miles.

Open: All year.

Directions

From M6 exit 35 take the A601M to roundabout and follow signs to Morecambe. Continue through Carnforth and after mini-roundabout look for site sign (at main entrance) in 500 yds. on the right. GPS will take you to rear entrance, which is less accessible. GPS: 54.11602, -2.78791

Charges guide

Per unit with 2 persons, car and electricity	£ 22.00 - £ 27.00

Chester
Manor Wood Country Caravan Park
Coddington, Chester CH3 9EN (Cheshire) T: 01829 782990. E: info@manorwoodcaravans.co.uk
alanrogers.com/UK5220

Arranged on well maintained grass, on farmland with views towards the Welsh hills, this family owned and orientated site has a small swimming pool for use in the summer months. There are 67 level touring pitches with 16A electricity, accessed via tarmac roads. Fifty-six have hardstandings and 47 have water and drainage. The footpaths and bridle paths from the park will appeal to those with an interest in nature, walking and cycling. Pools on the site allow for a range of activities from serious fishing to pond dipping. Chester and its zoo are nearby and the seaside can be reached in an hour.

Facilities

Heated sanitary unit with showers and washbasins in cubicles. Family room also for disabled campers. Laundry. Basics can be purchased. Small swimming pool (heated May-Sept), adventure play area (6-14 yrs). Games room. Tennis. Security barrier with unrestricted card access. WiFi (free). Dog walk (2 dogs per pitch). Fishing. Separate, central car parking for a number of pitches. Off site: Restaurant within 1 mile. Golf 1.5 miles.

Open: All year.

Directions

From A41 Whitchurch to Chester Road, take the A534 towards Wrexham, pass Carden Park Hotel and turn opposite Cock o'Barton. After a short distance through Barton the road narrows, bear left and continue for 500 yds. to find the site on the left. Do not rely on sat nav. GPS: 53.08731, -2.83033

Charges guide

Per unit incl. 2 persons and electricity	£ 13.50 - £ 25.00

Chester
Lady Heyes Touring Caravan Park
Kingsley Road, Frodsham WA6 6SU (Cheshire) T: 01928 788557. E: enquiries@ladyheyespark.com
alanrogers.com/UK5235

Lady Heyes is a new site situated on Frodsham Hill with views over the Cheshire Plain, just two miles from the old town of Frodsham with its Thursday market. The site is very open and although there are many small trees, very little shade is available at present. There are 135 slightly sloping, good sized pitches, of which 85 are on hardstandings for caravans and motorcaravans, all with 16A electricity, water and drainage. The 40 grass tent pitches, all with 10A electricity, are in a separate area some way from the main facilities. The site is in the same grounds as the Lady Heyes Craft Centre, a micro brewery, a bar with indoor play area, a restaurant and several other small shops and workshops.

Facilities

Very good, clean, heated toilet block with preset showers, baby bath and en-suite unit for disabled campers (code access). Motorcaravan services. Bar/snack bar with indoor play area and TV. Restaurant. Breakfast. Football field. Playgrounds. WiFi over site (charged). Off site: Bus stop at site entrance. Frodsham with some shops and bars 2 miles. Chester with shopping outlet 10 miles.

Open: 16 February - 14 January.

Directions

Leave M56 at exit 12 and take A56 to Frodsham. In town at traffic lights turn left on B5152 (Kingsley). Site on left in 2 miles. GPS: 53.276772, -2.697449

Charges guide

Per unit incl. 2 persons and electricity	£ 18.50 - £ 26.00
extra person	£ 5.00

Knutsford
Royal Vale Caravan Park
London Road, Allostock, Knutsford WA16 9JD (Cheshire) T: 01565 722355. E: canistay@royalvale.co.uk
alanrogers.com/UK5245

This new family run site for adults only is located in countryside close to Knutsford, with Tatton Park and other attractions nearby. Expect a relaxed stay all year round on 52 all-weather pitches, each with water, electricity and drainage, attractively arranged around a fully appointed, heated, modern central sanitary unit. There are a further ten grass pitches for tents. Access to the level, gravel and solid hardstandings is via compacted gravel roadways, landscaped on grass with mature and developing hedges and trees. The River Peover borders the park and a pleasant walk takes you along the valley to Lower Peover.

Facilities

The modern sanitary units include automatic lighting and the eco theme sees low level site lighting and reed beds servicing waste water. Facilities for disabled visitors include separate wet room and a toilet in each of the sanitary units. Laundry. WiFi (charged). Gas available. Off site: Golf 3 miles. Knutsford 3 miles. Tatton Park 6 miles. Little Moreton Hall.

Open: All year excl. 8 January - 6 February.

Directions

From south on M6 take exit 18 and follow A5 towards Holmes Chapel where you turn north on A50 for 4 miles. At Allostock continue 1.2 miles, passing an Alfa Romeo garage on the right and turning left into the park at Equiport Equestrian Supplies. GPS: 53.25144, -2.37009

Charges guide

Per unit incl. 2 persons and electricity	£ 24.00 - £ 27.00
extra person	£ 5.00

For latest campsite news visit
alanrogers.com

Lancaster
Moss Wood Caravan Park

Crimbles Lane, Cockerham, Lancaster LA2 0ES (Lancashire) T: 01524 791041. E: info@mosswood.co.uk
alanrogers.com/UK5272

Moss Wood is a well established park in a secluded rural location near the village of Cockerham. You can be sure of a friendly welcome from the park wardens Ian and Sandra when you arrive. A sheltered field has 25 touring pitches on level hardstandings (steel pegs required) with 16A electricity. Most also have water and drainage. Screened from the touring area by a high fence, so not visually intrusive, are 175 privately owned holiday homes. A purpose-built log cabin houses reception and a shop which sells basic supplies. There is a large field for ball games and a fenced fishing lake. Although there are passing places, the approach road to the park is narrow so care should be taken. The quiet seclusion of Moss Wood makes it most suitable for couples and younger families.

Facilities

New centrally located sanitary block (key entry) is kept spotlessly clean and provides vanity style washbasins and roomy, preset showers. Fully equipped facilities for disabled visitors. Undercover food preparation area, dishwashing and laundry facilities. Adventure playground. Large field for ball games. Fishing lake (fenced). Woodland dog walking. WiFi throughout (charged). Off site: Pubs at Cockerham 1 mile. Riding 3 miles. Beach 5 miles. Golf 6 miles. Garstang, historic Lancaster, seaside town of Morecambe and the Lune Valley all within easy reach. Local buses stop at end of lane.

Open: 1 March - 31 October.

Directions

Park is 1 mile west of Cockerham on the A588. Leave M6 at exit 33 joining the A6 southbound and follow signs for Cockerham. A588 is 4 miles. Site is signed on the left. GPS: 53.94095, -2.82761

Charges guide

Per unit incl. 2 adults, 2 children and electricity	£ 21.00 - £ 24.10
extra person	£ 3.10
awning	£ 3.10

Lytham Saint Annes
Eastham Hall Caravan Park

Saltcotes Road, Lytham-Saint Annes FY8 4LS (Lancashire) T: 01253 737907. E: info@easthamhall.co.uk
alanrogers.com/UK5295

Eastham Hall is a well established, family run park set in rural Lancashire between the Victorian town of Lytham and the pretty village of Wrea Green. Entering by an electronic barrier system, one sees an area of 150 caravan holiday homes. Quite separate are about 173 pitches on open plan, mostly level grass, with 10A electricity. Of these, 30 are for touring units, the remainder let on a seasonal basis. They include 57 super pitches on hardstanding and grass with full services, including 16A electricity. Tents are not accepted. A further five extra large pitches are on grass (units up to 28 feet can be taken). Mature trees border the park and shrubs and bushes separate the various areas. The park has no bar or clubhouse but Lytham is just five minutes by car or a pleasant twenty-minute walk.

Facilities

Two toilet blocks are kept clean and are being updated to include solar panels for heating and private cubicles. Laundry. Excellent facilities for disabled visitors. Gas supplies. Shop. Adventure play area and large sports field. Dog exercise field. Barrier (£10 deposit). WiFi throughout (charged). Off site: Local bus stops at park entrance. Excellent pub in Wrea Green. Golf and riding 1 mile. Boat launching 2 miles. Shops and restaurants in Lytham, fishing 2.5 miles. Blackpool 6 miles.

Open: 1 March - 1 December.

Directions

From M55 take exit 3 and turn left for Kirkham. At roundabouts follow signs for Wrea Green and Lytham. Continue on B5259 passing Grapes pub and village green. After 1.5 miles cross level crossing (Moss Side) and park is 1 mile on left. GPS: 53.75375, -2.94225

Charges guide

Per unit incl. 2 persons and electricity	£ 15.00 - £ 35.00
extra person	£ 3.00
child (5-11 yrs)	£ 2.00
dog	£ 2.00

For latest campsite news visit
alanrogers.com

Northwich

Lamb Cottage Caravan Park

Dalefords Lane, Whitegate, Northwich CW8 2BN (Cheshire) T: 01606 882302. E: info@lambcottage.co.uk

alanrogers.com/UK5240

At this peaceful, family run, adults only park set in the midst of the lovely Vale Royal area of Cheshire, emphasis is placed on attention to detail. Seasonal and touring caravan pitches are arranged separately on 41 large, landscaped pitches, all with 16A electricity, gravel hardstandings, water and drainage. There are an additional four motorcaravan pitches with hardstandings and electricity. Only breathable groundsheets are permitted and tents are not accepted. Nearby are Delamere Forest with walking and mountain biking trails, Whitegate Way walking trail, Oulton Park Motor Racing Circuit, castles at Peckforton and Beeston and, within 12 miles, the city of Chester.

Facilities

En-suite toilets, showers and washbasins are maintained to the highest standards and include facilities for disabled guests. Laundry room. Motorcaravan services. Fenced dog walk (max. 2 dogs). Chalet with books, magazines and DVDs to loan and tourist information to take away. WiFi (charged). Off site: Pub serving food within 1 mile. Riding 1.5 miles. Golf 2 miles. Supermarket 3 miles.

Open: 6 March - 31 October.

Directions

From M6 exit 19 take A556 towards Chester. After 12 miles turn left at traffic lights (signed Winsford and Whitegate) into Dalefords Lane. Continue for 1 mile and site entrance is on right between a white house and a bungalow. GPS: 53.218244, -2.578655

Charges guide

Per unit incl. 2 persons and electricity	£ 22.00 - £ 30.00

Ormskirk

Abbey Farm Caravan Park

Dark Lane, Ormskirk L40 5TX (Lancashire) T: 01695 572686. E: abbeyfarm@yahoo.com

alanrogers.com/UK5280

This quiet, well equipped, family park beside the Abbey ruins has views over open farmland. It is an ideal base for a longer stay with plenty of interest in the local area. The park is divided into small paddocks, one of which is for privately owned seasonal units, one for tents, the other for touring units. The 60 touring pitches, all with 16A electricity, 12 of which have water and waste water, are on hardstanding, separated by small shrubs and colourful flower borders. Mature trees provide shade in parts. A member of the Countryside Discovery group.

Facilities

The main sanitary block is modern, heated and spotless, providing controllable hot showers. Family bathroom that includes facilities for disabled visitors. A second smaller unit has individual cubicles with WC, washbasin and shower. Laundry room. Small shop at reception. Indoor games room. Small adventure playground and large field for ball games. Fishing lake. WiFi over site (charged). Off site: Local market on Thursday and Saturday.

Open: All year.

Directions

From M6 exit 27 take A5209 (Parbold) road. After 5 miles turn left (just before garage) onto B5240, and then first right into Hob Cross Lane, following signs to site. GPS: 53.5698, -2.85665

Charges guide

Per unit incl. 2 persons and electricity	£ 19.20 - £ 20.70
extra person	£ 3.50
child (5-15 yrs)	£ 2.00

Preston

Royal Umpire Caravan Park

Southport Road, Croston, Preston PR26 9JB (Lancashire) T: 01772 600257. E: reception@royalumpire.co.uk

alanrogers.com/UK5290

Royal Umpire is a spacious park near the coast and the M6 for overnight or longer stays. Comprising 60 acres, the park has 195 pitches, almost all with 10A electricity. Six new pitches with their own WC and shower cubicles, and five grass pitches with electricity have been added. About 75 per cent of the pitches have gravel hardstanding, some have TV and water connections. Four camping pods are for rent. A large proportion of the touring pitches are taken for seasonal use. There are unfenced ponds on the site.

Facilities

Two modern, heated, toilet blocks, one beside reception, the other centrally situated. Laundry. Very good facilities for disabled visitors that are shared with baby facilities (key access, £20 deposit). Adventure playground. Field for ball games. Rally field. Dog exercise area. Picnic area. Free WiFi over part of site. Charcoal barbecues are not permitted. Off site: A short walk takes you to the nearby river for fishing, and the conservation village of Croston. Shop and pubs nearby. Riding 3 miles. Golf 5 miles.

Open: All year.

Directions

From north use M6 exit 28 joining A49 going south (parallel to M6) for 2 miles. Then right at second mini-roundabout on A581 to Croston (4 miles). From south use M6 exit 27 onto A5209 but immediately right on B5250 and follow towards Eccleston, joining A581 at Newtown (5 miles). Site is clearly signed. GPS: 53.66669, -2.74827

Charges guide

Per unit incl. 2 adults, 2 children and electricity	£ 15.00 - £ 35.00

For latest campsite news visit

alanrogers.com

Southport
Willowbank Holiday Home & Touring Park

Coastal Road, Ainsdale, Southport PR8 3ST (Mersey) T: 01704 571566. E: info@willowbankcp.co.uk

alanrogers.com/UK5360

Well situated for the Sefton coast and Southport, Willowbank Park is set on the edge of sand dunes amongst mature, wind swept trees. Entrance to the park is controlled by a barrier with a pass-key issued at the excellent reception building which doubles as a sales office for the substantial, high quality caravan holiday home development. There are 87 touring pitches, 30 on gravel hardstandings, 24 on grass and a further 33 pitches, all with 10A electricity; these are on grass hardstanding using an environmentally friendly reinforcement system. Large units are accepted by prior arrangement. The owners are very well supported by the reception team which has considerable experience in managing the touring park. There could be some noise from the nearby main road. This is a good area for cycling and walking with the Trans Pennine Way being adjacent. The attractions of Southport with its parks, gardens, funfair and shopping are four miles away. The area is famous for its golf courses including the Royal Birkdale championship links. Latest arrival time is 21.00.

Facilities

The purpose built, heated toilet block is of a high standard including an excellent bathroom for disabled visitors, although the showers are rather compact. Baby room. Laundry. Motorcaravan services. Play area. Field for ball games. Bicycle hire. Beauty treatments. WiFi throughout (charged). Off site: Golf and riding 0.5 miles. Beach 1.5 miles. Fishing 4 miles. Martin Mere nature reserve.

Open: 1 March - 31 January.

Directions

Park is 4 miles south of Southport. From Ainsdale on A565 travel south for 1.5 miles to second traffic lights (Woodvale) and turn right into Coastal Road to site on left in 150 yds. From south pass RAF Woodvale and turn left at second set of lights. GPS: 53.5888, -3.044

Charges guide

Per unit incl. 2 persons	
and electricity	£ 15.70 - £ 19.10
hardstanding	£ 1.70
extra person	£ 4.00
child (5-16 yrs)	£ 2.55
dog (max. 2)	£ 1.35

Southport

Riverside Holiday Park

Southport New Road, Banks, Southport PR9 8DF (Lancashire) T: 01704 228 886.

E: reception@harrisonleisureuk.com **alanrogers.com/UK5285**

Situated by a busy road on the outskirts of the Lancashire coastal town of Southport, Riverside Holiday Park covers 80 acres and has a total of 620 pitches. Of these, 200 are for touring units and tents, 70 with 10A electricity, some with hardstanding. The park is level and open with little shade. A narrow unfenced river runs through the park where fishing in season is possible (licence required). Apart from an outdoor play area for younger children, most of the activities on the park centre around the indoor games room with live entertainment, a pool room, and a large amusement arcade. Riverside is undergoing a programme of upgrading including the installation of an ATM (cards are not accepted). In high season, a family club provides games, fancy dress, discos etc. Children must be accompanied by an adult at all times on the park.

Facilities

Three heated toilet blocks (key entry) only one of which has showers. At busy times these could be stretched, although it was clean at the time of our visit. Facilities for babies and disabled visitors. Laundry. Well stocked shop. Large bar with TV. Café. Indoor swimming pool (booking system). Games room. Pool room. Large amusement arcade. Play area. River fishing (with licence). Family club in high season with games, fancy dress, discos etc. Dog walking area. Bus route. WiFi in café. Off site: Shops and botanical gardens in Southport, Splash World swimming complex, Martin Mere wetland wildlife reserve. Golf and riding 1 mile. Bicycle hire and beach 5 miles.

Open: All year excl. 1-13 February.

Directions

From the south, M6 exit 26 take M58 to the end, take A59 north towards Preston. From the north, M6 exit 31 take A59 south towards Liverpool/Southport. Both directions, just south of Tarleton, turn west on A565 towards Southport. Park on left in 3 miles. GPS: 53.666955, -2.901056

Charges guide

Per unit incl. 2 adults	
and 3 children	£ 20.00 - £ 30.00
extra person	£ 5.00
child	£ 2.50
dog	£ 1.50

Thornton-Cleveleys

Kneps Farm Holiday Park

River Road, Stanah, Thornton-Cleveleys FY5 5LR (Lancashire) T: 01253 823632.

E: enquiries@knepsfarm.co.uk **alanrogers.com/UK5300**

A well established park with modern facilities, Kneps Farm is still operated by the family who opened it in 1967. Next to Wyre Country Park, it makes an excellent base from which to explore the area. A VNPR-operated barrier system flanks the reception building which also houses a well stocked shop. The 40 marked and numbered touring pitches are on hardstanding, all with 16A electricity and accessed from tarmac roads. They include eight pitches with full services. A separate area accommodates 50 caravan holiday homes (most privately owned) and six camping pods to rent. Recent additions to the park include a new playground for children and an outdoor fitness centre for adults. A path leads through a gate at the back of the site into the country park.

Facilities

The large, centrally heated sanitary building is warm and inviting with ten individual family bathrooms, each providing a WC, basin and bath/shower. Separate toilet facilities with electric hand wash units for men and women. Well equipped room for disabled visitors. Combined baby care/first aid room. Laundry room. Small, well stocked shop. New playground. Outdoor fitness centre. Up to two dogs are accepted per unit. WiFi throughout (free). Off site: Sailing 300 yds. Beach and golf 2.5 miles. Fishing 4 miles.

Open: 1 March - 15 November.

Directions

From M55 exit 3, take A585 towards Fleetwood. Turn left at lights, then right at lights by Shell station (for Thornton-Cleveleys), straight across next lights, then right at the next roundabout by River Wyre Hotel. After one mile (past school) turn right at mini-roundabout into Stanah Road, continue across second mini-roundabout and eventually into River Road. Do not use sat nav. GPS: 53.87903, -2.98506

Charges guide

Per unit incl. 2 persons	
and electricity	£ 20.00 - £ 24.50
incl. 2 children	£ 25.50 - £ 31.00
extra person	£ 3.50 - £ 4.00
extra child or senior	£ 2.75 - £ 3.25

For latest campsite news visit

alanrogers.com

With spectacular lakes, undulating fells, impressive mountains and lush green valleys, Cumbria is ideal for those who wish to get away from it all and unwind in peaceful, natural surroundings, or for the more active who want to participate in a range of outdoor pursuits.

Cumbria is best known for the beautiful Lake District National Park with the picturesque valleys and lakes of Windermere, Ullswater and Derwentwater, each with its own distinctive character. Windermere offers no shortage of watersports, whereas Ullswater mainly attracts peaceful sailing boats. While the Lake District is well known, there are also many quiet, undiscovered areas in the region including the wild, rugged moors of the north Pennines and the beautiful Eden Valley, an ideal place for a casual stroll along the riverside footpaths. The western lakes and fells offer more tranquillity. Here the fells drop down to a long and spectacular coastline, with many undiscovered corners from Ennerdale and Eskdale to the sandstone cliffs of St. Bees Head, now part of a designated Heritage Coast. The Lake District peninsulas along the southern coast of Cumbria also display beautiful scenery and are home to a cluster of ancient ruins such as Furness Abbey and the medieval castle built by monks on Piel Island. Rich in heritage, the historic city of Carlisle, which was sited on the Roman-built Hadrian's wall, boasts an impressive castle, Cumbria's only cathedral, a superb Victorian covered market and an array of speciality shops.

Places of interest

Barrow-in-Furness: South Lakes Wild Animal Park; Dalton Castle; Furness Abbey; Piel Island; indoor market.

Carlisle: Citadel and old courts; Tullie House museum and art gallery; cathedral.

Ravenglass: Muncaster Castle with gardens and owl centre; Ravenglass and Eskdale Railway;

Ulverston: the world's only Laurel and Hardy museum.

Kendal: historic riverside town famous for its mint cake and castle ruins; Abbot Hall Art Gallery; Sizergh Castle.

Ambleside: Beatrix Potter museum; 17th-century Bridge House built over the river.

Windermere: Blackwell Arts & Crafts House; World of Beatrix Potter; Grizedale Forest.

Grasmere: Dove Cottage and Wordsworth Museum; Helm Crag; Gingerbread shop.

Did you know?

Cumbria has the steepest road in England, the Hardknott Pass.

The Lake District was the inspiration for many poets, writers and artists, including William Wordsworth, Beatrix Potter and John Ruskin.

Windermere is Britain's largest natural lake at 10.5 miles long.

Bassenthwaite is the only real lake in the Lake District! All the others are either meres, (Windermere) or waters (Derwentwater, Coniston Water and Ullswater).

Stretching 73 miles, Hadrian's Wall was built by Romans in the second century.

Kendal's famous mint cake is popular with walkers and was taken on the Transarctic Expedition of 1914-1917.

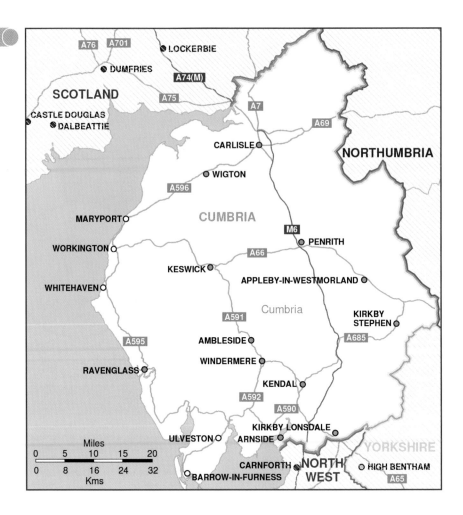

Ambleside
Skelwith Fold Caravan Park

Ambleside LA22 0HX (Cumbria) T: 01539 432277. E: info@skelwith.com

alanrogers.com/UK5520

Skelwith Fold has been developed in the extensive grounds of a country estate taking advantage of the wealth of mature trees and shrubs. The 300 privately owned caravan holiday homes and 120 touring pitches are absorbed into this unspoilt natural environment, sharing it with red squirrels and other wildlife in several discreet areas branching off the central, mile long main driveway. Touring pitches (no tents) are on gravel hardstanding and metal pegs will be necessary for awnings. Electricity hook-ups (10-16A) and basic amenities are available in all areas. Youngsters, and indeed their parents, will find endless pleasure exploring over 90 acres of wild woodland and, if early risers, it is possible to see deer, foxes, etc. at the almost hidden tarn deep in the woods.

Facilities

Three toilet blocks, well situated to serve all areas, have the usual facilities including laundry, drying and ironing rooms. Facilities for disabled visitors. Motorcaravan services. Well stocked, licensed shop. Battery charging, gas and caravan spares and accessories. Adventure play area. Astroturf sports pitch. Library with computer. E-bicycle hire. Family recreation area with picnic tables and goal posts in the Lower Glade. WiFi. Off site: Pubs within walking distance. Ambleside village 1.5 miles. Riding and sailing 3 miles. Fishing 5 miles.

Open: 1 March - 15 November.

Directions

From Ambleside take A593 towards Coniston. Pass through Clappergate and on far outskirts watch for B5286 to Hawkshead on left. Park is clearly signed 1 mile down this road on the right. Do not use sat nav to find this park – this will bring you to a locked gate! GPS: 54.41715, -2.995283

Charges guide

Per pitch	£ 21.50 - £ 30.10
incl. electricity	£ 25.00 - £ 33.60
awning	£ 3.50
dog	£ 2.00

For latest campsite news visit
alanrogers.com

Appleby-in-Westmorland

Wild Rose Park

Ormside, Appleby-in-Westmorland CA16 6EJ (Cumbria) T: 01768 351077. E: reception@wildrose.co.uk

alanrogers.com/UK5570

Set in the Eden Valley within easy reach of the Lake District and the Yorkshire Dales, Wild Rose is a well known park. The entrance is inviting with its well mown grass, trim borders and colourful flower displays. It is immediately apparent that this is a much loved park, and this is reflected throughout the site in the care and attention to detail. There are 135 touring pitches all with electricity, however 105 also provide water and waste water, plus the site boasts on-site wardens to ensure that everything is always neat and tidy. Wild Rose deserves its excellent reputation, which the owners strive to maintain and improve. There are five distinct areas on the park providing a variety of pitches and services.

Facilities

Three toilet blocks (two heated) of excellent quality and kept spotlessly clean. Most washbasins are in cubicles. Facilities for babies and for disabled visitors. Laundry facilities and drying rooms. Motorcaravan services. Exceptionally well stocked shop incl. gas (1/4-1/11). Licensed restaurant with takeaway (weekends only in low season). Outdoor pool (late May-Sept, 10.00-18.00). Indoor playroom for under fives. Adventure playground. Games room. TV room. Cinema room. Tennis. Bicycle hire. Dog exercise area. WiFi. Off site: Fishing 2 miles. Golf and riding 3 miles.

Open: All year.

Directions

Park is signed south off B6260 road 1.5 miles southwest of Appleby. Follow signs to park, towards Ormside. GPS: 54.54893, -2.46422

Charges guide

Per unit incl. 2 persons and electricity	£ 24.00 - £ 34.00
'super pitch' incl. mains services and awning	£ 29.00 - £ 42.00
extra person (over 4 yrs)	£ 5.00

Less 10% for 7 nights or more and for over 60s. Special long-stay rates.

Arnside

Hollins Farm Caravan & Camp Site

Far Arnside, Arnside LA5 0SL (Cumbria) T: 01524 701508. E: Info@hollinsfarm.co.uk

alanrogers.com/UK5595

In a superb location overlooking Morecambe Bay, Hollins Farm lies between two of north Lancashire's most picturesque coastal villages, Silverdale and Arnside. The park comprises several fields divided by trees. There are 73 pitches in all, with 12 for touring units (all with 16A electricity, water and TV connections), plus 23 grass pitches for tents. The addition of two camping pods is planned. Large units may have some difficulty negotiating the narrow country lanes. The site's facilities block is built in local stone and provides visitors with high quality facilities, plus a games room and TV lounge. Visitors may also use the excellent facilities at Holgates' nearby Silverdale Park. These amenities include a bar, restaurant and leisure facilities with an indoor pool and gym. There is also entertainment in high season and sports activities for children. This is a designated Area of Outstanding Natural Beauty and it is very popular walking country. Leaflets may be obtained from reception. A 20 minute walk takes you to the nearest pub, or ten more minutes to reach Silverdale village where there are more pubs, village shops and a restaurant. The RSPB's Leighton Moss at Silverdale is home to some of the UK's rarest birds, including the elusive Bittern.

Facilities

Smart facilities block with underfloor heating. Facilities for disabled visitors. Launderette. Games room. TV lounge. Shop (1/3-31/10). Fridge hire. Play area. Caravan storage. Amenities at Silverdale Park (five minutes walk across a field): bar, restaurant, indoor pool, gym and other leisure facilities (some charged). Off site: Leighton Moss RSPB Nature reserve. Cross Bay walks. Golf 2 miles. Fishing 9 miles. Market town of Kendal 12 miles.

Open: 14 March - 4 November.

Directions

From M6 exit 35 take the A601(M). At first roundabout take second exit A6 North. In 2.5 miles turn left signed Yealand Redmayne, then follow site signs for Holgates Caravan Park through Silverdale. Hollins Farm is 0.5 miles beyond Holgates. GPS: 54.18077, -2.84352

Charges year

Per unit incl. 2 persons and services	£ 32.00
extra person	£ 8.00
child (2-17 yrs)	£ 4.00

For latest campsite news visit
alanrogers.com

Carlisle

Green Acres Caravan Park

High Knells, Houghton, Carlisle CA6 4JW (Cumbria) T: 01228 675418. E: info@caravanpark-cumbria.com

alanrogers.com/UK5640

Green Acres is a small, family run, adults only park. Situated in beautiful, rural surroundings, yet only two miles from junction 44 of the M6, it is perfect for an overnight stop or a longer stay to enjoy Cumbria, Hadrian's Wall and the delights of Carlisle city (four miles away). The Browns have developed Green Acres into an attractive, well maintained and level touring park. There are 30 numbered pitches, all on large hardstandings, arranged in a semicircle, with 10A electricity connections and four serviced pitches (16A). Divided by a long beech hedge is a large camping field, including on one side 12 new hardstanding super pitches for seasonal letting. There is a direct access to the woods for dog walking.

Facilities

New toilet block has free hot showers and two additional wet rooms with shower, washbasin and WC. (suitable for disabled visitors). Laundry room with washing machine and tumble dryer. Car/caravan wash area. Caravan storage. Off site: Shop. Golf 3 miles. Bicycle hire 4 miles. Fishing 8 miles. Riding 10 miles.

Open: 1 April - 31 October.

Directions

Leave M6 at exit 44 and take A689E signed Brampton for 1 mile. Turn left signed Scaleby (site signed) and site is 1 mile on left.
GPS: 54.94505, -2.90728

Charges guide

Per unit incl. 2 persons and electricity	£ 17.00
extra person	£ 5.00

Kendal

Waters Edge Caravan Park

Crooklands, Kendal LA7 7NN (Cumbria) T: 015395 67708. E: info@watersedgecaravanpark.co.uk

alanrogers.com/UK5645

Close to the M6 motorway, Waters Edge makes an ideal stopover. However, it is also well worth a longer stay, being centrally situated for visiting the Lake District and the Yorkshire Dales. Surrounded by farmland, the park is long and narrow with one road running down the centre and the pitches on either side. There are 26 level touring pitches, all with hardstanding. These are open and a little on the small side. At each end of the park there are ten privately owned caravan holiday homes. There is a play area for children but parents of young children would need to be vigilant here as there are well signed but unfenced fast-flowing streams at both sides of the park.

Facilities

Centrally located heated toilet block, although a little dated, is spotlessly clean and has showers and washbasins in cubicles. Facilities for disabled visitors. Laundry. No motorcaravan service point. Shop for basics. Bar with TV. Grassy play area. Off site: Restaurant 300 yds. Bicycle hire. Riding 3 km. Golf 8 km. Canal and boat trips. Kendal 15 minutes drive.

Open: 1 March - 14 November.

Directions

From M6 exit 36 take the A65 (east) signed Kirkby Lonsdale for 300 yds. At next roundabout take first exit (Crooklands). Park is 1 mile on the right at Crooklands Motor Co. GPS: 54.24697, -2.7162

Charges guide

Per unit incl. electricity	£ 17.90 - £ 25.90
awning	£ 1.25

Kendal

Ashes Exclusively Adult Caravan Park

New Hutton, Kendal LA8 0AS (Cumbria) T: 01539 731833. E: info@ashescaravanpark.co.uk

alanrogers.com/UK5650

The Ashes is a small, friendly, adults only park in an extremely peaceful setting in the rolling Cumbrian countryside, yet less than three miles from the M6, and only slightly further from Kendal. Thus it is not only a convenient night stop, but also a useful base from which to explore the Lake District and the Yorkshire Dales. There are 25 hardstanding gravel pitches, all with 10A electrical connections. These are neatly placed around the perimeter with an oval access road. The whole area slopes gently down from the entrance with some pitches fairly level and others with a little more slope (levelling system for caravans on all pitches). No tents are accepted other than trailer tents.

Facilities

A small, purpose built stone building with a slate roof houses two unisex shower rooms (underfloor heating) and the washing and toilet facilities. New facilities for disabled visitors. No shop. New electronic barrier. TV signal booster. Dog exercise area. WiFi (charged). Off site: Full information sheet with details of shopping, eating and many other local venues available from site. 24-hr supermarket 2 miles. Fishing 2 miles. Golf 3 miles.

Open: 1 March - 1 November.

Directions

From M6 exit 37 follow the A684 towards Kendal for 2 miles. Just past a white cottage turn sharp left at crossroads signed New Hutton. Site is on right in 0.75 miles at a left bend. Only approach and depart using this road. GPS: 54.313133, -2.675

Charges guide

Per unit incl. 2 persons and electricity	£ 19.50 - £ 22.50
extra person (over 18s only)	£ 5.50

Keswick
Castlerigg Hall Caravan & Camping Park

Castlerigg Hall, Keswick CA12 4TE (Cumbria) T: 01768 774499. E: info@castlerigg.co.uk

alanrogers.com/UK5660

This well laid out park was started in the late 1950s by the Jackson family who over the years have developed and improved the site whilst maintaining its character. Good use has been made of the traditional stone buildings to house the reception and shop, whilst another building houses a modern amenity block along with a really excellent campers' kitchen. Gently sloping with some shelter, the 120 pitches have fine views across Keswick, Derwentwater and the western Fells. Each terrace has a maximum of eight pitches with 10/16A electricity and almost all with water and drainage. The 65 hardstanding pitches, 52 of which are fully serviced, overlook the lake. Places to visit include Keswick (about 20 minutes walk), Derwentwater, Ullswater, Penrith, Carlisle, Hadrian's Wall, Rhegad (the village in the hill) and, quite close to the site, Castlerigg stone circle which is believed to be some 4,000 years old, and of course as much walking as you might want. The Jacksons are committed to conservation.

Facilities

The main toilet block is beautifully fitted out, fully tiled and heated, with showers, vanity style washbasins (2 in cabins) and hair care areas. Unit for disabled visitors (key). Baby area. Two other toilet blocks are older in style but newly decorated and clean. Fully equipped laundry. Sitting room and campers' kitchen. Restaurant with locally sourced food. Reception houses tourist information and a well stocked shop. WiFi (free). Arts and crafts gallery. Off site: Hotel/pub for meals adjacent to site. Fishing, golf, riding, bicycle hire and boat launching, all 2 km.

Open: 12 March - 7 November.

Directions

From Penrith take A66 towards Keswick and Cockermouth. Leave at first sign for Keswick (A591) and follow to junction (A5271). Turn left on A591 (Windermere) and after 1 mile, take small road on right (Castlerigg and Rakefoot). Park entrance is on the right after 400 yds. GPS: 54.5931, -3.112583

Charges guide

Per unit incl. 2 persons and electricity	£ 19.00 - £ 32.00
extra person (over 4 yrs)	£ 2.90 - £ 4.00
tent per adult	£ 6.95 - £ 9.50

Kirkby Lonsdale
Woodclose Caravan Park

Kirkby Lonsdale LA6 2SE (Cumbria) T: 01524 271597. E: info@woodclosepark.com

alanrogers.com/UK5605

Woodclose is an established, nine-acre park situated in the Lune Valley, just one mile from the market town of Kirkby Lonsdale. With two herds of alpaca and a pair of cashmere goats, this park offers a peaceful and secluded setting catering for walkers, tourers and people who just want to relax. The whole park has a very well cared for appearance. There are 43 pitches in total, 26 with hardstanding and all with 16A electricity and digital TV hook-ups. Screened by a hedge and placed around the perimeter are several seasonal pitches with touring units being placed in the centre. In the camping area, ten 'wigwam' pods provide facilities for luxury camping, one with access for disabled visitors.

Facilities

Two toilet blocks. Facilities are unisex in large, heated, individual rooms with washbasin and toilet or washbasin and shower, all well equipped and very clean. Laundry. Facilities for disabled visitors. Motorcaravan service point. Shop. Small adventure play area. Bicycle hire. Large motorcaravans accepted (limited space). WiFi throughout (charged). Off site: Golf 1 mile. Riding 5 miles. Fishing and beach 7 miles.

Open: 1 March - 1 November.

Directions

From M6 exit 36 take A65 to Kirkby Lonsdale. Site is off the A65 in 6 miles from the motorway. GPS: 54.19835, -2.585017

Charges guide

Per unit incl. 2 persons and electricity	£ 15.00 - £ 27.00
extra person	£ 4.00
child (6-16 yrs)	£ 2.25

For latest campsite news visit
alanrogers.com

Kirkby Stephen

Pennine View Caravan & Camping Park

Station Road, Kirkby Stephen CA17 4SZ (Cumbria) T: 01768 371717.

alanrogers.com/UK5600

Suitable for night halts or longer breaks to visit the Lake District or the Yorkshire Dales, Pennine View is a super small park, well managed and well maintained. With a very attractive rockery at the entrance, the whole site is very neat and tidy. Level, numbered pitches with gravel hardstanding are arranged around the perimeter with grass pitches in the centre. The pitches are of a good size (some being especially large) and all are supplied with 16A electricity. Pennine View was opened in 1990 and is built on reclaimed land from a former railway goods yard. One end of the park adjoins the River Eden.

Facilities

Built of local stone, the modern toilet block is accessed by a digital keypad and includes individual wash cubicles and deep sink for a baby bath. Both ladies and men have large en-suite units for disabled visitors. Well equipped laundry room. Gas. Play area. Off site: Nearby hotel offers bar meals. Bicycle hire 300 m. Kirkby Stephen 1 mile (on the picturesque Settle-Carlisle railway line). Golf 4 miles.

Open: 1 March - 31 October.

Directions

Park is on the A685 on the southerly outskirts of Kirkby Stephen (just under 1 mile from the town centre). Turn left at small site sign opposite the Croglin Castle hotel. Site is 50 yds. on right. GPS: 54.461667, -2.353367

Charges guide

Per person	£ 6.50 - £ 6.90
pitch	£ 7.00 - £ 8.00

Penrith

Troutbeck Camping & Caravanning Club Site

Hutton Moor End, Troutbeck, Penrith CA11 0SX (Cumbria) T: 01768 779149.

alanrogers.com/UK5500

Within easy reach of Keswick and Derwentwater and with impressive views of the surrounding fells, Troutbeck is open to members and non-members alike and is a great base from which to explore the northern Lakes. There are 54 pitches, 36 on hardstanding, the remainder on grass. Most have 16A electricity connections and four pitches have TV hook-ups. A shallow river runs close to the touring area (steep drop). Blencathra and Sharp Edge are both within easy reach of the campsite. The Coast2Coast cycle way passes by the campsite. Another popular mountain bike route is the Old Coach Road from which, in places, there are splendid views of Blencathra and Skiddaw.

Facilities

Toilet block is well equipped, with free hot showers and facilities for disabled visitors. Baby room. Laundry room. Motorcaravan services. Small play area. Designated dog walk. Small shop selling local free-range eggs, meat and real ales. Coffee machine. Holiday homes and lodges. WiFi (variable reception; charged). Off site: Weekly Farmers' Markets locally. Riding 2 miles. Fishing 3 miles.

Open: 1 March - 1 December, 26 December - 2 January.

Directions

Troutbeck is 10 miles west of Penrith. From M6 at exit 40 take A66 west towards Keswick and Workington for 9 miles. Turn south then west signed Waithwaite to site on left. GPS: 54.63521, -2.98528

Charges guide

Per person	£ 7.70 - £ 11.30
child (6-17 yrs)	£ 3.85 - £ 5.65
non-member pitch fee	£ 5.35 - £ 7.90

Penrith

Sykeside Camping Park

Brotherswater, Patterdale, Penrith CA11 0NZ (Cumbria) T: 01768 482239. E: info@sykeside.co.uk

alanrogers.com/UK5560

This small touring park is located in a really beautiful, quiet spot in the northern Lakes area, just 400 yards from Brotherswater. With views up the Dovedale valley, the park has 100 tent pitches on the valley floor in addition to 24 hardstanding pitches for caravans and motorcaravans, all with 10A electricity. Tent pitches are not marked and campers arrange themselves to best enjoy the superb views. The stone-built building, an original barn near the entrance, houses all the facilities. These include the Barn End bar which serves drinks on Fridays and Saturdays.

Facilities

The toilet block includes hot showers. A chemical disposal point is available. Small launderette and dishwashing room. Self-service shop with camping equipment, gas and an ice-pack service, doubles as reception. Bunkhouse accommodation for 36 persons in various groups. Fishing nearby. WiFi over part of site (charged). Off site: Bicycle hire 3 miles. Good sailing on Ullswater 4 miles. Riding 8 miles. Golf 10 miles. Boat launching 10 km. The Brotherswater Inn is adjacent.

Open: All year.

Directions

From M6 exit 40 take A66 towards Keswick. At first roundabout take A592 and follow signs for Ullswater and Glenridding, continue to Brotherswater and Sykeside is on the right of the A592. The entrance is just behind the Brotherswater Inn. GPS: 54.4985, -2.9255

Charges guide

Per unit incl. 2 persons and electricity	£ 17.50 - £ 25.00
tent incl. 2 persons and car	£ 13.50 - £ 23.00
Min. charge for motorcaravan £15 per night.	

For latest campsite news visit

alanrogers.com

Penrith
Westmorland Caravan Park
Tebay, Orton, Penrith CA10 3SB (Cumbria) T: 01539 711322. E: caravans@westmorland.com
alanrogers.com/UK5590

For caravans, motorcaravans and trailer tents only, this is the ideal stopover for anyone heading either north or south, close to the M6 motorway, but far enough away for the traffic noise not to be too disturbing. There are 80 level pitches on gravel, divided into bays of about six or seven units (25 are for touring units, five with water and drainage). All the touring pitches have 16A electricity. The bays are backed by grassy banks alive with rabbits and birds – a long list in the office describes the large variety of birds to be seen on the site. There is good site lighting and a late arrivals area.

Facilities

The heated toilet block is basic but kept very clean and includes washbasins and showers. Bathroom for disabled visitors with ramped access. Family room. Laundry. Reception sells gas. Dog walk. Large RVs must book (£5 supplement). Off site: Shops and restaurants five minutes walk at the motorway service area. Fishing 2 miles. Golf 17 miles. Within 30 minutes drive are the market towns of Appleby, Penrith and Kendal.

Open: 9 March - 4 November.

Directions

From the M6, exit for Tebay services (site signed) just north of exit 38. Site is accessible from the services travelling north or south.
GPS: 54.4477, -2.606467

Charges guide

Per unit incl. 4 persons and electricity	£ 20.00 - £ 22.00

Discount on café meals and farm shop.

Penrith
Waterfoot Caravan Park
Pooley Bridge, Ullswater, Penrith CA11 0JF (Cumbria) T: 01768 486302. E: enquiries@waterfootpark.co.uk
alanrogers.com/UK5610

Waterfoot is a quiet family park for caravans and motorcaravans only. It is set in 22 acres of partially wooded land developed in the fifties from a private estate. The 146 private caravan holiday homes are quite separate from the 36 touring pitches (all are on hardstanding and numbered and full services are planned for 2015). Most are level and all have 10/16A electricity. There are two teepees for hire. Lake Ullswater is only about 400 yards away and a half mile stroll through bluebell woods brings you to the village of Pooley Bridge. Waterfoot's touring pitches are arranged very informally in a large clearing.

Facilities

The heated toilet block includes washbasins and preset showers in cubicles. New facilities for disabled visitors. Laundry facilities. Small shop selling basics, gas and newspapers. Bar with strictly enforced, separate family room (weekend evenings low season, every evening high season). Bicycle hire. Large fenced field with play equipment and goal posts for football and a new play park. WiFi throughout (charged). Off site: Fishing 0.5 miles. Riding 1.5 miles. Golf 5 miles.

Open: 1 March - 14 November.

Directions

Do not use GPS. Please use following directions: From M6 exit 40, take A66 signed Keswick. After 0.5 miles at roundabout take A592 signed Ullswater and site is on right after 4 miles.
GPS: 54.614017, -2.83115

Charges guide

Per unit incl. all persons and electricity	£ 15.50 - £ 28.50
extra person	£ 3.00

Penrith
Cove Camping Park
Ullswater, Watermillock, Penrith CA11 0LS (Cumbria) T: 01768 486549. E: info@cove-park.co.uk
alanrogers.com/UK5620

Cove Camping is a delightful, small site, some of the 50 pitches having great views over Lake Ullswater. The grass is well trimmed, there are ramps to keep speeds down to 5 mph. and the site is well lit. There are 21 touring pitches with 10A electricity hook-ups and water, some with waste water, plus 29 tent pitches, seven of which have electricity. The rest of the park is quite sloping and some terracing has been carried out to create pitches with a lake view. Refuse and recycling bins are hidden behind wooden fencing. The park is well situated for walking, boating, fishing and pony trekking.

Facilities

The recently refurbished toilet block is immaculate and heated in cooler months, providing adjustable showers, some washbasins in cabins and, for ladies, a hairdressing area and a baby changing unit. Foyer containing a freezer (free) and tourist information. Laundry facilities. Gas supplies. Small, grass-based play area. Off site: Shop nearby. Fishing 1.5 miles. Riding 3 miles. Golf 6 mile. Bicycle hire 3 miles (will deliver).

Open: March - 31 October.

Directions

We advise using the following directions rather than GPS. From A66 Penrith-Keswick road, take A592 south (Ullswater). Turn right at Brackenrigg Inn and follow road uphill for 1.5 miles to park on left. This road is narrow, large units should telephone park for an alternative route. GPS: 54.604283, -2.881883

Charges guide

Per unit incl. 2 persons and electricity	£ 20.00 - £ 34.00
extra person	£ 4.00

For latest campsite news visit
alanrogers.com

Penrith
Lowther Holiday Park

Eamont Bridge, Penrith CA10 2JB (Cumbria) T: 01768 863631. E: alan@lowther-holidaypark.co.uk
alanrogers.com/UK5625

Sitting on the banks of the River Lowther, this holiday park occupies 50 acres of rural, wooded parkland, home to the rare red squirrel. There are 400 caravan holiday homes and lodges around the park together with 70 touring pitches. A proportion of these are taken by seasonal lets. Marked and numbered, on mostly level ground between mature trees, all have 10A electricity and hardstanding. A separate elevated grass area is available for tents and two pods have been added. There is a small touring office with 24-hour security adjacent to the holiday home sales office.

Facilities

Two clean toilet blocks provide large, preset showers. Bathroom with baby changing. Motorcaravan services. Laundry facilities. Full facilities for disabled visitors (Radar key). Licensed shop. Squirrel Inn with restaurant. Play areas. Fly fishing on river (permit from office). Activity weekends. Live entertainment and children's parties. Max. 2 dogs. Off site: Golf, riding and bicycle hire 2 miles.

Open: 2 March - 22 November.

Directions

From M6 exit 40 take A66 towards Scotch Corner (signed Brough) for 1 mile. At roundabout take A6 south for 1 mile (Shap). Lowther is on the right after Eamont Bridge. GPS: 54.647667, -2.737017

Charges guide

Per unit incl. 6 persons and electricity	£ 26.00 - £ 40.00
extra person	£ 3.00

Penrith
The Quiet Site Caravan & Camping Park

Watermillock, Penrith CA11 0LS (Cumbria) T: 07768 727016. E: info@thequietsite.co.uk
alanrogers.com/UK5630

The Quiet Site is a secluded, family run park operating as a carbon neutral company. It is situated on a hillside in the Lake District National Park, with views over the fells, just 1.5 miles from Lake Ullswater. There are 100 unmarked touring pitches, most with hardstanding and all with electricity. They have been terraced to provide level surfaces. The camping area is undulating. In a separate part of the park, screened by mature trees, there are 23 privately owned caravan holiday homes. There are two cottages to rent and recent additions are 14 timber built camping pods, pre-erected bell tents and a 'Hobbit Hole'.

Facilities

The toilet block provides preset showers and open style washbasins, three bathrooms and two private shower rooms. Bathroom with facilities for disabled visitors. Baby area. Laundry facilities. Motorcaravan services. Shop at reception. Gas supplies. Bar (weekends only in low season). TV and games room. Adventure play area. Caravan storage. WiFi. Unsuitable for very large units. Off site: Fishing 1.5 miles. Riding and bicycle hire 3 miles.

Open: All year.

Directions

We advise the following directions, rather than GPS. From M6, exit 40, take A66 (Keswick) for 1 mile, then A592 (Ullswater) for 4 miles. Turn right at Lake junction, still on A592 (Windermere). After 1 mile turn right (at Brackenrigg Inn) and follow for 1.5 miles to site on right (large units phone for alternative route). GPS: 54.604683, -2.882783

Charges guide

Per unit incl. 2 persons, awning and electricity	£ 15.00 - £ 35.00
extra person	£ 5.00

Penrith
Ullswater Caravan, Camping & Marine Park

Watermillock, Penrith CA11 0LR (Cumbria) T: 017684 86666. E: info@ullswatercaravanpark.co.uk
alanrogers.com/UK5635

Located within the Lake District National Park, Ullswater Holiday Park is centrally situated for touring the many attractions of this glorious area. It has 220 pitches, 58 for touring units, the remainder used for holiday homes. All have 10A electricity, 50 also have water and drainage. Some are situated very close to the bar and are also overlooked by mobile homes with little privacy. At the far end of the park other pitches are in a more wooded area. In between is a large grassy space for tents. Four pods have been added. There are occasional glimpses of the lake through the trees.

Facilities

Three toilet blocks, two heated, with family shower room and facilities for disabled visitors. Laundry. Reception and shop with off-licence. Bar and games room open to 20.00 at busy times. Well equipped playground for younger children. WiFi in café. Off site: Walks in the hills above the park. Steamer rides on the lake from Pooley Bridge 2 miles.

Open: 1 March - 14 November.

Directions

From M6 exit 40 take A66 west (Keswick). At first roundabout (Rheged) take second exit (Ullswater) on A592. At T-junction turn right, still on A592, and after Brackenrigg Inn continue downhill to telephone box on right, and sign for church. Turn right here and up to entrance on right. GPS: 54.5978, -2.87482

Charges guide

Per unit incl. 2 persons and electricity	£ 18.00 - £ 28.00

For latest campsite news visit
alanrogers.com

Penrith

Flusco Wood Touring Caravan Park

Flusco, Penrith CA11 0JB (Cumbria) T: 01768 480020. E: info@fluscowoodtouringpark.co.uk

alanrogers.com/UK5670

Flusco Wood Caravan Park is still being developed but everything is to a very high standard. Set amongst woodland with the 22 touring pitches in bays, this park will meet the needs of those requiring a quiet holiday (with plenty of walks from the site) and also those travelling up or down the M6 looking for a quiet night's rest. All pitches have electricity and water and are on hardstanding, with an area near reception with hardstandings for motorcaravans. Recent additions here include new log cabins (privately owned) with more planned. The area abounds with wildlife including deer and red squirrels.

Facilities

A log cabin style building houses very clean, heated facilities including preset showers and vanity style washbasins (1 cubicle). Large en-suite shower rooms for families and disabled visitors, one for ladies, one for men. Laundry, drying room and boot washing sink. Second log cabin serves as reception/shop with basic supplies, gas and daily newspapers. Play equipment. Grass area for ball games. Off site: Pub and P.O. store in Greystoke 2 miles. Fishing, bicycle hire and golf 4 miles. Riding 5 miles.

Open: 22 March - 31 October.

Directions

From M6 exit 40 take A66 west towards Keswick. Straight on at first roundabout, after 2.5 miles take right turn at top of hill (Flusco, Recycling Centre). After 0.5 miles road turns right up hill (narrow), site is on left at the top. GPS: 54.655408, -2.841346

Charges guide

Per unit incl. 2 persons
and electricity   £ 21.00 - £ 24.00
extra person (over 6 yrs)   £ 4.00

Ravenglass

Ravenglass Camping & Caravanning Club Site

Ravenglass CA18 1SR (Cumbria) T: 01229 717250. E: ravenglass.site@thefriendlyclub.co.uk

alanrogers.com/UK5530

Ravenglass is just 500 metres from the seafront. There are 56 pitches for touring units on level hardstanding with 16A electricity connections. A small grass area at the top and back of the park provides an attractive spot for 21 tents (15 with hook-ups), plus three pods, off a circular gravel road providing access. This is a Club site but non-members are welcome. A central courtyard complex includes completely refurbished amenities, maintained to a high standard by Sara and Martyn Merckel. This is a useful site for all sorts of walking – estuary, river or fell – or to explore the Cumbrian coast.

Facilities

Completely refurbished, the toilet block provides all the usual amenities and a laundry room. Motorcaravan services. Licensed shop sells local meat and beer. Cable TV around the park. WiFi (charged). Off site: Play area and ball field opposite. Fishing and boat launching 0.5 miles. Bicycle hire 7 miles. Golf 8 miles. Riding 10 miles.

Open: 1 February - 30 November and 22 December - 3 January.

Directions

Park is just off A595 (between Egremont and Millom) signed on road into village of Ravenglass. GPS: 54.355758, -3.406424

Charges guide

Per unit incl. 2 persons
and electricity   £ 20.70 - £ 34.90
Non-member prices are higher.

Wigton

Stanwix Park Holiday Centre

Greenrow, Silloth CA7 4HH (Cumbria) T: 01697 332666. E: enquiries@stanwix.com

alanrogers.com/UK5505

Stanwix Park is a family run holiday park with absolutely everything anyone could want for a memorable holiday all year round. The park has 111 caravan holiday homes and chalets for rent, together with 212 which are privately owned. These are mostly located around the central complex. In addition, at either end of the park, there are 121 fully serviced (10A electricity) pitches for touring units and tents, some on grass, some with hardstanding. A warm welcome awaits in the main reception with lots of local and tourist information. Motorcaravans over eight metres only accepted by prior arrangement.

Facilities

The two heated sanitary blocks are kept spotlessly clean. Large en-suite bathrooms, showers, vanity style washbasins and a unit in each for disabled visitors. Campers' kitchen. Laundry facilities. Shop (6/3-15/11). Restaurant with takeaway. Bars (adults only and family) with evening entertainment (6/3-15/11). TV and snooker room. Indoor leisure centre. Outdoor swimming pool (31/5-1/9). Ten-pin bowling centre. Amusement arcade. Soft play area. Minigolf. Tennis. Bicycle hire. Free WiFi over part of site. Dogs max. 2. Off site: Beach 1 mile.

Open: All year.

Directions

From the south, take exit 41 from the M6 and follow B5305 through Wigton to Silloth. From north on A74/M6 take exit 44 and the A595 and A596 to Wigton. On entering Silloth, turn left following signs for park. Entrance is on the right. GPS: 54.8614, -3.388333

Charges guide

Per person   £ 4.20 - £ 5.00
child (under 5 yrs)   £ 2.70 - £ 3.30
pitch   £ 12.90 - £ 16.20

For latest campsite news visit
alanrogers.com

Wigton

Hylton Caravan Park

Silloth, Wigton CA7 4AY (Cumbria) T: 01697 332666. E: ericstanwix@stanwix.com

alanrogers.com/UK5506

Hylton Caravan Park is owned and managed by the Stanwix family and although it is only a short walk away from the livelier Stanwix Park, it is a peaceful haven for people who prefer the 'quiet life'. The only activity is an adventure park for children which is not visible from the touring area. Divided by a circular road, the 170 privately owned caravan holiday homes are visible but not intrusive. There are 90 open plan, mostly level touring and tent pitches, all fully serviced and with 10A electricity. There is no shop on site as the town and Stanwix Park are both within walking distance. Club membership for the extensive leisure and entertainment amenities at Stanwix Park is free of charge for the duration of your stay.

Facilities

A high quality toilet block is superbly fitted out and includes toilets, showers, vanity style washbasins, extra large bathrooms and a separate cubicle for disabled visitors. Dishwashing under cover. Fully equipped laundry. Gas sales. Max. 2 dogs per pitch. Off site: Bus stop 1 mile. Entertainment and amenities at Stanwix Park. Silloth golf course. Bowling. Windsurfing, boat launching and fishing 1 mile. Riding 7 miles.

Open: 1 March - 15 November.

Directions

On entering Silloth, turn left following signs to Hylton Caravan Park. GPS: 54.868333, -3.39835

Charges guide

Per person	£ 4.20 - £ 5.00
child (under 5 yrs)	£ 2.70 - £ 3.30
pitch	£ 10.40 - £ 13.00

Wigton

The Larches Caravan Park

Mealsgate, Wigton CA7 1LQ (Cumbria) T: 01697 371379. E: thelarches@hotmail.co.uk

alanrogers.com/UK5510

Mealsgate and The Larches lie on the Carlisle-Cockermouth road, a little removed from the hectic centre of the Lake District, yet with easy access to it (and good views towards it) and to other attractions nearby. This quiet, family run, adults only park takes 45 touring units of any type, 42 of which have 10A electricity, water and drainage. These pitches are in grassy areas with tall, mature trees, shrubs and accompanying wildlife. Some are sloping and irregular, others on marked hardstandings. There are currently a few privately owned holiday homes and there are plans to extend this area of the park. The Elliott family provide a warm welcome at this peaceful, well organised park which is undergoing some redevelopment. This is an ideal haven for couples – only adult visitors are accepted.

Facilities

Recently refurbished toilet facilities provide en-suite facilities for both sexes. Separate unit for disabled visitors can be heated. Campers' kitchen with microwave (free). Laundry room. Small shop selling mainly camping accessories, gas and off-licence. Small indoor heated pool (June-Aug). Wildlife pond. Caravan storage. Off site: Riding 1.5 miles. Golf 3.5 miles. Bicycle hire 7 miles. Fishing 8 miles.

Open: 1 March - 31 October.

Directions

Park entrance is south off A595 (Carlisle-Cockermouth road) just southwest of Mealsgate. GPS: 54.763267, -3.2358

Charges guide

Per unit incl. 2 persons and electricity	£ 19.00 - £ 22.00
extra person	£ 4.00 - £ 5.00
awning or extra car	£ 2.50 - £ 3.50
backpacker	£ 8.50 - £ 9.50

No credit cards.

For latest campsite news visit

alanrogers.com

Windermere
Park Cliffe Camping & Caravan Estate
Birks Road, Windermere LA23 3PG (Cumbria) T: 01539 531344. E: info@parkcliffe.co.uk
alanrogers.com/UK5545

This beautiful park is situated in the heart of the Lake District National Park and is well managed and maintained by the welcoming staff. The 60 touring pitches are open and unshaded, on gravel hardstanding with 10A electricity, water and drainage. There are some seasonal units and three mobile homes available for hire. Seven pods have been sited. Tucked away in a valley are privately owned mobile homes. Two areas have been set aside for 80 tent pitches, 25 of which have 6A electricity hook-ups (steel pegs required). There is no automatic barrier, but the gates are closed to both campers and caravanners 23.00-07.30, with a warden on site for emergencies.

Facilities

Two blocks of toilets and showers are heated and very clean. Full facilities for disabled visitors and excellent baby room. Four private bathrooms are available for hire (min. 3 days) and one by the hour (with refundable deposit). Laundry. Motorcaravan services. Small well stocked shop. Bar, restaurant and takeaway (weekends only in low season). Refurbished games room. Large outdoor adventure play area (recently refurbished) is set secluded to one side of the tourers, not fenced as a public footpath runs through to Moor How. WiFi in bar and games room (free). Off site: Fellfoot Country Park with (sail) boat launching, walking, climbing, cycling and many other activities possible. Cruises on the lake.

Open: 1 March - 8 November.

Directions

From M6 exit 36 take A590 to Newby Bridge. Turn right on A592 for 3.6 miles and turn right. Site is signed shortly on the right. It is vital that caravans and trailers approach Park Cliffe only from the direction of Newby Bridge on A592 - extremely tight turn from north. The park does not advise the use of sat nav to reach it. GPS: 54.312517, -2.9375

Charges guide

Per unit incl. 2 persons	
and electricity	£ 26.00 - £ 32.00
extra person	£ 5.00
child (5-17 yrs)	£ 3.00
dog	£ 2.00

Windermere
Hill of Oaks Caravan Park
Tower Wood, Windermere LA12 8NR (Cumbria) T: 01539 531578. E: enquiries@hillofoaks.co.uk
alanrogers.com/UK5615

On the banks of Lake Windermere, this park lives up to its name. Set on a hillside in mature woodland, the park offers families a safe natural environment with nature walks through the managed ancient woodlands, as well as six jetties for boat launching and access to watersports activities (jet skis are not allowed). The road into the park passing the farmhouse is long, winding and narrow, so those with long units should ring ahead for alternative access, reception being about half a mile from the entrance. Although the park is situated on Lake Windermere, most of the touring pitches nestle within the trees, not actually by the lake. All 43 have 16A electricity, digital TV hook-up and hardstanding. Most are large enough to take a car and boat and three large super pitches also have water and a drain. Tents are not accepted at Hill of Oaks.

Facilities

The central tiled toilet block is clean and heated (key entry, £10 deposit). Vanity style washbasins, controllable showers and free hairdryers. Baby changing areas. Fully equipped laundry. Unit for disabled visitors (combination lock). Motorcaravan services. Shop for basics. Two fenced play areas, one for toddlers and adventure style for over fives. Picnic areas and nature trails. Fishing (licence required). Electric car for hire. WiFi (charged). Off site: Fell Foot Park and Gardens 1 mile, with rowing boat hire and ferry rides to Lakeside and Ambleside. Aquarium of the Lakes at Newby Bridge 3.5 miles. Golf 4 miles. Riding and bicycle hire 6 miles.

Open: 1 March - 14 November.

Directions

From M6 exit 36 head west on A590 towards Barrow and Newby Bridge. Follow A590 to roundabout signed Bowness and turn right on A592 for 3 miles. Site is signed on left. GPS: 54.30246, -2.9493

Charges guide

Per unit incl. all persons	
and electricity	£ 21.00 - £ 41.00
boat	£ 3.00 - £ 9.00

For latest campsite news visit
alanrogers.com

THE REGION COMPRISES: NORTHUMBERLAND, DURHAM, TYNE AND WEAR, AND TEESIDE

The most northerly region of England, Northumbria is steeped in history, full of ancient forts and fairytale castles. The great outdoors offers limitless walking with trails stretching across moorlands and beaches, encompassing views of the beautiful scenery.

The 400 square mile Northumberland National Park is one of the most peaceful and remote places in England. With endless walks across moorlands and hills, it stretches south from the Cheviot Hills, through the Simonside Hills, to the crags of Whin Sill where it engulfs a section of the historic Hadrian's Wall, built by the Romans to mark the northern limit of their empire. The Pennine Way was the country's first official long distance path and is still the longest. At 268 miles, it stretches from the Peak National Park to the border. The coastline is not to be forgotten with mile upon mile of deserted, sandy beaches, with resorts that still have an old fashioned feel to them, such as Whitley Bay, South Shields and Seaton Carew. The majestic castles of Bamburgh and Dunstanburgh can be seen for miles along the Northumberland coast. Surrounded on three sides by the River Wear, the small, historic city of Durham is dominated by England's greatest Norman cathedral. With cobbled medieval streets and restricted car access, it is a popular place with visitors. Further north is the bustling city of Newcastle. Home to an array of cosmopolitan restaurants and bars, music venues and fabulous architecture, it also boasts a lively nightlife.

Places of interest

Northumberland: Bamburgh Castle; Alnwick Castle and gardens; Berwick-upon-Tweed; Lindisfarne Priory on Holy Island; Newbiggin Maritime Centre; Dunstanburgh Castle; Corbridge Roman sites at Hadrian's Wall.

Durham: Durham Castle and Cathedral; Barnard Castle; Beamish Museum; Diggerland at Langley Park; Harperley POW Camp; Crook Hall and Gardens.

Tyne and Wear: New Metroland indoor theme park and shopping complex; 700-year-old Holy Jesus Hospital, Newcastle with Life Science Centre, Discovery Museum and Castle Keep; Gibside forest garden.

Teeside: Kirkleatham Owl Centre; Darlington Railway Centre and Museum; Guisborough Hall; Saltburn Smugglers Heritage Centre; Captain Cook Birthplace Museum, Marton.

Did you know?

Alnwick Castle was used as the setting for Hogwarts in the Harry Potter films.

Stretching from Wallsend to Bowness-on-Solway, Hadrian's Wall is 81 miles long.

Middlesbrough Teesside Transporter Bridge was built in 1911 and is the only one of its kind in England, with a gondola capable of carrying nine cars and 200 passengers.

In the past 300 years Berwick has changed hands between the Scottish and the English no less than 13 times.

Anthony Gormley's Angel of The North has a wingspan of 54 metres and is visited by 150,000 people every year.

Sir Malcolm Campbell's first speed record of 138 mph was set on Saltburn sands on 17 June 1922.

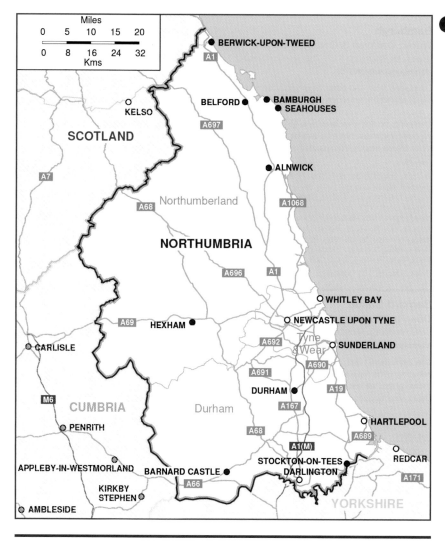

Alnwick
Dunstan Hill Camping & Caravanning Club Site
Dunstan Hill, Dunstan, Alnwick NE66 3TQ (Northumberland) T: 01665 576310.
alanrogers.com/UK5770

Off a quiet lane between Embleton and Craster, this is a rural site with a tree belt to shelter it from the north wind and has access to the beach via a level footpath through the fields, across the golf course and past the ruins of Dunstanburgh Castle. This is just over a mile by car. With gravel access roads, the peaceful site has 150 level, well spaced pitches, 80 with 16A electricity. Reception is manned by very helpful managers and there is an area for outside parking and late arrivals at the entrance. This site is not suitable for large American motorhomes.

Facilities

Two very clean and well maintained toilet blocks have some washbasins in cubicles, hairdryers (20p) and a washroom for children with deep sinks. Facilities for disabled visitors in one block, a laundry in the other. Small shop including gas. Newspapers can be ordered. Fish and chip van twice a week. Tourist information room. Small play area. Torches are useful. Dog walk. WiFi (charged). Off site: Buses pass the site entrance (request stop) and there are good eating places near. Pubs within 1 mile. Beach, fishing and golf 1.5 miles. Riding 8 miles.

Open: 17 March - 31 October.

Directions

From A1 just north of Alnwick take B1340 or B6347 (further north) for Embleton. Site is signed in Embleton village. Avoid signs to Dunstanburgh Castle and follow those for Craster. Site is (south) on the left after 0.5 miles. GPS: 55.4855, -1.6291

Charges guide

Per unit incl. 2 persons and electricity	£ 20.70 - £ 34.90
extra person	£ 7.90 - £ 13.30

No credit cards.
Non-member prices are higher.

For latest campsite news visit
alanrogers.com

Bamburgh
Waren Caravan & Camping Park
Waren Mill, Bamburgh NE70 7EE (Northumberland) T: 01668 214366. E: waren@meadowhead.co.uk
alanrogers.com/UK5750

Developed from 100 acres of privately owned, undulating heath and woodland, Waren Park is a large, family site with marvellous views over Northumberland's golden beaches and the sea. A large section of caravan holiday homes is separate from a compact, self-contained, four-acre touring area. Enclosed by sheltering banks, this provides 150 reasonably level pitches, 108 with 16A electrical connections. Wooden wigwams are also available for rent. As well as the spacious grounds to wander in, there is much to see nearby from castles and the Farne Islands to the Cheviot Hills and miles of sandy beaches.

Facilities

The older toilet facilities have been refurbished to a high standard and include four family en-suite shower rooms, a family bathroom and facilities for disabled visitors. A newer block in the static holiday home section also provides good facilities. Laundry room. Motorcaravan services. Licensed shop. Bar with terrace serving bar meals. Gaming machine room. Patio area. Play park and playing fields. Splash pool (June-Sept). WiFi on part of site. Off site: Beach 500 yds. Golf and riding 5 miles.

Open: 6 March - 31 October.

Directions

Follow B1342 from the A1 to Waren Mill towards Bamburgh. After Budle Bay turn right and follow signs. GPS: 55.60045, -1.75487

Charges guide

Per unit incl. 2 persons	
and electricity	£ 17.00 - £ 25.00
extra adult	£ 5.95
extra child (over 5 yrs)	£ 3.95
dog (max. 2)	£ 5.75

Barnard Castle
Doe Park Touring Caravan Park
Cotherstone, Barnard Castle DL12 9UQ (Co. Durham) T: 01833 650302. E: info@doepark.co.uk
alanrogers.com/UK5710

The Lamb family will make you very welcome and personally take you to your pitch at Doe Park. The camping fields have a lovely open aspect with wonderful views and the 70 pitches are spacious with well mown grass, all with 10A electricity, 60 with hardstanding. This is Hannah Hauxwell country and the Dales, less frequented than other upland areas, provide wonderful walking country; indeed part of the Pennine Way runs near this peaceful site. The park's reception is a new wooden cabin at the entrance to the pitch area and is well stocked with tourist information guides.

Facilities

With toilet facilities at the farmhouse, two well kept blocks are closer to the pitches (the newest one heated). Washbasins in cabins and adjustable showers. Unisex unit for disabled visitors. Small laundry. Eggs and milk are available from the farmhouse. No play area but a large grass area in front of some of the pitches can be used for ball games. River fishing on site. Notify park prior to arrival if taking pets. WiFi being considered. Off site: Reservoirs (sailing, water skiing and fishing) 3 miles. Golf 4 miles.

Open: 1 March - 31 October.

Directions

Follow B6277 from Barnard Castle towards Middleton in Teesdale. The farm is signed on the left just after Cotherstone village (there is no need to go into Barnard Castle). GPS: 54.578217, -1.99235

Charges guide

Per unit incl. 2 persons	
and electricity	£ 17.00 - £ 27.50
extra person (over 6 yrs)	£ 1.50 - £ 2.00
No credit cards.	

Barnard Castle
Barnard Castle Camping & Caravanning Club Site
Dockenflatts Lane, Lartington, Barnard Castle DL12 9DG (Co. Durham) T: 01833 630228.
alanrogers.com/UK5720

Welcoming non-members and tents, the Camping and Caravanning Club site at Barnard Castle was opened in 1996. There are 90 flat pitches, most on grass but including 35 hardstanding pitches (gravel base with room for both car and caravan and space for an awning on grass). There are 81 electricity hook-ups (16A). One side of the site is bordered by mature trees and there is an attractive woodland dog walking area leading to a riverside footpath which takes you into Barnard Castle. There are many footpaths and walks in the area and numerous local attractions.

Facilities

The centrally located toilet facilities can be heated and are of good quality and kept spotlessly clean. Washbasins are in cubicles and free, controllable showers are roomy. Baby room. Unisex unit for disabled visitors. Laundry facilities. Motorcaravan services. Small shop in reception area. Fish and chip van calls. Play area. WiFi (charged). Off site: Riding 200 m. Golf 2.5 miles. Fishing 4 miles. Bus from end of lane (flag down service).

Open: 3 March - 31 October.

Directions

Follow B6277 from Barnard Castle (towards Middleton in Teesdale) for 1 mile to Lartington. Turn left at club sign into narrow lane with passing places to site entrance on left (there is no need to go into Barnard Castle). GPS: 54.546883, -1.962583

Charges guide

Per unit incl. 2 persons	
and electricity (non-member)	£ 18.70 - £ 31.85
extra person	£ 7.15 - £ 12.15

For latest campsite news visit
alanrogers.com

Belford
South Meadows Caravan Park

South Meadows, Belford NE70 7DP (Northumberland) T: 01668 213326. E: info@southmeadows.co.uk
alanrogers.com/UK5755

South Meadows is set in the north Northumberland countryside, within walking distance of the village of Belford with its market cross and old coaching inn. The park is pleasantly landscaped and two short walks lead into the adjacent bluebell woods. Covering 40 acres of level grass, there are 87 hardstanding touring pitches, all with 16A electricity, water and TV aerial point. Help is available from a team who will position and level your caravan for you. A further area can accommodate about 50 tents. The manager is environmentally aware and encourages recycling. There is an area especially for disabled visitors with wider paths and safety features. This attractive, well maintained park is already popular with couples and young families and booking is advised.

Facilities

The fully tiled toilet block is excellent, heated in cool weather, with washbasins in cabins and roomy showers. Three family shower rooms. An additional prefabricated sanitary unit is open in one area for the summer months. Hairdryers. Full facilities for disabled visitors. Laundry with washing machines, dryers and iron plus a baby unit. Play area. Caravan storage and servicing. Free WiFi over site. Off site: Restaurant and farm shop adjacent to park. Village with pub and shops, golf 0.5 miles. Riding and beach 3 miles. Alnwick Castle of Harry Potter fame.

Open: All year.

Directions

Turn off A1 15 miles from Alnwick to Belford village and park is signed at the southern end. GPS: 55.590967, -1.822583

Charges guide

Per unit incl. 2 persons and electricity	£ 19.00 - £ 26.00
extra person	£ 6.00
child (2-16 yrs)	£ 4.00

Berwick-upon-Tweed
Chainbridge Touring Caravan Site

Bankhead Villa, Horncliffe, Berwick-upon-Tweed TD15 2XT (Northumberland) T: 07554 953697.
E: stay@chainbridgecaravansite.co.uk **alanrogers.com/UK5785**

This beautifully laid out L-shaped park is for adults only and quietly situated down a non-classified road which leads to a chain bridge over the River Tweed, linking Scotland and England. The owners are very welcoming and many visitors return time and time again. The park offers 16 hardstanding touring pitches off a gravel driveway. All have electricity (16A) and fresh water. With very little noise from all but the birds this is a very tranquil site. Berwick-upon-Tweed is on the doorstep, just four miles away, and just inland you'll find Northumberland's fine sandy beaches. The park is easily accessible from both north and south of the border. Fishing is possible in the River Tweed, just across the road.

Facilities

Three unisex toilets provide washbasins and showers with underfloor heating. No dedicated facilities for disabled visitors. Coin operated washing machine and dryers. Kitchen with sink, freezer and microwave. Motorcaravan services. TV room and lounge. Trout fishing. Riverside walks. Cycle paths. WiFi (limited area). Off site: Beach, bicycle hire and golf all within 4 km. Riding 5 km. Berwick-upon-Tweed 4 miles. Holy Island, Alnwick Castle and Gardens, Hadrian's Wall and the Scottish Borders.

Open: 1 March - 30 November.

Directions

From the A1 turn off onto A698, after approximately 2 miles turn right and follow brown tourist signs for Honey Farm. From the west turn off the A698 towards Horncliffe and follow signs for Honey Farm. Site is down a narrow road before road weight and width limits apply. GPS: 55.7474, -2.10489

Charges guide

Per unit incl. 2 persons and electricity	£ 20.00 - £ 24.00

No credit cards.

For latest campsite news visit
alanrogers.com

Berwick-upon-Tweed

Ord House Country Park

East Ord, Berwick-upon-Tweed TD15 2NS (Northumberland) T: 01289 305288. E: enquiries@ordhouse.co.uk

alanrogers.com/UK5800

Ord House is a 44-acre park for 260 privately owned holiday homes and 74 touring caravan and tent pitches. The park has a very well cared for appearance throughout with well mown grass and colourful arrays of flowering bushes. Ord House itself, an 18th-century mansion, has been tastefully converted to provide a bar, lounge bar and family room. The touring pitches (all with 16A electricity, 39 also with water and drainage) are on hardstandings, in small sections, some of which are sloping. Twelve level pitches are in the more secluded walled garden, separated by shrubs. A member of the Best of British group.

Facilities

The main, modern toilet building is of excellent quality and cleanliness and can be heated. Two family bathrooms. Two rooms for disabled visitors. Laundry. Motorcaravan services. Camping shop with gas supplies. Bar, bar meals and family room. Crazy golf. Draughts. Two play areas, one for ball games. No commercial vehicles. Dogs accepted by prior arrangement. WiFi (free in clubhouse, rest of site charged). Off site: Post office stores 50 yds. from the entrance. Beach 1.5 miles. Golf 2 miles.

Open: All year.

Directions

From A1 Berwick bypass take East Ord exit and follow signs. GPS: 55.7574, -2.0297

Charges guide

Per unit incl. up to 4 persons and electricity	£ 18.50 - £ 29.00
extra person (over 5 yrs)	£ 2.50
dog	£ 1.00

Discounts for 1- and 2-man tents and for longer stays.

Durham

Strawberry Hill Caravan Park

Running Waters, Old Cassop, Durham DH6 4QA (Co. Durham) T: 01913 723457. E: info@strawberryhf.co.uk

alanrogers.com/UK5700

This park is owned and managed by Howard and Elizabeth who are experienced caravanners. They have terraced their site to offer panoramic views over the fields and woodland from all the pitches. The park is licensed to accommodate more units but the owners prefer to offer space to visitors by providing generous pitches on either grass or hardstanding. There are 30 touring pitches (with 16A electricity), including ten on hardstanding, plus a separate terrace for tents. Nature corridors and the surrounding countryside make this a haven for nature lovers.

Facilities

The single toilet block can be heated and is kept immaculately clean. Free showers. Laundry. Facilities for disabled visitors incorporating a baby care area. Small but well stocked shop in reception. Gas. Off site: Buses (Durham-Hartlepool) from entrance. Country pub with meals 1 mile. Large hypermarket 3 miles. Riding 5 miles. Park and ride (07.00-19.00) into Durham city centre operates nearby.

Open: 1 March - 30 November.

Directions

From A1M exit 61 follow signs for Peterlee. At next roundabout take first left (A688). Straight on at next roundabout then right at the next (A181). Park is 2 miles on the left as you go up a hill on a dual carriageway. GPS: 54.75239, -1.47046

Charges guide

Per unit incl. 2 persons and electricity (meter)	£ 18.00 - £ 20.00
extra person	£ 4.00

Durham

Durham Grange Caravan Club Site

Meadow Lane, Durham DH1 1TL (Co. Durham) T: 01913 844778.

alanrogers.com/UK5705

Fully refurbished and landscaped, this park offers 76 level, spacious pitches, 51 of which are hardstanding and eight fully serviced. Easy access to the A1M and the A690 make it an ideal stopover for those travelling north or south, or for visiting the historic cathedral city of Durham, the Beamish Museum and shopping at the Gateshead Metro centre. A coppice of mature trees and newly planted shrubs mask most of the road noise. The park has been redesigned with attention to detail throughout, offering pockets of privacy and a central area with picnic tables and benches.

Facilities

The single sanitary block is a heated building with free showers, hairdryers and private cubicles. Larger cubicle for families. Laundry facilities. Baby area and facilities for disabled visitors. Shop in reception with essentials; bread, milk and newspapers to order. Play park. WiFi throughout (charged). Off site: Large supermarket 2 miles. Park and ride (07.00-19.00) into Durham city centre 800 yds. Buses run from Belmont and Carville. Fishing and golf 1 mile. Bicycle hire and riding 4 miles. Beach 10 miles.

Open: All year.

Directions

From A1M exit 62 turn left for Durham city (A690). After 20 yds. turn right (across dual carriageway A690) – a safer approach for large units, and continue along A690 to next exit 2 miles and return on A690 left hand turn (signed just before A1M). GPS: 54.79545, -1.53065

Charges guide

Per person	£ 5.70 - £ 7.90
pitch incl. electricity (non-member)	£ 15.80 - £ 19.80

For latest campsite news visit

alanrogers.com

Durham

Finchale Abbey Touring Park

Finchale Abbey Farm, Brasside, Durham DH1 5SH (Co. Durham) T: 01913 866528.

E: Godricawatson@hotmail.com **alanrogers.com/UK5715**

At the end of a very narrow no-through road is the Finchale Abbey (English Heritage). This adults only park is situated alongside it with the ruins forming a scenic backdrop. It offers 43 pitches, 34 of which are hardstanding, all with 10A electricity. There are also three large, fully serviced super pitches. Privately owned mobile homes are positioned on the upper level above the touring pitches. A tarmac road within the park allows for easy access to the pitches which are off to both sides. The River Wear runs along one side of the park.

Facilities

The single, heated toilet block includes facilities for disabled visitors. All facilities are modern and very clean. Motorcaravan services. Small shop for essentials. Small café with takeaway. River fishing (permits from shop). Swimming and canoeing in the river (guests to bring own equipment). Walks in the woods and along the river bank. WiFi in reception area. Off site: Golf 800 m. The Arnison Centre (1.5 miles) has a full range of shopping facilities.

Open: All year.

Directions

From A1 exit 63, turn onto A167 for approximately 4 miles, turn left at the roundabout, towards Arnison Centre. Follow signs for Finchale Abbey from there. Please note some signs say Finchale Abbey and some say Finchale Priory (both are same). GPS: 54.818101, -1.5423

Charges guide

Per unit incl. 2 persons and electricity	£ 28.00
extra person	£ 5.00

Hexham

Causey Hill Caravan Park

Causey Hill, Hexham NE46 2JN (Northumberland) T: 01434 602834. E: causeyhill@dalyparks.co.uk **alanrogers.com/UK5805**

Causey Hill Caravan Park is situated at the top of a steep hill overlooking Hexham. It is mainly occupied by mobile homes, in excess of 100, but also offers a small touring area which is well separated above them. There are 20 hardstanding pitches for touring, all with 16A electricity and water. Plenty of grassy areas surround the pitches and trees have been recently planted. Barbecue and picnic areas are provided and walks amongst wildflowers and wildlife are possible in the woodland.

Facilities

The heated toilet block is near reception and quite a walk from the touring area. Facilities for disabled visitors (key access). Laundry room. Small play area. Woodland walks. WiFi throughout (charged). Off site: Bicycle hire, fishing and golf all within 1 mile. Restaurants, supermarkets, swimming pool and theatre in Hexham just over 1 mile. Hexham Racecourse 800 m. Hadrian's Wall 5 miles. Newcastle and The Metro Centre 20 miles. Kielder Reservoir 30 miles.

Open: March - October.

Directions

From Hexham town centre, follow the B6306 Blanchland Road to Hexham Racecourse, turn right at the sign. GPS: 54.957128, -2.118709

Charges guide

Per unit incl. 2 persons and electricity	£ 25.00

No credit cards.

Hexham

Fallowfield Dene Caravan & Camping Park

Acomb, Hexham NE46 4RP (Northumberland) T: 01434 603553. E: info@fallowfielddene.co.uk **alanrogers.com/UK5810**

Although only 2.5 miles from Hexham, Fallowfield Dene Caravan Park is very secluded, situated in mature woodland at the end of a no-through road. Set in woodland glades (formerly a Victorian lead mine), each with a Roman name (Hadrian's Wall is close), are 118 seasonal pitches and 32 touring pitches, all with 16A electricity. A further ten tent pitches have been added, suitable for smaller tents. The park entrance, with a new reception and shop, is neat, tidy and very colourful. There is no play area or games field, but the surrounding woods are a paradise for children.

Facilities

Brick built toilet blocks (one for each sex) are central and heated in cool weather. Well tiled and kept very clean, there are washbasins in cabins and free hairdryers. Separate, fully equipped room for disabled visitors. Laundry room. Baby bath. Motorcaravan services. Small shop for essentials, including gas. Small coffee car. Barrier card £5 deposit. WiFi (charged; currently in reception area with plans to extend over site). Off site: Good restaurant 5 mins. walk. Supermarkets and shops at Hexham and Corbridge.

Open: 14 March - 2 November.

Directions

From A69 Newcastle-Carlisle road, take A6079 north signed Bellingham and Rothbury. At village of Acomb, site is signed to right. Follow site signs for 1.5 miles. Then turn left down a single track road with passing places. GPS: 55.00166, -2.09470

Charges guide

Per unit incl. 2 persons and electricity	£ 17.50 - £ 18.50
extra person	£ 3.50
child (5-15 yrs)	£ 2.00
dog	£ 0.50

For latest campsite news visit
alanrogers.com

Seahouses

Seafield Caravan Park

Seahouses NE68 7SP (Northumberland) T: 01665 720628. E: info@seafieldpark.co.uk

alanrogers.com/UK5745

The park is situated just across the road from the sea with its rock pools. The park provides lodges, caravan holiday homes and apartments to rent (or buy) and pitches for just 20 touring units (no tents). All the pitches have concrete squares, water, waste, sewerage and 16A electricity (but unfortunately none have sea views). The large park is attractively landscaped with gardens, pools and a stream among the privately owned holiday homes which are set apart from those for rent. The adjacent Ocean Club's facilities include a 20 m. swimming pool and children's pool. Small gates give immediate access to Seahouses with its excellent range of shops and eating places.

Facilities

The single, heated toilet block is housed in an old building but is of the highest standard inside with controllable showers, ample changing space, hair dryers and the latest in hand dryers. Facilities for disabled visitors and a family bathroom. Baby room. Laundry area. All facilities are accessed by a code. Snack bar/takeaway. Swimming pool, children's pool, spa, steam room, sauna, fitness suite and coffee shop at adjacent Ocean Club. Play area. Bicycle hire. WiFi throughout. Trailer tents are not permitted. Off site: Immediate access to the town of Seahouses with all amenities, local transport, and various trips available from the harbour. A good beach at Bamburgh just along the coast.

Open: All year excl. 10 January - 8 February.

Directions

On entering Seahouses from the south take the road to Bamburgh and the site is on the left, just past the road down to the harbour.
GPS: 55.583162, -1.657171

Charges guide

Per unit incl. 2 persons and electricity	£ 25.00 - £ 48.00
extra person	£ 8.00
child (2-15 yrs)	£ 5.00

Stockton-on-Tees

White Water Park Caravan Club Site

Tees Barrage, Stockton-on-Tees TS18 2QW (Teeside) T: 01642 634880.

alanrogers.com/UK5740

Adjacent to the multi-million pound development at the Tees Barrage, this pleasantly landscaped Club site caters for all tastes, especially watersports enthusiasts. The Tees Barrage has transformed 11 miles of the Tees, providing clean, non-tidal water for many activities. The site itself provides 109 pitches (14 hardstanding), all with 16A electricity connections, and includes 21 fully serviced pitches set within bays and hedges (fresh water and waste disposal). This is a neat and well maintained site with good lighting and a security barrier. The adjoining White-Water Course (Britain's largest purpose-built canoe course) provides facilities for both advanced and beginner canoeists.

Facilities

The central, heated sanitary block is of a high standard and includes washbasins in cubicles, baby changing facilities and a well appointed unit for disabled visitors. Laundry room. Motorcaravan services. Shop. Fish and chip van visits most Fridays. Play area. Heated family room with TV and pool table for wet weather. WiFi throughout (charged). Off site: Supermarket nearby. Restaurant near the entrance. Retail and leisure park, just across Barrage bridge, with 14-screen cinema, 10-pin bowling, shops and fast food outlets. Fishing and bicycle hire 2 miles. Golf and riding 3 miles. North York Moors and the Hartlepool Historic Quay within 40 minutes drive.

Open: All year.

Directions

From A1(M1) take A66 for Darlington and follow until you pick up signs for Teeside Retail Park and the Tees Barrage. Cross railway bridge and the Barrage bridge, then first right to site on left in 400 yds.
GPS: 54.5684, -1.28631

Charges guide

Per person	£ 5.50 - £ 6.70
child (5-17 yrs)	£ 0.01 - £ 2.30
pitch incl. electricity (non-member)	£ 15.20 - £ 17.90

Tent campers apply to site.

For latest campsite news visit

alanrogers.com

Land of ancient myths and Celtic legends, Wales is a small and compact country boasting a diverse landscape, from lakes and mountains, rivers and valleys to beautiful coastlines and rolling wooded countryside. It offers superb opportunities for an active holiday.

Wales' biggest asset is undoubtedly its countryside, home to three National Parks that make up almost a quarter of the country's total area. Snowdonia National Park in the north combines dramatic mountain scenery with glacial valleys, lakes and streams, while in the south the Brecon Beacons boast mountains, moorlands, forests and wooded gorges with deep caves. The surrounding area of the Wye Valley, on the borders with England, is a designated Area of Outstanding Natural Beauty; as are the Gower Peninsula, the Lleyn Peninsula, the Anglesey Coast and the Clwydian Range. The endless miles of largely unspoilt and beautiful Pembrokeshire coastline in the west have some of the finest long beaches in Europe, with pretty little bays plus the lively traditional seaside resorts of Tenby and Whitesand. Further inland is the secluded and pretty Gwaun Valley. The capital of Wales, Cardiff, has many attractions, including its newly developed waterfront, the Millennium Stadium. Castles can be seen all over Wales, ranging from tiny stone keeps to huge medieval fortresses; some of the best preserved are Caernarfon, Conwy and Harlech, all built by Edward I.

Places of interest

North: Isle of Anglesey; Portmeirion Italianate village; Llandudno; Colwyn Bay; Caernarfon, Conwy and Harlech castles; Ffestiniog and Welsh Highland railways.

West: Oakwood Park, Wales' only theme park; the National Botanic Gardens at Aberglasney; Dolaucothi Goldmines; historic, stone-walled Aberaeron.

Mid: Brecon Beacons National Park; the lakes of the Elan Valley; picturesque seaside town of Barmouth; Machynlleth, 'ancient capital of Wales' and the nearby Centre for Alternative Technology.

South: Caerphilly's enormous medieval castle; Cardiff, capital of Wales; seaside resorts of Tenby and Saundersfoot; National Botanic Garden of Wales, Llanarthne.

Did you know?

The origins of the Red Dragon flag may date back to the Roman period, when the dragon was used by military cohorts.

St. David's in Pembrokeshire is Britain's smallest city by virtue of its cathedral to the patron saint of Wales.

There are many sites in Wales linked to the legend of King Arthur: Castell Dinas Brân, near Llangollen, is reputed to be the resting place of the Holy Grail.

The Welsh name for Snowdon, Yr Wyddfa, means burial place.

The Welsh ruler, Owen Glendower, was the last native Welshman to be given the title Prince of Wales in 1400.

The Welsh language is one of Europe's oldest languages and shares its roots with Breton, Gaelic and Cornish.

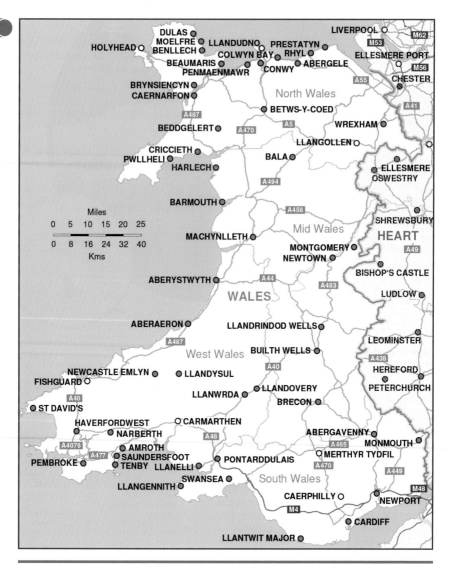

Aberaeron
Aeron Coast Caravan Park
North Road, Aberaeron SA46 0JF (Ceredigion) T: 01545 570349. E: enquiries@aeroncoast.co.uk

alanrogers.com/UK6280

Aeron Coast is a family holiday park with a wide range of recreational facilities, on the west coast of Wales. Although it has a high proportion of caravan holiday homes (200 privately owned), touring units of all types are provided for in two fields separated from the beach and sea by a high bank (although the best beach is on the south side of this traditional fishing village). Pitches are on level grass with all units regularly and well spaced in lines in traditional style. The main attraction of the park is its excellent provision for families, both in and out of doors.

Facilities

Two modern, heated toilet blocks offer excellent facilities including large family showers. Facilities for disabled visitors and babies are in one block. Basic motorcaravan service point. Heated swimming pools (1/6-15/9). Club house and bar (from Easter, 12.00-14.00 and from 19.00) with family room serving bar meals and takeaway in school holiday periods. Large entertainments room. Max. 1 dog per unit.

Open: 1 March - 31 October.

Directions

Park is on northern outskirts of Aberaeron village on A487, with entrance on the right-hand side of a petrol station. Brown signpost.
GPS: 52.2445, -4.254917

Charges guide

Per unit incl. 4 persons and electricity	£ 17.00 - £ 28.00
extra person (over 2 yrs)	£ 4.00
dog	£ 1.00

For latest campsite news visit
alanrogers.com

Abergavenny
Pont Kemys Caravan & Camping Park

Chainbridge, Abergavenny NP7 9DS (Monmouthshire) T: 01873 880688. E: info@pontkemys.com

alanrogers.com/UK5914

Pont Kemys is an attractive, peaceful touring park neatly arranged on the banks of the River Usk, only four miles from the town of the same name. There are 65 touring pitches, both on grass and with hardstanding, arranged around the perimeter of the park and within the central area. All have 16A electric hook-ups and TV connections. An adult only area provides 21 fully serviced pitches and a separate area is dedicated to tents. This is a quiet site with few amenities. Reception contains a small shop selling basic provisions, plus gas and camping supplies. The Chainbridge pub and a bar/restaurant at the local golf club are within walking distance.

Facilities	Directions
The modern sanitary block is neat and clean. Baby room. Toilet/shower for disabled visitors. Laundry room. Kitchen area with microwave. Basic provisions and camping items from reception. Gas. TV lounge. Max. 2 dogs per pitch. Separate dog walking area. WiFi (free). Off site: Pub and golf club bar/restaurant within walking distance. Golf 400 m. Fishing 4 miles. Usk 4 miles.	From Abergavenny follow one-way system (Monmouth), turn left on B4598 (do not join the A40 dual carriageway). After 4 miles turn right for Usk at Charthouse pub, then 2.5 miles to park. GPS: 51.746567, -2.946556

Open: March - October.

Charges guide

Per unit incl. 2 persons and electricity	£ 20.00
extra person	£ 4.00

Abergele
Hunters Hamlet Caravan Park

Sirior Goch Farm, Betws-yn-Rhos, Abergele LL22 8PL (Conwy) T: 01745 832237. E: huntershamlet@aol.com

alanrogers.com/UK6650

This small, family owned park is licensed for all units except tents (trailer tents are allowed). On a gently sloping hillside providing beautiful panoramic views, one area provides 15 well spaced pitches with hardstanding and 10A electricity, with access from a circular, hardcore road. An adjacent area of a similar design has 15 fully serviced super pitches (water, waste water, sewage, TV and 16A electricity). Shrubs and bushes at various stages of growth enhance both areas. A natural play area incorporating rustic adventure equipment set amongst mature beech trees with a small bubbling stream is a children's paradise. For added tranquillity, the site operates a no football policy.

Facilities	Directions
The heated toilet block has fully tiled facilities including showers en-suite with toilets for both sexes. New facilities include further showers, two wet rooms and a wet room for disabled visitors. Laundry and dishwashing, washing machine and dryer, freezer and fridge. Family bathroom (metered). Bread, milk and newspapers can be ordered. Play area. WiFi over site (free). Max. 2 dogs per pitch.	From Abergele take A548 south for almost 3 miles; turn onto B5381 towards Betws-yn-Rhos and park is on left after 0.5 miles. GPS: 53.24853, -3.60672

Open: 1 March - 31 October.

Charges guide

Per unit incl. 2 persons and electricity	£ 18.00 - £ 24.00
super pitch	£ 23.00 - £ 29.00
extra person	£ 4.00

Abergele
Ty Mawr Holiday Park

Towyn Road, Towyn, Abergele LL22 9HG (Conwy) T: 01745 832079. E: ty.mawr@park-resorts.com

alanrogers.com/UK6655

Ty Mawr Holiday Park is located close to the many attractions of the North Wales coast and the Snowdonia National Park. The Warren touring area has two modernised toilet blocks. The pool complex has an excellent indoor pool and flume with supervision and organised activities. There is some traffic noise from the road adjacent to the Meadow touring area, which is served by a portable toilet block. There is a large proportion of privately owned and rental caravan holiday homes, however this means that the site can provide extra entertainment and catering facilities for guests. Please check availability and pricing for very large units.

Facilities	Directions
Two clean, well maintained blocks, which can be heated, serve the main touring area, with prefabricated units on the open meadows. Open style washbasins, preset showers with curtain divider. Baby rooms. Spacious facilities for disabled visitors (key). Launderette. Ice pack service. Shop. Bar with meals, cafeteria and takeaway. Indoor pool. Multisports courts. Excellent play areas and children's clubs. Evening family entertainment. WiFi (free).	Take A55 westerly into North Wales and take exit 24 for Abergele. Follow signs for A548 Rhyl and Pensarn towards Towyn. Shortly after Pensarn turn right into site. GPS: 53.299980, -3.55351

Open: Mid March - end October.

Charges guide

Per unit incl. 4 persons and electricity	£ 11.00 - £ 35.00
Units over 6 m in length are charged for 2 pitches.	

For latest campsite news visit
alanrogers.com

Abergele

Plas Farm Caravan Park

Plas-yn-Betws, Betws-yn-Rhos, Abergele LL22 8AU (Conwy) T: 01492 680254.
E: info@plasfarmcaravanpark.co.uk **alanrogers.com/UK6685**

Siân and John have created an attractive and welcoming terraced site behind a former working farm. Situated on the edge of the Snowdonia National Park, Plas Farm perfectly blends the campsite into the beautiful surrounding countryside with different views afforded from each of the terraces. From the bottom terrace a woodland walk circles the site and is used as a dog walk. The 50 pitches all have 10/16A electric hook-ups and 46 are fully serviced. On a separate field there is provision for 30 tents, some with electricity. This is an ideal location for adults and children alike, with access to the beaches on the coast, and also offering opportunities for hill walking, golfing, rambling, tennis and watersports.

Facilities

Two modern toilet blocks have a mixture of cubicles and open washbasins, showers and toilets for both sexes. For disabled visitors there is a shower, toilet and washbasin. Family room with further facilities and baby changing. Laundry with washing machine, tumble dryer and ironing. Excellent kitchen facilities for campers. Motorcaravan services. Local takeaways will deliver. Play area with low-level climbing frame. WiFi over site (charged). Caravan storage. Off site: Pub within one mile of the site. Golf 1 mile. Fishing 4 miles. Beach and boat launching 5 miles.

Open: 1 March - 31 October.

Directions

Heading towards North Wales, leave A55 at exit 24 on A547 through Abergele town centre. Straight over mini-roundabout at Tesco, and next one. After 0.5 miles, turn left (Rhyd-y-Foel/Dolwen). In 3 miles at crossroads, turn left on B5381 for 0.5 miles and turn left signed Abergele and site in 200 yds. on left. Use directions not sat nav. GPS: 53.25259, -3.65084

Charges guide

Per unit incl. 2 persons and electricity	£ 17.50 - £ 19.50

Aberystwyth

Glan y Môr Leisure Park

Clarach Bay, Aberystwyth SY23 3DT (Ceredigion) T: 01970 828900. E: glanymor@sunbourne.com
alanrogers.com/UK6290

Follow the road to Clarach Bay and on the seafront is Glan y Môr, a busy, holiday-style park with an enviable situation. On a wet day you may not wish to go far with the comprehensive leisure centre on site – it is open eight months of the year with reduced entry fee for campers. Although the balance of pitches is very much in favour of caravan holiday homes (3:1) which dominate the open park and bay, there are 150 touring pitches, 46 with 10A electricity and four new super pitches. They are rather small and are pressed together in two small sections on the lower part of the park.

Facilities

One heated toilet block on the lower touring area has dishwashing and laundry plus a WC for disabled guests. A suite including shower for disabled visitors is on the upper static site, with further facilities at the leisure centre (Radar key). Motorcaravan services. Gas. Supermarket. Fun Factory. Play area for younger children. Large sports field. Swimming pool. Licensed restaurant and takeaway (from Easter). Dog walk. WiFi over site (charge).

Open: 1 March - 31 October.

Directions

Clarach is signed west from A487 (Aberystwyth-Machynlleth) in village of Bow Street (narrow bridge). Follow signs over crossroads to beach and park. Access for caravans from Aberystwyth on B4572 is difficult. GPS: 52.43625, -4.08025

Charges guide

Per unit incl. up to 6 persons and electricity	£ 15.00 - £ 32.00

Amroth

Pantglas Farm Caravan Park

Tavernspite, Pembrokeshire, Amroth SA34 0NS (Pembrokeshire) T: 01834 831618.
E: pantglasfarm@btinternet.com **alanrogers.com/UK5974**

A secluded, rural, family run park with a nice atmosphere and new owners, Pantglas Farm is four miles from the coast with extensive views over rolling countryside and down to the sea. Set in three gently sloping paddocks spread over 14 acres, there are 83 generously sized, fairly level touring pitches, all with 10A electricity and on gravel hardstanding. A further three fields, without electricity, are reserved for tents. This is a popular and attractive site close to main resorts but with a more tranquil atmosphere.

Facilities

Two toilet blocks (one can be heated) include large controllable showers and some washbasins in cubicles. Facilities for disabled campers. Laundry. Gas. Battery charging and freezer pack services (free). Licensed clubhouse (evenings only every day for B.Hs and peak season, weekends only low season). Playground. Games field. Games room. TV lounge. Dog exercise area. WiFi over site (charged). Caravan and boat storage.

Open: 27 March - 31 October.

Directions

Site is 3 miles southwest of Whitland. From A477 Tenby-Pembroke road turn right at Red Roses crossroads to Tavernspite for 1.25 miles. At the village pump take the middle road and site is 0.5 miles on left. GPS: 51.778317, -4.645417

Charges guide

Per unit incl. 2 persons and electricity	£ 22.00 - £ 24.00
extra person	£ 3.00

For latest campsite news visit
alanrogers.com

Bala
Pen-y-Bont Touring & Camping Park
Llangynog Road, Bala LL23 7PH (Gwynedd) T: 01678 520549. E: penybont-bala@btconnect.co.uk
alanrogers.com/UK6340

This is a pretty little park with 59 touring pitches, 47 of which have hardstanding. Connected by circular gravel roads, they are intermingled with trees and tall trees edge the site. Electricity connections (16A) are available, including 11 for tents, and there are 28 serviced pitches with hardstanding, electricity, water and drainage. There are also pitches for 25 seasonal units. The park entrance and the stone building that houses reception and the shop provide quite a smart image. With views of the Berwyn mountains, Pen-y-bont has a peaceful, attractive and useful location being the closest park to Bala town.

Facilities
The toilet block includes washbasins in cubicles and spacious hot showers. Two new cubicles with washbasin and WC. Separate laundry room and an en-suite unit for disabled visitors that doubles as a baby room, operated by key (£5 deposit). Motorcaravan services. Shop. Bicycle hire arranged. Caravan storage. WiFi (charged). Romany-style caravans for rent. Off site: Fishing 200 yds.

Open: 15 March - 27 October.

Directions
Park is 0.5 miles southeast of Bala village on the B4391. Bala is between Dolgellau and Corwen on the A494. GPS: 52.901717, -3.590117

Charges guide
Per unit incl. 2 persons and electricity	£ 22.00 - £ 24.00
tent pitch incl. 2 persons	£ 16.00 - £ 20.00
extra person	£ 7.50

Bala
Glanllyn Lakeside Caravan & Camping Park
Llanuwchllyn, Bala LL23 7ST (Gwynedd) T: 01678 540227. E: info@glanllyn.com
alanrogers.com/UK6345

This spacious 16-acre site lying alongside the southern end of Bala lake has its own small beach and boat launching area. The site is in a grassy, parkland setting, fairly open and reasonably level, but with natural terraces. There are 204 pitches, with 50 for seasonal units and 154 for touring; 150 have 10A electricity hook-up and there are 19 on hardstandings. A hardstanding area by the beach is a favourite with motorcaravanners. Many pitches have views of the lake or the surrounding hills.

Facilities
Three modern sanitary blocks (one heated) are fully equipped and have facilities for babies and disabled campers. Motorcaravan services. Small, well stocked shop. Gas supplies. Good, fenced play area by entrance. Lake swimming, fishing and small boat launching (permit). Only 1 dog per pitch. Breathable groundsheets only and only for min. 3-day stay. Off site: Bus stops outside gate. Ideal for exploring the southern part of Snowdonia National Park. Indoor swimming pool and golf 3 miles. Small steam train along lakeside. Riding 18 miles.

Open: Easter - mid October.

Directions
From Bala take A494 southwest towards Dolgellau for 3 miles, entrance on left, on right-hand bend. GPS: 52.877667, -3.64665

Charges guide
Per unit incl. 2 persons and electricity	£ 22.00 - £ 30.00
tent pitch incl. 2 persons	£ 16.00 - £ 36.00
extra person	£ 7.00
child (4-16 yrs)	£ 4.00
dog (max. 1)	£ 2.00

Barmouth
Hendre Mynach Touring Caravan & Camping Park
Llanaber, Barmouth LL42 1YR (Gwynedd) T: 01341 280262. E: info@hendremynach.co.uk
alanrogers.com/UK6370

A large family park, stretching out along the beach on the outskirts of Barmouth. Colourful flowers brighten the steep entrance to this site (help is available to get out if you are worried). Of the 240 pitches, all for touring, 60 are on hardstanding with 10A electricity and 39 are fully serviced. The beach is only 200 yards away but is separated from the park by a railway line. It can be crossed by pedestrian operated gates, which could be a worry for those with young children.

Facilities
Two traditional toilet blocks offer adequate facilities for the whole family, including those for disabled campers (a long way from some pitches). Motorcaravan services. Small shop (Easter-1/11). Play area. WiFi (charged). Off site: Beach 200 yds. Fishing 300 yds. Boat launching 1 mile. Riding 5 miles. Golf 9 miles.

Open: 1 March - 8 January.

Directions
Park is off the A496 road north of Barmouth. Entrance is on left down a steep drive. GPS: 52.73300, -4.06618

Charges guide
Per unit incl. 2 persons and electricity	£ 19.00 - £ 32.00
extra person	£ 4.00
child (2-14 yrs)	£ 2.00
dog	free

For latest campsite news visit
alanrogers.com

Barmouth

Trawsdir Touring Caravans & Camping Park

Llanaber, Barmouth LL42 1RR (Gwynedd) T: 01341 280999. E: enquiries@trawsdir.co.uk

alanrogers.com/UK6380

With sea views from almost every pitch and with a backdrop of hills, this campsite has something for everyone, young and old alike. Entrance and exit via the site barrier and access to the facilities are by a key fob. A well equipped children's play area with safety surface is close to reception. Of the 142 touring pitches, 70 are for tents (48 with electricity) while the remaining 72 are fully serviced and can take RVs. The campsite has a large dog walking field and from the corner of the site is a lit walk to the Wayside Inn, avoiding the main road. A member of the Best of British group.

Facilities

Two toilet blocks are equipped to a very high standard, however one is kept in reserve for when cleaning is being done, except at the busiest times. Facilities for disabled visitors with good access (Radar key). Baby changing in both male and female toilets. Fully equipped laundry. Shop. Playground. WiFi (charged). Off site: Pub 5 mins. walk. Sea fishing trips from Barmouth. Golf at Royal St Davids Golf Club is 20 minutes away in Harlech. A private beach is available at sister site across the road.

Open: 1 March - 6 January.

Directions

From Barmouth follow signs for Harlech (do not take beach road), pass through the town. After town, pass church, up the hill and leave the 40 mph speed limit. Pass Caerddaniel Holiday Park and Wayside Inn. Trawsdir entrance is just beyond on right hand side. GPS: 52.749871, -4.080361

Charges guide

Per unit incl. 4 persons and electricity	£ 18.00 - £ 38.00

Barmouth

Islawrffordd Caravan Park

Talybont, Barmouth LL43 2AQ (Gwynedd) T: 01341 247269. E: info@islawrffordd.co.uk

alanrogers.com/UK6385

If you like to park up and have all amenities within easy access, then this site is ideal. Family owned and run since being established in 1957, Islawrffordd Caravan Park offers the very best in quality, which is evident as you enter the park. There are 75 fully serviced touring pitches (some seasonal) and 30 tent pitches. The fully serviced pitches all have courtesy light, electricity, fresh and waste water points and chemical disposal. The site has private access to a sandy beach with slipway launching for small boats.

Facilities

The immaculate, modern toilet facilities have underfloor heating and climate control, a toilet for disabled visitors (Radar key) and baby changing room. Launderette. The toilet block and the entrance and exit of the park are activated by a key fob (deposit required). Well stocked minimarket. Bar/restaurant and takeaway. Indoor swimming pool with sauna, jacuzzi and tanning suite. Fully equipped playground with safety surface. WiFi over site (charged). Off site: Sea fishing trips from Barmouth. Golf at Royal St Davids Golf Club, Harlech 15 mins away.

Open: All year.

Directions

Approximately four miles north of Barmouth, turn off the main A496 on to Fford Glan Môr Road, over a narrow railway bridge, past the Talybont Railway Halt and neighbouring campsites. The park is almost at the end and is signed to the left. GPS: 52.772491, -4.100299

Charges guide

Per serviced pitch incl. 5 persons	£ 36.00
tent pitch incl. up to 5 persons	£ 29.50
dog	£ 2.00

Beaumaris

Kingsbridge Caravan & Camping Park

Camp Road, Llanfaes, Beaumaris LL58 8LR (Isle of Anglesey) T: 01248 490636.
E: info@kingsbridgecaravanpark.co.uk **alanrogers.com/UK6633**

Family owned and run, Kingsbridge is a haven for nature lovers and within easy reach of several beaches. It has both family and adult only areas to take full advantage of the spacious 14-acre site, and being in an Area of Outstanding Natural Beauty, there are many opportunities to observe wildlife, including owls and woodpeckers. Of the 90 level or gently sloping pitches, 55 are for tourers (all 10A electricity) and 35 for tents. Twenty-five hardstandings are included in the touring pitches and two mobile homes are available to rent.

Facilities

Two modern, clean, heated sanitary units serve the two touring areas and have controllable hot showers, some private cabins and baby room. No designated facilities for disabled visitors but access is good. Motorcaravan services (by arrangement with reception). Shop with basics, beach items and essential caravan accessories. Play area. Torches essential. WiFi (charged). Off site: Golf and fishing 1 mile. Beaumaris Castle 2 miles.

Open: 1 March - 31 October.

Directions

From Menai Bridge town, take A545 to Beaumaris, past castle and following coast road B5109. At crossroads (1.7 miles) on edge of Langoed take left turn (Kingsbridge). Site is 400 yds. down single track lane (arrive after 13.00). GPS: 53.28456, -4.09271

Charges guide

Per unit incl. 2 persons and electricity	£ 23.00 - £ 35.00
extra person	£ 5.00

For latest campsite news visit
alanrogers.com

Beddgelert
Camping in the Forest Beddgelert
Caernarfon Road, Beddgelert LL55 4UU (Gwynedd) T: 01766 890288. E: info@forestholidays.co.uk

alanrogers.com/UK6590

Camping in the Forest is a partnership between the Forestry Commission and The Camping and Caravanning Club. This spacious site is in the heart of Snowdonia, set in a marvellous, natural, wooded environment on the slopes of Snowdon. The 204 slightly sloping pitches are naturally laid out in clearings in the woods. There are 100 for caravans and motorcaravans and 104 for tents. The former are on hardstandings, well shaded and all have 10/16A electricity. The tent pitches are more open, in grassy glades, but only six have 6A electricity. Rock pegs are advised. No mobile phone signal.

Facilities

Two modern, fully equipped toilet blocks have all necessary facilities, including those for babies and disabled campers. Clothes drying lockers (charged). Motorcaravan services. Well stocked shop. Well equipped adventure playground. Log cabin common room. Off site: Pubs, shops and restaurants in Beddgelert 1 mile. Bicycle hire 1 mile.

Open: All year.

Directions

Site is clearly signed off A4085 to the left 1 mile northwest of Beddgelert on the A4085 Caernarfon road. GPS: 53.02075, -4.119767

Charges guide

Per unit incl. 2 persons and electrcity	£ 13.50 - £ 25.50
extra person	£ 4.00 - £ 8.00

Benllech
Penrhos Caravan Club Site
Brynteg, Benllech LL78 7JH (Isle of Anglesey) T: 01248 852617.

alanrogers.com/UK6634

Penrhos is a busy classical Caravan Club Site in a parkland setting in the beautiful and peaceful countryside on the island of Anglesey, yet only two miles from the small seaside resort of Benllech. The site is on a hillside surrounded by trees, though most pitches have little shade. There are 89 good sized, slightly sloping pitches, all for touring and with 16A electricity. Fifty-two pitches are on hardstandings and 32 are on grass. Tents are not accepted here. Advanced booking is advised, particularly for those with large outfits.

Facilities

Very clean, heated toilet block has all necessary facilities, but is dated and due for refurbishment. Washbasins in cubicles, controllable showers, baby bath with taps. En-suite unit for disabled visitors. Laundry. Basic shop with lending library. Large gated field for sports. Play area. Football and basketball. WiFi over site (charged). Off site: Fishing and seaside resort of Benllech 2 miles. Many walks including coastal paths, cycle tracks, beaches. Zoo, model village, gardens, museums, castles and nature reserves. Golf and riding 1 mile. Bus stop.

Open: 27 March - 12 October.

Directions

Leave A55 Chester-Anglesey road at exit 8, just after crossing the Menai Strait. Turn right, take A5025 through Benllech. About 1 mile after Benllech turn left B5110, signed Llangefni. Site on right just beyond Brynteg. B5108 not advised. GPS: 53.31241, -4.27062

Charges guide

Per person	£ 5.20 - £ 7.20
child (5-17 yrs)	£ 1.40 - £ 2.40
pitch incl. electricity (non-member)	£ 16.00 - £ 19.20

Benllech
Plas Uchaf Caravan & Camping Park
Benllech Bay, Benllech LL74 8NU (Isle of Anglesey) T: 01407 763012.

alanrogers.com/UK6636

This spacious, family run campsite is set in 16 acres of flat, well mown grass with 12 hardstandings. A separate area for 60 tents is provided. Within the park there are woodland walks and a play route for children to explore, an attractive play area with robust play equipment and a dog walk. All in an open, rural setting this park offers a safe haven for young families to enjoy. The pitches are set around the perimeter of six individual areas, each with picnic tables for communal use and all 80 touring pitches offer electricity (10/16A) and a water supply. Motorcaravans over 26 ft. are not accepted. Large outfits are advised to phone in advance.

Facilities

Four clean, traditional style sanitary blocks (1 new for 2015) have separate facilities for men and women, with hot showers (charged), open style washbasins, hairdryers and small baths. Baby changing. Facilities for disabled visitors in new block. Limited laundry. Large playing field, play equipment and dog walk. Freezer facilities.

Open: 14 March - 14 October.

Directions

From the Britannia Bridge take the A5025. In Benllech turn left onto the B5108. After the fire station on left, turn first right and the park is signed. GPS: 53.32676, -4.23956

Charges guide

Per unit incl. 2 persons and electricity	£ 18.00 - £ 22.00
No credit cards.	

For latest campsite news visit
alanrogers.com

Betws-y-Coed
Riverside Touring Park
Old Church Road, Betws-y-Coed LL24 0AL (Gwynedd) T: 01690 710310. E: riverside@morris-leisure.co.uk
alanrogers.com/UK6615

This is a delightful, peaceful, eight-acre caravan park owned and operated by the Morris Leisure Group. It is set just a few minutes' walk away from the beautiful village of Betws-y-Coed, a perfect location to visit the stunning Snowdonia National Park. Betws-y-Coed is widely acclaimed as one of the most attractive villages in Great Britain. There are a total of 120 spacious pitches, 61 for mobile homes and 59 for tourers (all hardstanding; 45 are super pitches and there are a few grass tent pitches). All have 16A electricity and digital TV. The area has something for everyone – sportsmen, anglers, walkers, nature lovers and families. Listen for the owls hunting at night.

Facilities

The heated sanitary block (key access) has walk-in style shower cubicles. Separate cubicles with WCs for men and similar for women. Facilities for children and disabled visitors. Washing machine and dryer. Dishwashing sinks. Motorcaravan services. Digital TV booster system. Dog walk (max. 2 per unit). No arrivals before 13.00. Gazebos are not allowed. Off site: Supermarket in village.

Open: 17 February - 3 January.

Directions

From southeast turn right off A5 (Llangollen-Betws-y-Coed) in Betws village and follow signs Riverside, Railway Museum. Site entrance on left just after railway station. GPS: 53.093264, -3.799234

Charges guide

Per unit incl. 2 persons	
and electricity	£ 25.20 - £ 28.30
extra person	£ 7.50 - £ 7.90

Brecon
Pencelli Castle Caravan & Camping Park
Pencelli, Brecon LD3 7LX (Powys) T: 01874 665451. E: pencelli@tiscali.co.uk
alanrogers.com/UK6040

This high quality park is on the edge of Pencelli village. Set in the grounds of an old castle amidst the Brecon scenery, the park has both atmosphere and character. It offers excellent facilities in peaceful, rural tranquillity. The owners, Liz and Gerwyn Rees, have retained the country charm but have added an all-embracing range of spacious, heated, luxury facilities, attractively enhanced by potted plants etc. There are three touring fields housing 80 pitches, half with electricity (16A); The Orchard has some fully serviced pitches with hardstanding, amongst shrubs, fruit trees and a stone cider mill; The Oaks takes a mixture of motorcaravans, caravans and tents, and The Meadow is for tents only (with boot and bike wash). The park is bordered by majestic trees and the Monmouthshire and Brecon Canal.

Facilities

The toilet block is very well designed and includes some private cubicles, two large fully equipped rooms for families and disabled visitors with double showers, baby changing and bath facilities, all humorously decorated for the young at heart. Laundry. Drying room with lockers. Information room. Indoor dishwashing and food room. Motorcaravan services. Small shop (basics). Playground. Bicycle hire. Assistance dogs only. WiFi over site (free).

Open: 15 February - 27 November.

Directions

From A40 south after Brecon bypass take B4558 at signs for Llanfrynach then Pencelli (narrow bridge). If travelling north on A40, approach via Tal-y-Bont. Site at south end of Pencelli. GPS: 51.914783, -3.317867

Charges guide

Per unit incl. 2 persons	
and electricity	£ 23.20 - £ 28.80
extra person	£ 7.35 - £ 8.40

Brynsiencyn
Fron Caravan & Camping Park
Brynsiencyn, Anglesey LL61 6TX (Isle of Anglesey) T: 01248 430310. E: mail@froncaravanpark.co.uk
alanrogers.com/UK6635

A traditional, all touring campsite in a peaceful rural location, Fron has panoramic views over the surrounding countryside. From the entrance gate, a tarmac drive passes through a two-acre, level, grassy paddock, which is reserved for 35 large sized tent and trailer tent pitches. The drive leads up to the old farmhouse which houses reception, a well stocked shop and plenty of tourist information. Behind the farmhouse is another two-acre, sloping paddock with 40 caravan and motorcaravan pitches, 19 with hardstandings, and 57 electricity hook-ups (10A).

Facilities

Toilet facilities are in three units of varying ages and designs located at both sides of the farmhouse. These include a unit for ladies with some washbasins in cubicles, good hot showers (40p), hairdryers, a baby area and a suite for disabled campers. Laundry. Motorcaravan services. Heated swimming pool (30x14 ft; May-Sept). Playground. Gas. Max. 2 dogs per pitch. Torches useful.

Open: Easter/1 April - end September.

Directions

Cross Britannia Bridge, take 1st slip road (A4080), then next left (Newborough). Continue on A4080 for 5 miles, turning right in village at Groeslon Hotel. Continue through Brynsiencyn for 1 mile to site at western end of village. GPS: 53.17693, -4.28944

Charges guide

Per unit incl. 2 persons and 2 children	£ 25.00
extra person	£ 6.00

For latest campsite news visit
alanrogers.com

Builth Wells

Fforest Fields Caravan & Camping Park

Hundred House, Builth Wells LD1 5RT (Powys) T: 01982 570406. E: office@fforestfields.co.uk
alanrogers.com/UK6320

This secluded park is set on a family hill farm within seven acres in the heart of Radnorshire. This is simple country camping and caravanning at its best, with no clubhouse, swimming pool or games room. The facilities include 80 large pitches on level grass on a spacious and peaceful, carefully landscaped field by a stream. Electrical connections (6-16A) are available and there are 17 hardstanding pitches, also with electricity. Several additional areas without electricity are provided for tents. There are two new lakes, one for boating and fly fishing, the other for coarse fishing.

Facilities

The toilet block is spotlessly clean and has underfloor heating, family rooms, drying rooms, laundry and spacious controllable showers. Reception stocks essentials. Room for campers with fridges and freezers, microwave, table and chairs. Fishing. Torches are useful. Free WiFi over site. Off site: Pub at Hundred House village 1 mile. Bicycle hire and golf 5 miles. Riding 7 miles.

Open: 1 March - 3 January.

Directions

Park is 4 miles east of Builth Wells near the village of Hundred House on A481. Follow brown signs. Do not use postcode on sat nav. GPS: 52.17121, -3.31621

Charges guide

Per unit incl. 2 persons and electricity	£ 15.00 - £ 24.00
extra person (over 3 yrs)	£ 1.00 - £ 3.00
dog (max. 2)	free

Discounted low season rates for senior citizens. No credit cards.

Caernarfon

Bryn Gloch Caravan & Camping Park

Betws Garmon, Caernarfon LL54 7YY (Gwynedd) T: 01286 650216. E: eurig@bryngloch.co.uk
alanrogers.com/UK6600

Bryn Gloch is a tranquil, well maintained, family owned touring park in the impressive Snowdonia area. An unusual feature is the mountain railway which runs along one side of the park. Six flat, spacious meadows accommodate 231 units and afford some breathtaking views of the surrounding landscape. Tarmac access roads serve 151 touring pitches with 131 having hardstandings, 10A electricity, water and drainage. In addition, there are four caravan holiday homes and 24 serviced pitches for tents. The park has a barbecue and picnic area, a children's play area, and a large field for ball games, dog walks and fishing borders the river. Tourist information is provided in the complex by the reception/shop and the park is very popular with walkers and cyclists. Caernarfon, with its famous castle, is five miles away. This is a beautiful site with the mountains and lakes surrounding you and the seaside just a short drive away. It offers convenient access to the leisure and outdoor activities of this Area of Outstanding Natural Beauty. There are many walks possible to access the nearby peaks.

Facilities

Two very clean, modern main toilet blocks include washbasins in cabins, large showers, a heated family bathroom (hot water £1), baby room and complete facilities for visitors with disabilities (coded access). The far field has a prefabricated unit containing all facilities, for use in peak season. Well equipped laundry and separate drying room. Motorcaravan services and car wash. Shop (1/3-31/10). TV and games rooms with computer and pool tables. Minigolf. Entrance barrier (code). WiFi throughout (free). Dog walks. Off site: Pub 1 mile. Riding 2.5 miles. ATM at garage in Ceathro 3 miles. Bicycle hire and golf 5 miles.

Open: All year, limited facilities 1/11 - 28/2.

Directions

From Caernarfon take A4085 signed Beddgelert. Park is just beyond Waunfawr, 5.6 miles southeast of Caernarfon. After crossing river bridge, the entrance is immediately on the right, opposite St Garmon church. GPS: 53.09513, -4.18802

Charges guide

Per unit incl. 2 persons and electricity	£ 19.00 - £ 31.00
extra person	£ 4.00
child (3-16 yrs)	£ 2.00
dog (max. 2)	£ 2.00

For latest campsite news visit
alanrogers.com

Caernarfon

Tafarn Snowdonia Parc Brewpub & Campsite

Waunfawr, Caernarfon LL55 4AQ (Gwynedd) T: 01286 650409. E: info@snowdonia-park.co.uk

alanrogers.com/UK6605

Set on the banks of the River Gwyrfai and amongst spectacular scenery, this no-frills campsite is adjacent to the station for the Welsh Highland Railway. There are 32 grass pitches of varying sizes, 20 with 16A electricity). They are set in an open field and serviced by two clean sanitary blocks. You can enjoy riverside walks and free fishing (licence required) before calling in at the adjoining pub with its own microbrewery (listed in the CAMRA Good Beer Guide) and home cooked food. Children are well catered for with a family room in the pub, two gardens (one safe for toddlers) and a playground.

Facilities

One small toilet block in main camping field. A second block with separate showers and toilets for men and ladies, together with laundry facilities, is reached via a footbridge over the railway track. Both have been upgraded, but may become stretched when site is full. Full bar, restaurant and takeaway facilities. TV. Games room. Playground. Free fishing (licence required). Off site: Riding 800 yds. Golf 3 miles. Beach 5 miles.

Open: All year.

Directions

From Caernarfon take the A4085 for 4 miles and campsite is on the left. The entrance is at the far end of pub/railway station car park. GPS: 53.10611, -4.20176

Charges guide

Per unit incl. 2 persons and electricity	£ 22.00
extra person	£ 4.00
child	free

Caernarfon

Plas Gwyn Caravan & Camping Park

Llanrug, Caernarfon LL55 2AQ (Gwynedd) T: 01286 672619. E: info@plasgwyn.co.uk

alanrogers.com/UK6620

In a beautiful location, this traditional, family run touring site is within the grounds of a house that was built in 1785 in the Georgian style with a colonial style veranda. The 30 touring caravan pitches are set around the perimeter of a slightly sloping grass field and there are eight hardstandings for motorcaravans. There are 36 pitches with 16A electricity hook-ups, of which 17 also provide water and waste water. A separate tent field has ten pitches. Two 'timber tents' offer a touch of luxury camping. Please note there is minimal site lighting on the caravan field and none on the tent field, so a torch is handy. A separate field houses holiday caravans to rent. A member of the Countryside Discovery group.

Facilities

A new sanitary block opened in 2015 equipped with free hot showers and dishwashing sinks. Good laundry room (by reception). Drive-over motorcaravan service point. Gas stocked. Reception stocks basic food items, etc. Breakfast 'butties' made to order and delivered. WiFi. Off site: Golf 1 mile. Llanberis and Snowdon Mountain Railway 2.5 miles. Riding 2.5 miles. Bicycle hire 3 miles.

Open: 1 March - 31 October.

Directions

Site is on A4086, 3 miles from Caernarfon, and 2.5 miles from Llanberis, well signed with easy access. GPS: 53.146733, -4.212233

Charges guide

Per unit incl. 2 persons and electricity	£ 17.50 - £ 21.00
extra person	£ 3.00
child (0-15 yrs acc. to age)	£ 1.00 - £ 2.50

Cardiff

Cardiff Caravan Park

Pontcanna Fields, via Sophia Close, Cardiff CF11 9XR (Cardiff) T: 02920 398362. E: cardiffcaravanpark@cardiff.gov.uk **alanrogers.com/UK5925**

Run by the city council, this popular site is set within acres of parkland, one mile from the city centre, ideal for visiting the many attractions of the city of Cardiff. The campsite has 61 touring pitches which are on a fairly open area, with 43 on a grasscrete surface with 16A electric hook-ups, the remainder are on grass. There is a public right of way through the site. Security is good with an on-site warden 24 hours a day, and security cameras (infrared) constantly scanning the whole area. Large units should phone ahead to arrange for access.

Facilities

Two heated buildings each with key code entry systems, the one by reception has a laundry with washer and dryer, and facilities for disabled campers. Both have controllable hot showers. Café near reception run by Pedal Power (a cycling charity). Baby facilities. Bicycle hire (the site specialises in bicycles adapted for disabled visitors). Riding can be arranged. Off site: The Millennium Stadium, Glamorgan County Cricket Ground, Cardiff Bay. Local shops and services within easy walking distance.

Open: All year.

Directions

From A48 turn south on A4119 (Cardiff Road). Pass church on left following signs for SWALEC Stadium and at next traffic lights turn onto Sophia Close and Gardens. Turn left at Institute of Sport and pass County Cricket Ground on right. Continue along avenue to site on left. GPS: 51.49155, -3.20313

Charges guide

Per unit incl. 2 persons and electricity	£ 30.00
extra person	£ 6.00
child	£ 2.00
dog	£ 1.00

For latest campsite news visit
alanrogers.com

Colwyn Bay

Bron-Y-Wendon Touring Caravan Park

Wern Road, Llanddulas, Colwyn Bay LL22 8HG (Conwy) T: 01492 512903.
E: stay@northwales-holidays.co.uk **alanrogers.com/UK6690**

Bron-Y-Wendon is right by the sea between Abergele and Colwyn Bay on the beautiful North Wales coast. This is a quiet park which, by its own admission, is not really geared up for the family unit – there is no playground here, although there is a games room with table tennis and a TV. The park is maintained to the highest standards and caters for a large number of seasonal caravans on pitches with gravel bases which are kept very tidy. There are a further 65 grass based, and 85 hardstanding, touring pitches, all with 16A electricity and tarmac access roads; 75 also with water and waste water. All pitches have coastal views and the beach is just a short walk away. Trailer tents are accepted but not other tents.

Facilities

Two main toilet blocks, both with heating, provide excellent facilities including three shower blocks, separate from the toilets and washbasins. Third smaller, but roomier, shower block with underfloor heating. Good facilities for disabled visitors. Laundry with washing machines and dryers. Mobile shop visits daily. Gas supplies. WiFi (charged). Access to coastal cycle paths. Off site: Llanddulas village with shops and several good pubs is very close. Fishing 1 mile. Golf 4 miles.

Open: All year.

Directions

From A55 Chester-Conwy road turn at Llanddulas interchange (A547), exit 23. Turn right opposite Shell garage and park is 400 yds, signed on coast side of the road. GPS: 53.29142, -3.64656

Charges guide

Per unit incl. 2 persons	
and electricity	£ 21.00 - £ 25.00
extra person	£ 2.00 - £ 3.00
child (2-12 yrs)	£ 1.00 - £ 2.00

Conwy

Bron Derw Touring Park

Llanrwst, Conwy LL26 0YT (Conwy) T: 01492 640494. E: info@bronderw-wales.co.uk
alanrogers.com/UK6644

Nestling between the mountains and the edge of the small village of Llanrwst, Bron Derw has two camping areas, one for adults only and one for families. The 43 pitches (all with 16A electricity) are well spaced on hardstandings around the edge of the site, giving a feeling of spaciousness which matches the surrounding countryside. It is a family run site and this shows in the level of service and welcome which is received. Larger outfits can be accommodated but it is advisable to phone ahead to make sure an adequate pitch is available.

Facilities

Two very modern and well apportioned blocks, one in each area. The adults only block has high quality fittings. The other block was refurbished at the same time. Both have facilities for disabled visitors and laundry facilities at the rear. Motorcaravan services. Utility room. Public telephone. WiFi. Off site: Within the Snowdonia National Park and only 20 mins. drive to the coastal resorts of North Wales. Fishing within 1 mile.

Open: 1 March - 31 October.

Directions

From coast follow A55 on to A470 for Betws-y-Coed and Llanrwst, in Llanrwst turn left into Parry Road then left again at T-junction. Take first farm entrance on the right signed Bron Derw and continue up drive to campsite. GPS: 53.143639, -3.797126

Charges guide

Per unit incl. 2 persons	
and electricity	£ 21.00 - £ 23.00
extra person	£ 4.00

Criccieth

Llanystumdwy Camping & Caravanning Club Site

Tyddyn Sianel, Llanystumdwy, Criccieth LL52 0LS (Gwynedd) T: 01766 522855.
alanrogers.com/UK6580

Overlooking mountains and sea, Llanystumdwy is one of the earliest Camping and Caravanning Club sites. It is an attractive, sloping site with well manicured grass areas surrounded by trees and with good facilities. The wardens are very helpful and know their site and can advise on the most suitable pitch and even have a supply of chocks. There are 70 pitches in total (20 ft. spacing), 45 with 10A electricity connections, spaced over two hedged fields with caravans in the top field and four hardstandings for motorcaravans, while tents are sited lower down (some road noise can be heard here). Most pitches are sloping so chocks are recommended. A small library with tourist information is by the small reception.

Facilities

A purpose built toilet block to one side includes excellent, full facilities for disabled visitors including access ramp, one washbasin each in a cubicle for male and female and extra large sinks. Facilities for babies. Laundry (taps with fitting for disabled campers). Gas supplies. WiFi over site (charged). Off site: Riding and fishing 0.5 miles.

Open: 24 March - 3 October.

Directions

Follow A497 from Criccieth west and take second right to Llanystumdwy. Site is on the right. GPS: 52.920867, -4.27885

Charges guide

Per unit incl. 2 persons	
and electricity	£ 16.90 - £ 28.70

Non-member prices are higher.

For latest campsite news visit
alanrogers.com

Dulas

Tyddyn Isaf Caravan & Camping Park

Lligwy Bay, Dulas LL70 9PQ (Isle of Anglesey) T: 01248 410203.

alanrogers.com/UK6637

This warm, welcoming family site cascades down the hillside from the bar/restaurant at the top of the site to the beach. The site has had the same owners for over 40 years. Lligwy Bay, with its sandy beach and sheltered waters, is ideal for children to play on and is accessible from the site. There are 80 touring pitches (of which 40 are seasonal) all with 16A electricity. The tent pitches (some with 10A electricity) are on separate fields. Children are catered for with a play area arranged neatly on one of the slopes which make up the site. The site has been influenced by the clientèle who have visited over the years. The owners insist that all visitors are escorted to their pitch and, if required, helped with siting.

Facilities

Two toilet blocks with free electric showers (timed; activated by a key-fob) and hairdryers. Dishwashing sinks with plenty of hot water. Laundry room with washing machine and tumble dryer in lower toilet block. The upper toilet block can be overstretched in peak times. A third toilet block is next to the bar. Shop selling basics. Bar serving snacks and main meals, takeaway (mid May-mid Sept). WiFi (free). Off site: Golf is a short drive away. Sea and freshwater fishing. Numerous cycle paths and walks including the coastal walk to Moelfre.

Open: 20 March - 30 September.

Directions

From A55 drive over Britannia bridge onto Anglesey. Look for turning for Benllech and Amlwch. Drive to roundabout and follow A5025 through Pentraeth then Benllech, at 2nd roundabout turn left. Continue to Brynrefail and turn right opposite gift shop and follow signs for Tyddyn Isaf, half a mile down short narrow lane. GPS: 53.3625, -4.27545

Charges guide

Per unit incl. 2 adults, 2 children and electricity	£ 23.00 - £ 31.00

No credit cards.

Harlech

Barcdy Caravan & Camping Park

Talsarnau, Harlech LL47 6YG (Gwynedd) T: 01766 770736. E: anwen@barcdy.co.uk

alanrogers.com/UK6350

Barcdy is partly in a sheltered vale, partly on a plateau top and partly in open fields edged by woods. There are fells to the rear and marvellous views across the Lleyn peninsula in one direction and towards the Snowdon range in another. The Roberts family opened to their first visitors over 60 years ago and still welcome them today. The park provides for all tastes with level or sloping grass pitches, either secluded in the valley or enjoying the view from the plateau or the lower field. There are 110 pitches in total, including 40 fully serviced for touring caravans with electricity (10/16A) and 40 for tents, eleven with 10A electricity, plus 30 caravan holiday homes. A member of the Countryside Discovery group.

Facilities

Two toilet blocks, the one at the top of the valley opened at weekends and in high season, include spacious showers, that open direct to the outside. Two family shower rooms at each block, one for each sex. Hot water is free to the washbasins, dishwashing sinks and showers. WiFi over site (charged). Dogs are not accepted.

Open: 1 April or Easter - 31 October.

Directions

Park is just off A496 between Llandecwyn and Talsarnau, 4 miles north of Harlech. If coming from Porthmadog do not attempt to use toll road if towing or over 2 tons. GPS: 52.912983, -4.0524

Charges guide

Per unit incl. 2 persons and electricity	£ 22.50 - £ 25.50

Harlech

Woodlands Caravan Park

Harlech LL46 2UE (Gwynedd) T: 01766 780419. E: info@woodlandsparkharlech.com

alanrogers.com/UK6355

This delightful little site is lovingly tended by its owners and has just 18 pitches for touring units, all with gravel hardstanding and 10A electric hook-ups, for caravans and motorcaravans only. Tents are not accepted. There are also 22 privately owned holiday homes and three holiday cottages. However, the location of this site certainly makes up for its diminutive size, nestling under the massive rock topped by Harlech Castle, now a designated World Heritage Site. The narrow lane running alongside the site up to the old town above is the steepest hill in Britain.

Facilities

The modern stone built toilet facilities are heated, clean and tidy with controllable showers (50p), vanity style washbasins, a small laundry with a baby changing area, but with no dedicated facilities for disabled visitors. Chemical disposal point but no motorcaravan service point. WiFi. Off site: Golf 0.25 miles. Steam train pleasure trips (July/Aug). Harlech Castle. Fishing and riding 3 miles.

Open: 1 March - 31 October.

Directions

From Barmouth A496 to Harlech, go downhill past Royal St David's Golf Course. Fork right just before railway crossing and site is 200 yds. on right. DO NOT turn towards narrow and congested town centre on B4573. GPS: 52.86155, -4.107633

Charges guide

Per unit incl. 2 persons and electricity	£ 18.00 - £ 25.00

No credit or debit cards.

For latest campsite news visit

alanrogers.com

Harlech
Min-y-Don Holiday Home & Touring Park

Beach Road, Harlech LL46 2UG (Gwynedd) T: 01766 780286. E: manager@minydonholidayhomepark.co.uk
alanrogers.com/UK6365

Set within the Snowdonia National Park, this excellent Caravan Club affiliated park was totally rebuilt for the 2009 season to a standard that others will strive to achieve. It is a level site with first class facilities and has 100 well drained touring pitches, all on hardstanding and fully serviced. Tents are not accepted. In a separate area there are 112 caravan holiday homes. The site has three miles of golden sand beaches nearby and the Snowdon mountain range as a backdrop. It overlooks the famous Royal St David's Golf Course and Harlech town, dominated by its 13th-century castle, is within walking distance.

Facilities

New superb toilet facilities with underfloor heating. Large separate unit for disabled visitors. Two private bathrooms for rent. Motorcaravan services. Laundry facilities. Play area. Football pitch. Putting green. WiFi (free). Off site: Supermarket and leisure centre 800 yds. Walking distance to shops, pubs and restaurants in Harlech. Beach nearby. Coastal train. Bus service. Ffestiniog steam railway. Portmeirion. Snowdonia.

Open: 1 March - 31 October.

Directions

From Barmouth go north on the A496 to Harlech. Just beyond level crossing, turn left into Beach Road. From the north on the A496 in Harlech, right into Beach Road before level crossing. Park is on the right in 400 yds. GPS: 52.862366, -4.11526

Charges guide

Per unit incl. 2 persons	
and electricity (non-member)	£ 19.50 - £ 44.00
child (5-15 yrs)	£ 2.50 - £ 3.75

Haverfordwest
South Cockett Caravan & Camping Park

Broadway, Broad Haven, Haverfordwest SA62 3TU (Pembrokeshire) T: 01437 781296.
E: esmejames@hotmail.co.uk **alanrogers.com/UK5991**

South Cockett is an attractive and well maintained park which is personally run by the James family (Stephen, Esme and Will). The park provides 70 caravan pitches, all with electricity and 20 tent pitches, some with electricity. They are all grass (no hardstandings) and laid out over five separate areas which are separated by high, well maintained hedges. There is, however, no separation between pitches and very little shade. A bus service to Broad Haven and Haverfordwest is only 300 yards from the site. A well stocked shop can be found in nearby Broad Haven along with its Blue Flag beach.

Facilities

Two toilet blocks, one with showers (20p), and although basic and a little dated, they are kept very clean. Separate laundry and dishwashing area. Plenty of open space for children to play. Small reception with information about local places of interest. WiFi (charged). Torches useful. Off site: Blue Flag beach at Broad Haven and harbour at Little Haven both within 1.5 miles. Shop, fishing, windsurfing and swimming all 1.5 miles. Pony Trekking 5 miles. Golf 6 miles.

Open: 11 April - 12 October.

Directions

From Haverfordwest take B4341 to Broadway. At Broadway turn left at brown caravan site sign. Site is 300 yards on the right. GPS: 51.77899, -5.07593

Charges guide

Per unit incl. 2 persons	
and electricity	£ 13.00 - £ 16.00
extra person	£ 4.00
child (under 12 yrs)	£ 3.00

Haverfordwest
Creampots Touring Caravan & Camping Park

Broadway, Broad Haven, Haverfordwest SA62 3TU (Pembrokeshire) T: 01437 781776.
E: creampots@btconnect.com **alanrogers.com/UK5992**

This peacefully located and beautifully manicured, garden-like park is ideal for couples and families, and is a convenient base within easy reach of beaches or for touring the local area. Creampots has 62 spacious, level pitches all with 10A electric hook-ups, including 21 with gravel hardstanding, and ten pitches for tents. There is a separate field and an overflow area taking 32 tents for the August peak holiday time. This is an ideal location for the local attractions.

Facilities

The single small, white-washed sanitary unit is a modern building which can be heated. Two free hot showers per sex, open style washbasins. Washbasin and WC for disabled campers. These facilities were clean and tidy but may come under pressure at peak times. Tiny laundry room with just about space for one person at a time but with washing machine, dryer and sink. Outside are four covered dishwashing sinks at each end of the block. Gas supplies. Free WiFi over site. Off site: Shop, post office, pub with hot food in Broad Haven 1 mile.

Open: March - October.

Directions

Site is 5 miles west of Haverfordwest. From Haverfordwest take B4341 to Broad Haven, at Broadway follow brown tourist sign on left. GPS: 51.777333, -5.072283

Charges guide

Per unit incl. 2 persons	
and electricity	£ 15.50 - £ 19.95
extra person	£ 4.50
dog	free

For latest campsite news visit
alanrogers.com

Haverfordwest

Redlands Touring Caravan & Camping Park

Hasguard Cross, Little Haven, Haverfordwest SA62 3SJ (Pembrokeshire) T: 01437 781300.
E: info@redlandstouring.co.uk **alanrogers.com/UK5994**

This peaceful, family run site is located in the heart of the Pembrokeshire countryside, close to many lovely sandy beaches. Redlands takes around 80 touring units in three areas divided by banks topped with pine trees, 32 hardstandings and 69 with 10A electricity. The first two areas take 60 caravans or motorcaravans and include 32 hardstandings, the third takes 19 tents on a level grassy meadow. There are fine sea views across rolling countryside to Saint Brides Bay. Reception has a small shop which is open only in peak periods. Breathable groundsheets should be used. American RVs – advance booking only. A sandy beach and the Pembrokeshire Coastal Path are 1.5 miles away. The countryside around here is made for walking, with lots of small villages dotted along the coastline. Haverfordwest is just a short drive away for any shopping needs. The area is perfect for get-away holidays.

Facilities

The traditional style toilet block is well kept and heated early and late season. It has all the usual requirements including two extra shower, basin and WC suites. Large utility room with washing machine, dryer and spin dryer. Ironing is free and there are sinks for laundry and dishes. Shop. Freezers. Wet suit washing area. Dogs are welcome (max. 2 high season) but must be kept on lead. WiFi over part of site (free). Off site: Summer bus service. Fishing and boat launching 1.5 miles. Shops and ATM in Broad Haven 2 miles. Riding and sailing 5 miles. Golf 6 miles. Coastal bus service.

Open: 1 March - 9 January.

Directions

Site 6.5 miles southwest of Haverfordwest. From Haverfordwest take the B4327 road towards Dale and site is on the right at Hasguard Cross. N.B. Do not approach via Broad Haven. GPS: 51.755567, -5.112383

Charges guide

Per unit incl. 2 persons	
and electricity	£ 18.90 - £ 22.95
extra person	£ 4.50
dog (max. 2, 1st free)	free - £ 1.00

No credit cards.
Special offer for couples in low season.

Llandovery

Rhandirmwyn Camping & Caravanning Club Site

Rhandirmwyn, Llandovery SA20 0NT (Carmarthenshire) T: 01550 760257.
alanrogers.com/UK6070

This is a popular site with those who like a peaceful life with no on-site entertainment, just fresh air and beautiful countryside. The site is only a short drive from the magnificent Llyn Brianne reservoir and close to the Dinas RSPB nature reserve, where a two mile trail runs through oak and alder woodland alongside the River Tywi, and the wildlife includes many species of birds such as red kites. The site is in a sheltered valley with 90 pitches on level grass, 51 electricity hook-ups (16A) and 21 hardstandings. The village is within walking distance although there is a fairly steep hill to negotiate (but the return is much easier), and you can take a short cut through the woodland grove dedicated to John Lloyd, a former Chairman of the Club.

Facilities

The single heated sanitary block is kept very clean and tidy and includes facilities for disabled visitors. Some washbasins in cubicles, dishwashing sinks and fully equipped laundry. Drive-over motorcaravan service point. Shop for essentials. Small playground with rubber base. Payphone (no mobile signal). WiFi. Lodges for sale and for rent. Off site: The Royal Oak Inn in the village serves good value meals. Farmers' market in Llandovery twice a month. Fishing 6 miles. Golf and bicycle hire 7 miles. Riding 11 miles.

Open: 24 March - 31 October.

Directions

From centre of Llandovery take A483 towards Builth Wells, after a short distance turn left by the fire station, signed Rhandirmwyn, continue for 7 miles along country lanes. Do not use sat nav for directions. GPS: 52.077017, -3.783833

Charges guide

Per unit incl. 2 persons	
and electricity	£ 15.05 - £ 25.70
extra person	£ 5.75 - £ 9.80
child (6-18 yrs)	£ 2.87 - £ 4.90

Non-member prices are higher.

For latest campsite news visit
alanrogers.com

Llandovery
Erwlon Caravan & Camping Park

Brecon Road, Llandovery SA20 0RD (Carmarthenshire) T: 01550 721021. E: enquiries@erwlon.co.uk

alanrogers.com/UK5955

Just outside Llandovery and on the edge of the Brecon Beacons National Park, Erwlon is an attractive and welcoming campsite. Of the 110 pitches, seven are used for privately owned caravan holiday homes, 33 have seasonal caravans and 70 are for touring units. Fifty are on hardstanding with electricity connections and 12 have water and drainage as well. There is a flat field for tents at the bottom of the park with some electrical outlets; an open-sided, covered area for eating, food preparation and bicycle storage is at the planning stage. The site has a relaxed atmosphere where consideration for others minimises the need for formal rules. It is ideal for young families, walkers, cyclists and fishermen. Gold mines and the National Showcaves Centre for Wales (including dinosaur park) are within an easy drive. A member of the Best of British group.

Facilities

New heated toilet block with washbasins in cabins, four family rooms (basin, shower, toilet) and a room for families and disabled visitors which includes a baby unit. Combined, well equipped laundry and dishwashing room. Motorcaravan services. Fridge freezer. Fishing. WiFi over site (charged). Off site: Supermarket 500 yds. Town amenities (shops, pubs, restaurants and indoor pool) within 1 mile. Golf and bicycle hire 1 mile. Riding 8 miles. Beaches about 25 miles.

Open: All year.

Directions

Park is half a mile outside the town boundary of Llandovery on the A40 to Brecon.
GPS: 51.99325, -3.78023

Charges guide

Per unit incl. 2 persons	
and electricity	£ 16.00 - £ 20.00
extra person	£ 1.50 - £ 2.00
dog	free

No credit cards.

Erwlon is a family run park with a warm welcome and excellent award winning facilities including a heated amenity block, family rooms, laundry, super pitches, a motor caravan service point and plenty of landscaped pitches available.

Erwlon Caravan & Camping Park Llandovery
Brecon Road | Llandovery Carmarthenshire SA20 0RD
Phone: 01550 721021 / 720332
Email: enquiries@erwlon.co.uk

www.erwlon.co.uk

Llandrindod Wells
Dolswydd Caravan Park

Dolswydd, Pen-y-Bont, Llandrindod Wells LD1 5UB (Powys) T: 01597 851267.
E: Hughes@dolswydd.freeserve.co.uk **alanrogers.com/UK6250**

Dolswydd is on the edge of a pretty, traditional working farm. A tranquil site with excellent views of the Welsh hills and surrounding area, it has modern facilities and 30 good spacious pitches, mainly on hardstandings, all with 16A electricity connections. The Hughes family extends a warm and friendly welcome to their little park surrounded by hills and wandering sheep, which is ideal as a touring base or for a one night stop, but booking is recommended, especially at peak times, Bank Holidays and during the Victorian Festival (last week in August). A footpath leads from the back of the site to the rear of the local pub which offers good, home cooked food.

Facilities

One modern toilet block includes lots of hot water, dishwashing, laundry, and a WC/washroom for disabled campers. Fishing in the river alongside the site (free, but licence required). Off site: Within walking distance are the local pub and garage. Riding 1 mile. Golf and bicycle hire 5 miles.

Open: Easter - end October.

Directions

Pen-y-Bont is 2 miles east of the junction of the A44 and A483 roads at Crossgates. Take A44 (Kington). Go through Pen-y-Bont and immediately after crossing cattle grid, site is on right. On arrival drive across farm cattle grid and reception is at second farmhouse. GPS: 52.15857, -3.18773

Charges guide

Per unit incl. 2 persons and electricity	£ 14.00
extra person	£ 1.00

For latest campsite news visit
alanrogers.com

Llandysul
Brynawelon Touring & Camping Park
Sarnau, Llandysul SA44 6RE (Ceredigion) T: 01239 654584. E: info@brynaweloncp.co.uk
alanrogers.com/UK6005

Paul and Liz Cowton have turned Brynawelon into a friendly, attractive and well appointed campsite. It is in a stunning rural location within two miles of the Ceredigion coast with its beaches, and close to the River Teifi with plenty of water based activities. All 40 pitches have electricity hook-ups and of these, 25 also have water and drainage and hardstanding. Ten all-weather pitches for tents have been added. The remainder are on level grass. The park has ample room for children to play, an enclosed play area, an indoor games room with TV and a sauna next to reception. Buzzards, red kites, owls and the occasional eagle can be seen from the park. There is also a wide variety of small birds.

Facilities

Modern toilet block with toilets, showers, washbasins in cabins, two full suites in each side and a separate room for families and disabled visitors. Laundry/kitchen with washing machine, tumble dryer, ironing board and iron, fridge/freezer, microwave, kettle and toaster. Enclosed play area. Games room with TV and library. Sauna (charged). Dog walking area. WiFi (charged). Off site: Beach 1 mile. Shops 2 miles. Golf 3 miles.

Open: March - 31 October.

Directions

Travelling north on the A487 from Cardigan turn right (southeast) at the crossroads in Sarnau village, signed Rhydlewis. Site is on the left after 650 yds. Note: the cross-country approach is not advised. GPS: 52.13001, -4.45401

Charges guide

Per unit incl. 2 persons and electricity	£ 15.00
incl. 4 persons, hardstanding and services	£ 25.00
extra person	£ 6.00

Llandysul
Pencnwc Holiday Park
Cross Inn, New Quay, Llandysul SA44 6NL (Ceredigion) T: 01545 560479. E: holidays@pencnwc.co.uk
alanrogers.com/UK6015

Pencnwc Holiday Park is a family owned holiday park with a wide range of recreational facilities, close to the Cardigan Bay coastline and only two miles from the seaside town of New Quay. There are 377 pitches, 150 for touring, of which 70 have 16A hook-up and 36 are hardstandings. They are in the centre of the site, away from the static and seasonal vans. Tents are welcome and an area without electricity has been set aside for them.

Facilities

Toilet blocks throughout are clean and have facilities for disabled visitors. Launderette. Two bars (entertainment centre with top class singers etc.) and a smaller, quiet bar. Fish and chip shop. Indoor heated swimming pool and paddling pool (small charge). Kids' club. Coarse fishing lake. Free WiFi in clubhouse. No dogs at B.Hs.

Open: 1 March - 31 October.

Directions

From A487 Cardigan-Aberaeron road turn northwest onto A486, signed New Quay and Honey Farm. The entrance to the park is 2 miles on the left. GPS: 52.18798, -4.35402

Charges guide

Per unit incl. 4 persons and electricity	£ 17.50 - £ 27.00

Llanelli
Pembrey Country Park Caravan Club Site
Pembrey, Llanelli SA16 0EJ (Carmarthenshire) T: 01554 834369.
alanrogers.com/UK5940

Set on the edge of a 520-acre country park, this popular Caravan Club site enjoys a wonderful location with a vast range of outdoor activities, including the use of a seven-mile stretch of safe, sandy beach a mile away. Well sheltered, the site is set in 12-acre grounds and provides 125 touring pitches, of which 68 are on hardstanding for caravans and motorcaravans. All are equipped with 16A electricity. Thoughtful landscaping has included the planting of many species of trees and a circular, one-way tarmac road provides easy access. Sensibly placed service points provide fresh water and waste disposal of all types. RAF jets do practise in this area (although becoming less frequent and generally not flying at the weekend). Tents are not accepted.

Facilities

The sanitary block is of an excellent standard with washbasins in cubicles, facilities for disabled visitors and a baby room. Fully equipped laundry room. Dishwashing room and further sinks under cover. Motorcaravan services. Gas available. Small shop in reception for essentials. Local tradesmen visit each morning selling milk and bread. Play area. Riding. Dry ski slope. Toboggan ride. Late arrivals area (with electricity). WiFi.

Open: 20 March - 4 January.

Directions

Leave M4 at exit 48 onto A4138 (Llanelli). After 4 miles turn right onto A484 at roundabout (Carmarthen). Continue for 7 miles to Pembrey. Follow country park signs off A484 in Pembrey village; site entrance is on right 100 yds. before park gates. GPS: 51.6823, -4.2979

Charges guide

Per person	£ 6.40 - £ 8.80
child (5-17 yrs)	£ 0.01 - £ 3.40
pitch incl. electricity (non-member)	£ 16.80 - £ 20.80

For latest campsite news visit
alanrogers.com

Llangennith

Kennexstone Camping and Touring Park

Kennexstone Farm, Llangennith, Swansea SA3 1HS (Swansea) T: 01792 386790.
E: kennexstone@btconnect.com **alanrogers.com/UK5876**

Set alongside a working organic farm, mainly arable during the summer months, this ten-acre campsite covers three level, well manicured fields. The 251 pitches, 72 with 16A electricity hook-up, are all on well drained and reasonably level grass. Each pitch is separated by posts and rope which is in keeping with the rural feel to the site. Hedges separating the fields are left undisturbed to encourage the wildlife that is so abundant in the area. The whole site has been preserved with both the wildlife and the visitor in mind. The birdlife thrives in the wood that forms a backdrop to the older part of the farm.

Facilities

One unisex toilet block with separate shower rooms, pushbutton showers on a timer, dishwashing and laundry area. Disabled toilet/shower room doubles as a baby changing room (key from reception with £5 deposit). Separate wet suit shower area. Water is supplied to a single point on each field. Shop in reception stocks basics. WiFi over site (charged). Off site: Several beaches within 2 miles, one has some of the best surfing in Wales, another borders a National Trust Nature Reserve. Six country pubs/hotels within 3 miles, all serving meals.

Open: 23 March - 30 September.

Directions

From M4 exit 47, at flyover take second exit A483, at roundabout turn right onto A484. At second roundabout, turn left onto B4296. After 0.5 miles (at first lights), turn right onto B4295. Follow road through Burry Green. Turn right onto Kyfts Lane, signed. Entrance is 200 m. on left. Do not use postcode for sat nav. GPS: 51.60154, -4.23950

Charges guide

Per unit incl. 4 persons and electricity	£ 21.00 - £ 24.00
extra person	£ 3.00 - £ 4.00

Llantwit Major

Happy Jakes Caravan Park

1 New Barn, Flemingston CF62 4QL (Vale of Glamorgan) T: 01446 750174. E: info@happyjakes.co.uk
alanrogers.com/UK5926

Happy Jakes is a quiet, well laid out site with 46 grass touring pitches, 30 of which are for caravans and motorcaravans (16A electricity hook-ups). There is one fully serviced, super pitch for an RV-type vehicle, and 15 pitches have been left for tents. The site name reflects that of the owner's little boy, who inspired them to create a campsite with facilities for visitors with disabilities, and many of the features were created with children in mind. An example of this is 'Rachel's Walk', a sensory experience for campers who are blind or partially sighted. There is some aircraft noise from the nearby airport.

Facilities

Small, fully tiled, heated toilet block with small laundry room and dishwashing area for campers. Two large rooms with preset showers for disabled visitors. Very small shop for basics. Hot food and drink to take away. Playground. Dog walking area. Information room. WiFi (deposit required). Off site: The Vale of Glamorgan has many attractions including Ogmore Castle, fine beaches and many small towns and villages.

Open: All year.

Directions

Follow signs for Cardiff Airport, take A4226 past airport onto B4265. Turn right into St Athan Road and look for brown site sign. Continue to next brown sign and turn left towards Llanmaes. In 0.5 miles turn left at final sign and site is 500 yds. Do not approach from Cowbridge. GPS: 51.421308, -3.433024

Charges guide

Per unit incl. 2 persons and electricity	£ 21.00
extra person	£ 4.00

Llantwit Major

Acorn Camping & Caravanning

Ham Lane South, Llantwit Major CF61 1RP (Vale of Glamorgan) T: 01446 794024.
E: info@acorncamping.co.uk **alanrogers.com/UK5927**

A peaceful, family owned, rural site, Acorn is situated on the Heritage Coast, one mile from the beach and the historic town of Llantwit Major. The 105 pitches are mostly on grass, with a few private mobile homes at the far end, leaving around 90 pitches for touring units, including eight gravel hardstandings and 71 electric hook-ups (10A). There is a separate area for tents. Reception houses a very well stocked shop which includes groceries and essentials, souvenirs, children's toys, camping gear and takeaway meals cooked to order. There is occasional aircraft noise.

Facilities

A warm, modern building houses spacious shower cubicles with washbasins, ample WCs, a family/baby room and a suite for disabled campers. Laundry facilities. Takeaway meals. Shop. Gas. TV lounge. Games room (charged). Play area with free trampoline. WiFi (free). Off site: Glamorgan Heritage Coastal Footpath. Llanerch Vineyard. Cosmeston Lakes Country Park at Penarth.

Open: 1 February - 30 November.

Directions

From east on M4 exit 33 follow signs to Cardiff airport, take B4265 for Llantwit Major. Turn left at lights, through Broverton and left into Ham Lane East, finally left into Ham Manor Park and signs to site. GPS: 51.40409, -3.48181

Charges guide

Per unit incl. 2 persons and electricity	£ 17.00 - £ 21.50

For latest campsite news visit
alanrogers.com

Llantwit Major

Llandow Caravan Park

Llandow, Cowbridge CF71 7PB (Vale of Glamorgan) T: 01446 794527. E: info@llandowcaravanpark.com

alanrogers.com/UK5928

Llandow Caravan Park is in a fairly secluded rural area in the beautiful Vale of Glamorgan. You will receive a very warm welcome from the park wardens, Julie and Alan. The site is divided into two areas separated by a road. The main area comprises 100 level pitches, some on hardstanding, whilst across the road is the new area with 73 mainly grass pitches. This is a quiet site suitable for couples, families and visitors with disabilities. The owners work very hard to maintain the highest standard of cleanliness for all facilities.

Facilities	Directions
Two sanitary blocks, one new on the new field. Coin-operated showers. New facilities for disabled visitors. Good quality laundry facilities. Well stocked shop in reception. Play area. Dog walking area. Tourist information leaflets. Free WiFi throughout. Off site: Llandow Motor Racing Circuit adjoining site. Pub 2.5 miles. Beaches 3 miles. Supermarket 3 miles.	From the west leave M4 at exit 33 and follow A48 to Cowbridge. Bypass Cowbridge and take left turn at Pentre Meyrick onto B4270 towards Llantwit Major. Continue for approx. 3 miles. Turn right just past the Ford garage (follow brown signs) then left after the motor racing circuit. GPS: 51.43156, -3.50292

Open: 1 February - 30 November.

Charges guide

Per unit incl. 2 persons and electricity	£ 17.50 - £ 21.50
extra person	£ 4.00

Llanwrda

Springwater Lakes

Harford, Llanwrda SA19 8DT (Carmarthenshire) T: 01558 650788. E: bookings@springwaterlakes.com

alanrogers.com/UK5880

Set in 20 acres of Welsh countryside, Springwater offers a selection of fishing lakes to keep even the keenest of anglers occupied. However, it is not just anglers who will enjoy this site – it is a lovely base to enjoy the peace and tranquillity of this part of Wales. Springwater offers 40 spacious, flat pitches either on grass or 30 gravel hardstanding, all with 16A electricity and ten fully serviced pitches, plus ten tent pitches. Malcolm and Shirley Bexon are very proud of their site and welcome all visitors with a smile. This is not a site for children unless they enjoy fishing (no play areas). If you want to learn about fishing, Malcolm or Mark will be happy to help.

Facilities	Directions
The heated toilet block is very clean and includes facilities for disabled visitors (there is also wheelchair access to the lakes for fishing). Fishing. Tackle/bait shop (also sells ice-creams and confectionery). Free WiFi around shop. Off site: Spar shop and garage 500 yds. (other shops 5 miles). Riding 2 miles. Golf 4 miles.	From A40 at Llanwrda take A482 to Lampeter. After 6 miles go through village of Pumsaint and site is 2 miles further on the left, just before garage shop. GPS: 52.067417, -3.98225

Open: 1 March - 31 October.

Charges guide

Per unit incl. 2 persons and electricity	£ 18.25 - £ 25.85
extra person	£ 8.00

Machynlleth

Morben Isaf Touring & Holiday Home Park

Derwenlas, Machynlleth SY20 8SR (Powys) T: 01654 781473. E: manager@morbenisaf.co.uk

alanrogers.com/UK6245

Morben Isaf provides 26 touring pitches with multi-services, all with 16A electricity, water tap, waste water drain and a satellite TV hook-up. There is further grassy space below the touring pitches, beyond the fishing lake, which is normally used as a playing field and football pitch but can accommodate around ten tents which do not need any services. On a lower level, behind the site manager's bungalow and barely visible from the touring site, are 87 privately owned caravan holiday homes. There is a new play area suitable for children up to ten years old. Also on the site is an unfenced coarse fishing lake, which campers are free to use, a bird hide and a dog walk.

Facilities	Directions
Small but well equipped, heated modern toilet block includes spacious controllable showers, baby changing and child seats in both ladies' and men's. Facilities for disabled campers. Well equipped laundry. Internet access (free). Off site: Pub serving hot food 1.5 miles. Leisure Centre, shops and services in Machynlleth 3 miles (market on Wed). Dyfi Osprey Project visitor centre adjacent.	Site is 3 miles southwest of Machynlleth beside A487. GPS: 52.570067, -3.91145

Charges guide

Per unit incl. 4 persons and electricity	£ 22.00 - £ 26.00
extra person	£ 2.00

Open: Mid March - 31 October.

For latest campsite news visit

alanrogers.com

Moelfre
Home Farm Caravan Park

Marian-glas, Anglesey LL73 8PH (Isle of Anglesey) T: 01248 410614. E: enq@homefarm-anglesey.co.uk

alanrogers.com/UK6640

A tarmac drive through open fields and a barrier/intercom system leads to this neatly laid out, quality park, with caravan holiday homes to one side. Nestling below what was once a Celtic hill fort, later decimated as a quarry, the park is edged with mature trees and farmland. A circular, tarmac access road leads to the 102 well spaced and numbered touring pitches. With five types available, there are pitches for everyone; ranging from grass without electricity, to oversized, deluxe hardstandings with electricity, water tanks/taps, waste water drain and TV hook-ups. All electricity is 16A and there are separate well maintained grass fields/areas for tents. Some areas are slightly sloping. The 'pièce de résistance' must be the children's indoor play area, large super adventure play equipment, complete with tunnels and bridges on safe rubber matting, not to mention an outside fenced play area and fields available for sports, football, etc. and walking. Various beaches, sandy and rocky, are within a mile. A member of the Best of British group.

Facilities

Two purpose built toilet blocks, one part of the reception building, are of similar design, can be heated and are maintained to a high standard. En-suite provision for visitors with disabilities (key access). Excellent small bathroom for children, with baby bath and curtain for privacy. Family room (key access). Laundry room. Motorcaravan services. Ice pack service. A new reception building with shop provides basic essentials, gas and some caravan accessories. Indoor and outdoor play areas. TV and pool table. Small library. Hard tennis (extra charge) with racquet hire. WiFi (charged). Off site: Beach 1 mile. Restaurants, shops and ATM at Benllech 2 miles. Fishing and golf 2 miles. Riding 8 miles.

Open: April - October.

Directions

From the Britannia Bridge take second exit left signed Benllech and Amlwch on the A5025. Two miles after Benllech keep left at roundabout and park entrance is 300 yds. on the left beyond the church. GPS: 53.33877, -4.26056

Charges guide

Per unit incl. 2 persons and electricity	£ 21.50 - £ 36.00
extra person	£ 4.00 - £ 6.50
child (3-15 yrs)	£ 2.50 - £ 4.50
dog (max. 2)	£ 1.50 - £ 2.50

An **award winning family run park** within landscaped gardens situated in a perfect setting to explore the wonderful Isle of Anglesey. Ideal for couples and families who seek a peaceful and relaxing holiday in beautiful surroundings. Immaculate facilities include shop, inside/outside play areas, tennis court and an extensive dog walk.

Marian-glas • Anglesey • Ynys Môn • LL73 8PH • North Wales • Tel: 01248 410614
www.homefarm-anglesey.co.uk • enq@homefarm-anglesey.co.uk

Monmouth
Glen Trothy Caravan & Camping Park

Mitchel Troy, Monmouth NP25 4BD (Monmouthshire) T: 01600 712295. E: enquiries@glentrothy.co.uk

alanrogers.com/UK5890

Glen Trothy is a pretty park on the banks of the River Trothy and visitors are greeted by an array of colourful flowerbeds and tubs around the entrance and reception area. Three fields provide level touring and tent pitches. The first and largest field has a circular gravel road with seasonal pitches arranged on the outer side and touring pitches on the inner side. These have slabs for vehicle wheels and electricity hook-ups. The second field, just past the toilet block, has pitches for trailer tents and tents only (16 with electricity), whilst the camping field is for tents only (no cars are allowed on this area). The friendly owners are working hard on their site bringing its facilities up-to-date, recently adding security barriers at the entrance. This is a neat and well maintained park in a lovely location.

Facilities

Neat and clean sanitary block with facilities for disabled visitors. Laundry facilities. Token-operated showers (40p). Tourist information in hut opposite reception. Small play area. Free fishing (from the camping field only). Dogs are not accepted. Off site: Golf, canoeing, shopping and supermarkets at the historic town of Monmouth 1.5 miles. The Wye Valley and the Forest of Dean are nearby.

Open: 1 March - 31 October.

Directions

At Monmouth, take A40 east to Abergavenny. Exit at first junction and at T-junction, where site is signed, turn left onto B4284. Follow signs for Mitchel Troy. Site is on right just past village sign. GPS: 51.790967, -2.7341

Charges guide

Per unit incl. 2 persons and electricity	£ 16.00
extra person (over 5 yrs)	£ 3.00

£2 surcharge for stays of only one night.
Min. stay of 3 nights on B.Hs.

For latest campsite news visit
alanrogers.com

Montgomery
Smithy Park

Abermule, Montgomery SY15 6ND (Powys) T: 01584 711280. E: info@smithypark.co.uk

alanrogers.com/UK6305

Smithy Park is set in four acres of landscaped grounds bordered by the River Severn and the Shropshire Union Canal, in the tranquil rolling countryside of central Wales. It does have 60 privately owned caravan holiday homes, but beyond these is a separate touring area which has the benefit of being closest to the river with the best views and a small picnic and seating area on the bank. This area has 26 fully serviced hardstanding pitches (16A electricity, water, waste water and satellite TV hook-ups). A timber chalet provides all the sanitary facilities and is located in one corner of the touring area.

Facilities

The heated, timber-clad chalet building provides two good sized showers per sex, washbasins in cubicles, a family room doubling as disabled facilities (there is a step up to the building). Additional toilet and washbasin in a new building by reception. Utility room housing a laundry with washing machine, dryer and dishwashing sink. Fishing in the River Severn. Fenced playground. Gas stocked. WiFi.

Open: 1 March - 31 October.

Directions

Site is 3 miles north of Newtown in the village of Abermule. Turn off the A483 into village, and turn down the lane beside the Waterloo Arms, opposite the village shop and Post Office. Site is at end of lane. GPS: 52.544217, -3.238717

Charges guide

Per unit incl. 2 persons and electricity	£ 23.00 - £ 26.00
extra person	£ 4.00

Montgomery
Daisy Bank Touring Caravan Park

Snead, Montgomery SY15 6EB (Powys) T: 01588 620471. E: enquiries@daisy-bank.co.uk

alanrogers.com/UK6330

For adults only, this pretty, tranquil park in the Camlad Valley has panoramic views and is an ideal base for walkers. Attractively landscaped with traditional English flower beds and many different trees and shrubs, this small park has been carefully developed. The Welsh hills to the north and the Shropshire hills to the south overlook the three fields which provide a total of 84 pitches. The field nearer to the road (perhaps a little noisy) is slightly sloping but there are hardstandings for motorcaravans, while the second field is more level. All pitches have 16A electricity, water and waste water drainage and TV hook-up. Camping pods are also available for hire.

Facilities

Two well equipped, heated toilet blocks now incorporate modern, en-suite units and facilities for disabled visitors. One has four en-suite units and two WCs. Covered dishwashing area. Laundry facilities. Shop in reception (honesty policy at certain times). Gas supplies. Barbecues. Small putting green (free loan of clubs and balls). Bicycle hire. Small library. WiFi. Off site: Supermarket 2 miles.

Open: All year.

Directions

Site is by the A489 road 2 miles east of Churchstoke towards Craven Arms. GPS: 52.529917, -3.0297

Charges guide

Per unit incl. 2 persons and all services	£ 19.00 - £ 28.00
extra person	£ 5.00
tent incl. 2 persons	£ 20.00 - £ 22.00

Narberth
Little Kings Park

Amroth Road, Ludchurch, Narberth SA67 8PG (Pembrokeshire) T: 01834 831330.
E: littlekingspark@btconnect.com **alanrogers.com/UK5975**

This superb family run park has a number of attributes to make your stay both comfortable and memorable. There are stunning views over Carmarthen Bay to the Gower and beyond to the coast of Somerset and North Devon. At night no fewer than seven lighthouses can be seen blinking out their warnings. A touring field provides 55 well spaced, large touring pitches all with 16A electricity, 21 with gravel hardstanding and most fully serviced. A new attractive playground is in the central open grass area. There are 60 pitches for tents in an adjoining paddock with 31 electricity hook-ups (10A).

Facilities

The two toilet blocks are modern and well equipped, including controllable hot showers, open style washbasins, a family shower room and a full suite for disabled visitors. Laundry rooms. Gas supplies. Shop with bakery. Tavern with conservatory (from 27/3). Covered, heated swimming pool. Games rooms. Playground. Area for ball games. Free WiFi around pool and tavern. Off site: Supermarket and ATM at Kilgetty 2.5 miles. Fishing 1.5 miles. Riding 4 miles. Tenby 7 miles.

Open: 1 March - 1 November.

Directions

Site is 5 miles southeast of Narberth. From A477 Carmarthen to Pembroke road, 2 miles after Llanteg at petrol station, turn left towards Amroth, Wiseman's Bridge, Ludchurch. After 1 mile, at crossroads, turn right (signed Ludchurch, Narberth) and park is 800 yds. GPS: 51.751517, -4.6879

Charges guide

Per unit incl. 2 persons and electricity	£ 16.00 - £ 28.00
extra person (over 3 yrs)	free - £ 2.20

For latest campsite news visit
alanrogers.com

Newcastle Emlyn
Cenarth Falls Holiday Park
Cenarth, Newcastle Emlyn SA38 9JS (Ceredigion) T: 01239 710345. E: enquiries@cenarth-holipark.co.uk
alanrogers.com/UK6010

The Davies family has developed an attractively landscaped, part wooded holiday home park with 89 units (one for rent). A neat, well cared for, sheltered area at the top of the park provides 29 touring pitches, accessed via a tarmac road. All are on shingle hardstanding with 16A electricity. A sunken, kidney shaped outdoor pool with landscaped surrounds and sunbeds is a focal point. The Coracles Health and Country Club provides an indoor pool, spa, sauna and steam rooms and fitness suite (reduced rates for campers). It also has a bar with pizzas, an adults only lounge and a large function room where live entertainment is organised during the main season. Everything is of a high quality.

Facilities	Directions
The excellent sanitary block has easy ramped access. Accessed by key, it uses a 'P.I.R.' system that controls heating, lighting, water and air freshener on entry – very efficient. Provision for disabled visitors (doubles as family room), spacious, well equipped showers and one of the washbasins in a roomy private cabin. Laundry room. Gas supplies. Outdoor pool (late May-late Aug). Play area. Games room. WiFi over site (charged).	Follow A484 Cardigan-Newcastle Emlyn road and park is signed before Cenarth village. GPS: 52.0499, -4.531717

Charges guide

Per unit incl. up to 4 people and electricity	£ 18.00 - £ 28.00
extra person (over 2 yrs)	£ 2.00
dog	£ 2.00

Open: 1 March - mid-November.

Newport
Cwmcarn Forest Drive Campsite
Cwmcarn, Crosskeys, Newport NP11 7FA (Newport) T: 01495 272001. E: cwmcarn-vc@caerphilly.gov.uk
alanrogers.com/UK5930

This forest site, run by Caerphilly Council, is set in a narrow, sheltered valley with magnificent wooded slopes. The park is not only central for the many attractions of this part of Wales, but there is also much of the natural environment to enjoy including a small fishing lake. The site offers 23 pitches, these include seven all-weather pitches for tents on pea shingle and six hardstandings for touring units, all with 16A electricity. Ten timber camping pods have also been added and are available to hire. Wardens are on hand daily. The entrance barrier is locked between 22.00 and 07.00.

Facilities	Directions
The single, heated toilet block includes toilet facilities for disabled visitors. Wet room (£5 deposit for key). Laundry facilities. Small hob, microwave and freezer. The Visitor Centre has a coffee shop selling refreshments and meals daily. Guided walks and the popular Twrch (9 miles) and Cafell (9 miles) mountain bike trails. Timber camping pods. Dogs accepted by prior arrangement. Large units (over 24 ft) not accepted due to access. Off site: Shops, leisure centre and takeaway food in village less than 1 mile.	Cwmcarn Forest Drive is well signed from exit 28 on the M4. From the Midlands and the 'Heads of the Valleys' road (A465), take A467 south to Cwmcarn. Follow campsite and Visitor Centre signs. (Note: many speed bumps along driveway to site). GPS: 51.63771, -3.11877

Charges guide

Per unit incl. 2 persons and electricity	£ 15.00 - £ 19.00
extra person	£ 4.50 - £ 6.50

Open: All year excl. 23 December - 2 January.

Newport
Tredegar House Country Park Caravan Club Site
Tredegar House, Coedkernew, Newport NP10 8TW (Newport) T: 01633 815600.
alanrogers.com/UK6060

This immaculate Caravan Club site is ideally situated for breaking a journey or for longer stays. It can accommodate 79 units, all with 16A electricity hook-up and 68 with gravel hardstanding, four fully serviced. A further grass area is allocated for tents, with its use limited to families and couples – no single sex groups are accepted. The site is set within the gardens and park of Tredegar House, a 17th-century house and country park, which is open to the public to discover what life was like 'above and below stairs'. The park entrance gates are locked at dusk so contact the site reception for details of latest arrival times. Some road noise may be expected at times, but otherwise this is an excellent site.

Facilities	Directions
The sanitary block is of an excellent standard with a digital lock system. It includes washbasins in cubicles. Facilities for disabled visitors. Baby and toddler bathroom. Laundry. Good motorcaravan service point. Calor gas available. Tredegar House visitors' centre with tea rooms, gift shop and craft workshops (open Easter-Sept). Adventure play area in the park. WiFi (charged).	From M4 take exit 28 or from A48 junction with the M4 follow brown signs for Tredegar House. The caravan park is signed to the left at the house entrance. GPS: 51.56148, -3.03341

Charges guide

Per person	£ 4.80 - £ 7.00
pitch incl. electricity (non-member)	£ 15.40 - £ 19.10

Open: All year.

For latest campsite news visit
alanrogers.com

Newtown
Cringoed Caravan Park
Cringoed, Llanbrynmair, Newtown SY19 7DR (Powys) T: 01650 521237. E: enquiries@cringoed.co.uk
alanrogers.com/UK6240

Cringoed is a pleasant, peaceful, small park with a river to one side, hills on the other and trees at either end. There are 30 spacious pitches available for touring and these are in a level open field, each with hardstanding and 16A electricity. About 36 caravan holiday homes are placed at either end of the site, some amongst trees and some in a newer, more open area. There are also ten tent pitches, some with electricity. This is a relaxing base where you can sit and listen to the river and watch the wildlife, but it is also within easy reach of some of mid-Wales' best scenery and not far from the coast.

Facilities	Directions
The single toilet block is neat, modern and quite adequate. Laundry and dishwashing. Adventure play area. Small tourist information room. WiFi (free). Off site: Shops 1 mile (ATM at Spar in Carno 6 miles). Bicycle hire 1 mile. Fishing 5 miles. Golf 8 miles. Riding 12 miles.	From A470 between Newton and Machynlleth in the Llanbrynmair take B4518 signed Staylittle. After 1 mile just before bridge turn right, go over bridge and turn right. GPS: 52.598333, -3.644383

Open: 17 March - 30 November.

Charges guide

Per unit incl. 2 persons
and electricity £ 18.00 - £ 21.00
No credit cards.

Pembroke
Freshwater East Caravan Club Site
Trewent Hill, Freshwater East, Pembroke SA71 5LJ (Pembrokeshire) T: 01646 672341.
E: freshwatereast@caravanclub.co.uk alanrogers.com/UK5990

Located within the Pembrokeshire Coast National Park, this Caravan Club site is open to non-members (for all units). The park is flanked by trees on one side with a mix of grass and hardstanding tiered pitch areas to choose from. There is a total of 128 pitches, 65 hardstanding, all with 16A electricity hook-ups. There are five pitches for tents. The beach and the Pembroke Coastal Path are just a few minutes' walk. This is an excellent area for walking with magnificent cliff views and birdwatching. You will find Saint David's, the smallest cathedral city, well worth a visit. Note: TV aerial connections are available, but you will need your own extension cable.

Facilities	Directions
The two heated sanitary blocks have washbasins in cubicles and free hairdryers. Facilities for disabled visitors in a dedicated area (RADAR key). Fully equipped laundry rooms. Waste point for motorcaravans. Gas supplies. Reception keeps basic food items. Information kiosk. Small play area. Public telephone (no mobile signal). WiFi (charged). Off site: Beach 400 yds. Shop 2 miles. Public transport 1 mile. Fishing 5 miles.	From east on A477, fork left 1.25 miles past Milton onto A4075. In Pembroke immediately (after railway bridge) turn sharp left at roundabout on A4139 Tenby road. In Lamphey turn right onto B4584. In 1.75 miles turn right (Stackpole, Trewent) and after 400 yds. right into lane at Club sign. Do not tow to the beach area. GPS: 51.64514, -4.87185

Open: 20 March - 12 October.

Charges guide

Per person £ 5.10 - £ 7.00
pitch incl. electricity (non-member) £ 16.00 - £ 19.00

Penmaenmawr
Tyddyn Du Touring Park
Conwy Old Road, Penmaenmawr LL34 6RE (Conwy) T: 01492 622300. E: stay@tyddyndutouringpark.co.uk
alanrogers.com/UK6695

This attractively landscaped, adults only, five-hectare campsite is conveniently situated close to the A55 and positioned on a hillside with panoramic views across Conwy Bay to The Great Orme at Llandudno and Puffin Island. Offering peace and quiet in a superb location between mountains and the sea, and being within easy reach of Conwy, Snowdonia National Park and many historic regions of north Wales, this is an ideal base for exploring the area. Tarmac roads connect the three levels which are tiered to maximise the views for everyone. There are 87 touring pitches on either grass or hardstanding and all have 16A electricity. Chocks may be required. No arrivals before 14.00 please and no visitors under 18.

Facilities	Directions
Two well maintained sanitary blocks provide showers, open style washbasins and hairdryers. En-suite facilities for disabled visitors (Radar key). Motorcaravan services (care needed to access). Well equipped laundry room. Small library. £5 (cash only) refundable deposit for entry card. WiFi (charged). Off site: Golf 0.5 mile. Pub at entrance to park. Shops and restaurants within 1 mile.	From the A55 take exit 16 and at roundabout signed Penmaenmawr turn immediately sharp left into Ysguborwen Road. Entrance to park is 300 yds. on the right. GPS: 53.27425, -3.90632

Open: 22 March - 31 October.

Charges guide

Per unit incl. 2 adults
and electricity £ 23.00 - £ 26.00

For latest campsite news visit
alanrogers.com

Pontarddulais

River View Touring Park

The Dingle, Llanedi, Pontarddulais SA4 0FH (Carmarthenshire) T: 01269 844876.
E: info@riverviewtouringpark.com **alanrogers.com/UK5945**

Nestling in the valley of the River Gwili, River View is an attractive, quiet and friendly park made up of three fields: one by the river which is kept for adults only and two on a plateau up a steep slope on the opposite side of the lane. Particular care has been taken to protect the natural environment. There are 60 level, generously sized pitches, all with 16A electricity, 44 have hardstanding and 12 are fully serviced. This is a popular rural retreat for young families and older couples. The park is close to the end of the M4. This allows easy access and there is plenty to do or see in the near vicinity, including castles, gardens, beaches, wildfowl reserves and a water park.

Facilities

Modern and immaculate toilet block, including an en-suite family room with baby changing facilities and one for disabled visitors, equipped to a very high standard with underfloor heating and automatic lighting. Laundry. Small shop in reception for basics and local fresh produce. Large grassy recreation area on main field. Fishing. Dog walk area. Short woodland walk. Off site: Golf, shop, bar and restaurant 1 mile. Bicycle hire 5 miles. Beach 12 miles.

Open: 4 March - 20 November.

Directions

From M4 exit 49 take A483 signed Llandeilo. Take the first turn left (after layby) and park is on left after 300 yds. Do not use sat nav from Carmarthen direction. GPS: 51.75817, -4.06288

Charges guide

Per unit incl. 2 persons and electricity	£ 17.00 - £ 21.00
extra person	£ 3.00 - £ 4.00

No credit cards.

Prestatyn

Nant Mill Family Touring Caravan & Tenting Park

Gronant Road, Prestatyn LL19 9LY (Denbighshire) T: 01745 852360. E: nantmilltouring@aol.com
alanrogers.com/UK6660

This traditional style, family owned and run park of around seven acres, takes some 115 units arranged over four fields. There are some distant sea views to be had from many pitches. These are carefully allocated to ensure that the largest, central, sloping field is reserved for families. A smaller more intimate field for tents only is to one side of this and two small paddocks on the other side are for couples who might prefer a quieter, more level location. There are 85 electricity connections (10A) but tents are not permitted on pitches with hook-ups. The pitches nearer the road may experience some noise.

Facilities

The main toilet block is older in style but very well kept, with showers, an ample number of open style washbasins and baby changing in both ladies' and men's rooms. Extra showers are in a small modern prefabricated unit alongside. Showers are free, with a £1 deposit for the cubicle key (return after each shower). A prefabricated unit with ramp provides services for disabled visitors. Large laundry and dishwashing room. Playground. WiFi (free).

Open: 28 March - 18 October.

Directions

Site entrance is 0.5 mile east of Prestatyn on A548 coast road. GPS: 53.33765, -3.3932

Charges guide

Per unit incl. 2 persons and electricity	£ 19.00 - £ 22.00
extra person (over 3 yrs)	£ 2.00
dog (max. 1)	free

No credit/debit cards.

Pwllheli

Hafan y Môr Holiday Park

Pwllheli LL53 6HJ (Gwynedd) T: 07949 642534. E: enquiries@haven.com
alanrogers.com/UK6575

One of Haven's flagship parks, Hafan y Môr has substantially redeveloped the touring site and activity area. The park is set on the coast with direct access to the beach. A full range of clubs is provided for toddlers to teens and there is a popular splash zone and adventure playground. This is a large park with 700 caravan holiday homes, either for rent or privately owned. The site has been well designed with hedges, trees, planting, green spaces and lakes. The 74 hardstanding touring pitches are in a separate area and all have 16A electricity. Tents are not accepted on this site.

Facilities

Superb new toilet block with underfloor heating, open washbasins and large, preset showers. Facilities for babies and disabled visitors. Washing machines and dryers. Well stocked supermarket with bakery, off licence, coffee shop and bars. Gift shop. Restaurant and takeaway. Indoor pool complex with flumes and slides. Sporting facilities and coaching. Entertainment. Activity programmes and clubs for children. WiFi (charged).

Open: March - 2 November.

Directions

In Porthmadog take A497 west towards Pwllheli. Park is on the left at roundabout 3 miles beyond Criccieth. GPS: 52.906137, -4.334579

Charges guide

Contact the park for details.

For latest campsite news visit
alanrogers.com

Pwllheli

Bolmynydd Camping Park

Llanbedrog, Pwllheli LL53 7UP (Gwynedd) T: 07882 850820. E: info@bolmynydd.co.uk

alanrogers.com/UK6585

The drive to Bolmynydd is not for the faint hearted. The roads are extremely narrow with plenty of bends, and are accessible only by cars and small VW-style camper vans; the site is not licensed for touring caravans or motorcaravans. However, those who do make the drive are rewarded with spectacular views and a campsite which is ideal for tents and those who wish for peace and quiet in a wonderful rural setting. One field is available for tents and other fields offer safe play areas for young children. With 16 seasonal caravan pitches and 40 tent pitches, the owners request that you telephone ahead to discuss access and availability.

Facilities	Directions
One clean sanitary block, maintained to a high standard (may be under pressure in peak season). Separate modern showers, toilets and open style washbasins. Baby bath in well equipped laundry room. No motorcaravan services. WiFi over site. Off site: Ten minutes walk to small supermarket and pub. Riding, beach and sailing 400 yds. Fishing 1 mile. Golf 3 miles.	From Pwllheli take the A499 toward Abersoch. After 4 miles pass through Llanbedrog and at the campsite sign turn sharp left. Continue for half a mile, site is on the left. Do not follow sat nav into the village of Llanbedrog, instead proceed past and turn at the brown sign. GPS: 52.85231, -4.48844

Open: 1 April - 31 October.

Charges guide

Per unit incl. 2 persons and electricity	£ 25.00 - £ 27.00

No credit cards. Must phone prior to arrival to discuss access and availability.

Pwllheli

Yr Helyg - The Willows Touring Caravan Park

Mynytho, Abersoch, Pwllheli LL53 7RW (Gwynedd) T: 01758 740676. E: thewillowsabersoch@gmail.com

alanrogers.com/UK6587

The Willows is a charming, small but spacious site run by a very friendly family and only three miles from the seaside village of Abersoch. It has magnificent views over the Snowdonia mountains to the east, and the coast to the south. You are sure of a very warm welcome here. This is an immaculate site with superb toilet facilities. The generous, reasonably level pitches are laid out around the perimeter of four small fields. There are 44 touring pitches, with 20 on hardstandings for caravans, all with 16A electricity, plus 22 grass pitches without electricity. Large groups and motorcaravans over 7 m. are not accepted.

Facilities	Directions
Superb, modern, very clean, heated toilet block with some washbasins in cubicles, controllable showers and a family room that doubles as a room for disabled visitors. Some local produce. Separate playing field. Dog walk field. Bicycle hire. Free WiFi over site. Off site: Small shop 500 yds. Fishing, beach and riding 2 miles.	From Pwllheli take A499 southwest to Llanbedrog. In village turn right uphill, B4413, to Mynytho. Just beyond 30 mph sign turn right (signed) to site in 400 yds. GPS: 52.854308, -4.516102

Open: 1 March - 31 October.

Charges guide

Per unit incl. 2 persons and electricity	£ 25.00 - £ 38.00

Rhyl

The Little Paddock Caravan Park

30 Gwellyn Avenue, Kinmel Bay, Rhyl LL18 5HR (Conwy) T: 01745 351607. E: info@thelittlepaddock.com

alanrogers.com/UK6654

This three-acre family run park has 20 touring pitches for caravans and motorcaravans and 15 static caravans. There are no pitches for tents at the moment. Little Paddock is located on the edge of Kinmel Bay with the town on the one side of the site and open, flat fields to the rear, behind the static caravans. All of the pitches are level and the majority are grass, although there are some hardstandings. Most have 16A electricity hook ups, with a few at 10A. The touring pitches are situated either side of the road leading to the static caravans, so some vehicle noise may be heard.

Facilities	Directions
The sanitary block is new and very well maintained, with hot showers (20p/4 mins) and open style washbasins. Washing machines and dryer. Adventure playground. Off site: Beach, sea fishing, golf, town with supermarkets, shops, services and gas supplies all 1 mile. A bus stop is in Denbigh Circle, a short walk from the site.	From the north exit A55 at J27 for Rhyl. Take A525 (Rhyl). At first traffic island turn onto A547 (Abergele), at next traffic island turn right (Kinmel Bay). Just after 30 mph sign turn right into Gwellyn Ave. Site is 500 m. on right. Ignore sat nav directions for Gipsy Lane, where site cannot be accessed. GPS: 53.29753, -3.5103

Open: March - mid October.

Charges guide

Contact park for details.

Saundersfoot
Moreton Farm Leisure Park

Moreton, Saundersfoot SA69 9EA (Pembrokeshire) T: 01834 812016. E: moretonfarm@btconnect.com

alanrogers.com/UK5980

Moreton Farm has been developed in a secluded valley, a 10-20 minute walk from Saundersfoot and four miles from Tenby. It provides 36 caravan pitches (all with 10A electricity, including 22 fully serviced hardstanding pitches) plus 24 tent pitches on two sloping, neatly cut grass fields. There are 12 pine holiday lodges and four cottages for rent occupying another field. The site is approached under a railway bridge (height 10 ft. 9 ins, width across the top 6 ft. 6 ins, but with alternative access over the railway line for slightly larger vehicles just possible). There are a few trains during the day, none at night. This is a quiet family site. An attractive lake at the bottom of the valley is home to ducks, geese and chickens (no fishing). Pembroke and Carew castles and a variety of visitor attractions are close by.

Facilities

The toilet blocks (which can be heated) are light and airy, providing free preset hot showers. Unit for disabled visitors with ramp (shower, toilet and washbasin). Baby bath. Laundry facilities. Fenced, outside clothes drying area. Playground. WiFi over site (charged). No animals are accepted. Off site: Fishing and riding 1 mile. Golf 4 miles.

Open: 1 April - 31 October.

Directions

From A477 Carmarthen-Pembroke road take A478 for Tenby at Kilgelly. Park is signed on left after 1.5 miles. Watch for sign and park is 0.5 miles along new tarmac road and under bridge. Large units should phone in advance for alternative access avoiding low bridge. GPS: 51.71158, -4.72635

Charges guide

Per unit incl. 2 persons and electricity	£ 26.00 - £ 30.00
extra person	£ 3.00

St Davids
Caerfai Bay Caravan & Tent Park

Caerfai Road, St Davids SA62 6QT (Pembrokeshire) T: 01437 720274. E: info@caerfaibay.co.uk

alanrogers.com/UK5995

About as far west as one can get in Wales, St Davids is Britain's smallest city, noted for its cathedral and Bishop's Palace. This cliff-top park in west Wales has direct access to the Pembrokeshire Coastal Path and a magnificent sandy beach is just a few minutes away, down a path from the car park by the site entrance. Altogether there are 105 touring pitches (including 78 for tents) and 45 electric hook-ups (10A), with 16 hardstandings. Main access roads are tarmac. The camping area is spread over three open and sloping fields (chocks are often necessary). All have magnificent views over Saint Brides Bay. The caravan field also has a small number of holiday homes and is closest to reception. The second and third fields are for tents and motorcaravans, almost all on grass with a few hardstandings available. Caerfai farm shop is across the lane (opens at the end of May) and other shops and services are just a mile away. Site lighting is deliberately minimal, so a torch would be useful.

Facilities

Three main heated buildings house the sanitary facilities, one by reception contains facilities for disabled visitors and families, dishwashing, laundry, cooking facilities (hot plate, microwave and fridge). Adjacent a small block offers 3 unisex cubicles (WC and basin). The third, in the tent field, includes 4 family rooms, dishwashing, microwave, fridge, toaster, wet suit washing and drying area. Motorcaravan services. Bicycle storage. Gas. Barbecue stands for hire. Dog walking area (dogs not accepted in the tent field in high season). WiFi (charged). Charging points for phones and tablets (in secure lockers). Off site: Walk the Pembrokeshire coastal path, visit Ramsey Island Bird and Grey Seal Reserve. St Davids Cathedral and Oriel Y Parc Visitor Centre/Gallery. Sea fishing 400 yds. Boat launching 1.5 and 3 miles. Golf 2 miles. Riding 10 miles.

Open: 1 March - 14 November.

Directions

From Haverfordwest take the A487 to St Davids. On passing the city boundary, turn left into lane immediately before the Oriel Y Parc Visitor Centre and Gallery (site signed), and continue on for 0.75 miles to site entrance on right. GPS: 51.872983, -5.2569

Charges guide

Per unit incl. 2 persons and electricity	£ 19.00 - £ 24.00
extra person	£ 5.00
child (3-12 yrs)	£ 3.50
dog	£ 1.00
Discounts for early payment, and for senior citizens in low season.	

For latest campsite news visit
alanrogers.com

Swansea

Three Cliffs Bay Holiday Park

North Hills Farm, Penmaen, Swansea SA3 2HB (Swansea) T: 01792 371218. E: info@threecliffsbay.com

alanrogers.com/UK5874

This site is in an ideal situation for beach lovers or those who simply want to enjoy a superb coastal view. A large courtyard with a small row of holiday cottages provides the backdrop to the campsite that lies beyond. The pitches are on two fields, with 21 hardstandings (10A electricity hook-up) and 100 grass pitches (five 10A hook-ups), some overlooking the Three Cliffs Bay. Although predominantly a touring site, there are six luxurious, wooden shepherd's huts plus a 'timber tent' for rent. A well laid out and attractive site, but with some steep slopes near the edge overlooking the bay (levelling blocks required). The final access road is narrow with passing places.

Facilities

A centrally located toilet block is kept exceptionally clean. Facilities for disabled visitors serve as a second family room in peak season as required. Kitchen with dishwashing facilities. Laundry room by site entrance. Small shop in reception sells groceries, takeaway tea and coffee. Mobile phones and laptops can be charged at the shop (small charge). Free WiFi. Off site: The Gower Inn (dogs accepted) 1 mile. Pony trekking and archery just over 1 mile. Surfing at Llangenith beach. Excellent shopping and LC2 indoor pool in Swansea.

Open: Week before Easter - October.

Directions

From M4 exit 42 take A483 towards Swansea, bear left onto A4067 for 3.5 miles. Turn right at lights (B4436) signed South Gower and Port Eynon. After 4 miles turn right by Pennard Church, then next left onto A4118 for 2.5 miles. Penmaen is between the villages of Parkmill and Nicholston. Park is signed on left as you enter Penmain. GPS: 51.57714, -4.11335

Charges guide

Per unit incl. 4 persons and electricity	£ 26.00 - £ 30.00

Tenby

Trefalun Park

Devonshire Drive, Saint Florence, Tenby SA70 8RD (Pembrokeshire) T: 01646 651514. E: trefalun@aol.com

alanrogers.com/UK5982

Only four miles from Tenby and the beaches of Carmarthen Bay, Trefalun Park is an open, well laid out campsite with a friendly atmosphere engendered by the owners. There are 90 touring pitches here which are mainly level, although the park has gentle slopes. The pitches are generously sized with 10/16A electricity available. Hardstandings have been created for 64 pitches, some with full services. This park will suit those, particularly families, looking for a quiet holiday and also the more active who favour walking, cycling or watersports. A large fenced recreational area has a variety of adventure type play equipment and a football pitch. A wildlife park is about 600 yards away opposite the turning to Trefalun Park. Pembroke and Manorbier with their respective castles are only four and five miles away and there are many other historic monuments close by.

Facilities

Modern heated sanitary block with showers and some washbasins in cubicles. Separate, fully equipped suite for disabled visitors and families. Separate baby room. Laundry. Motorcaravan services. Gas. Play area. WiFi (charged). Off site: Fishing, riding and wildlife park 600 yds. Shop, pub (with food) and outdoor pool 1.5 miles. Golf 3 miles. Tenby with all town facilities, beach, boat launching and sailing 4 miles.

Open: April - October.

Directions

From the A477 at Sageston (4 miles east of Pembroke) turn southeast just to the east of the village on B4318 signed for the Wildlife Park. Trefalun Park is signed to the left after 2.5 miles, opposite the entrance to the Wildlife Park. GPS: 51.69326, -4.75340

Charges guide

Per unit incl. 2 persons and electricity	£ 15.00 - £ 24.00
with services	£ 17.00 - £ 27.00
extra person (over 3 yrs)	£ 2.50

Wrexham
Plassey Leisure Park
Eyton, Wrexham LL13 0SP (Wrexham) T: 01978 780277. E: enquiries@plassey.com
alanrogers.com/UK6670

Plassey Leisure Park has been carefully developed over the past 50 years. Improvements include landscaping, car parking and low level lighting installed around the park. A new area for 15 privately owned holiday homes has been recently created. Originally a dairy farm, the park is set in 247 acres of the Dee Valley and offers an extensive range of activities. It has been divided into discreet areas with 120 pitches around the edges. There are 90 touring pitches with 16A electrical connections, 30 pitches are fully serviced and 50 have hardstanding. Five further areas accommodate 120 seasonal caravans. There is much to do and to look at in the rural setting at Plassey. A member of the Best of British group.

Facilities

Some refurbished toilet facilities are supplemented by a newer heated block with individual washbasin cubicles, a room for families and disabled visitors. Laundry. Motorcaravan services. Shop. Club room with games room for children. Heated indoor pool with sunbed and sauna (charged). Adventure play area. 9-hole golf course. Fishing lakes. Bicycle hire. No skateboards or footballs permitted. Luxury holiday home for hire. WiFi throughout (charged). Off site: Riding 2 miles.

Open: February - November.

Directions

Follow brown and cream signs for The Plassey from the A483 Chester-Oswestry bypass onto the B5426 and park is 2.5 miles. Also signed from the A528 Marchwiel-Overton road. GPS: 52.997883, -2.966317

Charges guide

Per unit incl. 2 persons and electricity	£ 18.70 - £ 36.90

Includes club membership, coarse fishing, badminton and table tennis (own racquets and bats required).

Wrexham
Emral Gardens Caravan Park
Holly Bush, Bangor-on-Dee, Wrexham LL13 0BG (Wrexham) T: 01948 770401. E: info@emralgardens.com
alanrogers.com/UK6675

Emral Gardens is located on the edge of Bangor on Dee. It sits in a small valley and is surrounded by ancient woodland and undulating fields. A small family run caravan park for adults only, it has just 20 fully serviced touring pitches for caravans and motorcaravans. All are flat and equipped with 16A electricity hook-ups, water, waste water and TV connection. There are some hardstandings and some additional grass pitches are planned. The pitches surround a quaint pond in the middle of the site.

Facilities

The heated sanitary block, in the style of a log cabin, is new and very well maintained, with hot showers, open style washbasins. Laundry facilities. Fishing. WiFi (free). Off site: Bangor on Dee Racecourse. National Trust properties Erddig Hall and Chirk Castle are just a short drive away. Llangollen with its canal and railway and the famous Pontcysyllte Aqueduct are 15 minutes' drive.

Open: 1 March - 1 November.

Directions

From Bangor on Dee take A525 southeast towards Whitchurch. After 1.5 miles turn left at crossroads (Worthenbury and Tallarn Green). After 0.75 miles turn right (by Emral Lodge). Follow hardcore track for 0.5 miles to site. GPS: 52.99219, -2.86671

Charges guide

Per unit incl. 2 persons and all services	£ 20.00 - £ 30.00
extra person	£ 5.00

Wrexham
James' Caravan Park
Ruabon, Wrexham LL14 6DW (Wrexham) T: 01978 820148. E: ray@carastay.demon.co.uk
alanrogers.com/UK6680

Open all year, James' has attractive, park-like surroundings with mature trees and neat, short grass. However, edged by two main roads it is subject to some road noise. The park has over 40 pitches, some level and some on a slope, with informal siting giving either a view or shade. Electricity (6/10A) is available all over, although a long lead may be useful. Being so conveniently positioned, this is an ideal stopover site with easy access from the A483 Wrexham-Oswestry road. The park is close to a number of man-made and natural attractions.

Facilities

The heated toilet block offers roomy showers but would benefit from updating. Foyer contains tourist information and free freezer. Cleaning variable. En-suite facilities for disabled campers complete with special 'clos-o-mat' toilet! Motorcaravan services. Gas available. Payphone. Off site: The village is a 10 minute walk with a Nisa shop, fish and chips, a restaurant, launderette and four pubs. Golf 3 miles.

Open: All year.

Directions

Park is at junction of A483/A539 Llangollen road and is accessible from the westbound A539. GPS: 52.98305, -3.04081

Charges guide

Per unit incl. 2 persons and electricity	£ 17.00
extra person	£ 5.00
awning	£ 2.00

No credit cards.

For latest campsite news visit
alanrogers.com

From gentle rolling hills and rugged coastlines, to dramatic peaks, punctuated with beautiful lochs, Scotland is a land steeped in history that provides superb opportunities to enjoy wild, untamed and spectacular scenery.

Probably the most striking thing about Scotland is the vast areas of uninhabited landscape. Southern Scotland boasts beautiful fertile plains, woodlands and wild sea coasts. It also has a rich heritage with ancient castles, abbeys and grand houses. Further north are the Trossachs with their heather-clad hills, home of Rob Roy, the folk hero. The Highlands and Islands, including Skye, Mull and Islay, have some of the most dramatic landscapes in Europe, dominated by breathtaking mountain ranges such as Ben Nevis and the Grampians, plus deep glistening lochs, the largest being Loch Ness where the monster reputedly lives. And lying at the very edge of Europe, the islands of the Inner and Outer Hebrides share a rugged, natural beauty with unspoilt beaches and an abundance of wildlife. The two largest cities, Edinburgh and Glasgow, have their own unique attractions. The capital, Edinburgh, with magnificent architecture, comprises the edieval Old Town and the Georgian New Town, with the ancient castle standing proudly in the middle. A short distance to the west, Glasgow has more parks and over 20 museums and galleries, with works by Charles Rennie Mackintosh scattered around the city.

Places of interest

Lowlands: National Gallery of Scotland and Edinburgh Castle; Glasgow Science Centre; Stirling Castle; New Lanark World Heritage Site; Kelso Abbey.

Heart of Scotland: fishing town of Oban; Stirling Castle and Wallace Monument; Loch Lomond; Pitlochry; university town of St Andrews; Aberdeen; Dunfermline Abbey; fishing villages of Crail and Anstruther; Famous Grouse Experience in Crieff.

Highlands and Islands: Fort William; 600 ft. Eas a Chual Aluinn waterfall near Kylesku; the Cairngorms; Highland Wildlife Park at Kingussie; Inverness; Aviemore; Lochalsh Woodland Gardens; Malt Whisky Trail, Moray; Dunvegan Castle on the Isle of Skye.

Did you know?

Dunfermline Abbey is the final resting place of 22 kings, queens, princes and princesses of Scotland, including Robert the Bruce.

Whales can be seen off the west coast of the Highlands, and the Moray Firth is home to bottle-nosed dolphins.

Many famous ships were built at Clydebank, including the Cutty Sark and the Lusitania.

Since 1861, every day (except on Sundays), the one o'clock gun has boomed out from Edinburgh castle.

Charles Rennie Mackintosh, famous architect and designer, was born in Glasgow in 1868.

The first organised fire brigade was established in Edinburgh in 1824.

The Forth Railway Bridge is 8,296 ft. long.

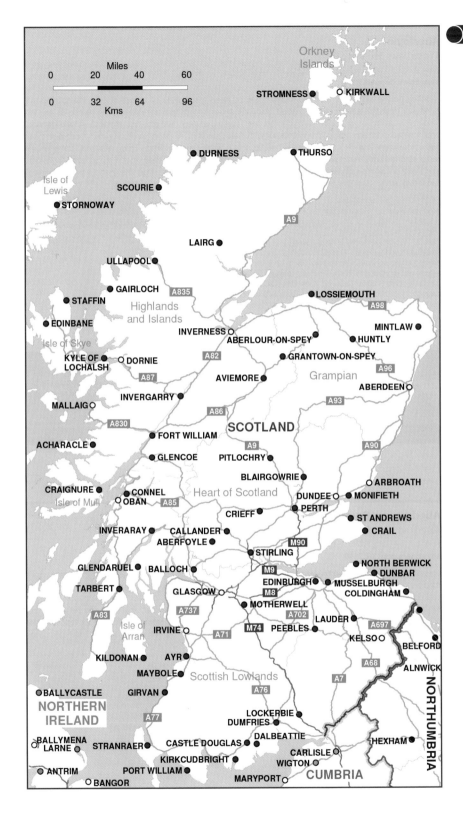

Aberfoyle

Trossachs Holiday Park

Aberfoyle FK8 3SA (Stirling) T: 01877 382614. E: info@trossachsholidays.co.uk

alanrogers.com/UK7230

Nestling on the side of a hill, three miles south of Aberfoyle, this is an excellent base for touring this famously beautiful area. Lochs Lomond, Ard, Venachar and others are within easy reach, as are the Queen Elizabeth Forest Park and, of course, the Trossachs. Very neat and tidy, there are 45 well laid out and marked pitches arranged on terraces with hardstanding. All have electricity and most also have water, drainage and TV connections. There is also a large area for tents. There are trees between the terraces and lovely views across the valley. The adjoining oak and bluebell woods are a haven for wildlife and there are some wonderful walks. You will receive a warm welcome from the friendly staff at this well run family park.

Facilities

A timber building houses sanitary facilities providing a satisfactory supply of toilets, showers and washbasins, the ladies' area being rather larger with two private cabins. Two private family shower suites (deposit required). Laundry room. Well stocked shop (all season). Motorcaravan services. Games room with TV. Play equipment (on gravel). Off site: Fishing 1 mile. Golf and boat launching 3 miles. Sailing 6 miles. Discount scheme arranged with a local leisure centre provides facilities for swimming, sauna, solarium, badminton, tennis, windsurfing, etc.

Open: 1 March - 31 October.

Directions

Park is 3 miles south of Aberfoyle on the A81 road, well signed. GPS: 56.140133, -4.3555

Charges guide

Per unit incl. 2 persons	
and electricity	£ 19.00 - £ 25.00
child (0-15 yrs)	£ 2.00
tent pitch incl. 2 persons	£ 15.00 - £ 21.00
extra person	£ 4.00

TROSSACHS HOLIDAY PARK - ABERFOYLE STIRLING FK8 3SA
www.trossachsholidays.co.uk Tel: 01877 382614

One of the finest Environmental Holiday Parks on the edge of the National Park area
• 40 Exclusive Touring Pitches - ALL fully serviced and on Hard-Standing
• Motorhome Driveover service point • Family Shower suite available
• Internet cafe • Visit Scotland 5 Star Holiday Park

Aberlour-on-Spey

Aberlour Gardens Caravan & Camping Park

Aberlour-on-Spey AB38 9LD (Moray) T: 01340 871586. E: info@aberlourgardens.co.uk

alanrogers.com/UK7540

This pleasant park is within the large walled garden of the Aberlour Estate on Speyside. The owners have made many improvements to the sheltered, five-acre, family run park which provides a very natural setting amidst spruce and Scots pine. Of the 73 level pitches, 35 are for touring units leaving the remainder for holiday homes and seasonal units. All pitches have 10A electrical connections and 16 are all-weather pitches. This is an ideal area for walking, birdwatching, salmon fishing or for following the only Malt Whisky Trail in the world, while Aberlour has a fascinating old village shop. A member of the Best of British group.

Facilities

The toilet facilities are now a little dated (there are plans for refurbishment). Facilities for visitors with disabilities can also be used as family or baby changing room. Laundry facilities. Motorcaravan services. Small shop stocking basics and with an information area. Play area. Bicycle hire. WiFi throughout (charged). Off site: Swimming 1 mile. Fishing 1 and 5 miles. Golf 4 miles.

Open: 1 March - 27 December.

Directions

Turn off A95 0.5 miles east of Aberlour onto unclassified road (Bluehill Quarry). Site signed in 500 yds. Vehicles over 10 ft. 6 in. high should use the A941 Dufftown road (site signed). GPS: 57.47485, -3.1986

Charges guide

Per unit incl. 2 persons	
and electricity	£ 20.15 - £ 25.10
extra person (over 5 yrs)	£ 2.50
backpacker and tent (per person)	£ 9.00 - £ 10.65
dog	free

For latest campsite news visit

alanrogers.com

Acharacle
Resipole Farm Holiday Park
Loch Sunart, Acharacle PH36 4HX (Highland) T: 01967 431235. E: info@resipole.co.uk
alanrogers.com/UK7800

This quiet, open, five-hectare park is marvellously set on the shores of Loch Sunart, eight miles from Strontian, on the Ardnamurchan peninsula. It is a must for anyone seeking peace and tranquillity and really worth the journey. With wonderful views across the water and regularly visited by wild deer, Resipole Farm offers a good base for exploring the whole of this scenic area or, more locally, for fishing, boating (launching from the site's own slipway) and walking in the unspoilt countryside. There are 48 level and well drained touring pitches here, 40 with 10/16A electricity. Tents are sited by the hedges.

Facilities

The central, modern sanitary block can be heated and is kept very clean. Excellent provision for disabled visitors. Laundry facilities. Motorcaravan services. Caravan storage. Art gallery and studios. Fishing. WiFi in some areas (free).

Open: Easter/1 April - 31 October.

Directions

From A82 Fort William road, take Corran ferry 5 miles north of Ballachulish and 8 miles south of Fort William. Leaving ferry, turn south along A861. Park is on north shore of Loch Sunart, 8 miles west of Strontian. Single track road for 8 miles towards Resipole. GPS: 56.710933, -5.720217

Charges guide

Per unit incl. 2 persons and electricity	£ 23.00
extra person	£ 4.00

Aviemore
Camping in the Forest Glenmore
Aviemore PH22 1QU (Highland) T: 01479 861271. E: info@forestholidays.co.uk
alanrogers.com/UK7680

Forest Holidays is a partnership between the Forestry Commission and The Camping and Caravanning Club. This site is attractively laid out in a fairly informal style in several adjoining areas connected by narrow, part gravel, part tarmac roads, with access to the lochside. One of these areas, the Pinewood Area, is very popular and has 28 hardstandings (some distance from the toilet block). Of the 206 marked pitches on fairly level, firm grass, 78 have 16A electricity. This site, with something for everyone, would be great for family holidays. The Glenmore Forest Park lies close to the sandy shore of Loch Morlich amidst conifer woods and is surrounded on three sides by the impressive Cairngorm mountains.

Facilities

Heated toilet and shower blocks include facilities for disabled visitors. Next to the site is a range of amenities including a café serving a variety of meals and snacks, and a Forestry Commission visitor centre. Barbecues are not permitted in dry weather. Bicycle hire. Fishing. Sandy beach (Blue Flag). Off site: The Aviemore centre with a wide range of indoor and outdoor recreation activities including skiing 7 miles. Golf within 15 miles. Boat trips.

Open: All year.

Directions

Immediately south of Aviemore on B9152 (not A9 bypass) take B970 then follow sign for Cairngorm and Loch Morlich. Site entrance is on right past the loch. If travelling in winter, prepare for snow. GPS: 57.167033, -3.694717

Charges guide

Per unit incl. 2 persons and electricity	£ 15.00 - £ 28.50
extra person	£ 5.00 - £ 9.50

Ayr
Sundrum Castle Holiday Park
Coylton, Ayr KA6 5JH (South Ayrshire) T: 01292 570057. E: siobhanstevenson@parkdeanholidays.com
alanrogers.com/UK7005

Sundrum Castle Holiday Park, part of the Parkdean Group, is situated in rolling countryside close to historic castles and miles of Ayrshire beaches. This is a large park with 285 caravan holiday homes. There is also provision for 45 touring units on open pitches around the main complex, including 30 on hardstanding pitches with 16A electricity connections. A further sloping grass area is available for tents. The extensive site facilities are arranged around the entrance with a large reception and leisure complex including an indoor pool. An entertainment programme is arranged for all the family.

Facilities

The clean, heated sanitary block has vanity style washbasins and small preset showers. Facility for disabled visitors (bath, no shower). Laundry room. Motorcaravan services. Well stocked shop. Bar/restaurant. Takeaway. Indoor heated swimming pool (March-Nov). Solarium. Arcade games and pool table. Mini 10-pin bowling. Evening entertainment. Outdoor adventure play area. Crazy golf. Basketball. Free WiFi over site.

Open: 23 March - 6 November.

Directions

Four miles east of Ayr take A70. Just before Coylton village, park is on left hand side. GPS: 55.4533, -4.523533

Charges guide

Per unit incl. 4 persons and electricity	£ 14.00 - £ 36.00
extra person	£ 3.50
child	£ 2.50

For latest campsite news visit
alanrogers.com

Balloch

Lomond Woods Holiday Park

Tullichewan, Old Luss Road, Balloch G83 8QP (West Dunbartonshire) T: 01389 755000.

E: lomondwoods@holiday-parks.co.uk **alanrogers.com/UK7240**

A series of improvements over the last few years has made this one of the top parks in Scotland. Almost, but not quite, on the banks of Loch Lomond, this landscaped, well planned park is suitable for both transit or longer stays. There are 110 touring units on well spaced, numbered pitches on flat or gently sloping grass. All have hardstanding and 10A electrical connections and 27 have water and waste water too. Watersports activities and boat trips are possible on Loch Lomond, with a visitor attraction, Lomond Shores, nearby.

Facilities

The large, heated, well kept toilet block includes some showers with WCs, baths for ladies, a shower room for disabled visitors and two baby baths. Covered dishwashing sinks. Launderette. Motorcaravan services. Games room with TV, table tennis and pool table. Playground. Caravan storage. American motorhomes accepted with prior notice. WiFi over site (charged). Glamping style pods are available for rent.

Open: All year.

Directions

Turn off A82 road 17 miles northwest of Glasgow on A811 Stirling road. Site is in Balloch at southern end of Loch Lomond and is well signed.
GPS: 56.00155, -4.592233

Charges guide

Per unit incl. up to 2 persons	
and electricity	£ 21.00 - £ 25.00
incl. mains services and awning	£ 24.00 - £ 28.00
extra person	£ 3.00

Blairgowrie

Nethercraig Caravan Park

By Alyth, Blairgowrie PH11 8HN (Perth and Kinross) T: 01575 560204. E: info@nethercraig.com
alanrogers.com/UK7280

Nethercraig is a family run touring park, attractively designed and beautifully landscaped, with views across the Strathmore valley to the long range of the Sidlaw hills. The 50 large touring pitches are accessed from a circular, gravel road, all with 10A electrical connections and 40 on hardstanding (for awnings too). In addition, there are five large pitches for tents on flat grass. There is a personal welcome for all visitors at the attractive modern reception building and shop which provides the necessary essentials, gas and tourist information. The owners have arranged discounts with three local golf courses. A one mile circular woodland walk from the park has picnic benches and a leaflet is provided.

Facilities

The central, purpose built toilet block is well equipped and maintained and can be heated. Unit for disabled visitors (entry by key). Laundry room with washing machine, dryer, iron and clothes line. Shop. Play area. Small football field. Fishing. Bicycle hire. Caravan storage. WiFi throughout. Off site: Golf within 4 miles. Riding 4 miles. Boat launching 6 miles.

Open: 15 February - 15 January.

Directions

From A926 Blairgowrie-Kirriemuir road, at roundabout south of Alyth join B954 (Glenisla). Follow caravan signs for 4 miles and turn right onto unclassified road (Nether Craig). Park is on left after 0.5 miles. GPS: 56.6614, -3.1998

Charges guide

Per unit incl. up to 4 persons and electricity	£ 22.00
extra person	£ 1.00

No credit cards.

Callander

The Gart Caravan Park

Stirling Road, Callander FK17 8LE (Perth and Kinross) T: 01877 330002. E: enquiries@theholidaypark.co.uk
alanrogers.com/UK7220

Gart Caravan Park is situated within the Loch Lomond and Trossachs National Park, just a mile from the centre of Callander. Surrounded by mature trees, this attractive, family run park is peaceful and spacious. All is kept in a pristine condition and a very warm welcome awaits on arrival with a superb information pack given to all. The 128 all grass touring pitches are reasonably level, open plan and marked, with 16A electricity, water and drain. Tents and pup tents are not accepted, groundsheets are not permitted. Privately owned caravan holiday homes are located away from the touring section near the river which runs for 200 yards along the park boundary.

Facilities

Modern heated central facilities are immaculate, kept spotlessly clean with toilets and showers, plus extra areas with showers, baby changing and hair washing basins. Separate facilities for disabled visitors. Laundry. Drive-over motorcaravan service point. Gas sales. Breakfast car arrives at 09.00 with papers and basics. Large adventure play area, part undercover. Separate field for ball games.

Open: 1 April - 15 October.

Directions

From the south take M9. Near Stirling, leave at exit 10 and follow A84 through Doune. Park is on the left, 1 mile before Callander town centre.
GPS: 56.2365, -4.1891

Charges guide

Per unit incl. services	£ 24.00 - £ 26.00
awning	£ 2.00

Reduced rates for the over 50s. Loyalty card.

For latest campsite news visit
alanrogers.com

Castle Douglas
Mossyard Caravan Park

Gatehouse of Fleet, Castle Douglas DG7 2ET (Dumfries and Galloway) T: 01557 840226.

E: enquiry@mossyard.co.uk **alanrogers.com/UK6890**

Mossyard is a family run park set within a working farm right beside the sea in a sheltered bay. The park and farmhouse appear together suddenly over the horizon as you approach, with some breathtaking views across the Solway where the waters of Fleet Bay meet. There are 37 grass touring pitches, 12 for caravans and motorcaravans on an elevated area that slopes in parts. The remaining 25 pitches for any unit are on a level field which adjoins the beach but is a little way from the sanitary facilities. Electrical connections (16A) are available to all.

Facilities

Some of the farm buildings around the main farmhouse have been utilised for the sanitary facilities, which are of traditional design. Showers are coin-operated (20p). Roomy facilities for disabled visitors can also be used as a family bathroom. Building with laundry, dishwashing area and information room with freezer and fridge for visitors' use. No shop, but supermarkets deliver. Off site: Gatehouse of Fleet with pubs, restaurants and shops 4 miles. Riding 1 mile. Bicycle hire and golf 5 miles.

Open: 1 April - 31 August.

Directions

Take A75 road from Dumfries towards Stranraer and park is signed to the left, 4 miles west of Gatehouse of Fleet, 1 mile down a single track farm road. GPS: 54.840183, -4.26015

Charges guide

Per unit incl. 2 persons and electricity	£ 15.00 - £ 17.00
extra person	£ 2.00

Castle Douglas
Loch Ken Holiday Park

Parton, Castle Douglas DG7 3NE (Dumfries and Galloway) T: 01644 470282.

E: office@lochkenholidaypark.co.uk **alanrogers.com/UK6940**

Loch Ken Holiday Park is a very well maintained site on the shore of the loch, opposite the RSPB bird reserve and the Galloway Forest Park – it is a peaceful haven in an Area of Outstanding Natural Beauty. This is a family owned park with 40 touring pitches and 34 caravan holiday homes, 11 of which are for rent. The touring pitches, all with 16A electricity, are separate and arranged in an open plan way with loch views, on good sized hardstandings, with three on neatly mown grass. There is a separate tent field offering some pitches with electricity. Mature trees border the park and provide a dog walking area.

Facilities

The heated toilet block has been completely refurbished to modern standards and was exceptionally clean when we visited. Separate facilities in a modern prefabricated unit are provided in the tent field. Facilities for disabled visitors. Laundry room. Gas supplies. Well stocked shop. Two play areas. Outdoor chess. Herb garden. Bicycles, canoes, pedaloes and dinghies for hire. Boat launching (permit from reception). Fishing (permit). WiFi (free).

Open: 1 March - 10 November.

Directions

From Castle Douglas take the A713 north for 7 miles. Site entrance is on left in Parton. GPS: 55.01017, -4.05630

Charges guide

Per unit incl. 2 persons, 2 children and electricity	£ 18.00 - £ 22.00
tent, no electricity	£ 14.00 - £ 17.00
extra person	£ 2.00

Castle Douglas
Barlochan Caravan Park

Palnackie, Castle Douglas DG7 1PF (Dumfries and Galloway) T: 01557 870267.

E: info@gillespie-leisure.co.uk **alanrogers.com/UK6945**

Barlochan Caravan Park is situated on a hillside overlooking the Urr Estuary on the Solway Coast close to Dalbeattie and Castle Douglas, with the small village of Palnackie being a short walk away. Set on terraces, level, marked and numbered, most of the touring and tent pitches are on grass with a limited number of hardstandings available. There are 16 with 16A electrical connections. In addition, there are two new hikers' pods and 60 holiday homes (five for hire) are positioned on terraces high above the touring areas and screened by mature shrubs and trees. Just to the left of the entrance there is a minigolf course and an adventure play area screened from the park with mature trees.

Facilities

The heated sanitary facilities are kept spotlessly clean. Shower cubicles have recently been made larger, suitable for wheelchair entry, but if required there is also a separate unit with WC and basin. Fully equipped laundry with outside drying area. Reception and well stocked shop. Heated small outdoor swimming pool and terrace. Large games room and TV room. Minigolf.

Open: Easter/1 April - 31 October.

Directions

From Dumfries take A711 west to Dalbeattie. Continue through Dalbeattie for 0.5 miles and bear left at T-junction signed Auchencairn. Site is 2 miles on the right. GPS: 54.895023, -3.842564

Charges guide

Per unit incl. 2 persons and electricity	£ 17.00 - £ 22.00
extra person	£ 2.00

For latest campsite news visit
alanrogers.com

Coldingham

Scoutscroft Holiday Centre

Saint Abbs Road, Coldingham, Eyemouth TD14 5NB (Borders) T: 01890 771338.
E: holidays@scoutscroft.co.uk **alanrogers.com/UK7070**

Scoutscroft Holiday Centre is a family run park surrounded by low banks and trees, situated in the picturesque village of Coldingham. A tarmac road passes through the mobile home section to the 80 fairly level, hardstanding touring pitches. All are numbered and have 13A electricity. There is a steep drop to an unfenced stream that runs alongside the touring area, and the road to the beach can be accessed from this area (but not by vehicles). There is no shop on site, but a well stocked Spar is nearby. There is entertainment every evening in high season and every Friday and Saturday outside this period.

Facilities

A modern heated toilet block (key access) is approached via a bridge over the stream. It is clean and well equipped with controllable showers. Separate family room with baby changing area, also used for disabled visitors. A second block is by the touring area and houses the launderette. Bar, restaurant and takeaway. Snooker lounge. Play area with indoor arcade. Dive shop with tackle and hire and repair equipment. TV booster aerials for hire. Off site: Spar shop 5 mins. walk. Safe, sandy beach nearby.

Open: 1 March - 30 November.

Directions

From south take A1107 off A1 and continue to Coldingham. Take B6438 towards St. Abbs. The site is on your right. From north leave A1 at Reston junction and take B6438 into Coldingham, then as above. GPS: 55.888484, -2.151126

Charges guide

Per unit	£ 21.00 - £ 25.00
awning	£ 5.00

Connel

Oban Camping & Caravanning Club Site

Barcaldine, By Connel PA37 1SG (Argyll and Bute) T: 01631 720348.
alanrogers.com/UK7810

Owned by The Camping and Caravanning Club, this site at Barcaldine, 12 miles north of Oban, is a small, intimate site taking 75 units. Arranged within the old walled garden of Barcaldine House, it has some protection from the wind which makes it quite a sun trap. There are 23 level, fairly small pitches with hardstanding and 52 electrical hook-ups (16A). It can be wet underfoot in bad weather. Being a small site, it has a very cosy feel to it, due no doubt to the friendly welcome given to new arrivals. There is a new entrance barrier (code access).

Facilities

The excellent new central toilet block can be heated and is kept very clean with free hot showers, hairdryers and plenty of washbasins, some in cubicles, and WCs. Two excellent units for disabled visitors (one doubles as family room) with ramped access. Laundry. Motorcaravan services. Small shop open a few hours each day for basic provisions and gas. Small play area with effective safety base. WiFi over site (charged). Off site: Marina and small beach opposite. Sea Life Centre 2 miles.

Open: 24 March - 24 October.

Directions

Entrance is off the A828 road on south side of Loch Creran, 6 miles north of Connel Bridge. From the south, go past Barcaldine House and site is 300 yds. on right. Entrance height restriction: 3.4 m. GPS: 56.5265, -5.309933

Charges guide

Per unit incl. 2 persons and electricity	£ 15.05 - £ 25.70
extra person	£ 5.75 - £ 9.80
Non-member prices are higher.	

Craignure

Shieling Holidays

Craignure, Isle of Mull PA65 6AY (Argyll and Bute) T: 01680 812496.
alanrogers.com/UK7825

This lovely site looks across the Sound of Mull to the mainland, and on a clear day, Ben Nevis can be seen from the tent pitches. There are 31 hardstanding pitches for tourers, all with 13A electricity hook-ups, plus 59 tent pitches. The tent pitches are astroturf and strong pegs and a hammer are available from reception if required. Rental accommodation is in two cottages and 13 Shielings (tents made of a very thick white plastic material). Some are en-suite, carpeted and have gas and electricity. Most pitches have wonderful views.

Facilities

The modern, clean toilet block can be heated and has free showers and hairdryers. Two Sheiling toilet blocks are in the tent area, along with baths and facilities for disabled visitors. Family shower room. Laundry. Motorcaravan services. Games room. Bicycle hire and boat launching. Free WiFi in reception and common room (open 24 hours; no mobile signal). Off site: Play area by entrance.

Open: 6 March - 2 November.

Directions

Take a ferry crossing to Mull. Take the A849 to Craignure. The site is at the far end of the village looking across to the jetty. GPS: 56.469235, -5.698278

Charges guide

Per unit incl. 2 persons and electricity	£ 24.50

For latest campsite news visit
alanrogers.com

Crail
Sauchope Links Park

Crail KY10 3XJ (Fife) T: 01333 450460. E: info@sauchope.co.uk

alanrogers.com/UK7285

Sauchope Links Park is a member of the Largo Leisure Parks group with a good range of facilities on offer, notably a heated swimming pool, an indoor recreation room and a play area for children. The coastal location is very attractive with miles of rocky shore to be explored and the Fife Coastal Path traverses the site. Pitches here are grassy and of a good size. A number of fully serviced pitches are available and also hardstandings. Sea front pitches provide views of the Isle of May. Alternatively, a number of mobile homes and micro lodges (small wooden chalets) are available for rent.

Facilities

Heated sanitary block with hot showers and facilities for disabled visitors. Laundry facilities. Small shop. Outdoor swimming pool (June-Sept). Games room. Play areas. Mobile homes and other accommodation for rent. WiFi throughout (charged). Off site: Top class golf at Crail golf club, the seventh oldest in the world and the Royal and Ancient club at St Andrews needs little introduction. Walking and cycle tracks. Fishing. Riding. Scone Palace.

Open: 20 March - 31 October.

Directions

Approaching from St Andrews on the A917, on entering Crail at a sharp right hand corner, turn left down an unclassified road. Site is signed 400 yds. on right. Follow signs to the site, which is down by the sea. GPS: 56.261606, -2.612724

Charges guide

Per unit incl. 2 persons	
and electricity	£ 19.00 - £ 40.00
fully serviced	£ 21.00 - £ 45.00

Crieff
Braidhaugh Holiday Park

South Bridgend, Crieff PH7 4DH (Perth and Kinross) T: 01764 652951. E: info@braidhaugh.co.uk

alanrogers.com/UK7275

Braidhaugh is a member of the Largo Leisure Parks group and is situated on the banks of the River Earn among the scenic surroundings of Perthshire. There are 39 touring pitches, all with electricity, water and drainage. The site is well located for exploring central Scotland, as well as being within walking distance of shops, restaurants, places of interest and many sporting facilities. The Earn is renowned for its salmon and trout fishing and permits can be purchased from the reception. The small shop stocks the essentials and a larger supermarket is close at hand. Other on-site amenities include a games room with TV. For younger children there is an outdoor play area and the public playground next to the park provides a larger play area and space for ball games.

Facilities

Sanitary block with power showers and hairdryer in ladies' (20p) Separate room with shower and WC for disabled visitors. Small shop. Games room. Play areas. Fishing. WiFi (charged). Mobile homes and other accommodation for rent. Off site: Top class golf (courses at Muthill, Crieff and Comrie). Walking and cycle tracks. Fishing. Riding. Leisure centre.

Open: All year.

Directions

Approaching from Perth, drive through Crieff and turn left onto the A822 (Stirling). At the bottom of the hill cross a bridge over the River Earn. Turn right immediately after the bridge and take the first right to enter park. GPS: 56.366771, -3.853455

Charges guide

Per unit incl. 2 persons	
and electricity	£ 21.00 - £ 26.00

Dalbeattie
Glenearly Caravan Park

Dalbeattie DG5 4NE (Dumfries and Galloway) T: 01556 611393. E: glenearlycaravan@btconnect.com

alanrogers.com/UK6870

Rurally located, Glenearly has been tastefully developed from farmland into a touring and mobile home, all year park. There are 115 marked, open pitches (39 for touring), all with 16A Europlug and TV, most on hardstandings. Seasonal units use some pitches. Walls and shrubs divide the touring section from the caravan holiday homes (two for rent), with mature trees around the perimeter. There are attractive views over the hills and forest of Barhill and buzzards, yellow wagtails, woodpeckers and goldfinch are some of the birds that can be seen, along with the park's own donkeys and ponies. This is a very well kept and well designed park, which would suit those looking for a quiet site in the country.

Facilities

Situated in the centre of the touring area, the toilets and showers are fitted out to a high standard. Unit for disabled visitors and families. Laundry room with washing machines and dryer and an outside drying area. Motorcaravan services. Large games room. Play area. Max. 2 dogs accepted. Off site: Shops, pubs, restaurants, WiFi etc. at Dalbeattie (10 mins. walk). Golf 1 mile.

Open: All year.

Directions

From Dumfries take A711 towards Dalbeattie. 6 miles beyond Beeswing, after passing sign for Edingham Farm, park is signed with entrance on right (beside a bungalow). GPS: 54.94218, -3.82016

Charges guide

Per unit incl. 2 persons	
and electricity	£ 19.00 - £ 20.50
extra person (over 5 yrs)	£ 2.50

255

For latest campsite news visit
alanrogers.com

Dalbeattie

Sandyhills Bay Leisure Park

Sandyhills, Dalbeattie DG5 4NY (Dumfries and Galloway) T: 01387 780257. E: info@gillespie-leisure.co.uk

alanrogers.com/UK6880

Sandyhills Bay is a small, quiet park beside a sheltered, sandy beach. Reception is on the left through a car park used by visitors either walking the hills or enjoying the beach. Beyond is a large flat camping area, above which, divided by a tree lined hedge, are 60 pitches, 35 taken by holiday homes situated around the perimeter. The 24 touring pitches, most with 16A electricity connections are in the centre of the flat grass area. Wooden wigwams with a terrace and picnic bench are available to rent. This is an excellent family park with the beach and a children's play area.

Facilities

The sanitary facilities are of traditional design, situated in one central block to the side of the touring area. Laundry room (tokens from reception). Shop. Snack bar/takeaway (Easter-30/9). Adventure play area by the beach. Visitors can also use the facilities at Brighouse Bay, the largest park in the Gillespie Group. Barrier at entrance and beach car park (returnable deposit). Off site: Clifftop walk from Sandyhills to Rockcliffe 10 miles. Golf and riding 500 yds.

Open: Easter/1 April - 31 October.

Directions

From Dumfries take A710 Solway coast road (about 16 miles). Site is on left just after signs for Sandyhills. GPS: 54.87901, -3.73103

Charges guide

Per unit incl. 2 persons and electricity	£ 18.00 - £ 23.00
extra person	£ 2.00
dog	£ 1.50

Dumfries

Southerness Holiday Village

Southerness, Dumfries DG2 8AZ (Dumfries and Galloway) T: 01387 880256.
E: enquiries@parkdeanholidays.co.uk **alanrogers.com/UK6875**

Set beside a two mile stretch of sandy beach, at the foot of the beautiful Galloway Hills, is Southerness Holiday Village. Part of the Parkdean Group, it is a large park with the main emphasis on caravan holiday homes. However, there are also 100 open plan pitches for caravans, motorcaravans and tents. Set away from the static units, these are divided into two areas, some on level hardstanding with water connection, others on grass and all with 16A electrical connections. The light and airy reception office displays local information including a weekly 'What's On' programme as the main leisure complex is located a short walk from the touring area.

Facilities

A modern toilet block provides en-suite facilities throughout (key entry). Well maintained, it is kept very clean by on-site wardens. Excellent unit for disabled visitors. Well equipped laundry. Shop. Bar with large TV. Bistro, takeaway and coffee shop. Indoor swimming pool. Indoor soft play area. Amusement arcade. Comprehensive evening entertainment programme in the Sunset Show bar. Outdoor adventure play area. Nature trails. Beach. Off site: Golf course adjacent. Fishing 2.5 miles.

Open: Before Easter - 31 October.

Directions

From Dumfries take A710 Solway Coast road for 10 miles. Sign for Holiday Village is on the left. GPS: 54.87613, -3.60037

Charges guide

Per unit incl. 4 persons	£ 14.00 - £ 35.00
incl. services	£ 16.00 - £ 39.00
extra person	£ 2.50 - £ 3.50
dog	£ 2.00 - £ 3.00

Dunbar

Belhaven Bay Caravan & Camping Park

Belhaven Bay, West Barns, Dunbar EH42 1TU (East Lothian) T: 01368 865956.
E: belhaven@meadowhead.co.uk **alanrogers.com/UK7065**

Located in the John Muir Country Park, Belhaven Bay Caravan Park is just one mile from the historic town of Dunbar, where the ancient castle ruin stands guard over the town's twin harbours. This is an excellent family park with easy access to the beach and to the clifftop trail which has spectacular views capturing the beauty of the countryside and seascapes. The park's 66 caravan holiday homes (five for rent) are located quite separately from the touring and tent areas. These are surrounded by mature trees and are arranged in large open bays. There is a new tent and touring area with electricity points so now there are 60 reasonably level, mostly grass touring pitches, 48 with 10A electricity available.

Facilities

Facilities are central and include a unit for disabled visitors. Laundry room. Motorcaravan services. Reception also has a small shop and tourist information. Cyber Café and WiFi. Play area and ball game area. Off site: Bus stop at entrance. Golf 1 mile. Riding and boat launching 2 miles.

Open: 13 March - 31 October.

Directions

From A1 exit at the Thistley Cross roundabout west of Dunbar. Park is 1 mile down the A1087 towards Dunbar. GPS: 55.996767, -2.545117

Charges guide

Per unit incl. 2 persons and electricity	£ 19.50 - £ 29.80
extra person (over 5 yrs)	£ 5.95

For latest campsite news visit
alanrogers.com

Dunbar
Thurston Manor Leisure Park

Innerwick, Dunbar EH42 1SA (East Lothian) T: 01368 840643. E: info@thurstonmanor.co.uk

alanrogers.com/UK7075

In a rural setting and nestling at the foot of the Lammermuir hills, this holiday park offers either a restful or a lively stay. It is close to historic Dunbar with its beaches, harbour and ruined castle. The 129 touring pitches are set away from the 510 holiday homes. All have 10A electricity connections. Thirty of these are super pitches with electricity, water and drainage. The indoor heated swimming pool and leisure complex offer space to relax and work out. There are woodland walks, safe play areas for children and fishing in a well stocked pond.

Facilities	Directions
The clean, well equipped and fully heated sanitary block provides constant hot water for showering, dishwashing and family bathing. Shop. Restaurant and sports bar. Leisure centre with heated swimming pool (10x6 m), sauna, steam room, fitness room and solarium. Play areas. Function room with live family entertainment. WiFi. Off site: Riding and beach 2 miles. Bicycle hire and sailing 4 miles. Golf 5 miles. Open: 1 March - 7 January.	From north or south on the A1 take the Innerwick turnoff (near Dunbar). Follow the road for half a mile. Thurston Leisure Park is on the right hand side. GPS: 55.959847, -2.46221

Charges guide	
Per unit incl. 2 persons and electricity	£ 23.50 - £ 25.50
extra person	£ 2.00
dog	£ 3.00

Durness
Sango Sands Oasis Caravan & Camping Site

Sangomore, Durness via Lairg IV27 4PZ (Highland) T: 01971 511726. E: keith.durness@btinternet.com

alanrogers.com/UK7735

Sango Sands Oasis is a quiet, ten-acre site overlooking the beautiful Sango Bay, a Blue Flag beach. The site was established by the family in 1978 and they continue to work hard improving the facilities each year. There are 82 pitches for tents and touring caravans, 70 with 16A electricity. The land is well drained and fairly level. It is possible to see whales, porpoise, dolphins and seals from the site plus a variety of sea birds which nest nearby. An ideal area for walkers, including the less adventurous, there are numerous marked paths and there is an excellent variety of angling, from rivers to the sea.

Facilities	Directions
The renovated toilet and shower blocks are lit at night but a torch may be useful. Free showers with curtains (Apr-Oct). Showers and toilets are separate. With the beach so close don't be surprised to find sand in the showers. En-suite facilities for disabled visitors. Laundry. Campers' kitchen. Motorcaravan services. Café, bar and licensed restaurant. TV. Games room. Barbecues permitted off ground. WiFi (charged). Two caravans for hire. Only WCs and electric hook-ups available Nov-Mar. Open: All year (Nov-March very limited facilities).	From Ullapool follow A835 north to Ledmore Junction and turn left on A837. After 8 miles turn right onto A894 to Laxford Bridge. Turn left on A838. Durness is 19 miles further. Site is on the left going through the village. GPS: 58.56449, -4.74221

Charges guide	
Per person	£ 7.00
child (5-15 yrs 3rd child free)	£ 3.00 - £ 5.00
electricity	£ 4.00

Edinbane
Skye Camping & Caravaning Club Site Loch Greshornish

Edinbane, Portree IV51 9PS (Isle of Skye) T: 01470 582230. E: skye.site@thefriendlyclub.co.uk

alanrogers.com/UK7740

On the banks of Loch Greshornish, the location of this site is both scenic and peaceful. The owners look after the site themselves and everything is very well cared for, clean and attractive. There are 105 pitches, 59 with 16A electricity and of these, 38 are on hardstanding. Most pitches are level and have loch views. The atmosphere is very welcoming, from the first greeting at reception to the wave goodbye. Facilities are modern, warm and clean. There is much wildlife in the area and we were lucky enough to see and hear a golden eagle just above the site. The site owns the adjoining loch shore, which is fenced and gated, so fishing (without a licence) is possible.

Facilities	Directions
Well maintained sanitary block with underfloor heating in the cooler months, separate provision for campers with disabilities, and a separate family room. Small laundry. Dog shower. Motorcaravan services. Camper's shelter with seating, cooking and eating area. Good shop with bread and fresh eggs. Gas. Fishing. Island trips. Two camping pods for rent. WiFi throughout (charged). Open: 2 April - 9 October.	Site is 12 miles northwest of Portree on the A850 Dunvegan road by Edinbane. GPS: 57.4868, -6.4308

Charges guide	
Per person	£ 7.90 - £ 9.65
child	£ 2.75 - £ 3.00
pitch (non-member)	£ 7.20

For latest campsite news visit
alanrogers.com

Edinburgh
Mortonhall Caravan & Camping Park

38 Mortonhall Gate, Frogston Road East, Edinburgh EH16 6TJ (Edinburgh) T: 01316 641533.
E: mortonhall@meadowhead.co.uk **alanrogers.com/UK6990**

Mortonhall Park makes a good base to see the historic city of Edinburgh and buses to the city leave from the park entrance every ten minutes (parking in Edinburgh is not easy). Although only four miles from the city centre, Mortonhall is in quiet mature parkland in the grounds of the Mortonhall estate, and easy to find with access off the bypass. There is room for 250 units, mostly on numbered pitches on a slight slope with nothing to separate them, but marked by jockey wheel points. Over 180 places have 10/16A electricity, several with hardstanding, water and drainage as well, and there are many places for tents.

Facilities
Two modern toilet blocks with covered, outdoor dishwashing sinks, but the only cabins are in the third excellent facility at the top of the park, which has eight unisex units incorporating shower, washbasin and WC. Facilities for disabled visitors. Laundry. Motorcaravan services. Bar/restaurant. Self-service shop (all season). Games and TV rooms. Play area. Internet at reception (£1/30 mins). WiFi (£5/day). Glamping style pods for rent.
Open: 20 March - 4 January.

Directions
Park is well signed south of city, 5 mins from A720 city bypass. Take Mortonhall exit from Straiton junction and follow camping signs. Entrance road is by Klondyke Garden Centre.
GPS: 55.902889, -3.181705

Charges guide
Per unit incl. 2 persons and electricity	£ 16.00 - £ 30.95

Edinburgh
Linwater Caravan Park

West Clifton, East Calder, Edinburgh EH53 0HT (Edinburgh) T: 01313 333326. E: queries@linwater.co.uk
alanrogers.com/UK7045

This delightful, small, family run park is set in the countryside but is still close to the city of Edinburgh. The park is level and the 60 large touring pitches are a mixture of grass and hardstanding; 49 have 16A electricity connections. Parts of the park are screened off by trees and fences. Two sides are sheltered by trees and shrubs and one side is open with views over fields. With just the occasional sound of aircraft from the airport, it is difficult to believe that you are so close to a major city. Linwater is a useful park for visiting Edinburgh and areas outside the city.

Facilities
The modern and well maintained heated sanitary block has private cabins. Facilities for disabled visitors. Laundry. Motorhome services. Gas supplies. Milk, bread and newspapers to order (by 21.00 for the next morning). Home produced free range eggs and bacon from reception. Sand pit. Four timber tents for hire. One new self catering lodge. Free WiFi in reception area.
Open: Mid March - early November.

Directions
From A720 Edinburgh bypass, leave at sign for Wilkieston on A71. In Wilkieston turn right at traffic lights (park signed). Continue to next sign indicating left and site 1 mile further on right. Also signposted from J1 of M9. GPS: 55.91104, -3.43588

Charges guide
Per unit incl. 2 persons and electricity	£ 18.00 - £ 23.00

Edinburgh
Edinburgh Caravan Club Site

35-37 Marine Drive, Edinburgh EH4 5EN (Edinburgh) T: 01313 126874.
alanrogers.com/UK7050

Situated as it is, on the northern outskirts and within easy reach of the city of Edinburgh, this large, busy Caravan Club site (open to non-members) provides an ideal base for touring. Enter the site through rather grand gates to find the visitors' car park and reception to the left. There are 146 large, level pitches, 142 on hardstanding, all with 16A electricity hook-ups and TV aerial. Twelve have a water tap and waste water disposal also. There is provision for 50 tents in a separate field (hook-ups available) with a covered cooking shelter and bicycle stands nearby.

Facilities
Two well kept, heated sanitary blocks provide washbasins in cubicles, hairdryers and hand dryers, an en-suite room for disabled campers, a baby and toddler room with child size facilities. Each block houses a dishwashing and vegetable preparation area and a laundry. Drying room. No shop, but milk, bread and newspapers to order, with ice-creams and gas from reception. Fenced play area. Boules. Dog walk in the only natural wood in Edinburgh (part of the site). WiFi. Off site: Bicycle hire nearby. Health club 400 yds. – ask at site for introduction card.
Open: All year.

Directions
Turn right off A720 at Gogar roundabout at end of bypass (A8). Turn left onto A902 (Forth Rd Bridge), then right onto A90. At Blackhall junction lights, left into Telford Rd (A902). At Crewe Toll roundabout left (B9085) and at T-junction (after bridge) turn right at lights Leith (A901). Turn left at lights (Silverknowes). In 0.5 miles at roundabout turn right into Marine Dr. Site in 0.5 miles on the left. GPS: 55.97764, -3.2651

Charges guide
Per person	£ 5.70 - £ 7.80
pitch incl. electricity (non member)	£ 15.90 - £ 20.00

For latest campsite news visit
alanrogers.com

Fort William
Glen Nevis Caravan & Camping Park
Glen Nevis, Fort William PH33 6SX (Highland) T: 01397 702191. E: holidays@glen-nevis.co.uk

alanrogers.com/UK7830

Just outside Fort William, in a most attractive and quiet situation with views of Ben Nevis, this spacious park is used by those on active pursuits as well as sightseeing tourists. It comprises eight quite large fields, divided between caravans, motorcaravans and tents (steel pegs required). It is licensed for 150 touring caravans but with no specific tent limits. The large touring pitches, many with hardstanding, are marked with wooden fence dividers, 174 with 13A electricity and 80 also have water and drainage. The park becomes full in the peak months but there are vacancies each day. If reception is closed (possible in low season) you site yourself. There are regular security patrols at night in busy periods. The park's own modern restaurant and bar with good value bar meals is a short stroll from the park, open to all. A well managed park with bustling, but pleasing ambiance, watched over by Ben Nevis. Around 1,000 acres of the Glen Nevis estate are open to campers to see the wildlife and explore this lovely area.

Facilities

The four modern toilet blocks with showers (extra showers in two blocks) and units for disabled visitors. An excellent block in Nevis Park (one of the eight camping fields) has some washbasins in cubicles, showers, further facilities for disabled visitors, a second large laundry room and dishwashing sinks. Motorcaravan services. Shop (Easter-mid Oct), barbecue area and snack bar (1/4-31/10). Play area on bark. WiFi over site (charged). Off site: Fishing 1 mile. Golf and bicycle hire 4 miles. Riding 4.5 miles.

Open: 15 March - 31 October.

Directions

Turn off A82 to east at roundabout just north of Fort William following camp sign. GPS: 56.804517, -5.073917

Charges guide

Per unit incl. 2 persons and electricity	£ 15.50 - £ 25.50
extra person	£ 3.50
child (5-15 yrs)	£ 2.00
dog	free

Perfectly located amidst beautiful Highland scenery at the foot of Ben Nevis

Fort William
Bunroy Park
Roy Bridge PH31 4AG (Highland) T: 01397 712332. E: info@bunroy.co.uk

alanrogers.com/UK7667

Bunroy Park is set in nine acres of secluded parkland on the banks of the River Spean. It is surrounded by breathtaking mountains and glens, yet within easy reach of Fort William, Ben Nevis and the countless attractions of the Scottish Highlands. All year round, you can relax and enjoy the magnificent scenery and wildlife, and take advantage of the numerous things to see and do. The site comprises level grass areas surrounded by sheltering woodland. All the touring pitches are hardstanding with 10A electricity hook-ups. Accommodation for rent includes eight wooden lodges and three camping pods.

Facilities

Sanitary block with hot showers, hot and cold water and shaver points. Covered dishwashing and vegetable preparation sinks. Laundry room with iron. Drying room. Fridge and freezer. WiFi throughout (20 mins. free then charged). Canoe launching is possible from the site (subject to river conditions). Off site: Railway station, small shop and two pubs serving food in Roy Bridge, a short walk away. Spean Bridge with larger shop, woollen mill with café, restaurants and 9-hole golf course.

Open: 26 March - 24 October.

Directions

Roy Bridge is 115 miles from Glasgow. At Roy Bridge turn off A86 directly opposite Stronlossit Inn and go straight ahead down lane until you get to Bunroy. Care needed crossing hump back bridge over railway line. GPS: 56.88503, -4.83384

Charges guide

Per unit incl. 2 persons and electricity	£ 17.00 - £ 19.00
extra persons	£ 4.00
child (5-14 yrs)	£ 3.00

Scotland

For latest campsite news visit
alanrogers.com

259

Fort William

Linnhe Lochside Holidays

Corpach, Fort William PH33 7NL (Highland) T: 01397 772376. E: relax@linnhe-lochside-holidays.co.uk

alanrogers.com/UK7850

This quiet well run park has a very peaceful situation overlooking Loch Eil, and it is beautifully landscaped with wonderful views. There are individual pitches with hardstanding for 66 touring units (12 seasonal) on terraces leading down to the water's edge. All have 10A electricity connection, water and drainage. A separate area on the lochside takes 15 small tents (no reservation). There are also 60 caravan holiday homes and 14 centrally heated pine chalets for hire. Fishing is free on Loch Eil and you are welcome to fish from the park's private beach or bring your own boat and use the slipway and dinghy park.

Facilities

Toilet facilities are excellent, heated in the cooler months and include baths (£1). Dishwashing room. Laundry. Outdoor clothing drying room (charged). Licensed shop (end May-end Sept). Gas supplies. Barbecue area. Toddlers' play room and two well equipped play areas on safe standing. Large motorcaravans are accepted but it is best to book first. Caravan storage. Up to two dogs per pitch are accepted. WiFi over site (charged).

Open: 15 December - 31 October.

Directions

Park entrance is off A830 Fort William-Mallaig road, 1 mile west of Corpach. GPS: 56.847817, -5.16025

Charges guide

Per unit incl. 2 persons	
and electricity	£ 18.35 - £ 21.70
extra person	£ 3.35
child (3-15 yrs)	£ 2.00
dog	£ 1.30

Gairloch

Sands Caravan & Camping

Gairloch IV21 2DL (Highland) T: 01445 712152. E: info@sandscaravanandcamping.co.uk

alanrogers.com/UK7645

Sands Caravan and Camping is located just three miles west of Gairloch on the North West coast of Scotland. It is directly adjacent to a magnificent stretch of white sandy beach and most pitches have spectacular views of the Isle of Skye. Here you can combine the feeling of 'wild' camping with first class site facilities. The park offers 125 tent pitches on mown grass in hollows to the rear of the beach and 75 pitches with electric hook-up for touring units. These are more formally arranged at a higher level. There are four hardstandings for motorcaravans and the remaining pitches are on grass. Wigwams and static caravans are available for hire, all with extensive sea views. The site shop is very well stocked with groceries and camping equipment. The Barn restaurant on site offers freshly cooked food using ingredients from local suppliers. Some glamping-style pods are available to rent.

Facilities

Three heated sanitary blocks include family bathrooms, wet rooms and facilities for disabled visitors. Laundry. Motorcaravan service point. Restaurant/café (open until 21.00 in high season). Very well stocked, licensed shop. Well equipped indoor campers' dining room/kitchen. Adventure playground. Games room with TV. Bicycle and kayak hire. Sea fishing. WiFi throughout (charged).

Open: 1 April - 25 October.

Directions

Site is signposted three miles west of Gairloch village on the B8021. Turn off the A832 onto the B8021 at McColls supermarket. GPS: 57.74078, -5.76504

Charges guide

Per unit incl. 2 persons	
and electricity	£ 19.50 - £ 21.50
extra person	£ 5.50 - £ 6.50
child (5-15 yrs)	£ 2.50

Girvan

Turnberry Holiday Park

Turnberry, Girvan KA26 9JW (South Ayrshire) T: 01655 331288. E: enquiries@turnberryholidaypark.co.uk

alanrogers.com/UK7009

Turnberry is a static caravan park on the Ayrshire coast, open for ten months of the year. There is a wide range of modern mobile homes available to buy and rent. Accommodation options are also available for disabled visitors. The park is located between Turnberry and Girvan along Scotland's popular west coast route, close to sandy beaches and in the heart of truly beautiful countryside. Historic attractions, which include the birthplace of Robert Burns and Culzean Castle, are close by. The world-class golf course at Turnberry Hotel, which has been home to the Open Championship, is nearby.

Facilities

Launderette. Convenience shop. Bar and restaurant with live music and entertainment in the evenings. Snacks and takeaway. New indoor heated swimming pool. Play areas with sand-pit, swings, slide and climbing frames. Amusement arcade with pool tables, video games and table football. WiFi throughout (charged).

Open: March - January.

Directions

Turnberry is 18 miles south of Ayr via the A77. Park is signed to the left one mile after passing Turnberry. Look for brown tourist signs. GPS: 55.291674, -4.82502

Charges guide

Contact the site for details.

For latest campsite news visit

alanrogers.com

Glencoe

Invercoe Caravan & Camping Park

Invercoe, Glencoe PH49 4HP (Highland) T: 01855 811210. E: holidays@invercoe.co.uk

alanrogers.com/UK7790

On the edge of Loch Leven, surrounded by mountains and forest, Iain and Lynn Brown are continually developing this attractively located park in its magnificent historical setting. It provides 63 pitches for caravans, motorcaravans and tents on level grass (can be a bit wet in bad weather) with gravel access roads (some hardstandings). You choose your own numbered pitch, those at the loch side being very popular. The only rules imposed are necessary for safety because the owners prefer their guests to feel free and enjoy themselves. This is a park you will want to return to again and again.

Facilities

The well refurbished toilet block can be heated. Excellent laundry facilities with a drying room. New large covered eating area. Motorcaravan services. Shop (Easter-end Oct). Play area with swings. Fishing. New fore-shore hardstanding with slipway. WiFi. Off site: Pub and restaurant within walking distance.

Open: All year.

Directions

Follow A82 Crianlarich-Fort William road to Glencoe village and turn onto the B863; park is 0.5 miles along, well signed. GPS: 56.686567, -5.105983

Charges guide

Per unit incl. 2 persons and electricity	£ 23.00
extra person	£ 4.00
child (3-15 yrs)	£ 2.00

Glendaruel

Glendaruel Caravan Park

Glendaruel PA22 3AB (Argyll and Bute) T: 01369 820267. E: mail@glendaruelcaravanpark.com

alanrogers.com/UK7860

Glendaruel is in South Argyll, in the area of Scotland bounded by the Kyles of Bute and Loch Fyne, yet within two hours by road of Glasgow and serviced by ferries from Gourock and the Isle of Bute. There is also a service between Tarbert and Portavadie. Set in the peaceful wooded gardens of the former Glendaruel House, in a secluded glen surrounded by the Cowal hills, it makes an ideal base for touring this beautiful area. The park takes 35 units on numbered hardstandings with 16A electricity connections, plus 15 tents on flat oval meadows bordered by over 50 different species of mature trees. In a separate area are 28 privately owned holiday homes, plus two holiday homes and a small camping lodge to rent.

Facilities

The toilet block is ageing but kept very neat and can be heated. It has modern showers. Washing machine and dryer. A covered area has dishwashing sinks and picnic tables for use in bad weather. Shop (limited hours in low season). Gas available. Games room with pool table, table tennis and video games. Behind the laundry is a children's play centre for under 12s and additional play field. Fishing. Free WiFi by reception. Torches advised. Off site: Sea fishing and boat slipway 5 miles, adventure centre (assault courses, abseiling and rafting) and sailing school close by.

Open: 28 March - 26 October.

Directions

Entrance is A886 road 13 miles south of Strachur. Alternatively by Gourock to Dunoon ferry, then on B836 which joins A886 4 miles south of the park (not recommended for touring caravans). Ignore sat nav which takes you down narrow back roads. Note: contact park for discount arrangements with Western Ferries (allow 7 days for postage of tickets). GPS: 56.033967, -5.212833

Charges guide

Per unit incl. 2 persons and electricity	£ 19.00
extra person	£ 3.50

Grantown-on-Spey

Grantown-on-Spey Caravan Park

Seafield Avenue, Grantown-on-Spey PH26 3JQ (Highland) T: 01479 872474. E: warden@caravanscotland.com **alanrogers.com/UK7670**

This excellent park is peacefully situated on the outskirts of the town with views of the mountains in the distance. There are 125 well tended gravel and grass pitches for caravans and motorcaravans, all with 10/16A electricity and 69 offer fresh and waste water facilities. In addition to this, a number of super pitches also offer 16A electricity, WiFi and individual Freesat TV box. A further 12 pitches are used for seasonal occupation and there is space for 50 or more tents. The park is affiliated to the Caravan Club. Trees and flowers are a feature of this attractive, landscaped location. The wardens escort visitors to their pitch and will help to site caravans if necessary. Caravan holiday homes are in a separate area.

Facilities

A modern sanitary block complete with laundry and drying room. A further block provides good, clean toilet facilities, with new washing cabins for ladies. Facilities for disabled visitors. Laundry. Motorcaravan services. Gas, ice-cream, cold drinks and camping accessories at reception. Games room with pool table. WiFi over site (charged).

Open: All year incl. Christmas and New Year.

Directions

Enter the town. Turn north at Bank of Scotland. Park straight ahead 0.5 miles. GPS: 57.3348, -3.618617

Charges guide

Per unit incl. 2 persons and 10A electricity	£ 19.50 - £ 26.00
fully serviced	£ 22.50 - £ 30.00
extra person	£ 1.00 - £ 3.00

For latest campsite news visit
alanrogers.com

Huntly

Huntly Castle Caravan Park

The Meadow, Huntly AB54 4UJ (Aberdeenshire) T: 01466 794999. E: enquiries@huntlycastle.co.uk

alanrogers.com/UK7550

Huntly Caravan Park was opened in '95 and its hardworking owners, the Ballantynes, are justly proud of their neat, well landscaped 15-acre site that is affiliated to the Caravan Club (non-members welcome). The 10 level grass and 50 hardstanding touring pitches are separated and numbered, with everyone shown to their pitch. Arranged in three bays with banks of heathers and flowering shrubs separating them, most pitches have 16A electrical hook-ups and 15 are fully serviced with water and waste water. Two bays have central play areas and all three have easy access to a toilet block, as has the camping area. The area abounds with things to do, from forest trails to walk or cycle, a falconry centre, malt whisky distilleries and an all year Nordic ski track.

Facilities	Directions
The three heated toilet blocks are well designed and maintained with washbasins (in cubicles for ladies) and large showers. Each block also has a family shower room, dishwashing sinks and a room for disabled visitors. Laundry room. Milk and papers may be ordered at reception. Activity centre (charged and facilities are also open to the public; open weekends and all local school holidays). WiFi (charged). Off site: Huntly is 10 mins. walk.	Site is well signed from A96 Keith-Aberdeen road. GPS: 57.45205, -2.7916

Open: 26 March - 28 October.

Charges guide

Per unit incl. 2 persons and electricity	£ 19.15 - £ 24.95
extra person	£ 5.80 - £ 7.50
child (5-16 yrs)	£ 1.70 - £ 2.85

Inveraray

Argyll Caravan Park

Inveraray PA32 8XT (Argyll and Bute) T: 01499 302285. E: enquiries@argyllcaravanpark.com

alanrogers.com/UK7255

This peaceful park, some two miles south of Inveraray and just a 90 minute drive from Glasgow, sits on the shores of Loch Fyne and is part of the Duke of Argyll's Estate. It has been welcoming campers since 1953, and many return year after year to this beautiful area of Scotland. There are 100 pitches here, and the 40 level, hardstanding touring pitches all have 16A electricity, water and lighting. They are well kept, have some shrubs and enjoy views of the hills across the loch, although they are not close to the water's edge. No tents are accepted at this site. Dogs are permitted by prior arrangement.

Facilities	Directions
An older prefabricated toilet block is kept very clean and has vanity-style washbasins and controllable hot showers. Facilities for babies and disabled visitors in a modern building (key access, some gravel outside). Launderette. Motorcaravan services. Shop for basics. Bar, restaurant and takeaway. Play area. Occasional entertainment and fun days. Games room. Free WiFi in reception.	The park is 2 miles south of Inveraray on A83. From Lochgilphead sign is not visible. GPS: 56.201233, -5.105517

Open: April - October.

Charges guide

Per unit incl. 4 persons and electricity	£ 25.00

Invergarry

Faichemard Farm Camping Site

Faichem, Invergarry PH35 4HG (Highland) T: 01809 501314. E: enquiries@faichemard-caravancamping.co.uk

alanrogers.com/UK7782

Faichemard Farm is an adult only site, idyllically located on the outskirts of Invergarry in the Scottish Highlands. It has been run by the same family since 1935 and visitors can expect a very warm and helpful welcome. There is stunningly beautiful scenery from the 15 level touring pitches, many on hardstanding and all with 10A electricity and its own picnic table. A few pitches look across a pond towards one of the toilet blocks, while a second block is further up the hillside. There is an abundance of wildlife here and deer, pine martins, red squirrel and even the occasional golden eagle can be seen.

Facilities	Directions
Two modern, heated and well equipped toilet blocks have very large showers, shaver points and hairdryers. One block also has an en-suite unit for disabled visitors. Close to reception is a large undercover area with a laundry and a fridge/freezer. Free WiFi over site. Dogs are welcome on a short lead. Off site: Fishing 2 miles. Golf, riding and bicycle hire 7 miles. Fort Augusta for the Caledonian Canal and Loch Ness monster! Fort William for a trip on the gondola up Aonach Mor. Culloden Battlefield.	From Fort Augusta or Fort William turn off A82 at Invergarry onto A87. Go through village. The sign for Faichemard Farm points to a right turn up a slope. becoming a single track road. Follow this good road uphill passing a number of entrances until you see site sign on right. GPS: 57.074783, -4.826633

Open: 1 April - late October.

Charges guide

Per unit incl. 2 persons and electricity	£ 17.00
extra person	£ 4.00

For latest campsite news visit
alanrogers.com

Kildonan

Seal Shore Camping & Touring Site

Kildonan, Isle of Arran KA27 8SE (North Ayrshire) T: 01770 820320. E: enquiries@campingarran.com
alanrogers.com/UK7025

A warm welcome awaits here on the island of Arran from the resident owner, Maurice Deighton and his daughter. Located on the southernmost point of the island, this is a quiet and peaceful park situated along its own private beach with wonderful sea views. The open, grassy area, sloping in parts, takes caravans, motorcaravans and tents with ten electricity connections (16A). The reception doubles as a shop selling basics with a TV room adjacent. There are communal picnic and barbecue areas. The Kildonan Hotel is next door serving restaurant and bar meals. Permits are available for loch fishing and charters are available from the owner, a registered fisherman. Golfers can choose from seven courses.

Facilities

The good toilet block is clean and tidy and includes full facilities for disabled visitors that double as a baby room. Laundry room with washing machine, dryers and iron. Indoor dishwashing with fridge and freezer. Shop. Camping gas. Beach. Fishing. Sailing. Covered barbecue area. Off site: Nearest golf course at Whiting 6 miles. Heritage Museum in Brodick and to the North of the island, Lochranza castle and distillery.

Open: March - October.

Directions

From Brodick take A841 south for 12 miles to sign for Kildonan. Site is downhill, on the seashore, next to the Kildonan Hotel. GPS: 55.44100, -5.11397

Charges guide

Per unit incl. 2 persons and electricity	£ 20.00 - £ 21.00
extra person	£ 6.00
child (5-15 yrs)	£ 4.00
tent pitch	£ 1.00 - £ 4.00

Kirkcudbright

Brighouse Bay Holiday Park

Brighouse Bay, Borgue, Kirkcudbright DG6 4TS (Dumfries and Galloway) T: 01557 870267.
E: info@gillespie-leisure.co.uk **alanrogers.com/UK6950**

Hidden away within 1,200 exclusive acres, on a quiet, unspoilt peninsula, this spacious family park is only some 200 yards through bluebell woods from an open, sandy bay. It has exceptional all-weather facilities, as well as golf and pony trekking. Over 90 percent of the 210 touring caravan pitches have 10/16A electricity, some with hardstanding and some with water, drainage and TV aerial. The three tent areas are on fairly flat, undulating ground and some pitches have electricity. There are 120 self-contained holiday caravans and lodges of which about 30 are let, the rest privately owned. On-site leisure facilities include a golf and leisure club with 16.5 m. pool, water features, jacuzzi, steam room, fitness room, games room (all on payment), golf driving range, bowling green and clubhouse bar and bistro. The 18-hole golf course extends onto the headland with superb views over the Irish Sea to the Isle of Man and Cumbria. This is a well run park of high standards.

Facilities

The large, well maintained main toilet block includes 10 unisex cabins with shower, basin and WC, and 12 with washbasin and WC. A second, excellent block next to the tent areas has en-suite shower rooms (one for disabled visitors) and bathroom, separate washing cubicles, showers and baby room. Laundry facilities. Motorcaravan services. Gas supplies. Licensed shop. Bar, restaurant and takeaway (all year). Golf and Leisure Club with indoor pool (all year). Play area (incl. toddlers' area). Pony trekking. Quad bikes, boating pond, 10-pin bowling, playgrounds, putting. Nature trails. Coarse fishing ponds plus sea angling and an all-tide slipway for boating enthusiasts. Caravan storage. WiFi over site, free in bistro. Purpose built chalet for tourist information and leisure facility bookings. Glamping style pods are available for rent. Off site: Small sandy beach nearby.

Open: All year.

Directions

In Kirkcudbright turn onto A755 and cross river bridge. In 400 yds. turn left onto B727 at the international camping sign. Or follow Brighouse Bay signs off A75 just east of Gatehouse of Fleet. GPS: 54.7875, -4.1291

Charges guide

Per unit incl. 2 persons and electricity	£ 19.50 - £ 26.00
extra person	£ 3.00
child (5-15 yrs)	£ 2.00
dog	£ 2.00

Contact park for full charges.
Golf packages in low season.

For latest campsite news visit
alanrogers.com

Kirkcudbright

Seaward Caravan Park

Dhoon Bay, Kirkcudbright DG6 4TJ (Dumfries and Galloway) T: 01557 870267. E: info@gillespie-leisure.co.uk
alanrogers.com/UK6900

Seaward Caravan Park is little sister to the much larger Brighouse Bay Holiday Park, 3.5 miles away. Set in an idyllic location overlooking the bay, this park is suitable for all units. The terrain is slightly undulating, but most of the numbered pitches are flat and of a good size. There are 35 pitches (21 hardstandings) designated for caravans and motorcaravans, a further 14 for tents, plus 43 caravan holiday homes (six for hire). All of the pitches for touring units have electricity connections and 12 are also serviced with water and drainage. This is a quiet park with excellent views over the sea, ideally suited for that relaxing holiday or for touring the region. The unspoilt country lanes are ideal for cycling.

Facilities

The principal, fully equipped sanitary block is to the rear of the touring area. Four rooms with en-suite facilities are also suitable for disabled campers. Well equipped baby room. Laundry . No motorcaravan services but manager can lift a manhole cover to empty tanks. Small shop in reception. Heated outdoor swimming pool (1/5-30/9). Central play area with bark surface, rocking horse, table tennis and picnic tables. Games room. Pitch and putt (charged). WiFi throughout (charged). No mobile signal.

Open: 1 March - 31 October.

Directions

In Kirkcudbright turn onto A755 (Borgue). Go over river bridge and after 400 yds. turn left onto B727 at international camping sign. Take care when turning right into site entrance as the turn is tight. GPS: 54.819767, -4.082117

Charges guide

Per unit incl. 2 persons and electricity	£ 18.00 - £ 23.00
extra person	£ 2.00

Kyle of Lochalsh

Reraig Caravan Site

Balmacara, Kyle of Lochalsh IV40 8DH (Highland) T: 01599 566215. E: warden@reraig.com
alanrogers.com/UK7760

This is a small, level park close to Loch Alsh with a wooded hillside behind (criss-crossed with woodland walks). Set mainly on well cut grass, it is sheltered from the prevailing winds by the hill and provides just 45 numbered pitches. There are 10A electrical connections and 35 hardstandings (two without electricity). Tents you can stand in are not accepted. Small tents are permitted at the discretion of the owner so it would be advisable to telephone first if this affects you. Reservations are not taken so it may be best to arrive before late afternoon in July and August.

Facilities

The single sanitary block is kept immaculately clean. Children have their own low washbasins. Controllable hot showers (10p/2 mins). Sinks for laundry and dishwashing. A slope replaces the small step into the ladies and sink rooms. Motorcaravan drainage point. WiFi throughout (charged). Off site: Balmacara Hotel (with bar), shop (selling gas), post office and off-licence.

Open: 1 May - 30 September.

Directions

On A87, park is 2 miles west of the junction with the A890, beside the Balmacara hotel. GPS: 57.283133, -5.626517

Charges guide

Per unit incl. 2 persons and electricity	£ 16.90
extra person (13 yrs or over)	£ 3.00
awning (May, June, Sept only)	£ 3.00

Lairg

Woodend Camping & Caravan Park

Achnairn, Lairg IV27 4DN (Highland) T: 01549 402248.
alanrogers.com/UK7720

Woodend is a delightful, small park overlooking Loch Shin and perfect for hill walkers and backpackers. Peaceful and simple, it is owned and run single-handedly by Mrs Cathie Ross, who provides a warm Scottish welcome to visitors. On a hill with open, panoramic views across the Loch to the hills beyond and all around, the large camping field is undulating and gently sloping with some reasonably flat areas. The park is licensed to take 55 units and most of the 30 electrical hook-ups (16A) are in a line near the top of the field.

Facilities

The sanitary facilities are of old design but kept very clean and are quite satisfactory. Laundry with a washing machine and a dryer. Kitchen with dishwashing sinks and eating room for tent campers. Reception is at the house, Sunday papers, daily milk and bread may be ordered. Fishing licences for the Loch (your catch will be frozen for you). Off site: Mountain bikes can be hired in Lairg 5 miles. Several scenic golf courses within 20-30 miles.

Open: 1 April - 30 September.

Directions

Achnairn is near southern end of Loch Shin. Turn off A838 single track road at signs for Woodend. From A9 (north) take A836 at Bonar Bridge, 11 miles northwest of Tain. GPS: 58.080267, -4.44705

Charges guide

Per unit incl. electricity	£ 10.00 - £ 12.00
tent	£ 8.00 - £ 10.00

No credit cards.

For latest campsite news visit
alanrogers.com

Lauder

Thirlestane Castle Caravan Park

Thirlestane Castle Park, Lauder TD2 6RU (Borders) T: 01578 718884. E: info@thirlestanecastlepark.co.uk

alanrogers.com/UK7029

Family run Thirlestane Castle Park is beautifully situated on the outskirts of the Royal Burgh town of Lauder, within the historic parklands of Thirlestane Castle. It is just five minutes' walk from local shops and hotels, and equally well located for those wishing to find a central base for exploring the Scottish Borders. The park was established over twenty years ago and has an enviable reputation as a quiet, friendly and welcoming site. The 50 touring pitches, 22 on hardstanding, are fairly level and all have electricity connections (10A). Very large motorcaravans cannot be accommodated but twin-axle caravans are welcome. There are numerous activities in the area including fishing and golf, and the Southern Upland Way is only 300 m. away. There is a direct bus service to Edinburgh (1 hour).

Facilities

The modern toilet block can be heated and has controllable showers, but currently no facilities for disabled visitors. Washing machine. Motorcaravan services. A torch might be useful. Off site: Golf and riding 2 miles. Public transport in Lauder. Historic border towns such as Melrose, Selkirk, Galashiels and Jedburgh. Historic buildings – Melrose Abbey and Traquair House.

Open: 1 April - 3 October.

Directions

The site is located on the southeast fringe of Lauder. From the A68 take the B6382 just southeast of Lauder. The park is on the left shortly after turning onto the B road. GPS: 55.715436, -2.738203

Charges guide

Per unit incl. 2 persons and electricity	£ 16.00 - £ 21.00
extra person	£ 3.50
dog	free

Lossiemouth

Silver Sands Holiday Park

Covesea West Beach, Lossiemouth IV31 6SP (Moray) T: 01343 813262.

alanrogers.com/UK7535

Silver Sands is in a peaceful location on the Moray Firth in the north east of Scotland. It is close to the seaside town of Lossiemouth which has a bustling marina and a good selection of shops and restaurants. This popular holiday park has a wealth of amenities, including a heated indoor pool, playground and games arcade, restaurant, fish and chip shop and plenty of entertainment for the whole family. There is a choice of grass or hardstanding touring pitches, many fully serviced. With direct access to a beautiful sandy beach, this is a good choice for a lively family holiday. The site is very close to an RAF base, so some aircraft noise can be expected.

Facilities

Sanitary block with hot showers. Launderette. Shop stocks essentials. Bar. Café. Restaurant. Fish and chips to take away. Heated indoor swimming pool with sauna and steam room. Gym. Playground. Children's club. Games room. Activity and entertainment programme. WiFi. Direct beach access. Off site: Riding. Two golf courses. Boat tours. Elgin.

Open: 1 April - 31 October.

Directions

Site is 7 miles north of Elgin. From A96 at Elgin, proceed onto A941 (signed for Moray Motor Museum). After approx. 3 miles, take left turn for RAF Lossiemouth. Straight on at roundabout, then left onto B9040 (site signed). Silver sand is on the right just after golf course. GPS: 57.72126, -3.33506

Charges guide

Per unit incl. 5 persons, electricity and water	£ 18.00 - £ 27.00
extra person	£ 1.00
dog	£ 1.00

For latest campsite news visit
alanrogers.com

Lockerbie

Hoddom Castle Caravan Park

Hoddom, Lockerbie DG11 1AS (Dumfries and Galloway) T: 01576 300251. E: enquiries@hoddomcastle.co.uk
alanrogers.com/UK6910

The park around Hoddom Castle is landscaped, spacious and well laid out on mainly sloping ground with many mature and beautiful trees, originally part of an arboretum. The drive to the site is just under a mile long with a one way system. Many of the 91 numbered touring pitches have good views of the castle and have gravel hardstanding with grass for awnings. Most have 16A electrical connections. In front of the castle are level fields used for tents and caravans, with limited electricity hook-ups. The oldest part of Hoddom Castle itself is a 16th-century Borders Pele Tower, or fortified keep.

Facilities

The main toilet block can be heated and is very well appointed. Washbasins in cubicles, three en-suite cubicles with WC and basin (one with baby facilities) and an en-suite shower unit for disabled visitors. Two further blocks provide washbasins and WCs only. Well equipped laundry room at the castle. Motorcaravan services. Licensed shop at reception (gas available). Bar, restaurant and takeaway (Easter-Oct). Games room. Large, grass play area. Crazy golf. Mountain bike trail. Fishing. Golf. Guided walks (high season). WiFi in bar. Caravan storage.

Open: 1 April - 30 October.

Directions

Leave A74M at exit 19 (Ecclefechan) and follow signs to park. Leave A75 at Annan junction (west end of Annan bypass) and follow signs.
GPS: 55.041367, -3.311

Charges guide

Per unit incl. 2 persons and electricity	£ 17.50 - £ 24.50
extra person	£ 5.00

Maybole

Culzean Castle Camping & Caravanning Club Site

Maybole KA19 8JX (South Ayrshire) T: 01655 760627.
alanrogers.com/UK7010

With wonderful views of the Firth of Clyde and over to the Isle of Arran from some pitches, this quiet Camping and Caravanning Club site is next door to Culzean Castle (pronounced Kullayne). Visitors can buy tickets to walk in the grounds (when open) with their 17 miles of footpaths. The campsite has 90 pitches, some level, others slightly sloping, and 60 have 10A electrical hook-ups. A few level pitches are suitable for motorcaravans and 20 pitches have hardstanding. American-style motorhomes (more than 25 ft) must contact the site prior to arrival as large pitches are limited.

Facilities

The toilet blocks, kept very clean, can be heated and include some washbasins in cubicles. Unit for disabled visitors has a WC, washbasin and shower – an excellent facility. Well equipped laundry. Small shop for basics opens for short periods morning and evening. Adventure playground. WiFi in some areas (charged). Off site: Riding 2 miles. Beach 3 miles. Golf 4 miles. Fishing 8 miles. Buses pass the gate.

Open: 24 March - 24 October.

Directions

From Maybole follow signs for Culzean Castle and Country Park, turning in town on B7023 which runs into the A719. Entrance to caravan park is on right in Country Park drive. GPS: 55.35345, -4.76945

Charges guide

Per unit incl. 2 persons and electricity	£ 4.90 - £ 7.20
extra person	£ 7.15 - £ 12.15

Non-member prices are higher.

Maybole

The Ranch Holiday Park

Culzean Road, Maybole KA19 8DU (South Ayrshire) T: 01655 882446.
alanrogers.com/UK7015

This holiday park is situated in the Ayrshire countryside, a mile from the small town of Maybole. The Ranch, a Caravan Club affiliated site, is managed by the McAuley family. The park is well set out with 65 spacious touring pitches, all with 16A electricity connections and on level hardstanding. There are also 100 caravan holiday homes with one for rent. The superb facilities include a private leisure centre with an indoor heated pool, sauna, solarium and well equipped gym. This is complete with changing room, toilets, shower and hairdryers. Adjacent is a small, fenced play park for toddlers and to the rear an enclosed play area for older children. The laundry room has a book and magazine exchange library.

Facilities

Clean, modern sanitary facilities, recently rebuilt, are well located and equipped with washbasins in cubicles and large showers. Facilities for disabled visitors. Good laundry with dishwashing area. Small shop for basics in reception with good information area. Indoor heated pool, sauna and well equipped gym. WiFi throughout (charged).

Open: All year.

Directions

From Maybole turn onto B7023 (signed Culzean Maidens) for 1 mile and site is signed on left.
GPS: 55.3559, -4.7061

Charges guide

Per unit incl. 2 persons and electricity	£ 16.00 - £ 22.00
extra person	£ 4.90 - £ 6.70

Mintlaw

Aden Country Park Caravan Park

Station Road, Mintlaw AB42 5FQ (Aberdeenshire) T: 01771 623460.

alanrogers.com/UK7530

Aden Country Park is owned by the Aberdeenshire local authority and is open to the public. The caravan and camping site is on one side of the park. Beautifully landscaped and well laid out with trees, bushes and hedges, it is kept very neat and tidy. It provides 48 numbered pitches for touring units with varying degrees of slope (some level) and all with 16A electrical hook-ups, plus an area for tents. There are also 12 caravan holiday homes. The campsite is also leased by the council to private owners. The park is in a most attractive area and one could spend plenty of time enjoying all it has to offer.

Facilities	Directions
The modern toilet block is clean with good facilities for disabled visitors. It can be heated and provides free, preset hot showers, hairdryer for ladies and a baby bath, but no private cabins. Dishwashing and laundry facilities (metered). Motorcaravan services. Gas supplies. Small shop in reception area. Restaurant in the Heritage Centre. Games areas. Play equipment (safety surfaces). Dog exercise area. Off site: Shops in Mintlaw 0.5 miles. **Open:** Easter - 25 October.	Approaching Mintlaw from west on A950 road, park is shortly after sign for Mintlaw station. From east, go to the western outskirts of village and entrance is on left – Aden Country Park and Farm Heritage Centre. GPS: 57.52475, -2.026117

Charges guide

Per unit incl. 1 person electricity	£ 15.36 - £ 17.08
extra person	£ 5.13 - £ 5.70
awning	free

Monifieth

Riverview Holiday Park

Marine Drive, Monifieth DD5 4NN (Angus) T: 01382 535471. E: info@riverview.co.uk

alanrogers.com/UK7410

A quiet, family park, Riverview overlooks a long sandy beach and has magnificent views over the estuary of the River Tay towards the Kingdom of Fife. It is a short walk to the shops and facilities of Monifieth. The park is neatly set out with flowering shrubs and bushes and some of the 40 numbered touring pitches enjoy estuary views. They are grassy and level, each with 16A electricity and two also with water and drainage. Bordering the park are 46 privately owned caravan holiday homes and four to rent. At the entrance to the park is a small reception office, a separate tourist information room and a leisure suite with sauna, steam baths and gym (charged). A member of the Best of British group.

Facilities	Directions
The spotlessly clean amenity block (key entry) has open washbasins, one in a cabin with WC, and preset showers. Baby bath. Facilities for disabled visitors. Well equipped laundry. Leisure suite. Games room and play area. Adventure play area. WiFi over site (charged). Off site: Picnic areas and small boat slipway adjacent. Opposite, the Riverview recreation park offers football pitches, putting, crazy golf, tennis, bowling and an adventure play park. Golf 800 yds. Fishing 2 miles. **Open:** 1 April - 31 October.	From Dundee follow signs for Monifieth on A930. After passing Tesco, turn right at sign for golf course and right again under narrow railway bridge (3.2 m. height limit). Park is signed on the left. GPS: 56.47995, -2.811533

Charges guide

Per unit incl. 2 adults and 2 children	£ 24.00
extra person	£ 12.00
awning	£ 3.00

Motherwell

Strathclyde Country Park Caravan Club Site

Bothwellhaugh Road, Bothwell, Glasgow G71 8NY (North Lanarkshire) T: 01698 853300.

E: strathclydepark@northlan.gov.uk **alanrogers.com/UK7000**

The 1,200-acre Strathclyde Country Park is a large green area less than 15 miles from the centre of Glasgow. This Caravan Club site has been entirely rebuilt and features 107 all-weather, hardstanding pitches. There are 12 serviced pitches and additional space for 45 tents, all off tarmac roads. The warden's accommodation and sanitary blocks are attractively clad in wood to blend in with their surroundings. This site is suitable as a stopover or for a longer holiday (max. 14 days) and it is ideal as a base for visiting the numerous attractions in and around Glasgow. As the site is close to the motorway, there may be some traffic noise.

Facilities	Directions
Two brand new sanitary blocks with all facilities. Enclosed sinks for dishwashing and food preparation. Provision for babies and disabled visitors. Laundry. Motorcaravan services. Shop in reception sells basic provisions. Play areas for young children. Woodland walk. WiFi. Off site: Bar and restaurant facilities (100 yds) in country park. Fishing 400 yds. Bus 1 mile. **Open:** All year.	From the M74 take exit 5 signed A275 Edinburgh and Country Park. At roundabout follow sign for the Country Park, then first left. Site entrance is 200 yds. on the left. GPS: 55.803917, -4.046733

Charges guide

Per person	£ 5.70 - £ 7.80
pitch incl. electricity (non-member)	£ 15.90 - £ 20.00

For latest campsite news visit
alanrogers.com

Musselburgh

Drum Mohr Caravan Park

Levenhall, Musselburgh EH21 8JS (East Lothian) T: 01316 656867. E: bookings@drummohr.org

alanrogers.com/UK6980

This family owned, attractively laid out touring park is on the east side of Edinburgh. It is a secluded, well kept modern park, conveniently situated for visits to Edinburgh, the Lothian and Borders regions. It has been carefully landscaped and there are many attractive plants, flowers and hedging. There are 120 individual pitches, 40 with hardstanding, for touring units of any type, well spaced out on gently sloping grass in groups of 12 or more, marked with white posts. All have electric hook-ups and 13 are fully serviced with water and waste water connections. Free space is left for play and recreation.

Facilities

The two toilet blocks are clean, attractive, of ample size and can be heated. Free hot water to washbasins (one cabin for men, two for ladies in each block) and to showers and laundry sinks. Baby changing facilities. Laundry facilities in each block. Motorcaravan services. Well stocked, shop (gas available, bread and papers to order). Playground on sand. Excellent dog walk. Caravan storage. Security barrier with code access. No late night arrivals area. WiFi (charged). Bothy for hire.

Open: All year.

Directions

From Edinburgh follow A1 signs for Berwick-upon-Tweed for 6-7 miles. Turn off for Wallyford and follow camp and Mining Museum signs. GPS: 55.950033, -3.011667

Charges guide

Per unit incl. 2 persons and electricity	£ 18.00 - £ 25.00
extra person	£ 3.00
child (5-15 yrs)	£ 2.00

North Berwick

Tantallon Caravan & Camping Park

Tantallon Road, North Berwick EH39 5NJ (East Lothian) T: 01620 893348. E: tantallon@meadowhead.co.uk

alanrogers.com/UK7060

Tantallon is a large park with views over the Firth of Forth and the Bass Rock. The park has 147 quite large, grass touring pitches in two lower, more sheltered areas (Law Park), with the rest having good views at the top (Bass Park). Many have some degree of slope. There are 75 electrical connections (10A) and ten pitches also with water and waste water. Each area has its own sanitary facilities, the top block a little way from the end pitches. About 55 caravan holiday homes for sale or hire are in their own areas. Wooden wigwams are also available. This is a mature, well managed park with good facilities.

Facilities

Bass Park has 8 unisex units with shower, washbasin and toilet. The other areas have open washbasins. Two heated units for disabled visitors. Good launderette. Motorcaravan services. Reception sells ices, chocolate bars, cold drinks and newspapers at weekends. Games room with TV. Internet access in reception. WiFi. Play area. Putting green. Dogs only by prior arrangement.

Open: 13 March - 31 October.

Directions

Park is beside the A198 just to the east of North Berwick, which is between Edinburgh and Dunbar. It is easily accessible from the A1. GPS: 56.05575, -2.690833

Charges guide

Per unit incl. 2 persons and electricity	£ 19.45 - £ 31.15
extra person (over 5 yrs)	£ 5.85

Peebles

Crossburn Caravan Park

Edinburgh Road, Peebles EH45 8ED (Borders) T: 01721 720501. E: enquiries@crossburncaravans.co.uk

alanrogers.com/UK6960

A peaceful, friendly, small park, suitable as a night stop, Crossburn is on the south side of the A703 road, half a mile north of the town centre. The entrance has a fairly steep slope down to reception and the shop which also sells a very large selection of caravan and camping accessories. Passing the caravans for sale and the holiday homes you might think that this is not the site for you, but persevere as the touring area is very pleasant with attractive trees and bushes. Of the 40 pitches, all have 16A electricity, 20 have hardstanding and eight are fully serviced. There is also a sheltered area for tents.

Facilities

Main toilet block has washbasins in cubicles, hairdryers and spacious, controllable showers. A second older block has been refurbished. Kitchen (key at reception) with free use of an electric hot plate, kettle and fridge. Shop. Large games room with snooker table and games machines. Good play area on bark chippings. Riverside dog walk. Card-operated barrier (£10 deposit). Glamping-style wooden camping lodges for rent.

Open: Easter/1 April - October.

Directions

Park is by the A703 road, 0.5 miles north of Peebles. GPS: 55.662167, -3.193333

Charges guide

Per pitch	£ 24.00 - £ 26.00
hiker or cyclist plus tent	£ 9.00
dog (max. 2)	free

For latest campsite news visit

alanrogers.com

Peebles

Rosetta Holiday Park

Rosetta Road, Peebles EH45 8PG (Borders) T: 01721 720770. E: info@rosettaholidaypark.com

alanrogers.com/UK6965

Within walking distance of the unspoilt market town of Peebles, in the heart of the Scottish Borders, Rosetta Holiday Park is set on 50 acres in the grounds of a Georgian mansion. There are approximately 140 touring pitches, some on grass, some hardstanding, all with electricity connections. They are screened from the permanent units by tall hedges and have lovely views of the Venlaw Hills. There is a bar and restaurant serving home-cooked food and breakfast is available. The strong point of Rosetta is its close proximity to Peebles, a historic town with a good range of independent shops, and the River Tweed – one of Scotland's best rivers for salmon fishing.

Facilities

Two basic sanitary blocks have hot showers and washbasins in cubicles. Baby changing. Laundry facilities. Small shop. Bar/café and restaurant (w/e only after 29/9, no food served). Breakfast service. Playground. TV/games room. Off site: Town centre 10 mins. walk. Mountain bike trails in Glentress Forest. Edinburgh 40 mins. by car.

Open: 20 March - 31 October.

Directions

Site is 0.5 miles north east of Peebles. From A72, follow campsite signs as you enter Peebles. Turn into Young St, then straight on to Rosetta Rd. Pass police station on right, then look out for park on left by lodge house. GPS: 55.65879, -3.19938

Charges guide

Per unit incl. electricity	£ 18.00 - £ 24.00

Family holidays in the heart of the Scottish Borders

Whether you want to get out and about and explore or just sit back and relax on park you'll have a fabulous time at Rosetta Holiday Park.

To book your short break or holiday Tel: 01721 720770 or visit rosettaholidaypark.com

Perth

Noah's Ark Caravan Park

Newhouse Farm, Perth PH1 1QF (Perth and Kinross) T: 01738 580661. E: info@perthcaravanpark.co.uk

alanrogers.com/UK7265

Noah's Ark Caravan Park is situated on the outskirts of Perth and enjoys panoramic views over the surrounding Grampian mountains. This is a good base for a golfing break with no less than five excellent courses within a short distance, including Saint Andrews and Gleneagles. There are 46 touring pitches here. These are grassy and of a good size. All have electrical connections. A further eight tent pitches are available (some with electricity). The site also has a number of Microlodge Hobbit Houses. These are unique wooden chalets, fully equipped to a high standard (even including a TV). Adjacent to the site is a play barn for children, which also houses a restaurant, karting, bowling and a golf driving range.

Facilities

Two sanitary blocks are adjacent in one corner of the park, one of wood construction, the other prefabricated. Family shower and bathrooms. Facilities for disabled visitors. Motorcaravan services. Gas. Noah's Galley café. Karting. Golf driving range. Bowling. Minigolf. Local takeaway meals are delivered. WiFi throughout (free). Microlodges for rent. Off site: Play barn for children adjacent. Golf (5 courses including Gleneagles and St Andrews). Perth (bus service). Fishing. Walking and mountain biking.

Open: All year.

Directions

The site is on the outskirts of Perth. Approach from south or north on the A9 and turn east at the Broxden roundabout. Follow signs for Broxden Park and Ride, then signs for Noah's Ark and Golf Driving Range. GPS: 56.397285, -3.49119

Charges guide

Per unit incl. 2 persons and electricity	£ 22.00 - £ 24.00
backpacker (1 person)	£ 12.00
extra person	£ 2.00
child (under 5 yrs)	free

No credit cards.

For latest campsite news visit
alanrogers.com

Pitlochry
The River Tilt Park
Golf Course Road, Blair Atholl, Pitlochry PH18 5TB (Perth and Kinross) T: 01796 481467.
E: stuart@rivertilt.co.uk **alanrogers.com/UK7295**

This good quality, family owned park is set on the banks of the River Tilt, a short walk from the village of Blair Atholl, where the 16th-century Blair Castle stands proud. There are 54 privately owned caravan holiday homes. Two central areas have been set aside for touring caravans, motorcaravans and tents, with 31 pitches mostly with hardstanding. Divided by mature shrubs and hedges, all have 10A electricity connections, 18 have water and a drain. One of the areas is reserved for dog owners and their pets. The Steadings Spa provides an indoor pool, solarium, steam room, spa pool and multigym, plus a hair salon.

Facilities

The purpose built toilet block is centrally situated (with key entry) and provides en-suite toilet and washbasin cabins and individual large preset showers, one suitable for disabled visitors. Baby facilities. Well equipped laundry. Motorcaravan services. Bar and restaurant. Leisure spa complex with indoor pool, etc. Hair salon. Tennis. WiFi throughout (free). Max. 2 dogs per pitch. Off site: Private fishing and golf adjacent. Bicycle hire 0.5 miles. Riding 1.5 miles. Pitlochry with its famous salmon leap 6 miles.

Open: Two weeks before Easter - 10 November.

Directions

From the A9 just north of Pitlochry, take B8079 into Blair Atholl, turn left after the Spar shop, then follow signs for River Tilt. GPS: 56.76538, -3.83962

Charges guide

Per unit incl. 2 persons	
and electricity	£ 22.00 - £ 25.00
extra person	£ 1.50
child	£ 1.00
dog (max. 2)	£ 2.00

Pitlochry
Blair Castle Caravan Park
Blair Atholl, Pitlochry PH18 5SR (Perth and Kinross) T: 01796 481263. E: mail@blaircastlecaravanpark.co.uk
alanrogers.com/UK7300

This attractive, well kept park is set in the grounds of Blair Castle, the traditional home of the Dukes of Atholl. It has a wonderful feeling of spaciousness with a large central area left free for children's play or for general use. There is space for 250 touring units, all with 10/16A electricity connections, 63 with hardstanding and 44 fully serviced pitches with water and waste water facilities. Caravan holiday homes, 85 privately owned and 18 for hire, are in separate areas along with five woodland lodges also available for hire. A quality park, quiet at night and well managed. The castle is open to the public, its 30 fully furnished rooms showing a picture of Scottish life from the 12th century to the present day, while the beautiful grounds and gardens are free to those staying on site.

Facilities

The five toilet blocks can be heated and are of excellent quality and very clean. Large hot showers, some with WC and washbasin, further cubicles with WC and washbasin. Facilities for disabled visitors. Baby changing. Laundry. Motorcaravan services. Shop. Beauty treatments and hair salon. Games room. WiFi throughout. Gas. American motorhomes accepted (max. length 20 m. or 5 tons).

Open: 23 February - 26 November.

Directions

From A9 just north of Pitlochry take B8079 into Blair Atholl. Park is in grounds of Blair Castle, well signed. Site entrance immediately north side of River Tilt bridge. GPS: 56.767039, -3.845791

Charges guide

Per unit incl. 2 persons	
and electricity	£ 23.00 - £ 29.00
extra person (over 5yrs)	£ 2.50

Pitlochry
Tummel Valley Holiday Park
Tummel Bridge, Pitlochry PH16 5SA (Perth and Kinross) T: 01882 634221.
E: enquiries@parkdeanholidays.co.uk **alanrogers.com/UK7305**

Set in the Tay Forest Park on the banks of the River Tummel, this large family holiday park is part of the Parkdean Group. Divided into two areas by the roadway, the main emphasis is on chalets to let on the side that overlooks the river. Privately owned caravan holiday homes and touring pitches are on the other, quieter side. The 26 touring pitches, open plan with hardstanding, electricity hook-up and a shared water point, overlook a small fishing lake, which is an added attraction for all the family. On arrival, you should turn right and park, then cross back to book in.

Facilities

The very clean toilet block has vanity style washbasins, preset showers and a bathroom in each section. Good facilities for disabled visitors. Laundry. Shop. Riverside entertainment complex with bar and terrace, restaurant and takeaway. Indoor heated pool and toddlers' splash pool. Solarium and sauna. Amusements. Play area. Crazy golf. Nature trails. Bicycle hire. Fishing. Max. 2 dogs.

Open: Late March/Easter - 31 October.

Directions

Travel through Pitlochry. After 2 miles turn left on B8019 to Tummel Bridge (10 miles). Park is on both sides. Touring units should turn right and park, then return to reception on left. GPS: 56.70742, -4.02002

Charges guide

Per unit incl. 4 persons	
and electricity	£ 14.00 - £ 34.00
dog	£ 2.00 - £ 3.00

Port William

Kings Green Caravan Park

South Street, Port William DG8 9SG (Dumfries and Galloway) T: 01988 700489.

E: kingsgreencaravanpark@gmail.com **alanrogers.com/UK6885**

Kings Green Caravan Park is now owned and run by the Port William Community Association with regular warden visits. Kept very natural and situated beside the sea overlooking Luce Bay and the Mull of Galloway, it is situated on the southern fringes of Port William, well known for its harbour and fishing community. The all grass, open site provides 30 marked and numbered pitches for caravans, motorcaravans and tents (21 with 16A electricity). On arrival visitors are given a welcome pack which includes a guide on the history of the area and local information.

Facilities

The small toilet block (key entry) is kept very clean and has vanity style washbasins, free electric showers and hairdryers. Facilities for disabled visitors include WC and washbasin (Radar key). New laundry area with dishwashing. Information room always open. Large play and ball game area adjacent. WiFi (free). Off site: Shops, restaurants and bars in Port William. Local walks and cycle routes. Fishing and rocky beach 50 yds.

Open: 1 March - 31 October.

Directions

From Dumfries, take A75 to Newton Stewart. Follow A714 to Wigtown, then B7085 to Port William. GPS: 54.755967, -4.581533

Charges guide

Per unit incl. 2 persons and electricity	£ 15.00
extra person	£ 2.00
child	free
dog	free

Saint Andrews

Craigtoun Meadows Holiday Park

Mount Melville, Saint Andrews KY16 8PQ (Fife) T: 01334 475959. E: info@craigtounmeadows.co.uk

alanrogers.com/UK7290

This attractively laid out, quality park has individual pitches and good facilities and although it is dominated by caravan holiday homes, the touring section is an important subsidiary. Its facilities are both well designed and comprehensive. There are 58 level touring pitches on hardstandings with grass area for awnings (only breathable groundsheets may be used) and hardstanding area for cars on most. All caravan pitches are large (130 sq.m) and are equipped with 16A electricity, water and drainage. There are 15 larger patio pitches with summer house, barbecue patio, picnic table and chairs, partially screened. Tents are taken on a grassy meadow at one end, also with electricity available.

Facilities

An excellent, centrally heated, luxury sanitary building serves the touring area. All washbasins are in cabins and each toilet has its own basin. Showers are unisex, as are two bathrooms, with hand- and hairdryers. Facilities for disabled visitors and babies. Launderette. Licensed restaurant (restricted hours in low seasons). Games room. Well equipped playground, play field and eight acres of woodland. Information room. WiFi throughout (charged). Pets are not accepted. Off site: Golf next to park.

Open: 15 March - 31 October.

Directions

From M90 exit 8 take A91 to St Andrews. Just after sign for Guardbridge (to left, A919), turn right at site sign and sign for Strathkinness. Go through village, over crossroads at end of village, left at next crossroads, then 0.75 miles to park. GPS: 56.324617, -2.83745

Charges guide

Per unit incl. electricity	£ 23.00 - £ 28.50
tent	£ 19.00 - £ 23.00

Scourie

Scourie Caravan & Camping Park

Harbour Road, Scourie IV27 4TG (Highland) T: 01971 502060. E: info@scouriecampsitesutherland.com

alanrogers.com/UK7730

The Mackenzie family run this park, which has a number of firm terraces with 60 pitches, giving it an attractive layout – there is nothing regimented here. Perched on the edge of the bay in an elevated position, practically everyone has a view of the sea and a short walk along the shore footpath leads to a small sandy beach. The park has tarmac and gravel access roads, with well drained grass and hardstanding pitches, some with 10A electricity hook-ups. A few are on an area which is unfenced from the rocks (young children would need to be supervised here).

Facilities

The toilet facilities can be heated. Showers have no divider or seat. Laundry. Motorcaravan services. The Anchorage restaurant at the entrance to the park (used as reception at quiet times) serves meals at reasonable prices, cooked to order (1/4-30/9). Boat launching. Fishing permits can be arranged. Off site: Village with shop and post office, gas is available at the petrol station.

Open: Easter/1 April - 30 September, but phone first to check.

Directions

Park is by Scourie village on A894 road in northwest Sutherland. GPS: 58.351417, -5.156767

Charges guide

Per unit incl. 2 adults and electricity	£ 23.00
extra adult	£ 5.00

No credit cards.

For latest campsite news visit
alanrogers.com

Staffin

Staffin Caravan & Camping Site

Staffin IV51 9JX (Isle of Skye) T: 01470 562213. E: staffincampsite@btinternet.com

alanrogers.com/UK7750

This site is just outside the village of Staffin on the east coast of Skye. There are 50 touring pitches, 26 with 16A electricity and hardstanding and 24 on grass without electricity. Pitches on the upper terrace enjoy lovely views of the sea. The entrance to the site from the main road is by a single track road. A marked walk from the site across the headland leads to the seashore and slipway (good for walking dogs). Skye has many activities to offer and for the truly dedicated walker the Cuillins are the major attraction, while the hills above Staffin are demanding in places!

Facilities	Directions
The sanitary block includes large, controllable showers. There are some hot water dishwashing sinks and a laundry. Small campers' kitchen with microwave, table and seating. Bicycle hire. WiFi throughout (charged). Off site: Staffin village with a licensed shop (open six days a week) and a restaurant 15 mins. walk. The Columbia centre in the village provides Internet access. Fishing and boat launching 2 miles. Riding 9 miles.	Site is 15 miles north of Portree on A855 just before 40 mph. signs on the right. GPS: 57.622017, -6.196

Directions

Site is 15 miles north of Portree on A855 just before 40 mph. signs on the right. GPS: 57.622017, -6.196

Charges guide

Per unit incl. 2 persons and electricity	£ 16.50
extra person	£ 4.00
child (5-12 yrs)	£ 2.50 - £ 3.00

No credit cards.

Open: One week before Easter - first week in October.

Stirling

Witches Craig Caravan Park

Blairlogie, Stirling FK9 5PX (Stirling) T: 01786 474947. E: info@witchescraig.co.uk

alanrogers.com/UK7320

Witches Craig is a neat and tidy park, nestling under the Ochil Hills. All 60 pitches have 10A electricity and hardstanding, seven of these being large (taking American-style motorhomes easily). Reasonably level, the park covers five well maintained acres with the grass beautifully manicured. Being by the A91, there is some daytime road noise. Trees have been planted to try to minimise this but the further back onto the park you go, the less the traffic is heard. The area has a wealth of historic attractions, starting with the Wallace Monument which practically overlooks the park. Its 220 ft. tower dominates the surrounding area and the climb up its 246 steps is rewarded by spectacular views.

Facilities	Directions
The modern, heated toilet block is well maintained and includes one cubicle with washbasin and WC each in ladies' and men's. Free controllable showers. Baby bath and mat. Good unit for disabled campers. Drive-over motorcaravan services. Laundry with free fridge/freezer facilities. Bread, milk, drinks and papers available daily (supermarket 2.5 miles). Large fenced play area. Field for team games. Free WiFi. Off site: Golf 1 mile. Riding and bicycle hire 2 miles. Fishing 3 miles. Bus stop 400 m.	Park is on the A91, 3 miles northeast of Stirling. GPS: 56.148033, -3.898667

Directions

Park is on the A91, 3 miles northeast of Stirling. GPS: 56.148033, -3.898667

Charges guide

Per unit incl. 2 persons and electricity	£ 21.00 - £ 24.00
extra person	£ 2.50
child (2-13 yrs)	£ 1.50
awning (no groundsheet)	£ 2.00

Open: 1 April - 31 October.

Stornoway

Laxdale Holiday Park

6 Laxdale Lane, Stornoway HS2 0DR (Isle of Lewis) T: 01851 706966. E: info@laxdaleholidaypark.com

alanrogers.com/UK7920

Whilst not in the most scenic of locations, this good park is well placed for touring. Surrounded by trees, it is on the edge of Stornaway (ferry port) and is well laid out with a tarmac road running through the centre. A level area has 18 touring pitches, all with electricity hook-ups (10A), plus five for tents, and a grassy area (no electricity) for tents gently slopes away to the trees and boundary. There is a choice of rental accommodation on offer: caravans, wigwams, a lodge, a bungalow and a bunkhouse. The site is centrally situated in an ideal spot for touring the Isle of Lewis with easy access to all parts of the island.

Facilities	Directions
The well maintained and modern sanitary block is heated and raised above the hardstanding area. Access is via steps or a gravel path to the ramp. Good (but narrow) showers with dividing curtain (on payment). Well equipped laundry with washing machine, dryer, iron and board, sink and clothes line. Telephone. WiFi in reception (charged). Glamping style pods are available for rent.	From Stornoway take the A857 for 1 mile then take the second turning on the left past the hospital. GPS: 58.22738, -6.39254

Directions

From Stornoway take the A857 for 1 mile then take the second turning on the left past the hospital. GPS: 58.22738, -6.39254

Charges guide

Per unit incl. 2 persons and electricity	£ 22.00
extra person	£ 3.50
child (5-15 yrs)	£ 2.50

Credit cards accepted (over £50).

Open: 1 March - 31 October.

For latest campsite news visit

alanrogers.com

Stranraer
Aird Donald Caravan Park

London Road, Stranraer DG9 8RN (Dumfries and Galloway) T: 01776 702025. E: enquiries@aird-donald.com
alanrogers.com/UK7020

Aird Donald is a good stopping off point when travelling to and from the Irish ferries, but it is also useful for seeing the sights around Stranraer. This tidy park comprises 12 acres surrounded by conifers, flowering trees and shrubs, and the 300-yard drive is lit and lined with conifers. There are grass areas for caravans and tents, and hardstandings with electricity hook-up. A small play area caters for young children, but the local leisure centre is only a walk away and provides swimming, table tennis, gym, bar and theatre that hosts everything from country and western to opera. The friendly owners, Mr and Mrs Cassie, made this campsite 53 years ago and keep it clean and well tended.

Facilities

Two toilet blocks, the newer one modern and heated (key deposit £5), are kept very clean. Electric showers are metered (50p) and others are free (strange, because they are all excellent). Unit for disabled visitors has washbasin and WC. The original block has been renovated but is more basic with free showers. Laundry. Motorcaravan services. Play area. WiFi over part of site (charged).

Open: All year.

Directions

Enter Stranraer on A75 road. Watch for narrow site entrance on left entering town, opposite school. GPS: 54.90185, -5.006217

Charges guide

Per unit incl. 2 persons
and electricity   £ 15.00 - £ 19.00
No credit cards.

Stromness
Point of Ness Caravan & Camping Site

Well Park, Ness Road, Stromness KW16 3DN (Orkney) T: 01856 873535. E: recreation@orkney.gov.uk
alanrogers.com/UK7950

This quiet site is in an idyllic position bounded by the sea on one side (an entrance to the harbour). It is sheltered by the land from the open sea and has views to the mountains and the island of Hoy. There is a rocky beach close by and walks from the site. There are 27 pitches (12 with 10A electricity hook-ups) on this level, firm grassy site, protected from the small drop to the sea by a low fence. Access to the steps to the sea is via a gate in the fence. Whilst being located at one end of Orkney, it is still easy to visit the Churchill Barriers and the Italian Chapel as well as the closer Maes Howe and Skara Brae sites.

Facilities

The well maintained traditional style toilet block has good sized showers (on payment) with curtains separating the changing area. Well equipped laundry. Lounge for campers is at one end of the block. Off site: Fishing, golf and bicycle hire all nearby.

Open: 1 April - 30 September.

Directions

Site is just west of Stromness and is signed from the town. Campers can walk along the narrow high street to site on edge of town. Caravans and motorcaravans are advised to take road at back of town (c. 2 miles). GPS: 58.95443, -3.30041

Charges guide

Per unit incl. 4 persons and electricity   £ 17.30
extra person   £ 6.10
No credit cards.

Tarbert
Muasdale Holiday Park

Muasdale, Tarbert PA29 6XD (Argyll and Bute) T: 01583 421207. E: enquiries@muasdaleholidays.com
alanrogers.com/UK7250

Muasdale Holiday Park has a beach-side location with fine views of the sea and islands, between Campbeltown and Tarbert on Kintyre's west coast. This is a small, friendly site with just ten pitches for touring units, five for tents and one used for a caravan holiday home to rent. The pitches are situated on a level, grass field, all with unobstructed sea views. All have electrical connections. You are advised to anchor tents and awnings securely as the winds are sometimes strong and gusty. The beach is a magnificent expanse of white sand with rock pools and an abundance of wildlife. The sunsets are frequently breathtaking. Sea canoeing and sea fishing are both popular.

Facilities

The single prefabricated toilet block is clean, heated and adequate. No specific facilities for disabled visitors or babies. Laundry facilities. Games room. Direct beach access. Sea swimming and fishing. Canoeing. WiFi (free). Accommodation to rent. Off site: Well stocked shop 100 yds. Kintyre Way walking trail. Whisky distilleries. Golf.

Open: April - end September.

Directions

From Glasgow (Erskine Bridge), take A82 towards Crianlarich, past Loch Lomond. At Tarbet take A83 towards Campbeltown, via Inveraray, Lochgilphead and Tarbert (Loch Fyne) and on to Muasdale Village, then site is signed. GPS: 55.597307, -5.686058

Charges guide

Per unit incl. 2 persons
and electricity   £ 17.50 - £ 20.00
extra person   £ 2.00

For latest campsite news visit
alanrogers.com

Tarbert

Port Bán Holiday Park

Kilberry, Tarbert PA29 6YD (Argyll and Bute) T: 01880 770224. E: info@portban.com

alanrogers.com/UK7880

Port Bán is in a fairly remote location on the peaceful coastline of the Knapdale Peninsula. Access to the site is via 15 miles of single track road with passing places. However, once you have arrived, you will appreciate the very tranquil setting, spectacular sunsets over Islay and Jura and the amazing variety of wildlife found here. There are just six pitches for touring units, four of which are on level grass with 10A electricity and direct frontage to a small beach. A camping field provides a further 30 pitches which are well marked out for tents and electricity is available for 26 of these. The main part of the site is occupied by caravan holiday homes, 20 of which are available for hire.

Facilities	Directions
Two sanitary blocks, one older in style and one modern block in the camping field with well equipped facilities, including those for disabled visitors. Laundry facilities. Shop (1/4-31/10). Café (flexible opening acc. to demand). Games room. Games field with football nets. Volleyball court. Tennis. Crazy golf and putting green. Bowling green. Play park. Beach suitable for launching small boats. Sea fishing. Bicycle hire. WiFi throughout.	Approach from the north on A83 from Lochgilphead. 3 miles south of Ardrishaig turn right onto B8024. Follow this single track road (with passing places) for 15 miles. Site signed on right via a short private lane. GPS: 55.82801, -5.66067

Open: 1 March - 31 October.

Charges guide

Per unit incl. 2 persons and electricity	£ 22.00 - £ 27.00
extra person	£ 4.00

Thurso

Dunnet Bay Caravan Club Site

Dunnet, Thurso KW14 8XD (Highland) T: 01847 821319. E: dunnetbay@caravanclub.co.uk

alanrogers.com/UK7745

Close to the village of Dunnet and next to a lovely sandy beach, Dunnet Bay is situated between the A836 and the sand dunes, looking out to Dunnet Head, the most northerly point of mainland Britain. There are 56 fairly level, grass touring pitches (two for tents), all with 16A electricity hook-ups. It is an ideal location for birdwatchers (a ferry trip around the Stacks of Duncansby is possible) and anglers, who can enjoy both sea- and freshwater fishing. There is no late arrivals area, so outfits over 8.5 m. should call the site.

Facilities	Directions
The beautifully clean, modern, heated sanitary block has controllable showers, hairdryers and cubicles. Well equipped en-suite unit for disabled visitors. Washing machine and dryer. Vegetable preparation area. Ice blocks frozen on request. Motorcaravan services. Essentials available in reception. Off site: Beach adjacent. Public telephone in Dunnet village (mobile reception limited). Fishing 2 miles. Shops in Castletown 3 miles.	Site can be found just west of Dunnet on A836. GPS: 58.61549, -3.34484

Open: 27 March - 5 October.

Charges guide

Per person	£ 6.30
child (5-17 yrs)	£ 1.30
pitch incl. electricity (non-member)	£ 15.40

Ullapool

Ardmair Point Caravan Park

Ardmair Point, Ullapool IV26 2TN (Highland) T: 01854 612054. E: sales@ardmair.com

alanrogers.com/UK7710

This spectacularly situated park, overlooking the little Loch Kanaird, just around the corner from Loch Broom, has splendid views all round. It is now run by new people who are really making a difference. The 68 touring pitches are arranged mainly on grass around the edge of the bay, in front of the shingle beach. Electricity hook-ups (10A) are available and some gravel hardstandings are on the other side of the access road, just past the second toilet block. Tent pitches, together with cheaper pitches for some touring units are in a large field behind the other sanitary facilities. Scuba diving is popular at Loch Kanaird because the water is so clear.

Facilities	Directions
Two toilet blocks, both with good facilities. One block has wonderful views from the large windows in the launderette and dishwashing rooms. Large en-suite rooms for disabled visitors. Motorcaravan services. Shop. Ardmair Bay Café in reception area serves breakfast and light meals (9.00-16.30; open to public). Play area. Fishing. Sailing and boating (with your own boat).	Park is off the A835 road, 3 miles north of Ullapool. GPS: 57.933967, -5.197017

Open: 1 April - late September, depending on the weather.

Charges guide

Per unit incl. 2 persons and electricity	£ 19.00 - £ 22.00

NORTHERN IRELAND COMPRISES THE FOLLOWING COUNTIES: ANTRIM, ARMAGH, DOWN, FERMANAGH, LONDONDERRY AND TYRONE

With a diversity of unspoilt landscapes, ranging from wild coastlines to green valleys, rugged mountains and shimmering lakes, to the natural phenomenon of the Giant's Causeway, Northern Ireland, though small, is crammed full of sights offering something for everyone.

The rugged coastline of the Causeway Coast and the nine Glens of Antrim in the north, is an Area of Outstanding Natural Beauty, with white sandy shores and little bays, tranquil forests and romantic ruins and castles, full of tales of the ancient Irish Giants and other myths and legends. At over 60 million years old, with a mass of 4,000 tightly packed basalt columns, each a polygon shape, the Giant's Causeway is a great attraction. One of the most beautiful regions is in the west around Londonderry, a delightful walled city set on a hill on the banks of the Foyle estuary. Further south is the beautiful region of Fermanagh with glistening lakes and little islands all surrounded by lush green fields, hillsides and forests. The large lake of Lough Erne is to be found here: made up of two channels, the lower and upper Loughs, the meeting point of these channels is Enniskillen, a town steeped in history, boasting numerous preserved buildings including a castle. Across to the eastern shores lies the ancient Kingdom of Down, with its endless miles of spectacular coastline, little fishing villages, country parks and the Mountains of Mourne. And, ringed by hills, sea lough and river valley is Belfast, a bustling city full of theatres, concert halls, art galleries and restaurants.

Places of interest

Antrim: Antrim Lough Shore Park; Rathlin Island; Giant's Causeway; Dunluce Castle near Portrush; Carrick-a-Rede Rope Bridge.

Belfast & environs: Belfast zoo and castle; Irish Linen Centre in Lisburn; Carrickfergus Castle; Crown Liquor Saloon.

Armagh: Gosford Forest Park near Markethill; Lough Neagh Discovery Centre on Oxford Island; Ardress House.

Down: County Museum and Downpatrick Cathedral; Mourne Mountains; Tollymore and Castlewellan forest parks; Ballycopeland Windmill near Millisle.

Fermanagh: Enniskillen Castle and Castle Coole; village of Belleek; Marble Arch Caves, near Lough Macnean; Devenish Island on Lough Erne.

Londonderry: St Columb's Cathedral; Tower Museum; Mural Tours; Foyle Valley Railway Centre in Derry.

Tyrone: Omagh; Beaghmore stone circles near Cookstown; Dungannon; Sperrin Mountains.

Did you know?

Northern Ireland measures 85 miles from north to south and is about 110 miles wide.

The world's most famous ship, the Titanic, was built in Belfast.

Legend has it that the rugged Giant's Causeway was built by Finn McCool, the legendary Irish Giant, when he travelled to Scotland to bring back his sweetheart.

At 2,240 yards, an Irish mile is 480 yards longer than a standard English mile.

Mountsandel near Coleraine is where Ireland's first known house was built 9,000 years ago.

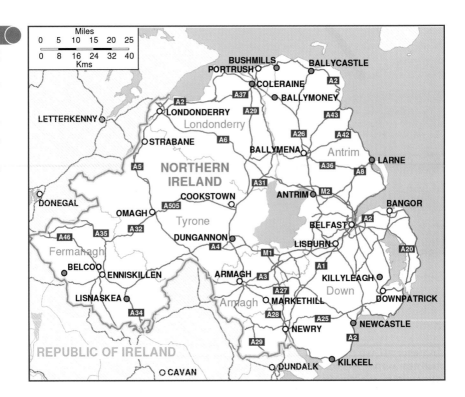

Antrim

Six Mile Water Caravan & Camping Park

Lough Road, Antrim BT41 4DG (Co. Antrim) T: 028 9446 4963. E: sixmilewater@antrim.gov.uk

alanrogers.com/UK8330

Six Mile Water is located at the Lough Shore Park and is adjacent to the Antrim Forum leisure complex, a major amenity area that includes swimming pools, a bowling green, an adventure playground for children, fitness and health gyms and sports fields. Managed by Antrim Borough Council, the park is easily accessible when travelling to and from the ports of Belfast and Larne, making it perfect for stopovers. There are now 37 pitches with 13A electricity, arranged in a herringbone layout of hardstandings with grass for awnings, a grass area for eight tents to one side, plus picnic and barbecue areas. Advance booking is advisable. Six Mile Water is central for sightseeing in the area including the Antrim Castle Gardens and Clotworthy Arts Centre, and for shopping in Antrim town. The Lough Shore Park offers visitors boating and water activities and boat launching on the beautiful Lough Neagh, as well as walking and cycling the Lough Shore Trail which takes in 25 places of interest along its 128-mile cycle route. The nearby golf club also offers a 20 bay driving range.

Facilities

The small, modern sanitary block provides toilets, washbasins and showers, with facilities for disabled campers. Baby changing unit. Laundry room. Restaurant and takeaway. TV lounge and games room. Fishing and boat launching. WiFi throughout. Off site: The facilities of Lough Shore Park, including a café, open all year round. Antrim Forum leisure centre. Bus service 1 mile. Shops, pubs and restaurants within 1.5 miles. Golf 1.5 miles. Riding 6 miles.

Open: 6 February - 29 November.

Directions

Site is 1 mile south of the city centre. Follow signs for Antrim Forum and Lough Shore Park. On the Dublin road, turn off into Lough Road. Pass Antrim Forum and park is at the end of the road (with speed bumps). Do not follow sat nav directions. GPS: 54.71533, -6.23375

Charges guide

Per unit incl. electricity	£ 21.00 - £ 23.00
tent	£ 15.00 - £ 18.00

For latest campsite news visit
alanrogers.com

Ballycastle

Glenmore Caravan and Camping Park

94 White Park Road, Ballycastle BT54 6LR (Co. Antrim) T: 028 2076 3584. E: glenmorehouse@lineone.net

alanrogers.com/UK8365

John and Valerie Brown run Glenmore Caravan and Camping Park on the beautiful Antrim Coast near the seaside town of Ballycastle. There are 27 hardstanding pitches for touring units which are spaced around the site in groups of four and five. The views from the easily accessible top field are spectacular. The restaurant/takeaway is open all year as is the bar with its covered terrace and live music at weekends. The creation of an on-site nature reserve makes this an ideal choice for birdwatching and nature lovers seeking a quiet and relaxing break. Those with an interest in fly fishing will enjoy the opportunity to catch brown and rainbow trout from one of three lakes, free of charge.

Facilities

One central, heated toilet block is basic but clean and tidy and offers hot showers operated by £1 coins. Washing machine and dryer. Restaurant/takeaway. Bar with covered terrace. Small playground on grass. Three lakes, free to use for fly fishing. Free WiFi in bar area. Off site: Beach, boat launching and golf within 2.5 miles. Riding 9 miles.

Open: All year.

Directions

From Ballycastle take the B15 towards Ballantoy. The site is 2.5 miles on the left. Do not follow sat nav as you will be directed down a very narrow lane unsuitable for caravans and motorcaravans. GPS: 55.220321, -6.31222

Charges guide

Per unit incl. electricity	£ 20.00

No credit cards.

Ballymoney

Drumaheglis Caravan Park

36 Glenstall Road, Ballymoney BT53 7QN (Co. Antrim) T: 028 2766 0280. E: drumaheglis@ballymoney.gov.uk

alanrogers.com/UK8340

A caravan park which continually maintains high standards, Drumaheglis is popular throughout the season. Situated on the bank of the lower River Bann, approximately four miles from the town of Ballymoney, it appeals to watersports enthusiasts and makes a very good base for exploring this scenic corner of Northern Ireland. This attractive site with 54 pitches is well laid out with trees, shrubs, flower beds and tarmac roads. There are 35 serviced pitches for touring units with hardstanding, 16A electricity, water points and drainage. The marina offers facilities for boat launching, water skiing, cruising, canoeing and fishing.

Facilities

Three modern toilet blocks are very clean and well maintained. Facilities for disabled visitors. Baby changing facilities and four en-suite shower rooms. Washing machine and dryer. Basic shop. Play area. Barbecue and picnic areas. Barrier with key system. Fishing. Boat launching. WiFi throughout. Off site: Marina. Bus service from park entrance. Bicycle hire and golf 4 miles. Riding 6 miles. Beach 10 miles.

Open: 17 March - end October.

Directions

From A26/B62 Portrush-Ballymoney roundabout continue for 2 miles on the A26 towards Coleraine. Site is clearly signed; follow international camping signs. GPS: 55.07212, -6.59082

Charges guide

Per unit incl. electricity	£ 24.00 - £ 25.00
tent pitch	£ 17.00

Belcoo

Rushin House Caravan Park

Holywell, Belcoo, Enniskillen BT93 5DU (Co. Fermanagh) T: 028 6638 6519.

E: enquiries@rushinhousecaravanpark.com **alanrogers.com/UK8515**

Although situated in Northern Ireland, this park, opened in 2007, is almost on the border with the Republic of Ireland. It has been carefully landscaped from farmland that sloped down to the tranquil Lough MacNean. There are 38 fully serviced, terraced pitches on hardstanding. They form a friendly circle surrounding a fairy thorn tree and have an added bonus of a wonderful view of the loch. There is also a small camping area. The toilet block, boat jetty, picnic tables and play areas are only a short walk away from the pitches. The helpful owners live on site and are on call most of the time. This park provides a peaceful haven to relax after returning from days out in lovely Fermanagh.

Facilities

Heated toilet block, beautifully appointed, with laundry and adjoining kitchen area. Separate facilities for disabled campers. Motorcaravan services. Payphone. Boat jetty. Play area. All-weather sports facility. Picnic area. WiFi throughout. Off site: Golf course nearby. Twin border towns of Belcoo and Blacklion are charming and well provided with shops and restaurants.

Open: 11 March - 31 October.

Directions

From Enniskillen follow the A4 for 13 miles to Belcoo. Turn right on to the B52 towards Garrison and in 1 mile you will see the signs for Rushin House. GPS: 54.306584, -7.89505

Charges guide

Per unit incl. 2 persons fully serviced	£ 25.00
extra person (over 16 yrs)	£ 3.00
tent	£ 15.00 - £ 22.00

For latest campsite news visit
alanrogers.com

Bushmills

Ballyness Caravan Park

40 Castlecatt Road, Bushmills BT57 8TN (Co. Antrim) T: 028 2073 2393. E: info@ballynesscaravanpark.com

alanrogers.com/UK8360

Ballyness is immaculately cared for and is designed with conservation in mind. In keeping with the surrounding countryside, it is extensively planted with native trees and shrubs. A pathway encircles several ponds which attract local wildlife and birds. The overall appearance of this eight-hectare park, with its black stone pillared entrance gate and broad tarmac drive, is attractive. There are 50 hardstanding pitches all with electricity (16A), water and drainage. Privately owned caravan holiday homes are placed away from the touring pitches. The village of Bushmills, with its famous whisky distillery, is within walking distance. The Giant's Causeway and the majestic Antrim coast are only a short drive.

Facilities

One spotlessly clean and well decorated, cottage-style heated sanitary block (key coded). Facilities for disabled visitors (toilet and shower). Shop for basic food supplies, gas and camping essentials. Family room with bath. Games and TV room. Laundry room. Play area and play park. Free WiFi throughout. Off site: Bus service 0.5 miles (between April and September the Causeway Rambler bus comes to the park). Bicycle hire and fishing 1 mile. Beach and boat launching 1.5 miles. Riding 5 miles. Championship golf courses 6 miles.

Open: 16 March - 2 November.

Directions

From M2 follow A26. At Ballymoney turn right on B66 towards Dervock and turn left at sign for Bushmills. Stay on B66 and site is 5.5 miles on right. GPS: 55.20121, -6.52096

Charges guide

Per unit incl. 2 persons, fully serviced	£ 25.00
extra person	£ 2.00
child (6-17 yrs)	£ 1.00

Coleraine

Tullans Farm Holiday Park

46 Newmills Road, Coleraine BT52 2JB (Co. Londonderry) T: 028 7034 2309. E: info@tullans.com

alanrogers.com/UK8590

A well run family park, convenient for the Causeway coast, Tullans Farm has a quiet, heart of the country feel, yet the university town of Coleraine is within a mile, the seaside resorts of Portrush and Portstewart five miles and a shopping centre a five minute drive. The toilet block is clean and attractive flower displays add to the park's well cared for appearance. Around the park, roads are gravel and the 36 pitches are on hardstanding; all with 10A electricity, water and drainage. A further 80 pitches are occupied by privately owned mobile homes/chalets. In season the owners organise barbecues, barn dances and line dancing (raising funds for charity).

Facilities

The toilet and shower rooms, including a family shower unit, are spacious, modern and include facilities for visitors with disabilities. Laundry and washing up room with sinks, washing machine, dryers and fridge. Play areas. TV lounge. Games room. Barn used for indoor recreation. Snooker room for adults. Caravan storage. WiFi over site. Off site: Public transport in Coleraine 1 mile. Fishing and riding 1.5 miles. Golf, beach and bicycle hire 5 miles.

Open: March - 30 September.

Directions

From the Lodge Road roundabout (south end of Coleraine) turn east onto A29 Portrush ring road and proceed for 0.5 miles. Turn right at sign for park and Windy Hall. Park is clearly signed on left. GPS: 55.12557, -6.63923

Charges guide

Per unit incl. 2 persons, fully serviced	£ 20.00 - £ 22.00

For latest campsite news visit
alanrogers.com

Dungannon

Dungannon Park

Moy Road, Dungannon BT71 6DY (Co. Tyrone) T: 028 8772 8690. E: dpreception@dungannon.gov.uk
alanrogers.com/UK8550

This small touring park nestles in the midst of a 70-acre park with a multitude of tree varieties, brightly coloured flower beds and a charming 12-acre fishing lake. The 12 touring pitches, some with lake views, are on hardstanding, each with dedicated water, waste and 16A electricity connections. Hedging provides some separation. There is also an unmarked grass area for tents. Run by Dungannon Council, the park, which also incorporates tennis courts, football and cricket pitches, lies about one mile south of Dungannon town.

Facilities

Sanitary facilities are to the rear of the Amenity Centre and include showers (by token), washbasins, baby changing mat and spacious unit for disabled visitors. Laundry room with washing machine and dryer. Excellent play area. TV lounge. Tennis. Fishing. Walking. Orienteering. Off site: Bus stop and shop at main entrance to park. Restaurants, shops, leisure facilities in Dungannon. Interesting walking and cycling in Clogher Valley.

Open: 1 March - 31 October.

Directions

From M1 exit 15 join A29 towards Dungannon. Turn left at second traffic lights signed Dungannon Park. GPS: 54.390217, -6.757967

Charges guide

Per unit incl. 2 persons and electricity	£ 19.00

No credit cards.

Kilkeel

Cranfield Caravan Park

123 Cranfield Road, Cranfield West, Kilkeel BT34 4LJ (Co. Down) T: 028 4176 2572.
E: jimchestnut@btconnect.com **alanrogers.com/UK8405**

On the shores of Carlingford Lough, with direct access to a Blue Flag beach, this friendly, family run park immediately impresses with its well cared for flower beds, neat hedging, cordyline palms and the elegant building which incorporates the family home and reception. Despite the many privately owned caravan holiday homes on site, 40 touring pitches are kept separate and are situated towards the park entrance. Most pitches have a sea view, hardstanding and all have tower units providing 10A electricity hook-ups, water, waste water point and TV outlet. Tents are not accepted.

Facilities

The modern, heated toilet block (entrance by key) is well maintained with tiled walls/floors, preset showers (token) and open style washbasins. Excellent suite for disabled visitors doubles as a family room, also a night WC (by key). Well equipped laundry in a separate building. Sea fishing, boat launching and beach (with lifeguard). WiFi (charged). Off site: Play area. Kilkeel town 3.5 miles. Golf, hill walking in the Mournes. Anglo Norman castle.

Open: 17 March - 27 September.

Directions

Travelling southeast on A2 Newry-Kilkeel Road turn right 5.5 miles after passing through Rostrevor onto local road, signed Cranfield/Greencastle. If approaching from Kilkeel follow signs for Cranfield West. Site signed at end of road. GPS: 54.029933, -6.0683

Charges guide

Per unit incl. all persons and electricity	£ 20.00 - £ 23.00
awning	£ 2.00

Kilkeel

Sandilands Caravan Park

30 Cranfield Road, Cranfield East, Kilkeel BT34 4LJ (Co. Down) T: 028 4176 3634.
E: info@chestnutholidayparks.com **alanrogers.com/UK8407**

In the very popular area of Cranfield, Sandilands is set slightly apart from its neighbours, looking south east over the Irish Sea rather than Carlingford Lough. The park largely comprises privately owned caravan holiday homes, but has an attractive and enclosed area for 31 touring units. It makes the most of its coastal plain situation to the immediate south of the Mourne Mountains. Kilkeel and the mountain foothills can be reached in a few minutes by car. Sandilands is pleasantly laid out with an inviting entrance and may be just the answer for those seeking a quieter location whilst visiting the area.

Facilities

Laundry and toilet block (entrance to all facilities by key) is well maintained. Preset showers (token) and open style washbasins and a night WC. Toilet only for disabled visitors. Play area and small football pitch. WiFi throughout (charged). Off site: Sea fishing and boat launching nearby. Pretty village of Rostrevor, well known for its ceilidhs and Irish music 7 miles. Kilkeel and Annalong are interesting fishing towns.

Open: Easter - 30 September.

Directions

From the north leave the A2 in the middle of Kilkeel and follow signs for Cranfield East until the sign for Sandilands appears on the left. From Newry pass through Rostrevor and after 6 miles turn right to Cranfield East. Follow signs for Sandilands Holiday Park. GPS: 54.029932, -6.058391

Charges guide

Per unit incl. services	£ 22.00

For latest campsite news visit
alanrogers.com

Kilkeel

Chestnutt Holiday Park

3 Grange Road, Kilkeel, Newry BT34 4LW (Co. Down) T: 028 4176 2653. E: info@chestnuttholidayparks.com
alanrogers.com/UK8410

Chestnutt Holiday Park is one of the best in the southernmost corner of Northern Ireland. There are two areas designated for touring units, one on each side of the entrance road and all pitches have electricity, light, water and waste. The park is surrounded by dramatic scenery and unspoilt countryside and is an attractive choice for a beach based holiday. The adjacent beach, with lifeguard, tennis court, small football pitch and play park will keep youngsters happy all day. The backdrop of the Mourne Mountains to the north gives the area shelter. Since the introduction of more facilities for children, Easter is becoming popular at this site.

Facilities

Each touring section has its own toilet block with token operated showers. The large well equipped laundry (also token operated), toilets and full facilities for disabled campers have been completely refurbished. Shop and restaurant (open Easter weekend, July/Aug). Takeaway (open as restaurant and also w/ends in low season). Tennis court. Small football pitch. Play area. Adventure summer camps (8-16 yrs). Saturday club (5-14 yrs). WiFi throughout (charged).

Open: Easter - mid September.

Directions

From the north follow the A2 from Newcastle and at Kilkeel follow signs for Cranfield West and then Chestnutt Holiday Park. From Newry, pass through Rostrevor and 6 miles further you will see signs for Cranfield and the site. GPS: 54.030864, -6.068868

Charges guide

Per unit incl. awning and electricity	£ 22.00

Killyleagh

Delamont Country Park Camping & Caravanning Club Site

Delamont Country Park, Downpatrick Road, Killyleagh BT30 9TZ (Co. Down) T: 028 4482 1833.
E: delamont.site@thefriendlyclub.co.uk **alanrogers.com/UK8460**

This is Northern Ireland's first Camping and Caravanning Club site and is now one of the country's more popular sites. Facilities on the campsite itself are excellent and it has an orderly, neat and tidy appearance. Reception stands beside the entrance, with the sanitary block towards the rear. The 63 hardstanding pitches on level terrain all have electricity, plus water and waste hook-ups. There are no grass-only pitches and campers with tents should contact the site. The site is surrounded by trees and the rich vegetation of the country park, and the shrubs and trees around the pitches are now mature.

Facilities

The single modern toilet block, with heating, has wash cubicles and a baby bath. En-suite facilities for disabled visitors. Laundry sinks, washing machine and dryer. Small shop area selling basics. Adventure playground and miniature railway in country park. Free admittance to country park for campers. WiFi on part of site (charged). Off site: Fishing and riding 1 mile. Tyrella beach 7 miles.

Open: 10 March - 31 October.

Directions

From Belfast follow A22 southeast to village of Killyleagh. Pass through village and site entrance is on left after 1 mile. GPS: 54.38656, -5.67657

Charges guide

Per unit incl. 2 persons and services	£ 18.70 - £ 31.75
extra person	£ 7.15 - £ 12.15
Non-member prices are higher.	

Larne

Carnfunnock Country Park Caravan Park & Campsite

Coast Road, Ballygally, Larne BT40 2QG (Co. Antrim) T: 028 2827 0541.
E: carnfunnock@midandeastantrim.gov.uk **alanrogers.com/UK8310**

In a magnificent parkland setting overlooking the Irish Sea and Scotland, what makes this touring site popular are its scenic surroundings and convenient location. It is 3.5 miles north of the market town of Larne on the famed Antrim Coast Road and offers 31 level super pitches, including three extra long pitches, all with hardstanding, water, 16A electricity, drainage, individual pitch lighting and ample space for an awning. The site has a neat appearance with a tarmac road following through to the rear where a number of pitches are placed close together in a circular position with allocated space for tents. Run by the Borough Council and supervised by a manager, the surrounding Country Park is immaculately kept.

Facilities

A small building beside the entrance gates houses the toilet facilities (key) which have had a major refurbishment and are kept very clean. Shower units, family bathroom and facilities for disabled visitors. Baby room. Shop (Easter- 31/10). Restaurant and takeaway. WiFi over site. Off site: Facilities of the adjacent Country Park including gift shop, restaurant and coffee shop.

Open: 27 March - 1 October.

Directions

From ferry terminal in Larne, follow signs for Coast Road and Carnfunnock Country Park; well signed on A2 coast road. GPS: 54.888193, -5.845231

Charges guide

Per unit incl. 2 persons and services	£ 22.00 - £ 25.00
tent incl. 2 persons	£ 13.50 - £ 14.50

For latest campsite news visit
alanrogers.com

Larne
Curran Caravan Park
131 Curran Road, Larne BT40 1DD (Co. Antrim) T: 028 2827 3797. E: info@caravanparksni.com
alanrogers.com/UK8320

Attractive garden areas add to the charm of this small, neat park which has recently been purchased by the owner of the garage/shop opposite. It is very conveniently situated for the ferry terminal and only a few minutes walk from the sea. The new owner has been making some upgrades and now provides four hardstanding pitches for motorcaravans. The 34 pitches, all with 14A electricity connections, give reasonable space off the tarmac road and there is a separate tent area of 1.5 acres. Larne market is on Wednesdays. You may consider using this site as a short term base for discovering the area as well as an ideal overnight stop, especially for early or late ferry crossings.

Facilities

The toilet block is clean and adequate without being luxurious but there are no facilities for disabled visitors. Laundry room with dishwashing facilities. Bowls and putting adjacent and also play areas with good equipment and safety surfaces. Late arrivals can call at the garage if open. WiFi. Off site: Train station and bus stop within a few mins. walk. Shop 100 yds. Restaurants, tennis and a leisure centre with swimming pool 300 yds.

Open: Easter - 31 October.

Directions

Immediately after leaving the ferry terminal, turn right and follow camp signs. Site is 400 yds. on the left. GPS: 54.84995, -5.80818

Charges guide

| Per unit incl. 2 persons, electricity and awning | £ 20.00 |
| tent incl. 2 persons | £ 16.00 |

Lisnaskea
Mullynascarthy Caravan Park
Gola Road, Lisnaskea BT92 0NZ (Co. Fermanagh) T: 028 6772 1040.
alanrogers.com/UK8510

This is a well kept touring site with 43 pitches, situated on the banks of the Colebrooke River. It has instant appeal, for the setting at Mullynascarthy is more like a mature garden. The pitches to the right of reception, which are grass on hardstanding, are interspersed with flowering shrubs and partly hedged. To the left of the facility block additional pitches are spread over meadow-like terrain and all have electric hook-ups. Sanitary facilities, although not ultra modern, are kept clean and housed alongside reception, which doubles up as a sub-post office and small shop.

Facilities

The toilet block has showers, open style washbasins, facilities for visitors with disabilities (washbasin/WC), laundry room and dishwashing sinks. Games and sports area. Open play area. River fishing (licences and permits available in Enniskillen). Off site: Bus service 1.5 miles. Golf and bicycle hire 10 miles.

Open: 17 March - 31 October.

Directions

From Enniskillen take A4 towards Dungannon for 8 miles, then turn right on A34 signed Lisnaskea. Continue on A34 for 2.5 miles and turn right onto B514 and right again after 400 yds. where site is signed Mullynascarthy. GPS: 54.26842, -7.48343

Charges guide

| Per unit incl. 2 persons and electricity | £ 20.00 |
| tent | £ 14.00 - £ 18.00 |

No credit cards.

Newcastle
Tollymore Forest Caravan Park
178 Tullybrannigan Road, Newcastle BT33 0PW (Co. Down) T: 028 4372 2428.
alanrogers.com/UK8420

This popular park, for touring units only, is located within the parkland of Tollymore Forest which is noted for its scenic surroundings. The forest park is approached by a majestic avenue of Himalayan cedars and covers an area of almost 500 hectares. Situated two miles from the beaches and resort of Newcastle, it is backed impressively by the Mourne mountains. The open grassy site is attractively laid out with 71 hardstanding pitches, all of which have 10A electricity. The Forestry Service Rangers are very helpful and ensure that the caravan site is efficiently run and quiet, even when full.

Facilities

The timbered toilet blocks have wash cubicles, showers, dishwashing and laundry area. Fishing (permit required, available from the Four Seasons Tackle Shop in Newcastle). Off site: Confectionery shop and tea room nearby (high season). Small grocery shop a few yards from the exit gate of the park, with gas available.

Open: All year.

Directions

Approach Newcastle on A24. Before the town, at roundabout, turn right onto A50 (Castlewellan), left onto B180 and follow Tollymore Forest Park signs. Do not use sat nav as you will be directed via a very narrow lane. GPS: 54.22630, -5.93449

Charges guide

| Per unit incl. electricity | £ 12.10 - £ 17.30 |

No credit cards.

For latest campsite news visit
alanrogers.com

IRELAND IS MADE UP OF FOUR PROVINCES: CONNAUGHT, LEINSTER, MUNSTER AND ULSTER, COMPRISING 32 COUNTIES, 26 OF WHICH FALL IN THE REPUBLIC OF IRELAND

Famed for its folklore, traditional music, and friendly, hospitable people, the Republic of Ireland offers spectacular scenery contained within a relatively compact area. With plenty of beautiful areas to discover, and a relaxed pace of life, it is an ideal place to unwind.

Ireland is the perfect place to indulge in a variety of outdoor pursuits while taking in the glorious scenery. There are plenty of waymarked footpaths which lead through woodlands, across cliffs, past historical monuments and over rolling hills. The dramatic coastline, with its headlands, secluded coves and sandy beaches, is fantastic for watersports: from sailing to windsurfing, scuba diving and swimming; or for just simply relaxing and watching the variety of seabirds that nest on the shores. The Cliffs of Moher, in particular, is a prime location for birdwatching and Goat Island, just offshore, is where puffins make their nesting burrows. Fishing is also popular; the country is full of streams, rivers, hidden lakes and canals, which can all be explored by hiring a boat. In the south, the beautiful Ring of Kerry is one of the most visited regions. This 110-mile route encircles the Inveragh Peninsula, and is surrounded by mountains and lakes. Other sights include the Aran Islands, home to some of the most ancient Christian and pre-Christian remains in Ireland, and the Rock of Cashel, with its spectacular group of Medieval buildings; not to mention the bustling cities of Dublin, Galway and Cork.

Places of interest

Connaught: Boyle Abbey; Connemara National Park; Céide Fields at Ballycastle; Kylemore Abbey; Aran Islands; Galway city; Westport; Sligo Abbey; megalithic tombs of Carrowmore.

Leinster: Wicklow Mountains National Park; Rock of Cashel; Killkenny Castle; Guinness brewery, Trinity College and National Museum in Dublin; Dunmore Cave at Ballyfoyle; Wexford Wildfowl Reserve.

Munster: harbour towns of Kinsale and Clonakilty; Blarney Castle in Cork; historical city of Limerick with 13th-century castle fortress and old town; Ring of Kerry; Bunratty Castle; Cliffs of Moher; Killarney National Park.

Ulster: Glenveagh National Park; Slieve League, the highest sea cliffs in Europe; Donegal Castle; Newmills Corn and Flax Mills in Letterkenny.

Did you know?

The official currency of the Republic of Ireland is the Euro.

The international dialling code for the Republic of Ireland is 00 353 (then drop the first '0' of the number).

The Blarney Stone, reputedly cast with a spell by a witch to reward a king who saved her from drowning, is said to bestow the gift of eloquence on all those who kiss it.

The harp is a symbol of the Irish people's love of music: since Medieval times it has been the official emblem for Ireland.

Hurling is the oldest native sport.

On display in Trinity College, the Book of Kells is one of the oldest books in the world, written around the year 800 AD.

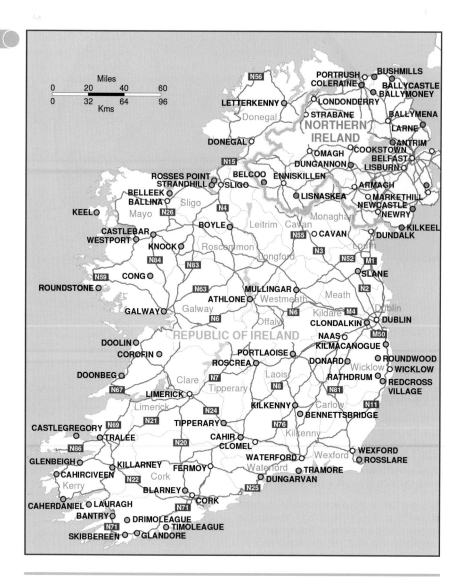

Athlone

Lough Ree (East) Caravan & Camping Park

Ballykeeran, Athlone (Co. Westmeath) T: 090 647 8561. E: athlonecamping@eircom.net

alanrogers.com/IR8960

This touring park is alongside the Breensford river, screened by trees but reaching the water's edge. The park is discreetly located behind Ballykeeran's main street. The top half of the site is in woodland and after the reception and sanitary block, Lough Ree comes into view and the remaining pitches run down to the shoreline. There are 60 pitches, most on hardstanding and all with 6A electricity. With fishing right on the doorstep there are boats for hire locally and the site has its own private mooring buoys, plus a dinghy slip and harbour. A restaurant and 'singing' pub are close by.

Facilities

The toilet block is clean and the recently refurbished ladies' toilets, unisex showers (€ 1) and facilities for disabled visitors are all excellent. Dishwashing sinks outside. Laundry room (wash and dry € 8). A wooden chalet houses a pool room with open fire and campers' kitchen (no cooking facilities). Off site: Riding 4 km. Bicycle hire 5 km. Golf 8 km.

Open: 1 April - 30 September.

Directions

From Athlone take N55 towards Longford for 4.8 km. (2 km. from exit 10 of M6). Park is in the village of Ballykeeran. Prepare to take a left turn on a sharp, right-hand curve, the park is then clearly signed. GPS: 53.44815, -7.88992

Charges guide

Per unit incl. 2 persons and electricity	€ 23.00
extra person	€ 4.00

No credit cards.

For latest campsite news visit

alanrogers.com

Bantry

Eagle Point Caravan & Camping Park

Ballylickey, Bantry (Co. Cork) T: 027 506 30. E: eaglepointcamping@eircom.net

alanrogers.com/IR9510

Midway between the towns of Bantry and Glengarriff, the spectacular peninsula of Eagle Point juts into Bantry Bay. The first impression is of a spacious country park rather than a campsite. As far as the eye can see this 20-acre, landscaped, part-terraced park, with its vast manicured grass areas separated by mature trees, shrubs and hedges, runs parallel with the shoreline providing lovely views. Suitable for all ages, this is a well run park mainly for touring units, with campers pitched mostly towards the shore. It provides 125 pitches with 6A electricity, although many are seasonally occupied.

Facilities

Three well maintained, well designed toilet blocks are of a high standard. Laundry. Motorcaravan services. Play area. Tennis. Football field, well away from the pitches. Fishing. Boat launching. Supermarket at park entrance. Dogs are not accepted. WiFi on part of site. Off site: Golf 2 km. Bicycle hire 6 km. Riding 10 km.

Open: 17 April - 21 September.

Directions

Take N71 to Bandon, then R586 Bandon to Bantry. From Bantry take N71 to Glengarriff. 6.4 km. from Bantry; or N22 Cork to Macroom, R584 to Ballylickey Bridge, right onto N71 to Glengarriff. Entrance opposite Cronins petrol station. GPS: 51.718333, -9.455278

Charges guide

Per unit incl. 2 persons and electricity	€ 29.00 - € 32.00
extra person	€ 10.00

Belleek

Belleek Park Caravan & Camping

Belleek, Ballina (Co. Mayo) T: 096 715 33. E: lenahan@belleekpark.com

alanrogers.com/IR8750

Belleek has a quiet woodland setting, only minutes from Ballina, a famed salmon fishing centre. With excellent pitches and toilet block, the family owners are committed to ensuring that it is immaculate at all times. From the entrance gate, the park is approached by a drive that passes reception and leads to 80 well spaced pitches. With a very neat overall appearance, 50 pitches have hardstanding and electricity hook-ups, and you may choose your spot. Sports facilities within a short distance of the park include a swimming pool, tennis and bicycle hire. There is a Blue Flag beach at Ross.

Facilities

Spotlessly clean, tastefully decorated toilet block providing showers (€ 1 token). Baby bath. Facilities for disabled campers. Laundry facilities. Reception includes a shop and a tea room also serving breakfast. Campers' kitchen and emergency accommodation with beds provided. TV room. Games room. Play area. Ball game area. Tennis. Free WiFi over site. Off site: Bar and restaurant 1.5 km.

Open: 1 March - 1 November, by arrangement all year.

Directions

Take R314 Ballina-Killala road. Park is signed on right after 3 km. GPS: 54.1345, -9.1585

Charges guide

Per unit incl. 2 persons and electricity	€ 20.00 - € 24.00
extra person	€ 3.00
child	€ 1.50
hiker/cyclist and tent	€ 8.00 - € 9.00

Bennettsbridge

Nore Valley Park

Bennettsbridge, Kilkenny (Co. Kilkenny) T: 056 772 7229. E: norevalleypark@eircom.net

alanrogers.com/IR9230

This lovely site is set on a grassy hill overlooking the valley of the River Nore, with a woodland setting behind. Situated on a working farm, it offers 70 touring pitches, 60 of which have 6A electricity. There is an additional area for tents and four mobile homes for rent. The owners, Samuel and Isobel, are proud of their park and her baking and jams must be sampled. An attractive courtyard houses several unusual facilities including a sand pit and a straw loft play area for wet weather. Animal park, outdoor chess, tractor rides and go-karts in the fields.

Facilities

The modern toilet block is kept clean and can be heated. Two units suitable for disabled visitors. Laundry room with washing machine and dryer. Motorcaravan services. The original block in the courtyard is used mainly in the low season. Shop (basic items such as milk, bread and camping gaz) and café (June-Aug). Comfortable lounge. Games room. Play area. Minigolf. WiFi (free).

Open: 1 March - 31 October.

Directions

From Kilkenny take R700 to Bennettsbridge. Just before the bridge turn right at sign for Stoneyford and after 3 km. site is signed Nore Valley Park. GPS: 52.56307, -7.19506

Charges guide

Per unit incl. 2 persons and electricity	€ 24.00
extra person	€ 4.00

For latest campsite news visit
alanrogers.com

Blarney

Blarney Caravan & Camping Park

Stone View, Blarney (Co. Cork) T: 021 451 6519. E: info@blarneycaravanpark.com

alanrogers.com/IR9480

There is a heart of the country feel about this 'on the farm' site, yet the city of Cork is only an 8 km. drive. What makes this friendly, family run park so appealing is the welcome you receive on arrival and the friendliness throughout your stay. Its secluded location and neat spacious pitches add to its appeal. The terrain on the three-acre park is elevated and gently sloping, commanding views towards Blarney Castle and the surrounding mountainous countryside. The 80 pitches, 40 of which have hardstanding and 10A Europlug, are with caravans near the entrance with tents pitched slightly further away. There are gravel roads, well tended young shrubs and a screen of mature trees. Tidy hedging marks the park's perimeter.

Facilities	Directions
Excellent toilet facilities are housed in converted farm buildings. Reception and small shop are now at entrance. Good facilities for disabled visitors. Laundry. Campers' kitchen. Motorcaravan services. Shop (1/6-31/8). TV lounge. Playground. WiFi throughout (free). Delightful 18-hole golf and pitch-and-putt course. Off site: Bar 100 m. Restaurants in Blarney village 2.5 km. Open: 24 March - 31 October.	Site is 8 km. northwest of Cork, just off the N20. Take N20 from Cork for 6 km. and then left on R617 to Blarney. Site clearly signed at Maxol petrol station in village, in 2 km. GPS: 51.94787, -8.54622

Charges guide

Per unit incl. 2 persons and electricity	€ 25.00 - € 27.00
extra person	€ 7.00

Boyle

Lough Key Caravan & Camping Park

Lough Key Forest Park, Boyle (Co. Roscommon) T: 071 966 2212. E: info@loughkey.ie

alanrogers.com/IR8825

This caravan and camping park is set deep in the 320 hectares of the Lough Key Forest Park. Comprising mixed woodland including giant red cedar, beech, ash and oak trees, the forest is bounded by Lough Key and incorporates several of its islands. The rustic design of the main building on the park (which houses reception, a campers' kitchen, a lounge and the sanitary and laundry facilities) blends well with the wooded environment. The well landscaped, five-hectare site provides space for 52 touring units with electricity connections and ample water points, and many of the pitches are within woodland. There is a separate area for tents.

Facilities	Directions
The main toilet block includes metered hot showers (€ 2). Facilities for disabled campers (key required). Campers' kitchen and sheltered eating area. Laundry. Play area in the centre of the park with adventure type play equipment in a hedged area, plus seating for parents. Forest walks and trails. Boat tours and boat hire. Site security patrol. Off site: Local shop will deliver to site. Restaurant at Rockingham harbour. Amenities in Boyle 3 km. Open: 1 April - mid-September.	Park is 4 km. east of Boyle on the N4 Dublin-Sligo Road. Note: there is a height restriction (3 m) on the signed exit from the park towards Boyle, but there is an alternative route to the N4. GPS: 53.98125, -8.235167

Charges guide

Per unit incl. 2 persons and electricity	€ 22.00
No credit cards.	

Caherdaniel

Wave Crest Caravan & Camping Park

Caherdaniel (Co. Kerry) T: 066 947 5188. E: wavecrest@eircom.net

alanrogers.com/IR9560

It would be difficult to imagine a more dramatic location than Wave Crest's on the Ring of Kerry coast. Huge boulders and rocky outcrops tumble from the park entrance on the N70 down to the seashore which forms the most southern promontory on the Ring of Kerry. There are spectacular southward views from the park across Kenmare Bay to the Beara peninsula. Sheltering on grass patches in small coves that nestle between the rocks and shrubbery, are 40 hardstanding pitches and 23 on grass offering seclusion. Electricity connections are available (13A). This park would suit older people looking for a quiet, relaxed atmosphere.

Facilities	Directions
Two blocks house the sanitary and laundry facilities and include hot showers on payment (€ 1). Small shop, restaurant and takeaway service (June-Sept). Small play area. Fishing and boat launching. WiFi throughout (charged). Boat trips from the site. Off site: Small beach nearby and Derrynane Hotel with bar and restaurant. Open: All year.	On the N70 (Ring of Kerry), 1.5 km. east of Caherdaniel. GPS: 51.75881, -10.09112

Charges guide

Per unit incl. 2 persons and electricity	€ 28.00
extra person	€ 2.00

For latest campsite news visit

alanrogers.com

Cahir
The Apple Camping & Caravan Park
Moorstown, Cahir (Co. Tipperary) T: 052 744 1459. E: con@theapplefarm.com
alanrogers.com/IR9410

This fruit farm and campsite combination offers an idyllic country holiday venue in one of the most delightful situations imaginable. For touring units only, it is located off the N24, midway between Clonmel and Cahir. The park has 32 pitches in a secluded situation behind the barns, set among trees and shrubs. They are mostly grass with 14 hardstandings and 28 electricity connections (13A Europlug). Entrance is by way of a 300 m. drive flanked by the orchard fields and various non-fruit tree species which are named and of interest to guests who are free to spend time walking the paths around the farm. Apples, raspberries and strawberries were picked while we were there – the best we had tasted all season – and these are available to purchase.

Facilities

Heated toilet facilities, kept very clean, comprise showers, washbasins with mirrors, electric points, etc. in functional units occupying two corners of the large floor space. Facilities for disabled visitors. Also in the barn are dishwashing sinks, washing machine and a fridge/freezer for campers to use. Good drive-on motorcaravan service point. Good tennis court (free). Play area. Dogs are not accepted. WiFi (free). Off site: Golf and riding 6 km.

Open: 1 May - 30 September.

Directions

Park is 300 m. off main N24, 9.6 km. west of Clonmel, 6.4 km. east of Cahir. From M8 motorway take exit 10 and follow signs for Clonmel. GPS: 52.37663, -7.84262

Charges guide

Per unit incl. 2 persons and electricity	€ 16.50
extra person	€ 7.00
child	€ 4.50

Cahirciveen
Mannix Point Camping & Caravan Park
Cahirciveen (Co. Kerry) T: 066 947 2806. E: mortimer@campinginkerry.com
alanrogers.com/IR9610

A tranquil, beautifully located seashore park, it is no exaggeration to describe Mannix Point as a nature lovers' paradise. Situated in one of the most spectacular parts of the Ring of Kerry, overlooking the bay and Valentia Island, the rustic seven-acre park commands splendid views in all directions. The park road meanders through the level site and offers 42 pitches of various sizes and shapes, many with shelter and seclusion and all with 10A electricity. A charming, old flower bedecked fisherman's cottage has been converted to provide facilities including reception, excellent campers' kitchen and a cosy sitting room with turf fire. This is also an ideal resting place for people walking the Kerry Way.

Facilities

Toilet and shower facilities were clean when we visited. Modern and well equipped campers' kitchen and dining area. Comfortable campers' sitting room. Laundry facilities with washing machines and dryer. Motorcaravan services. Picnic and barbecue facilities. Fishing and boat launching from site. Playing field. WiFi throughout. Off site: Bicycle hire 800 m. Pubs, restaurants and shops 15 mins. walk.

Open: 15 March - 15 October.

Directions

Park is 300 m. off the N70 Ring of Kerry road, 800 m. southwest of Cahirciveen (or Cahersiveen) on the road towards Waterville. GPS: 51.941517, -10.24465

Charges guide

Per unit incl. 2 persons and electricity	€ 29.00
extra person	€ 6.00

No credit cards.

Castlebar
Carra Caravan & Camping Park
Belcarra, Castlebar (Co. Mayo) T: 094 903 2054. E: post@mayoholidays.com
alanrogers.com/IR8790

This is an ideal location for those seeking a real Irish village experience in a 'value for money' park. Small, unpretentious and family run, it is located in Belcarra, a regular winner of the Tidiest Mayo Village award. Nestling at the foot of a wooded drumlin, it is surrounded by rolling hills and quiet roads which offer an away from it all feeling, yet Castlebar, the county's largest town, is only an 8 km. drive. On the pleasant 1.5-acre park, the 20 unmarked touring pitches, 15 with electric hook-up (13A Europlug), are on flat ground enclosed by ranch fencing and shaded in parts by trees.

Facilities

The new toilet block has well equipped showers (€ 1). En-suite facility for disabled visitors. Combined kitchen with fridge/freezer, sink, table, chairs, washing machine and dryer. Comfortable lounge with TV, books and magazines at reception. Horse-drawn caravans for hire. Off site: Village shops, a post office and 'Flukies' cosy bar with traditional Irish music most Friday nights.

Open: 18 January - 22 November.

Directions

From Castlebar follow the N84 towards Ballinrobe. On the outskirts of Castlebar, 300 m. after the railway bridge turn left for Belcarra (Ballycarra) 8 km. Site is at south end of village by a garage and a plumber's merchant. GPS: 53.79950, -9.21699

Charges guide

Per unit incl. all persons and electricity	€ 18.00

No credit cards.

For latest campsite news visit
alanrogers.com

Castlebar
Lough Lannagh Caravan Park
Old Westport Road, Castlebar (Co. Mayo) T: 094 902 7111. E: info@loughlannagh.ie
alanrogers.com/IR8810

Lough Lannagh is an attractive holiday village on the lake shore, comprising quality accommodation, self-catering cottages and a caravan park. A new lakeside path takes you into Castlebar (15 minute stroll) with its many restaurants, pubs, theatres and shops. County Mayo's main attractions are also within a short drive. The caravan park has 20 touring pitches, well laid out in a separate dedicated corner of the village, all on hardstanding with electric connections. There is a separate grass area for tents. One reception area serves all and is situated to the right of the security barrier; check in prior to 18:00.

Facilities

One modern heated sanitary block provides washbasins and well equipped, preset showers. En-suite unit for disabled visitors (has a bath but no shower). Laundry room with sink, washing machines and dryers near reception. Café serving breakfast (daily), snacks, lunch etc. Two play areas. Boules. Badminton. Tennis. Lakeside circular walk. Dogs accepted by prior arrangement. Off site: Fishing lake (pike and trout) two minute walk.

Open: 3 April - 31 August.

Directions

To get to Castlebar take the N5, N60 or N84. At Castlebar ring road follow directions for Westport. Site is signed on all approach roads to the Westport roundabout. GPS: 53.8491, -9.3119

Charges guide

Per unit incl. 2 persons, electricity and hardstanding	€ 21.00 - € 25.00
tent incl. 2 persons (no car at pitch)	€ 15.00 - € 20.00

Castlegregory
Anchor Caravan Park
Castlegregory (Co. Kerry) T: 066 713 9157. E: anchorcaravanpark@eircom.net
alanrogers.com/IR9550

Of County Kerry's three long, finger like peninsulas which jut into the sea, Dingle is the most northerly. Anchor Caravan Park is 20 km. west of Tralee, the main town, and under 4 km. south of Castlegregory on Tralee Bay. Its situation, just 150 m. from a fine sandy beach, provides ideal opportunities for safe bathing, boating and shore fishing. A secluded and mature, five-acre park, it is enclosed by shrubs and trees that give excellent shelter. There are 30 pitches, most with electricity and 13 also with drainage and water points. Although there are holiday homes for hire, these are well apart from the touring pitches. The approach roads to the park are narrow and may be difficult for larger units.

Facilities

Sanitary facilities (entry by key) are kept very clean and provide showers on payment (€ 0,50), two private cabins, some low level washbasins and a WC with handrail. No facilities for disabled campers. Laundry facilities. Campers' kitchen with fridges, freezers and seating. Motorcaravan services. Two play areas. Games and TV rooms. Electric barbecues are not permitted. WiFi throughout. Off site: Beautiful sandy beach 2 minutes.

Open: Easter - 30 September.

Directions

From Tralee follow the N86 Dingle coast road for 15 km. At Camp take the R560 towards Castlegregory. Park is signed from Camp junction. Approach road is narrow and crosses a steep humpback bridge. The site entrance is narrow. GPS: 52.24393, -9.98579

Charges guide

Per unit incl. 2 persons and electricity	€ 20.00 - € 22.00
No credit cards.	

Clondalkin
Camac Valley Tourist Caravan & Camping Park
Green Isle Road, Clondalkin Dublin 22 (Co. Dublin) T: 014 640 644. E: reservations@camacvalley.com
alanrogers.com/IR9100

Opened in 1996, this campsite is not only well placed for Dublin, but also offers a welcome stopover if travelling to the more southern counties from the north of the country, or vice versa. Despite its close proximity to the city, and the constant noise from the dual carriageway, being located in the 300-acre Corkagh Park gives it a 'heart of the country' atmosphere. There are 113 pitches on hardstanding for caravans, laid out in bays and avenues, all fully serviced (10A Europlug). Maturing trees and shrubs separate pitches and roads are of tarmac. Beyond the entrance gate and forecourt stands an attractive, timber-fronted building housing the site amenities.

Facilities

Heated sanitary facilities include good sized showers (token). Facilities for disabled visitors. Baby room. Laundry. Shop (for basics) and coffee bar. Playground with wooden play frames and safety base. Fishing. Electronic gate controlled from reception and 24-hour security. WiFi (free). Off site: Golf 1.5 km. Riding 9 km.

Open: All year.

Directions

Site is in Corkagh Park, 4 km. west of M50 exit 9, just off N7 Nass Road on the north side. It is clearly signed from both directions at the new R136 turnoff. GPS: 53.30445, -6.41533

Charges guide

Per unit incl. 2 persons and electricity	€ 26.00 - € 28.00

For latest campsite news visit
alanrogers.com

Cong
Cong Caravan & Camping Park
Lisloughrey, Quay Road, Cong (Co. Mayo) T: 094 954 6089. E: info@quietman-cong.com
alanrogers.com/IR8740

It would be difficult to find a more idyllic and famous spot for a caravan park than Cong. Situated close to the shores of Lough Corrib, Cong's scenic beauty was immortalised in the film, The Quiet Man. This well kept park is 1.6 km. from the village of Cong, near the grounds of the magnificent and renowned Ashford Castle. Reception, shop and the hostel, stand to the fore of the site. Toilet facilities and the holiday hostel accommodation are entered from the courtyard area. The 40 grass pitches, 36 with electricity, are placed at a higher level to the rear, with the sheltered tent areas below and to the side. The park can be crowded and busy in high season.

Facilities

Toilet facilities are kept clean and are heated when necessary. Hot showers with curtains (€ 1 charge). Good facilities for disabled visitors. Campers' kitchen. Launderette service. Shop. Catering is a feature – full Irish and Continental breakfast, dinner and packed lunch may be ordered, and home baked bread and scones purchased in the shop. Barbecue, games room and extensive play area. TV lounge. WiFi (free).

Open: All year.

Directions

Leave N84 road at Ballinrobe to join R334/345 signed Cong. Turn left at end of the R345 (opposite entrance to Ashford Castle), slow down take next road on right (about 300 m) and the park is on right (200 m). GPS: 53.53945, -9.27263

Charges guide

Per unit incl. 2 persons
and electricity   € 23.00 - € 27.00

Corofin
Corofin Village Camping & Caravan Park
Main Street, Corofin (Co. Clare) T: 065 683 7683. E: info@corofin.camping.com
alanrogers.com/IR9460

This compact green oasis in the centre of the village of Corofin occupies one acre and adjoins the family's hostel. The owners, Jude and Marie Neylon, live on the site and have a policy of always having a family member on hand at all times. They are very environmentally aware and have excellent recycling facilities. There are 25 touring pitches, 18 with electricity and there are ample water points. The site now includes a small separate tent area which is quite private and well sheltered. A campers' kitchen, laundry room and the TV and games room are separate to the hostel facilities. This little site is neat and well maintained and makes an ideal base for sightseeing throughout Clare. Site is not suitable for large units.

Facilities

The sanitary block is bright and clean with free hot showers. Separate facilities for disabled campers. Laundry room with washing machine and dryer. Campers' kitchen. TV and games room. CCTV security. Free throughout (free). Torches only. Off site: Fishing and boat launching 2 km. Riding 5 km. Golf 8 km. Bicycle hire 10 km. Beach 20 km.

Open: 1 April - 30 September.

Directions

Corofin village is 12 km. from Ennis, from where you take the N85 towards Ennistymon and after 2 km. (well signed) turn right onto R476. Site is in the centre of the village. GPS: 52.9407, -9.058933

Charges guide

Per unit incl. 2 persons and electricity   € 25.00
extra person   € 5.00
No credit cards.

Donard
Moat Farm Caravan & Camping Park
Donard (Co. Wicklow) T: 045 404 727. E: moatfarmdonard@gmail.com
alanrogers.com/IR9160

Providing a true feel of the countryside, this park is part of a working sheep farm. It offers incredible vistas across a scenic landscape, yet is within driving distance of Dublin and Rosslare. Driving into the village of Donard you little suspect that alongside the main street lies a pleasant, well cared for and tranquil five acre campsite. The entrance is approached by way of a short road where the ruins of a medieval church sit high overlooking the forecourt and reception. There are 40 pitches for caravans and tents. Spacious pitches with hardstanding line both sides of a broad avenue, incorporating ample space for awnings and all with 10A Europlug. The entrance road is very narrow and requires great care.

Facilities

The toilet block is kept very clean and includes spacious showers. Facilities for visitors with disabilities. Well equipped laundry room. Good quality campers' kitchen. Large recreation/entertainment room with open fire. Three large barbecues and patio area. Caravan storage. WiFi. Off site: Shop and bars serving food just outside site. Fishing 3 km. Golf and riding 13 km. Bicycle hire 15 km.

Open: 17 March - 14 September.

Directions

Leave M50 Dublin ring motorway at exit 10 to join N81 southwest for 19 km. to Blessington. Continue on N81 for a further 16.5 km. and turn left at Old Toll House pub onto local road and follow signs to park in Donard village (3.5 km). GPS: 53.0212, -6.61562

Charges guide

Per unit incl. 2 persons and electricity   € 23.00
No credit cards.

For latest campsite news visit
alanrogers.com

Doolin

Nagle's Doolin Camping & Caravan Park

Doolin (Co. Clare) T: 065 707 4458. E: ken@doolincamping.com

alanrogers.com/IR9465

This neat and tidy seaside site is located just one kilometre from the cliffs of Moher, and a short ferry ride from the sparsely populated Aran Islands. The nearby village of Doolin, famed for its traditional music, has good shops, restaurants and pubs. The four-hectare site, which enjoys spectacular views over the bay to Conemara, has 99 pitches, including 76 level hardstandings (all with 10A electricity, and 21 also with water and drainage) and grass pitches for tents. They are not separated by hedges, but the site is divided into bays by limestone walls. Three new camping pods are available to hire. There is excellent WiFi coverage over the whole site.

Facilities

One modern, well equipped toilet block is unheated but has good facilities including hot showers (€ 1) and en-suite unit for disabled visitors. Laundry facilities. Kitchen with cooking rings (charged), fridge/freezer and sinks with hot water. Motorcaravan services. Shop (June-Aug). Gas. Games room. Play area. WiFi over site. Off site: Pitch and putt, boat launching and ferry to Aran Islands all 300 m. Fishing, riding, bicycle hire, shops, hot food and bars within 1-2 km. Golf 10 km.

Open: Mid March - mid October.

Directions

From Limerick take N85 round Ennis to Ennistymon, then N67 towards Lisdoonvarna. After 11 km. turn left onto R478 and then onto the R479 for Doolin and then Doolin Pier. Site signed. From Galway take N18 and then in 20 km. N67 to Lisdoonvarna and follow signs as above. GPS: 53.01677, -9.402

Charges guide

Per unit incl. 2 persons and electricity	€ 22.00 - € 24.00
extra person	€ 7.00

Doonbeg

Strand Camping

Killard Road, Doonbeg (Co. Clare) T: 065 905 5345. E: strandcampingdoonbeg@gmail.com

alanrogers.com/IR9462

This small site was taken over by the present owners in 2014, and they are making great improvements. It is a friendly site, opposite the sea on the beautiful Doonbeg Bay and just a short walk from Doonbeg village. The 20 level pitches, some with sea views, vary in size and are mainly on hardstanding. They are separated by shrubs and wild flowers and each has a 16A electricity hook-up; there are four water points on site. The village has a choice of bars, restaurants and takeaways. The site owners are happy to advise on walking routes and book fishing and dolphin watching trips, and the Trump Golf Complex is just a short drive away.

Facilities

One heated sanitary block has free hot showers. No facilities for disabled visitors. Well equipped laundry block. Motorcaravan services (chemical disposal planned). Small dishwashing and kitchen area. Bicycle hire. WiFi over site (free). Offsite: Shops, bars and restaurants a short walk away. Bicycle hire, pedalos and zorbing in nearby village. Boat trips from pier 1 km. Blue flag beach 3 km.

Open: 1 March - 31 October.

Directions

From Ennis take N68-7 to Doonbeg. Site is located at South end of village and is well signed. GPS: 52.73535, -9.53414

Charges guide

Per unit incl. 2 persons and electricity	€ 21.00
extra person	€ 9.00

No credit/debit cards.

Drimoleague

Top of the Rock Pod Páirc & Walking Centre

Ar an Carraig, Rockmount, Drimoleague (Co. Cork) T: 028 31547. E: david@topoftherock.ie

alanrogers.com/IR9515

This family site is located in the heart of West Cork, near Ireland's Atlantic coast amid nine miles of wonderful walking trails in an area rich in folklore, history and culture. The working farm provides an area to pitch tents (six 6A Europlug electricity sockets and water) and a purpose-built quarter of an acre for six camper vans (no caravans), on gravel, with full access to facilities. There are seven pods to rent, dispersed throughout the farm, their design inspired by early Christian structures. A well placed centre to explore a beautiful rural environment of farmland, woodland, water, flora and fauna.

Facilities

Sanitary facilities with provision for disabled visitors (showers 5 mins. for € 1). Laundry room. Campers' kitchen with fridge, cookers, kettles etc. Breakfast delivered to pitches. Campfire area. Playground. Games field. Games room with table tennis, pool (€ 1), board games. Barbecue and grill for hire. WiFi in reception (free).

Open: All year (excl. Christmas and own holidays).

Directions

Top of the Rock Pod Pairc and Walking Centre is west of Cork. From Cork travel west towards Drimoleague on R586 and then follow signs. GPS: 51.66875, -9.26105

Charges guide

Contact the site for details.

For latest campsite news visit
alanrogers.com

Dungarvan
Casey's Caravan & Camping Park
Clonea, Dungarvan (Co. Waterford) T: 058 419 19.
alanrogers.com/IR9330

This is a very large park by Irish standards. Set on 20 acres of flat grass, edged by mature trees, this family run park is well managed and offers 284 pitches which include 103 touring pitches, 75 with electrical hook-ups (10A Europlug) and 53 with hardstanding. There is even a large, open and flat field without services for high season overspill arrivals. The remainder are occupied by caravan holiday homes. There is direct access from the park to a sandy, Blue Flag beach with a resident lifeguard during July and August. A highly recommended leisure centre is adjacent should the weather be inclement. The park is 5.5 km. from Dungarvan, a popular town for deep sea angling, from where charter boats can be hired and three, 18-hole golf courses are within easy driving distance. Suggested drives include the scenic Vee, the Comeragh Mountain Drive and the coast road to Tramore – the latter having a series of magical coves and the remains of old copper mines. The pretty 'English' village of Lismore and the picturesque and historic town of Youghal, once home to Sir Walter Raleigh, are about a 30 km. drive.

Facilities

The central toilet block (key system), has good facilities kept spotlessly clean. Showers on payment (€ 1). Small laundry with washing machine and dryer. A further modern block provides an excellent campers' kitchen, laundry room and toilet for disabled visitors. Large adventure play area. Large, well equipped games room. TV lounge. Minigolf. Gas supplies. Full time security staff in high season. Play area for under 4s. Bicycle hire. Free WiFi throughout. Off site: Two village stores by the beach.

Open: 17 March - 31 October.

Directions

From Dungarvan centre follow R675 east for 3.5 km. Look for signs on the right to Clonea and site. Site is 1.5 km. GPS: 52.094767, -7.546167

Charges guide

Per unit incl. 2 persons and electricity	€ 25.00
extra person	€ 2.00
child (0-14 yrs)	€ 2.00
hiker, biker, cyclist	€ 10.00

No credit cards.

Galway
Salthill Caravan Park
Knocknacarra, Salthill (Co. Galway) T: 091 523 972. E: info@salthillcaravanpark.com
alanrogers.com/IR8870

Salthill Caravan Park was first opened in 1960, and has been run by the O'Malley family ever since. The park comprises five acres of mobile homes and a three-acre campsite, near the water's edge. The park has superb views over Galway Bay and has access to a shingle beach, just 100 m. distant. The 49 touring pitches are grassy and open, all with 10A electrical connections and 35 hardstanding. Adjacent to the site, there is a pleasant coastal pathway which leads to Galway City and sandy beaches, while a friendly pub and a large, well stocked supermarket are within walking distance.

Facilities

One (unheated) sanitary block in the middle of the touring pitches also contains a washing machine and dryer (€ 5 each), sinks (hot water on payment). Showers by reception (on payment). No facilities for disabled visitors. Limited grocery items in reception. New playground. Games room. WiFi throughout (free). Off site: Watersports. Pub 200 m. Fishing, beach and golf 500 m. Supermarket 600 m. Bicycle hire 3 km. Riding 4 km.

Open: 1 April - 29 September.

Directions

The site is 1 mile west of Salthill. From N6 (bypassing Galway City) follow signs to Clifden, R338 to its junction with R337 at traffic lights. Turn right and follow R337 (large supermarket on right) to its junction with R336, turn left (south) and site is 200 m. on left. GPS: 53.256798, -9.104914

Charges guide

Per unit incl. 2 persons	
and electricity	€ 25.00 - € 32.00
extra person	€ 8.00

Glandore
The Meadow Camping Park
Glandore (Co. Cork) T: 028 332 80. E: meadowcamping@eircom.net
alanrogers.com/IR9500

The picturesque stretch of coast from Cork to Skibbereen reminds British visitors of Devon before the era of mass tourism. This is rich dairy country with green meadows all around and thanks to the warm and wet Gulf Stream climate, it is also a county of gardens and keen gardeners. The Meadow is best described not as a site but as a one-acre garden surrounded, appropriately, by lush meadows. The owners, who live on the park, have arranged accommodation for 19 pitches, 14 with 6A electric hook-ups (12 Europlugs), among the flower beds and shrubberies of their extended garden. There are ten hardstandings. The site is not suitable for large units.

Facilities

Facilities are limited but well designed and maintained with brand new solar panels. Showers on payment. Washing machine and dryer. Larger units may be accepted depending on length and available space; contact park before arrival. Football and cycling are not permitted on the park. No electric barbecues. WiFi over site. Off site: Fishing and watersports at Glandore 2 km.

Open: Easter - 15 September.

Directions

Park is 1.5 km. east of Glandore, off N71 road, on R597 midway between Leap and Rosscarbery (coast road). Approach roads are very narrow and therefore unsuitable for large units. GPS: 51.56693, -9.09702

Charges guide

Per unit incl. 2 persons and electricity	€ 23.00
extra person	€ 6.00

No credit cards.

Glenbeigh
Glenross Caravan & Camping & Motor Home Park
Ring of Kerry, Glenbeigh (Co. Kerry) T: 087 137 6865. E: glenross@eircom.net
alanrogers.com/IR9600

Its situation on the spectacular Ring of Kerry and the Kerry Way footpath gives Glenross an immediate advantage and scenic grandeur around every bend of the road is guaranteed as you approach Glenbeigh. Quietly located before entering the village, the park commands stunning views of Rossbeigh Strand, (within walking distance) and the Dingle Peninsula. On arrival, a good impression is created with the park being well screened from the road, with a new stone entrance and gates. With 30 touring pitches, 27 with hardstanding and all with 10A electricity (Europlug), and six caravan holiday homes, the park is attractively laid out. Dedicated small tent area.

Facilities

Well maintained and modern sanitary block with refurbished showers (€ 1) includes laundry facilities. Motorcaravan services. Shelter for campers and dining area. Bar, restaurant and takeaway (all year). Games room. Free WiFi throughout. Off site: Playground at Blue Flag Rossbeigh beach (5 mins). Riding and fishing 200 m.

Open: 3 April - 30 September.

Directions

Park is on N70 Killorglin-Glenbeigh road, on right just before entering village. GPS: 52.05887, -9.93198

Charges guide

Per unit incl. 2 persons and electricity	€ 29.00 - € 30.00
extra person	€ 8.00

No credit cards.

Keel
Keel Sandybanks Caravan & Camping Park
Keel, Achill Island (Co. Mayo) T: 098 432 11. E: info@achillcamping.com
alanrogers.com/IR8730

This is a park offering a taste of island life and the opportunity to relax in dramatic, scenic surroundings. Achill, Ireland's largest island, is 24 km. long and 19 km. wide and is connected to the mainland by a bridge. The wide open site is situated beside the Blue Flag beach near Keel village. Although there are static holiday mobile homes on this site, the 84 touring pitches are kept separate. There are 50 pitches with hardstanding and some are located at the perimeter fence overlooking the beach. Although sand based, the ground is firm and level. Roads are tarmac and there is direct access to the beach which is supervised by lifeguards. Occasionally, a traditional music evening is organised on the site.

Facilities

Two modern toilet blocks serve the site, one at the entrance gate beside reception and the other in a central position. Heated facilities include WCs, washbasins and hot showers (on payment). Hairdryers. Laundry with irons and ironing boards. En-suite facilities for disabled visitors at reception block. Campers' kitchen and dining room. Motorcaravan services. Play area. TV/games room. Fishing trips can be arranged. WiFi throughout (charged).

Open: Easter - mid September.

Directions

From Achill Sound follow the R319 for 13 km. Site is on the left before Keel village. GPS: 53.97535, -10.0779

Charges guide

Per unit incl. 2 persons and electricity	€ 19.00 - € 22.00
child	€ 2.00
extra person	€ 5.00

For latest campsite news visit
alanrogers.com

Kilkenny
Tree Grove Caravan & Camping Park

Danville House, Kilkenny (Co. Kilkenny) T: 056 777 0302. E: treecc@iol.ie

alanrogers.com/IR9240

This park appeals to many because of its proximity to the impressive and historic town of Kilkenny. It is terraced with the lower terrace to the right of the wide sweeping driveway laid out with 20 hardstanding pitches for caravans. All pitches have 10A electricity hook-ups and plenty of water points are to be found. There are 13 full service pitches. On the higher level is a grass area for hikers and cyclists, with further caravan and tent pitches sited on grass near the elevated sanitary block. There is some road noise which can be distracting.

Facilities	Directions
Family room with shower, WC and washbasin which can be used by disabled campers. Laundry room. Open, covered kitchen for campers with fridge, worktop, sink and electric kettle adjoins a comfortable games/TV room with pool table, and easy chairs. Bicycle hire. Riding. Tents to rent. Free WiFi. Off site: Fishing 500 m. Riding 1 km. Golf 2 km.	Turn south off Kilkenny ring road at roundabout showing R700 to Thomastown. Signs for park show it 150 m. on the right. GPS: 52.63998, -7.22955

Charges guide

Per unit incl. 2 persons and electricity	€ 18.00 - € 23.00
extra person	€ 5.00

No credit cards.

Open: 1 March - 15 November.

Killarney
Fossa Caravan & Camping Park

Fossa, Killarney (Co. Kerry) T: 064 663 1497. E: fossaholidays@eircom.net

alanrogers.com/IR9590

This park is in the village of Fossa, ten minutes by car or bus (six per day) from Killarney town centre. Fossa Caravan Park has a distinctive reception building and hostel accommodation. The park is divided in two – the touring caravan area lies to the right, tucked behind the main building and to the left is an open grass area mainly for campers. The 83 compact touring pitches, with 10/15A electricity and drainage, have hardstanding and are angled between shrubs and trees in a garden setting. To the rear at a higher level and discreetly placed are 30 caravan holiday homes, sheltered by the thick foliage of the wooded slopes which climb high behind the park.

Facilities	Directions
Modern toilet facilities include showers on payment. En-suite unit for campers with disabilities. Laundry room. Campers' kitchen. TV lounge. Tennis. Play area. Picnic area. Games room. Security patrol. WiFi on part of site. Off site: Fishing and golf 2 km. Riding 3 km. Bicycle hire 5 km. Woodland walk into Killarney. A visit to Killarney National Park is highly recommended.	Approaching Killarney from all directions, follow signs for N72 Ring of Kerry/Killorglin. At last roundabout join R562/N72. Continue for 5.5 km. and Fossa is second park to the right. GPS: 52.07071, -9.58573

Charges guide

Per unit incl. 2 persons and electricity	€ 22.00 - € 26.00
extra person	€ 6.00

Open: 1 April - 30 September.

Killarney
Fleming's White Bridge

Ballycasheen Road, Killarney (Co. Kerry) T: 064 663 1590. E: info@killarneycamping.com

alanrogers.com/IR9620

The main road from Cork to Killarney (N22) runs through the gentle valley of the River Flesk. Between the two sits Fleming's White Bridge camping park. Its ten-hectare site is within comfortable walking distance of Killarney centre. Surrounded by mature, broad-leafed trees, the park is flat, landscaped and generously adorned with flowers and shrubs. It comprises 92 pitches, the majority for touring caravans, on well kept grass pitches with electricity hook-ups, although some have concrete hardstanding and some pitches are reserved for tents.

Facilities	Directions
Three toilet blocks are of a high standard. Motorcaravan services. Campers' drying room and two laundries. Small shop (1/6-1/9). Two TV rooms. Games room. Fishing (advice and permits provided). Canoeing (own canoes). Bicycle hire. Woodland walks. WiFi. Off site: Swimming pool and leisure centre 500 m. Kayaking 1.5 km. Golf 2 km. Riding and Killarney National Park 3 km. Beach 30 km.	From Cork and Mallow: at N72/N22 junction continue towards Killarney and take first turn left (Ballycasheen Road). Continue 300 m. to archway entrance on left. GPS: 52.05595, -9.47458

Charges guide

Per unit incl. 2 persons and electricity	€ 25.00 - € 30.00
extra person	€ 8.00

No credit cards.

Open: 13 March - 26 October.

For latest campsite news visit

alanrogers.com

Killarney
Donoghues White Villa Farm Caravan & Camping Park

Lissivigeen, Killarney-Cork Road (N22), Killarney (Co. Kerry) T: 064 662 0671.
E: killarneycamping@eircom.net **alanrogers.com/IR9630**

This is a very pleasing, small touring park, surrounded by green fields, yet only five minutes away from Killarney town. There are many trees and shrubs around the park, but dominant is a magnificent view of the MacGillicuddy's Reeks. There are 30 pitches for caravans and tents, 30 with hardstanding and a grass area for awnings, electricity (10A Europlug), water points and night lighting. One pitch is designated for disabled campers with a specially adapted en-suite facility. Unusually, old school desks are placed in pairs around the site as picnic tables, plus an antique green telephone box. One can enjoy walking through the oak wood, fishing on the Flesk or visiting the site's own National Farm Museum.

Facilities

The toilet block is kept spotlessly clean and houses showers (€ 1), a good toilet/shower room for disabled visitors (key). Laundry room. Motorcaravan services. Campers' kitchen with TV. Play area. Max. 2 dogs (not certain breeds). Daily coach tours from park to Ring of Kerry and Dingle Peninsula. WiFi (free). Off site: Pub with restaurant 1 km. Bicycle hire 3 km. Riding and golf 4 km. and Killarney town 5 mins. National Park is 10 mins.

Open: 20 May - 25 September.

Directions

From Killarney take N22 Cork road, through Park Road roundabout, pass Supervalu and go downhill. Continue on N22 up next hill to N22/N72 roundabout. Take second exit and park is 200 m. on the right. GPS: 52.04724, -9.45358

Charges guide

Per unit incl. 2 persons and electricity	€ 22.00 - € 24.00
extra person	€ 6.00

No credit cards.
Seven nights for the price of six (if pre-paid).

Killarney
Killarney Flesk Caravan & Camping Park

Muckross Road, Killarney (Co. Kerry) T: 064 663 1704. E: info@killarneyfleskcamping.com
alanrogers.com/IR9640

At the gateway to the National Park and Lakes, near Killarney town, this family run, seven-acre park has undergone extensive development and offers high quality standards. Pitches vary in size and spacing and have 10A electricity. Many pitches have a good grass area for awnings and 21 also have dedicated electricity, water and drainage. The grounds are neat and tidy with a feeling of space. The toilet block is central to most pitches and camp security appears to be tight. A well located site for the centre of Killarney and the famous Ring of Kerry.

Facilities

Modern, clean toilet blocks are well designed and equipped. Baby room. En-suite facility for disabled campers (key operated). Laundry room. Campers' kitchen. Night time security checks. WiFi throughout. Off site: Adjacent hotel (same ownership) with bar and restaurant. Fishing 300 m. Boat launching 2 km.

Open: 16 April - 30 September.

Directions

From Killarney follow the N71 and signs for Killarney National Park. Site is 1.5 km. on the left beside the Victoria House Hotel. GPS: 52.04304, -9.49954

Charges guide

Per unit incl. 2 persons and electricity	€ 30.00 - € 31.00
extra person	€ 8.50

Kilmacanogue
Valley Stopover & Caravan Park

Killough, Kilmacanogue (Co. Wicklow) T: 012 829 565. E: rowanbb@eircom.net
alanrogers.com/IR9140

In a quiet, idyllic setting in the picturesque Rocky Valley, this small, neat, family run park is convenient for the Dublin ferries. Situated in the grounds of the family home, covering under an acre, it can be used either as a transit site or for a longer stay. It will appeal to those who prefer the small, certificated type of site. There are grassy pitches, eight hardstandings and a total of ten electricity hook-ups, a separate area for three tents, two water points, night lighting and a security gate. Staying here, you are only minutes from Enniskerry which lies in the glen of the Glencullen river.

Facilities

Sanitary facilities, clean when we visited, are housed in one very small unit and consist of two WCs with washbasins, mirrors, etc. and a shower (free). Laundry sink, spin dryer. Campers' kitchen. Full cooked Irish breakfast in the family house. Off site: Riding 3 km. Golf 7 km. Fishing 8 km.

Open: Easter - 31 October.

Directions

Turn off N11 Dublin-Wexford road at Kilmacanogue, following signs for Glendalough. After 1.6 km. take right fork (Waterfall). Park is 2nd opening on left in 200 m. Narrow entrance off road requires care and is unsuitable for large units. GPS: 53.1671, -6.1634

Charges guide

Per unit incl. 2 persons and electricity	€ 20.00
extra person	€ 1.25

For latest campsite news visit
alanrogers.com

Knock

Knock Caravan & Camping Park

Main Street, Knock (Co. Mayo) T: 094 938 8100. E: caravanpark@knock-shrine.ie

alanrogers.com/IR8780

This park is in a sheltered, landscaped area immediately south of the world famous Shrine that receives many visitors. Comfortable and clean, the park has neatly trimmed lawns with tarmac roads and is surrounded by clipped trees. The 70 touring pitches are of average size on hardstanding and 52 have 15A electricity connections. There is also an overflow field. Because of the religious connections of the area, the site is very busy in August and there are unlikely to be any vacancies at all for 14-16 August.

Facilities

Two heated toilet blocks, one dated, have good facilities for disabled visitors and a nice sized rest room attached, hot showers and adequate washing and toilet facilities. Laundry room. Gas supplies. TV rooms. Playground. Free WiFi over site. Off site: The Shrine and Basilica are adjacent with a restaurant in the grounds. Fishing 5 km. Golf and riding 11 km.

Open: 1 April - 31 October.

Directions

Exit from the N17 at the Knock bypass and from the roundabout follow signs to the site which is just south of the village. GPS: 53.79391, -8.91387

Charges guide

Per unit incl. 2 persons and electricity	€ 23.50 - € 25.50
extra person	€ 2.00 - € 2.50

No credit cards.

Lauragh

Creveen Lodge Caravan & Camping Park

Healy Pass, Lauragh (Co. Kerry) T: 064 668 3131. E: info@creveenlodge.com

alanrogers.com/IR9570

The Healy Pass is the well known scenic summit of the R574 road that crosses the Beara Peninsula, shortening the original journey from Kenmare Bay in the north to Bantry Bay in the south by nearly 70 km. As this narrow coast road starts to climb steeply, on the mountain foothills you will arrive at Creveen Lodge, a working hill farm with a quiet, homely atmosphere. The park provides 20 attractive pitches, 10 with 10A electricity and an area of hardstanding for motorcaravans. To allow easy access, the steep farm track is divided into a simple one-way system. Creveen Lodge, commanding views across Kenmare Bay, is divided among three gently sloping fields separated by trees.

Facilities

Well appointed and maintained, the small toilet block provides token operated showers (€ 1). Communal room with cooking facilities, a fridge, freezer, TV, ironing board, fireplace, tables and chairs. Reception is in the farmhouse. Play area. Cottages and caravans for rent. Off site: Watersports, riding, cruises and a shop nearby.

Open: Easter - 31 October.

Directions

Park is on the Healy Pass road (R574) 1.5 km. southeast of Lauragh. GPS: 51.75562, -9.76193

Charges guide

Per unit incl. 2 persons and electricity	€ 22.00
extra person	€ 3.00
child (under 10 yrs)	€ 1.00

No credit cards.

Letterkenny

Rosguill Holiday Park

Melmore Road, Downings, Letterkenny (Co. Donegal) T: 074 915 5766. E: rosguillholidaypark@yahoo.ie

alanrogers.com/IR8635

Rosguill Park is a quiet, family owned caravan and camping site, located on a stunning peninsula that forms part of the rugged and beautiful North West Donegal coast. The site is surrounded by six long, clean, sandy beaches, all within walking distance, plus a number of other beaches nearby all in Downings. The site is predominantly occupied by privately owned mobile homes but offers 26 touring pitches, 12 of which have concrete hardstanding, 10A electricity and water, the remainder are on grass without services. All of the touring pitches face the beautiful Mulroy Bay and enjoy amazing views.

Facilities

New, well appointed en-suite sanitary block in the touring area. Facilities for disabled visitors. Family shower rooms. Campers' kitchen. Laundry facilities. Tennis. Multisports field. Pitch and putt. Bicycle hire. Play area. Off site: Golf. Riding and pony trekking. Fishing. Diving. Hill walking. Martial arts.

Open: 1 May - 30 September.

Directions

Park is 45 km. north of Letterkenny. Turn right at junction before Letterkenny centre (Ramelton, Milford and Carrickart). Take right hand turn after Carrickart towards Downings. After 1 km. turn right at sign for park and follow road for about 6 km. past Singing Pub on left. The park is located just over the hill. Do not use sat nav. GPS: 55.230394, -7.793083

Charges guide

Per unit incl. electricity and water	€ 25.00

No credit cards.

For latest campsite news visit

alanrogers.com

Mullingar
Lough Ennell Camping & Caravan Park

Tudenham Shore, Mullingar (Co. Westmeath) T: 044 934 8101. E: eamon@caravanparksireland.com
alanrogers.com/IR8965

Natural, rustic charm is the visitor's first impression on arrival at Lough Ennell Caravan Park. Set in 18 acres of mature woodland beside a Blue Flag lake, Eamon and Geraldine O'Malley run this sheltered and tranquil park with their family, who live on the site. They receive a blend of visitors – seasonal residents in camping holiday homes (private and to rent), caravanners and motorcaravanners and there are ample areas for tents. Pitches are varied, sheltered with trees and natural shrubbery, and with gravel or gravel and grass combinations. There are 44 touring pitches with electricity (7A Europlug) available on 25 hardstanding and grass pitches, with water points on or nearby all pitches; there are also 80 tent pitches. The site is a paradise for fishermen, with brown trout, rainbow trout, pike, tench, roach, perch, rudd and bream available. There is also one lake stocked with carp. Just an hour from Dublin, it provides a good holiday base or a useful stopover en-route to the West of Ireland. The watersports permitted on the lake include canoeing, sailing, windsurfing, boating, water skiing, fishing and safe swimming. The woodlands offer ample opportunities for walking and cycling. The site has several other lakes within a 10 to 15 minute drive. Some are coarse fishing only, while others are stocked lakes with multiple varieties of fish. Other activities might include tennis, riding, golf, dog racing and, of course, forest walks.

Facilities

The toilet block provides toilets, washbasins and hot showers (€ 1 coin). Additional dishwashing areas are around the park. Laundry. Small shop (all season). Café and coffee shop with takeaway. TV and games room. Play areas and area for ball games. Small lakeside beach. Fishing. Late arrivals area outside. Security including CCTV. Some breeds of dog are not accepted. Off site: Golf 1.5 km. Riding 4 km. Bicycle hire 6 km. Bus service 8 km. Boat hire on Lough Ennell and other lakes.

Open: Easter/1 April - 30 September.

Directions

From N4 take the N52. Follow signs for Belvedere House and take turn 300 m. south of Belvedere House (signed for site). Continue to the shores of Lough Ennell and turn left. If in difficulty, telephone the site. GPS: 53.466111, -7.375278

Charges guide

Per unit incl. 2 persons and electricity	€ 25.00
extra person	€ 5.00
child	€ 3.00

No credit cards.

Portlaoise
Laois Caravan and Camping

Clondouglas, Mountrath Road, Portlaoise (Co. Laois) T: 086 339 0867. E: ti.brenn1@gmail.com
alanrogers.com/IR9040

Opened in 2011 and set on a family run farm, this small site is conveniently situated for the Dublin to Limerick M7 motorway. It is less than 15 km. from the Slieve Bloom mountains, a Mecca for walkers, and 6 km. from the centre of Portlaoise. There are seven touring pitches with hardstanding, 16A electricity and water set to one edge of a camping field. Children can enjoy farm animals such as sheep, goats, chickens and pigs, and perhaps help feed lambs and find eggs (even chocolate ones at Easter). There is some distant noise from the motorway, and mainline trains pass behind the farm. It would make a good stopover between Dublin and Cork or Limerick. Local activities include karting, angling, horse-drawn caravans and guided walks in the Slieve Bloom mountains.

Facilities

A new timber-clad toilet block is tiled and heated and has three family rooms with WC and shower. One also has a bath and is equipped for disabled visitors. Laundry room. Kitchen/lounge with cooking and dishwashing facilities, satellite TV, extensive library, comfortable seating and table tennis. Motorcaravan services. Off site: Karting and angling 14 km. Horse-drawn caravans, guided walking tours 25 km.

Open: March - September.

Directions

From motorway M7 take exit 18 head southwest on R445 (signed Castletown-Mountrath). Site is on left in 1.5 km. GPS: 53.0082, -7.372083

Charges guide

Per unit incl. 2 persons and electricity	€ 24.00
extra person	€ 10.00
child (3rd free)	€ 4.00

For latest campsite news visit
alanrogers.com

Rathdrum
Hidden Valley Caravan & Camping Park
Rathdrum (Co. Wicklow) T: 086 727 2872. E: hiddenvalleyholidays@gmail.com
alanrogers.com/IR9155

This pleasant, level park occupies over seven hectares on both banks of the pretty Avonmore River near the small town of Rathdrum. It has 110 pitches arranged around a boating pond. The pitches are mostly concrete hardstandings with a few on grass. All have 16A Europlugs and close access to a water tap and waste drainage. Across a fine footbridge is a large, flat area for tents – most of them used by families at holiday time. This site now boasts one of the finest adventure play areas in Ireland. Recent additions are archery, digital paintballing and crazy golf.

Facilities

Well equipped and very modern toilet block finished in local slate. Facilities for visitors with disabilities. Motorcaravan services. Laundry. Hobs for cooking. Small shop, bar, restaurant and takeaway (all April-Sept). Fishing in the river may be arranged. Impressive play park. Canoes and boats for hire on lake. Bicycle hire. Log cabins for rent. Dogs must be kept on a lead. WiFi. Off site: Golf and riding within 5 miles. Beach within 15 miles. The open moorland of the Wicklow Mountains.

Open: 17 March - 30 September.

Directions

Leave M11 at exit signed Rathnew. From this village follow signs for Rathdrum (c.15 minutes). Over the bridge approaching Rathdrum turn right immediately at large new apartment building. Take care over speed humps for 100 m. Park gate is on the right. GPS: 52.938693, -6.22898

Charges guide

Per unit incl. 2 persons and electricity	€ 26.00 - € 28.00
extra person	€ 6.00

Redcross Village
River Valley Caravan & Camping Park
Redcross Village (Co. Wicklow) T: 040 441 647. E: info@rivervalleypark.ie
alanrogers.com/IR9150

In the small country village of Redcross, in the heart of County Wicklow, you will find this first rate, family run park. It is within easy reach of beauty spots such as the Vale of Avoca (Ballykissangel), Glendalough and Powerscourt, plus the safe beach of Brittas Bay. The 160 touring pitches are divided into separate, well landscaped areas with an adults-only section. All have 6/10A electricity connections and offer a choice of hardstanding or grass – you select your pitch. A late arrivals area has electricity hook-ups, water and night lighting.

Facilities

All sanitary blocks are of the highest quality, modern and well designed. Excellent facilities for disabled visitors. Showers are on payment (€ 1 token). Laundry area. Campers' kitchen. Motorcaravan services. Gas supplies. Full bar and restaurant, entertainment twice a week. TV and games room. Three tennis courts. Beer garden with entertainment for children (July/Aug). Sports complex. New foot-golf course. Go-kart track. Movie nights. Adventure and toddlers' playgrounds. WiFi (free).

Open: 11 March - 4 November.

Directions

From Dublin follow N11 Wexford road south, bypassing Ashford and Rathnew. After The Beehive pub look out for Doyle's pub on right. Turn right at pub and continue for 5 km. to park at top of Redcross village. GPS: 52.8884, -6.14528

Charges guide

Per unit incl. 2 persons and electricity	€ 25.00 - € 27.00
extra person	€ 6.00

Roscrea
Streamstown Caravan & Camping Park
Streamstown, Roscrea (Co. Tipperary) T: 050 521 519. E: info@tipperarycaravanpark.com
alanrogers.com/IR9420

This family run site, set on a dairy farm in the centre of Ireland, has been open for over 40 years. It is conveniently situated off the M7 Dublin-Limerick road and makes a good overnight halt or for a longer stay if you are seeking a quiet, restful location with little to disturb the peace. There are 26 touring pitches (10A Europlug), ten with hardstanding and separated by low hedges. The remainder are on grass and more suitable for units with awnings. This is a working farm and the owners, who are friendly and welcoming, have made some attractive improvements. What impresses most here, as well as the tidy overall appearance with neatly trimmed hedging, is the simplicity – no 'bells and whistles'.

Facilities

The sanitary facilities are very clean and housed in a modern block. Showers (free), toilets and washbasins (two in cubicles). Facilities for disabled visitors in family shower room. Laundry room. Motorcaravan services. Good campers' kitchen with fridge/freezer, electric cooker and TV. Small play area. TV, pool table and games room. Accommodation to rent. A torch would be useful.

Open: Easter - 1 October (other times phone in advance).

Directions

Leave M7 at Roscrea exit. From Roscrea follow signs for R491 Shinrone. Continue towards Shinrone following site signs for 2.5 km. and site entrance is on left. GPS: 52.95720, -7.83937

Charges guide

Per unit incl. 2 persons and electricity	€ 29.00
extra person	€ 5.00
child (under 14 yrs)	€ 2.00

For latest campsite news visit
alanrogers.com

Rosses Point
Greenlands Caravan & Camping Park
Rosses Point (Co. Sligo) T: 071 917 7113. E: noelineha@eircom.net
alanrogers.com/IR8690

Just off the N15 road and 8 km. west of Sligo town, this is a well run park at Rosses Point, in the sand hills adjoining a championship golf course. The 120 pitches (100 for touring units, all with 10A electricity) are thoughtfully laid out with small tents placed to the front of reception and the hardstanding touring pitches separated from the trailer tent pitches which occupy the rear. The ground is undulating and adds interest to the overall appearance. Your view depends on where you are pitched – look towards Coney Island and the Blackrock lighthouse which guards the bay, take in the sight of Benbulben Mountain or appreciate the seascape and the water lapping the resort's two bathing beaches.

Facilities

Modern toilet facilities are kept exceptionally clean, with hot showers (€ 1 token). Washing machine, dryer and iron. Motorcaravan services. Campers' kitchen. Information point and TV room beside reception. Play area and sand pit for children. Outdoor chess and draughts sets. Internet in reception. Night security.

Open: Easter - 14 September.

Directions

From Sligo city travel 800 m. north on N15 road, turn left onto R291 signed Rosses Point. Continue for 6.5 km. and park is on right after village. GPS: 54.30628, -8.56889

Charges guide

Per unit incl. 2 persons and electricity	€ 25.00
extra person	€ 5.00

Rosslare
Saint Margaret's Beach Caravan & Camping Park
Lady's Island, Rosslare Harbour (Co. Wexford) T: 053 913 1169. E: info@campingstmargarets.ie
alanrogers.com/IR9170

'This park is loved', was how a Swedish visitor described this family run, environmentally friendly caravan and camping park, the first the visitor meets near the Rosslare ferry port. Landscaping with flowering containers and maze-like sheltered camping areas and a pretty sanitary block all demonstrate the Traynor family's attention to detail. The 27 touring pitches all have 6/10A electricity, are sheltered from the fresh sea breeze and ferries can be seen crossing the Irish sea. Just metres away, the safe, sandy beach (part of the Wexford coastal path) curves around in a horseshoe shape ending in a small pier and slipway. Tourist information on the area is provided in the well stocked shop.

Facilities

The toilet block is spotless. Laundry room. Campers' kitchen including toaster, microwave and TV. Shop (June-Aug). Fresh milk and bread daily. Mobile homes for rent. Sun/TV room. Free WiFi over site. Courtesy bicycles. Off site: Walking, beach and fishing. Boat slipway 2.5 km. Pitch and putt 2 km. Riding 6 km. Pubs and restaurants. The JFK Arboretum, Johnstown Castle and Gardens, the Irish National Heritage Park, Kilmore Quay and Marina.

Open: 1 April - 30 September.

Directions

From the N25 south of Wexford town, outside village of Tagoat, follow signs for Lady's Island and Carne. After 3 km. pass Butler's Bar and take next left and continue for 2.5 km. Site is well signed. GPS: 52.206433, -6.356417

Charges guide

Per unit incl. 2 persons and electricity	€ 24.00 - € 26.00
extra person	€ 3.00

Roundstone
Gurteen Bay Caravan and Camping Park
Roundstone (Co. Galway) T: 095 358 82. E: gurteenbay@eircom.net
alanrogers.com/IR8860

Gurteen Bay Caravan and Camping Park is situated just 50 m. from the beach and the sea, with wonderful views out over the bay and a beautiful surrounding area. It offers 80 touring pitches which occupy three sections throughout the site. All have 6A electricity and water taps are provided all over the site. The white, sandy beach, with lifeguard on duty in July and August, is great for all the family and the site owners organise group activities. If you are looking for a beach holiday without the 'all singing, all dancing' facilities of a large resort, this park is a good choice.

Facilities

Spotlessly clean, central toilet block includes hot showers (token operated) and washbasins. Campers' kitchen. Laundry facilities. Motorcaravan services. Shop (May-Sept) selling groceries, ice-cream and beach toys with a games and TV room at the rear. Bicycle hire. Organised group activities. WiFi throughout. Off site: Recently introduced 'cycle loops' are all around the area. Bars, restaurants and shops and Sun. market in Roundstone.

Open: March - November.

Directions

From Galway take N59 west towards Clifden. Then left to Cashel (R340) and right onto R342 following signs to Roundstone. Go through village and park is 2 km. on left (use the 2nd entrance, the first is too narrow for touring units). GPS: 53.38381, -9.95354

Charges guide

Per unit incl. 2 persons and electricity	€ 25.00
extra person	€ 5.00
No credit cards.	

For latest campsite news visit
alanrogers.com

Roundwood
Roundwood Caravan & Camping Park

Roundwood Village, Bray Co Wicklow (Co. Wicklow) T: 012 818 163. E: info@dublinwicklowcamping.com

alanrogers.com/IR9130

In the heart of the Wicklow mountains, the hospitable owner of this park maintains high standards. It is neatly laid out with rows of trees dividing the different areas and giving an attractive appearance. There are 42 hardstanding pitches for caravans and motorcaravans, some sloping, all with electricity (16A), plus 30 pitches for tents, arranged off tarmac access roads. There are excellent walks around the Varty Lakes and a daily bus service to Dublin city. Close by are the Wicklow Mountains and the Sally Gap, Glendalough, Powerscourt Gardens, plus many other places of natural beauty. Apart from its scenic location, this site is well placed for the ferry ports.

Facilities

The sanitary block is kept clean, with adequate washing and toilet facilities, plus spacious showers on payment (€ 1). Good laundry facilities, but ask at reception as machines are not self-service. Motorcaravan services. Campers' kitchen and dining room. TV room. Adventure playground. WiFi (charged). Bicycle hire. Off site: Roundwood village has shops, a supermarket with ATM, pubs, restaurants, takeaways and Sun. market.

Open: 1 May - 5 September.

Directions

Turn off N11 Dublin-Wexford road at Kilmacanogue (exit 8), towards Glendalough and then 15 km. to Roundwood. Park is on the north side of the village. GPS: 53.06924, -6.22269

Charges guide

Per unit incl. 2 persons and electricity	€ 30.00
extra person	€ 8.00
child (under 14 yrs)	€ 4.00
dog	free

Skibbereen
The Hideaway Camping & Caravan Park

Skibbereen (Co. Cork) T: 028 222 54. E: skibbereencamping@eircom.net

alanrogers.com/IR9505

A sister park to The Meadow at Glandore, The Hideaway is ideally situated as a touring base for the West Cork region. It is a well run site under the supervision of the owners and although it enjoys tranquil surroundings, including preserved marshland, it is only ten minutes walk from the busy market town of Skibbereen. The Hideaway is a two-hectare, touring only park with 60 pitches, including 50 with hardstanding and 6A electricity hook-up. The remainder are for tents. Shrubs and low hedges divide the park giving an open feel overall and commanding views across the fields and hills. One long building houses reception, the toilet facilities and a games room.

Facilities

The modern toilet block has non-slip floors, well equipped showers (on payment). Baby room with bath. En-suite unit for disabled visitors. Laundry. Campers' dining room. Motorcaravan services. Adventure play area. Football and cycling not permitted on the park. Electric barbecues are not permitted. WiFi on part of site.

Open: Easter - 15 September.

Directions

From Skibbereen town centre take R596 (signed Casteltownsend). Site is on the left after 1 km. GPS: 51.54167, -9.26008

Charges guide

Per unit incl. 2 persons and electricity	€ 23.00
extra person	€ 6.00

No credit cards.

Slane
Slane Farm Camping

Harlinstown House, Slane (Co. Meath) T: 041 988 4985. E: info@slanefarmhostel.ie

alanrogers.com/IR8900

Slane Farm Camping is a friendly, family run campsite situated on a large working farm, in a rural setting in the heart of the historic Boyne valley, 16 km. west of Drogheda. This small campsite has a sunny field for tents and a separate stony area for motorcaravans and caravans. Electricity (6A Europlug) is available, but long leads may be needed. It is an ideal base for pop concerts in the grounds of Slane Castle, only 5 minutes walk away, so can be quite busy. A well equipped kitchen is available for use by campers and the reception area is well stocked with local information. The owners are always on hand to offer help and advice about the area.

Facilities

Well maintained, but very basic toilet facilities in nearby farm building. Kitchen. Laundry room. Barbecue. Bicycle hire (delivered to site). WiFi (free). 6 cottages for rent. Hostel accommodating 42 people in private rooms. Twin-axle caravans are not accepted. Off site: Visits to farm dairy and animals. Bicycle hire and fishing 2 km. Riding and golf 9 km. Marked walking, cycling routes.

Open: 1 March - 31 October.

Directions

Leave the north-south M1 motorway at exit 10 near Drogheda. Take N51 west through Slane for just under 12 km. Turn northwest on R163, site on right in 600 m. GPS: 53.71575, -6.57334

Charges guide

Per person	€ 10.00
child (6-12 yrs)	€ 5.00

For latest campsite news visit
alanrogers.com

Strandhill

Strandhill Caravan & Camping Park

Strandhill (Co. Sligo) T: 071 916 8111. E: strandhillcvp@eircom.net

alanrogers.com/IR8695

This seaside park is located on 20 acres of undulating grass on a sandy base, with natural protection from the onshore breezes of the famous Strandhill beach. There are 55 hardstanding pitches for caravans and motorcaravans with electricity and ample water points, and two camping areas for tents, one with views of the sea and the second more sheltered. Throughout the site many hollows provide ideal pitches for tents. Strandhill, world recognised as a surfing Mecca, also provides activities for all the family. There are miles of sandy beach and dunes and the Knocknarea Mountain is popular with walkers.

Facilities

The toilet block (keys provided on deposit) is clean and fresh with hot showers (token €1.50), electric hand dryers and hairdryer. New reception building including TV room, games room, campers' kitchen, laundry and a well equipped facility for disabled visitors. WiFi over part of site (charged). Automatic gate and door control. Off site: Shops, restaurants, takeaway, pubs and ATM are just beyond the park's boundary in the village.

Open: Easter - 25 September.

Directions

Strandhill is 8 km. west of Sligo city on the R292. Site is on the airport road. GPS: 54.27242, -8.60448

Charges guide

Per unit incl. 2 persons and electricity	€ 25.00
plus 2 children	€ 27.00
extra person	€ 3.00 - € 5.00

Timoleague

Sextons Caravan & Camping Park

R600 Timoleague-Clonakility Road, Clonakility (Co. Cork) T: 023 884 6347. E: info.sextons@gmail.com

alanrogers.com/IR9490

Sextons is an unpretentious site that has been in existence for over 40 years. The park, which is just under two hectares, offers just 30 pitches for touring. Gravel hardstandings are available for touring units and 18 tent pitches are on well kept grass. Along with a fairly new reception, the old shop has been converted into a comfortable lounge area for campers. Although convenient for the Cork Ferry Terminal, Sextons is situated on a quiet road between Clonakilty and Timoleague. It is well placed for those who like unspoilt countryside and discovering for themselves small hideaway cove beaches and country pubs with traditional music.

Facilities

Two small toilet blocks with free showers are in old farm buildings. En-suite facility for disabled visitors. Small shop (1/5-30/9). Gas. Small but comfortable camp kitchen with local TV. Sitting room for campers. Laundry. Small playground, football field and games room. Bicycle hire can be arranged. No electric barbecues. WiFi throughout (charged). Off site: Beaches, riding, boat launching, fishing and golf, all within 6 km.

Open: 15 March - 31 October.

Directions

N71 into Clonakilty, then follow R600 towards Timoleague for 5 km. – site on right. Look for 'Cornelius' the chicken guarding the entrance. GPS: 51.635006, -8.800821

Charges guide

Per unit incl. 2 persons and electricity	€ 25.00 - € 27.00
tent incl. 2 persons	€ 21.00 - € 22.00
No credit cards.	

Tipperary

Ballinacourty House Caravan & Camping Park

Glen of Aherlow, Tipperary (Co. Tipperary) T: 062 565 59. E: info@camping.ie

alanrogers.com/IR9370

Ballinacourty House and its cobble-stoned courtyard form the centrepiece of this south facing park with views of the Galtee Mountains. Accessed by a tree-lined lane, the reception area is in part of the renovated 18th-century building, as is the adjoining restaurant. The park is level with 38 touring pitches with 6A Europlugs and seven grassy pitches for tents. Some areas are shaded and there are open spaces to accommodate rallies and larger groups. Self-catering cottages and B&B are also available. This tranquil site appeals to families with young children. It is an excellent base from which to tour the Rock of Cashel, the Mitchelstown Caves, Swiss Cottage and the towns of Tipperary, Cahir and Cashel.

Facilities

Sanitary facilities provide free hot water and showers. Baby room. Laundry with ironing facilities. Campers' kitchen. Ice pack freezing. Licensed restaurant (early booking advised). Motorcaravan services. Gas supplies. Frisbee golf. TV and games rooms. Picnic benches. Tennis. Play area. WiFi (free). Off site: Fishing 1 km. Riding 4 km. Golf 5 km. Bicycle hire 8 km.

Open: 1 April - 28 September.

Directions

Follow the N24 from Tipperary or Cahir to Bansha. Turn on to R663 for 11 km, passing Glen Hotel after 10 km. Follow signs for Ballinacourty House. GPS: 52.41614, -8.21047

Charges guide

Per unit incl. 2 persons and electricity	€ 22.00 - € 25.00
extra person	€ 5.00

For latest campsite news visit
alanrogers.com

Tipperary
The Glen of Aherlow Caravan & Camping Park

Newtown, Glen of Aherlow (Co. Tipperary) T: 062 565 55. E: rdrew@tipperarycamping.com

alanrogers.com/IR9400

The owners of one of Ireland's newest parks, George and Rosaline Drew, are campers themselves and have set about creating an idyllic park in an idyllic location. This three-hectare park is set in one of Ireland's most picturesque valleys and is open all year. There are beautiful views of the wooded and hilly areas of Slievenamuck and the Galtee Mountains. There are 42 large and level touring pitches, on both hardstanding and grass, each pair sharing a double 10A Europlug post and water point. The Drew family is happy to welcome large groups and rallies, and large units can be accommodated. The stone-built reception and shop beside the gate is a super addition to the site and includes a coffee shop.

Facilities	Directions
The modern toilet block includes free showers and facilities for disabled visitors. Motorcaravan services. Laundry room with ironing. Campers' kitchen. Recreation and TV rooms. Shop. Coffee shop. Bicycle hire (delivered to site). WiFi (free). Off site: Holiday homes to rent 300 m. Pub nearby. Outdoor activities. Fishing in Aherlow River.	From Tipperary town take N24 to Bansha, then R663 to Newtown. Continue through village and pass Coach Road Inn to park in 300 m. GPS: 52.419981, -8.187867

Open: All year.

Charges guide

Per unit incl. 2 persons and electricity	€ 26.00
extra person	€ 6.00

Tralee
Woodlands Park Touring Caravan & Camping Park

Dan Spring Road, Tralee (Co. Kerry) T: 066 712 1235. E: woodlandstralee@gmail.com

alanrogers.com/IR9650

This family run park is located in the heart of Kerry, on the gateway to the Dingle peninsula and just north of the Ring of Kerry and Killarney. Woodlands is an ideal base, only ten minutes' walk from Tralee town centre via the town park and famous rose garden. Located on a 16-acre elevated site approached by a short road and a bridge that straddles the River Lee; once on site the town seems far removed with a countryside environment taking over. Hedging, trees, grazing fields and the distant Slieve Mish Mountain create the setting. There are 135 pitches including 85 super pitches with hardstanding, electricity (10A), water and drainage and a grass area.

Facilities	Directions
Excellent, heated sanitary facilities include sizeable showers (€ 1 token) and provision for disabled guests. Campers' kitchen. Laundry room with washing machines and dryer. Gas for sale. Motorcaravan services. Club house serving hot and cold drinks. Shop (Easter-30/9). Games room. TV and adult only room. Free WiFi over part of site. Fenced adventure play area. Off site: Aqua Dome nearby (discounted family pass for campers). Golf 6 km.	Site is 1 km. southwest of Tralee town centre. From N21/N69/N86 junction south of Tralee follow site signs for 2.4 km. to park, 200 m. off the N86 Tralee-Dingle road. Site is 300 m. east of the Aqua Dome. GPS: 52.26157, -9.70338

Open: 1 February - 30 November.

Charges guide

Per unit incl. 2 persons, electricity, water and drainage	€ 25.00 - € 27.00
extra person	€ 6.00

Tralee
Green Acres Caravan Park

Aughacasla, Castlegregory, Tralee V92 TK40 (Co. Kerry) T: 066 713 9158. E: info@greenacrespark.com

alanrogers.com/IR9660

This small, family run site is situated close to the village of Castlegregory, Co. Kerry. With direct access to an Atlantic Coast beach just metres away, it is ideal for campers who enjoy watersports as well as those just wishing to relax in a coastal setting. There are 27 unmarked, level, grassy pitches for tourers, each with a 10A electricity hook-up and a water point. Three extra large pitches are available for American-style motorhomes. There are some 70 privately owned units on the site. This is a friendly, simple site, within walking distance of shops and restaurants; the local bar has live music twice a week.

Facilities	Directions
Basic sanitary facilities include hot showers (€ 1.50 for 6 mins). Baby changing. No facilities for disabled visitors. Laundry room with washing machine and dryer. Fridge/freezer. TV/games room with pool table and air hockey. Adventure-style play area (2-12 yrs). Direct beach access. Excursions can be organised in reception. Dogs are not accepted. Multi Universal Games Area on beach. WiFi over site (charged).	From Cork take N22 to Tralee, N86 to Dingle (14 km), then R560 towards Castlegregory for 5.5 km. Site is on right before village and well signed. GPS: 52.23813, -9.97128

Open: Easter - 2 October.

Charges guide

Per unit incl. 2 persons and electricity	€ 20.00 - € 25.00
extra person	€ 4.00
child	€ 2.00

For latest campsite news visit
alanrogers.com

Tramore

Newtown Cove Camping & Caravan Park

Newtown Road, Tramore (Co. Waterford) T: 051 381 979. E: info@newtowncove.com

alanrogers.com/IR9340

Well run and friendly, this very attractive small park is only five minutes walk from the beautiful Newtown Cove. It has views of the famous and historic Metal Man and is 2.5 km. from Tramore beach and 11 km. from Waterford. Neatly set out on gently sloping grass are 40 pitches, with the abundance of shrubs and bushes reflecting the efforts of the owners. All pitches have 10A Europlug, 30 with hardstanding also, and access is by well lit, tarmac roads. There are some 56 privately owned caravan holiday homes. A modern building at the entrance houses reception, the amenities and additional sanitary facilities.

Facilities

The main sanitary block at the bottom end of the site provides good, clean facilities including a bathroom. Showers on payment (token from reception). Additional toilet facilities in reception. Excellent motorcaravan services. Campers' kitchen with cooking facilities, sheltered eating area, lounge and small laundry. Small shop (July/Aug). TV room. Games room. Small play area. WiFi throughout (charged). Off site: Beach 400 m.

Open: 2-6 April and 1 May - 27 September.

Directions

To Tramore on R675 coast road to Dungarvan. Turn right at 2nd roundabout in Tramore and follow signs for site. Turn left at roundabout after golf club, then immediately right at next junction. After 400 m. take left fork to site just on left. GPS: 52.14763, -7.17274

Charges guide

Per unit incl. 2 persons	
and electricity	€ 24.00 - € 29.00
extra person	€ 6.00

Westport

Westport House Caravan & Camping Park

Westport House Country Park, Westport (Co. Mayo) T: 098 277 66. E: camping@westporthouse.ie

alanrogers.com/IR8770

Located in the grounds of an elegant country estate, this is a popular park. In an attractive, sheltered area of the parkland, set in the trees, are 95 pitches, 70 with hardstanding and 10/12A electricity. Outside the peak season, the site may not be fully open and some facilities such as the bar and café may not be available. Westport House and an adventure park are nearby on the estate and campsite visitors get a 20 per cent discount on all tickets. There are also special family rates for three days camping, along with an annual pass to the adventure park.

Facilities

Toilet facilities are provided at various points on the site, plus a 'super-loo' located in the farmyard buildings. Facilities for disabled visitors. Laundry facilities. Café and bar with food and musical entertainment at weekends. Fishing. Westport House and Pirate Park. Dogs are not accepted in July/Aug. Bell tents available to rent. Free WiFi over site. Off site: Within 5 km. of the estate are an 18-hole golf course and deep sea angling on Clew Bay.

Open: 1 April - 8 September, but contact site first.

Directions

New entrance to park. Follow signs to N59 north to Achill/Newport, turn left at Teagasc building onto the Golf Course Road. Westport House is the second left. Continue through estate following signs for camping. GPS: 53.8053, -9.5395

Charges guide

Per unit incl. 2 persons	
and electricity	€ 27.00 - € 30.00
extra person	€ 5.00

For latest campsite news visit

alanrogers.com

THE CHANNEL ISLANDS ARE MADE UP OF THE ISLANDS OF: JERSEY, GUERNSEY, SARK, HERM AND ALDERNEY

A visit to the Channel Islands offers a holiday in part of the British Isles, yet in an area which has a definite continental flavour. All the islands have beautiful beaches and coves, pretty scenery and fascinating histories.

The largest of the Channel Islands is Jersey, which is also the most commercial with more entertainment on offer. It has long stretches of safe beaches for swimming and water-based activities such as windsurfing and banana rides. Caravans and motorcaravans are allowed on Jersey but with a number of limitations (for example, length of stay, the width and length of the unit). A permit is required, which is obtained as part of the booking procedure with the campsite of your choice. You must book in advance but the campsite owner will advise you on all aspects of your visit.

Guernsey will suit those who prefer a quieter, more peaceful holiday. Motorcaravans are now allowed here, but not caravans as yet. Guernsey too has wide, sandy beaches plus sheltered coves. The historic, harbour town of St Peter Port has steep and winding cobbled streets, with plenty of shops, cafés and restaurants.

For total relaxation, one of the smaller islands – Sark or Herm – would be ideal. No cars are permitted on either of these islands. Explore on foot, by bicycle or horse-drawn carriage.

Shopping on all the islands has the advantage of no VAT – particularly useful when buying cameras, watches or alcohol.

Places of interest

Jersey: St Helier; Jersey Zoo; Jersey war tunnels; Elizabeth Castle; German Underground Hospital in St Lawrence; Samarès Manor in St Clement; Shell Garden at St Aubin; Battle of Flowers Museum in St Ouen.

Guernsey: Castle Cornet at St Peter Port Harbour; Victor Hugo's House; Guernsey Folk Museum; German Occupation Museum; Fort Grey Shipwreck Museum; Saumarez Park.

Sark: La Coupée; La Seigneurie, with old dovecote and gardens; Gouliet and Boutique Caves; Le Pot on Little Sark; Venus Pool; Little Sark Village.

Herm: This tiny island has beautiful, quiet, golden beaches and a little harbour village and hotel. Arrive by ferry from Guernsey for a wonderful day out.

Did you know?

Jersey has been associated with knitting for nearly 400 years.

The Channel Islands were the only part of the British Isles to be occupied by the Germans during the Second World War.

Herm island is just one and a half miles long and only half a mile wide.

Le Jerriais is the native language of Jersey, a blend of Norse and Norman French.

Note: The reciprocal health services agreement between the British Government and the Channel Islands ended in April 2009. The EHIC card does not cover emergency health care as the Channel Islands are not part of the EU. Travel insurance is now essential.

Saint Martin

Rozel Camping Park

Rozel, Saint Martin JE3 6AX (Jersey) T: 01534 855200. E: enquiries@rozelcamping.com

alanrogers.com/UK9710

Family owned and run for over forty years, this attractive park has some wonderful views across the sea to the coast of France. The famous Durrell Wildlife Park is within walking distance, as are the pretty harbour and fishing village of Rozel. The campsite provides four terraced, grass camping areas, all with differing characteristics – open and with views, sheltered at a lower level or with pitches in groups in hedged bays. The welcoming owners will help you decide which will suit you best. In total, there are 130 touring pitches, all with access to 16A electricity. A further 20 are used for fully equipped tents to hire. The site has provided easy access for caravans and motorcaravans and the Germains will meet you at the ferry to help you navigate to the park. The thoughtful amenities on the park include an appealing swimming pool with sheltered surrounds for sunbathing, free crazy golf, a TV room, a quiet room for relaxing and reading, plus a play barn with pool tables and other games. Play equipment is provided in an open area of the park with plenty of space for children to run around. The surrounding countryside is quieter than many areas of the island, and the Green Lane network of tree-lined narrow lanes is perfect for walking or cycling. A car is probably necessary to reach the main island beaches, although a bus service does run to Saint Helier from close by.

Facilities

Two bright, heated sanitary buildings are kept clean and include some washbasins in cubicles. Facilities for disabled visitors. Family shower rooms. Motorcaravan drain point (grey water only). Fully equipped laundry, also with hairdryers. Shop (opened and stocked acc. to season). Solar-heated swimming pool (June-Sept) with children's pool and sunbathing areas. Play area. Crazy golf. Games, reading and TV rooms. Torches useful. Fully equipped tents to rent. WiFi near reception (free). Off site: Takeaway food can be delivered to site. Pub and restaurants within walking distance in Rozel village. Fishing 1 mile. Beach 2 miles. Riding 3 miles. Golf 4 miles.

Open: 7 May - 10 September.

Directions

Leave harbour by Route du Port Elizabeth, take the A1 east through tunnel and A17. At traffic lights turn left on A6 (Five Oaks). Continue to Five Oaks and on to St Martin's church. Turn right, then immediately left at The Royal pub on B38 to Rozel, continue to end of road, turn right and park is on right.
GPS: 49.23841, -2.05058

Charges guide

Per unit incl. 2 persons and electricity	£ 23.00 - £ 24.00
extra person	£ 10.50 - £ 11.50
child (3-12 yrs)	£ 7.00
dog	£ 2.00

Credit cards 2.5% surcharge.

Saint Martin

Beuvelande Camp Site

Beuvelande, Saint Martin JE3 6EZ (Jersey) T: 01534 853575. E: info@beuvelandecampsite.com

alanrogers.com/UK9720

Beuvelande is a family owned and run campsite, set amongst the 'Ruettes Tranquilles' (narrow, tree-lined lanes) of northwest Jersey. There is a warm welcome here and the site offers all the necessary amenities for a happy family holiday, including a swimming pool, a well stocked shop and a bar and café with an outdoor eating area. There are around 100 pitches for all types of unit, a mixture of standard (6x10 m) and super (6x16 m), all with 5/10A electricity. These are arranged on a series of flat, hedged meadows and cars may be parked next to your unit. On further fields, ready erected tents, some attractive bell tents and a safari tent are available for rent. On arrival you will receive a welcome pack of brochures covering activities on the island. Car and bicycle hire can be arranged. Families are particularly welcome, with TV and games rooms, as well as the heated outdoor pool and modern play area. The bar, café and covered outdoor sitting area provide a popular social hub for the site. This family run park prides itself on quality, cleanliness and hospitality.

Facilities

The sanitary block is fully tiled, with controllable showers, facilities for disabled visitors, family shower room and a baby facilities (a long walk from some pitches). Dishwashing facilities. Laundry. Shop (hours acc. to season). Licensed restaurant. Outdoor heated swimming pool (41x17 ft, May-Sept. acc. to the weather) with a sun terrace and small waterslide. Play area and large playing field. Games room. TV room. Evening entertainment (high season). Ice pack and battery charging services (small charge). Car and bicycle hire by arrangement. WiFi (free in restaurant). Tents for rent. Torches useful. Off site: Bus service on the main road. Beach and sailing 1.5 miles. Fishing, golf and riding within 2 miles.

Open: 1 April - 30 September.

Directions

On leaving the harbour by Route du Port Elizabeth, take A1 east through tunnel and A17. At second set of traffic lights turn left signed Five Oaks. Continue to Five Oaks and on to St Martin's RC church, then right into La Longue Rue (watch carefully for the sign), right again Rue de L'Orme then left to site. Access roads are narrow. Do not use sat nav.
GPS: 49.21294, -2.05615

Charges guide

Per unit incl. 2 persons and electricity	£ 22.00 - £ 26.00
extra adult	£ 10.00
child (2-14 yrs)	£ 8.00

Single sex groups not accepted.

For latest campsite news visit

alanrogers.com

Castel
Fauxquets Valley Campsite
Candie Road, Castel GY5 7QL (Guernsey) T: 01481 255460. E: info@fauxquets.co.uk
alanrogers.com/UK9780

Situated in the rural centre of the island, Fauxquets is in a pretty sheltered valley, hidden down narrow lanes away from busy roads and run by the Guille family assisted by friendly collie, Lottie. Originally part of a dairy farm, the valley side has now been developed into an attractive campsite. Plenty of ornamental trees, bushes and flowers have been planted to separate pitches and to provide shelter around the various fields which are well terraced. The 100 pitches are of a good size, mostly marked, numbered and with 6-32A electricity, offering a choice of pitches for tents and motorcaravans. There is lots of open space and some friendly farm animals in surrounding enclosures. The site has fully equipped tents for hire and two comfortable log cabins. Reception at the entrance includes a small shop and coffee and drinks are served here. A covered outdoor area provides somewhere to relax (with free WiFi) and a centre for regular organised gatherings with pizza or barbecues. There is plenty of room to sit around the heated swimming pool, including a large grassy terrace with sunbeds provided. A car would be useful here to reach the beaches, Saint Peter Port and other attractions, although there is a bus service each day (20 minutes walk). The German Military Underground Hospital is nearby.

Facilities

Good toilet facilities have controllable showers, some washbasins in private cabins with a shower, baby bath and changing unit. Dishwashing facilities under cover and a tap for free hot water. Laundry room with free irons, boards and hairdryers. Well stocked shop with fresh produce, bread delivered daily, snacks and camping essentials. Off licence. Heated swimming pool (13x6 m) with paddling pool (10:00-19:00). TV and games rooms. Small play area and play field. Farm animals. Bicycle hire arranged. Torches useful. WiFi in reception (free). Off site: Small supermarket 2 miles. Riding and golf 2 miles. Fishing, sailing and boat launching 3 miles.

Open: 1 April - 7 September.

Directions

From harbour take second exit from roundabout. At top of hill, turn left at 'filter in turn' into Queens Road, then right at next filter. Follow straight through traffic lights and down hill past hospital, through pedestrian lights and straight on at next lights at top of hill. Continue for 0.75 miles, then turn right opposite sign for German Hospital. Fourth left is pedestrian entrance, cars carry on for 400 yds. to gravel entrance on left. GPS: 49.46812, -2.58843

Charges guide

Per unit incl. 2 persons and electricity	£ 23.00 - £ 28.00
child (0-14 yrs)	£ 4.00 - £ 9.00
extra person	£ 9.50 - £ 12.00

Saint Sampson's
Vaugrat Camping
Route de Vaugrat, Saint Sampson's GY2 4TA (Guernsey) T: 01481 257468. E: enquiries@vaugratcampsite.com **alanrogers.com/UK9770**

Vaugrat Camping is a neat, well tended site, close to the beach in the northwest of the island. Owned and well run by the Lainé family, it is centred around attractive and interesting historic granite farm buildings dating back to the 15th century, with a gravel courtyard and very pretty flower beds. It provides 150 pitches (with 10A electricity available) on flat, grassy meadows that are mostly surrounded by trees, banks and hedges to provide shelter. Tents and motorcaravans are arranged around the edges of the fields, giving open space in the centre, and while pitches are not marked, there is sufficient room and cars may be parked next to tents. Only couples and families are accepted. The site also offers fully equipped tents for hire and they are considering the addition of glamping-style units. Housed in the old farmhouse, now a listed building, are the reception area and small shop. Upstairs is the Coffee Barn/TV room with views across the site to the sea. Restaurants, cafés, takeaways and a supermarket are all within walking distance, as is the nearby beach.

Facilities

Well kept sanitary facilities are in two buildings. The first block is in the courtyard, with hot showers on payment (20 p/3 mins). Unit for disabled visitors with shower, basin and toilet (6 in. step into building). Laundry facilities. Second block near the camping fields provides toilets, washbasins and dishwashing facilities. Shop with ice pack hire and gas (open at certain times by arrangement). Coffee barn with TV and free WiFi access. Dogs are not accepted. Torches would be useful. Fully equipped tents to hire (details from site). Off site: Bus service nearby. Car and bicycle hire by arrangement. Beach 500 yds. Fishing, riding and golf within 2 miles. Hotel and bar, restaurant, takeaway and supermarket nearby.

Open: 1 May - 14 September.

Directions

On leaving St Peter Port, turn right onto coast road for 1.5 miles. At filter turn left into Vale Road. Straight over at two sets of lights then first left turn by church. Follow to crossroads (garage opposite) turn right. Carry on past Peninsula Hotel, then second left, signed for site. Site on left after high stone wall (400 yds) with concealed, narrow entrance. GPS: 49.49584, -2.55433

Charges guide

Per unit incl. 2 persons and electricity	£ 30.00
extra person	£ 12.00
child (3-13 yrs)	£ 8.25

Families and couples only.

For latest campsite news visit
alanrogers.com

Vale

La Bailloterie Camping

Vale GY3 5HA (Guernsey) T: 01481 243636. E: info@campinginguernsey.com

alanrogers.com/UK9790

Arranged on a series of spacious, grassy meadows, each surrounded by attractive trees, La Bailloterie is a long-established Guernsey campsite run by friendly and welcoming owners, Richard and Caryl. It is a very peaceful setting down a narrow, rural lane but is just minutes from the shops and services of Vale and the beach. Said to take around 150 tents or motorcaravans, there is always plenty of room and 48 electricity connections are available (16A). Choose your own pitch. Also provided are hire tents and simple log cabins to rent. The site's amenities are housed in a large, converted granite barn with sanitary facilities on the ground floor and reception, a simple shop and a lounge with a relaxing balcony area where you can enjoy a coffee overlooking the play area. The barn provides a social centre for the site too, as meals and snacks are served here and barbecues are arranged twice weekly in season. With a good supermarket just three minutes walk away, the site shop is not large, but pre-ordered baguettes, etc. can be delivered to your pitch by bike each morning. A footpath to the nearest beach at Pembroke Bay ten minutes away, and a bus service is in Vale for access to most places of interest on the island.

Facilities

Sanitary facilities are modern and kept clean. Showers are free. Facilities for disabled visitors. Baby room. Washing machine and dryer. Motorcaravan emptying point. Basic shop (pre-order bread). Coffee lounge and café with TV (17/7-20/8). Organised barbecues and meals (twice weekly in high season). Play area. Tea garden and boules pitch. Bicycle hire. WiFi in café area (free). Tents and log cabins to rent. Off site: Supermarket 3 mins. walk. Beach 10 mins. walk. Peninsula Hotel restaurant. Golf.

Open: 15 May - 15 September.

Directions

From the harbour drive up to the main roundabout and take the third exit heading along the seafront. Go over mini-roundabout at Red Lion Hotel. At next filter in turn, bear left for Pembroke Bay. At third set of traffic lights turn right, then first left. Site is signed straight ahead. GPS: 49.48926, -2.5311

Charges guide

Per unit incl. 2 persons and electricity	£ 24.00 - £ 28.00
extra person	£ 9.00 - £ 11.00
child	£ 7.00 - £ 8.00

Herm Island

Seagull Campsite

The Administration Office, Herm Island GY1 3HR (Herm) T: 01481 750000. E: reservations@herm.com

alanrogers.com/UK9830

This tiny site, and indeed the island of Herm, will certainly appeal to those who are looking for complete tranquillity and calm. Reached by boat from Guernsey (20 minutes), this beautiful, 300-acre island allows no cars, only tractors, on its narrow roads and paths (no bicycles either). The 'tents only' campsite is a twenty minute uphill walk from the harbour, although your luggage will be transported for you by tractor. Just 80 pitches are arranged in three small meadows with a variety of trees to provide shelter. A wide open field with amazing views provides further camping pitches with plenty of space. There are no electricity hook-ups. There are 29 ready erected tents for rent and about 20 seasonal units. Bring your own tent and equipment or hire both (but not bedding, crockery and lighting) from the site. Campsite wardens can be contacted at all times by phone. Walk down the hill to the harbour village and there is a pub with good meals, a restaurant and two small shops. One is free to stroll around the many paths, through farmland, heath and around the coast, where there are stunning beaches. Visit Shell Beach to gather a wonderful variety of shells or walk down to Belvoir Bay and spend the day swimming and sunbathing. Herm is definitely not for those who like entertainment and plenty of facilities, but for total relaxation, with the absence of any bustle and noise, it takes some beating!

Facilities

Small, wooden toilet block. Hot showers (£1) open from the outside. Laundry facility and small kitchen area. Freezer for ice-packs. Public phone. Mobile phone charging points and air bed inflating point. Groceries to order. No dogs or pets are allowed. Torches essential. Ready erected tents to rent. Off site: Beach 500 yds. The harbour village, about 10 mins. walk downhill, with small shop, gas, a post office, pub, restaurants and café. Fishing on the island. Holiday cottages and log cabins to rent.

Open: Early May - late September.

Directions

Reached by boat from St Peter Port – report to Administration Office at port on arrival. Do not take your car as it is very unlikely you will be able to park long term in St Peter Port. GPS: 49.46997, -2.445745

Charges guide

Per person	£ 8.50
child (under 14 yrs)	£ 4.25
transportation of luggage	£ 8.00

Single-sex groups not accepted.

For latest campsite news visit
alanrogers.com

Sark
Pomme de Chien Campsite

Sark GY9 0SB (Sark) T: 01481 832316. E: rangjill@hotmail.com

alanrogers.com/UK9870

'The island where time stands still' is an apt description of Sark, one of the smallest inhabited Channel Islands, some 45 minutes from Guernsey by boat. Bicycles, horsedrawn carriages and tractors provide the only transport on the island. Situated five minutes from the shops and ten from the beach, the Pomme de Chien campsite is small with only 50 pitches, some of which are occupied by fully equipped tents for rent (May-September). The remainder are for campers with their own tents (no caravans, motorcaravans or trailer tents, of course). The pitches are large, on fairly level grass; there are no electricity hook-ups. Visit with your own small tent or hire one of the site's own (equipment includes everything you're likely to need except bedding and a torch). On arrival by boat at the La Masseline Jetty, take the 'toastrack' tractor-bus up the hill, then follow the track with its flower-filled banks to the site. You can arrange to have your luggage transported by a local carter for a small fee. Call at the owners' home to check in. Enjoy the total tranquillity of the island which has recently been recognised as the world's first 'Dark Sky Island'. All you are likely to need for a peaceful stay is provided, with several small shops, pubs, hotels, restaurants, a Tourist Office and even a bank.

Facilities

Small sanitary block with free hot showers (bench and hook), toilets and washbasins. Fridge and freezer (free). Dishwashing sinks and washing line. Eggs for sale. Book swap. Dogs are not accepted. Torches are necessary. Baggage transfer on payment. No camp fires. Hire tents. Off site: Shop, pub, restaurants and bicycle hire 5 mins. walk. Dixcart Bay beach and fishing 10 mins. walk. Boat trips. Folk festival in early July.

Open: All year.

Directions

Take the small ferry from Guernsey (www.sarkshippingcompany.com). On arrival catch the tractor-drawn 'bus' up Harbour Hill (you can walk but it is a ten minute hike). Once at the top take road leading off left, then second right, and follow the lane to the site entrance. Reception is at house with white gates. GPS: 49.43665, -2.36331

Charges guide

Per person	£ 8.50
child	£ 5.00

No credit cards.

Sark
La Valette Campsite

Sark GY10 1SE (Sark) T: 01481 832202. E: lavalette@yahoo.co.uk

alanrogers.com/UK9880

La Valette is one of just two options for simple camping on this wonderful island. Bring your own tent (baggage will be transported for you to and from the harbour) or rent a ready erected tent or one of four smart, new camping pods. With stunning sea views across to Alderney and France, the large open field slopes in places, although it should always be possible to find a level spot and there is some shelter from hedges if preferred. There are no electricity hook-ups and the only amenity is a purpose built toilet block. One of the joys of this car-free island is that children can experience a wonderful freedom and everyone can explore the island on foot or by bike. Mrs Adams, the owner, provides a friendly welcome and can provide a fascinating insight into Sark and the history of her beautiful granite farmhouse. La Valette is the only Sark 'tenement' never to have been sold and, since 1565, has been passed down through the family. The small shops, pubs and restaurants of the island are an easy stroll. Walking amongst the flora and fauna of the island is a delight or you could rent a bike. Sandy coves are accessible down cliff paths. The site overlooks Grève de la Ville Bay which is ideal for a refreshing morning swim when the sun hits the beach on this side of the island. Above all, this car-free island provides ample opportunities to totally relax and recharge your batteries.

Facilities

Purpose built, small toilet block (quite a walk from the far corners of the site). Unisex facilities including two showers (on payment, £1 for four minutes), two washbasins in cabins and four WCs. Shaver points. Dishwashing sink. Torches essential. Camping pods and ready erected tents with equipment (bring sleeping bags and lighting). Luggage transportation. Off site: Small shops, cafés, restaurants and pub within walking distance (0.5 miles). Bicycle hire. Fishing. Boat trips. Star-gazing (the world's first Dark Sky Island).

Open: March - October (camping pods all year).

Directions

Take small ferry from Guernsey (www.sarkshippingcompany.com). On arrival catch the tractor-drawn 'bus' up Harbour Hill (you can walk but it is a ten minute, steep hike). Once at the top take road leading off right and follow the lane and signs to the farmhouse. GPS: 49.43359, -2.35141

Charges guide

Per person	£ 8.00
child	£ 4.00

No credit cards.

For latest campsite news visit
alanrogers.com

Holiday Caravans and Chalets

Over recent years, many of the campsites featured in this guide have added large numbers of high quality caravan holiday homes, chalets and lodges. Many park owners believe that some former caravanners and motorcaravanners have been enticed by the extra comfort this type of accommodation can now provide, and that maybe this is the ideal solution to combine the freedom of camping with all the comforts of home.

Quality is consistently high and, although the exact size and inventory will vary from park to park, if you choose any of the parks detailed here, you can be sure that you're staying in some of the best quality and best value caravan holiday homes or chalets available.

Home comforts are provided and typically these include a fridge with freezer compartment, gas hob, proper shower – often a microwave and CD player too, but do check for details. All caravan holiday homes and chalets come fully equipped with a good range of kitchen utensils, pots and pans, crockery, cutlery and outdoor furniture. Many even have an attractive wooden sundeck or paved terrace – a perfect spot for outdoors eating or relaxing with a book and watching the world go by. An efficient heating system is invariably included and some models may also incorporate air conditioning.

Regardless of model, colourful soft furnishings are the norm and a generally breezy décor helps to provide a real holiday feel.

Although some parks may have a large number of different accommodation types, we have restricted our choice to one or two of the most popular accommodation units (either caravan holiday homes or chalets) for each of the parks listed.

The caravan holiday homes here will be of modern design, and recent innovations such as pitched roofs undeniably improve their appearance.

Design will invariably include clever use of space and fittings/furniture to provide for comfortable holidays – usually light and airy, with big windows and patio-style doors, fully equipped kitchen areas, a shower room with shower, washbasin and WC, cleverly designed bedrooms and a comfortable lounge/dining area (often incorporating a sofa bed).

In general, modern campsite chalets incorporate all the best features of caravan holiday homes in a more traditional, wood-clad structure, sometimes with the advantage of an upper mezzanine floor for an additional bedroom.

Our selected parks offer a massive range of different types of caravan holiday home and chalet, and it would be impractical to inspect every single accommodation unit. Our selection criteria, therefore, primarily takes account of the quality standards of the campsite itself.

However, there are a couple of important ground rules:

- Featured caravan holiday homes must be no more than five years old.

- Chalets no more than ten years old.

- All listed accommodation must, of course, fully conform with all applicable local, national and European safety legislation.

For each park we have given details of the type, or types, of accommodation available to rent, but these details are necessarily quite brief. Sometimes internal layouts can differ quite substantially, particularly with regard to sleeping arrangements, where these include the flexible provision for 'extra persons' on sofa beds located in the living area.

These arrangements may vary from accommodation to accommodation, and if you're planning a holiday which includes more people than are catered for by the main bedrooms you should check exactly how the extra sleeping arrangements are to be provided!

Charges

An indication of the tariff for each type of accommodation featured is also included, indicating the variance between the low and high season tariffs. However, given that many parks have a large and often complex range of pricing options, incorporating special deals and various discounts, the charges we mention should be taken to be just an indication. We strongly recommend therefore that you confirm the actual cost when making a booking.

We also strongly recommend that you check with the park, when booking, what (if anything) will be provided by way of bed linen, blankets, pillows etc. Again, in our experience, this can vary widely from park to park.

On every park a fully refundable deposit (usually between £100 and £250) is payable on arrival. There may also be an optional cleaning service for which a further charge is made. Other options may include sheet hire (typically £20 per unit) or baby pack hire (cot and high chair).

UK4520 Flower of May Holiday Park

▶ see report page 186

Lebberston Cliff, Scarborough YO11 3NU, Yorkshire

AR1 – 4 BERTH GOLD – Mobile Home

Sleeping: 2 bedrooms, sleeps 4: 1 double, 2 singles, pillows and blankets provided

Living: heating, TV, shower, WC

Eating: fitted kitchen with hobs, oven, microwave, grill, fridge, freezer

Pets: not accepted

AR2 – 6 BERTH GOLD – Mobile Home

Sleeping: 3 bedrooms, sleeps 6: 1 double, 4 singles, pillows and blankets provided

Living: heating, TV, shower, WC

Eating: fitted kitchen with hobs, oven, microwave, grill, fridge, freezer

Pets: not accepted

Other (AR1 and AR2): cot, highchair to hire

Open: 2 April - 2 November

Weekly Charge	AR1	AR2
Low Season (from)	£ 380	£ 430
High Season (from)	£ 640	£ 690

UK4640 Goosewood Holiday Park

▶ see report page 194

Carr Lane, Sutton-on-the-Forest, York YO61 1ET, Yorkshire

AR1 – ELM – Mobile Home

Sleeping: 2 bedrooms, sleeps 4: 1 double, 2 singles, pillows and blankets provided

Living: heating, TV, shower, WC, separate WC

Eating: fitted kitchen with hobs, oven, microwave, grill, dishwasher, fridge, freezer

Outside: table & chairs

Pets: accepted (with supplement)

AR2 – LAUREL/WILLOWS – Lodge

Sleeping: 3 bedrooms, sleeps 6: 1 double, 4 singles, pillows and blankets provided

Living: heating, TV, shower, WC, separate WC

Eating: fitted kitchen with hobs, oven, microwave, grill, dishwasher, fridge, freezer

Outside: table & chairs

Pets: accepted (with supplement)

Open: 1 March - 2 January

Weekly Charge	AR1	AR2
Low Season (from)	£ 340	£ 380
High Season (from)	£ 610	£ 1048

Open All Year

The following parks are understood to accept caravanners and campers all year round. It is always wise to phone the park to check as the facilities available, for example, may be reduced.

England

South West England
Cornwall

Bodmin	UK0270	Mena	16
Bodmin	UK0306	Ruthern Valley	17
Bude	UK0370	Budemeadows	18
Bude	UK0385	Pentire Haven	18
Looe	UK0006	Tencreek H.P.	23
Newquay	UK0540	Carvynick	30
Newquay	UK0165	Monkey Tree	26
Padstow	UK0430	Padstow	31
Redruth	UK0114	Globe Vale	35
Saint Ives	UK0030	Ayr	38
St Martins-Looe	UK0320	Looe Country Park	39
Saltash	UK0440	Dolbeare	40
Truro	UK0180	Carnon Downs	43
Truro	UK0185	Cosawes	44
Truro	UK0012	Killiwerris	41

South West England
Devon

Braunton	UK0710	Hidden Valley	49
Dawlish	UK0970	Cofton	55
Dawlish	UK1010	Lady's Mile	54
Drewsteignton	UK1250	Woodland Springs	56
Ilfracombe	UK0690	Stowford Farm	58
Modbury	UK0820	Moor View	60
Newton Abbot	UK0980	Lemonford	62
Paignton	UK0870	Beverley	65
Plymouth	UK0810	Riverside	66
South Molton	UK0745	Riverside	68
Tavistock	UK0795	The Old Rectory	69

South West England
Somerset, Wiltshire, Dorset

Bishop Sutton	UK1510	Chew Valley	76
Martock	UK1420	Southfork	87
Minehead	UK1301	Westermill Farm	87
Salisbury	UK1655	Church Farm	91
Salisbury	UK1650	Coombe	90
Salisbury	UK1640	Greenhill Farm	90
Sparkford	UK1500	Long Hazel	92
Taunton	UK1340	Cornish Farm	93
Taunton	UK1350	Quantock Orchard	93
Taunton	UK1520	Waterrow	94
Wareham	UK2030	Wareham Forest	96
Weston-s-Mare	UK1305	West End Farm	98
Weymouth	UK1820	Bagwell Farm	99

Southern England

Banbury	UK2600	Barnstones	103
Bletchingdon	UK2590	Greenhill Farm	105
Burford	UK2620	Wysdom	105
Cowes	UK2530	Waverley	106
Fordingbridge	UK2290	Sandy Balls	106
Oxford	UK2595	Diamond Farm	111

South East England

Ashford	UK3040	Broadhembury	117
Bexhill-on-Sea	UK2955	Kloofs	118
Brighton	UK2930	Brighton	119
Canterbury	UK3070	Canterbury	120
Chertsey	UK2810	Chertsey	120
Dover	UK3100	Hawthorn Farm	122
Folkestone	UK3090	Black Horse Farm	124
Horsham	UK2940	Honeybridge	125
Horsham	UK2935	Sumners Ponds	125
Marden	UK3030	Tanner Farm	126
Redhill	UK2800	Alderstead Heath	127
Sevenoaks	UK3038	Thriftwood	127
Washington	UK2950	Washington	128

London

Abbey Wood	UK3260	Abbey Wood	130
Crystal Palace	UK3270	Crystal Palace	131
Edmonton	UK3230	Lee Valley	132

East of England

Beccles	UK3380	Waveney River	135
Bury St Edmunds	UK3345	The Dell	135
Cambridge	UK3562	Cherry Hinton	136
Great Yarmouth	UK3485	Clippesby	140
Great Yarmouth	UK3382	Rose Farm	139
Hunstanton	UK3525	Deepdale	141
Hunstanton	UK3520	Searles	141
King's Lynn	UK3465	King's Lynn	143
Norwich	UK3455	Deer's Glade	145
Peterborough	UK3580	Ferry Meadows	145
Pidley	UK3575	Stroud Hill	146
Swaffham	UK3470	Breckland	147
Woodbridge	UK3322	Run Cottage	148

Heart of England

Bridgnorth	UK4400	Stanmore Hall	155
Buxton	UK3845	Clover Fields	156
Coventry	UK4075	Hollyfast	157
Grantham	UK3775	Wagtail C.P.	159
Grantham	UK3765	Woodland Waters	159
Ludlow	UK4395	Ludlow T.P.	163
Lutterworth	UK3890	Stanford Hall	163

Quick Reference - Open All Year

Market Bosworth	UK3898	Bosworth	164
Market Rasen	UK3660	Walesby Woodlands	164
Matlock	UK3815	Lickpenny	165
Melton Mowbray	UK3895	Eye Kettleby	165
Meriden	UK4070	Somers Wood	166
Moreton-in-Marsh	UK4130	Moreton-in-Marsh	166
Newark	UK3945	Milestone	167
Newark	UK3950	Orchard Park	167
Newark	UK3940	Smeaton's Lakes	166
Nottingham	UK3935	Thornton's Holt	167
Oakham	UK3903	Rutland	168
Oswestry	UK4405	Oswestry	168
Peterchurch	UK4300	Poston Mill	169
Ripley	UK3865	Golden Valley	169
Scunthorpe	UK3755	Brookside	171
Shrewsbury	UK4410	Beaconsfield	171
Shrewsbury	UK4430	Oxon Hall	172
Skegness	UK3730	Skegness Sands	172
Slimbridge	UK4170	Tudor	173
S.port-on-Severn	UK4210	Lickhill Manor	173
Worksop	UK3920	Riverside	176

Yorkshire

Bridlington	UK4504	Bridlington	179
Selby	UK4635	Cawood	189

North West England

Bury	UK5265	Burrs Park	196
Carnforth	UK5270	Bay View	197
Carnforth	UK5350	Silverdale	197
Chester	UK5220	Manor Wood	198
Ormskirk	UK5280	Abbey Farm	200
Preston	UK5290	Royal Umpire	200

Cumbria

Appleby	UK5570	Wild Rose	205
Penrith	UK5560	Sykeside	208
Penrith	UK5630	The Quiet Site	210
Wigton	UK5505	Stanwix Park	211

Northumbria

Belford	UK5755	South Meadows	217
Berwick-on-Tweed	UK5800	Ord House	218
Durham	UK5705	Durham Grange	218
Durham	UK5715	Finchale Abbey	219
Stockton-on-Tees	UK5740	White Water Park	220

Wales

Barmouth	UK6385	Islawrffordd	226
Beddgelert	UK6590	Beddgelert	227
Caernarfon	UK6600	Bryn Gloch	229
Caernarfon	UK6605	Tafarn Snowdonia	230
Cardiff	UK5925	Cardiff	230
Colwyn Bay	UK6690	Bron-Y-Wendon	231
Llandovery	UK5955	Erwlon	235
Llantwit Major	UK5926	Happy Jakes	237
Montgomery	UK6330	Daisy Bank	240
Newport	UK6060	Tredegar House	241
Wrexham	UK6680	James'	247

Scotland

Aviemore	UK7680	Glenmore	251
Balloch	UK7240	Lomond Woods	252
Crieff	UK7275	Braidhaugh	255
Dalbeattie	UK6870	Glenearly	255
Durness	UK7735	Sango Sands	257
Edinburgh	UK7050	Edinburgh	258
Glencoe	UK7790	Invercoe	261
Grantown-on-Spey	UK7670	Grantown	261
Kirkcudbright	UK6950	Brighouse Bay	263
Maybole	UK7015	The Ranch	266
Motherwell	UK7000	Strathclyde	267
Musselburgh	UK6980	Drum Mohr	268
Perth	UK7265	Noah's Ark	269
Stranraer	UK7020	Aird Donald	273

Northern Ireland

Ballycastle	UK8365	Glenmore	277
Newcastle	UK8420	Tollymore	281

Republic of Ireland

Caherdaniel	IR9560	Wave Crest	289
Clondalkin	IR9100	Camac Valley	288
Cong	IR8740	Cong	294
Drimoleague	IR9515	Top of the Rock Pod Páirc	287
Tipperary	IR9400	Glen of Aherlow	297

Channel Islands

Sark	UK9870	Pomme de Chien	307

Dogs

For the benefit of those who want to take their dogs with them or for people who do not like dogs at the parks they visit, we list here the parks that have indicated to us that they do not accept dogs. If you are planning to take your dog we do advise you to phone the park first to check – there may be limits on numbers, breeds, etc. or times of the year when they are excluded.

Never – these parks do not accept dogs at any time:

UK0065	Wayfarers	32	UK4165	Little Wood	156
UK0115	Tehidy	34	UK4498	South Cliff	178
UK0250	Pentewan Sands	31	UK5890	Glen Trothy	239
UK0302	South Penquite	16	UK5980	Moreton Farm	245
UK0306	Ruthern Valley	17	UK6040	Pencelli Castle	228
UK0870	Beverley	65	UK6350	Barcdy	232
UK1150	Ruda	52	UK7290	Craigtoun Meadows	271
UK1490	Greenacres	92	UK9770	Vaugrat	305
UK1953	Lookout	94	UK9830	Seagull	306
UK2130	Grove Farm	84	UK9870	Pomme de Chien	307
UK2160	Harrow Wood	84	IR9410	The Apple	298
UK2300	Ashurst	103	IR9510	Eagle Point	287
UK3060	Canterbury Fields	120	IR9660	Green Acres	292
UK3120	Gate House Wood	128			
UK4100	Hoburne Cotswold	157			

Sometimes – these parks do not accept dogs at certain times of the year or have other restrictions, contact park:

UK0010	Chacewater	41	UK3520	Searles	141
UK0030	Ayr	38	UK4496	Skipsea Sands	190
UK0215	Sun Haven Valley	28	UK4520	Flower of May	186
UK0485	Franchis	23	UK5350	Silverdale	197
UK1540	Batcombe Vale	91	UK5995	Caerfai Bay	245
UK2270	Oakdene Forest	112	UK6280	Aeron Coast	222
UK2510	Whitecliff Bay	104	UK6345	Glanlynn	225
UK2572	Swiss Farm	109	UK6660	Nant Mill	243
UK2590	Greenhill Farm	105	UK6990	Mortonhall	258
UK3095	Little Satmar	124	UK7060	Tantallon	268
UK3110	Quex	119	IR8770	Westport House	294
UK3485	Clippesby	140	IR8810	Lough Lanagh	295

Fishing

We are pleased to include details of parks which provide facilities for fishing on site. Many other parks, particularly in Scotland and Ireland, are in popular fishing areas and have facilities within easy reach. Where we have been given details, we have included this information in the reports. It is always best to contact parks to check that they provide for your individual requirements.

England

UK5280	Abbey Farm	200
UK0784	Appledore	63
UK3680	Ashby Park	161
UK1540	Batcombe Vale	91
UK4410	Beaconsfield	171
UK2610	Bo Peep	103
UK2965	Brakes Coppice	118
UK4320	Broadmeadow	170
UK1630	Brokerswood	96
UK4500	Burton Constable	182
UK1665	Burton Hill	86
UK3855	Callow Top	153
UK4635	Cawood	189
UK5785	Chainbridge	217
UK1545	Cheddar Bridge	82
UK2810	Chertsey	120
UK2875	Chichester Lakeside	121
UK3845	Clover Fields	156
UK0970	Cofton	55
UK2755	Cosgrove Park	110
UK1125	Crealy Meadows	57
UK4150	Croft Farm	175
UK3455	Deer's Glade	145
UK5710	Doe Park	216
UK1590	Exe Valley	85
UK3895	Eye Kettleby	165
UK2915	Fairfields Farm	123
UK4380	Fernwood	158
UK5715	Finchale Abbey	219
UK1780	Freshwater Beach	79
UK3970	Glencote	161
UK1740	Golden Cap	78
UK1075	Golden Coast	71
UK3865	Golden Valley	169
UK4640	Goosewood	194
UK1640	Greenhill Farm (Salisbury)	90
UK2590	Greenhill Farm (Bletchingdon)	105
UK2130	Grove Farm	84
UK0790	Harford Bridge	68
UK2160	Harrow Wood	84
UK3371	Heathland Beach	144
UK2360	Hill Cottage	107
UK5615	Hill of Oaks	213
UK4100	Hoburne Cotswold	157
UK1480	Home Farm	80
UK3300	Homestead Lake	136
UK3055	Hop Farm	126
UK2900	Horam Manor	125
UK2820	Horsley	123

UK2700	Hurley	109
UK4090	Island Meadow	160
UK3430	Kelling Heath	147
UK4190	Kingsgreen	164
UK4720	Knight Stainforth	189
UK3210	Lee Valley	132
UK4210	Lickhill Manor	173
UK3480	Little Lakeland	141
UK5625	Lowther	210
UK4310	Lucksall	160
UK5220	Manor Wood	198
UK0415	Meadow Lakes	37
UK0270	Mena	16
UK3945	Milestone	167
UK0750	Minnows	70
UK0165	Monkey Tree	26
UK4610	Moorside	193
UK5272	Moss Wood	199
UK0425	Mother Ivey's Bay	30
UK0685	Newberry Valley	51
UK2465	Ninham	114
UK1570	Northam Farm	76
UK3400	Old Brick Kilns	139
UK1390	Old Oaks	86
UK5600	Pennine View	208
UK0250	Pentewan Sands	31
UK4300	Poston Mill	169
UK3850	Rivendale	152
UK0950	River Dart	48
UK4715	Riverside (Lancaster)	182
UK0745	Riverside (South Molton)	68
UK5285	Riverside (Southport)	202
UK4080	Riverside (Stratford-upon-Avon)	174
UK1150	Ruda	52
UK4480	Sand le Mere	191
UK2290	Sandy Balls	106
UK3520	Searles	141
UK4588	Sleningford Watermill	185
UK3940	Smeaton's Lakes	166
UK0302	South Penquite	16
UK3890	Stanford Hall	163
UK3575	Stroud Hill	146
UK2935	Sumners Ponds	125
UK2572	Swiss Farm	109
UK3685	Tattershall Lakes	175
UK4510	Thorpe Hall	179
UK3655	Thorpe Park	157
UK4345	Townsend	162
UK0530	Trethiggey	29
UK0170	Trevella	25

Wales

Scotland

Northern Ireland

Republic of Ireland

Bicycle Hire

We understand that the following parks have bicycles to hire on site or can arrange for bicycles to be delivered. However, we would recommend that you contact the park to check as the situation can change.

England

UK1415	Alpine Grove	80
UK2300	Ashurst	103
UK4410	Beaconsfield	171
UK0110	Calloose	23
UK3855	Callow Top	153
UK5660	Castlerigg Hall	207
UK3485	Clippesby	140
UK3525	Deepdale	141
UK3455	Deer's Glade	145
UK3390	Dower House	138
UK1590	Exe Valley	85
UK3895	Eye Kettleby	165
UK4560	Golden Square	181
UK1490	Greenacres	92
UK1640	Greenhill Farm	90
UK3371	Heathland Beach	144
UK0210	Hendra	27
UK3430	Kelling Heath	147
UK1010	Lady's Mile	54
UK3210	Lee Valley	132
UK0415	Meadow Lakes	37
UK0750	Minnows	70
UK3330	Moat Barn	149
UK2270	Oakdene Forest	112
UK1350	Quantock Orchard	93
UK0950	River Dart	48
UK2050	Rowlands Wait	75
UK0306	Ruthern Valley	17
UK4540	Saint Helens	188
UK2290	Sandy Balls	106
UK5745	Seafield	220
UK3520	Searles	141
UK2120	South Lytchett Manor	89
UK5505	Stanwix Park	211
UK0255	Sun Valley	24
UK3685	Tattershall Lakes	175
UK3655	Thorpe Park	157
UK0220	Trevornick	27
UK5610	Waterfoot	209
UK3380	Waveney River	135
UK2510	Whitecliff Bay	104
UK5570	Wild Rose	205
UK5360	Willowbank	201
UK5605	Woodclose	207
UK3500	Woodhill	138
UK0805	Woodovis	70

Wales

UK5925	Cardiff	230
UK6330	Daisy Bank	240
UK6040	Pencelli Castle	228
UK6340	Pen-y-Bont	225
UK6670	The Plassey	247
UK6587	Yr Helyg The Willows	244

Scotland

UK7540	Aberlour	250
UK6950	Brighouse Bay	263
UK7680	Glenmore	251
UK6940	Loch Ken	253
UK7280	Nethercraig	252
UK7880	Port Bàn	274
UK7645	Sands Caravan & Camping	260
UK7825	Shieling Holidays	254
UK7750	Staffin	272
UK7000	Strathclyde Caravan Club Site	267
UK7230	Trossachs	250

Republic of Ireland

IR9620	Flemings	291
IR9600	Glenross	290
IR8860	Gurteen Bay	288
IR9155	Hidden Valley	302
IR9640	Killarney Flesk	291
IR8965	Lough Ennell	300
IR8635	Rosguill Holiday Park	287
IR9130	Roundwood	301
IR9490	Sextons	286
IR9240	Tree Grove	293

Channel Islands

UK9780	Fauxquets	305
UK9790	La Bailloterie	306

Golf

We understand that the following parks have facilities for playing golf on site. Where facilities are within easy reach and we have been given details, we have included this information in the individual reports. However, we recommend that you contact the park to check that they meet your requirements.

England

UK2920	Bay View	124
UK0540	Carvynick	30
UK0720	Easewell Farm	72
UK1750	Highlands End	78
UK3230	Lee Valley	132
UK3320	Moon & Sixpence	148
UK1020	Oakdown	67
UK4300	Poston Mill	169
UK4710	Rudding	180
UK3520	Searles	141
UK4070	Somers Wood	166
UK0690	Stowford Farm	58
UK3685	Tattershall Lakes	175
UK3655	Thorpe Park	157
UK0220	Trevornick	27
UK2510	Whitecliff Bay	104
UK0380	Wooda Farm	17
UK1070	Woolacombe Bay	71

Wales

| UK6670 | The Plassey | 247 |
| UK6655 | Ty Mawr | 223 |

Scotland

UK6950	Brighouse Bay	263
UK6910	Hoddom Castle	266
UK7265	Noah's Ark	269

Northern Ireland

| UK8310 | Carnfunnock | 280 |

Republic of Ireland

| IR9155 | Hidden Valley | 302 |
| IR9150 | River Valley | 302 |

Adults Only

We list here the parks that have indicated to us that they do not accept children at any time during the year, at certain times, or in certain areas of their park.

England

UK4410	Beaconsfield	171
UK1770	Bingham Grange	79
UK3470	Breckland	147
UK3755	Brookside	171
UK0010	Chacewater	41
UK5785	Chainbridge	217
UK1545	Cheddar Bridge	82
UK3650	Cherry Tree	173
UK1510	Chew Valley	76
UK3845	Clover Fields	156
UK3646	Delph Bank	173
UK1590	Exe Valley	85
UK3895	Eye Kettleby	165
UK5715	Finchale Abbey	219
UK4580	Foxholme	181
UK5640	Green Acres	206
UK0012	Killiwerris	41
UK5240	Lamb Cottage	200
UK4165	Little Wood	156
UK3695	Long Acres	154
UK1500	Long Hazel	92
UK1355	Lowtrow Cross	94
UK3330	Moat Barn	149
UK0820	Moor View	60
UK1390	Old Oaks	86
UK4534	Overbrook	184
UK1680	Plough Lane	84
UK5245	Royal Vale	198
UK4070	Somers Wood	166
UK3575	Stroud Hill	146
UK5650	The Ashes	206
UK5510	The Larches	212
UK3420	Two Mills	144
UK1520	Waterrow	94
UK0065	Wayfarers	32
UK0900	Widdicombe Farm	64
UK1250	Woodland Springs	56
UK0915	Woodville	62
UK4609	York (Stockton Lane)	192

Wales

| UK6330 | Daisy Bank | 240 |
| UK6695 | Tyddyn Du | 242 |

Scotland

| UK7782 | Faichemard | 262 |

Horse Riding

We understand that the following parks have horse riding stables on site. Where facilities are within easy reach and we have been given details, we have included this information in the individual reports. However, we recommend that you contact the park to check that they meet your requirements.

England

UK1370	Burrowhayes	88
UK2900	Horam Manor	125
UK0360	Lakefield	19
UK1306	Mill Farm	77
UK2290	Sandy Balls	106
UK0690	Stowford Farm	58
UK1060	Yeatheridge	52

Scotland

UK7300	Blair Castle	270

Republic of Ireland

IR9240	Tree Grove	293

Boat Launching

We understand that the following parks have boat slipways on site. Where facilities are within easy reach and we have been given details, we have included this information in the individual reports. However, we recommend that you contact the park to check that they meet your requirements.

England

UK4500	Burton Constable	182
UK2810	Chertsey	120
UK2755	Cosgrove Park	110
UK4150	Croft Farm	175
UK3290	Fen Farm	136
UK5615	Hill of Oaks	213
UK3055	Hop Farm	126
UK2700	Hurley	109
UK4210	Lickhill Manor	173
UK4310	Lucksall	160
UK0750	Minnows	70
UK0250	Pentewan Sands	31
UK4080	Riverside Stratford upon Avon	174
UK3685	Tattershall Lakes	175
UK3380	Waveney River	135
UK2510	Whitecliff Bay	104

Wales

UK6345	Glanlynn	225
UK6385	Islawrffordd	226

Scotland

UK7710	Ardmair Point	274
UK7255	Argyll	262
UK6950	Brighouse Bay	263
UK7850	Linnhe Lochside	260
UK7740	Loch Greshornish	257
UK6940	Loch Ken	253
UK6890	Mossyard	253
UK7250	Muasdale	273
UK7880	Port Bàn	274
UK7800	Resipole	251
UK7410	Riverview	267
UK7645	Sands Caravan & Camping	260
UK7025	Seal Shore	263
UK7825	Shieling Holidays	254

Northern Ireland

UK8405	Cranfield	279
UK8340	Drumaheglis	277
UK8515	Rushin House	277
UK8407	Sandilands	279
UK8330	Sixmilewater	276

Republic of Ireland

IR9510	Eagle Point	287
IR8860	Gurteen Bay	288
IR8965	Lough Ennell	300
IR8960	Lough Ree	300
IR9610	Mannix Point	290
IR9560	Wave Crest	289

Regions of Britain & Ireland

Scotland
page 248

Northern
Ireland
page 275

Northumbria
page 214

Cumbria
page 203

Yorkshire
page 177

North West
England
page 195

Republic of Ireland
page 283

Heart of England
page 150

Wales
page 221

East of England
page 133

Southern
England
page 101

South West England
page 14

South East
England
page 116

London
page 129

Channel Islands
page 303

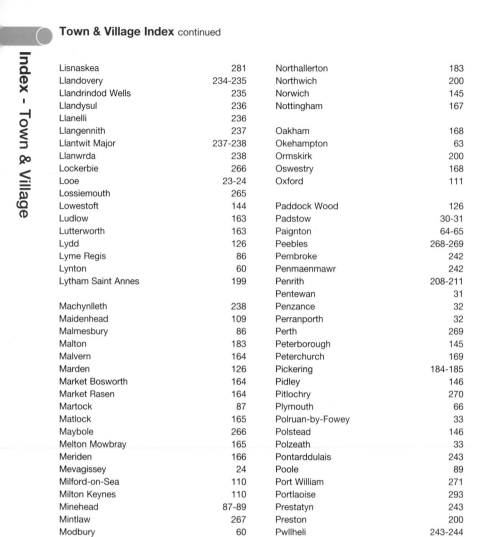

Index by Campsite Region, County & Name

Channel Islands